Economics of Federalism
Volume I

Economic Approaches to Law

Series Editors: Richard A. Posner
*Judge, United States Court of Appeals for the Seventh Circuit
and Senior Lecturer, University of Chicago Law School, USA*
Francesco Parisi
*Professor of Law, University of Minnesota Law School, USA
and Professor of Economics, University of Bologna, Italy*

A full list of published and future titles in this series is printed at the end of this volume.

Wherever possible, the articles in these volumes have been reproduced as originally published using facsimile reproduction, inclusive of footnotes and pagination to facilitate ease of reference.

For a list of all Edward Elgar published titles visit our site on the World Wide Web at
www.e-elgar.com

Economics of Federalism Volume I

Edited by

Bruce H. Kobayashi

Professor of Law
School of Law, George Mason University, USA

and

Larry E. Ribstein

Mildred Van Voorhis Jones Chair in Law
College of Law, University of Illinois, USA

ECONOMIC APPROACHES TO LAW

An Elgar Reference Collection
Cheltenham, UK • Northampton, MA, USA

Published by
Edward Elgar Publishing Limited
Glensanda House
Montpellier Parade
Cheltenham
Glos GL50 1UA
UK

Edward Elgar Publishing, Inc.
William Pratt House
9 Dewey Court
Northampton
Massachusetts 01060
USA

A catalogue record for this book is available from the British Library

Library of Congress Control Number: 2007921146

ISBN: 978 1 84542 527 2 (2 volume set)

Printed and bound in Great Britain by MPG Books Ltd, Bodmin, Cornwall

Contents

Acknowledgements

The editors and publishers wish to thank the authors and the following publishers who have kindly given permission for the use of copyright material.

American Economic Association for articles: Robert P. Inman and Daniel L. Rubinfeld (1997), 'Rethinking Federalism', *Journal of Economic Perspectives*, **11** (4), Fall, 43–64; John D. Donahue (1997), 'Tiebout? Or Not Tiebout? The Market Metaphor and America's Devolution Debate', *Journal of Economic Perspectives*, **11** (4), Fall, 73–81; Paul W. Rhode and Koleman S. Strumpf (2003), 'Assessing the Importance of Tiebout Sorting: Local Heterogeneity from 1850 to 1990', *American Economic Review*, **93** (5), December 1648–77.

Cambridge University Press for excerpts and article: Geoffrey Brennan and James M. Buchanan (1980), 'Open Economy, Federalism, and Taxing Authority', in *The Power to Tax: Analytical Foundations of a Fiscal Constitution*, Chapter 9, 168–86, 219; Albert Breton (1996), 'A Retrospective Overview' and 'The Organization of Governmental Systems', in *Competitive Governments: An Economic Theory of Politics and Public Finance*, Chapters 7 and 8, 181–95, 196–227 and references; Jonathan Rodden (2003), 'Reviving Leviathan: Fiscal Federalism and the Growth of Government', *International Organization*, **57** (4), Fall, 695–729.

Copyright Clearance Center and *Virginia Law Review* for article: Jonathan R. Macey (1990), 'Federal Deference to Local Regulators and the Economic Theory of Regulation: Toward a Public-Choice Explanation of Federalism', *Virginia Law Review*, **76** (2), March, 265–91.

Duke University School of Law for article: Richard A. Epstein (1992), 'Exit Rights Under Federalism', *Law and Contemporary Problems*, **55** (1), Winter, 147–65.

Elsevier for article: Robert P. Inman and Daniel L. Rubinfeld (1996), 'Designing Tax Policy in Federalist Economies: An Overview', *Journal of Public Economics*, **60** (3), June, 307–34.

Edmund W. Kitch for his own excerpt: (1980), 'Regulation and the American Common Market', in A. Dan Tarlock (ed.), *Regulation, Federalism, and Interstate Commerce*, 9–55.

Oxford University Press for article: Barry R. Weingast (1995), 'The Economic Role of Political Institutions: Market-Preserving Federalism and Economic Development', *Journal of Law, Economics and Organization*, **11** (1), April, 1–31.

Springer Science and Business Media for article: Gordon Tullock (1969), 'Federalism: Problems of Scale', *Public Choice*, **6**, Spring, 19–29.

University of Chicago Press for articles: Charles M. Tiebout (1956), 'A Pure Theory of Local Expenditures', *Journal of Political Economy*, **64** (5), October, 416–24; Susan Rose-Ackerman (1981), 'Does Federalism Matter? Political Choice in a Federal Republic', *Journal of Political Economy*, **89** (1), February, 152–65; Dennis Epple and Allan Zelenitz (1981), 'The Implications of Competition among Jurisdictions: Does Tiebout Need Politics?', *Journal of Political Economy*, **89** (6), December, 1197–1217; Edward M. Gramlich and Daniel L. Rubinfeld (1982), 'Micro Estimates of Public Spending Demand Functions and Tests of the Tiebout and Median-Voter Hypotheses', *Journal of Political Economy*, **90** (3), June, 536–60; Dennis Epple and Thomas Romer (1991), 'Mobility and Redistribution', *Journal of Political Economy*, **99** (4), August, 828–58.

Every effort has been made to trace all the copyright holders but if any have been inadvertently overlooked the publishers will be pleased to make the necessary arrangement at the first opportunity.

In addition the publishers wish to thank the Marshall Library of Economics, University of Cambridge, UK, the Library at the University of Warwick, UK, and the Library of Indiana University at Bloomington, USA, for their assistance in obtaining these articles.

Introduction

Bruce H. Kobayashi and Larry E. Ribstein

Federal political systems have a hierarchy of at least two distinct levels, referred to here as "state" and "central", each with a well-defined scope of authority so that each level is autonomous within its scope (Riker 1964). Federal structures are used in many countries (Riker 1964). The primary economic question is how to allocate government functions and means of carrying out these functions among governments at different levels of the hierarchy. One main branch of the economic literature, the literature on competitive federalism, focuses on the horizontal structure of federalism. These articles examine jurisdictional competition between state governments for mobile individuals and resources (Tiebout 1956, Volume I, Chapter 1). A second main branch of the literature is that on fiscal federalism (Oates 1972; Breton 1998). These papers examine how the provision of public services and taxing power should be divided between the central and state governments – that is, federalism's vertical structure. The central government should use fiscal policy to correct spillovers and other distortions that result from uncoordinated state policymaking. Any study of federalism ideally should cover both the horizontal and vertical structures of government (Keen and Kotsogiannis 2002). But because this may not be practicable, analysts often have focused on one or the other.

The Tiebout theory

The economic theory of federalism began with a study of taxes and provision of public goods. The modern literature on the economics of federalism is often traced back to Tiebout's (1956) article on state public expenditures. Tiebout argued that Samuelson's (1954) hypothesis that governments would under-produce public goods did not necessarily apply to the provision of public goods by competing state governments. Tiebout, in effect, viewed these governments as markets in which individuals, like consumers, choose the jurisdictions that best satisfy their preferences for public goods and taxes. Under this view, public goods would be efficiently allocated when; (1) people and resources are mobile; (2) the number of jurisdictions is large; (3) jurisdictions are free to select any set of laws they desire; and (4) there are no spillovers (Oates 1972).

Numerous articles have tested empirically the assumptions and hypotheses that the Tiebout model generates. Early tests of the hypothesis postulated that housing prices would correlate negatively with local government tax rates and positively with local government spending levels. Oates (1969) found that housing prices negatively related to the effective tax rate and positively with public school expenditures per pupil. However, critics noted that no such relationship should exist in full Tiebout equilibrium, when taxes equal the price of efficiently provided local government services (Hamilton 1976). Thus, the rejection of the null hypothesis of no relationship between housing prices and fiscal variables indicated that such a Tiebout equilibrium did not exist. Epple et al. (1978) showed that correlations between housing prices and local government fiscal variables cannot test a more refined hypothesis based on the Tiebout theory.

A second set of papers testing the Tiebout theory used sub-county data to examine whether lower mobility costs were associated with greater Tiebout sorting. Gramlich and Rubinfeld (1982, Volume I, Chapter 7) estimated public spending demand functions and found that variance in local spending demand within communities was significantly lower than the statewide variance. This finding is consistent with Tiebout sorting of individuals with similar demands for public spending. Gramlich and Rubinfeld also found that estimated preferences for median voters in urban areas were consistent with actual levels of local government services provided. However, the results were weaker in rural areas, where mobility costs are higher. These results are consistent with local jurisdictions providing the desired level of services in the presence of low mobility costs. On the other hand, Rhode and Strumpf (2003, Volume I, Chapter 8) found that decreased mobility costs over time were not associated with increases in intercommunity heterogeneity in local taxation and service levels, which is inconsistent with Tiebout sorting. This suggests that forces reducing cross-community heterogeneity overwhelmed Tiebout forces over time.

Other benefits of federalism

The literature on the economics of federalism since Tiebout has articulated several benefits of federal systems in addition to the sorting and matching theorized by Tiebout. While many of these benefits are supported by exit rights and mobility, some are not dependent upon such mobility (Oates 1972, 1999).

Exit Rights and Voice

By letting a voter supplement his "voice" with an option to "exit" the jurisdiction, exit rights under federalism can powerfully check state governments' powers to tax and regulate (Epstein 1992, Volume I, Chapter 2). Exit rights effectively bring market forces to bear on political structures. While the literature on competitive federalism largely has focused on exit rights, some have pointed out that there is an optimal balance of exit and voice. These tradeoffs can be complex, as ease of exit theoretically can reduce use of voice to a suboptimal level. Hirschman (1970) analyzes these tradeoffs generally in the context of firms and of unitary governments, but does not explicitly address federalism issues. Decentralized federal political structures may be optimal even in the absence of viable exit rights because reducing the size of the jurisdiction may enhance the exercise of voice (Brennan and Buchanan 1980, Volume I, Chapter 15).

The Promotion of Economic Growth and Development

Federal systems can increase economic growth and development. The theory known as "market-preserving federalism" sets out several conditions under which a federal system will effectively preserve markets and provide incentives for economic growth and development

(Weingast 1995, Volume I, Chapter 12; Qian and Weingast 1997). Under this theory, a nation adopts political institutions that credibly commit it to a self-enforcing structure of limited government. Under this self-enforcing design, state units have primary regulatory responsibility, there are no barriers to trade, and state governments face "hard" budget constraints in the sense that they can neither print money nor engage in unlimited borrowing. Under these conditions, property rights will be respected and contracts enforced primarily at the state level. The self-enforcing design also must constrain the power of the federal government. Thus, the central government would have authority only over national issues and could not undo state protections, and states would not have incentives to defect from this agreement by free-riding. The jurisdictions would interact through a common market, which fosters growth and development.

Federalism, Innovation and Information

A federal system has the potential advantage over a unitary system that the state jurisdictions can be laboratories to experiment with various mixes of laws, taxes and services (Oates 1999). The notion of the states as laboratories has great intuitive appeal and therefore has influenced the legal treatment of federalism. For example, Justice Brandeis, in his oft quoted dissent in *New State Ice Co. v. Liebmann*, 285 U.S. 262, 311 (1932), noted that "it is one of the happy incidents of the federal system that a single courageous State may, if its citizens choose, serve as a laboratory; and try novel social and economic experiments without risk to the rest of the country." State by state determination of issues is less likely than federal government determination to result in nationwide uniform policy choices, especially if individuals sort themselves according to their heterogeneous preferences. The advantages of state variation over centralized uniformity are emphasized by the competitive federalism literature and underlie the "decentralization theorem" of the fiscal federalism literature (Oates 1999).

The central government theoretically can conduct limited policy experiments even without a federal system (Oates 1999). But a partitioned federal system at least increases the likelihood such experimentation may occur. State governments are better informed than the central government as to their constituents' needs (Oates 1999, 1972). Because decentralized governments are presumably closer to their constituents, they are much more likely to possess superior knowledge of local preferences and cost conditions (Hayek 1945). And while the central government theoretically can employ local agents, local government agents have stronger political incentives than those of the central government to take their constituents' preferences into account (Oates 1999). These information and political advantages suggest that states will have a comparative advantage over the central government in producing variation and experimentation. On the other hand, state politicians may under-produce costly innovation if those in other states can free-ride on them (Rose-Ackerman 1980; Strumpf 2002), unless quasi-property rights or other institutional mechanisms are available to address this free-riding (Ribstein 2004).

The Optimal Scale of Government

State governments may be able to operate closer to the optimal scale than a unified government (Tullock 1969, Volume I, Chapter 3). Although central government provision of services can internalize spillovers, at some point of expansion the costs of political bargaining among individuals and groups may exceed internalization benefits. These costs are likely to increase with the size of government for several reasons. First, governments operating with a larger scope or scale cannot use the sorting and matching function, and thus must offer larger bundles of services to a larger and more heterogeneous set of constituents. This may dissatisfy individual constituents on a larger number of issues. Optimal division between the federal and local governments therefore requires balancing the internalization of spillovers with these scale effects. Federal structures also can enhance the exercise of voice by decreasing the size of the political unit (Brennan and Buchanan 1980). Thus, even if the central government would more efficiently carry out some activities, considerations of "political efficiency" may justify assigning such functions to the states.

Problems of federalism

The literature on federalism has identified several problems with decentralizing government authority.

Spillovers

Public goods and costs may spill over from one state jurisdiction into others (Sandler and Culyer 1982). This would give each jurisdiction suboptimal incentives to provide public goods, or incentives to permit harmful activities whose effects are felt mainly in other jurisdictions. For example, a subordinate jurisdiction has little incentive to provide for the nation's defense because other jurisdictions could free-ride on these defense costs. A jurisdiction might have incentives to engage in tax exportation by taxing activities whose main benefits are felt elsewhere or revenues earned elsewhere (Gordon 1983; Oates and Schwab 1988; Inman and Rubinfeld 1996, Volume I, Chapter 14, Shaviro 1992, Volume II, Chapter 9). Jurisdictions also may choose to permit activities such as pollution and gambling that cause harm in other jurisdictions (Donahue 1997, Volume I, Chapter 17).

Distribution Issues

Mobility within a federal system may affect the distribution of resources (Buchanan 1952). States competing for business and capital may have incentives to levy lower or more regressive taxes to attract the more mobile wealthy while providing fewer services for the less mobile poor (Epple and Romer 1991, Volume I, Chapter 18). This may particularly be a problem if the central government devolves welfare responsibilities to the state governments, as has been occurring in the US (Donahue 1997). More generally, the presence of both mobile and non-mobile resources can cause states' tax policies to favor mobile resources and thereby distort factor prices and utilization. Factor mobility may decrease welfare under certain circumstances (Flatters et al. 1974).

Constraints on Mobility

Many of the advantages of federalism depend on an optimal level of mobility of citizens and resources that does not always exist. State jurisdictions may impose taxes and tariffs or exit restrictions that impede movement between jurisdictions (Epstein 1992). Mobility also may be constrained by jurisdictional differences in legal rights, cultural and ethnic affinities, language barriers and family ties.

Constrained mobility may have distributional implications because some groups of citizens are less mobile than others. For example, retirees and childless individuals may be more mobile, resulting in state policies designed to attract them at the expense of the less mobile. Businesses generally may be more mobile than individuals, as business is becoming increasingly national and international and states therefore increasingly fungible as business environments (Donahue 1997).

Mobility can also create problems when some factors are not mobile. As noted in Part B, for example, when capital is mobile but individuals are not (Oates and Schwab 1988), mobility can distort both the fiscal and policy decisions of heterogeneous local jurisdictions. Similar distortions will occur when individuals are mobile but capital (e.g. land) is not (Epple and Zelenitz 1981, Volume I, Chapter 10; Buchanan and Goetz 1972).

Using Grants to Solve Problems of Fiscal Federalism

Some of the spillover problems discussed above can be solved through grants by the central to state governments (Inman and Rubinfeld 1996, 1997, Volume I, Chapter 13; Gordon 1983; Oates 1972, 1999; Epple and Romer 1991). The central government could make conditional grants to be spent in particular ways if the purpose of the grant is to provide incentives for the production of public goods that otherwise would be subject to free-rider problems. On the other hand, the grant could be unconditional as to use if it is intended to solve distributional inequities between jurisdictions (Buchanan 1952).

Much of the discussion of grants ignores public choice issues concerning what lower level jurisdictions do with the grant money. There may be "flypaper" effects, as grants intended to induce voters to finance public goods that have benefits outside the jurisdiction actually may "stick" at the central level, thereby expanding the size of government (Oates 1972; Brennan and Buchanan 1980; Hines and Thaler 1995; Fisher 1982; Brennan and Pincus 1996).

The central government has other mechanisms at its disposal to deal with inter-jurisdictional issues, including directly providing the service (as with national defense), reducing tax rates, or providing deductions for taxes paid in the disadvantaged states (Inman and Rubinfeld 1997). Again, this discussion often ignores the public choice issues concerning whether or not the central government will use available fiscal policies to counter these spillover effects (Inman and Rubinfeld 1996). There is little evidence that federal grant-in-aid policies and other vertical intergovernmental transfers are consistent with reducing inter-jurisdictional spillovers (Inman 1988).

Even without central government intervention, state governments could minimize inter-jurisdictional problems through the form of taxation (Krelove 1992; Meyers 1990). For example, states could discourage jurisdiction-shopping for tax rates, facilitate redistribution of income or avoid externalizing tax burdens by relying on taxes tied to in-state benefits, taxes on immobile property or taxes based on residence (head taxes) (Oates 1999; Oates and Schwab 1988). However, an efficient result may hold only in limited circumstances (Inman and Rubinfeld 1996). Where individuals have homogeneous preferences and taxes are limited to head taxes, a decentralized economy with mobile individuals and capital will achieve tax efficiency (Tiebout

1956). Tax efficiency can be achieved in such an economy when states use source-based taxes (taxes that tax factors where they are employed and tax goods and services where they are purchased) in addition to head taxes. However, tax efficiency in the presence of source taxes requires that states do not act myopically when setting these taxes (that is, the states' tax-setting decisions must recognize the effect these decisions will have on equilibrium taxes) (Inman and Rubinfeld 1996).

The Size, Shape and Existence of Federal Systems

Which countries are likely to be, and to remain, federal systems, and how these systems will be organized geographically, depend to some extent on the costs and benefits of federalism for a particular country. Under the "decentralization theorem" (Oates 1972), it is more efficient to provide public goods through the state than the central government if consumption levels depend on geography, assuming that the costs of providing the public goods are the same for the central as for the state government. Although the desirability of heterogeneity may justify smaller state jurisdictions, such a division entails offsetting costs, including more inter-jurisdictional spillovers and higher costs of collective decision-making because of the need to maintain multiple government units (Tullock 1969).

Competition between jurisdictions theoretically can check the size and scope of individual jurisdictions, and thereby reduce the overall size of government (Grossman 1989; Brennan and Buchanan 1980; Hayek 1948; Persson and Tabellini 2000; Weingast 1995). Brennan and Buchanan's "Leviathan theory" views the central government as a tax-maximizing monopolist constrained only by the possibility that individuals will withhold their labor. In contrast, decentralized government forces politicians to compete for mobile individuals and capital. Thus, under this theory, "total government intrusion into the economy should be smaller, *ceteris paribus*, the greater the extent to which taxes and expenditures are decentralized" (*id.* at 185). On the other hand, rent-seeking competition between local governments can increase the size of government (Anderson and Tollison 1988).

Numerous articles have empirically examined the Leviathan hypothesis, with mixed results. For example, Oates (1985) found little evidence of correlation between measures of decentralization and the size of government based on cross-sectional data. Zax (1989) found that decentralization that increases competition between local governments decreased the size of government, while decentralization that sacrificed scale economies increased the size of government. Rodden (2003, Volume I, Chapter 16) tested the Leviathan hypothesis using panel data and additional explanatory variables and found that decentralized governments funded by autonomous local taxation have smaller public sectors. In contrast, decentralization funded by revenue-sharing grants or centrally regulated state taxation is associated with larger government.

The existence and shape of federal systems also depend on political considerations. For example, the US has jurisdictions of many sizes and shapes that do not seem to mesh with demographic or other characteristics and that have not changed significantly despite changes in underlying costs and benefits. Thus, Riker (1964) emphasizes the "military condition" – the objective of the central government to expand, coupled with offering a threat or opportunity to the lower level jurisdictions. In addition, the institutional economics theory of federalism discussed below may offer at least a partial explanation for the observed structure of federal systems.

Constraints on the Federal Government

A viable federal system requires a central government to deal with free-riding and other refusals to cooperate by state governments (Riker 1964; Persson and Tabellini 1996a, b; de Figueiredo and Weingast 2005). But there is a danger that the central government will eliminate the benefits of diverse jurisdictions by exercising too much power (Riker 1964). A fundamental dilemma of federalism is how to have a central government that is strong enough to provide a check on the lower level governments but is not so strong that it overwhelms the states (Riker 1964). This dilemma is a difficult one, because state governments cannot easily prevent the central government from seizing power other than by seceding, which would destroy the union, or by refusing to empower the central government at the outset. Thus, federalism must be self-enforcing (de Figueiredo and Weingast 2005).

One prominent theory holds that durable, market-preserving federalism (see discussion above) is self-enforcing (Weingast 1995; Qian and Weingast 1997; McKinnon 1997). Borrowing from institutional economics and the theory of the firm, these writers argue that institutional constraints prevent the central authority from "overawing" the state units. The equilibrium is maintained because the nation's constitution coordinates and enforces citizens' views about the appropriate limits on government. In the absence of such a consensus, the central government would form coalitions that defeat state governments' power. For example, federalism in England was built on powerful state justices of the peace who cared about state prosperity. After the Glorious Revolution the country reached consensus on the need to limit the monarch's power. In the US, Jacksonian democrats held power by establishing various constraints on the national government, including a 2/3 rule for nominating candidates for presidency, which gave southerners a veto over national policy. Critics of the theory note several shortcomings, including the lack of empirical support and uncertainty as to the conditions necessary for the creation and maintenance of a federal system (Rodden and Rose-Ackerman 1997).

Another theory rests on national politicians' incentives to maximize political support, which may sometimes require not alienating state interest groups (Macey 1990, Volume I, Chapter 6). This theory explains why the federal government has not sought to seize power on several issues, such as corporate law, despite its constitutional power to do so.

Supply-Side Considerations

The advantages of federalism depend significantly on the individual incentives of political actors. As explained immediately above, these incentives help explain why central government politicians respect the power of state governments. But it is also necessary to explain why state government politicians would have an incentive to engage in jurisdictional competition. It has been argued that they may not, since they are not rewarded for successful innovations and may suffer political penalties for unsuccessful innovations (Rose-Ackerman 1980). However, this ignores the incentives of citizens and interest groups, particularly including lawyers, to supply innovations (Ribstein 2004; Sitkoff and Schanzenback 2005).

Effect of Federalism on Political Structure

The above discussion focuses on issues relating to allocating power between the central and state governments. There is a further question of how federalism matters to decisions made by the central government – that is, whether those decisions depend on whether the country is federalist or unitary. There are theoretical reasons to believe that they do, and some anecdotes to support the theory (Rose-Ackerman 1981). Citizens may vote against national laws that restrict their states' ability to export costs and support laws that reduce other jurisdictions' ability to export costs on them. National support for a law therefore may depend on whether the nation has a unitary or federal structure. For example, a state's residents may support a national law that bans gambling if their own state can allow it, or may support a national law that bans gambling everywhere, thereby preventing neighboring states from imposing on them the costs of legalized gambling. Also, citizens in states adopting minimum wage and pollution laws may favor federal preemption to prevent other states from imposing costs on them, but states without these laws may benefit from national diversity, particularly as more states adopt the laws. Thus, it is not clear that a state consensus points the way to a national law. Moreover, federalism creates interest groups based on geographical location that might not exist under a unitary system (Oates 1999; Grossman 1989).

Coordination among Subordinate States

As discussed above, state jurisdictions may have incentives to externalize costs, inadequate incentives to produce public goods with extra-territorial benefits, or an inability to effect socially desirable redistribution because of the mobility of citizens and resources. The central government may be able to remedy some of these problems, but the remedies may be ineffective and may lead to giving excessive powers to the central government. This raises the question of whether there are more cost-effective ways to reduce inter-jurisdictional costs.

One possible approach is through design of the decision rule at the central government level. Under a system of "cooperative federalism" the central government can act only upon a unanimous vote of the states' representatives (Inman and Rubinfeld 1997). However, a unanimity rule would entail high decision costs and might impede effective central government action (Buchanan and Tullock 1962). Agreement might be secured by compensating jurisdictions that would lose through a central government decision, provided the states can agree on allocations (Inman and Rubinfeld 1997). The problems of cooperative federalism are reflected in the failure of the Articles of Confederation in the US and in Europe's difficulties in coordinating fiscal policies (Inman and Rubinfeld 1997).

Other alternatives include compacts (Oates 1999) and voluntary coordination among the states. One possible mechanism of cooperation is the central promulgation of "uniform" law proposals. However, coordination problems remain, combined with political costs at the uniform lawmaking level (Ribstein and Kobayashi 1996, Volume II, Chapter 2).

The states can coordinate through courts' application of choice-of-law rules (Baxter 1963). State A's courts have incentives to apply State B's laws in order to encourage State B lawmakers to reciprocate by enforcing State A's law. States may apply laws other than their own to achieve a variety of goals, including predictability and decision-making by the courts with knowledge about state conditions (O'Hara and Ribstein 2000, Volume II, Chapter 4). State lawmakers have incentives to enforce contracts to apply the law of a particular state and provide for adjudication in that state. If states do not enforce such contracts, parties may completely avoid contacts with the state, thereby inflicting costs on interest groups in the state (Ribstein 2003). These choice-of-law rules do not, however, fully solve coordination problems as long as the federal constitution does not prevent state legislatures from over-riding them (see discussion on the legal constraints on federalism, below).

Federalism and Individual Rights

The above discussion focuses on fiscal federalism. But there are also important federalism issues regarding problems of social policy. For example, should the states be permitted to decide issues regarding abortion, the right to die and same sex marriage? Many of these issues involve individual rights that are embodied in the national constitution. Recognition of some fundamental rights may be necessary to ensure popular acceptance of a federal system. For example, if federalism favors racists, and "if in the US one disapproves of racism, one should disapprove of federalism" (Riker 1964 at 155). It arguably follows that citizens' acceptance of devolving authority to the states can be increased by protecting some individual rights from erosion by the states. Also, central government recognition and enforcement of individual rights enables the mobility among jurisdictions that is essential to a federal system. On the other hand, national recognition of rights undercuts the competition and diversity advantages of a federal system. In some situations, including marriage, the federal system might reach an efficient compromise by permitting affected parties to contract for the law of a particular state (Buckley and Ribstein 2001).

Legal Constraints on Federalism

The federal constitution sets out the relationship between the central government and state governments. The constitution may not determine the actual relationship between government units, or may be significant mainly in representing a consensus rule with which the parties have expressed willingness to comply. This Part will focus on the US Constitution as an example of the types of rules that deal with the above problems.

The federal constitution must give the central government some power to regulate spillovers among the states. Thus, the "Commerce Clause" of the US Constitution, article I, § 8, clause 3, provides that Congress has the power "[t]o regulate Commerce ... among the several states". The problem is limiting the federal government's power to the spillover situation (Kitch 1980, Volume I, Chapter 5). For example, in *Gonzales v. Raich*, 125 S.Ct. 2195 (2005), the Supreme Court held that the Commerce Clause authorized regulation of intrastate growing of marijuana because the marijuana might enter interstate commerce, although the effect of its doing so was probably minimal.

If the federal government lawfully exercises power, its statutes must take precedence over state law to the extent they conflict. The "Supremacy Clause", US Constitution article VI, § 3, clause 2, so provides. The courts must then interpret the statutes to determine whether they permit avoidance by inconsistent state law. Again, the courts can significantly expand federal government power, consistent with the language of the Constitution, by broadly interpreting federal statutes.

The federal constitution may not only empower the central government to act, but also may forbid the states from engaging in regulation that has spillover effects. The Commerce Clause of the US Constitution has been held to imply a "negative" version that restricts state power to regulate interstate commerce (*Cooley v. Board of Wardens*, 53 U.S. (12 How.) 299 (1851)). The Supreme Court has endorsed a theory of the negative Commerce Clause that is consistent with the economic theory of federalism in holding that state statutes are unconstitutional if their costs fall mostly on interest groups outside the state while groups inside the state reap the benefits (Fischel 1987; Levmore 1983, Volume II, Chapter 1). However, the Court has applied this theory inconsistently, except to the extent that states clearly *discriminate* against interstate commerce. Challenges under the Full Faith and Credit Clause and Due Process Clauses of the U.S. Constitution to state regulation that effects spillovers also generally have been unsuccessful (Ribstein 1993).

Specific Applications

This Part discusses a few specific legal areas where federalism issues have been particularly important.

Corporate Law

Significant federalism issues are raised by regulation of the internal governance of corporations and other business firms. Particularly to the extent that these firms have owners throughout the country, it would be costly to apply different state laws to the owners who reside in each state. The owners may agree to apply the law of a single jurisdiction, as by incorporating there. Strict application of this rule would give corporations significant ability to choose from among all state laws without regard to their physical location, thereby providing an example of federalism under conditions of complete mobility. The US is a prominent example of a federal system that applies this "incorporation-state" choice of law rule.

On the other hand, many countries in Europe and elsewhere apply a "real situs" rule that applies the law of the corporation's home office. This rule provides less mobility because it is more costly for firms to change home office than their legal state of incorporation, this rule permits less mobility. However, the European Union appears increasingly willing to apply the incorporation rule (Case C-212/97, *Centros Ltd. v. Erhvervs-og Selskabsstyrelsen*, 1999 E.C.R. I-1459 (1999), 2 C.M.L.R 551 (1999); Case C-167/01, *Kamer van Koophandel en Fabrieken voor Amsterdam v. Inspire Art Ltd.*, September 30, 2003), 2003 E.C.R. I-10155 (2003)).

The choice among these rules depends significantly on the extent to which the incorporation rule permits states to export regulatory costs or the situs rule discourages efficient jurisdictional competition. In the US, the inventor of the term "race to the bottom" argued that the incorporation rule permitted the leading state of Delaware to export the costs of inefficiently lax regulation (Cary 1974). However, the stock markets promote a "race to the top" by capitalizing the costs of inefficient rules in the price of the shares (Winter 1977). Romano (1985,

Volume II, Chapter 5, 2005) further developed the theory by applying institutional economics to show how Delaware could entrench its lead in incorporations by offering an efficient legal system. Other writers have argued that defects in the market for incorporations enable Delaware to win the incorporation race despite adopting laws that favor corporate managers over share-holders (Bebchuk 1992, Volume II, Chapter 6; Bebchuk and Ferrell 1999; Bebchuk and Hamdani 2002). Macey and Miller (1987) argue that Delaware wins the race by offering laws superior to those in other jurisdictions, but that much of the advantage is dissipated in rents to lawyers who influence the lawmaking process. Ribstein (2004) also emphasizes lawyers' role in the lawmaking process. Finally, there is reason to believe that state competition has been influenced by the threat of federal regulation (Roe 2003).

Antitrust and Regulation

The antitrust laws illustrate the coordination problems associated with multiple jurisdictions in a federal system (Epstein and Greve 2004). Easterbrook (1983, Volume II, Chapter 7) hypothesized that the US Supreme Court's state action doctrine might foster regulatory competition by forcing firms that demand industry-specific anticompetitive legislation to accept the most stringent form of regulation. However, states may thwart this approach by externalizing regulatory costs.

Antitrust legislation also consists of rules that apply to firms generally (Sherman Act, EC Competition Laws). Large firms operating in multiple jurisdictions may be subject to multiple and inconsistent regulations, and therefore may have to decide between complying with the most stringent regulations and avoiding these jurisdictions altogether. A central government theoretically may address these coordination problems. However, central government regulation may simply be added to regulation at the state level (Epstein and Greve 2004; Inman and Rubinfeld 1997). Moreover, except in limited cases, there is little evidence of coordination between central governments.

The problem of regulation by overlapping jurisdictions is not limited to antitrust law. Similar issues arise in other contexts, including the regulation of contracts (Ribstein and Kobayashi 2002). In these contexts, such problems may be solved by enforcing contracts that specify the applicable law and jurisdiction.

Environmental Law

Environmental law seems to offer a good example of state coordination problems because of states' ability to export costs and incentives to free ride on regulation in other states. However, Revesz (2001, Volume II, Chapter 8) has shown that public choice theory does not necessarily predict that the state rather than central government regulation would under-protect the environment. Environmental interest groups may face greater free-rider problems than business groups in obtaining federal regulation, but may have more power at the state level. Moreover, states have incentives to protect the environment in order to compete for firms and citizens on the basis of environmental quality. There are data that US states effectively protect the environment and that citizens' heterogeneous preferences can account for regulatory differences among the states. There is also evidence that federal regulation often has inappropriately targeted intra- rather than interstate environmental issues (Adler 2005).

Property and Trust Law

There is a developing literature on the federalism of property laws. A study of the demise of the US "rule against perpetuities", which restricts the terms of trust instruments, shows an active, lawyer-driven state competition (Sitkoff and Schanzenback 2005). Bell and Parchamovsky (2005) propose enabling a corporate-type state competition for real property rules.

Welfare Reform

Welfare reform exemplifies the tradeoffs between providing a "laboratory" for development of policy and facilitating export of costs beyond state borders (Donahue 1997; Oates 1999; Brown and Oates 1987, Volume II, Chapter 10; Levine and Zimmerman 1999; Gramlich and Laren 1984). These tradeoffs are being tested in the US as welfare reform at the federal level has devolved responsibility to the states. Although states competed to be "welfare magnets" prior to federal welfare reform, the dynamic may have changed in recent years.

Takings

Federalism presents a potentially interesting perspective from which to examine state takings. Competition in the market for development may constrain state governments from engaging in exactions, thereby rendering less necessary constitutional protection (Been 1991). Resolution of this issue depends on the costs of mobility.

Marriage and Other Social Policy Issues

One of the most important modern federalism issues is the extent to which federal constitutional and statutory law is appropriate to protect individual rights from erosion by the states. As discussed above, protection of such rights may be important in ensuring mobility within a federal system and citizens' willingness to accept devolution to the states. On the other hand, devolution to the "laboratory" of the states may be the best way both to develop social policy and to satisfy heterogeneous preferences. This may be particularly true for same sex marriage, where many of the relevant issues are in the nature of contract enforcement and therefore arguably can be left to resolution by the parties to the relationship (Buckley and Ribstein 2001). There are also contract-type issues with regard to the right to die, particularly in regard to promulgation of "durable powers of attorney" that leave medical instructions when one becomes incompetent. Abortion involves a clearer conflict between state policy and individual preferences. Nevertheless, there are questions as to whether the right to an abortion is the sort of fundamental right that should be protected at the federal level, or instead is an issue that can be devolved to the state governments.

The difficulty of these issues is indicated by the fact that federal systems have adopted differing responses to questions of allocation of authority. For example, while the Supreme Court of Canada has clearly recognized a constitutional right to same sex marriage (Klarman 2005), it is unclear whether the Supreme Court of the US would go that far (*Lawrence v. Texas*, 539 U.S. 558 (2003)).

Law and Development

A critical modern federalism issue is the extent to which federalism should be promoted for developing countries. The success of federalism in developed countries in encouraging markets and property rights suggests that this approach would also work in developing countries. On the other hand, the Tiebout conditions arguably cannot be met in many such countries because of citizens' lack of mobility resulting from, among other factors, the presence of community-specific public goods, cultural and language differences and strong norms limiting acceptance of outsiders. Also, state governments often have weak information, accounting and account-ability and low-quality public bureaucrats as compared with the central government (Bardhan 2002; Oates 1999 at 1144; Martin and Lewis 1956; Shah 1998).

Criminal Law

Criminal law also presents federalism issues. A voluminous literature has examined the grow-ing application of new federal criminal laws to areas traditionally enforced by the states. Increased federal criminal enforcement may be justified by an overall increase in interstate crime. On the other hand, critics of the increased federalization of the criminal law point out the costs associated with this federal expansion. These costs include interfering with the proc-ess of experimentation that occurs as individual states try different approaches to controlling crime, and over-riding policy choices made by individual states, especially regarding a state's choices on capital punishment. This literature generally assumes that federal enforcement serves to increase the level of enforcement above that provided by the states. This is achieved through an increase in law enforcement resources and by the application of higher criminal sanctions under federal law. However, in the absence of federal coordination, the individual states may have an incentive to adopt criminal laws that are too harsh in order to divert crime to neighbor-ing states (Epstein 1996). Thus, given the states' incentive to externalize crime to other states, the proper role of the federal government may be to preempt overly harsh state criminal laws (Teichman 2005, Volume II, Chapter 11).

Conclusion

Federalism will continue to be important as rapidly developing technologies and business practices raise questions about the appropriate locus of taxation and regulation. Some govern-ment functions inevitably will continue to be provided at the local level, while others need to be provided by the central government. A form of government that both promotes local serv-ices and enforcement of property rights and deals with coordination problems has obvious benefits. The problem lies in devising mechanisms and structures that maintain the appropriate balance between central and local government power.

Bibliography

Adler, Jonathan (2005), 'Jurisdictional Mismatch in Environmental Federalism', *NYU Environmental Law Journal*, 14, pp. 130–78.

Anderson, Gary M. and Robert D. Tollison (1988), 'Legislative Monopoly and the Size of Government', *Southern Economic Journal*, 54, pp. 529–45.

Bardhan, Pranab (2002), 'Decentralization of Governance and Development', *Journal of Economic Perspectives*, 16, pp. 185–205.

Bebchuk, Lucian A. and Allen Ferrell (1999), 'Federalism and Corporate Law: The Race to Protect Managers from Takeovers', *Columbia Law Review*, 99, pp. 1168–99.

Bebchuk, Lucian A. and Assaf Hamdani (2002), 'Vigorous Race or Leisurely Walk: Reconsidering Competition Over Corporate Charters', *Yale Law Journal*, 112, pp. 553–615.

Been, Vicki (1991), 'Exit as a Constraint on Land Use Extractions: Rethinking the Unconstitutional Conditions Doctrine', *Columbia Law Review*, 91, pp. 473–545.

Bell, Abraham and Gideon Parchamovsky (2005), 'Of Property and Federalism', U. Penn. Working Paper.

Brennan, Geoffrey and Jonathan J. Pincus (1996), 'A Minimalist Model of Federal Grants and Flypaper Effects', *Journal of Public Economics*, 61, pp. 229–46.

Breton, Albert (1987), 'Mobility and Federalism', *University of Toronto Law Journal*, 37, pp. 318–26.

Brueckner, Jan (1982), 'A Test for the Allocative Efficiency in the Local Public Sector', *Journal of Public Economics*, 19, pp. 311–31.

Buchanan, James M. (1995), 'Federalism as an Ideal Political Order and an Objective for Constitutional Reform', *Publius*, 25, pp. 19–27.

Buchanan, James M. (1952), 'Federal Grants and Resource Allocation', *Journal of Political Economy*, 60, pp. 208–21.

Buchanan, James M. (1950), 'Federalism and Fiscal Equity', *American Economic Review*, 40, pp. 583–99.

Buchanan, James M. and Charles J. Goetz (1972), 'Efficiency Limits of Fiscal Mobility: An Assessment of the Tiebout Model', *Journal of Public Economics*, 1, pp. 25–43.

Buchanan, James M. and Gordon Tullock (1962), *The Calculus of Consent*, U. Mich. Press.

Buckley, Frank H. and Larry E. Ribstein (2001), 'Calling a Truce in the Marriage Wars', *University of Illinois Law Review*, 2001, pp. 561–610

Cary, William L. (1974), 'Federalism and Corporate Law: Reflections Upon Delaware', *Yale Law Journal*, 83, pp. 663–705.

De Figueiredo, Rui J.P. and Barry R. Weingast (2005), 'Self-Enforcing Federalism', *Journal of Law, Economics, and Organization*, 21, pp. 103–35.

Elliot, E. Donald, Bruce A. Ackerman and John C. Millian (1985), 'Toward a Theory of Statutory Evolution: The Federalization of Environmental Law', *Journal of Law, Economics, and Organization*, 1, pp. 313–40.

Epple, Dennis, Alan Zelenitz and Michael Visscher (1978), 'A Search for Testable Implications of the Tiebout Hypothesis', *Journal of Political Economy*, 86, pp. 405–25.

Epstein, Richard A. (1996), 'Constitutional Faith and the Commerce Clause', *Notre Dame Law Review*, 71, pp. 167–91.

Epstein, Richard A. and Michael S. Greve (2004), *Competition Laws in Conflict: Antitrust Jurisdiction in the Global Economy*, AEI Press.

Farber, Daniel A. (1997), 'Environmental Federalism in a Global Economy', *Virginia Law Review*, 83, pp. 1283–319.

Fischel, Daniel R. (1987), 'From MITE to CTS: State Antitakeover Statues, the Williams Act, and the Commerce Clause, and Insider Trading', *Supreme Court Review*, 1987, pp. 47–95.

Fischel, William A. (1992), 'Property Taxation and the Tiebout Model: Evidence for the Benefit View from Zoning', *Journal of Economic Literature*, 30, pp. 171–7.

Fisher, R. (1982), 'Income and Grant Effects on Local Expenditures: The Flypaper Effect and Other Difficulties', *Journal of Urban Economics*, 12, pp. 324–45.

Flatters, Frank, Vernon Henderson and Peter Mieszkowski (1974), 'Public Goods, Efficiency, and Regional Fiscal Equalization', *Journal of Public Economics*, 3, pp. 99–112.

Gordon, Roger H. (1983), 'An Optimal Taxation Approach to Fiscal Federalism', *Quarterly Journal of Economics*, 98, pp. 567–86.

Gramlich, Edward M. and Deborah Laren (1984), 'Migration and Income Distribution Responsibilities', *Journal of Human Resources*, 9, pp. 489–511.

Gramlich, Edward M., Henry J. Aaron and Michael C. Lovell (1982), 'An Econometric Examination of the New Federalism', *Brookings Papers on Economic Activity*, 2, pp. 327–70.

Grossman, Phillip J. (1989), 'Federalism and the Size of Government', *Southern Economic Journal*, 55, pp. 580–93.

Hamilton, Bruce W. (1976), 'The Effects of Property Taxes and Local Public Spending on Property Values: A Theoretical Comment', *Journal of Political Economy*, 84, pp. 647–50.

Hayek, Friedrich (1948), 'The Economic Conditions of Interstate Federalism', reprinted in *Individual and Economic Order*, pp. 255–72, University of Chicago Press.

Hayek, Friedrich (1945), 'The Use of Knowledge In Society', *American Economic Review*, 35, pp. 519–30.

Hines, J. and R. Thaler (1995), 'The Flypaper Effect', *Journal of Economic Perspectives*, 9, pp. 217–26.

Hirschman, Albert O. (1970), *Exit, Voice, and Loyalty: Responses to Decline in Firms, Organizations, and States*, Harvard University Press.

Hochman, Oded, David Pines and Jacques-Francios Thisse (1995), 'On the Optimal Structure of Local Governments', *American Economic Review*, 85, pp. 1224–40.

Inman, Robert P. (1988), 'Federal Assistance and Local Services in the United States: The Evolution of a New Federalist Fiscal Order', in Harvey Rosen ed., *Fiscal Federalism: Quantitative Studies*, pp. 33–74, Chicago: University of Chicago Press.

Inman, Robert P. and Daniel L. Rubinfeld (1979), 'The Judicial Pursuit of Local Fiscal Equity', *Harvard Law Review*, 92, pp. 1663–750.

Inman, Robert P. and Michael A. Fitts (1990), 'Political Institutions and Fiscal Policy: Evidence from the U.S. Historical Record', *Journal of Law, Economics, and Organization*, 6, pp. 79–132.

Keen, Michael J., and Christos Kotsogiannis (2002), 'Does Federalism Lead to Excessively High Taxes?', *American Economic Review*, 92, pp. 363–70.

Klarman, Michael J. (2005), 'Brown and Lawrence (and Goodridge)', *Michigan Law Review*, 104, pp. 431–89.

Kollman, Ken, John H. Miller and Scott E. Page (1997), 'Political Institutions and Sorting in a Tiebout Model', *American Economic Review*, 87, pp. 977–92.

Krelove, R. (1992), 'Efficient Tax Exportation', *Canadian Journal of Economics*, 25, pp. 145–55.

Levine, Phillip B. and David Zimmerman (1999), 'An Empirical Analysis of the Welfare Magnet Debate using the NLSY', *Journal of Population Economics*, 12, pp. 391–409.

Macey, Jonathan R. and Geoffrey P. Miller (1987), 'Toward an Interest Group Theory of Delaware Corporate Law', *Texas Law Review*, 65, 469–523.

Martin, Alison W. and Arthur Lewis (1956), 'Patterns of Public Revenue and Expenditure', *Manchester School of Economics Social Studies*, 24, pp. 203–44.

McKinnon, Ronald I. (1997), 'The Logic of Market-Preserving Federalism', *Virginia Law Review*, 83, pp. 1573–80.

Meyers, G. (1990), 'Optimality, Free Mobility, and the Regional Authority in a Federation', *Journal of Public Economics*, 43, pp. 107–21.

Muller, Dennis C. (1997), 'Federalist Government and Trumps', *Virginia Law Review*, 83, pp. 1419–32.

Musgrave, Richard A. (1997), 'Devolution, Grants, and Fiscal Competition', *Journal of Economic Perspectives*, 11, pp. 65–72.

Musgrave, Richard A. (1959), *The Theory of Public Finance*, McGraw-Hill.

Oates, Wallace E. (1999), 'An Essay on Fiscal Federalism', *Journal of Economic Literature*, 37, pp. 1120–49.

Oates, Wallace E. (1985), 'Searching for Leviathan: An Empirical Study', *American Economic Review*, 75, pp. 748–57.

Oates, Wallace E. (1972), *Fiscal Federalism*, Harcourt Brace Jovanovich.

Oates, Wallace E. (1969), 'The Effects of Property Taxes and Local Public Spending on Property Values: An Empirical Study of Tax Capitalization and the Tiebout Hypothesis', *Journal of Political Economy*, 77, pp. 957–71.

Oates, Wallace E. (1968), 'A Theory of Public Finance in a Federal System', *Canadian Journal of Economics*, 1, pp. 37–54.

Oates, Wallace E. and Robert M. Schwab (1991), 'The Allocative and Distributive Implications of Local Fiscal Competition', in Daphne Kenyon and J.K. Kincaid, eds. *Competition Among States and Local Governments: Efficiency and Equity in American Federalism*, pp. 127–45, Urban Institute.

Oates, Wallace E. and Robert M. Schwab (1988), 'Economic Competition Among Jurisdictions: Efficiency Enhancing or Distortion Inducing?', *Journal of Public Economics*, 35, pp. 333–54.

Olson, Mancur (1969), 'The Principle of "Fiscal Equivalence": The Division of Responsibility Among Different Levels of Government', *American Economic Review*, 59, pp. 479–87.

O'Hara, Erin and Larry E. Ribstein (2000), 'From Politics to Efficiency in Choice of Law', *University of Chicago Law Review*, 67, pp. 1151–232.

Olson, Mancur (1986), 'Toward A More General Theory of Governmental Structure', *American Economic Review*, 76, pp. 120–5.

Parikh, Sunita and Barry R. Weingast (1997), 'A Comparative Theory of Federalism: India', *Virginia Law Review*, 83, pp. 1593–615.

Pauly, Mark V. (1973), 'Income Redistribution as a Local Public Good', 2 *Journal of Public Economics*, pp. 35–58.

Persson, Torsten and Guido Tabellini (2000), *Political Economics*, MIT Press.

Persson, Torsten and Guido Tabellini (1996a), 'Federal Fiscal Constitutions: Risk Sharing and Moral Hazard', *Econometrica*, 64, pp. 623–46.

Persson, Torsten and Guido Tabellini (1996b), 'Federal Fiscal Constitutions: Risk Sharing and Redistribution', *Journal of Political Economy*, 104, pp. 979–1009.

Qian, Yingyi and Barry R. Weingast (1997), 'Federalism as a Commitment to Preserving Market Incentives', *The Journal of Economic Perpectives*, 11, pp. 83–92.

Qian, Yingyi and Gerard Roland (1998), 'Federalism and the Soft Budget Constraint', *American Economic Review*, 88, pp. 1143–62.

Ribstein, Larry E. (2004), 'Lawyers as Lawmakers: A Theory of Lawyer Licensing', *Missouri Law Review*, 69, pp. 299–364.

Ribstein, Larry E. (2003), 'From Efficiency to Politics in Contractual Choice of Law', *Georgia Law Review*, 37, pp. 363–471.

Ribstein, Larry E. (1998), 'Federalism and Insider Trading', *Supreme Court Economic Review*, 6, pp. 123–71.

Ribstein, Larry E. (1993), 'Choosing Law By Contract', *Journal of Corporation Law*, 18, pp. 245–300.

Ribstein, Larry E. and Bruce H. Kobayashi (2002), 'State Regulation of Electronic Commerce', *Emory Law Journal*, 51, pp. 1–82.

Ribstein, Larry E. and Bruce H. Kobayashi (1996), 'An Economic Analysis of Uniform State Laws', *Journal of Legal Studies*, 25, pp. 131–99.

Rodden, Jonathan and Susan Rose-Ackerman (1997), 'Does Federalism Preserve Markets?', *Virginia Law Review*, 83, pp. 1521–72.

Roe, Mark (2003), 'Delaware's Competition', *Harvard Law Review*, 117, pp. 588–646.

Romano, Roberta (2005), 'The States as Laboratory: Legal Innovation and State Competition for Corporate Charters', *Yale University IFC Working Paper* No. 05-08.

Romano, Roberta (1985), 'Law as Product: Some Pieces of the Incorporation Puzzle', *Journal of Law, Economics and Organization*, 1, pp. 225–83.

Rose-Ackerman, Susan (1983), 'Cooperative Federalism and Co-optation', *Yale Law Journal*, 92, pp. 1344–8.

Rose-Ackerman, Susan (1980), 'Risk Taking and Re-election: Does Federalism Promote Innovation?', *Journal of Legal Studies*, 9, pp. 593–616.

Rubinfeld, Daniel L. (1997), 'On Federalism and Economic Development', *Virginia Law Review*, 83, pp 1581–92.

Samuelson, Paul (1954), 'The Pure Theory of Public Expenditure', *Review of Economics and Statistics*, 36, pp. 387–9.

Sandler, Todd and A.J. Culyer (1982), 'Joint Products and Multijurisdictional Spillovers', *Quarterly Journal of Economics*, 97, pp. 707–16.

Shah, Anwar (1988), 'Fostering Fiscally Responsive and Accountable Governance: Lessons from Decentralization', in *Evaluation and Development: The Institutional Dimension*, Robert Picciotto and Eduardo Wiesner, eds., pp. 83–96, World Bank.

Sitkoff, Robert H. and Max Schanzenbach (2005), 'Jurisdictional Competition for Trust Funds: An Empirical Analysis of Perpetuities and Taxes', *Yale Law Journal*, 115, pp. 356–436.

Steinberg, Richard (1987), 'Voluntary Donations and Public Expenditures in a Federalist System', *American Economic Review*, 77, pp. 24–36.

Stewart, Richard B. (1985), 'Federalism and Rights', *Georgia Law Review*, 19, pp. 917–80.

Strumpf, Koleman S. (2002), 'Does Government Decentralization Increase Policy Innovation?', *Journal of Public Economic Theory*, 4, pp. 207–41.

Winter, Ralph K., Jr. (1977), 'State Law, Shareholder Protection, and the Theory of the Corporation', *Journal of Legal Studies*, 6, pp. 251–9.

Wooders, M. (1980), 'The Tiebout Hypothesis: Near Optimality in Local Public Good Economics', *Econometrica*, 48, pp. 1467–85.

Zax, Jeffrey S. (1989), 'Is There a Leviathan in Your Neighborhood?', *American Economic Review*, 79, pp. 560–7.

Part I
Basics

A
Multiple Jurisdictions Are a Solution to the Public Good Problem

[1]

A PURE THEORY OF LOCAL EXPENDITURES[1]

CHARLES M. TIEBOUT

Northwestern University

ONE of the most important recent developments in the area of "applied economic theory" has been the work of Musgrave and Samuelson in public finance theory.[2] The two writers agree on what is probably the major point under investigation, namely, that no "market type" solution exists to determine the level of expenditures on public goods. Seemingly, we are faced with the problem of having a rather large portion of our national income allocated in a "non-optimal" way when compared with the private sector.

This discussion will show that the Musgrave-Samuelson analysis, which is valid for federal expenditures, need not apply to local expenditures. The plan of the discussion is first to restate the assumptions made by Musgrave and Samuelson and the central problems with which they deal. After looking at a key difference between the federal versus local cases, I shall present a simple model. This model yields a solution for the level of expenditures for local public goods which reflects the preferences of the population more adequately than they can be reflected at the national level. The assumptions of the model will then be relaxed to see what implications are involved. Finally, policy considerations will be discussed.

THE THEORETICAL ISSUE

Samuelson has defined public goods as "*collective consumption goods* $(X_n + 1, \ldots, X_n + n)$ which all enjoy in common in the sense that each individual's consumption of such a good leads to no subtraction from any other individual's consumption of that good, so that $X_n + j = X_n^i + j$ simultaneously for each and every ith individual and each collective good."[3] While definitions are a matter of choice, it is worth noting that "consumption" has a much broader meaning here than in the usual sense of the term. Not only does it imply that the act of consumption by one person does not diminish the opportunities for consumption by another but it also allows this consumption to be in another form. For example, while the residents of a new government housing project are made better off, benefits also accrue to other residents of the community in the form of the external economies of slum clearance.[4] Thus many goods that appear to lack the attributes of public goods may

[1] I am grateful for the comments of my colleagues Karl de Schweinitz, Robert Eisner, and Robert Strotz, and those of Martin Bailey, of the University of Chicago.

[2] Richard A. Musgrave, "The Voluntary Exchange Theory of Public Economy," *Quarterly Journal of Economics*, LII (February, 1939), 213–17; "A Multiple Theory of the Budget," paper read at the Econometric Society annual meeting (December, 1955); and his forthcoming book, *The Theory of Public Economy;* Paul A. Samuelson, "The Pure Theory of Public Expenditures," *Review of Economics and Statistics*, XXXVI, No. 4 (November, 1954), 387–89, and "Diagrammatic Exposition of a Pure Theory of Public Expenditures," *ibid.*, XXXVII, No. 4 (November, 1955), 350–56.

[3] "The Pure Theory . . . ," *op. cit.*, p. 387.

[4] Samuelson allows for this when he states that "one man's circus may be another man's poison," referring, of course, to public goods ("Diagrammatic Exposition . . . ," *op. cit.*, p. 351).

A PURE THEORY OF LOCAL EXPENDITURES   417

properly be considered public if consumption is defined to include these external economies.[5]

A definition alternative to Samuelson's might be simply that a public good is one which should be produced, but for which there is no feasible method of charging the consumers. This is less elegant, but has the advantage that it allows for the objections of Enke and Margolis.[6] This definition, unfortunately, does not remove any of the problems faced by Musgrave and Samuelson.

The core problem with which both Musgrave and Samuelson deal concerns

the mechanism by which consumer-voters register their preferences for public goods. The consumer is, in a sense, surrounded by a government whose objective it is to ascertain his wants for public goods and tax him accordingly. To use Alchian's term, the government's revenue-expenditure pattern for goods and services is expected to "adapt to" consumers' preferences.[7] Both Musgrave and Samuelson have shown that, in the vertically additive nature of voluntary demand curves, this problem has only a conceptual solution. If all consumer-voters could somehow be forced to reveal their true preferences for public goods, then the amount of such goods to be produced and the appropriate benefits tax could be determined.[8] As things now stand, there is no mechanism to force the consumer-voter to state his true preferences; in fact, the "rational" consumer will understate his preferences and hope to enjoy the goods while avoiding the tax.

The current method of solving this problem operates, unsatisfactorily, through the political mechanism. The expenditure wants of a "typical voter" are somehow pictured. This objective on the expenditure side is then combined with an ability-to-pay principle on the revenue side, giving us our current budget. Yet in terms of a satisfactory theory of public finance, it would be desirable (1) to force the voter to reveal his preferences; (2) to be able to satisfy them in

[5] There seems to be a problem connected with the external-economies aspect of public goods. Surely a radio broadcast, like national defense, has the attribute that A's enjoyment leaves B no worse off; yet this does not imply that broadcasting should, in a normative sense, be a public good (the arbitrary manner in which the level of radio programs is determined aside). The difference between defense and broadcasting is subtle but important. In both cases there is a problem of determining the optimal level of outputs and the corresponding level of benefits taxes. In the broadcasting case, however, A may be quite willing to pay more taxes than B, even if both have the same "ability to pay" (assuming that the benefits are determinate). Defense is another question. Here A is not content that B should pay less. A makes the *social judgment* that B's preference *should* be the same. A's preference, expressed as an annual defense expenditure such as $42.7 billion and representing the majority view, thus determines the level of defense. Here the A's may feel that the B's *should pay* the same amount of benefits tax.

If it is argued that this case is typical of public goods, then, once the level is somehow set, the voluntary exchange approach and the benefit theory associated with it do not make sense. If the preceding analysis is correct, we are now back in the area of equity in terms of ability to pay.

[6] They argue that, for most of the goods supplied by governments, increased use by some consumer-voters leaves less available for other consumer-voters. Crowded highways and schools, as contrasted with national defense, may be cited as examples (see Stephen Enke, "More on the Misuse of Mathematics in Economics: A Rejoinder," *Review of Economics and Statistics*, XXXVII [May, 1955], 131–33; and Julius Margolis, "A Comment on the Pure Theory of Public Expenditure," *Review of Economics and Statistics*, XXXVII [November, 1955], 247–49).

[7] Armen A. Alchian, "Uncertainty, Evolution, and Economic Theory," *Journal of Political Economy*, LVIII (June, 1950), 211–21.

[8] The term "benefits tax" is used in contrast to the concept of taxation based on the "ability to pay," which really reduces to a notion that there is some "proper" distribution of income. Conceptually, this issue is separate from the problem of providing public goods and services (see Musgrave, "A Multiple Theory . . . ," *op. cit.*).

the same sense that a private goods market does; and (3) to tax him accordingly. The question arises whether there is any set of social institutions by which this goal can be approximated.

LOCAL EXPENDITURES

Musgrave and Samuelson implicitly assume that expenditures are handled at the central government level. However, the provision of such governmental services as police and fire protection, education, hospitals, and courts does not necessarily involve federal activity.[9] Many of these goods are provided by local governments. It is worthwhile to look briefly at the magnitude of these expenditures.[10]

Historically, local expenditures have exceeded those of the federal government. The thirties were the first peacetime years in which federal expenditures began to pull away from local expenditures. Even during the fiscal year 1954, federal expenditures on *goods and services exclusive of defense* amounted only to some 15 billions of dollars, while local expenditures during this same period amounted to some 17 billions of dollars. There is no need to quibble over which comparisons are relevant. The important point is that the often-neglected local expenditures are significant and, when viewed in terms of expenditures on goods and services only, take on even more significance. Hence an important question arises whether at this level of govern-

ment any mechanism operates to insure that expenditures on these public goods approximate the proper level.

Consider for a moment the case of the city resident about to move to the suburbs. What variables will influence his choice of a municipality? If he has children, a high level of expenditures on schools may be important. Another person may prefer a community with a municipal golf course. The availability and quality of such facilities and services as beaches, parks, police protection, roads, and parking facilities will enter into the decision-making process. Of course, non-economic variables will also be considered, but this is of no concern at this point.

The consumer-voter may be viewed as picking that community which best satisfies his preference pattern for public goods. This is a major difference between central and local provision of public goods. At the central level the preferences of the consumer-voter are given, and the government tries to adjust to the pattern of these preferences, whereas at the local level various governments have their revenue and expenditure patterns more or less set.[11] Given these revenue and expenditure patterns, the consumer-voter moves to that community whose local government best satisfies his set of preferences. The greater the number of communities and the greater the variance among them, the closer the consumer will come to fully realizing his preference position.[12]

---

[9] The discussion that follows applies to local governments. It will be apparent as the argument proceeds that it also applies, with less force, to state governments.

[10] A question does arise as to just what are the proper expenditures to consider. Following Musgrave, I shall consider only expenditures on goods or services (his Branch I expenditures). Thus interest on the federal debt is not included. At the local level interest payments might be included, since they are considered payments for services currently used, such as those provided by roads and schools.

[11] This is an assumption about reality. In the extreme model that follows the patterns are assumed to be absolutely fixed.

[12] This is also true of many non-economic variables. Not only is the consumer-voter concerned with economic patterns, but he desires, for example, to associate with "nice" people. Again, the greater the number of communities, the closer he will come to satisfying his total preference function, which includes non-economic variables.

A PURE THEORY OF LOCAL EXPENDITURES   419

A LOCAL GOVERNMENT MODEL

The implications of the preceding argument may be shown by postulating an extreme model. Here the following assumptions are made:

1. Consumer-voters are fully mobile and will move to that community where their preference patterns, which are set, are best satisfied.

2. Consumer-voters are assumed to have full knowledge of differences among revenue and expenditure patterns and to react to these differences.

3. There are a large number of communities in which the consumer-voters may choose to live.

4. Restrictions due to employment opportunities are not considered. It may be assumed that all persons are living on dividend income.

5. The public services supplied exhibit no external economies or diseconomies between communities.

Assumptions 6 and 7 to follow are less familiar and require brief explanations:

6. For every pattern of community services set by, say, a city manager who follows the preferences of the older residents of the community, there is an optimal community size. This optimum is defined in terms of the number of residents for which this bundle of services can be produced at the lowest average cost. This, of course, is closely analogous to the low point of a firm's average cost curve. Such a cost function implies that some factor or resource is fixed. If this were not so, there would be no logical reason to limit community size, given the preference patterns. In the same sense that the average cost curve has a minimum for one firm but can be reproduced by another there is seemingly no reason why a duplicate community cannot exist. The assumption that some factor is fixed

explains why it is not possible for the community in question to double its size by growth. The factor may be the limited land area of a suburban community, combined with a set of zoning laws against apartment buildings. It may be the local beach, whose capacity is limited. Anything of this nature will provide a restraint.

In order to see how this restraint works, let us consider the beach problem. Suppose the preference patterns of the community are such that the optimum size population is 13,000. Within this set of preferences there is a certain demand per family for beach space. This demand is such that at 13,000 population a 500-yard beach is required. If the actual length of the beach is, say, 600 yards, then it is not possible to realize this preference pattern with twice the optimum population, since there would be too little beach space by 400 yards.

The assumption of a fixed factor is necessary, as will be shown later, in order to get a determinate number of communities. It also has the advantage of introducing a realistic restraint into the model.

7. The last assumption is that communities below the optimum size seek to attract new residents to lower average costs. Those above optimum size do just the opposite. Those at an optimum try to keep their populations constant.

This assumption needs to be amplified. Clearly, communities below the optimum size, through chambers of commerce or other agencies, seek to attract new residents. This is best exemplified by the housing developments in some suburban areas, such as Park Forest in the Chicago area and Levittown in the New York area, which need to reach an optimum size. The same is true of communities that try to attract manufacturing industries by setting up certain facilities and getting an optimum number of firms to move into the industrially zoned area.

The case of the city that is too large and tries to get rid of residents is more difficult to imagine. No alderman in his right political mind would ever admit that the city is too big. Nevertheless, economic forces are at work to push people out of it. Every resident who moves to the suburbs to find better schools, more parks, and so forth, is reacting, in part, against the pattern the city has to offer.

The case of the community which is at the optimum size and tries to remain so is not hard to visualize. Again proper zoning laws, implicit agreements among realtors, and the like are sufficient to keep the population stable.

Except when this system is in equilibrium, there will be a subset of consumer-voters who are discontented with the patterns of their community. Another set will be satisfied. Given the assumption about mobility and the other assumptions listed previously, movement will take place out of the communities of greater than optimal size into the communities of less than optimal size. The consumer-voter moves to the community that satisfies his preference pattern.

The act of moving or failing to move is crucial. Moving or failing to move replaces the usual market test of willingness to buy a good and reveals the consumer-voter's demand for public goods. Thus each locality has a revenue and expenditure pattern that reflects the desires of its residents. The next step is to see what this implies for the allocation of public goods at the local level.

Each city manager now has a certain demand for n local public goods. In supplying these goods, he and $m - 1$ other city managers may be considered as go-

ing to a national market and bidding for the appropriate units of service of each kind: so many units of police for the ith community; twice that number for the jth community; and so on. The demand on the public goods market for each of the n commodities will be the sum of the demands of the m communities. In the limit, as shown in a less realistic model to be developed later, this total demand will approximate the demand that represents the true preferences of the consumer-voters—that is, the demand they would reveal, if they were forced, somehow, to state their true preferences.[13] In this model there is no attempt on the part of local governments to "adapt to" the preferences of consumer-voters. Instead, those local governments that attract the optimum number of residents may be viewed as being "adopted by" the economic system.[14]

A COMPARISON MODEL

It is interesting to contrast the results of the preceding model with those of an even more severe model in order to see how these results differ from the normal market result. It is convenient to look at this severe model by developing its private-market counterpart. First assume that there are no public goods, only private ones. The preferences for these goods can be expressed as one of n patterns. Let a law be passed that all persons living in any one of the communities shall spend their money in the particular pattern described for that community by law. Given our earlier assumptions 1 through 5, it follows that, if the consum-

---

[13] The word "approximate" is used in recognition of the limitations of this model, and of the more severe model to be developed shortly, with respect to the cost of mobility. This issue will be discussed later.

[14] See Alchian, *op. cit.*

ers move to the community whose law happens to fit their preference pattern, they will be at their optimum. The *n* communities, in turn, will then send their buyers to market to purchase the goods for the consumer-voters in their community. Since this is simply a lumping together of all similar tastes for the purpose of making joint purchases, the allocation of resources will be the same as it would be if normal market forces operated. This conceptual experiment is the equivalent of substituting the city manager for the broker or middleman.

Now turn the argument around and consider only public goods. Assume with Musgrave that the costs of additional services are constant.[15] Further, assume that a doubling of the population means doubling the amount of services required. Let the number of communities be infinite and let each announce a different pattern of expenditures on public goods. Define an empty community as one that fails to satisfy anybody's preference pattern. Given these assumptions, including the earlier assumptions 1 through 5, the consumer-voters will move to that community which *exactly* satisfies their preferences. This must be true, since a one-person community is allowed. The sum of the demands of the *n* communities reflects the demand for local public services. In this model the demand is exactly the same as it would be if it were determined by normal market forces.

However, this severe model does not make much sense. The number of communities is indeterminate. There is no reason why the number of communities will not be equal to the population, since each voter can find the one that exactly fits his preferences. Unless some sociological variable is introduced, this may

[15] Musgrave, "Voluntary Exchange . . . ," *op. cit.*

reduce the solution of the problem of allocating public goods to the trite one of making each person his own municipal government. Hence this model is not even a first approximation of reality. It is presented to show the assumptions needed in a model of local government expenditures, which yields the same optimal allocation that a private market would.

THE LOCAL GOVERNMENT MODEL RE-EXAMINED

The first model, described by the first five assumptions together with assumptions 6 and 7, falls short of this optimum. An example will serve to show why this is the case.

Let us return to the community with the 500-yard beach. By assumption, its optimum population was set at 13,000, given its preference patterns. Suppose that some people in addition to the optimal 13,000 would choose this community if it were available. Since they cannot move into this area, they must accept the next best substitute.[16] If a perfect substitute is found, no problem exists. If one is not found, then the failure to reach the optimal preference position and the substitution of a lower position becomes a matter of degree. In so far as there are a number of communities with similar revenue and expenditure patterns, the solution will approximate the ideal "market" solution.

Two related points need to be mentioned to show the allocative results of this model: (1) changes in the costs of one of the public services will cause changes in the quantity produced; (2) the

[16] In the constant cost model with an infinite number of communities this problem does not arise, since the number of beaches can be doubled or a person can find another community that is a duplicate of his now filled first choice.

CHARLES M. TIEBOUT

costs of moving from community to community should be recognized. Both points can be illustrated in one example.

Suppose lifeguards throughout the country organize and succeed in raising their wages. Total taxes in communities with beaches will rise. Now residents who are largely indifferent to beaches will be forced to make a decision. Is the saving of this added tax worth the cost of moving to a community with little or no beach? Obviously, this decision depends on many factors, among which the availability of and proximity to a suitable substitute community is important. If enough people leave communities with beaches and move to communities without beaches, the total amount of lifeguard services used will fall. These models then, unlike their private-market counterpart, have mobility as a cost of registering demand. The higher this cost, *ceteris paribus*, the less optimal the allocation of resources.

This distinction should not be blown out of proportion. Actually, the cost of registering demand comes through the introduction of space into the economy. Yet space affects the allocation not only of resources supplied by local governments but of those supplied by the private market as well. Every time available resources or production techniques change, a new location becomes optimal for the firm. Indeed, the very concept of the shopping trip shows that the consumer does pay a cost to register his demand for private goods. In fact, Koopmans has stated that the nature of the assignment problem is such that in a space economy with transport costs there is *no* general equilibrium solution as set by market forces.[17]

[17] Tjalling Koopmans, "Mathematical Groundwork of Economic Optimization Theories," paper read at the annual meeting of the Econometric Society (December, 1954).

Thus the problems stated by this model are not unique; they have their counterpart in the private market. We are maximizing within the framework of the resources available. If production functions show constant returns to scale with generally diminishing factor returns, and if indifference curves are regularly convex, an optimal solution is possible. On the production side it is assumed that communities are forced to keep production costs at a minimum either through the efficiency of city managers or through competition from other communities.[18] Given this, on the demand side we may note with Samuelson that "each individual, in seeking as a competitive buyer to get to the highest level of indifference subject to given prices and *tax*, would be led as if by an Invisible Hand to the grand solution of the social maximum position."[19] Just as the consumer may be visualized as walking to a private market place to buy his goods, the prices of which are set, we place him in the position of walking to a community where the prices (taxes) of community services are set. Both trips take the consumer to market. There is no way in which the consumer can avoid revealing his preferences in a spatial economy. Spatial mobility provides the local public-goods counterpart to the private market's shopping trip.

[18] In this model and in reality, the city manager or elected official who is not able to keep his costs (taxes) low compared with those of similar communities will find himself out of a job. As an institutional observation, it may well be that city managers are under greater pressure to minimize costs than their private-market counterparts—firm managers. This follows from (1) the reluctance of the public to pay taxes and, what may be more important, (2) the fact that the costs of competitors—other communities—are a matter of public record and may easily be compared.

[19] "The Pure Theory . . . ," *op. cit.*, p. 388. (Italics mine.)

A PURE THEORY OF LOCAL EXPENDITURES   423

EXTERNAL ECONOMIES AND MOBILITY

Relaxing assumption 5 has some interesting implications. There are obvious external economies and diseconomies between communities. My community is better off if its neighbor sprays trees to prevent Dutch elm disease. On the other hand, my community is worse off if the neighboring community has inadequate law enforcement.

In cases in which the external economies and diseconomies are of sufficient importance, some form of integration may be indicated.[20] Not all aspects of law enforcement are adequately handled at the local level. The function of the sheriff, state police, and the FBI—as contrasted with the local police—may be cited as resulting from a need for integration. In real life the diseconomies are minimized in so far as communities reflecting the same socioeconomic preferences are contiguous. Suburban agglomerations such as Westchester, the North Shore, and the Main Line are, in part, evidence of these external economies and diseconomies.

Assumptions 1 and 2 should be checked against reality. Consumer-voters do not have perfect knowledge and set preferences, nor are they perfectly mobile. The question is how do people actually react in choosing a community. There has been very little empirical study of the motivations of people in choosing a community. Such studies as have been undertaken seem to indicate a surprising awareness of differing revenue and expenditure patterns.[21] The general disdain with which proposals to integrate municipalities are met seems to

reflect, in part, the fear that local revenue-expenditure patterns will be lost as communities are merged into a metropolitan area.

POLICY IMPLICATIONS

The preceding analysis has policy implications for municipal integration, provision for mobility, and set local revenue and expenditure patterns. These implications are worth brief consideration.

On the usual economic welfare grounds, municipal integration is justified only if more of any service is forthcoming at the same total cost and without reduction of any other service. A general reduction of costs along with a reduction in one or more of the services provided cannot be justified on economic grounds unless the social welfare function is known. For example, those who argue for a metropolitan police force instead of local police cannot prove their case on purely economic grounds.[22] If one of the communities were to receive less police protection after integration than it received before, integration could be objected to as a violation of consumers' choice.

Policies that promote residential mobility and increase the knowledge of the consumer-voter will improve the allocation of government expenditures in the same sense that mobility among jobs and knowledge relevant to the location of industry and labor improve the allocation of private resources.

Finally, we may raise the normative question whether local governments *should*, to the extent possible, have a fixed revenue-expenditure pattern. In a large, dynamic metropolis this may be

[20] I am grateful to Stanley Long and Donald Markwalder for suggesting this point.

[21] See Wendell Bell, "Familism and Suburbanization: One Test of the Choice Hypothesis," a paper read at the annual meeting of the American Sociological Society, Washington, D.C., August, 1955. Forthcoming in *Rural Sociology*, December, 1956.

[22] For example, in Cook County—the Chicago area—Sheriff Joseph Lohman argues for such a metropolitan police force.

impossible. Perhaps it could more appropriately be considered by rural and suburban communities.

CONCLUSION

It is useful in closing to restate the problem as Samuelson sees it:

However, no decentralized pricing system can serve to determine optimally these levels of collective consumption. Other kinds of "voting" or "signaling" would have to be tried. . . . Of course utopian voting and signaling schemes can be imagined. . . . The failure of market catallactics in no way denies the following truth: given sufficient knowledge the optimal decisions can always be found by scanning over all the attainable states of the world and selecting the one which according to the postulated ethical welfare function is best. The solution "exists"; the problem is how to "find" it.[23]

It is the contention of this article that, for a substantial portion of collective or public goods, this problem *does have* a

[23] "The Pure Theory . . . ," *op. cit.*, pp. 388–89.

conceptual solution. If consumer-voters are fully mobile, the appropriate local governments, whose revenue-expenditure patterns are set, are adopted by the consumer-voters. While the solution may not be perfect because of institutional rigidities, this does not invalidate its importance. The solution, like a general equilibrium solution for a private spatial economy, is the best that can be obtained given preferences and resource endowments.

Those who are tempted to compare this model with the competitive private model may be disappointed. Those who compare the reality described by this model with the reality of the competitive model—given the degree of monopoly, friction, and so forth—*may* find that local government represents a sector where the allocation of public goods (as a reflection of the preferences of the population) need not take a back seat to the private sector.

B
Exit and Federalism

[2]

EXIT RIGHTS UNDER FEDERALISM

RICHARD A. EPSTEIN*

I

INTRODUCTION AND OVERVIEW

A. The Government Monopolist

Defenders of federalism, among whom I count myself, have long been attracted by the analogy to the market. When any individual is on the opposite side of the market from a large number of independent parties, then he is not dependent on any single party for any set of goods and services. The diffuse distribution of power allows everyone to search the market in order to obtain the lowest price for goods and services of any given quality. In competitive equilibrium, the price of these goods and services will equal their marginal cost, and everyone will emerge the happier. All goods that should be produced in the open market will be produced, and no goods that should not be produced will be produced. There will be neither unwarranted subsidy on the one hand, nor foregone opportunities on the other. Who could ask for more?

The rise of modern transaction cost economics has forced us, as defenders of markets, to moderate our optimism about the capacity of markets to clear in such an advantageous fashion. Today no one thinks that these market forces invariably will first find the perfect equilibrium and then maintain it over time. Rather, the argument is one of constrained optimism. There are persistent and powerful incentives that will draw market participants in the correct direction. It hardly matters that perfection is unobtainable, so long as the deviations from the ideal are as small as human institutions can make them. The best is not allowed to become the enemy of the good, and we embrace markets for the promise that they hold, and do not condemn them for the occasional disappointment that they yield.

The antithesis of a well-functioning market is of course the monopoly power of the government. When it comes to certain forms of critical goods and services, including those most closely related to self-preservation and defense, we have to turn to government. The story for that dependence is an old and well-told one, which lies at the root of the English social contract

    * James Parker Hall Distinguished Service Professor of Law, The University of Chicago.

    This paper was originally presented at the conference on Canadian and American constitutional law held at Duke University, April 4-6, 1991.

148   LAW AND CONTEMPORARY PROBLEMS   [Vol. 55: No. 1

theories,[1] and need not be rehearsed here. The alternative to a state with monopoly power over the use of force is a constant conflict of wills and clash of arms in which every person has the power to be a judge in his own cause. The abuses of a monopoly power are thought to be a small price to pay for the elimination of the greater difficulties of anarchy and the uncontrolled use of force.

But with all that said, the price that is involved is quite high; for monopolists, especially those who can eliminate or suppress rivals by force, are known to behave in a way that generates huge gains for those who control the tools of power at the cost of still greater losses to those who are subject to that power. The social inefficiency results in the excess of losses over gains. Yet, even if the naked force of government officials is effectively constrained, these parties still possess a fair measure of monopoly power. These officials will therefore have every incentive to behave like monopolists in other markets—by providing too little service at too high a price, the very vice that antitrust laws attack. The exact source of misbehavior in government is difficult to predict because power within government is divided among many persons and is partially checked by constitutional restraint. Small changes in the initial positions of public officials and private actors, and subtle differences in the individual strategies of these players, could lead to marked differences in outcomes. But these uncertainties in the process do nothing to negate the corrosive effect that government abuse can have on the operation of a well-functioning society, even if these uncertainties make it difficult to identify in advance how that abuse will manifest itself. All too often aggressive individuals and groups engage in relentless efforts to gain subsidies for themselves, or to impose taxes or regulations upon rivals, and this bewildering array of economic regulation of all sorts and descriptions cannot be explained by any optimistic public interest model of regulation.[2] The forces of self-interest are all too often able, by a combination of influence and power, to commandeer and control the instruments of government. It is to guard against these risks that constitutions are established.

---

1. Thomas Hobbes, *Leviathan* (J.M. Dent & Sons, 1973)(first published 1651); John Locke, *A Second Treatise of Civil Government: An Essay Concerning the True Original, Extent, and End of Civil Government,* in Thomas I. Cook, ed, *Two Treatises of Government* 121 (Hafner, 1947).

2. The suspicion of state power and democratic excesses was a familiar theme in the Federalist Papers.

> The sober people of America are weary of the fluctuating policy which has directed the public councils. They have seen with regret and indignation that sudden changes and legislative interferences in cases affecting personal rights, become jobs in the hands of enterprising and influential speculators, and snares to the more-industrious and less-informed part of the community. They have seen, too, that one legislative interference is but the first link of a long chain of repetitions, every subsequent interference being naturally produced by the effects of the preceding. They very rightly infer, therefore, that some thorough reform is wanting, which will banish speculations on public measures, inspire a general prudence and industry, and give a regular course of the business of society.

Federalist 44 (Madison), in Roy P. Fairfield, ed, *The Federalist Papers* 126, 128-29 (speaking of the Article I, § 10 limitations on the power of states, including a prohibition of the impairment of obligations of contract).

There are three well-known strategies to counter these possibilities of government abuse. The first of these is separation of powers, and involves an effort to break up government power into constituent parts so that no individual or group gains access to all the monopoly levers. The second involves the protection of individual rights and liberties through a constitution and bill of rights that contains, most notably for these purposes, some form of property protection, although in other contexts protections of speech, press, and religion, and procedural due process may prove every bit as important. And the third is federalism, a system in which there are separate states or provinces that can be set into competition with one another. The individuals who are subject to state regulation need not be content with a "voice" in the political process but can protect their interests through the right of "exit," that is, through the ability to avoid the difficulties of further association by picking up stock and going elsewhere.[3] The central focus of this paper is the role of federalism, with its attendant exit right for private individuals and firms, in checking the monopoly power of state or provincial government.

B. Federalism as a Check on State Power

There is some evident irony in viewing federalism as a check on the power of state governments. The system was not created by conscious design in the original constitution. Instead, it was an historical outgrowth of the previous institutional arrangement in which the separate colonies each had power over their internal affairs subject only to the external review by the English Parliament and Crown. At the original founding, the states were the dominant players and the federal government was their creature, conceived as a government with delegated powers specifically enumerated in Article I of the Constitution.[4] The major impulse for the original constitutional design was to protect the states and their citizens against federal domination, that is, domination by a government so far removed from the people that it was likely to be insensitive to their liberties and concerns. There was less concern with the limitation of the powers of the state against its own citizens, and that those substantive provisions directed toward that end were cast as explicit substantive limitations on the power of the state.[5] Instead, the major fear of

---

3. Albert Hirschman, *Exit, Voice, and Loyalty: Responses to Decline in Firms, Organizations and States* (Harvard U Press, 1970), the now obligatory citation. For its application to antitrust law, see Frank H. Easterbrook, *Antitrust and the Economics of Federalism*, 26 J L & Econ 23, 28-50 (1983), and to land use decisions, see Carol Rose, *Planning and Dealing: Piecemeal Land Contracts as a Problem of Local Legitimacy*, 71 Cal L Rev 837, 901-12 (1983).

4. See US Const, Art I, § 1 ("All legislative Powers herein *granted* shall be vested in a Congress of the United States which shall consist of a Senate and a House of Representatives." (emphasis added)).

5. See id at § 10. It is the provisions that are contained in this section that were the subject of Madison's attack on state power contained in Federalist 44, from which the brief passage was quoted in note 2. Unfortunately, Madison's discussion contains relatively little about the scope of the contracts clause, even though it does go into some length about the risks associated with allowing the states to coin their own money.

state abuse was discrimination that any state might practice against the citizens of other states—a theme that is as important today as it was at the founding.[6]

The insight that federalism offered the prospects of structural limitations against the abuse of state power against its own citizens was not, as far as I can determine, part of the original constitution plan, but instead ranks only as a necessary and happy byproduct of that design. It is not possible therefore to find any early commentary that elaborates on the importance of federalism as a limitation on state power, so the arguments on the importance of federalism must be regarded as a modern reinterpretation of a fundamental constitutional structure in light of what we know to be the risks of government misconduct. Nonetheless, this element of competition between distinct states is an inseparable part of any federal system. It is important therefore to assess the role of federalism in preserving and organizing individual rights.

My conclusion is that while exit rights under federalism offer an important, indeed indispensable, safeguard against government abuse, the institution of federalism, without the rigorous enforcement of substantive individual rights, will not be equal to the formidable task before it. The great virtue of federalism is that it introduces an important measure of competition between governments. Federalism works best where it is possible to vote with your feet. The state that exploits its productive individuals runs the risk that they will take their business elsewhere. The exit threat therefore enforces the competitive regime. The weakness of federalism, standing alone, is that, in certain circumstances the presence of separate states within a federal union may not foster a competitive situation.

C.   Three Structural Weaknesses of Federalism

There are three types of situations in which federalism provides insufficient protection for market institutions. First, certain assets are tied to particular locations for which jurisdictional competition and the exit threat are not sufficient to discipline state governments. Second, there are certain transactions in which an individual or firm cannot choose among states, but must enlist the cooperation of *all* states in order to carry on its business. Third, states may adopt counterstrategies, most notably exit taxes of various kinds, that can neutralize the exit threat that federalism normally affords to private individuals. These three risks are not trivial, for they cover a large percentage of the situations that arise within a federalist system.

In looking at these three structural problems, it is important to note that each has its precise analogue in the analysis of ordinary markets for goods and services. These private markets tend to work well until the monopoly element is injected. This monopoly problem can arise in either of two ways: first, when one party commits specific capital to a venture, as with investments that

---

6. See id at Art IV, § 2 ("The Citizens of each State shall be entitled to all Privileges and Immunities of Citizens in the several States."). The diversity jurisdiction of Article III, § 2 was also designed to counter local prejudice.

are nonsalvageable at the conclusion of the venture by either abandonment, liquidation, or sale; or, second, when the coordination of multiple parties is necessary for any given project to be successful, as with a real estate developer that has to assemble many separate parcels of land in order to build. In both cases, the right to refuse to do business (the entrepreneur's analogue to the exit right) has certain major advantages in that it protects parties from outright confiscation of their assets by potential trading partners. The existence of the refusal to deal, therefore, will certainly influence the bargaining strategies of the private parties, and through it the level of goods and services that are produced and the prices at which they trade. In bankruptcy, for example, the ability of a trustee to gain an automatic stay against secured creditors who would otherwise liquidate their claims has enormous influence both on the shape of reorganization proceedings and the percentage of satisfaction of creditors' claims.[7] Even the best bankruptcy rules will yield inferior outcomes in at least some cases, for it may well be that if the secured creditor with exit rights can remove and sell the secured property, the going concern value of the business will be lost unless the trustee and creditor can agree to a reconfiguration of rights after costly renegotiations. The same difficulty applies with individual exit rights within federalism, for there are cases in which their exercise could create dislocations as well.[8] But these points are not decisive against federalism. Whatever its failings, federalism is an institution that improves the odds of forestalling government misconduct, even thought it cannot eliminate the entire risk of its occurrence.

In order to see both the strengths and limits of exit rights, the plan of action is as follows. The remainder of this paper is divided into four parts. Part II discusses two situations—the market for corporate control and the problem of environmental harm—in which exit rights are of value in constraining government power. The proposals to limit exit rights, or to encourage national solutions, to counteract "destructive" competition are generally misplaced. With that point first established, I turn next to some limitations on exit rights. Part III deals with the first of the limitations, the case in which exit rights are unable to protect specific investments within a given state. Part IV then deals with the coordination problem, where the ability to engage in business depends on the ability to do business in *all* states simultaneously. Finally, Part V considers state-imposed limitations on exit rights, a back-handed compliment for the indispensable place that exit rights have in any system of law.

---

7. For bankruptcy, see Douglas G. Baird & Randal C. Picker, *A Simple Noncooperative Bargaining Model of Corporate Reorganizations*, 20 J Legal Studies 311, 312-13, 321-24 (1991).

8. See Lucian Ayre Bebchuk, *Federalism and the Corporation: The Desirable Limits on State Competition in Corporate Law*, 105 Harv L Rev (forthcoming 1992)(sections III and IV of the draft on file with author).

II

SOME USES OF EXIT RIGHTS

A. State Incorporation Law

The question of competition between states arises in those areas in which states retain the primary power of regulation. One such area is the state power of incorporation, which is a source of extensive competition between the states. At present, major firms that do business in many states may pick a single state of incorporation. Incorporation is generally regarded as a good for the state of incorporation for the tax revenues it generates and the general business it provides. The battle between different states often centers on the inducements each could offer to promoters of new businesses to incorporate within their jurisdiction. Firms that do not like incorporation in one state can leave and reincorporate somewhere else. In some circles, this competition between states has been deplored as a "race to the bottom," on the ground that the managers will seek out that jurisdiction that is most favorable to their interests and, by implication, most adverse to the interests of prospective shareholders.[9] On balance, however, incorporation is an area in which the exit right operates as a powerful instrument for the public welfare.

The "race to the bottom" claim is flawed because it misses the central point that the protection individual investors receive under a system of federalism is derived from their ability to withhold their consent. If the state incorporation laws allow the officers and directors of a corporation effectively to expropriate the wealth of shareholders, then, in the first instance, the original promoters of the new venture will have to bear the costs of those inferior rules. The rules are a matter of public knowledge, and if they are skewed in the way in which proponents of the race to the bottom believe, then initial investors (including institutional investors with great sophistication) will demand at incorporation more favorable terms to compensate themselves for the additional legal risks they are asked to assume. As that additional compensation will cost the promoters of the new venture more than compliance to a superior set of rules, the promoters will modify *by contract* any rules that facilitate the exploitation of shareholders. I am skeptical that there should be any mandatory terms within corporate charters, but if such are required, then competition between states within a federal system should spur states to identify those restrictions that are required and to reject those that are superfluous.[10] The empirical evidence seems to be in accord with this

---

9. See, for example, id. For earlier contributions to the literature, see Ralph Nader, Mark Green & Joel Seligman, *Taming the Giant Corporation* (W.W. Norton & Co., 1976); William L. Cary, *Federalism and Corporate Law: Reflections upon Delaware*, 83 Yale L J 663 (1974) (arguing for federal chartering of corporations). The opposition to their position is developed in Ralph K. Winter, Jr., *Government and the Corporation* (Am Enterprise Inst for Pub Policy Research, 1978); Daniel R. Fischel, *The "Race to the Bottom" Revisited: Reflections on Recent Developments in Delaware Corporation Law*, 76 Nw U L Rev 913 (1982).

10. For an extensive debate over these provisions, see Symposium, Lucian Ayre Bebchuk, et al, *Contractual Freedom in Corporate Law*, 89 Colum L Rev 1395 (1989).

optimistic view, for those businesses that announce an intention to shift their state of incorporation to Delaware see significant advances in the value of their shares.[11] In this situation, therefore, the exit right offers incentives for states to find the right mix between contractual freedom and state regulation.

Professor Bebchuk in his recent contribution on this issue notes that a shift in the place of doing corporate business could lead to risks to minority shareholders or to various creditors, both by tort and by contract.[12] As regards dissident shareholders, the risk is surely there when majority vote and not unanimous consent is all that is necessary for reincorporation to take place. An additional requirement that no identifiable class of shareholders be left worse off after the reincorporation—a just compensation requirement for minority shareholders—could go a long way to prevent the abuses that might otherwise be allowable under majority voting. As regarding creditors, it is likely to be only the rare situation in which the reincorporation will benefit shareholders as a group, but at the same time will subject outside creditors (who otherwise benefit from the increased asset cushion) to greater risks than they sustained previously. If most shareholders are risk averse, it is unlikely they will support, even by a simple majority vote, any reincorporation in another state that increases the volatility of their holdings, the scenario most likely to prejudice any creditors. Since any federal law is so unlikely to represent a sensible response to any question of corporate governance, it seems best to rely on competition across states, notwithstanding the occasional case in which it might work more harm than good.

B. Environmental Regulations

The situation with respect to environmental regulation is more complicated, as there are elements of external harms that cannot be counted by ordinary markets, even in the absence of federalism. Thus, if state A induces a firm to locate within its borders by allowing it to pollute the air and water of state B, then the legal system has surely malfunctioned. But it is a mistake to insist that federalism solve a set of problems for which competition itself is not the answer. In the environmental context, the federalism option is no better than a rule that allows two private parties by agreement to inflict pollution losses upon a third party. A system of competition presupposes that goods and services are sold to third parties. It does not suppose that these third parties will be beaten or deceived. The problem of environmental spillovers across states is therefore one that the exit right cannot address, but for which alternative solutions are required. One possible solution under these circumstances is to allow the state in which the pollution has been discharged to maintain suit on behalf of its own citizens, either against the polluting firms or the states that have authorized the pollution in question.

---

11. Peter Dodd & Richard Leftwich, *The Market for Corporate Charters: "Unhealthy Competition" versus Federal Regulation*, 53 J Bus 259 (1980). Note that those commentators who believe in the race to the bottom generally favor federal regulation.

12. Bebchuk, 105 Harv L Rev (cited in note 8)(section IV B2 of the draft on file with author).

Still another solution is federal regulation of interstate pollution, as is now done under the Clean Water Act.[13] The relative desirability of these two systems of social control is far beyond the scope of this paper. For these purposes, where the regulation of private conduct is justified under traditional tort principles, then the exit option—if relevant at all—should not be allowed to permit a firm to escape the consequences of its actions.

Even here, a word of caution is necessary, for the exit right assumes a far more attractive profile when one state seeks to attract new businesses, or to retain old ones, by excusing them from paying for purely local environmental damage. Under these circumstances, individual victims of environmental pollution may well be entitled to redress for the harm they have suffered, perhaps even as a matter of individual constitutional right, but rival firms in other states should not be entitled to intervene if the state does not exceed its constitutional powers relative to its own citizens. If local citizens are prepared, for example, to tolerate higher levels of pollution in exchange for their ability to manufacture goods at lower prices, then disappointed out-of-state competitors should not be allowed to undo that decision in order to improve their relative competitive position. The danger of too much environmental regulation (as with excessive cleanups)[14] is often as severe as the risk of too little regulation. The increased competition is of course galling to the aggrieved competitor, but federal regulation dealing with purely local pollution (for example, strip mining) is no more justified than is federal regulation preventing one state from adopting right-to-work laws on the ground that this form of state labor regulation provides local firms with a competitive advantage in the open market. Where all environmental losses are concentrated within the state, the exit option again has important virtues, for it permits firms to migrate away from states that have embarked on excessive programs of regulation. Subject therefore to the vital constraint of harms external to the state, the exit option does impose some valuable constraint on what local and state governments can do.

III

SPECIFIC ASSETS WITHIN INDIVIDUAL STATES

In principle, then, there is no reason why one should be suspicious of the exit right in its own terms. While the right might not be sufficient to protect against all the various forms of state misconduct, it is surely an aid toward that direction. As the previous section pointed out some of the familiar strengths of the exit remedy, the next three sections point out some of its limitations.

---

13. Clean Water Act, Pub L No 92-500 (1972), codified at 33 USC §§ 1251 et seq (1990).
14. Keith Schneider, *U.S. Backing Away from Saying Dioxin is a Deadly Peril*, NY Times A1 col 6 (Aug 15, 1991).

A. Exit Rights of Developers and Landowners

The first weakness of the exit right under the federalist system concerns cases with specific assets tied to a single jurisdiction. Consider the situation in which a plot of land is subject to comprehensive regulation by a zoning authority which has the power to decide whether certain land development projects should be allowed to go forward. The question arises what social losses, if any, can be caused by the zoning authority (which for these purposes we can assume will operate at a state-wide level) if it exercises its general power in an unwise fashion. In dealing with this question, it is often customary to examine the situation from the point of view of a developer and to conclude that the power of the zoning board is sharply limited because of local competition.[15] If there were many different towns in which the development could take place, then the developer, who was faced with a set of powerful restrictions in the one town, could pack his bags and sell the project to some other location that desires the services in question. Where the power of regulation is vested in local governments, the distances that have to be moved are quite small so that the range of alternatives available to any single developer could be quite extensive. When the relevant unit of government is a state, the costs of exit are higher, but the exit threat can still be quite powerful. For example, it is generally recognized that state taxes are less progressive than national taxes because of the exit option, and several states have repealed their estate tax in order to stem the flow of retirees out of the jurisdiction.[16]

Yet it is also necessary to stress the limitations of the exit threat. To return to the real estate example again, it may well be that the developer has options to take the project elsewhere (a point to which I will come back to), but it surely does not follow that the landowner who wishes to sell to the developer has the same level of mobility or the same level of choices.[17] Thus a decision by the local board to limit development to fancy houses on ten acre plots may cause only limited consternation to a developer, but the regulation can reduce

---

15. See, for example, Charles M. Tiebout, *A Pure Theory of Local Expenditures*, 64 J Pol Econ 416 (1956). Tiebout's argument was that so long as local governments had to compete for taxpayers, each would seek to find a niche that will allow consumers to locate the right mix of services and taxes. Some local governments could specialize in quality education, and others in facilities for retirees, so that individuals could gravitate to where they were most welcome. Thus, governments could be made to act at least a little like a market.

16. Prohibition of Gift and Death Taxes, 1982 Cal Stat ch 1535, § 13,301, codified at Cal Rev and Tax Code § 13,301 (West 1970 & Supp 1991).

17. The fundamental difference in the position of the two parties is not taken into account in Vicki Been, *"Exit" As a Constraint on Land Use Exactions: Rethinking the Unconstitutional Conditions Doctrine*, 91 Colum L Rev 473, 500-04 (1991), discussing *Nollan v California Coastal Commission*, 483 US 825 (1987), criticizing my views on the case and commenting on Richard A. Epstein, *Foreword: Unconstitutional Conditions, State Power, and the Limits of Consent*, 102 Harv L Rev 4 (1988). Professor Been notes that the exit right will protect developers in land use contexts. Been, 91 Colum L Rev at 511 (cited in this note). However, *Nollan* involved a homeowner without an exit right, and, in any event, Professor Been overstates the value of the exit remedy.

market value of the land by perhaps eighty or ninety percent.[18] But the landowner is tied to the location, and so long as the political forces are aligned against him—nothing can stop the losses. Nothing, that is, unless there is some explicit takings protection against zoning—protections which, while available in principle, are not extensive against most forms of regulatory takings.[19] These losses suffered by landowners are social losses, and by any measure the situation is an unfortunate one if the losses are greater than the gains that are obtained by the neighboring landowners who have imposed the regulation in the first place, which will typically be the case with large lot zoning and similar restrictions. The point here is not that all zoning restrictions should be regarded as improper as a matter of course; it is easy to think of certain restrictions on the location of signs, or for the payment of sewers and off-site improvements, for example, that are fully justified even under a system with a strong protection against takings.[20] The negotiations between regulators and developers over these issues is often vexed, and some of the risk of expropriation, while reduced, still remains, for once matters have gone this far, the exit right is a threat that will prove of value only in rare situations.

It is important to stress, however, that the losses to the local landowners are not the only losses that will in fact take place. The developer in this instance has the right of exit and therefore is not trapped. But it should not be assumed that an exit right is every bit as good as an entrance right into a certain community. Quite the opposite. Exit serves only to mitigate the damages that are sustained by regulation. Yet to say that damages are mitigated is not to say that they have not occurred at all; nor is it to say that the damages that remain after mitigation are small. It may well be that the best counterstrategy available to a victim still leaves him bearing a very large loss. Presumably, the developer in question had some reason to prefer a site located in town A instead of town B. There may have been experience in dealing with local boards, or the developer may have established good connections with local contractors or suppliers, or have assembled marketing studies that allowed him to tailor a project to this locale. All of these local advantages are quickly lost if the landowner is blocked in his effort to make the deal with the outsider. The developer's opportunity cost of having to make do with the second best alternative, or perhaps third best alternative, is not trivial, given that the total cost involved in the project is usually a multiple of the value of the unimproved land. The usual model of competition

---

18. See, for example, the regulations sustained in *HFH, Ltd. v Superior Court of Los Angeles County,* 15 Cal3d 508, 125 Cal Rptr 365, 542 P2d 237 (1975), where the value of the land with a commercial designation was $400,000, but with a single family residential designation, it was only $75,000.

19. See *Euclid v Ambler Realty Co.,* 272 US 365 (1926), a case that set the stage for extensive regulation of land use in the United States, which has not been altered since that time. *Euclid* allows for virtually any form of "reasonable" land use regulation so long as it leaves the owner with some profitable use of the land. Today, the Supreme Court asks the wrong question: how much is left after regulation, rather than how much was taken by regulation?

20. See Richard A. Epstein, *Takings: Private Property and the Power of Eminent Domain* 266-67 (Harvard U Press, 1985).

assumes that there are many suppliers of fungible goods in the market. But let the uniqueness of land be taken into account, and even partial fungibility cannot be assured. The developer who has invested in soil tests or marketing studies has a site-specific investment in a particular prospect even if he has no ownership claim to that land at all. He should be required to bear the risks that the owner will not sell the property, but he can protect himself against some portion of that risk through option contracts with the landowner. Let the zoning ordinances change the minimum lot size, however, and the exit option does nothing at all to protect the developer's site-specific investments.

Nor do the losses stop there, as there are potential customers of the potential developer who also might prefer this location to any other that is made available to them. Again being able to leave is not the same as being able to stay. The right to back out of a contract when the other side breaches should not be deprecated, but it offers far less protection than a remedy for expectation damages when the other side is in breach. To say that the exit remedy is sufficient is to say that walking away from a winning contract provides the promisee with the ideal remedy. In the contract context, some damage remedy is required to prevent misconduct by the parties, even if the damages are difficult to value and calculate.[21] The same principle holds in the case of local regulation. The parallel between just compensation for the economic loss occasioned by the restriction on use, and expectation damages for the breach of contract is too close to be ignored. Both are one-time lump sum damages that are designed to leave the party paid indifferent between the continuation and termination of his particular project. The elimination of the contract remedy will lead to excessive breach; the elimination of the just compensation remedy will lead to excessive condemnation and regulation.

Carrying over these remedial ideals to the regulatory context is not easy. The just compensation principle should protect the expectations of both parties to the extent the expectations are realizable by the parties' combined actions. Yet it is difficult to quantify the losses, especially any that are borne by the developer. The precise details of these calculations, however, are not of concern here. What is evident is that the exit right does nothing to protect the losses of either landowner or developer. And where local governments can make their political decisions without internalizing the costs thereby imposed on the regulated parties, they will enact regulations desirable from the point of view of their electorate, but not necessarily from the point of view of the larger society.

---

21. For two studies of contract damage remedies under conditions of uncertainty, see Richard Craswell, *Performance, Reliance, and One-Sided Information*, 18 J Legal Studies 365 (1989); Steven Shavell, *Damage Measures for Breach of Contract*, 11 Bell J Econ 466 (1982). Shavell's work accepts as axiomatic the utility of damage measurements, but his first footnote lists several prior works on the economic role of damage measures.

B. Public Utilities

Thus far I have stressed the problem of specific rents[22] in connection with zoning, which is normally a local and not a state function. But the argument can be easily extended to other forms of regulation that are normally done at the state level. Regulation of utility rates and insurance markets are two obvious examples of such regulation, and each of them poses the same difficulty. Suppose that a power company invests heavily in order to develop a power plant to supply electricity or heat to a community, and that its rates and activities are subject to regulation by a Public Utility Commission ("PUC"). Here the PUC is normally given continuous power to regulate the activities of the utility, so that there is no once and for all contract that exists at the time the regulator starts its activities. Indeed there is early authority to the effect that the state could not contract away its police power (including the power of rate regulation) even if it tried to do so.[23] Once the utility has committed its resources to the region, however, then there is the same risk of opportunistic behavior[24] by government that is available to private parties whose trading partners have made initial investments. Unless there is specific protection against exploitation, the trading partner will try to expropriate quasi-rents from the party whose investment is complete, and will pay a price that is just large enough to keep that party in place (that is, to cover variable costs with a little something left over) without providing compensation for the initial front-end investment. Again the parallel between the contract situation and the eminent domain situation seems clear, and while there is much disagreement over the proper formula that should be used to determine the minimum rate of return made available to a public utility, everyone agrees that some compensation is required.[25] The necessary implication is clear. The governments are part of the federal system, but the exit remedy is manifestly insufficient. Some explicit takings protection is required as well. The problem here is one of sufficient universality that it cannot be treated as a peculiarly American issue; it is equally applicable to Canada or any other modern industrial democracy. Just as competitive conditions do not hold when two firms have made contract-specific investments on the strength of a special relationship, so too the exit remedy loses much of its punch when a firm has invested heavily in specific resources within a given region.

---

22. For a concise definition of "rents" in the economic context, see John Eatwell, Murray Milgate & Peter Newman, eds, *The New Palgrave: A Dictionary of Economics* 141 (Stockton Press, 1987).

23. See *Stone v Mississippi*, 101 US 814 (1879); see also dicta in *Boyd v Alabama*, 94 US 645, 650 (1876).

24. See, for example, Timothy J. Muris, *Opportunistic Behavior and the Law of Contracts*, 65 Minn L Rev 521 (1981).

25. *Duquesne Light Co v Barasch*, 488 US 299, 310-12 (1989). The Court upheld Pennsylvania's retroactive disallowance of the recovery of $43 million in "reasonable and prudent" costs for a cancelled nuclear power plant. The Court noted that even with this recovery disallowed, the utility company was allowed a fair and reasonable return on its overall investment, which is all that the formula in *Federal Power Comm. v Hope Natural Gas*, 320 US 591, 602 (1944), requires.

IV

COORDINATION PROBLEMS ACROSS JURISDICTIONS

A. The Land Assembly Problem

The use of market analogies also offers insight into a second limitation of the exit remedy. Recall that in ordinary markets the best results are obtained only when an individual purchaser is in a position to choose a contract with any one of a number of separate suppliers. There are certain situations, however, when it is necessary to have the cooperation of all the people on the opposite side of a transaction for it to go forward. In private markets, one common illustration of the problem is the land assembly question. A business wants to develop a unique site that is currently owned by a number of different individuals, but can only do so if all the plots are acquired. The value of the real estate in its unassembled form, when held by ten independent landowners, may be worth $100 per plot, or $1,000 altogether. But if all the plots can be brought under unified ownership, then for this particular project, the land has a value of $5,000. Faced with this situation, the developer will take extraordinary precautions to keep hidden the nature of the ultimate project in order to keep the landowners ignorant of the value of the project to the developer.[26] But if one of the landowners should find out, he could exact a price of up to $4,100 for his plot of land without making the project unprofitable for the developer.[27] If two or more landowners find out, then there could be elaborate strategic jockeying, with each seeking to hold out for the largest sum for his own parcel, knowing that other landowners have the same intentions. The combined demands of the present owners could easily exceed the $4,000 in assembly value that the project promises, and if no one is prepared to mitigate demands, a profitable deal could be lost to everyone's detriment.

In these circumstances, one possible use of the eminent domain power is to allow the developer to acquire all the plots by a forced purchase at a price equal to, or even in excess of, market value. Without the forced purchase, strategic behavior by individual landowners could doom the project. With the forced purchase at the right price, the deal can go forward, and all parties can share the gains. The Mill Act disputes in the nineteenth century showed how important these issues have been in the development of the law of eminent domain.[28] These statutes resolved the problem by allowing a landowner, typically with local approval, to flood the land of his neighbors upon payment of compensation for the land lost, often with some bonus value added. These Mill Acts, if operable at acceptable administrative costs, can work when ordinary market solutions are apt to fail because unanimous consent is

---

26. For the general rule that there is no duty to disclose, see *Guaranty Safe Deposit and Trust Co. v Liebold*, 207 Pa 399, 404-05, 56 A 951, 953 (1904).

27. See, for discussion, Lloyd Cohen, *Holdouts and Free Riders*, 20 J Legal Studies 351 (1991).

28. See generally *Head v Amoskeag Mfg Co.*, 113 US 9 (1885). I have discussed the Mill Act cases in some detail in Epstein, *Takings* at 170-76 (cited in note 20).

necessary for a deal to go through. The ultimate irony is that the existence of a large and diffuse number of persons on the other side of the market is a sign of health when a large number of distinct, two-party contracts can yield substantial social gains. But the multiplicity of persons on one side of the market is a sign, and source, of genuine bargaining obstacles when the concurrence of *all* parties is necessary for a beneficial deal to go forward.

The problems of coordination and holdout can arise with great frequency within the federalism context. The most important nineteenth century illustration of the issue concerns the building and pricing on the transcontinental railroads, both in Canada and the United States. In order to build the long lines, it is necessary to acquire rights of way in many jurisdictions. Additionally, once the projects are built, there is a risk of regulation along each sector by a state or provincial government that will be able to expropriate the wealth of the railroad developer, who, in this situation, stands in an analogous position to the party who wants to assemble land for a new project. If any single state can impose restrictions on the part of the business that is located within its jurisdiction, then each state can seek to squeeze out the profits that are associated with the overall venture. Where there is no coordination among competing states, their inconsistent demands could easily exceed the net present value of the project, a form of total confiscation. Knowing that this possibility may await them, some entrepreneurs will avoid making the kinds of investments that will expose them to this sort of risk, or, if they do go forward, they alter their pattern of investment to minimize exposure.

B. Multistate Coordination Problems

The same sort of issue can arise in other more modern contexts as well. Many large firms are able to service their clients only if they are entitled to do business in all states or provinces. The decision by any state to exclude them will make it impossible to handle national clients. The insurance industry, for example, is often called upon to write insurance for risks that could occur anywhere in the country—workers' compensation for a major insured is one example. If the insurer cannot do business in a single state, then it cannot follow and adequately service its national risks. A policy that allowed any individual state to regulate or tax in a fashion that garnered all the profits from this line of business opens up the coordination and holdout problems of the land assembly case with a vengeance. It is quite possible that the sum total of the demands will exceed the gains from running the business, so that the competition of federalism becomes the destroyer and not the protector of markets.

Against this evident form of peril, it should be clear that the exit remedy is of no assistance whatsoever. Leaving the jurisdiction will not allow a bank, a broker, or an insurance company to service all the risks of its clients. Needing the cooperation of every state or every province, the firm cannot do its job simply by leaving those states that accord it a frosty welcome. The firm has to be able to force its way into states. At this point, the same type of solutions that are thought of for the assembly problem have to be considered. The state may be thought of as a common carrier with a monopoly position, which is therefore obligated to take all comers on a nondiscriminatory basis if they can meet certain minimum standards of conduct. Translated into practical terms, it means that a corporation licensed to do business in one jurisdiction should be able to receive, as of right, a license to do business in another jurisdiction so long as it renders itself amenable to service within the jurisdiction and satisfies the capital requirements that are imposed upon local firms.[29] The basic principle is no longer one that allows states to turn down parties at will. Instead, like the obligations of a common carrier, a powerful nondiscrimination principle governs the entire field. The state is under a duty to treat the outsider on the same terms and conditions as its local firms.

This principle of nondiscrimination is applicable not only to the entry problem, but also to the question of state or provincial taxation of multi-state firms.[30] If everyone thought that the exit remedy were sufficient for the occasion, then there would be no need to develop an elaborate set of rules that limit the way in which states may tax these far flung enterprises. The articulation of the extensive doctrine that has grown up in the opposite direction shows that exit is not enough. Thus, think of the business that has costs of $100 in each of ten jurisdictions and profits of $10,000 that can be made only if business is carried on simultaneously in all these states. To hold that discriminatory taxes are permissible is to allow each state to impose taxes up to $9,000, which could well doom a profitable enterprise. Again the theory of government failure tracks the theory of market failure. The individual firm has to be able to force itself into the jurisdiction on even terms with its local competitors so that its going concern profit is not dissipated by the conduct of rival states. Here, too, the exit remedy is not enough.

V

STATE-IMPOSED LIMITS ON EXIT RIGHTS

The burden of the previous two sections has been to show that exit rights are insufficient to protect property rights over a broad range of circumstances. Nonetheless, it does not follow that these exit rights are of no importance in governing the relationships between the citizen and the state. The critical point is that exit rights do have an important role to play in a world in which the direct protection of property rights is, as it always will be, insufficient. The availability of exit limits the degree of exploitation that is possible by the

29. For early cases that applied this principle, see *Western Union Telegraph Co. v Kansas*, 216 US 1 (1910); *Southern Railway v Greene*, 216 US 400 (1910). There are exceptions to the nondiscrimination rule, see, for example, *Western & Southern Life Insurance Co. v Board of Equalization*, 451 US 648, 652-55 (1981) (Congress waived commerce clause protection for insurance company). I have analyzed the doctrine in Epstein, 102 Harv L Rev at 31-40 (cited in note 17).

30. See, for example, *Complete Auto Transit, Inc. v Brady*, 430 US 274 (1977); for an exhaustive analysis, see Walter Hellerstein, *State Taxation of Interstate Business: Perspectives on Two Centuries of Constitutional Adjudication*, 41 Tax Lawyer 37 (1987).

state. But all too often when exploitation is attempted through regulation, the power of the exit remedy is revealed by indirection, in the willingness of the state to limit it by taxation or regulation.

The problem may be illustrated by the following example, drawn from the situation as it exists in the automobile insurance industry both in New Jersey and Massachusetts.[31] In stylized form, the state has a system of rate regulation that promises a rate of return that the regulated industry regards as insufficient. The regulated firms challenge those state regulations in court and lose on some substantive or procedural ground. A company then decides to leave the jurisdiction and is willing to abandon specific capital located within the state and to lose the benefit of all business that requires it to be within the state. The state, however, does not wish to see the firm go, for if the insurer leaves two things will happen: a large portion of the state's market will not be serviced and the absent firm will be unable to make contributions that are necessary to prop up an assigned risk pool of drivers who cannot obtain insurance in the voluntary market. Given the existing level of regulation, it is highly unlikely that any new insurance firm will decide to do business within the state. So it is a question of how the insurer can be kept doing business within the state against its will.

A.   Effect of Exit Taxes

It is here that the exit tax becomes critical. Suppose that without the exit tax the decision to leave the state will cost the firm $1,000. The firm will then decide to stay in the state so long as the present value of the confiscation it will suffer in future years under regulation is in the aggregate kept below $999. The exit right thus limits the amount of loss that will be suffered, even if it will not prevent the abuse from occurring. But now suppose that a $500 exit tax is imposed, which is an amount that the state says it will need to fund the firm's share of the assigned risk pool over some future period. If the tax itself is valid, then it may never be collected directly, because the firm will decide to stay if the present value of its future losses under regulation are anticipated to be lower than $1,499. If the firm leaves, with the tax being valid, the state will be the better by $500, even though the state can hardly claim to be providing services or benefits to the firm that has decided to leave the jurisdiction. Either way, therefore, if the tax is effective, it operates as a partial nullification of the exit right and as an increase in the scope of confiscation that is possible under the regulatory scheme.

---

31.   See New Jersey Fair Automobile Insurance Reform Act of 1990, NJ Stat Ann §§ 17:33 B-1 et seq (West 1985 & Supp 1991); Mass Ann Laws, ch 175, § 22H (Michie/Law Coop 1987). The Commonwealth Automobile Reinsurers ("CAR") Rule 11 B.3, propagated under the authority of § 22H of chapter 175, provides that any insurer that wishes to abandon its license to sell automobile insurance and retain its other state licenses must make payments into the assigned risk pool for eight years after it withdraws from that market. See *Aetna Casualty and Surety Co. v Gailey,* 753 F Supp 46 (D Mass 1990), refusing to dismiss Aetna's challenge to Rule 11 B.3 on ripeness grounds. I have been involved in the litigation in New Jersey as a consultant to Allstate Insurance Company.

In making this point, it should be noted that the exit tax could take many forms. In addition to a simple cash levy that is based upon some volume of past business, it is also possible to impose obligations in kind. For example, the firm's departure could be delayed until the firm was able to secure some other firm to cover its business for some period of future years.[32] During the period of transition, the insurer might be required to write coverage at the old regulated rates or the firm could be expected to pay a successor corporation some sum of money in order to pick up that which is otherwise a losing book of business.[33] But these details are not relevant to the central theme: if the exit tax is allowed to compromise the exit right, then the prospect of exploitation against which federalism guards is thereby increased.

The solution seems clear enough. There ought to be a categorical rule against these exit taxes, so that the firms that do choose to leave can do so without the fear of facing extensive litigation and penalties for exercising their choices. Ever since Ex parte Young,[34] if not before, it has been widely recognized that it is intolerable to require a firm to break a law in order to test the law's constitutionality. In many circumstances a declaratory judgment action is the way to avoid the difficulty, but the case law with respect to takings is emphatic on the point that these anticipatory challenges to state regulations are not allowed. Administrative remedies, no matter how cumbersome and slow, must be exhausted before the administrative relief will be provided, for there are no facial challenges to comprehensive regulatory schemes.[35] Here the form of relief does nothing to ease the sting. So long as the previous regime continues in place until the judgment is obtained, there is an increased loss from having to operate under the impermissible scheme. The exit right exerts its greatest effects on local governments where a firm is allowed to pick up stakes and leave at will, without having to demonstrate the unreasonableness of local regulations to the state that promulgated them or to a court that never has had to live under their yoke.

The case for having that categorical exit right is very strong once it is recalled that no firm has ever exploited its consumers by seeking to go out of business. By exiting, a firm is announcing that it regards the regulated rate of return as negative. More concretely, the firm views its losses under regulation as greater than its losses through leaving, which are equal to its losses on existing assets plus the loss of any future business opportunities within the

---

32. See, for example, Cal Ins Code § 1861.03(c) (West 1972 & Supp 1991) (requiring renewal except for nonpayment of premium or substantial increase in insurable risk).

33. See the California decision in *Travelers Indemnity Co. v Gillespie*, 50 Cal3d 82, 266 Cal Rptr 117, 785 P2d 500 (1990), which, in its interpretation of California Proposition 103, held that Travelers was entitled to exit the state so long as it found a successor corporation that was prepared to assume its liabilities for renewal for a *single* year. The decision did not pass on the question whether the perpetual obligation to renew could be imposed.

34. 209 US 123, 147-48 (1908).

35. See, for example, *Hodel v Virginia Surface Mining & Reclamation Association*, 452 US 264, 297 (1981); *State Farm Insurance Co. v State of New Jersey*, 124 NJ 32, 590 A2d 191 (1991) (sustaining NJ Stat Ann § 17:33 B-51 against a facial constitutional challenge).

state. No firm will easily make the decision to exit if it is in fact making a decent return on its invested capital.

The game here thus differs fundamentally from that which is played where a firm under regulation challenges its rate structure but still is willing to provide the necessary service. In that case, it is quite possible that the firm is seeking nothing more than a disguised monopoly rent. So long as the firm is prepared to stay in the state, that possibility cannot be ruled out in principle. It is of course possible that the firm's claim of confiscation is valid, but at a limited level where it is more prudent to stay and fight than it is to leave. But the relevant judgment that the regulation is oppressive is far easier to make whenever the firm is prepared to vote with its feet, for now there is no scenario that allows it to make a profit under regulation. As that is the case, the categorical prohibition against exit taxes is an effective way to prevent the abuses that now abound in state regulatory processes.

B.   Exit Rights and Existing Liabilities

There is still one further complication, however. Suppose that the firm has decided to exit the state because it is worried about the firm's liabilities under existing contracts, and wishes to leave to avoid paying those liabilities when they come due. That problem always exists, for example, under insurance contracts where the obligation of the insured to pay premiums is incurred by the insured before the insurance company comes under its obligation to pay out losses. Indeed the early systems of regulation were justified, and rightly justified, to make sure that companies did not engage in strategic behavior to avoid their contractual liabilities. To guard against this prospect, insurers are required to establish reserves for their anticipated losses, and should not be able to defeat the reserve requirements by exercising any constitutionally protected exit option.

But those reserve requirements only clarify that the state could require the firm to remain within the state in order to answer claims on existing contracts. Perhaps the firm might be required to place some money on deposit within the state so that in-state plaintiffs are not required to bring suit in a foreign jurisdiction to vindicate a contract right established within the state. The obligations here are hardly novel. They are not different from those that are imposed when any other company wants to liquidate before its contract obligations are discharged. But if the question is whether the firm must continue to write new contracts at a loss, then there is no risk of taking money today and not paying out tomorrow. The basic theme still remains compelling. The exit option should be preserved against that form of taxation. No firm that has achieved a just rate of return will choose to leave. Federalism and exit rights under it therefore form an essential backstop against state exploitation, one that becomes ever more important as the direct protections against confiscation through regulation become weaker. It is probably a sign of the times, at least on the American side, that the toleration of exit taxes becomes greater as the concern over confiscation diminishes.

Indeed one way to understand this problem is to recognize that any state claim to impose an exit tax (or even a requirement to keep the firm doing business within the state) will rest as ever on the operation of the police power, which is here said to be sufficient to allow the state to take steps to maintain an orderly market when the withdrawal is threatened.[36] This claim would have a certain sense if it were assumed that the breakdown in the market were attributable to sudden and unforeseen events that are beyond the power of the state to prevent—war and famine come most quickly to mind. But the breakdown in the market is a direct function of the system of regulation that chokes off profitability and innovation in competitive markets. To have the state first create the crisis with a set of stringent regulations and then use that crisis to justify still more extensive state regulation is an open invitation for government irresponsibility. The restrictions on profits, and the obligations to fund an assigned risk pool, induce existing firms to reduce their market share and operate as a storm signal that induces other firms to stay out of the market. The capacity shortage in the automobile insurance industry is related directly to the limitations on price.

VI
CONCLUSION

The great advantage of the exit remedy is its self-help nature, which may make it preferable to legal remedies (such as a regulatory decision to grant an appropriate rate increase) that in principle may offer more substantial relief, but which also cost more to achieve. To say that federalism remedies may be cut off by a state whenever there is no clear declaration of a substantive government wrong is to carry over the relaxed views on individual property rights to another arena and to compound a major problem. Exit rights are to federalism as the right to reject defective goods is to the law of sales. Neither remedy places the injured party in the place he would have enjoyed if a fully adequate set of remedies had been provided. The buyer armed only with the right of rejection cannot recover her lost profits on a contract of sale.[37] The individual armed only with the right to leave the state cannot get a just rate of return on the investment in the state. Thus both self-help and legal remedies are worthy of enforcement in both the private and the public context. Our courts, both state and federal, should not allow the state or provincial governments to fritter away these important protections of individual property rights.

---

36. See, for example, Fair Automobile Insurance Reform Act of 1990, § 72, 1990 NJ Sess Law Serv 8 (West), codified at NJ Stat Ann § 17:33 B-30.
37. See, for example, UCC § 2-711 (Am L Inst, 1990).

C
Optimal Jurisdiction Size

[3]

FEDERALISM: PROBLEMS OF SCALE

Gordon Tullock
Virginia Polytechnic Institute

The modern explanation of Democratic government is based firmly on the theory of economic externalities. Individual choices in a situation in which externalities are important may lead to highly inefficient resource use. Government is one way, and frequently the most convenient way, to deal with this problem. This approach also gives a idea of the optimal size of the government or governments. It may be said that the governmental unit chosen to deal with any given activity should be large enough to "internalize" all of the externalities which that activity generates. It would appear that most students do not really aim at totally internalizing all external effects of the given action, but merely internalizing most of them, say 90 per cent. The reason that I am confident that this is so is that they almost never discuss local border effects. Any geographically delimited governmental unit must have a border, and if its function is to deal with an externality producing activity, then its actions just inside the border will normally produce an externality just outside the boundary. Thus total internalization would normally require boundaries which ran along some very impressive natural barrier. Such a minor matter as street-cleaning might require a continental or even world-wide governmental unit to totally internalize its effects.

If we assume, however, that it is not (for some reason) desirable to internalize all externalities, only most of them, then the existence of externalities even when handled in this very crude way, does give a guide for governmental size. National defense would require larger units to internalize 90 per cent of the externalities than would garbage removal. The exact percentage of externalities which are to be internalized, however, is not normally discussed. A policy of internalizing 99 per cent of the externslities would produce much larger governmental units than would a policy of internalizing 80 per cent. We will later see that this is not an insoluable problem.

A second factor traditionally considered in discussion of the size of governmental units is the optimal scale of production for the governmental service. Economies of scale, of course, can be regarded as externalities, but let us discuss them either as a special kind of externality or as a separate phenomenon. There is, in fact, a good deal of literature dealing with local government which simply seeks the most efficient operating unit in terms of scale economies. If costs of providing governmental services do vary as the size of the operating unit is changed, this should somehow be taken into account in designing an optimal system of

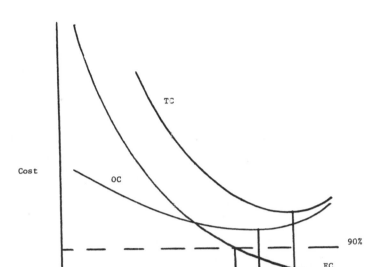

FIGURE 1

governmental units. Assuming that the governmental unit is to provide its own facilities, then there would be arguments for choosing the governmental unit in such a way as to give the most efficient production unit. This might or might not be the same size as would be chosen on straight externality grounds. The two considerations, however, can be easily combined. In Figure 1, I have put the cost of choice of some governmental unit on the vertical axis, and the absolute size on the other. The external cost (EC) line shows the cost inflicted by the continued existence of noninternalized externalities, and it slopes down to the right throughout its range. If we arbitrarily aim at an internalization of 90 per cent of the externalities, then the optimal governmental size would be A. If, on the other hand, we were only interested in efficency in producing the governmental service, then we would choose a governmental unit which minimized the operating cost (OC), and this would be at B. Geometrically summing these two cost lines (TC) gives us C as the optimal size of the governmental unit. Note that the optimum size in terms of total cost must always lie to the right of the optimum from the point of view of economies of scale. This is a simple consequence of the fact that the external cost line is continuously downsloped to the right while the "scale" cost comes down and then goes up.

But although I have drawn a correct conclusion from assumptions which a short time ago had been accepted as the modern tradition, the work of our host, Dr. Ostrom, has fairly conclusively demonstrated that there is a hidden, and untrue, assumption in the reasoning. The economies of scale are relevant to the choice if a governmental unit itself must produce the particular governmental service. If it can purchase it from a specialized producer, then the economies of scale cease to have relevance to the decision as to the size of the governmental unit. I need not repeat here the work of Dr. Ostrom, but I take it that we can agree that only conservatism and organizational rigidities prevent widespread purchase of services by governmental units of any size from organizations large enough to obtain the full benefit of any economies of scale which may exist. Thus the "optimal size" of the government as a producer of services can be dropped from the rest of this paper even though it has played a notable role in the recent literature about local governments.

But this leaves us only with the externality criteria, which provides no maximum size for the governmental unit at all. I have introduced an ad hoc assumption that we only try to internalize something like 95 per cent of the externalities from each activity, but this is clearly arbitrary. Not only is it arbitrary, but I have been unable to find[1] any previous example of its use. My only excuse for introducing it is that externality arguments are used in a way which implies that something like this is at the back of the mind of their authors. Clearly, however, it is an inadequate criterion. If there is not a counterbalancing factor, the more of the externality that is internalized the better. That there are other factors, I presume we all agree. Clearly continental or even world governmental agencies for street cleaning or fire protection are not desirable.

There are, in fact, factors which lead to the optimal size of the governmental unit normally being smaller than is necessary to internalize *all* externalities. The first of these is simply that the smaller the governmental unit the more influence any one of its citizens may expect to exert, consequently, the smaller the unit, the closer it will come to fitting the preference patterns of its citizens. This is true of all forms of government, although it is easier to analyze the matter formally when we consider democratic governments.

That the average level of adjustment of government to its citizens desires must increase as the size of the government is reduced, can be very readily proved by a technique invented by   Pennock.[2] Suppose   some governmental unit

---

[1] In an admittedly rather cursory survey of the literature.

[2] "Federal and Unitary Government-Disharmony and Frustration," BEHAVIOURAL SCIENCE, IV (April, 1959), 147-57.

makes its decisions by majority rule. A majority of its citizens prefer policy A to $\overline{A}$. The government therefore carries out policy A which pleases the majority and displeases the minority. Suppose the area is now divided into two units, and each of these units votes on the issue. There may be a majority for A in both of the new, smaller units, and there certainly will be such a majority in at least one of them. If both new units have majorities for A, then A will be applied in both areas and there is no change in satisfaction. If, however, one of the new units has a majority for $\overline{A}$, then the total number of people in the society who are getting their wish in the matter must go up.[3] Although Pennock developed this argument for simple majority voting, it may readily be extended to any voting rule.

This principle is perfectly general, and clearly indicates that the individual will suffer less cost from governmental activities of which he disapproves the smaller the government. This cost would probably take the form shown on Figure 2.

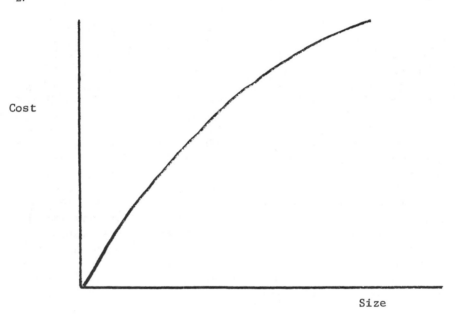

Cost

Size

FIGURE 2

[3] A numerical example may be helpful. Suppose the original unit had a voting population of 10,000, of whom 6,000 favored A and 4,000 favored $\overline{A}$. It is broken into two units of 5,000 voters, and in one of these we find a majority, say 3,000 to 2,000, for $\overline{A}$. The other small unit would have 4,000 for A and 1,000 for $\overline{A}$. Before the division 6,000 voters got what they wanted, under the new arrangement 7,000 do.

Surely this cost is a strong offset to gains which can be made by expansion of the governmental unit. We could add this line on to those of Figure 1 to get an improved optimum size, but there are othere costs of governmental expansion.

Suppose you normally eat in restaurants and that there are a considerable number of competitive restaurants to choose among. For the first stage of our model assume that all of these restaurants have a la carte menus. The customer thus chooses each item separately. Let us now assume that all of the restaurants, perhaps as the result of an unwise law, shift to a system under which they list a number of complete meals on their menus, and you must choose from among these without any substitution being permitted. Let us carry this procedure further and assume that the restaurants begin requiring their customers to purchase meals for a full day as a bloc. The restaurants publish daily menus in which you can choose among a dozen or so full menus for the day. Menu A, for example, would consist of toast and coffee for breakfast, vegetable soup and cottage cheese salad for lunch, and roast beef, spinach and carrots for dinner. One cup of coffee being served with each meal. Menu B, on the other hand, might be less obviously aimed at people who intend to reduce, and so on through menus C . . .N. The individual is still exercising freedom of choice in a competitive market, but I think it would be agreed that his satisfaction would have declined. We can extend the example by assuming fixed weekly menus among which choice is to be made; monthly, or even yearly menus.

The declining degree of satisfaction as the unit of choice is raised comes from two interrelated factors. In the first place it is harder to provide as wide a total range of choice if the unit of choice is large. Consider the breakfast menus of a typical restaurant, for example. If they offered nothing but fixed breakfasts, and simply presented all of the possible combinations which could be made from their present menu, they would have a book instead of a page or two. Further, the customer obviously would not wade through the innumerable combinations in search of his optimum. He would look at the first page or so and make his choice from this restricted set of choices.

The second problem is related to communication theory. When you choose an item to buy, among other things, you give the restaurant owner information about your tastes which will permit him to adjust his offerings so as to please you and get a competitive advantage over the other restaurants. By restricting the number of choices you can made, the information content of the total "communication" between you and the restaurant manager is reduced. As a consequence it is less likely that the choices with which you will be presented in subsequent periods will be as desirable as they would be if the solution process were more highly segmented. People who have unusual combinations of tastes would be

24   PUBLIC CHOICE

particularly disadvantaged by the procedure of grouping decisions into large bundles.

The relevance of all of this to the scale of government may not be obvious, but the selection of a governmental unit involves a decision on the size of the bundles of alternatives which will be chosen among in future elections. The situation is depicted in Figure 3.

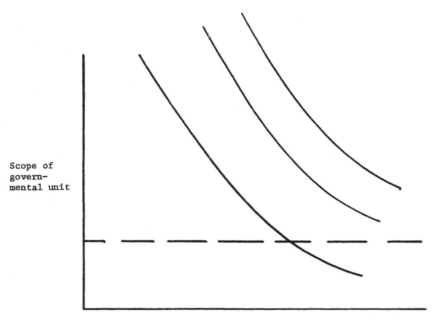

Scope of
govern-
mental unit

Size of governmental unit or
number of citizens

FIGURE 3

On the vertical axis the scope of the governmental unit is shown. This means, quite simply, the number of activities that it carries out with respect to any citizen or group of citizens. On the horizontal axis is shown the number of citizens for which it performs these activities. The total number of activities, thus, increases as you move up and to the right. Since the governmental unit will be elected to deal with all of the activities covered, the farther to the right and up on the figure, the higher the cost imposed by the necessity of making choices in large bundles. If the scope of governmental activities is held constant and the size of it is increased, as along the dotted line, then the cost of the increase would be shown by a cross-section of Figure 3 which would look like Figure 2.

There is a final cost associated with enlarging government units which is extremely popular these days; this is the cost of bureaucracy. The New Left and other groups which we may loosely call "Libertarian" are deeply distressed at the amount of bureaucracy in our society. It is certainly true that the longer the chain of officials that runs between the voter making the choice and the actual provision of the product, the more noise is introduced into the process by the individual bureaucrats who have their own preference functions and by the problems of information transmission.[4] This cost, like the others, steadily increases as the size of bureaucracy grows, in fact it might well increase at the increasing rate — i.e. it might be an exponential function of the size of the government unit. Here again, this function could be represented by a figure like 3. Figure 3 could also represent the sum of all of the costs we have been discussing.

Note that the figure says nothing at all about the total size of "government," taking that term to mean the sum of all governmental organizations. Many American cities and states have numerous different elected officials dealing with different governmental functions. If people actually made independent choices instead of voting a party ticket, then the scope of each governmental agency chosen by the voter might be quite small while the total scope of "government" was very large.

Now, having three costs which vary with the governmental unit dealing with any particular activity, we might simply add them and find the minimum total cost point and choose that as the optimum size for the governmental unit dealing with that particular problem. It should be noted that if you have a large number of government activities being carried on by different governmental units, presumably there will be externalities generated by the individual government activities which affect the others. As a simple example, the fire department in many ways makes traffic control difficult. These externalities, external effects of one government agency on another, would themselves be dealt with by other government agencies which would have the specific purpose of providing through taxes and subsidies for internalizing these externalities in the actual operating units.

The end product of our reasoning, if we stop now, would be a genuinely Rube Goldberg arrangement in which the individual citizen would be a member of a vast collection of governmental units, each of these governmental units being to some respect of a different geographical coverage than the others and each one dealing with a separate activity. The reason for this would be simply that each type of government activity has slightly different externality from the others and as a

---

[4]See Oliver E. Williamson, "Hierarchical Control and Optimum Firm Size," THE JOURNAL OF POLITICAL ECONOMY (April 1967), 123-38.

consequence each one requires a different size. Some of these governmental agencies would be engaged in providing services for the citizen and others would be engaged in internalizing the externalities generated by the individual agencies on each other.

It is, I presume, reasonably clear that this system would not be an optimum government organization. With each individual a member of 5,000 or perhaps 50,000 different governmental units it would be quite impossible for him to engage in the most rudimentary supervision of his servants. It is, indeed, unlikely that the average citizen would even know the names of the people who are running for office in many of these "governments." If we contemplate an actual voter attempting to deal with this multitude of governmental units, it is fairly certain that he would not even bother to participate in the elections which controlled very many of them. The bulk of them then would be, from this standpoint, quite uncontrolled. It is clear that this pattern would be very, very far from optimum.

In actual economic life we also deal with situations in which the individual cannot hope to make rational decisions for himself. I do not make even the slightest effort to decide the detailed specifications of the automobile that I buy; I leave that to other people and choose among the alternative packages of characteristics that are presented to me. In some cases I hire the services of a specialized consultant, a doctor for example, who will give me advice on what type of unit I should consume. Clearly the same method would be suitable when purchasing government services.

So far we have not specified how individuals choose the government service which is performed. It might, for example, be arranged so that each of our multitudinous governmental units submits all its detailed administrative decisions to a public plebiscite. Clearly, this not what we normally observe and we would be surprised if it would be optimum. What we normally do is simply appoint an agent to deal with government activities. Here again, the resemblance to the private economy is considerable. The difference is largely that we appoint our agents in a different manner -- through elections instead of through contract. If then, we assume that the government agencies which we have set up to deal with these specific problems will be controlled by some kind of a special agent or board of agents and the voter selects these agents or boards of agents, let us say at the end of the year, we have greatly simplified the task the voter has in making decisions about these services. Similarly the private economy greatly simplifies *its* purchasing decisions by grouping the characteristics of automobiles and letting individuals choose among baskets of such characteristics. But though this greatly simplifies matters we still find ourselves with some five to ten thousand decisions for the voter to make. Clearly the grouping of the process should be carried further. We

SCALE   27

must appoint agents to deal not with the individual government activities but with whole clusters of such activities.

How, then, would we determine the optimum site of such clusters? There is a fairly simple analytical answer to this question, unfortunately actually applying it may be extremely difficult. On Figure 4 the horizontal axis represents the degree of dispersion of governmental activities. It is assumed that as you move to the right the government is first halved and then each of the halves cut in half and etc. Somehow this process is assumed to be continuous in order to give us smooth curves. Curve C represents the cost inflicted on the voter through poor control as the scale of government organizations are shifted. At the left where he faces a single choice, let us say once a year a package of policies covering all government policies in the whole of the country, his costs are quite high. As the government is broken into smaller fragments his costs go downward. After a while, however, it begins to be difficult for him to make individual choices for each of the fragments and at this point his cost begins to go up again. Eventually in the Rube Goldberg model of a few paragraphs back they might well be much higher in this highly differentiated government then they are in a monolithic government.

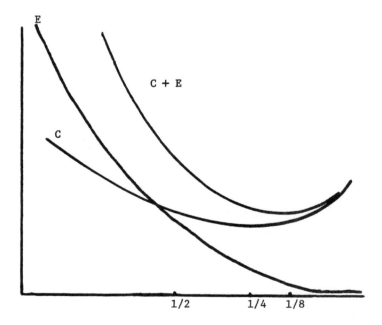

FIGURE 4

Line E is the cost that will imposed through grouping governmental units in nonoptimum ways, the optimum way being defined in the way we have done before. We assume that, as you move from left to right, not only is the government split into smaller and smaller pieces, but that all of the splitting of the government is done in such a way as to be the " most efficient" arrangement for that particular degree of differentiation in government.[5]

This curve falls monotonically from the left to the right and eventually reaches a point of zero when the differentiation of the government functions has exhausted the full possibilities of the economies by this method -- that is when every government function is at its most efficient size. The total costs then of having any particular degree of division of governmental functions can be shown by summing costs C and E as on the diagram. The low point on this curve would be the optimum degree of differentiation of the government. It will always lie to the right of the low point on the C curve simply because E is monotonically decreasing. It might not lie very much to the right.

The division of the functions of the government, if it is to be efficient, will take a good deal of care. You can't just randomly allocate several functions to one bureau; there are efficiency considerations here too. In general we need not concern ourselves with the details of these efficiency considerations here but one point should be made. It is not necessarily true that all functions in a given geographic area should be run by the same unit. One can well imagine, let us say, the voters of the state of Indiana instead of voting for the state of Indiana government and a city government voting for two governments for the Indiana area, each of which dealt with a different aspect of affairs.

We have now what appears to be a theoretical structure for deciding the degree to which the government should be federalized. A society actually applying our solution would require a good deal of empirical research which has not yet been down. If I may be permitted to offer a guess, I would imagine that it would end up with each individual being a member of somewhere between five and eight separate government units. These government units would not necessarily bear any particular resemblance to our present governments. It is, for example, quite possible theoretically that we would have two "national" governments. One of which, let us say, dealt with national defense and the other with all other activities which required nationwide organization.

---

[5]In practice of course, splitting the government evenly into two parts or evenly into four parts or evenly into eight parts would be unlikely to be the efficient arrangement. You might find 65 per cent in one group and 35 per cent in another.

SCALE 29

We should, of course, make every effort to make the voting itself an efficient choice process. As to one example, we could use what used to be called the Soviet system. Voters can elect small governments which themselves elect the next higher unit(s) of government. A scheme in which small government units create larger government units is far more efficient than one which large government units subdivide their control. The city of Chicago, for example, would be better off controlling its own destiny and participating in electing a government of Illinois than if the government of Illinois had two subdivisions, one of which dealt with the city of Chicago and one of which dealt with the rest of the state. The reason being simply that the down state voters would have less influence on the city of Chicago under the former system.

Another rather simple method of improving efficiency of the voting process is to arrange that people defeated, in the election process, but who nevertheless do reasonably well are given an opportunity to act as sort of public auditors over the behavior of the people who win. As is rather well known I am a proponent of proportional representation. If we have proportional representation, and if, let us say, five members were elected to duty on a govering board, whatever that board is, making the sixth highest ranking candidate auditor and giving him full access to all records would provide an excellent control without much burden on the voters. Today we have auditors but we usually elect them separately, thus requiring an additional vote and complicating the election process.

In sum, many students seem to think that a highly centralized government is the most efficient government. It would be more accurate to say that centralized government is the most orderly government. If we want the voters wishes to be served by the government, then a system under which the voters are able to communicate those wishes to the government through the voting process in a more detailed and particular way is more efficient. We cannot carry this detailed voting, however, to its logical extreme because the information costs put on the voter are too great. Still it is probable that we could rearrange things in the United States so that the voter had to know less in order to cast an intelligent vote than he now does – i.e. we could get rid of the long ballot. At the same time we could give the voter considerably more control over his future and his fortunes. The most efficient government is not the most orderly looking government but the government that comes closest to carrying out the wishes of its masters.

D
Twin Dilemmas of Federalism:
Free Riding, Spillovers and Agency Costs

[4]

The origin and purposes
of federalism

I₍ₙ ₜₕₑ₎ previous chapter I interpreted federal-
ism as a bargain between prospective national leaders and officials of constituent governments for the purpose of aggregating
territory, the better to lay taxes and raise armies. This bargain
can be defined quite precisely so that, when presented with an
instance of a constitution, one can say whether or not it belongs
to the class of federalisms. The rule for identification is: A constitution is federal if (1) two levels of government rule the same
land and people, (2) each level has at least one area of action in
which it is autonomous, and (3) there is some guarantee (even
though merely a statement in the constitution) of the autonomy
of each government in its own sphere. Since such constitutions
have appeared frequently in the last century and three-quarters,
the class of federal bargains is large enough to admit of some
generalizations involving it. Because the class is both precisely
defined and relatively large, one can rise above the undisciplined
uniqueness characteristic of historical commentary, even though

Origin and purposes of federalism

each instance of a federal bargain is of course imbedded in a unique historical context.

I   CONDITIONS OF THE FEDERAL BARGAIN

As bargains, the acts of making federal constitutions should display the main feature of bargains generally, which is that all parties are willing to make them. Assuming that they do display this feature, one may ask what it is that predisposes the parties to favor this kind of bargain. From the theory set forth in the previous chapter, I infer the existence of at least two circumstances encouraging a willingness to strike the bargain of federalism:

1. The politicians who offer the bargain desire to expand their territorial control, usually either to meet an external military or diplomatic threat or to prepare for military or diplomatic aggression and aggrandizement. But, though they desire to expand, they are not able to do so by conquest, because of either military incapacity or ideological distaste. Hence, if they are to satisfy the desire to expand, they must offer concessions to the rulers of constituent units, which is the essence of the federal bargain. The predisposition for those who offer the bargain is, then, that federalism is the only feasible means to accomplish a desired expansion without the use of force.

2. The politicians who accept the bargain, giving up some independence for the sake of union, are willing to do so because of some external military–diplomatic threat or opportunity. Either they desire protection from an external threat or they desire to participate in the potential aggression of the federation. And furthermore the desire for either protection or participation outweighs any desire they may have for independence. The predisposition is the cognizance of the pressing need for the military strength or diplomatic maneuverability that comes with a larger and presumably stronger government. (It is not, of course, necessary that their assessment of the military–diplomatic circumstances be objectively correct.)

Conditions of the federal bargain 13

For convenience of abbreviation I shall refer to these two predispositions as (1) the expansion condition and (2) the military condition.

The hypothesis of this chapter is that these two predispositions are *always* present in the federal bargain and that each one is a necessary condition for the creation of a federalism. I am tempted, on the basis of my immersion in this subject, to assert that these two conditions are together sufficient. But, since I cannot possibly collect enough information to prove sufficiency, I am constrained to assert only the more modest hypothesis of necessity.

In order to prove this hypothesis, I have examined *all* the instances of the creation of a federalism since 1786, giving most detailed attention to the invention of centralized federalism in the United States. (More exactly, I have examined all the instances I have been able to discover. It is quite possible, however, that I have overlooked some obscure instances.) For those federalisms which have survived, I am able to show that the two conditions existed at the origin; and, for those which failed, I am able to show that either the conditions never existed or they existed only momentarily. Though such evidence does not constitute absolute proof of the hypothesis, it comes as close to a proof as a non-experimental science can offer.

Before this proof is undertaken, a word about the significance of this hypothesis. To those whose first acquaintance with the literature on federalism was the introductory chapter of this book, the hypothesis may seem obvious and trivial. But it is not; and to show why it is not I shall briefly examine two widely asserted fallacies about the origin of federalism.

One is the ideological fallacy, which is the assertion that federal forms are adopted as a device to guarantee freedom. Numerous writers on federalism, so many that it would be invidious to pick out an example, have committed this ideological fallacy. It is true, of course, that federalism does involve a guarantee of provincial autonomy and it is easy to see how some writers have confused this guarantee with the notion of a free society. Indeed, in certain circumstances, for example by encouraging provinces to have different policies or even simply to be inefficient, federalism may provide interstices in the social order in which personal liberties can thrive. And I suppose it is the observation of this fact that leads one to the ideological fallacy.

The worst error involved in this fallacy is the simple association of (1) federalism and (2) freedom or a non-dictatorial regime. Only the most casual observation of, for example, the Soviet Union or Mexico demonstrates, however, that even though all the forms of federalism are fairly scrupulously maintained, it is possible to convert the government into a dictatorship. In the two examples mentioned, the conversion has been accomplished by a strict one-party system, which suggests that the crucial feature of freedom is not a particular constitutional form, but rather a system of more than one party. (See Chapter 5, *infra*.) But in other countries, *e.g.*, Brazil, Argentine, imperial Germany, even federalism and a multi-party system have been unable to prevent dictatorships, so probably some even more subtle condition is necessary to maintain free government. What it is I cannot say, but I am certain that there is no simple causal relationship between federalism and freedom.

Even though it is objectively false that federalism preserves freedom, it is still possible that uninformed constitution-writers might believe they were providing for freedom simply by making the federal bargain. And if they did, then the ideological fallacy would be no fallacy at all. But there is almost no evidence that they have so believed, or at least no evidence that such a belief was a primary motivation. Theoretically, it is unlikely that writers of federal constitutions are so motivated. As men engaged in expanding a government, they are much more likely to be preoccupied with practical expedients for the moment than with provisions for the distant and not clearly foreseen future. As centralizers, they are much more likely to be concerned with centralization itself than with fears that centralization may go too far. Entirely apart from these theoretical considerations, however, there simply is almost no evidence that they have been motivated in the way the ideological fallacy asserts. Most so-called evidence for this proposition is essentially anachronistic in nature, *e.g.*, citations from *The Federalist* papers to indicate the motives of the framers six months previously, conveniently overlooking that the authors of *The Federalist* papers throughout the

Conditions of the federal bargain   15

Convention were in favor of unitary government and had almost nothing to do with the invention of centralized federalism. If one examines the debates of authors of federal constitutions and the political circumstances surrounding them, as is done in the rest of this chapter, it is abundantly clear that practical considerations of expansion rather than ideological considerations of safeguards for freedom animated framers of federalisms. Only in the instances of Latin American federalisms can even moderately convincing cases be made for the latter motivation and under close examination, as I will show, even these instances collapse.

Alongside the rather crude ideological fallacy is the subtler and initially more impressive reductionist fallacy, which is the assertion that federalism is a response to certain social conditions that create some sense of a common interest. On the basis of a theory of this sort, British colonial administrators have encouraged a number of federalisms, some successful, some not. It is the fact of some failures that is interesting — for they indicate the inadequacy of the theory. Perhaps the most exhaustive statement of this kind of theory is contained in the work of Deutsch and his collaborators,[1] who produced a list of nine "essential conditions for an amalgamated security-community" of which class the class of federalisms is a sub-class:

> (1) mutual compatibility of main values; (2) a distinctive way of life; (3) expectations of stronger economic ties or gains; (4) marked increase in political and administrative capabilities of at least some participating units; (5) superior economic growth on the part of at least some participating units; (6) unbroken links of social communication, both geographically between territories and sociologically between different social strata; (7) a broadening of the political elite; (8) mobility of persons at least among the politically relevant strata; and (9) a multiplicity of ranges of communications and transactions.

There are many defects in such a list. It is apparent that these conditions are not sufficient to bring about amalgamation for, if they were, federalisms like the Central American Federation would never have broken up or a pan-Arabic movement would

[1] Karl Deutsch, et al., Political Community in the North Atlantic Area (Princeton: Princeton University Press, 1957) p. 58.

reunite the Arabic parts of the former Turkish empire. Nor are all these conditions necessary, for a great many successful amalgamations have violated some or even all of them, *e.g.*, the Swiss confederation seems to have violated conditions (1) and (2) during most of its history and 19th-century colonial empires violated almost all conditions. If these conditions are neither jointly necessary nor sufficient, it is hard to imagine in what sense they are "essential."

The trouble with the Deutsch list is that it attempts to reduce the explanation of the political phenomenon of joining together to an explanation of the social and economic condition of the population. In bypassing the political, in bypassing the act of bargaining itself, it leaves out the crucial condition of the predisposition to make the bargain. What this list amounts to is a set of frequently observed conditions in which politicians can develop a predisposition to unite in some way or another. But it omits any mention of the political conditions in which, given some of these and other social and economic conditions, the actual predisposition to bargain occurs. The theory I have set forth, on the other hand, is confined to the political level entirely. It assumes some sense of common interest, of course, and then asserts the invariant conditions of forming one kind of larger political association, namely, federalism. (Incidentally, by confining the theory to a specific kind of amalgamation, the theory has a political focus that Deutsch and his collaborators failed to achieve.)

II THE INVENTION OF CENTRALIZED FEDERALISM

American historians have long disputed about the reason for the replacement of the peripheralized federalism of the Articles of Confederation by the centralized federalism of the Constitution. The traditional and long-prevailing explanation, which reached its most complete formulation in the writings of John Fiske (ca. 1890), was the teleological assertion that a more centralized union than the Articles could provide was needed for the United States to fulfill its destiny. This notion, however flattering to American readers, was, of course, chronological nonsense since the politicians of the 1780's could have at best a dim view of the "destiny" of the United States of 1890 or 1960.

Invention of centralized federalism   17

As against this mystical explanation, Charles Beard in 1913 offered a wholly naturalistic explanation that, however, so denigrated heroes and assumed so naive a theory of social causation that it continued to be a center of controversy for nearly 50 years. Beard called his explanation an *economic* interpretation, by which he meant that the motive of those who wrote and supported the Constitution as against the Articles was simply the desire to get rich or stay rich. Assuming that the central feature of politics was the struggle between the haves and the have-nots, Beard argued that the have-nots preferred the peripheralized federalism of the Articles to the centralized Constitution proposed by the haves. In some places he even goes so far as to argue that the evil rich succeeded in imposing their Constitution on the meek poor only by chicanery. Naturally, this oversimplified attribution of motives and morals is easy to challenge and in the last decade the so-called revisionist historians have in fact shown, *inter alia*, that in some states it was the rich who opposed and the poor who favored the Constitution.[2]

Mere revision of Beard's historical errors is not likely, however, to improve our understanding of the constitutional change. What is needed is a broader conception of the nature of politics than Beard's narrow progressivism. In the following paragraphs, therefore, I have outlined what I call the "Military Interpretation of the Constitution of the United States" and have demonstrated that it accounts for the total local, national, and international features of the process of constitution-writing.

The Military Interpretation of the Constitution. From the end of the War of 1812 until the manufacture of an atomic bomb by the Soviet Union, most Americans felt safe from European invasion. During that long period (in the latter part of which Beard wrote), it was difficult to conceive of the international situation of the American states in the 1780's, when European aggression seemed both imminent and inevitable. (Probably this continental security that permitted exclusive preoccupation with domestic affairs was

[2] Charles Beard, *An Economic Interpretation of the Constitution of the United States* (New York: Macmillan, 1913); Robert E. Brown, *Charles Beard and the Constitution* (Princeton: Princeton University Press, 1956).

a precondition of Beard's misinterpretation of history.) But in the 1950's and 1960's it is again easy to sympathize with the fears and calculations of politicians of the era of the Articles. Consider the objective international situation they found themselves in. The thirteen states concluded in 1783 a very uneasy peace with the imperial power, uneasy because significant politicians in Britain regretted the outcome and hoped to reopen the war, and uneasy because it appeared likely that some of the states would give them occasion to do so. The British occupied forts in the Northwest Territory, forts which they were obligated to surrender under the terms of the Treaty of Paris but which they refused to surrender until the states paid the arrears in the treaty-obligated indemnity for Tory property seized during the war. The English threat in the Northwest was matched by the Spanish threat in the Southwest, where New Orleans was a base for potential expansion into the Ohio and Tennessee valleys. The States had neither fleet to forestall invasion nor army to repel it. In such circumstances wise politicians could seldom be free of the fear of war and in fact they were not. The chief criticisms they made of the peripheralized federalism of the Articles was that the system as a whole, central and constituent governments together, was inadequate for war and the prospect of war. I cite three instances: (1) Washington in his semi-annual political surveys to Lafayette throughout 1785 to 1787 emphasized the military weakness of government under the Articles. He seemed especially disturbed by the possibility that Kentucky might even voluntarily go with Spain. The military emphasis of these summaries, which presumably give Washington's considered judgment of the total political situation, probably explains why he attended the Philadelphia convention and by his sanction gave it a chance of success; (2) Madison, who is often called the father of the Constitution in the sense that he came to Philadelphia with a considered plan of reform and succeeded, of course, with Washington's approval, in writing the substance of it into the Constitution, circulated in 1786 a manuscript criticism of the Articles. The first, the longest, and the most passionately argued items in the list of weaknesses of the Articles all refer to the military or diplomatic inadequacies of Congress. Indeed, five items out of eleven are on

Invention of centralized federalism 19

this subject. Because Madison subsequently wrote the tenth *Federalist* paper, with its interpretation of domestic conflict in economic terms, Beard and his followers have supposed that Madison, like them, saw the great issue of the times as a domestic conflict among a variety of economic interests. But Madison's own writings on the Articles say otherwise and, as I shall show in item (3), only a wilful misinterpretation of *The Federalist* can align Madison with Beard.[3] (3) *The Federalist* papers, the main propaganda document issued in support of the ratification of the Constitution, emphasizes the military–diplomatic advantages of centralized federalism. *The Federalist* has, I recognize, been used to prove many and contradictory propositions about the Constitution. Nevertheless I point out that the first five papers — and presumably the first papers were regarded by its authors as of primary importance — are concerned with military and foreign affairs and were written by John Jay, who was then regarded as the great specialist on diplomacy. The structure of *The Federalist* and the content of its first papers thus suggests the primacy of military considerations in the process of centralization, at least in the understanding of the authors of that work.

These three instances, chosen from the main writers and writings responsible for the Constitution, do strongly suggest the primacy of the military motive in the adoption of centralized federalism. The suggestion is in fact so strong that one wonders how Beard and his followers could ever have believed that the main issues at Philadelphia were domestic matters of the distribution of income. The conflict between the military and economic interpretations is over what was the "main" issue. Naturally, the fathers of the Constitution were interested in both international and domestic affairs and when they talked about a better army sometimes they referred to the international scene and sometimes to the maintenance of order at home (especially to the policing of revolts by poor farmers, such as Shays' rebellion). Unques-

---

[3] See for example J. Fitzpatrick, *Writings of George Washington* (Washington, D.C.: Government Printing Office) Vol. 29, pp. 260-261 (15 Aug. 1787, to Lafayette); G. Hunt, *Writings of James Madison* ᵀew York: G. P. Putnam and Sons, 9 vols., 1900-1910) Vol. 2, pp. 361-369, "Vices of the Political System of the United States."

tionably the Beardians were right when they said that some economic concerns were felt, but they were perversely wrong when they magnified the domestic concerns and ignored the foreign concerns almost entirely. Probably they did so because in their day foreign concerns were not very important anyway; but as I have shown, the preconceptions of their era were such that they could not easily sympathize with politicians who daily expected to be involved in European wars on the American continent. This is why they have distorted the message and the structure of *The Federalist*, why they have written incessantly of Shays' rebellion (which did indeed disturb Washington), but totally ignored Washington's much greater fear that the Kentuckians might join Spain, why they have emphasized the writings and views of provincial and insignificant leaders like Luther Martin, George Mason, *et. al.*, and largely ignored the writings of a really national and significant leader like Washington. It is almost as if some future historians of India were to interpret the history of constitution-making in that country with the words of Ambedekar and Narayan without discussing the words of Gandhi and Nehru.

The Bargain at Philadelphia. Taking it as proved that the fathers of the Constitution were primarily concerned with rendering their federalism better able to meet military and diplomatic threats, we may ask now how they proposed to improve its capabilities. This question leads us directly into the nature both of centralized federalism and of the bargain invented at Philadelphia in 1787.

The Virginia delegation at Philadelphia came prepared with a plan for a new constitution (presumably written by Madison and endorsed by Washington) which was essentially unitary in character. It provided that the people at large would elect the lower house of the national legislature and that this body in turn would choose all the remaining parts of a national government: an upper house, an executive, and a judiciary. Furthermore, it proposed to give an essentially unlimited grant of power to the national legislature

> to legislate in all cases to which the separate States are incompetent, or in which the harmony of the United States may be in-

Invention of centralized federalism   *21*

terrupted by the exercise of individual Legislation; to negative all
laws passed by the several States, contravening in the opinion of
the National Legislature the articles of Union; and to call forth
the force of the Union ag^st any member of the Union failing to
fulfill its duty under the articles thereof.[4]

This arrangement seems to be an adaptation of the unitary English constitution to fit a society lacking a formal aristocracy and
royalty. Had the Virginia Plan been adopted and successfully
imposed, federalism in North America would have ceased to
exist. But the Virginia Plan was far too extreme a change to win
acceptance in the Convention and so it was repeatedly modified. The invention of centralized federalism was thus a byproduct of modifications made to render the plan acceptable to ruling
factions in the states. One cannot say that the framers tried to in-
vent what they did — rather they tried to construct, by means of
ad hoc arrangements, a government that would work in their own
peculiar circumstances. By happenstance it embodied a principle
that could also work in numerous other circumstances.[5]

The general theme of the modifications in the Virginia Plan
was, as I have just indicated, to deviate from the unitary form just
enough to render the plan acceptable to ruling factions in the
states. In practice, this meant guaranteeing that the governments
of the states have something to say about the formation of the
central government and that they also have important areas of
governing left to themselves. The main deviations from the Virginia Plan were in the selection and structure of the upper house
of the legislature, the selection of the executive, and the grant of
legislative authority to the national government. In each instance,
the framers went just as far from the unitary form as they
thought necessary to obtain adherence of state-centered politicians and then backed sharply away from going further.

[4] M. Farrand, *Records of the Federal Convention of 1787* (New Haven:
Yale Univ. Press, rev. ed., 4 vols., 1937) Vol. 1, p. 21.

[5] For a demonstration of the *ad hoc* character of this federalism, see William H. Riker, "Dutch and American Federalism," *Journal of the History
of Ideas*, Vol. 18 (1956), pp. 495-526, where it is shown that the framers' invention owed nothing, either positively or negatively, to the most well-
known federalism then in existence.

22   *Origin and purposes of federalism*

The great debate, as every American school child knows, was over the representation of states in the national government. The essential modification that the proponents of the Virginia Plan were forced to accept was the equal representation of state governments in one house of the national legislature. The issue arose out of the fear of the nine small states that they would be swamped by the preponderant weight of the four large states. This was probably an unreasonable fear since the subsequent politics of the federation has seldom, if ever, seen the small states pitted directly against the large ones. Whether reasonable or not, however, the fear was real (possibly because the small states had generally been lax in their payments to the Congress whereas the large ones had not) and it led the small states to insist on some kind of equal representation. The large states acceded in order to keep the Convention in session and this modification rendered the states a formal part of the central government and ensured the retention of some of the federalism of the Articles.

Once the proponents of unitary government had made this one great concession, however, they were extremely loath to make additional ones. And it was this systematic resistance on their part that produced a federalism of an essentially different kind from the peripheralized federalism of the Articles.

Consider, for example, the way the framers handled the election of the executive, which was a problem with at least two dimensions. Given the traditions in the states, it was natural for the framers to suggest that the legislature elect the executive; but, since most of the framers were mild conservatives fearing too much authority in popularly elected legislatures, this natural method was undesirable. Given the existence of the federation of the Articles, the next most obvious method was election by some agency of the states; but, since the framers mostly wanted something approaching unitary government, state-controlled elections were also undesirable. Faced with this two-dimensional set of considerations, the framers had a terrible time. Twelve different methods of election were proposed, two of which were actually adopted in a preliminary way, before the electoral college was finally devised. Though this expedient was a poor one (for it had

Invention of centralized federalism   23

to be revised in the Twelfth Amendment and is still subject to constant criticism today), it satisfied them on both dimensions. From the point of view of the federal–unitary dimension, it is important to note that, however great the difficulty of decision, the proponents of unitary government managed to avoid giving the states a part in the process of election. Thus, having capitulated on the election of the upper house of the legislature, the proponents of centralism refused to capitulate further, even though the way out of their difficulty was hard to discover.[6]

Or consider, as a further illustration of the resistance of centralizers to peripheralization, the development during the course of the convention of the grant of legislative power to the national government. It started out in the Virginia Plan as the (previously quoted) unlimited grant. It reappeared just after the large states' capitulation on equal representation as substantially the list of the powers delegated to Congress by the Articles. Having capitulated on one thing, it appeared that the large states were capitulating on everything. But then revisions began to appear in debates and committee reports. For example, the first list gave the Congress simply the power to call the militia into its service. Then it was proposed to give Congress full authority to regulate and discipline the militia, which was then the only military force in existence and therefore of central importance to men who wanted a stronger central government for military reasons. This proposal failed quite probably because, as one delegate remarked, "If it be agreed to by the Convention, this plan will have as black a mark as was set on Cain." What resulted, however, was a compromise that allowed the Congress not only to call out the militia but also to "provide for organizing, arming, and disciplining" it and to govern "such Part of them as may be employed in the Service of the United States." This compromise, which seems quite weak to us today, was probably as far as the proponents of centralized government dared go, for, as it turned out, the militia provisions came under extremely heavy criticism in the ratifying conventions and the Second Amendment was tacked onto the Constitu-

[6] William H. Riker, *Democracy in the United States* (New York: Macmillan, 1953) pp. 146-49.

tion to ensure that the militia would never be fully transferred to the central authority.[7] For another example, the first list of delegated powers did go much beyond the Articles in that it enabled the Congress to "lay and collect" taxes. But in subsequent revisions this power was expanded almost into a general grant of power of the sort originally intended in the Virginia Plan by the addition of the phrase "to pay the Debts and provide for the common Defense and general Welfare of the United States." The meaning of this statement has always been ambiguous, for it is not clear whether the grant of power to provide for the general welfare is a grant for taxing or for all legislative purposes. The tradition of constitutional jurisprudence has been to assume the former, but the plain English of the sentence and the probable intent of the framers suggests that one ought to assume the latter. Under either interpretation, however, there occurred a considerable expansion of the power of the central government.

In short, the proponents of a centralized government made the concessions to federalism that they were obliged to make in order to keep the Convention in session and to offer a Constitution with a reasonable expectation of ratification. Beyond that they would not go and so resulted the centralized federalism of the new Constitution.

The foregoing description of the development of centralized federalism at the Philadelphia Convention of 1787 has demonstrated, I believe, the validity with respect to the United States of the hypothesis set forth at the beginning of this chapter. The military interpretation of the Constitution has demonstrated the existence of the military condition, whereas the determination of the centralizing framers to grant to the decentralizers only so much as was necessary to keep the convention in session and to produce an agreed-upon document demonstrates the expansion condition. In connection with the latter condition, I suppose it should be shown also that imperial expansion was impossible. It is conceivable that Virginia, Pennsylvania, and Massachusetts could have conquered some of their immediate neighbors; but no one thought of doing so probably because the cost would have been

[7] William H. Riker, *Soldiers of the States* (Washington, D.C.: Public Affairs Press, 1957) pp. 14ff.

Former British colonies as federalisms 25

thoroughly prohibitive. Hence there was but one means to centralize, namely to bargain rather than to conquer, and that is what the centralizers did.

The hypothesis has now been confirmed with respect to the first centralized federalism. It now remains to confirm it with respect to the eighteen other federalisms now in existence as well as the nine previous federalisms that failed. Space limitations prohibit a discussion of each of the 27 instances in the same detail as I have discussed the United States and, for that reason alone, I now relate the evidence from these 27 instances in summary fashion.

III   FORMER BRITISH COLONIES AS FEDERALISMS

Over one-third of the federalisms existent today have been constructed by uniting former British colonies. Besides the United States, where the ex-colonials invented centralized federalism, Canada, Australia, India, Pakistan, Malaysia, and Nigeria started out as groups of colonies. Furthermore, some federalisms that failed were started under British auspices: New Zealand, British West Indies, and Rhodesia. Of the large British colonies now self-governing only the Union of South Africa and Burma have not at least tried federalism; and in both these instances there was considerable pressure from London to give federalism a chance. All these facts suggest that there is something in the British political tradition that is especially conducive to the federal form. And I am sure there is, although I have never been able to identify what it is in a way that is satisfactory to me. Those who are hostile to the British interpret their fondness for suggesting federalism as a part of the strategy of "divide and rule." That is, they interpret the imperial creation of semi-autonomous constituent units of a federalism as a means of generating internal dissension in the freed government, dissension that can be mollified only by recourse to the former imperial master. In connection with India especially, incautious Tory politicians actually uttered publicly statements of this "divide and rule" strategy; and such incaution has led many to interpret all ex-British federalisms as the last-chance frauds of a dying imperialism. But this view is, I think, too cynical. It supposes that the entire British policy on the treatment of lost colonies has been dictated by Machiavellian colonial officers; and I find such a supposition hard to believe. A more sympathetic view of the British imperialism is: (1) by using the system of colonial governors who were supposed to be absolute executives over a given area, the British effectively limited the size of colonies to what could be efficiently governed by one man; and (2) the area ruled by a governor was seldom, if ever, large enough to be a viable nation in the modern world. By granting, as a prelude to full self-government, provincial autonomy to the area ruled by a governor, the British created provincial interests which might reasonably demand continued existence and which the British (as the creators of the interest) might reasonably expect to recognize. In recognizing the provincial interests, the British were probably doing no more than displaying a sympathetic concern for their own creations. Though that may have been somewhat selfish, viewed from the standpoint of the colonial peoples, it is a far cry from "divide and rule." And in seeking to centralize by means of federalism, the British also displayed an altruistic concern that the self-governing units would be large enough to succeed in the modern world.

Regardless of whether the British penchant for federalism is a devious strategy for future control or simply a complacent assurance that their own colonial boundary markers were wisely placed, there can be no doubt that the penchant existed. Given its existence, one might suppose, therefore, that a sufficient reason for the existence of some of these federalisms is merely the pressure from the colonial office for its own favorite expedient. But such is not the case. As the following survey demonstrates, federalism in former British colonial territories has occurred in precisely the fashion set forth in the hypothesis at the beginning of this chapter.

Canada. Although the unification and self-government of the Canadian provinces, especially of the present Ontario and Québec, was discussed in the 1830's (following the minor rebellions in that era) and for a generation thereafter, no specific action was taken until 1864-67. It was precisely then that relations between the United States and Canada were more strained than at any time from 1777 to the present. As the Civil War in the United States drew to a close, outstanding Republican leaders discussed the possibility of annexing Canada, a process that would have been quite easy with the large and war-trained federal army. Going far beyond mere talk, however, the Fenian movement of Irish-Americans was organized to invade Canada. Its quixotic intentions were to promote a Canadian rebellion that in turn might, hopefully, lead to a war between the United States and Britain, out of which might come freedom for Ireland. In 1866 the Fenians actually did invade, quite unsuccessfully. Such is the backdrop in which after a generation of discussion the Canadians drafted and ratified a federal constitution in less than a year, a constitution the British Parliament substantially enacted as the British North America Act of 1867 in just one more year. Quite clearly, the second condition about the cognizance of a pressing military need holds in this instance. As for the first condition, it was clear from the reaction to the Durham *Report* (1839), which proposed the gradual elimination of French culture, that the unitary government Durham contemplated could be achieved only by force. The fact that the Canadian leaders never seriously considered the use of such force indicates that the expansion condition also holds in this case.

Australia. Although Australian federation has often been interpreted as a bargain made for strictly economic reasons (*i.e.*, inter-colonial free trade) and although there was no immediate threat of war when the union was consummated, only a slight survey of the circumstances of union indicates the omnipresence of the military–diplomatic concerns. Though some had agitated for federation from the 1850's onward, the federation movement really gained momentum in the early 1880's coincident with the French expansion in the New Hebrides. The first convention on federation in 1890, which was called because of a British military investigation that had recommended the unification of the colonial defense forces, also coincided with a frustrated Australian imperialism toward Oceania that had failed to maintain Queensland's annexation of New Guinea. But the most important event of all was the swift Japanese victory in the Sino-Japanese War of 1894, which resulted in Japan's annexation of Korea. With substantial imperial ambitions of their own and faced with a proven imperial naval power close by, the Australian colonials who could not agree on a federation in 1890-91 found it possible to do so in 1897-1900. Along with these direct military concerns stands the great diplomatic concern over Chinese exclusion, a concern which reached its peak in the 1890's and which was satisfied by an immigration act passed almost as soon as the new government was established. Thus, although the recognized military need is not so obvious in the case of Australia as in most others, military concerns were the ostensible reason for the federation movement and were probably crucial to its consummation.

As in the case of Canada, no thought was ever given in Australia to a unitary government. The self-governing colonial institutions were well established and easily able to resist unification, especially since the motive of defense was not desperately pressing. Hence the Australians substantially and consciously followed the American technique of the federal bargain.

India. Nowhere have the British more elaborately and consciously prepared their ex-colonies for federalism than in India. Throughout the entire period of British occupation of India, in fact, the British operated a kind of federal system in that they governed the provinces directly and the princely states indirectly. Thus the states stood in a kind of federal relationship to each other and to the rest of India. When forced to concede some degree of self-government, the form in which the British naturally chose to grant it was federal. The Government of India Act of 1935 suited the British purposes very well, for it granted self-government in those subjects of legislation reserved for the provinces and retained imperial control of those subjects reserved for the central government. Although Congress, the largest Indian party, refused to take office in most of the states, some Indian politicians were found to fill the cabinets of the states. Hence from 1937 to

Former British colonies as federalisms 29

1947, when the British withdrew from India abruptly, the states were operating governments with a conscious political tradition. Of course, also, the princely states had always maintained the fiction of self-government. Hence, although India superficially appeared to be a unitary empire, it, like Canada in 1865 and Australia in 1900, was a collection of partially self-governing colonies in 1947.

When Indian independence was granted, it came in the form of a partition of the subcontinent into India and Pakistan, a partition that occasioned the great rioting, vast transfers of peoples, and an undeclared war between the two new nations over the possession of the princely state of Kashmir and Jammu. From the very beginning, therefore, the Indian nation has faced the prospect of immediate foreign war, especially since Pakistan was more warlike, better armed, and more resentful than India of the boundaries drawn in 1947. As in the instances already mentioned, therefore, the Indian federalism, though foreshadowed by the Government of India Act of 1935, was actually entered into at a time of real threat of foreign war.

That the Indians chose federalism as a means of reconciling some subsidiary governments to centralization is demonstrated by the difference in their acceptance of federalism in the former provinces and in the princely states. Within a few months after independence, Sardar Patel had, in a whirlwind campaign, cajoled, threatened, bribed, and forced all the princely states into the Indian Union in such a way that most of them lost their identity. Of those which survived the first integration only one, Mysore, still survives a decade and a half later as a constituent unit of Indian federalism. Thus the Indians accepted, with some subsequent territorial revision, the provinces, which had had some experience in self-government and a well-developed local tradition; but they refused to accept any sort of federalism for the princely states, which lacked such experience. In the one case, the bargain of federalism seemed reasonable in the face of the threat of war; but in the other case, force was preferred to bargaining and the Union expanded by conquest rather than federalism. This choice is particularly clear-cut evidence of the existence of the

expansion condition; and the widespread consciousness of the
threat from Pakistan is sufficient evidence of the existence of the
military condition.

Pakistan. All that has been said about the presence of the threat of
war at the time of constitution-making in India applies with additional force to Pakistan. In the east, Pakistan is almost wholly
encircled by India; in the west, one border faces India and the
other faces Afghanistan, with which Pakistan has had perpetual
though intermittent border warfare during its entire history.

But though the presence of the condition of recognized military needs is clearly confirmed in this instance, the evidence for
the first hypothesis on federalism as the alternative to forced
centralization is even clearer. After a prolonged period of constitution-making under an interim federal constitution, Pakistan
adopted a kind of peripheralized federalism that, furthermore,
under-represented East Pakistan. Shortly thereafter a military
dictatorship was established, presumably to maintain the Union
by force the better to face the Hindu enemy. What this experience
indicates is that the federal bargain was indeed made to avoid the
use of force, that the kind of bargain possible under the circumstances was inadequate for the military threat, and that it
turned out to be necessary to use force to keep the central
government militarily viable. Nevertheless the federal forms remain under the dictator so that, if he should no longer be necessary because the tensions with India lessen, federalism may again
be used.

Malaysia. In Malaysia the British used the technique of indirect rule almost exclusively, except for the colony of Singapore. Since indirect rule involves the retention of local insititu-
tions with puppet rulers, it amounts to an imperial version of
federalism and indeed, when it was a colony, the British called
this agglomeration of territory the Federated Malay States. This
federalism was spurious, of course, for the puppets were indeed
puppets; but it nevertheless conditioned the Malay peoples to an
expectation of federalism.

Naturally, therefore, the Malays in making their first free government adopted a federal form. The military condition was

Former British colonies as federalisms 31

present owing to the existence of communist guerillas, supported from China, whereas the expansion condition was present owing to the necessity of reconciling the previously federated states. Furthermore, faced with the prospect of Indonesian conquest of Borneo and outlying islands, the British engineered an expansion of Malaya into a genuine federation including Malaya proper, Singapore, and Borneo. The clearly discernible motive for this federalism was, therefore, a fear of Indonesian imperialism and a reluctance, on the part of Singapore, Borneo, *et. al.*, to accept Malayan domination. And this set of circumstances of course fulfills both conditions of the hypothesis.

Nigeria. Nigeria is the only one of the ex-British federalisms that does not display the unification of a number of separate colonies no one of which would have been viable alone. For most of its history under British rule, Nigeria had a unitary government. It was only as withdrawal became an immediate prospect that the British split Nigeria into three parts in anticipation of a future federalism. The justification for doing so was, of course, the existence of three geographically distinct and politically hostile cultures within the colony. The federal arrangements they made were highly peripheralized — subsequent political developments have peripheralized them even more[8] — and, owing to this peripheralization, it is surprising that the federation exists at all.

The only clear-cut reason — aside from the fact that the British prepared the way for it — that one can give for the continued existence of this federation during its first few years is the presence of Ghana and the pan-African (read: "imperial") propositions uttered by its leader, Nkrumah. During the time just before and during the Nigerian achievement of independence, Nkrumah's emphasis on pan-Africanism was at its height and no Nigerian leader could fail to be aware of the proximity of the western (and depressed and minority) region of Nigeria to Ghana. Nkrumah's personal pan-Africanism, that is, his personal

[8] According to John P. Mackintosh, "Federalism in Nigeria," *Political Studies,* Vol. X, pp. 223-47, the main political leaders prefer to govern the states and to send agents to the center, which is sufficient evidence of the highly peripheralized character of this federalism.

32   *Origin and purposes of federalism*

ambitions to unite at least West Africa under his leadership, seems
to have diminished in the last few years and with this diminution
the rationale of a federal Nigeria has diminished also. Only the
future can tell whether this initial threat was sufficient to create
a viable Nigeria federation or whether the peripheralization will
culminate in dissolution.

Because of the peripheralization, Nigeria is a marginal instance;
nevertheless the two conditions are verified for it: the second because of the Ghanaian threat and the first because of the unwillingness of Nigerian leaders to upset the bargain the British had
made for them.

Unsuccessful British Federations. British colonial officials as a
group never understood federalism. They failed to appreciate
that the bargain is feasible only if there exists in all the prospective
constituent governments both a sense of provincial integrity and
a recognized need for military centralization. In their ignorance
they have tended to organize federalisms on the basis of barely
relevant considerations such as cultural diversity coupled with
geographic contiguity. The Indian, Pakistani, and Nigerian federations, for example, were suggested on these bases, but came
into existence owing to the presence of a military threat. Several
other suggested federalisms, however, have failed to come to
fruition largely because the British colonial officials have planned
them on the basis of cultural or geographic diversity in the
absence of military considerations.

Chronologically, the first failure occurred in New Zealand
where, from the Constitution Act of 1852 until the Dominion's
deliberate reversion to unitary government in 1876, a federal
form existed. This federalism, of course, was based purely on
geographic and communicatory considerations, on the distance
between the north of North Island and the south of South Island.
It was, however, a culturally unified society with no problems of
foreign war, at least after the Maori had been pacified. Quite
reasonably, therefore, the New Zealanders concluded that the
federal bargain was both unnecessary and appallingly destructive
of efficient government and hence abolished it in 1876.

Subsequent failures of British federalisms have come after

World War II, but the reasons for failure are similar to the instance of New Zealand. The projected, but abandoned, British West Indian federation was intended to unite the British Caribbean island colonies. But, though such a federation might have made a viable state in a way that no single island might, still the colonies felt no compelling military reason to unite with each other and hence the richer islands refused to take on the burden of the poorer ones. Again the federation of Rhodesia and Nyasaland, which was proposed on purely geographic grounds, broke down because the several parts feared different and conflicting military threats. Southern Rhodesia feared black pan-Africanism and Northern Rhodesia and Nyasaland feared white hegemony. Since the proposed constituent governments feared antithetical things, the federation had no basis for cohesion in a mutual military threat.

The moral of these failures is that federalism must be based on some deeper emotion than mere geographic contiguity with cultural diversity. Political sociologists like Deutsch (whose work is cited earlier in this chapter) are often inclined to accept a set of sociological preconditions as a sufficient reason for federalism. In these failed federalisms, however, all or most of the preconditions existed, yet the federalism never came off. So I infer the *necessity* of the political as distinct from the sociological conditions: Federalism is feasible only if both the conditions stated in the beginning of this chapter exist. In the instances of Rhodesia and the West Indies the first condition was absent; and in all three instances the second condition was absent. Hence these proposed federalisms collapsed.

IV   EUROPEAN FEDERALISMS

Every national constitution originates of course in unique circumstances. The thesis of this chapter is, however, that the circumstances that have resulted in federal rather than unitary constitutions can be characterized by a recognized need for military–diplomatic unity and an unwillingness or inability of national leaders to impose centralization by force. Beyond these minimum characteristics, however, there seems to be little in common among the circumstances of origin of federal constitutions. In the previous discussion of federalism of the British Commonwealth, the origins showed additional common features: guidance from Britain and an adaptation of the main features of the United States' federalism to the parliamentary government encouraged by the British example. As we turn now to a discussion of the origins of European, Latin American, and other federalisms, this additional common feature disappears. One is again and again impressed that the only common feature of federal governments is that they are federal and that the only common features of their origins are the two characteristics the existence of which is here being confirmed.

Switzerland. The only survivor of the peripheralized leagues of late medieval and early modern times in Europe is the Swiss confederation. Yet it is not clearly a survival, except in popular tradition. The old confederation was replaced by Napoleon with a unitary Helvetic Republic and, although the Swiss returned to something of their old peripheralized federation after Napoleon's defeat, the desire for centralization, which the Republic had created, did not disappear. After several attempts, a reformed and centralized federal constitution, composed of elements of the old confederation and of borrowings from the United States Constitution, was adopted in 1848.

The old peripheralized confederation was formed at least as early as 1291 to resist the military encroachments of the Austrian Hapsburgs and served to maintain the political independence of the mountain cantons until Napoleon's conquest. This independence was, of course, far from absolute, for it existed only on the sufferance of the surrounding great powers, all of whom interfered frequently in internal cantonal affairs. In the period after 1815 such interference was increasingly regarded as offensive by Swiss nationalists and liberals, who espoused centralization as a device to minimize it. Their chance to centralize came at the end of the Sonderbund war, in which the liberal cantons defeated the so-called Sonderbund of conservative, Catholic cantons. The centralizers forced the liberalization of constitutions in the defeated cantons and then proceeded to reorganize the federation. Early in 1848 the conservative great powers (Austria, Prussia, France, Russia) forebade the constitutional revision; but owing to the revolutionary movement which swept Europe that spring, they were unable to interfere further in Swiss affairs. Hence followed the centralization of Swiss federalism in the Constitution of 1848 and, to an even greater degree, in the Constitution of 1874.

Both the old and the new confederations were therefore occasioned by the recognition of the need for military–diplomatic strength. But in neither the old nor the new was the desire for centralization strong enough to lead the centralizers to force a unitary government of the sort Napoleon had imposed. Even after the Sonderbund war the liberal centralizers wanted to conciliate the losers by retention of the federal form. So in the instance of Switzerland also the hypothesis is confirmed.

West Germany. The federalist tradition in Germany can be clearly traced as far back as the Confederation of 1815 and some say as far back as the Holy Roman empire. But the Confederation of 1815 was highly peripheralized and was used mainly as a device to frustrate liberal and nationalistic desires for unification. Hence the first appearance of something like modern centralized federalism came with the formation in 1871 of the German empire. Most commentators on the constitution of the empire have dismissed it as a "sham federalism." Nevertheless it displayed most of the characteristics usually mentioned in recent definitions of federalism: central and constituent governments each had unique and concurrent powers to govern the same people, guarantees of the integrity of constituent governments were given by the central government, and it originated in the circumstances of our two conditions. It was indeed more centralized than any federation up to that time had been, which is doubtless why it has been felt to be a sham; but it was considerably less centralized than subsequent federalisms with impeccable title to the name, and for that reason I have no reservations in asserting that it was the first German centralized federalism.

That the federation of 1871 originated under circumstances of

great foreign hostility and was therefore aimed at improving the
military–diplomatic position of the German states, especially of
Prussia, can hardly be doubted when one recalls the Austro-
Prussian War of 1866 and the Franco-Prussian War of 1870. Bis-
marck had pursued a policy of aggressive expansion and could
expect hostility not only from those he defeated but also from
those he threatened by his upsetting of the balance of power. His
answer to this anticipated hostility was the consolidation of the
peripheralized confederation into the centralized empire by means
of the federal bargain. Bavaria, Baden, Württemberg, etc., were
brought into the empire with a perpetual guarantee of their
dynasties (the Kings of Bavaria and Baden, for example, were
theoretically equal to the King of Prussia, except that he happened also to be the German emperor), with a second chamber to
represent constituent governments (except that Prussia was by
far the greatest government represented), and with a set of
duties reserved to constituent governments.

Thus the federalism of the empire originated in exactly the
circumstances set forth in the two conditions in the beginning of
this chapter. Its internal arrangements were somewhat different
from federalisms formed on the example of the United States in
that almost all the legislative power was retained by the central
government whereas much the greater part of the administration
of both national and local legislation was delegated to the constituents. But this local variation, which Arnold Brecht called
"horizontal" federalism in contrast to the "vertical" federalism
of the American–Commonwealth tradition, may be ascribed to
the unique circumstances of its creation without in any way
denying the existence of the general circumstances common to
all federalisms.[9]

Since the federalism of the empire, two new federal constitutions have been adopted in Germany, the Weimar constitution of
1921 and the Bonn constitution of 1949. Both have expressed the
main feature of the imperial federalism; *i.e.*, its horizontal nature,
and have thus not been "true" federalisms in the interpretation of
legalists of the United States–Commonwealth tradition like Pro-

[9] Arnold Brecht, *Federalism and Regionalism in Germany* (New York:
Oxford University Press, 1945) pp. 47ff.

fessor Wheare.[10] By their very continuation of this feature, however, they demonstrate that the crucial event in German federalism was the adoption of the imperial constitution.

By reason of the primacy of the imperial constitution, it is not necessary to show that the two conditions were present at the time of the adoption of the later constitutions. But to allay any doubts that may exist, I shall briefly show that they were present. In 1919, with the collapse of the empire, government in Germany substantially reverted to the constituent states of the former empire, which became republics in those troubled times. To organize a defeated Germany it was necessary to bring together again the constituents of the empire and this is precisely what the Weimar constitution accomplished in complete accord, therefore, with the two conditions. After World War II, constitution-making in Germany was dominated by American occupation forces who wished to impose federalism both as an alternative to the Morgenthau plan of Balkanizing Germany and as an expression of their provincial conviction that federalism was a "good thing." That the Bonn "fundamental law" was federal in nature may thus partially be attributed to the presence of Americans. But it may also be attributed to a deeper political circumstance: the hope and expectation of reuniting West and East Germany. What was written at Bonn was called a fundamental law rather than a constitution and was federal in nature because of the hope of attracting East Germany back into the federation. It was a proposed bargain in the face of the Soviet military threat and thus satisfies the conditions of the hypothesis.

Austria. As in the instance of Germany, centralized federalism in Austria appeared first in connection with the controversies in the 1860's over the nature of the peripheralized Confederation of 1815. Emperor Franz Joseph created the so-called Dual Monarchy of Austria-Hungary in 1867, after Austria's defeat in the Austro-Prussian War, as a device to strengthen the monarchy in its competition with Prussia for control of the German Confedera-

---

[10] K. C. Wheare, *Federal Government* (London: Oxford University Press, 1953) pp. 26ff. This is a characteristic example of Professor Wheare's provincialism in his fairly consistent misinterpretation of federalism.

tion. The Dual Monarchy provided for substantial local autonomy
to the Hungarian aristocracy and, after 1873, provided some
lesser measure of the same kind of autonomy to the Czechs.
Thus the creation of the Dual Monarchy, which was a curious
and wholly local kind of federalism, occurred in exactly those
circumstances set forth in the two conditions. As in Germany,
therefore, the federalism of 1867 provided the tradition to which
all subsequent federalisms in Austria have adhered. But, unlike
Germany, the federalism in Austria after World War I was not a
replication of an earlier federalism. Rather it was based on the
fact that, with the collapse of the monarchy, no governments
were left in Austria but the provincial ones. As Schlesinger remarks, "Under such conditions Austria *was*, virtually, a federation (unless she was about to lapse into a state of anarchy) . . ." [11]
Given the fact that some sections of even lesser Austria (by
"lesser Austria" I mean what was left of Austria after the collapse and dismemberment of the Austro-Hungarian empire) were
about to defect to Italy, the military–diplomatic reason for the
federal bargain among quasi-independent provinces is abundantly
clear. Thus the federalism of the first Austrian republic clearly
satisfies the hypothesis. As for the second Austrian republic after
the liberation of 1945, one can say that it repeated, under American auspices (perhaps one should say "dictation"), the institutions adopted after the World War I. And yet it too reflects something of the two conditions in a somewhat attenuated form. For
Austria the main political events of the period between the wars
were the attempt to create a unique Austrian nation and the
failure of that attempt in Hitler's *anschluss*. Back of the federal
bargain stands the fact of *anschluss*, the ever-present fear of an
aggressive Germany, and, owing to that fear, the intention to
give all parties and geographic areas a part in the government.

Soviet Union. The federalism of the Soviet Union, which is almost entirely indigenous, is as clearly the product of the two
conditions as are the United States and German federalisms. The

[11] Rudolph Schlesinger, *Federalism in Central and Eastern Europe* (London: Kegan Paul, 1945) p. 253. See also p. 259, where Schlesinger remarks,
"there could have been no alternative to federalism but civil war."

Russian revolution in February in Petrograd was accompanied by other nationalist revolutions elsewhere in the Russian empire so that the immediate end product of revolution in 1917 was a set of national governments in Russia, in the Baltic States, in Poland, in the Ukraine, in White Russia, in the Caucasus, in the trans-Caucasian region, and in central Asia. In some of these peripheral areas of the empire, such as the Caucasus, much the same sequence of events occurred as in Russia proper; that is, national revolutions were succeeded by left proletarian revolutions, whereas in others, such as the Baltic States, the national revolution was the end of the process. In Russia proper, during the period of civil war and war with Poland, Lenin sought to strengthen the Soviet government by the federal bargain with White Russia and some internal dissidents such as the Volga Germans. Thus he created autonomous units within the Russian Soviet Socialist Republic for the Volga Germans and later for the Kalmuks, the Bashkirs, the Tatars, the Kirghiz, the Daghestani, and the Crimeans. Autonomous governments such as these were clearly responses to the circumstances of the first condition; that is, they were a kind of bribe; but, since the dissidents conciliated did not necessarily feel any sympathy with the military objectives of the Soviet Union, these instances do not satisfy the second condition. But in the course of 1920–22 the left-wing governments of Armenia, Georgia, Transcaucasus, *et. al.*, all of which felt a genuine sympathy with the military objectives of the Soviet government in Russia, were persuaded to join with the Russian Soviet government. This juncture was formalized with the constitution of 1924, which joined Russia, White Russia, the Ukraine, and the Transcaucasus in the Soviet Union. It is true that the process of making this constitution started in 1922 and that by the time it was adopted the regional autonomy of the acceding governments had been abolished by means of Bolshevik domination of all the governments involved, but nevertheless when the process started the main governments involved agreed with Russia on military questions and gladly accepted the bribe of federalism to meet the military threat. Since 1923 the Soviet Union has been highly centralized and for that reason many scholars have refused to call it a federalism. This refusal is, however, merely the expression of the American–Commonwealth mythology that federalism ought to prevent tryanny. Since the Soviet Union preserves all the features of federalism, the mere fact that its federalism fails to prevent tyranny should not lead to casting it out of the class of federalisms. Rather it should lead to a re-evaluation of what federalism means and implies.

Yugoslavia. The federalism of Yugoslavia is based on three sources. One is the rather inchoate tradition of federalism from the Austrian empire; a second is the experience and example of the Soviet Union; and a third is the military–diplomatic ambitions of Marshal Tito. Apparently Tito attempted to use federalism for two purposes: (1) to satisfy resentful minorities within Yugo-slavia and (2) to serve as an attraction to other Balkan states in the creation of a great central European nation under Tito's leadership. In the Austrian empire the Slavic minorities felt (and in fact were) oppressed. And when Yugoslavia was formed in 1919 as a kind of greater Serbia those same minorities, especially Croats, continued to feel mistreated. Tito's federalism was par-tially at least aimed at alleviating the sense of national oppression by giving territorially based ethnic groups some slight measure of self-government (or at least government by Communists from the same ethnic origins as themselves). Beyond this, however, Tito's federalism was constructed so that it might accept new members. Along with Dimitrov of Bulgaria, Tito had planned, with Stalin's approval, a Balkan Union, presumably to include both Bulgaria and Albania as well as Yugoslavia, perhaps to in-clude Roumania, Greece, Hungary, and as Tito's ambitions grew, even Poland. At the same time Tito had plans to absorb at least Trieste and perhaps other areas of Italy and Austria. Federalism is an efficient form for such territorial expansion since new con-stituent units can be brought into the federation without losing either territorial identity or the jobs of their rulers.

In all the federalisms so far discussed (except possibly Ger-many, Austria, and Australia), the military need was to ward off or anticipate some expected aggression. In the case of Yugoslavia, however, the military need was imperialistic, for federalism there was clearly to prepare for aggression rather than defense. This seems clearly to have been the case also in the union of Ethiopia and Eritrea. But the variation in military objectives does not alter the fundamental relationship between federalism and military preparedness. Hence, although those prospectively imperial federalisms like Yugoslavia, Ethiopia, and possibly Australia and Austria and Germany initially may not seem quite the same as the rest, still these instances satisfy the conditions of the rather narrow military condition. And as prospective imperialisms, they also satisfy the expansion condition.

V SPANISH-AMERICAN FEDERALISMS

The essential features of the adoption of federalism in Spanish-American nations are so similar that these events can be considered together. All these federalisms originated in the military crisis of that prolonged and bitter warfare which seldom seemed to favor the revolutionists until near the very end. The wars started in 1810 and, at least in Bolívar's area (which was the militarily crucial one), were not completed until 1826. During that period Venezuela, Colombia, Argentina (including Uruguay), Mexico, and Central America adopted federal constitutions. Furthermore, for a short while Gran Colombia was a federation of what are now Ecuador, Colombia, and Venezuela. Thus, in 1826 much the greater part of Spanish America was governed by federalisms created during the course of revolution, presumably for the better prosecution of the wars.

An alternative interpretation of the motive for federalism in revolutionary Spanish America has nevertheless frequently been suggested. Federalism was often the rallying cry of the liberal parties, whereas conservatives as well as Rousseauesque military dictators like Bolívar and O'Higgins preferred unitary governments. Given this political division, it is easy to identify the movement for federalism as a movement for freedom. Thus, the origin of these federalisms can be interpreted as the adoption of a political ideal rather than, as I have previously interpreted it in every instance, as the adoption of a mere military–diplomatic expedient that is morally neutral.

Careful historians of Latin American thought are, however, thoroughly opposed to this romantic and idealistic version of the origin of Latin federalism. Speaking of "provincial sovereignty," Belaunde says:

> When the central authorities had been swept aside and the authority of the mother country was no longer recognized, the government fell necessarily into the hands of local oligarchies or of the *caudillos* who took the lead in the popular insurrection. So much for the fact. As for the doctrine, what we have is the logical result of the application of the principle of communal sovereignty when the Peninsular authorities had disappeared. This doctrine was exaggerated by Jacobin and federalist imitation.
>
> This is the true origin of American federalism . . . . In a general way, it is not badly applied ideology which created the movement or the tendency [*i.e.*, toward federalism] but the tendency supported by determined interests that encountered its ideology.[12]

In short, effective power, once Spanish authority was gone, lay in the hands of *caudillos* who were willing and eager to unite for revolutionary purposes but not for much else. This is, of course, the ideal setting for some kind of federalism, which in fact appeared over most of the former Spanish lands. That this interpretation is substantially correct is shown by the gradual disappearance of federalism once the pressing military need for it had disappeared. Chile prepared a federal constitution in 1826, adopted a highly centralized federalism in 1828, and abandoned federalism completely in 1833. Uruguay broke off from La Plata in 1828 and adopted a unitary government in 1830. In that same year Gran Colombia broke up into the constituent units of Ecuador, Venezuela, and New Granada (later Colombia). In 1839 the Central American Federation disbanded into Guatemala, Salvador, Honduras, Costa Rica, and Nicaragua. Finally, in 1886 the Colombian federation was revised into a highly centralized unitary government. So much for formal constitutional revision. In the post-revolutionary period, many federal constitutions have been operated (usually by dictators) as if they were unitary governments. Thus Mexico, for example, has retained a federal constitution through most of its history, although its federalism

---

[12] Victor Andrés Belaunde, *Bolívar and the Political Thought of the Spanish American Revolution* (Baltimore: Johns Hopkins Press, 1938) pp. 131-32.

has usually been as highly centralized as is the federalism of the Soviet Union. Only in Argentina and to a much lesser degree in Venezuela has the federalist tradition really survived — in both instances in a highly centralized form. The general interpretation of these events is that, once the fear of imperial reconquest subsided, the *caudillos* and local oligarchies had no motive to accept any kind of centralization. In some instances this changed state of mind led to the dissolution of the federation, whereas in others it led to centralizing dictatorships, some of which abandoned even the pretense of federalism.

All these remarks demonstrate that the second condition; namely, that the receivers of the federal offer be motivated by a military goal, applies to all Spanish American federalisms. And they demonstrate as well that the first condition also applies; namely, that the offerers of the federal bargain prefer federalism to conquest. When the concern over Spanish reconquest died down, federalism waned because few national leaders were willing to offer the necessary bargain to the *caudillos*. In those cases in which a strong national leader ultimately appeared (*e.g.*, Chile, Colombia), federalism was changed to unitary government. But when no strong national leader appeared, the federation simply dissolved into constituent units.

VI BRAZIL

It is customary to identify the origin of Brazil's federalism with the republican revolution of 1889.[13] But in fact the empire, like the later German and Austro-Hungarian empires, was itself a kind of federal government, the federal features of which originated in exactly the circumstances set forth in the hypothesis.

From the beginning there was a certain popular element in the Brazilian empire, an element epitomized in its very name, which was intended to recall the popularly acclaimed Roman *imperator* rather than a divinely chosen king. Furthermore, the heritage of Portuguese rule was decentralizing in character for the nation was from the beginning divided into coastal provinces,

[13] Herman G. James, *The Constitutional System of Brazil* (Washington, D.C.: The Carnegie Institution of Washington, 1923) pp. 1-8.

each of which acquired its own local traditions and ruling class.
The original constitution of the empire was substantially unitary
in nature, but in 1834 this constitution was revised by the Additional Act to create a kind of federalism, specifically a senate
based on selection by provincial legislatures.

The immediate motive for the Additional Act was clearly military–diplomatic in nature. In the revolutionary deeds of 1831,
Dom Pedro I had been expelled and the crown was given to his
infant son, Dom Pedro II. In the ensuing year, partly as a reaction against the conservatism of the central government of Dom
Pedro I and partly as an expression of the sense of independence
of local oligarchies, there was a series of revolts in, especially,
outlying provinces. In 1833 the constitutional revision of the Additional Act was proposed, chiefly to mitigate the conditions
that led to the local revolts for provincial autonomy. This fact
about its origin confirms the existence of the first condition that
the bargain-offerers must prefer a bargain to conquest. In the
next year, at just about the time of the passage of the Act, the
agitation intensified for the return of Dom Pedro I, possibly with
the support of European arms. Although the conservatives certainly did not intend this result, their agitation frightened the
legislature into the passage of the Additional Act, with its feder-
alistic reform of the senate, which theretofore had been the main
source of conservative power. Thus the facts in this case also indicate the occurrence of the military condition that the bargain
acceptors recognize a military danger. Subsequent elaboration of
federalism in 1889 and later are simply continuations of the tradition established in 1834 by the federal empire.

VII   NON-BRITISH FEDERALISMS IN AFRICA
         AND ASIA

              These constitute a heterogeneous group of fed-
eralisms (Ethiopia, Indonesia, the Mali Federation, and the Congo-
lese Federation), none of which is very strong, two of which
have already failed, and two more of which have dim futures.
Yet each in its way is an illustration of the validity of the hypothesis.

The strongest and apparently most stable is the Union of Ethi-

Non-British federalisms in Africa and Asia   45

opia and Eritrea, which is a kind of dual monarchy. Each nation has its own constitution and owes common allegiance to the Ethiopian monarchy. This federalism is a joint consequence (1) of the United Nations' effort to divest itself of trusteeship responsibilities for former Italian colonies and (2) of the expansionist ambitions of the Ethiopian monarch. The UN sought a solution to its responsibilities and Ethiopia provided the solution with its federal proposal. This union satisfies the first condition in that Ethiopia was willing to offer the bargain as the only feasible means of acquiring the territory and it satisfies the second condition since for Ethiopia it was a means of imperial expansion in which Eritrea acquiesced. In this respect the Ethiopian federalism is quite similar to the Yugoslavian, the more so since the Ethiopian government may have envisioned the ultimate absorption of the several Somalilands (also under UN trusteeship) by means of the same device.

Mali Federation. In the course of the dismantling of the French empire, the French colonial administration, otherwise totally inexperienced with federalism, experimented with a West African federation, which finally ended up in attenuated form as the Mali Federation with a life of several months. The first French response to a realization of the probable success of independence movements was to propose the French Union; *i.e.*, the integration of colonies with metropolitan France. Since this was no more than disguised colonialism, it never caught on; but under the guise of assisting the Union, some West African politicians, notably the Senegalese leader Leopold Senghor, promoted a federation for exactly the same presumed motives of personal aggrandizement that Nkrumah has for promoting pan-Africanism. Although several other colonies were originally included, by the time of the formal independence from the French Community, only Senegal and Soudan were included, the one only fairly Europeanized, the other barely touched culturally by French rule. In the ensuing few weeks of federation, the main political question was the selection of a president. As the coalition-formation progressed on this point, it became apparent that Senghor would lose, whereupon he dissolved the federation.

It is notable that neither of my conditions was present in this federation. Senghor was eager to offer the federal bargain as long as he thought he could control the federation. Indeed, that the federation existed at all was owing to his previous willingness to compromise. But Senghor's eagerness disappeared when it appeared that federation would not suit his purposes. Thus the first condition was lacking. And no military threat existed at any time. The only military–diplomatic goal was Senghor's expansionism and this goal disappeared when the Soudanese outmaneuvered him. Hence the second condition was also lacking. In the absence of both conditions this federalism could not succeed.

Congo. The Belgian government, when it resigned from the Congo, left its colony with a unitary constitution. The civil wars that followed were at least partially occasioned by provincial resentment of the unitary form, although the attempts by Belgium, the Soviet Union, the United States, and the UN to influence provincial attitudes and decisions have so obscured the desires of the provinces that it is difficult to say what the indigenous peoples and politicians want. As a result of UN military intervention something of a federalism now exists in the Congo, based entirely for the moment on UN force. It is therefore too early to say whether or not this federal notion will survive or, if it does, whether or not it will remain a federation. In any event, the expansion condition is present by reason of UN insistence and the military condition is present by reason of the persistent intervention of Belgium and the Soviet Union.

Indonesia. The federalism in Indonesia, which was rejected after a substantial civil war, is especially interesting as an example in which both conditions of the hypothesis were absent. The rejection of federalism therefore suggests in a negative way the validity of the hypothesis.

Federalism in Indonesia was planned by the Dutch administration as a means of transferring power in all the Dutch colonies in southeast Asia. The core was to be Netherlands Indies (Indonesia) in association with Timur, Sumatra, Borneo, Celebes, Moluccas, New Guinea, etc. A sympathetic interpretation of the Dutch motives is that the Dutch colonial officials believed (1) that the cultures of the several parts were so divergent as to require considerable local autonomy if they were to remain together and (2) that federalism was an adequate device to guarantee that autonomy. On the other hand, a hostile interpretation of Dutch motives is that the Dutch believed that they might continue to play a significant part in Indonesian affairs after independence if those parts of the Indies still friendly to the Dutch had extensive autonomy from Djakarta. In this view a Dutch-imposed federalism is a form of the policy of divide and rule.

Fortunately, we do not need to speculate about Dutch motives for the significant fact is that, rightly or wrongly, Javanese leaders adopted the hostile interpretation. Hence they rejected federalism as just another piece of Dutch craftiness. Further, they rejected the entire notion of a bargain, preferring to use military conquest to acquire all reluctant parts of the Dutch Asian empire. Thus the first condition of federalism, the willingness to bargain, was absent. So also was the second. The Dutch colonial system had been founded on a remarkably small metropolitan base and persisted as long as it did only because of the military immaturity of the colonials. The effect of the Japanese conquest in World War II was to destroy much of the Dutch military strength and at the same time to educate the Indonesians. Simultaneously the German conquest of the Netherlands weakened the Dutch even further. It was therefore apparent in 1949, when the federal constitution came into existence and independence was proclaimed, that no serious military threat to Indonesia existed. Hence there was no need for a federal bargain and the second condition was not satisfied. Within less than a year (by August, 1950), federalism in Indonesia was abolished in favor of a unitary government.

Thus, Indonesian federalism failed simply because it could not satisfy the necessary conditions for federalism in its origin. The main historian of Indonesian federalism remarks in retrospect, however:

> Recent writers have rightly recognized that opposition to the federal state in Indonesia was largely due to the fact that it was

"Dutch-inspired" or "Dutch-imposed," rather than because of any absence of intrinsic merit in the plan.[14]

But in the interpretation of federalism set forth here there was indeed an intrinsic defect in the plan. I have been arguing that constitutions are bargains that come out of specifiable political conditions. Any attempt to copy a particular bargain outside of the specified political context is surely an intrinsic defect of the plan itself. And this is what was wrong with federalism in Indonesia.

＊   ＊   ＊

On the basis of the evidence here set forth, we may conclude that the hypothesis is confirmed that the military and expansion conditions are necessary to the occurrence of federalism.

[14] A. Arthur Schiller, *The Formation of Federal Indonesia 1945-49* (The Hague: Van Hoeve, 1955) p. 9. Schiller cites George Kahin, *Nationalism and Revolution in Indonesia* (Ithaca, N.Y.: Cornell University Press, 1952) p. 450, in support of this view.

The maintenance of federalism: the administrative theory

Aʟᴛʜᴏᴜɢʜ ᴀ willingness to compromise and a recognized need for military unity are two necessary predisposing conditions for the federal bargain, they cannot have much to do with its survival. If they were the conditions of keeping the bargain as well as of making it, then remarkably few bargains would be kept. As military tensions eased, federal unions either would disintegrate or, if governed by determined centralizers, would become unitary. This is, of course, what happened to most of the peripheralized federalisms prior to 1787. And the few that survived for appreciable lengths of time (*e.g.*, the Swiss and Dutch confederations) were seldom without a dire military threat. Hence it may well be that the conditions necessary for keeping the bargain of a peripheralized federalism are the same as those for making it. But this surely cannot be true of centralized federalisms, for there are too many instances to the contrary. The United States has survived for a century and three-quarters, although the initial military conditions of its centralization disappeared within a generation after 1787. The Canadian federation

49

50   *The maintenance of federalism*

has survived for nearly a century, yet the military–diplomatic concerns that called it forth were passing away even as the federation was founded. The Brazilian and Argentinian federations are both much more than a century old and yet the military dangers from both Europe and each other had disappeared by 1850. Etc., etc. It must be, therefore, that the conditions of keeping the bargain are different from the conditions of making it, at least in centralized federalisms. My concern in this chapter and the next two is to identify some of these conditions for survival.

In general the reason for the survival of centralized federalisms is the fact that they are centralized; that the rulers of the federation can overawe and overrule, but not annihilate, the rulers of the constituent units. Unfortunately a general statement of this sort is not very useful for it is almost a tautology. What one wants for understanding the survival of centralized federalism is a detailed analysis of the devices for overawing and overruling and of the devices for moderating the overawing; and such analysis can come only from surveys of constitutional arrangements. Such an analysis is undertaken in the following three chapters, of which I offer a preview here.

Survival has, as I have just pointed out, two features: (1) centralization, which allows the central government to exploit the advantages of a larger base for taxes and armies, and (2) maintenance of guarantees to the constituent units, which prevents the transformation of federalism to a unitary government. The most frequently offered explanation of survival attempts to combine these features with the administrative system. It asserts that the gradual transfer of administrative duties to the center provides for centralization whereas the sharing of these duties between the center and the periphery maintains the guarantees. In this chapter this assertion is examined in detail with respect to the system of federalism in the United States, incidentally presenting a fairly detailed examination of the way in which at least one federalism works. The conclusion of this survey is, however, that the administrative theory, though initially attractive, does not hold for the United States. Since it does not hold for the system for which and from which it was inferred, it probably cannot be expected to hold elsewhere. Given this conclusion, one must look elsewhere for an

Administrative theory of federalism   *51*

explanation of survival and hence in Chapter 4 I survey the institutions and cultural conditions in the United States that serve the centralizing and guarantee-maintaining functions. Having identified these institutions and conditions for one federalism, in Chapter 5 the same kind of institutions and conditions are identified in seven others. The main conclusion from Chapters 4 and 5 is that the structure of the system of political parties is what encourages or discourages the maintenance of the federal bargain.

I   THE ADMINISTRATIVE THEORY OF FEDERALISM

Since the kinds of federalism have been distinguished by the division of areas of action between the central and constituent governments, the obvious way to investigate the degree of centralization is, according to the administrative theory of federalism, to look at the way in which the areas of action are in fact divided up. The traditional method is to examine the formal division in the Constitution and the gloss applied to it by judicial decision. (In most federalisms, courts interpret the exact meaning of the division; and in the United States it has been customary to refer to the Supreme Court as "the arbiter of federalism.") The fault in this method is that judicial decisions concern the boundaries of areas of action and do not in any way indicate their absolute size and importance. Yet most of the history and analysis of federalism has been written by constitutional lawyers using judicial decisions as their raw material. As a consequence the tradition provides us with a highly distorted picture of the relationship between the nation and the states.

In order to avoid the lawyers' distortion and to present the case for the administrative theory as fairly and completely as possible, one must look at the whole arrangement of authority over governmental functions,[1] which will be attempted in this chapter.

In order to survey the whole range of action in a systematic

---

[1] A step in this direction has been taken in Daniel J. Elazar, *The American Partnership* (Chicago: University of Chicago Press, 1962) which is an examination of the total picture of action by state and national government in several substantive areas. Unfortunately his picture is al somewhat distorted because of his avoidance of substantive areas not displaying the feature of cooperation he wished to emphasize.

way, we need some sort of distribution of functions into manageable categories. In Table 3.1 one possible categorization is set forth. It purports to be no more than a distillation of the common sense of the scholarly tradition about what governments in the United States do. Its usefulness, if it has any, is its completeness. And the test of completeness is: If some governmental action cannot be placed in a category except by an argument that scholarly common sense would regard as contrived, then a new category is needed and Table 3.1 is incomplete. If, on the other hand, and again in accordance with scholarly common sense, any given governmental action fits easily into one or more categories, then the table is complete. I have tested this table on a number of friends and, provisionally at least, I regard it as complete. Since it is offered only for the American tradition, however, it is clearly incomplete for others, although it probably fits the whole Western tradition fairly well. (Incidentally, it is not to be inferred that the categories are listed in order of importance for, quite obviously, importance varies over time and in accordance with unique historical events.)

Using this list, we now shall survey for each of the nineteen categories the division of action between federal and constituent governments from 1788 to the present.

II GETTING MONEY

Current Financing. The arrangements in the Constitution give almost unlimited taxing power to the central government, or so the first clauses of Article I, Section 8, have been interpreted in recent years. But given the kinds of taxes that had been invented in 1787 (*i.e.*, customs duties, excises on goods and services, capitation taxes, and taxes on real property), this grant is not nearly so generous as it appears. The right to impose excises, though granted, was not really expected to be used, as the response of the Whiskey Rebellion of 1793 indicates. Furthermore, the really productive tax was the one on real property, which the framers apparently intended to reserve for the states and localities by means of their confusing restriction on direct taxation by the central government (Article I, Section 9). By reason of wholly adventitious circumstances, however, this ap-

Getting money   *53*

Table 3.1   FUNCTIONAL AREAS OF GOVERNMENTAL ACTION

A. *Getting Money*
   1. By current financing, *e.g.*, tax collection, sales of public property, etc.
   2. By deferred financing, *e.g.*, borrowing
B. *Spending Money*
   1. On external affairs, *e.g.*, military and diplomatic affairs
   2. On activities related to internal order
     a. Maintenance of public safety, *e.g.*, enforcement of criminal law
     b. Supervision of property rights, *e.g.*, defining and protecting ownership of realty and personalty
     c. Supervision of civic rights and liberties, *e.g.*, defining and protecting the right to vote
     d. Supervision of public and private morality, *e.g.*, censorship, supervision of marriage
     e. Inculcation of patriotism, *e.g.*, provision of national holidays
   3. On activities related to trade
     a. Provision and supervision of money and credit, *e.g.*, central banking
     b. Provision and supervision of facilities for transportation and communication, *e.g.*, management of the post office
     c. Provision and supervision of utilities, *e.g.*, management of wells and atomic energy plants
     d. Supervision and regulation of production and distribution of goods and services, *e.g.*, supervision of labor-management relations
     e. Encouragement of economic development, *e.g.*, granting subsidies
     f. Supervision of irreplaceable resources, *e.g.*, conservation and management of forests
   4. On activities related to citizens' welfare
     a. Provision and supervision of education
     b. Provision of aid to the indigent or handicapped
     c. Provision for recreation and culture, *e.g.*, maintenance of parks, musical societies, etc.
     d. Provision of public health services, *e.g.*, supervision of drug manufacturing
     e. Encouragement of the acquisition of new knowledge, *e.g.*, granting patents and copyrights, supporting exploration, encouraging scientific societies.

54   *The maintenance of federalism*

parently generous but actually niggardly grant of support to the
center was soon augmented from another source: land sales. In
its early years the central government subsisted almost entirely
on excises and, especially, customs. But as the tempo of the west-
ward movement increased, the income from sales of western
lands outstripped all other sources of revenue. Indeed, it was
possible for Jacksonians to lower the tariff largely because of
surplus income from land — and it is not fanciful to suggest that
the original Republican policy of free land and high tariffs were
related: Once it started to give the land away, the central government was forced to rely on tariffs for revenue.

From 1815, the end of the second war with England, to 1865,
the end of the Civil War, the Union was at its weakest. The British failure to invade successfully removed the threat of foreign
war and thus removed one of the original conditions of federation. The failure of secession, on the other hand, ensured the
continuation of the Union. But in between these two situations,
the Union was weak. Quite probably one of the factors that allowed it to survive was the unanticipated income from land sales,
which relieved the central government of the necessity for invad-
ing the states for tax purposes.

Until the second decade of this century both central and constituent governments could live on their traditional resources,
although both kinds of governments, especially the central one,
were forced to amazing contrivances in excise taxes. But the expansion of functions of government at both levels has forced the
development of new kinds of taxes. The two major innovations
have been the income tax and the sales tax, each of which has
been adopted primarily by the kind of government best able to
collect it. The crucial feature of the income tax is that the taxing
authority must be able to collect on income earned in every
place, lest capital flee from an income-taxing jurisdiction to one
that is not. This the national government is able to do, especially
since by currency control, etc., it is even able to collect on income earned outside the United States. The crucial problem of
sales taxes is that the taxing authority must cover one territorial
area completely in order to minimize evasion. This also the national government is able to do best, but the states can do it almost

Getting money 55

as well. Hence the nation has been the primary user of the income tax and the states the primary users of the sales tax.

I suppose there is no necessary reason why the income taxes should produce far more revenue than sales taxes, but such has in fact been the situation. On the basis of resources for current financing, then, the central government has come in this century to have far greater resources than the states. The Sixteenth Amendment (1913) was required in order to bring this situation about, although the authority granted was not extensively used until the 1930's.

Summarizing: In the beginning, states probably had better tax resources than the nation, although revenue from land sales made up for national tax disabilities in the first half of the 19th century. In this century, the tax resources of the central government have been much greater than the resources of the states, largely because of the decision to concentrate income taxation at the center.

Borrowing. As long as it was believed that borrowing by all levels of government laid a charge on future generations for the sake of the present one, the constitutional authorization of borrowing for the federal government did not place it in a special position. It was no more than similar authorizations to state governments for the purpose of spreading the payment for capital assets over the life of the assets. But when it came to be understood that borrowing by the central government had an economic effect quite different from that of borrowing by lesser governments, then the way was opened for huge expenditures by central governments even in peacetime.

The difference in economic effect between borrowing by the two levels of government is that borrowing by the central government is a cost to the society at the time of borrowing and is thus a kind of current financing like taxation, whereas borrowing by lesser governments is a cost to the society at the time of repayment and is thus genuinely a deferred charge. That borrowing by the government that controls the system of money and credit is only a current economic cost can be shown thus: If the central government with citizens $A, B, \ldots, N$ borrows x

dollars from citizens I, J, and K in time period t, no citizens (neither those in the set $\{A, B, \ldots, N\}$ nor those in its subset $\{I, J, \text{and } K\}$) can use these x dollars in period t. If the amount of money available for the private sector in the absence of borrowing is Q, then this amount for period t is $(Q - x)$. Thus what is borrowed diminishes the size of funds in the private sector during the period in which the borrowing occurs. When the central government repays x in time period $(t + 20)$, it taxes A, B, $\ldots, N$ to raise x and pays x out to I, J, and K. Since $\{I, J, \text{and } K\}$ is a subset of $\{A, B, \ldots, N\}$ there is no effect on Q. Hence there is no economic cost, but merely redistribution, in the repayment of x. It is quite otherwise with borrowing by lesser governments, especially if one assumes that the persons who lend are not citizens of the jurisdiction they lend to. If a state government borrows x dollars from non-citizens in period t, there is no diminution of Q for the citizens of the state. But in period $(t + 20)$, when x is repaid, taxes in x amount are taken from citizens to repay non-citizens, so that citizens have only $(Q - x)$. Thus the economic cost is incurred only when the debt is repaid.

Borrowing by the central government may thus be regarded as a kind of selective taxation in which the taxpayer voluntarily foregoes the present use of his money for the sake of interest. Furthermore, the interest is socially costless since it is merely a redistribution from all taxpayers to bond holders. As a tax that costs the society nothing beyond what the self-chosen taxpayer chooses to forego, borrowing by the central government is thus an exceptionally attractive tool of current financing. Since the realization in the mid-1930's that central borrowing had this feature, it has become a widely used tool of fiscal policy and public finance. In the United States, it has provided the central government with a potent new fiscal resource, partly at the expense of lesser governments. The framers of the Constitution specifically granted the central government the authority to borrow money, probably with the intention of ensuring that the debts to England (incurred by the treaty of 1783 to recompense for revolutionary confiscations of Tory property) would be paid. But because the advance of economic science has shown the fallacy of regarding all borrowing as a deferred charge, this simple grant of a traditional (but not heavily used) power has turned into a potent new kind of current financing — but only for the central government, not for the states and localities.

III EXTERNAL AFFAIRS

As I have previously shown, one immediately necessary condition for the federal bargain in 1787 was the presence of a severe external threat. Hence one of the main concerns of the framers was to improve federal control of military–diplomatic affairs. They did so by authorizing the central government:

1. to maintain an army and navy
2. to organize and use the militia of the states
3. to maintain diplomatic relations, to make treaties, and to regard treaties as part of the fundamental law.

We are so accustomed today to think of foreign affairs as exclusively the function of the central government that it is difficult to imagine ourselves back into the situation of 1788. Today this list of powers seems to be adequate to guarantee full centralization. But it was not so assumed in 1788. Not only were the states presumably to have some indirect control over ambassadors and treaties through the medium of the Senate, but the training and officering of the militia was directly in the hands of the states. Furthermore, the Second Amendment was intended to guarantee that state control of the militia would be reinforced and perpetuated.

It seems to me that, in 1788, even though the control of foreign affairs had been centralized somewhat in comparison with the situation under the Articles, still the control of this function was more peripheral than central. The grant of authority to the central government to provide and maintain an army and navy was initially only good intention, for neither existed in 1788. The only military forces in the United States, aside from one battery of artillery and several small coastal vessels, were the militia, which the states controlled. Furthermore, it was expected that the militia would make up the main, if not the only, military force for the foreseeable future. Or so, at least, I infer from some of the circumstances involved in the whole process of constitution-writing. Much care was taken at the Philadelphia convention to centralize the control of the militia to just the right degree. The framers as a whole would have preferred to nationalize, but dared not; and so they carried the process as far as they felt they could, producing a highly unmilitary division of command. Judging by the reaction in the ratifying conventions, the framers carried the process too far. In the Virginia convention, for example, more criticism was directed at the militia provision than at any other part of the Constitution. The result of this criticism was the Second Amendment, which perpetually guaranteed the right of states to maintain militia, presumably because they expected it to be the chief military force for the future. The significance of the retention of a major portion of control over military decisions in the states is that the grant of diplomatic authority to the United States was thereby severely undercut. The Constitution did indeed confide diplomatic affairs exclusively to the national government, as had the Articles; but the independence of the diplomatic negotiator is necessarily conditioned by the apparent validity of his threats and promises and this validity is in turn dependent on the military force behind him. Thus the fact that the American diplomat was deprived of the assurance of the American military force transferred even diplomatic decisions back to state capitols. As late as the War of 1812 this transference was clearly visible both inside and outside the nation. Altogether, therefore, the military–diplomatic provisions of the Constitution, though centralized in appearance, were in fact quite peripheralized.

Centralization in military–diplomatic affairs could not occur until the militia was replaced by the army and navy as the chief military force. The replacement occurred in the period between the War of 1812 and the Mexican War, largely because of the failure of the militia in the War of 1812. An army and navy had been created in Washington's first administration and under Adams the military acadamy at West Point had begun to produce officers. But all this was on a very small scale and the War of 1812 was necessarily fought mostly with militia. This disastrous war taught Americans some lessons: that the most successful units, that is, the navy, were the most professional; and that the militia was

External affairs   59

unreliable in open battle, as at Bladensburg, although it was adequate when entrenched, as at New Orleans. As these lessons gradually pervaded the American mind, the army and navy were expanded far beyond their prewar size, and the service academies produced (apparently deliberately) a considerable oversupply of officers. At the same time the states allowed their militia to decay: militia duty had come to be regarded as onerous, doubtless because of the battlefield failures of the militia, and democratic politicians naturally shrank from imposing an onerous duty on voters. By the time of the Mexican War only a few New England and Middle Atlantic states had a viable militia; and hence that war was fought with nationally organized volunteers.

Once the states abandoned their military arm, they lost their voice in foreign affairs, a loss that can be illustrated by the differing behavior of New England governments in the War of 1812 and the Mexican War. New Englanders of the locally dominant Federalist–Whig tradition disapproved of both wars. In the first one, their recalcitrance had actual military and diplomatic effect. By withholding troops they contributed to specific failures on the battlefield and by threatening secession they embarrassed and weakened the government in Washington, which was thus driven to conclude a hurried and unsatisfactory peace. In the second war, their recalcitrance meant only that New England was not a very good area for recruiting.

The final blow to state participation in the management of external affairs was, of course, the federal victory in the Civil War. Had the attempted secession, with all its concomitant negotiations with other countries, been successful, then the states doubtless would have retained a strong voice in external affairs. But secession was not successful. Indeed its main long-term effect was to generate a need for a strong federal army and otherwise to centralize decision making in Washington.

From time to time since the Civil War, the states have attempted to revive their militia. And today they are undoubtedly better than ever, although presumably much inferior to similar federal forces; but the revival has not affected the federal relationship and the states have never regained a voice in foreign affairs. The revival of the militia started in 1877, when the industrial states of the Middle West and the Middle Atlantic raised local forces to put down the first nationwide strike (in the railroad industry). As I have shown elsewhere, the growth of the militia in the next decade is highly correlated with the spread of labor unrest.[2] Since the National Guard, as it then came to be called, had primarily an internal police function, it could not and did not affect state participation in external affairs. In order to get some federal funds for their internal police, however, the states generally pretended that the National Guard did have a military function. And since there has been a high degree of interlocking between the officer corps of the Guard and local political party organization, the states have been able to persuade Congress to finance special Guard activities. But the federal army, which also has had a powerful lobby, has consistently resisted the military use of, especially, National Guard officers. The repeated outcome of the conflict between the two lobbies has been a compromise in which the states surrender some additional kind of control over the Guard in return for additional federal financing. If the states had hoped that they might regain military significance by recreating a functioning militia, the very form of the compromises has prevented them from doing so. Hence what the states lost between 1815 and 1847 they have never regained. The management of external affairs is exclusively in the hands of the central government.

IV   ACTIVITIES RELATING TO INTERNAL ORDER

The initial and primary responsibility for activities in each of the five categories under this rubric lies with the constituent governments. Although by far the greater bulk of the work is done by the states, over the years the center has acquired some duties, especially in connection with marginal features, in these areas of action. Unfortunately for scholarly accuracy, the constitutional lawyers who study this control at the margin have given the impression that the federal government plays a larger role than it actually does.

[2] William H. Riker, *Soldiers of the States* (Washington, D.C.,: Public Affairs Press, 1957) pp. 41-66.

Internal order   61

There are two theses that I shall defend in the interpretation of the division of authority under this rubric:

1. It has been felt that duties in these categories are the function of the states.
2. When the central government has performed duties in this category, it has usually been assumed that such performance is either temporary or politically extraordinary.

Public Safety. This is the vast routine work of police and fire protection, criminal law enforcement (including the operation of penal institutions), and the mitigation of disasters, the great bulk of which is performed by state governments (and their creatures, the governments of cities and counties). The central government has, however, duplicated what the states do in the territory of the United States not subject to state jurisdiction. At times, indeed through most of the 19th century, this territory was large in area, though small in population. Some have suggested that the duties of the United States in fully governing initially the territory of states-to-be enhanced the national character of the Union and diminished state-oriented patriotism. But since central control of the territories was always felt to be temporary, it is unwise to force this argument very far. At most it can be said that the provision of internal order in the territories throughout the 19th century gave the central government something important to do at a time when its initially primary function of external relations had waned in significance. In the first half of the 20th century, when the United States was a minor imperial power, the central government was of course also responsible for the internal order of dependencies. But this responsibility too was regarded as temporary, as in fact it was. Further, since the United States had in this era much more to do than it had earlier, it is doubtful if the job of governing the Philippines in the 1920's contributed as much to the prestige of the central government then as did the job of governing Wisconsin in the 1840's. There is some territory, of course, which is assumed to be permanently within the jurisdiction of the United States alone, *e.g.*, the District of Columbia and permanent federal installations such as post offices and forts. These are regarded as extraordinary, however. Witness the persistent agitation to turn Washington, D.C., into something like another state. And the federal jurisdiction over special installations is regarded as an adjunct of other federal activities relating to external affairs and the regulation of trade. It is true that a federal criminal law exists for such territory, as well as federal prisons and special federal police (such as the F.B.I. and the Coast Guard); but all these permanent federal activities, though well-known, are but a drop in the bucket compared with the total maintenance of public safety by states and cities and counties.

The more significant federal activity in this area is, in contrast to the maintenance of order in territories, the supervision of order in the states. The Constitution requires the federal government to guarantee republican government in the states. But the federal government has made remarkably little use of this authority. By contrast with Latin American federalisms, India, etc., where a similar provision (copied, at least in the Latin case, almost directly from the United States) has often been used to centralize, the federal government in the United States has only infrequently intervened in the domestic affairs of states. Of course, the whole of Reconstruction after the Civil War constituted intervention, but the remarkable aspect of Reconstruction is that it did not set a pattern. Given the political situation of the mid-1860's — in which the central government was controlled by a party that had not yet won a national Presidential election by a majority — it is not surprising that Reconstruction occurred, nor is it surprising that it lasted ten years or until Republicans believed they could win without it. But this kind of intervention did not set a precedent, possibly because the basic situation of control of the central government by a party in the minority nationally has never recurred.

Lesser kinds of intervention have occasionally happened, usually at the request of state officials who find themselves unable to keep order, but occasionally over the opposition of state officials who sympathize with the disorder. Most such intervention in the past has occurred in connection with large-scale disputes between management and labor (from the railroad strikes of 1877 and

Internal order   63

1893 to the steel strikes of 1952). Recently, however, most intervention has occurred because of the reluctance of officials of a few Southern states to subdue disorders occasioned by U.S. enforcement of U.S. court orders concerning civil rights for Negroes. In both substantive areas of federal intervention to maintain public safety and order, it has clearly been assumed throughout that the intervention is an extraordinary effort and is to be abandoned as soon as the crisis is over.

Except for the mitigation of disaster, which has come to be a recognized federal function provided the disaster is large enough, but which involves mostly financial aid rather than the maintenance of domestic order, federal intervention in this fundamental function of government has never been regularized. It does occur sporadically, but it is nonetheless assumed that domestic order is really the function of the states.

Property Rights. The maintenance of property rights, which is closely related to the maintenance of public safety, has also been traditionally assigned mostly to the states. According to the Beardian view of the Constitution, however, one of its main purposes was to centralize the control of property rights, especially to permit the national courts to supervise state legislatures and courts on this matter. It is true that several provisions of the Constitution do seem to have this effect, *e.g.,* the supremacy clause (Article VI, Section 2) and the prohibitions on states manipulating currency or impairing the obligation of contracts (Article I, Section 10). But the supremacy clause is a general grant of authority to central government, not limited to property rights as such, and is merely another feature of the centralized federalism invented at Philadelphia. And the prohibitions on devaluing currency and contracts, clearly aimed at a specific abuse common in the 1780's, was a prohibition on what was felt to be the business of the states, not a grant of power to the national government. To read these provisions as intending national control of property rights is simply another of Beard's anachronistic fallacies.

But, though the original scheme assigned this function to states (except that the national government was to manage currency and bankruptcy, two subjects on which variation among states is

obviously unwise), still the nation does now partially govern
property directly because of two main developments: (1) the
emergence, in the post-Civil War period, of the Supreme Court
as a really powerful maker of national policy; and (2) the acquisition by the national government of great responsibility for the
soundness of the economy. The latter development, which will
be considered later in the chapter, inevitably invested some control over property rights in the center. The former development,
which came about as a basic structural change in the system, will
be considered here. From the very beginning some judges on the
Supreme Court aspired to make policy, especially in this area,
for the whole nation. But they were successful in only a limited
way until after the Civil War, at which time the judges' personal
motive of aggrandizement coincided with a national conservatism.
The first major attempt by the Supreme Court to define property
rights was abruptly rebuffed: the Court entertained a suit by a
citizen of one state against another state for alleged denial of
property rights and the Constitution was promptly amended to
deny the Court jurisdiction in such suits (Eleventh Amendment,
adopted in 1798). Soon thereafter John Marshall, who is usually
described as the great centralizer, came to lead the Supreme
Court. But Marshall's centralization consisted chiefly of the enun-
ciation of decisions that had little practical effect in their own
time and are important today chiefly as precedents for a later
centralization. (The lawyers' overemphasis on Marshall's work
has been one of the main anachronistic distortions of the development of American federalism.) Marshall's main effort to supervise state control of property rights in the *Dartmouth College*
case (1819) in which the Court held that a charter, as a kind of
contract, could not be directly revoked by a state. The main effect of this case was, of course, to induce state legislatures to insert a revocability clause in all subsequent charters. And Marshall's successor, Taney, who had less reason to aggrandize the
Court since he represented the leading party, restricted the effect
of the case even further. The Supreme Court in the pre-Civil
War period was a far less significant body politically than it subsequently became and hence it could not, even though some
judges wanted it to, supervise property. In the era of the Civil

War, however, the nation acknowledged the right of the Court to declare acts of Congress and the President void and this acknowledgement raised it to a new level in the system. One of the things the judges did with their new power was to supervise the substantive due process of acts of state legislatures and regulatory agencies. (Due process, once merely a protection of procedural fairness in court proceedings, was expanded in this era to mean fairness of the law or order under which the proceeding was initiated.) From the 1890's to the 1930's the Court made basic rules on property by means of this device. Since 1938, however, the Court has refused to use this doctrine to regulate property and this self-denial may constitute a basic regression in the over-all tendency toward centralization. Nevertheless, that control of property which came as a result of federal management of the economy has increased rather than abated so that the Supreme Court's self-denial may now be quite insignificant in the total view of federalism.

In summary, the control of property rights lay almost exclusively with the states until after the Civil War. By the 1890's the Supreme Court began to set some basic guidelines. Somewhat earlier the central government had begun to regulate the national economy, incidentally thereby regulating property in a basic way. Today the former activity is abated but the latter has regularly increased. The consequence is that today the maintenance of property rights is a shared activity. In my opinion, however, the states are dominant — for they define and regulate the ownership of both realty and personalty — but the federal government has now a significant role at the margin (*i.e.*, on some contested questions).

Civic Rights. These too have typically been regarded as the responsibility of the states. Until recently, only the right to vote has been significantly regulated by the national government. And even this regulation has taken the form of setting the boundaries of the policy of the states. In two amendments to the Constitution, the nation has stated that the states may not deny the vote to persons on account of color or sex. But it has set no positive standards. Indeed, it has shied away constantly from setting posi-

The maintenance of federalism

tive standards because, I assume, these are felt to be exclusively the province of the constituent governments.

In recent years, however, the central government has invaded this area more than any others under this rubric, again largely because of the aggrandizing tendencies of the Supreme Court. Throughout most of our history the Court had no rationale with which to supervise the states in this area. The first ten amendments, concerned as they are mostly with civil liberties, might be supposed to grant control of them to the central government. But in the case of *Barron v. Baltimore* (1833) it was held that these amendments regulated *only* the central government, not the states. (Incidentally, it was Marshall, the supposedly great centralizer, who wrote the opinion in this case.) Not until the 1920's did the Court find a rationale to insert itself in these matters, when it held that the due process clause of the Fourteenth Amendment applied some of the civil rights protections of the first ten amendments to the states. Gradually, in the last generation, the Court has undertaken to regulate states in these matters to a greater and greater degree. On the whole, the states have acquiesced. Today we have reached this point: The setting of the boundaries and many of the definitions of civil rights are now a function of the center; the day-to-day enforcement is a matter for the states; but on dramatic occasions the United States enforces also.

Public and Private Morality. Although the liberal tradition has always denied that private morality is of any concern to government, the fact is that governments have invariably regulated such matters as marriage, sexual behavior, the use of stimulants, sacrilege, etc. In our tradition the states fully control these things, although the Supreme Court sometimes has become peripherally involved via the full faith and credit clause (Article IV, Section 1). In exceptional instances the United States has indirectly controlled (*e.g.*, by refusing to admit Utah as a state until it prohibited polygamy and by prohibiting the insterstate transport of women for prostitution). The one great instance of direct federal control was the Eighteenth Amendment, which, however, was not passed until most of the states had themselves prohibited the sale of alcohol. The fact that this matter was handled by a constitutional amendment indicates the prevailing belief that the regulation of morality was believed to be basically a state matter.

Patriotism. Probably all levels of government have felt called upon to inculcate patriotism. Since the objects of inculcation are mostly children, the states with their function of education probably have the greater responsibility. On the other hand, the military forces are very much involved in patriotic displays and the inculcation of patriotism in young men.

V   ACTIVITIES RELATING TO TRADE

Money: Currency and Credit. Although the Constitution gives exclusive control of currency to the central government, one of the persistent political conflicts for well over the first century of this federation was whether the states or the nation would control credit, the more important form of money. The great controversy between Jefferson and Hamilton started over the chartering of the first Bank of the United States. Marshall's most famous pronouncement on national authority was uttered in *McCulloch v. Maryland* (1819), in which a state tax on the business of the second Bank was held void. And Jackson separated the Democrats and Whigs by means of the controversy over the rechartering of the second Bank. After Jackson it appeared that the states had won, but in the next generation the United States again developed a national banking system, without, however, a central bank.

A central bank, the Federal Reserve System, was established in 1913. And in the 1930's the remnants of the state banking system were brought under some federal control by the Federal Deposit Insurance Corporation and other specialized banking agencies. Though the dispute over banking has not always been couched directly in terms of the centralist–peripheralist dichotomy (Jackson, for example, fought the Bank as a private monopoly under government auspices), still the ultimate significance of the dispute has always been the effect on centralization. The issue is, of course, whether or not the federal government can use the banking system to try to control the basic course of trade. (The con-

verse is not in question, however, for a state-managed banking
system cannot control anything, least of all itself.) The history of the issue in the United States is simply that initially Hamilton asserted the power for the federal government, that his
opponents triumphed in the next generation, and that in this
century under Wilson and Roosevelt the control of banking has
been vested mainly in the central government.

Transportation and Communication. Like money, facilities for
transport and communication are basic instruments for trade;
and throughout recorded history, governments, once strong
enough to maintain external self-control and domestic order, have
turned to the promotion of these instruments as a means of promoting trade. In the tradition of the United States, where external
problems were minimal from 1815 to 1941 and where domestic
order has not been hard to keep except from 1861 to 1865, the
function of encouraging trade has been a major duty of governments at all levels. It is a paradox of American capitalism that,
although private industry has accomplished more here than anywhere else in the world, governments here have also promoted
private industry more than anywhere else in the world. Much of
this promotion has come in the guise of providing facilities for
transport and communication.

The usual rule (not always followed, of course) for the division
of labor on this function among the several levels of government
seems to have been: The smallest government that rules both
terminals of the proposed line of transport or communication is
the one to promote and supervise it. The operative effect of this
rule is that initially the states were the main promoters, whereas
in the last century or so the United States has become the main
one. Even in the beginning, however, the central government had
quite a bit to do and today the states have quite a bit to do. At no
point is there an exclusion of one kind of government from the
function. Rather, the function is fully shared. It is just that the
recognized rule of division gave the states the preponderance of
the task in the beginning and now gives the preponderance to
the nation.

The usual rule (again not always followed) for the division of

Trade   69

labor between private enterprise and the appropriate level of government (chosen according to the previous rule) has been: If the appropriate political authorities believe the line is justified by prospective needs of trade, then the line is built either (1) by a private capitalist under government supervision if a capitalist can be found to provide enough funds and to bear the risk, or (2) by a private capitalist under such subsidy and supervision from the appropriate government as is necessary to make him willing to bear the risk, or (3) by the appropriate government itself, especially if the amount of capital necessary is greater than most private organizations have.

What has resulted from these two rules is a very mixed system with elements of private enterprise (usually supervised by a government) and elements of governmental enterprise from village to nation.

In the beginning the central government ran the post office and supervised coastal shipping. States and localities maintained the road system, bridges, and ferries (often chartered to private entrepreneurs), and ports. As the nation expanded the main avenues were turnpikes and canals, which reached their zenith in the 1840's and 1850's. Except for the National Road and some small canals, the road and canal building was done by states. Even then the Corps of Engineers was improving navigable waterways, but still the system of water transport largely depended on state initiative. With the coming of the railroads, especially the transcontinental railroads, the balance of endeavor swung to the national government. Though the states subsidized and authorized many railroads in the East, the great subsidization was the federal land grants to western lines. Of the western states, only Texas made grants as large, in proportion to its size, as the United States. The federal authority over the railroad system was officially recognized with the establishment of the Interstate Commerce Commission in 1887. The railroads drove the canals out of business, but water transport survived on natural inland waterways, which were the child of the federal government also. By the end of the 19th century, however, the preponderance of effort in providing transport facilities had shifted from the states to the nation. In the ensuing few decades, it initially appeared that this relative weight might shift back again owing to the development of the automobile and truck, for which states provided paved roads. But it turned out eventually that states were not financially competent to provide all the roads necessary for this kind of transport. Gradually the United States has undertaken to control more and more roads, even in cities, so that today the road system is almost as much national as state. Something of the same thing happened with airlines, the initial subsidies for which (*i.e.*, airports) were provided by states; but as the business expanded, federal subsidies and control far outweighed state support and regulation.

With respect to communication, the post office has always been national and so has most of the subsidy and control of telegraph and cable communication. Telephone communication, however, which is primarily local in nature, has been subsidized and regulated mostly by states (except for interstate traffic) — a fact that is recognized in the structure of the subsidiaries of the American Telephone and Telegraph Company. Radio and television, which are interstate in structure, have been regulated and subsidized from the very beginning by the central government.

What this survey indicates is that all kinds of government have something to do with promoting traffic. Often the same industry, *e.g.*, telephone, is regulated and subsidized extensively by both levels of government. The present state of supervision of transport and communication can be indicated by Table 3.2.

Table 3.2 Supervision of Transportation and Communication

Industry	Primary provision or supervision	Substantial secondary provision or supervision
Road transport	states	United States
Railroad transport	United States	states
Inland waterways	United States	. . .
Marine transport	United States	. . .
Air transport	United States	states
Mail	United States	. . .
Telephone	states	United States
Telegraph	United States	. . .
Radio and television	United States	. . .

Utilities. Utilities have always attracted government supervision. Like transport facilities, utilities have a public character, for it is believed conventionally that they should be provided to everybody and that the market and exchange method of allocating resources does not guarantee such provision. Hence, presumably, political allocation is necessary.

Much the same rule for the division of the labor of allocation has been followed here as in transportation, *viz.*, if the area served by a utility is wholly within a state, it has been promoted and subsidized by states; if not, then by the central government. Until quite recently most utilities were necessarily local and hence were provided locally and supervised on a state level. Thus, the provision of fresh water, the disposal of sewage and garbage, the provision of warehouses, stockyards, grain elevators, and the like, and the provision of water power, electricity, gas, and heated air have been performed either directly by local governments or by private entrepreneurs under close state and local supervision. Only in this century has the United States entered the field in a significant way: (1) by promoting and regulating irrigation systems derived from interstate rivers, (2) by supervising and financing sewage disposal in interstate rivers, (3) by generating electricity and selling it on an interstate basis, (4) by financing rural electric cooperatives, and (5) by regulating interstate transport of gas and electricity. All of these activities are, however, simply supplemental to the task done by the states.

Regulation of Production and Distribution. Despite the supposed American adherence to economic liberalism, those who have been dissatisfied with the operation of the free market have repeatedly sought to modify market outcomes by political bargains. Regulation of wages, prices, working conditions, apprenticeship and entry into trades and professions, conspiracies to restrain trade, monopolies, etc. have, therefore, been a regular part of the functions of American governments at various levels throughout our history. The decision about which level of government should modify the market outcome is, of course, a practical one, entirely dictated by the size of the market. Until quite recently, the market for bread, for example, was entirely local, so that the regulation of bread prices, bakers' wages, etc. was undertaken by local, or, at the largest, state governments. But the market for

The maintenance of federalism

wheat and flour has always been larger than individual states so
that it has only been regulated successfully by the central government. Thus it is that in the early period of our history, indeed
until nearly the end of the 19th century, most markets were local
and hence most direct regulation of the economy was local
also. But the vast technological changes in transportation have
rendered most markets, at least most markets for goods, national.
So, gradually, the regulation of market outcomes has become a
national function, especially since the 1930's.

But not, of course, without intense resistance. Each act of regulation modifies a market outcome in such a way that one set of
persons gains more than the market would give it and another
set loses something it might otherwise have. Those who lose by
regulation of course resist and, in our circumstances for the last
75 years, their resistance has taken the form of denying the central government the right to regulate the market.

In this struggle the Supreme Court for about 50 years after
1890 sided with the losers from regulation and did nearly everything in its power to prevent national regulation of markets. It
systematically weakened the effect of national antitrust laws. By
defining "production" as something distinct from commerce, it
interpreted the federal authority to regulate commerce as a mere
grant to regulate transportation. It limited the plainly unlimited
federal authority to tax to merely taxation for support of those
substantive functions otherwise granted. Thereby it rendered national regulation of markets almost impossible. The older commentators on constitutional law interpreted this policy as a preference for laissez-faire economic theory; but this, I believe, grants
more philosophical sophistication than the narrowly trained lawyers on the Court then possessed. The main argument of those
who attribute motives of theory-realization is that simultaneously
the Court also restricted state and local regulation of markets by
means of the due process clause of the Fourteenth Amendment.
The effect of these simultaneous restrictions on both kinds of
government, a restriction that E. S. Corwin called "dual federalism," was that markets could not be regulated by any government,
state or national. And this result is, of course, what economic liberalism demands. But to a later generation this coincidence of

Trade   73

theory and practice appears purely accidental. It seems more likely that, having excluded national regulation of national markets out of a straightforward partiality for the people who would lose by regulation, the business-oriented lawyers on the Court recognized that local regulation of a national market would entail a disastrous relocation of industry and so simply saved states from the consequences of their own folly in attempting to regulate national markets. Whether philosophically or practically inspired, however, the fact is that for about 50 years regulation of national markets was rendered very difficult by the Supreme Court — and at a time when most markets were becoming national.

In the long run the potential losers from regulation; *i.e.*, chiefly traders from Wall Street to Main Street and mine and mill owners everywhere, could not hold out in a democracy based on "one-man, one-vote" against the much more numerous class who expected to benefit from modifications of the market; *i.e.*, the vast number of farmers who sold their produce to traders, the vast number of laborers who sold their services to entrepreneurs, and, under another aspect, the vast number of small-scale entrepreneurs who bought from semi-monopolistic producers. The dramatic conflict in 1937 between President Roosevelt and the Court, which resulted in a defeat for the President in his proposal to revise the Constitutional structure and in a victory for the President (by reason of the resignation of one judge and the self-reversal of another) over the Constitutional doctrine, was the beginning of the acceptance of national regulation of national markets. In that confrontation the Court backed down on the doctrinal issue to save its structural integrity and, as result of this outcome and the subsequent appointment over the next 25 years of judges sympathetic to national regulation, all the legal barriers to national regulation so carefully erected in the two generations before 1937 have been swept away. As might be expected, those who lost the legal battle have continued to fight a political one, but their heart has not really been in the struggle. The nation has been extraordinarily prosperous since 1937, perhaps because of these very modifications of market outcomes, perhaps because of adventitious factors, and this very prosperity has come to those who lost as much or more than to those who won. Naturally the losers have been reluctant to upset a system in which they win along with everybody else.

As a consequence, numerous markets are now federally regulated without much objection: many markets for agricultural commodities are directly regulated from the supply side and, in some, prices are fixed by executive action; the supply of labor has been regulated by the National Labor Relations Board and the price of labor has been almost directly regulated in numerous crisis instances in basic industries (such as railroads and steel) by executive action at the Presidential level; federal anti-monopoly legislation (with respect both to mergers and to direct conspiracies to set prices), which was originally enacted in 1890 and 1914, has been enforced generally for the first time in the 1950's and 1960's; securities markets have been regulated in detail since the 1930's; price maintenance by local retailers (a market modification to protect local retailers operating in a national market) usually has been enforced for the last generation; minimum wages and maximum hours have been set in an increasing number of markets since 1938; etc., etc. There is no necessary economic coherence in this regulation. Anti-monopoly legislation does not jibe with retail price maintenance, for example. But there is a political coherence in it all; namely, those who have sufficient political influence to bring about a market modification in their favor have done so — and they usually have done so through the medium of the central government with its present-day control of national markets.

This is not to say that significant markets are not still controlled by states. Indeed they are. When the supply of a commodity originates chiefly in one state, it is possible to control market outcomes by controlling production. Thus Texas can control gasoline prices and California can control the prices of certain fruits. All states regulate the building industry minutely and the function of supervising local markets lies chiefly with states. Most markets for services are state-supervised. The ambiguously named U.S. Employment Service is partly financed by the federal government but is operated and largely controlled by the states. Licensing of trades and professions, which is really a control of entry or supply, is under state regulation: *e.g.*, accounting, barbering, bricklaying, engineering, hacking, law, medicine, plumbing, teaching, etc., are all licensed trades or professions, the entry to which is still state-controlled. In a number of these the prices of services as well as entry are also state-controlled. But only the most local of these are really state-controlled — the professions, as distinct from the trades, tend to be national in character so that states lose control by competition with each other, and as a result regulation is self-defeating and is eventually abandoned.

On the whole, markets are national nowadays and hence economic regulation or the modification of market outcomes is national. And this is a remarkable change from the 19th century.

Economic Development. This function, unlike the one just discussed, is not necessarily tied to the nature of markets. Even when a market is completely national, a state may seek to aid its citizens in the market by helping them to produce more cheaply or more efficiently. Thus states have subsidized much agricultural research, pest control, etc. State universities have had research institutes added to them to serve local industry. In the mid-19th century, most states had geological surveys, the better to exploit land resources, etc., etc. Furthermore, when markets are national the location of producers is partially undetermined. States can, in such circumstances, affect the location of industry to their advantage by offering subsidies to producers. Of course, this kind of bidding can become self-defeating if all states participate; but so long as some are less active than others in subsidization, it continues to go on. Throughout our history states have subsidized entrepreneurs: initially mostly in transportation, but in this century in nearly all kinds of business.

Substantial as commercial research and subsidies by states are, still the United States has spent far more than the states during the last generation, even if one omits the field of transportation. (And of course throughout our history the protective tariff has been a national subsidy to selected industries, a subsidy that, however, has not directly cost the government.) There is no single reason why direct subsidies to producers have become a national function, except perhaps the fact of superior national re-

76   *The maintenance of federalism*

sources in recent years. Some subsidies, *e.g.*, to shipbuilders and
mineral producers, have been justified on military grounds. So
also have the vast contracts for weapons development and space
research, although in practical effect they are subsidies to air-
craft, electronics, and similar industries. Entirely aside from the
militarily justified subsidies, however, are subsidies to and
research for agriculture, not in the interest of market regulation,
but in the interest of greater productivity. Partly these are justified by the nature of the problem; corn borers, for example, do
not recognize state boundaries. Partly, however, the central government deals with these problems simply because it and they
are there. Something of the same may be said about subsidies like
cheap credit for small business. Any level of government could
handle this function, but the federal government does, partly because it has the money, partly because it is there. The census
function, originally purely political in nature, has expanded into a
business service and by example has spawned numerous data-gath-
ering activities in the Commerce and Labor Departments. There
is constitutional justification for the census, but many of its duties
are assigned simply because it is there.

Irreplaceable Resources. In the field of conservation, which has
been a governmental function only in the 20th century, much the
same principle holds as in other areas discussed under this rubric:
If the resource to be conserved can be protected by state action,
then the function is assigned to states; if it cannot be, then it goes
to the central government. Since much so-called conservation is
really covert regulation of a market and since most markets are
national, it follows that most conservation is also a national function. Soil, uranium, forests, wildlife, and gas and oil are the chief
regulated resources. Of these, only oil is fully regulated by a
state (and this is, of course, simply market regulation from the
supply side, a regulation possible only because of the large concentration of oil in Texas.) States participate in forest conservation and may even exceed the efforts of the United States in wildlife conservation. In sum, it appears, however, that the central
government probably does more conserving than do all the states
combined.

VI   ACTIVITIES RELATING TO CITIZENS' WELFARE

Education. Traditionally, education is the business of states and localities and it remains so today. There always has been, however, a substantial amount of federal aid indirectly and at the edges of the system. From 1787 onwards most federal arrangements for the sale of public lands have reserved some proceeds to support schools. During the 19th century the service academies formed a larger part of the system of higher education than they do today. Vocational education has been subsidized by the United States since 1917. Much educational research is done by the U.S. Office of Education. Children's lunches have been provided since 1946. National fellowship programs for graduate education are simply a regularization of subsidies given for research (by various scientific agencies such as the Public Health Service) but actually used to support graduate students. Grants to support schools in areas significantly affected by federal installations have been given since World War II, and recently the federal government has subsidized dormitory building for colleges. But these varied grants (most of which, in recent years at least, have been compromises resulting from the failure of a general aid to education bill) are all on the edges of the system; they do not involve any significant federal control of education at any level. The states are still in control of education.

Aid to the Indigent and Handicapped. In the American tradition, poor relief has traditionally been associated with local government, probably because the preceding way in which society handled the function — through the parishes of an established church — was also specifically local. Today, however, the function is thoroughly shared by the nation and the states, with the United States bearing by far the greater portion of the cost and labor. On their own initiative and at their own expense, the states still do much of what they have always done, *e.g.*, they operate hospitals and asylums. With the assistance of federal funds and usually with federal supervision, states continue to do (often in new ways) many traditional functions, *e.g.*, supporting widowed, orphaned, handicapped, and aged indigents. Under the fairly close

supervision of the United States, the states operate the unemployment insurance program. But the really large welfare program is
Old Age and Survivors' insurance, which is operated entirely by
the United States.

The history of the development of federal participation in poor
relief begins with a series of quite modest grant-in-aid programs
for special welfare problems involving women and children, as
well as a pension program for railroad employees. These began in
the second and third decades of this century. Had there been
no great depression, presumably these would have grown slowly
in response to state requests for financial help. But the depression
created welfare problems far beyond the financial capacity of the
states. As a temporary measure the central government undertook support for the unemployed; but as a permanent measure
the United States guided the states in forming unemployment insurance programs. Once it had accepted these welfare responsibilities it also seemed reasonable to support a general Old Age
and Survivors' insurance program that, because of the mobility
of Americans, could hardly be run by any government other than
the federal one.

Recreation and Culture. Despite a persistent myth about the ma-
terialism of American life and the cultural indifference of its governments, the fact is that Americans have for a long time pursued
culture with an avidity unparalleled in any other society. Governments have participated in this pursuit in appropriate ways,
not all of which, of course, have suited the most refined taste of
the period. I suppose it is the failure to suit the most refined
taste that has led many to overlook the support governments have
given to the arts. But the support has existed at all levels from the
early part of the 19th century onward and deserves mention. Because of the size of the country and the complexity of our governmental structure and because of our long-standing effort to
educate everybody, we have required an extraordinarily large
number of public buildings, the competitions for which have
done much to encourage architecture. The tradition has suggested
that buildings and parks be adorned with paintings and statuary,
which has meant a basic subsidy of these arts. Furthermore, al-

Citizens' welfare 79

most every metropolitan center with a population of 100,000 or more has art museums, some private, but many public. As for letters, the federal government during the 19th century subsidized some men of letters with political sinecures (though perhaps not as many as elsewhere in the world); but the great subsidy for letters is the free public library movement that spread throughout state and local governments in the late 19th century and thereby both subsidized authors and made their products available to the whole society. Next to letters, music has been the most heavily subsidized of the arts, from town bands (an almost universal feature of 19th-century and even 20th-century state subsidy) to symphony orchestras. Music has been incorporated generally into the secondary school curriculum, a major subsidy absent from most other nations. Of the performing and decorative arts, the only one not supported in depth by the several governments is the theater, yet even in this there is indirect support through the provision of buildings for performances. Typically, the support of the arts has come mostly from states or their subsidiaries rather than from the central government, although it too has participated where appropriate and the short-lived WPA program for unemployed artists during the 1930's subsidized decorative arts, letters, and even the performing arts.

The preponderance of the states is just about as great in the field of recreation, although here the federal government makes notable and expensive contributions. Cities began the development of their park systems in the mid-19th century and these today have become one of the most attractive features of American urbanism, distinguishing it rather sharply from European and Asiatic urbanism, which lack extensive park resources. In the 20th century, cities have established systematic recreation programs in their parks and playgrounds, supplementing these with zoos and gardens. But the federal government also has created parks. As a consequence of the conservation movement at the turn of the century vast wilderness areas (especially in the West) were set aside as national parks. On a lesser scale the state governments have followed a policy of preserving areas of special interest so that there is now also a large state park program. In short, both levels of government have extensive park resources. In area, the national system is probably greater; but measured by expenditure the state and local system probably surpasses the federal.

Public Health. Owing to the explosion of medical knowledge in the last century, public health has become a concern of all levels of government. Even before the explosion began, the provision of sewers (previously discussed as a utility) and asylums (previously discussed as an aid to the handicapped) was recognized as a public health function. But with the development of epidemiology, public health became a major political concern. Initially local and state governments undertook to report on deaths and to regulate the response to epidemics, *e.g.*, vaccination and isolation. Later, as the facts of disease-transmission were recognized, pure food and drug statutes were passed by most governments, including the federal. Since national markets existed for most foods and drugs, federal supervision of these matters largely superseded state supervision. As industrial diseases and hazards were recognized, safety programs were established to deal with them; and since most of the industries were national (*e.g.*, mining), so were the safety and health programs. As drug manufacturing came to be recognized as a major health factor, inspection and supervision programs were established, chiefly under federal aegis, since the drug market, too, is national in nature.

The present state of the division of labor in this area is hard to assess. Every locality has its public health officers; but the crucial programs seem to be in the hands of the national government. A paradigm: Two generations ago the control and therapy of tuberculosis was entirely in state control; a generation ago the control and therapy of syphilis was in joint state and federal hands; today the research on cancer, heart disease, and mental health is largely under federal auspices. The point is that the direction of medical energy on the main attackable diseases has gradually shifted from state to nation. To some degree the nature of diseases has been basic to the shifting; but even more basic has been the availability of financial support.

It would be difficult to say which level, state or national, now predominates in the field of public health. Perhaps the appropriate generalization is that, with some exceptions in each case, states and localities do most of the routine work, whereas the nation does most of the work on the frontiers of public health. Financially, state and local expenditures are probably greater.

New knowledge. Most governmental support for the acquisition of new knowledge comes under the rubric of economic development, but some patronage of pure research, of finding things out for the sake of finding them out, has always been undertaken by civilized governments. The system of patents, which is meant to encourage full disclosure, probably benefits economic development primarily, but the system of copyrights seems purely to encourage and reward the arts and sciences. These are, of course, federal by reason of the Constitution; but other patronage might conceivably come from either level, presumably from the more affluent level. Since the federal government has usually been the more affluent, it is the one that has supported the most pure research. It has sponsored scientific societies, supported exploration of remote places (not only on this continent but also at the poles), and in the period since World War II has directly supported a large amount of research in both physical and biological sciences that could at the moment have very little practical application. So far as I know, states have never done anything like this directly, though of course they do much indirectly by supporting universities.

VII   CENTRALIZED FEDERALISM IN THE
       UNITED STATES

This chapter contains an examination in nineteen categories of action of the degree of centralization (or peripheralization) of federalism in the United States. It is apparent that one theme running through these brief verbal descriptions is that the federal government has acquired more duties, in relation to the states, over the years. Both kinds of governments have grown with the nation, but the federal government seems to have become somewhat more conspicuous than that of the states.

This conclusion is summarized numerically in Table 3.3, which indicates, for each of the seventeen substantive areas of spending money, the relative position of federal and constituent governments at four time periods. The entries are defined thus:

1 The functions are performed exclusively or almost exclusively by the federal government.
2 The functions are performed predominantly by the federal government, although the state governments play a significant secondary role.
3 The functions are performed by federal and state governments in about equal proportions.
4 The functions are performed predominantly by the state governments, although the federal government plays a significant secondary role.
5 The functions are performed exclusively or almost exclusively by the state governments.
– The functions were not recognized to exist at the time.

The choice of a particular entry is, of course, my highly subjective judgment based only on my immersion in the study. Others might disagree with my assignments, but by keeping the discriminations crude, that is, by using only a five-point scale, disagreements are probably minimized. The last row of the table shows the average for each of the time points of all functions then recognized to exist. Since the seventeen (or fourteen, or fifteen) categories of functions are by no means of equal significance politically or socially, it may well be argued that the average is without meaning. Therefore, I have made the same kind of judgment for possibly equally significant groups of functions (external affairs, internal order, trade, and welfare) and the result is approximately the same.

But granted that the federal government has become administratively somewhat more conspicuous than the states, the question remains: Does this table of American experience support the administrative theory of federalism? I think not. Under this theory, administrative centralization is what is supposed to preserve and maintain the central government. But if one looks at the

Centralized federalism in the U.S. *83*

Table 3.3 THE DEGREE OF CENTRALIZATION IN THE UNITED STATES BY SUBSTANTIVE FUNCTIONS AND AT POINTS IN TIME

	Functions	ca. 1790	ca. 1850	ca. 1910	ca. 1964
1	External affairs	4	1	1	1
2	Public safety	5	4	4	4
3	Property rights	5	5	4	4
4	Civic rights	5	5	5	3
5	Morality	5	5	5	5
6	Patriotism	3	3	3	3
7	Money and credit	3	4	3	1
8	Transport and communication	4	4	2	2
9	Utilities	5	5	5	4
10	Production and distribution	5	5	4	2
11	Economic development	3	4	3	2
12	Resources	—	—	2	2
13	Education	—	5	5	4
14	Indigency	5	5	5	2
15	Recreation	—	4	4	3
16	Health	—	—	4	3
17	Knowledge	1	1	1	2
	Average	4.1	4.0	3.5	2.8

crucial period for the survival of federalism in the United States; that is, from 1790 to 1850, it appears that some functions were centralized and others were decentralized. Military centralization was matched by economic decentralization (cf. rows 1, 7, and 11). We have no easy way of knowing whether or not these reallocations were in areas of comparable importance; but we do know that the reallocations were not all in the same direction — as they have been since the Civil War. And since they are not all in the same direction we cannot affirm that administrative centralization is what preserved the federal bargain in the pre-Civil War era.

On the other hand, the sharing of administration is what is supposed to preserve the guarantees to the states. Yet, according to the table, sharing has declined notably in the last period (*i.e.*, from 1910 to the present) whereas the fundamental guarantees to the states seem as strong as ever. I conclude, therefore, that the administrative theory is totally inadequate to explain the main-

84   *The maintenance of federalism*

tenance of federalism. Unfortunately, most American students of
the subject have been deeply attracted to the theory; hence it
has tended to obscure constitutional realities. I will be content if
this essay has no other impact but to disabuse scholars of their
faith in the clearly false administrative theory of federalism.

E
Conditions for Federalism

[5]

Regulation and the American Common Market

Edmund W. Kitch

"Our system," wrote Mr. Justice Jackson, "is that every farmer and every craftsman shall be encouraged to produce by the certainty that he will have free access to every market in the Nation, that no home embargoes will withhold his exports, and no foreign state will by customs duties or regulations exclude them. Likewise, every consumer may look to the free competition from every producing area in the Nation to protect him from exploitation by

---

This paper has benefited from conversations with David P. Currie and from Walter Hellerstein, "Federal Limitations on State Taxation of Interstate Commerce in the United States" (paper presented at Conference on the Judicial Role in Economic Integration, Bellagio, Italy, July 16-21, 1979, forthcoming from Oxford University Press, edited by Eric Stein and Terrance Sandalowe), and from comments of Gerhard Casper and Philip B. Kurland. A different perspective on the nineteenth-century issues discussed here is provided by Harry N. Scheiber, "Federalism and the American Economic Order, 1789-1910," 10 *Law and Society Review 57* (1975). Scheiber concludes that "American federalism provided a benign framework favoring business institutions and fostering 'benevolent' promotional or supportive policies by rivalistic state governments. Equally important, federalism also threw serious structural obstacles in the way of timely, effective regulation of business by governmental authorities." *Id.,* pp. 117-118. Scheiber seems to confuse stringent regulations and higher taxes with "timely and effective regulation."

10 / Regulation, Federalism, and Interstate Commerce

any."[1] And Mr. Justice Holmes wrote: "I do not think the United States would come to an end if we lost our power to declare an Act of Congress void. I do think the Union would be imperiled if we could not make that declaration as to the laws of the several states. For one in my place sees how often a local policy prevails with those who are not trained to national views and how often action is taken that embodies what the Commerce Clause was meant to end."[2]

This paper reviews the theory, practice, and prospects of the American common market.

Four principal questions are addressed. First, has the Constitution, as interpreted by the Supreme Court, mandated an open national market? Second, has the United States in fact enjoyed an open national market? Third, should national law restrict the freedom of action of the states in order to further national free trade? And fourth, has national law and policy been the friend of free internal trade? The argument here is that all four questions should be answered in the negative. The answers are necessarily tentative. The law has a rich but formal literature on the Interstate Commerce Clause, a literature that is inevitably linked, and for these purposes contaminated, with the question of the scope of the national commerce power. Economists and historians have generally assumed rather than demonstrated that the internal American national economy is open.

The position argued here is not that the American states have not enjoyed a high degree of economic cooperation and integration. Rather, the position is that the existence of a system of paramount, national political integration has not demonstrably furthered free internal trade. In very recent years, it has in fact become an enemy of that integration. The traditional free trade literature, with its focus on reducing barriers to trade between nations, has commonly (and usually implicitly) assumed that free trade prevails within nations. The modern scholarship of regulation, however, shows that this is an assumption that cannot be made. One of the paradoxes of contemporary economic regulation is that with reductions in international barriers to trade there are simultaneous increases in intranational barriers.

The first section of this paper is a brief and elementary discussion of the theory of free trade, with special attention to what it does not say, and an application of the theory to the commercial experience under the Articles of Confederation. The second section reviews the Constitution and the derived set of rules governing the role of the states and the nation. The third section undertakes a preliminary assessment of the actual performance of the states and the nation within the Constitutional framework. A final section speculates briefly on what impact the Court has actually had in maintaining an open national market.

THE THEORY OF FREE TRADE AND THE EXPERIENCE UNDER THE ARTICLES OF CONFEDERATION

The power of the case for free trade lies in the argument that voluntary transactions must be welfare-enhancing for all participants—otherwise they would not join in the transaction. Given plausible assumptions about the effectiveness of property rights and the relative unimportance of externalities in many contexts, the argument has wide applicability to both international and intranational commerce.

The argument becomes more difficult when the need for a tax system is introduced. Any tax on a transaction distorts the equality between the costs of the transacting parties and generates a welfare loss. It is elementary price theory to demonstrate that the effects of monopoly and of an excise tax are the same. But in a world where government, and hence taxes, are found necessary, this is an inefficiency that must be accepted. The welfare theorist is therefore driven to argue that taxes should be applied evenly and broadly to transactions so that the tax system does not distort the choice among economic activities.

The choice of the optimal tax system will involve considerations of costs in collecting the tax and its effect on the transactions taxed. A tax that is simple to administer and whose evasion is easy to detect should be preferred to a tax that is difficult to administer and can be easily evaded. Under highly plausible assumptions, a duty has the first features, although its relative attractiveness may have declined over time. In an economy where written records are costly, where the suitable points for commercial import and export operations are few, where ships are easily detected, and where the goods of commerce are relatively simple, a uniform, *ad valorem* duty on imports will be a very attractive tax and its incidence will not be confined to a small sector of the economy. Through the effects of the duty on the prices of imports, the burden of the tax will be spread throughout the economy. Nor will the burden of the tax fall outside the country that imposes it. The tax will cause an offsetting

12 / Regulation, Federalism, and Interstate Commerce

rise in the value of the country's currency or, in other words, an offsetting fall in the price of the goods to be imported.

The existence of such a tax will, of course, be a political question
within the country that imposes it. The nature of the tax and the
details of its administration can affect the welfare of particular
groups and areas relative to the welfare of other groups and areas.
For example, if a group can direct the duty toward the products
that it produces and away from the products that it consumes, it
can benefit itself at the expense of other groups. How this will
occur will depend on the particular political system. The mechanism
that drives such phenomena in democratic systems has been the
subject of considerable study, speculation, and controversy. It need
only be recognized here what has been demonstrated—that it does
happen.

When discussion moves from explicit duties to the vast range
of taxes and regulation that can constitute indirect barriers to free
trade, the analysis remains the same. If decisions concerning health
and safety regulations, the rules of contract law, the price or quality
of goods, and the structure of taxation are efficient, they will maximize the position of the society; however, if they depart from
efficiency in this sense, their principal effect will be to reduce the
total net position of gains and losses and affect their distribution
within the society.

One line of public choice analysis has explored the issue of what
scope of governmental jurisdiction would be desirable.[3] Two basic
principles must be considered. First, the scope of jurisdiction should
be as small as possible in order to maximize diversity of choice as
well as to promote the maximum competition among jurisdictions
for laws, practices, and procedures that people prefer. Second, the
scope of governmental jurisdiction should be large enough so that the
jurisdiction's decisions do not produce important externalities and
allow significant economies of scale in legal administration to be
captured. An instant's reflection yields the result that different
governmental functions should be assigned to different levels of government, and this has been the universal practice within both formally federal and nonfederal countries. Thus responsibilities for foreign
relations and national defense are almost entirely national responsibilities, while matters such as land use controls, policing, and schooling have to a greater or lesser extent been assigned to "inferior"
levels of government. The "appropriate" level of assignment will be
affected by numerous factors: the size of the country; the density
of its population; the cultural diversity of its population; its history;

Regulation and the American Common Market / 13

its political traditions and practices; its relationships with adjoining countries; and the nature of the governmental policies it wishes to pursue.

In the area of commerce, these efficiency-driven principles would favor subnational jurisdiction. Issues of contract law, corporation law, government procurement, and the licensing of businesses, trades, and professions involve no significant economic externalities beyond the jurisdiction that makes the rules. In this area, the principle of maximum competition would be limited only by the principle of economy of scale. At some point the multiple administrative centers would generate conflicts from their differences in contract law, corporation law, licensing law, and so on, and the costs of this diversity would exceed the benefits. Even here, however, theory would predict that the incentives for uniformity and cooperation between jurisdictions would minimize the problem.

The relatively large size of the American states suggests that these principles would not support an argument that they are too small in size or volume of commerce to perform efficiently the law-making function in the area of commerce. Indeed, the historic argument against the exercise of state power in these areas has not been an efficiency argument; it has been an unfairness argument. Groups unhappy with outcomes of the marketplace have recognized that federal-level intervention would be necessary to implement change, as no single state would be willing to accept the costs of acting alone. A distinctive theme of federal intervention in the economy, from the founding of the republic to the present—from nineteenth-century tariff policy to the minimum wage, union and social welfare legislation of the progressives,[4] to contemporary proposals to handicap the Sunbelt—has been the claim by the northern states that southern economic competition is undesirable on grounds other than efficiency: it prevents the development of a national merchant marine, stifles home industry, or is unfairly based on the presence of a lower-cost, exploited, or non-unionized labor force. The southern states foresaw this problem at the Constitutional Convention;[5] it formed the basis of the South Carolina nullification resolutions of 1832,[6] it was a grievance in the Civil War, and it remains an important national issue today.[7]

This way of viewing jurisdiction by units of government results in a very different vision of free trade than the vision that has dominated constitutional scholarship. The fact that there is decentralized authority over the laws and government practices affecting commerce does not mean that there will not be free trade. Free trade

14 / Regulation, Federalism, and Interstate Commerce

among decentralized authorities will result from voluntary cooperation, motivated by the fact that free trade will produce greater wealth for all to share. In the short run, this approach to free trade may cause significant bargaining instability, as each jurisdiction tries to establish a bargaining position through bluff, threat, and implemented threat. But in the long run, this system may provide more free trade than centralized authority because it places stronger incentives on each jurisdiction to promulgate efficient rules for both its internal and external commerce.

In the United States, the constitutional debate of these questions has taken the form of advocates of national power versus advocates of state power—a form that has persisted from the debates over the drafting and ratification of the Constitution, to the Supreme Court decisions, to the Civil War, to the floor of Congress. A distinctive feature of this debate is that the advocates of national power have captured the free trade issue for their position. Of the argument here, the *Federalist* said: "It may perhaps . . . [be argued] that whether the States are united or disunited, there would still be an intimate intercourse between them which would answer the same ends; but this intercourse would be fettered, interrupted, and narrowed by a multiplicity of causes, which in the course of these papers may have been amply detailed. A unity of commercial, as well as political, interests, can only result from a unity of government."[8] Almost fifty years later, Madison wrote of the conditions leading to the Constitution: "The other source of dissatisfaction was the peculiar situation of some of the states, which having no convenient ports for foreign commerce, were subject to be taxed by their neighbors, thro whose ports, their commerce was carried on. New Jersey, placed between Phila. & N. York, was likened to a Cask tapped at both ends: and N. Carolina between Virga. & S. Carolina to a patient bleeding at both Arms."[9]

Crosskey, who worked out a fascinating tale of a "lost" Federalist constitution with plenary national power over commerce, was explicit about what he saw as the desirability of such a national power.

> [O]ne practical consequence [of the present understandings] of a very serious kind, is that acts by Congress to establish uniform law in the various commercial fields wherein such law has so long been desired are still beyond that body's competence. . . . [T]he practical situation is that there is no government, or governments, within the country, which can act effectively, singly or together, with respect to a great deal of badly needed lawmaking in the commercial field; lawmaking, it may be added, which is generally desired; which has long had widespread backing in the business world; and which is not known to have been opposed by any group in the community.[10]

Regulation and the American Common Market / 15

And Ernest Brown of Harvard, perhaps the last in this line of thought, explicitly compared Supreme Court invalidation of state taxing power to the case for free international trade.[11]

The opinion that national power is the friend of national free trade is not confined to lawyers. A leading text on American economic history advises its readers that "the formation of a federal government with the power—given to it by the Constitution or by the court decisions—to encourage and regulate economic behavior, was of far-reaching importance. Imagine the chaos if the separate states were permitted to restrict interstate trade, to coin their own currency, to set weights and measures, or to establish their own law of contract and property."[12] Such "chaos" would be easier to imagine if the states had not effectively exercised autonomous monetary power until the Civil War, and established the law of property and contract to the present day. Douglas North has, more equivocally, written,

> Regulation of interstate commerce was another area delegated to the federal government, a control that historically, to this day, has had an enormous impact. By prohibiting the states from erecting barriers to the interstate movement of goods, this clause not only encouraged the growth of a national market, but gave the federal government constitutional authority to exercise control and regulation over economic activity.[13]

The idea that the thirteen years of experience under the Articles of Confederation proved that decentralized authority over commerce would degenerate into restrictions on freedom of trade has played a central role in the American tradition.[14] The *Federalist* referred to "[t]he interfering and unneighborly regulations of some States, contrary to the true spirit of the Union, [that] have, in different instances, given just cause of umbrage and complaint to others." "It is to be feared," the *Federalist* continued, "that examples of this nature, if not restrained by a national control, would be multiplied and extended till they became not less serious sources of animosity and discord than injurious impediments to the intercourse between the different parts of the Confederacy."[15] Of the causes of friction between the states in the Articles' period. Allen Nevins has written, "Disputes over trade were the most constant and discreditable of all."[16]

Given this tradition, it may be surprising to some that the Articles forcefully stated that freedom of commercial intercourse was an objective of the Confederation, and that states were bound to observe the principle of granting to citizens of other states the same treatment

16 / Regulation, Federalism, and Interstate Commerce

they accorded to their own citizens, including a right of free ingress and regress, and "all the privileges of trade and commerce subject to the same duties, impositions, and restrictions, as the inhabitants thereof respectively."[17] However, it is important to keep in mind that the commerce of the states was largely a commerce of exporting raw materials to Europe and importing manufactured goods from Europe. This trade flowed directly by ship from each state to Europe. Interstate trade, in the modern sense, was relatively unimportant.

Problems concerning commerce that arose between the states under the Articles were related to three distinct issues. The first class of complaints involved the ability of the United States to engage in effective commercial negotiations with European powers.[18] Prior to the Revolution, Americans had enjoyed rights as citizens of the United Kingdom, under the English Navigation Acts. During and after the war, however, they met with discrimination in English ports, and the English West Indies trade and the Newfoundland fisheries were closed to them. Since the New Englanders had done well at sea and because their still-rich forests provided raw material for ship-building, they desired commercial agreements with other countries to widen their markets. The Articles created an awkward structure for negotiation of these matters. The United States, not the states, had the power to send and receive ambassadors and to enter into treaties, but national treaty power in the commercial area was circumscribed. Article IX provided that "no treaty of commerce shall be made whereby the legislative power of the respective States shall be restrained from imposing such imposts and duties on foreigners as their own people are subject to, or from prohibiting the exportation or importation of any species of goods or commodities whatsoever." When John Adams arrived at the Court of St. James after the treaty of peace, he was met with the position that his authority to negotiate on commercial matters would have to come directly from the states, an arrangement whose impracticality he immediately saw.[19] The difficulty of negotiating effectively on behalf of American commercial interests under these arrangements turned Adams into a strong advocate of national power over commerce, and he repeatedly argued that position in his dispatches to Jay.[20]

Adams also advocated legal retaliation by the states against the English government to get its attention. "The commerce of America will have no relief at present, nor, in my opinion, ever, until the United States shall have generally passed navigation acts. If this measure is not adopted, we shall be derided; and the more we suffer,

Regulation and the American Common Market / 17

the more will our calamaties be laughed at."[21] Although most states did enact restrictions on British shipping, the restrictions varied in their details. In 1784 Congress submitted to the states a request to have the power for fifteen years to forbid the import and export of goods in vessels of countries not having treaties with the United States and to forbid the subjects of foreign nations to import goods from other than their own countries, unless exempted by treaty.[22]

The *Federalist* switched the argument from the disadvantages of the Articles to that of the perils of disunity and exaggerated the helplessness of the United States under these arrangements.

> [I]n a state of disunion ... It would be in the power of the maritime nations, availing themselves of our universal importance, to prescribe the conditions of our political existence; and as they have a common interest in being our carriers, and still more in preventing our becoming theirs, they would in all probability combine to embarrass our navigation in such a manner as would in effect destroy it, and confine us to a PASSIVE COMMERCE. . . . That unequalled spirit of enterprise, which signalizes the genius of the American merchants and navigators, and which is in itself an inexhaustible mine of national wealth, would be stifled and lost, and poverty and disgrace would overspread a country which, with wisdom, might make herself the admiration and envy of the world.[23]

The second class of complaints under the Articles was raised against those ports in a position to extract tariff revenue from goods coming from points in other states. "The opportunities which some States would have of rendering others tributary to them by commercial regulations," argued the *Federalist*, "would be impatiently submitted to by the tributory States. The relative situation of New York, Connecticut, and New Jersey, would afford an example of this kind. New York, from the necessities of revenue, must lay duties on her importations. A great part of these duties must be paid by the inhabitants of the two other states, in the capacity of consumers of what we [New York] import. . . . Would Connecticut and New Jersey long submit to be taxed by New York for her exclusive benefit?"[24] Nevins reports that southern duties were generally low, but "in the smaller States of the North . . . resentment against the tariff exactions of selfish neighbors was greatest. New York's duties came to be regarded with indignation by all the surrounding commonwealths. . . . A recent historian has computed that one-third the Empire State's expenses were defrayed by this indirect tribute from the land of steady habits [Connecticut]."[25]

William Zornow has questioned this traditional view of state

18 / Regulation, Federalism, and Interstate Commerce

tariff policy that was established under the Articles. In four basically identical articles, published separately in the mid-1950s, he
analyzed tariff statutes of New York, Massachusetts, South Carolina
and Virginia.[26] Of the New York statutes, he wrote: "The law . . .
[provided] that when ships landed at a New York port with goods
aboard consigned to a person living in other states such goods were
to be allowed to pass duty free upon the giving of a sworn statement
as to their ultimate destination. There is a further provision that the
goods must be reexported in the same package, but there is no
specification that it must be reexported in the same vessel which
originally brought the goods."[27] Zornow found similar provisions
in the other state statutes he examined. Provisions for duty exemption of through or reshipped goods are, of course, a common feature
of national tariffs.

New York made such an exemption because the port's comparative advantage in handling through shipments was not very strong:
the marine technology of the day did not limit unloading to only a
few favored places. And since New Jersey had extensive shore within
New York Harbor, if New York raised the cost of through shipment,
it would risk a loss of business.

The exemption, of course, did not extend to shipped goods
that were bought by New York merchants and resold to buyers in
Connecticut and New Jersey. These New York merchants actually
performed a valuable economic function by buying in quantity,
holding supplies in inventory, providing credit, and selling in small
units. A duty on these imports would differ little from an *ad valorem*
property tax on inventory (or from, today, a business profits tax),
and the statute appears to follow the same dividing line that Marshall's constitutional Original Package doctrine does.[28]

The third class of complaints under the Articles related to barriers
on trade among the states. The *Federalist* repeatedly suggested
that this was a fundamental problem under the Articles, although
it never cited any domestic examples. (It either hypothesized or
referred to the policies of foreign governments.) But Zornow reports
that the state tariff laws of the period exempted American goods
from an duty.[29]

There is only one recorded instance of one state imposing a
restriction on commerce coming from other states. Nevins describes
it as follows:

> One pin prick by New York was especially irritating to her neighbors.
> In the spring of 1787 the Legislature, . . . extended the entrance and
> clearance fees to all vessels bound from or to Connecticut and New Jersey.

Regulation and the American Common Market / 19

This threw into the State treasury a share of the profits of the many boatmen who piled down the Sound and from eastern New Jersey with firewood and foodstuffs, while it was troublesome as well as expensive for every shallop and sailboat to clear at the customhouse just as if it had been a full-sized English or French ship. The New Jersey Legislature took the only retaliatory action possible. The city of New York had purchased four acres at Sandy Hook for the purpose of 'maintaining a lighthouse, public inn, and a kitchen garden thereon,' and the Assembly promptly taxed the lighthouse 30 lbs. a month.[30]

Zornow says of this episode:

The one example of discrimination which is most often cited in the case of New York tariff legislation arose over the matter of entrance and clearance fees. There was some irritation between New York and New Jersey because of the latter's refusal to discriminate against English ships and goods as other states had done. It was for this reason that New York had seen fit in 1785 to place higher duties on foreign goods imported from neighboring states unless it could be demonstrated that such goods came originally in non-British bottoms. . . . The clearance and entrance fees were altered substantially by the tariff laws of April 1787 as they applied to vessels from Connecticut and the eastern division of New Jersey. New Jersey became so incensed over what were regarded as discriminatory tactics that her Legislature placed a rent of £30 per month on the Sandy Hook light house. . . . In the final analysis, however, it was a teapot tempest. . . . The final revision in the entrance and clearance fees came in the tariff law of 1788 which absolved all vessels of less than fifty tons of having to pay the fees unless they had dutiable goods aboard.[31]

It appears from Zornow's analysis that New York "restricted" interstate commerce because it had joined Massachusetts in the campaign to discriminate against British shipping—in retaliation for the Navigation Acts—and it wanted to prevent the use of transhipment through New Jersey or Connecticut as a device for evading the discrimination.

The theoretical arguments that decentralized authorities should be expected to cooperate to facilitate freedom of trade appear to be confirmed by the experience under the Articles of Confederation. The argument that this experience demonstrated the opposite is based on a misreading of the *Federalist* and it has no support in primary source materials.

20 / *Regulation, Federalism, and Interstate Commerce*

THE CONSTITUTION AND THE
SUPREME COURT[32]

The Constitution did not, like the Articles of Confederation, explicitly grant to the people the right of free ingress and egress from every state and "all privileges of trade and commerce subject to the same duties, impositions, and restrictions, as the inhabitants thereof respectively." Therefore, any constitutional common market that exists must be constructed from a large number of clauses dispersed throughout the document. Those clauses will be reviewed here in summary form.

The arguably pertinent clauses are:

1. The Preamble ("to form a more perfect Union, . . . to promote the general Welfare.")
2. A series of grants of power to Congress in Article I, Section 8: the power to lay duties, imposts, and excises uniformly; the power to regulate commerce; the power to establish uniform rules for naturalization and for bankruptcies; the power to coin money, regulate its value, and fix standards of weights and measures; the power to establish post offices and post roads; the power to grant patents and copyrights; and the power to make all laws "necessary and proper for carrying into execution the foregoing powers."
3. A series of prohibitions on the federal government, contained in Article I, Section 8 (no tax or duty on Articles exported from any State, no preference shall be given to the Ports of one State over those of another).
4. A series of prohibitions on state governments in Article I, Section 10 (no law impairing the obligation of contract, no imposts or duties on Imports or Exports, no duty of tonnage, or interstate compact without the consent of Congress).
5. Article IV, Sections 1 and 2 (full faith and credit and privileges and immunities).[33]

These clauses in the Constitution did not result from a program to create a customs union, a free trade area, or a common market. Rather, they responded to a series of more limited and practical problems. First among these was the need to create a national government that could bargain effectively with European powers about U.S. rights of commerce and navigation. The *Federalist* had justified the interstate commerce power in part on this ground. The second problem addressed by the Constitution was the need to give the national government a reliable revenue base—the power to

Regulation and the American Common Market / 21

impose duties on imports. The third was the need to provide checks on the use of the first two powers in order to reassure the South that the North would not use them to favor itself at southern expense. The fourth need was to place constraints on the states so that they could not erode federal income from duties through overlapping taxes. Finally, there was a need to create a national system for naturalization. Thus, the Constitution was not designed to implement a common market; that task was left to Congress.

The constitutional clause that prohibits interstate compacts without the consent of Congress has had significance in the area of commercial relations. This clause was drafted to implement the common sense idea that states should not subvert the national government through the formation of subunions. Congressional approval of such interstate compacts has been sparing, and this has denied the states a device commonly available to national sovereignties—the long-term bilateral or multilateral trade agreement. Such arrangements were available to the states under the Articles. On the eve of the signing of the Constitution, Maryland and Virginia successfully negotiated a complex agreement governing the navigation of Chesapeake Bay and the Potomac estuary; more than one hundred years later the Supreme Court held that agreement to still be in force.[34] The relative unavailability of a binding interstate agreement under constitutional law has significantly restricted the ability of the states to coordinate their commercial policies.[35]

The national government that developed after ratification of the Constitution used its commercial powers sparingly. It established patent and copyright law and a post office, and it implemented a system of duties and a customs service to administer them. The duties remained for many years the principal source of federal revenue. The national government also established a program for the construction of post roads. However, it did not provide for extensive regulation of navigation and commerce, nor did it establish national bankruptcy law. The Bank of the United States became the principal political battleground for the issue of the commercial role of the national government until the 1830s, when the Jacksonians came into power and the concept of a national instrumentality to facilitate commercial transactions was abandoned.[36]

A review of the Constitution and the debates that surround commercial issues lead one to conclude that the federal commercial laws and policies that emerged after the signing of the Constitution varied greatly from what the Federalists had envisaged. They had looked toward an activist national government in the area of

22 / *Regulation, Federalism, and Interstate Commerce*

commercial promotion and development.[37] With the ascendency of the Republicans, however, commercial regulation was left to the states,[38] where it largely remained until the 1930s.

It fell to John Marshall to preserve the Federalist vision in *Gibbons* v. *Ogden*. Like a shipwrecked mariner placing a message in a bottle in the hope that it might make its way to a distant land, he there planted in the constitutional jurisprudence the notion that the Commerce Clause actually limited the scope of state power. The clause was an awkward vehicle for the purpose, but it was all there was at hand for a Supreme Court justice to use. Crosskey, who in his own way wished to recapture the Federalist vision, saw that the clause was not sufficient, and attempted to bend the Obligation of Contracts Clause to the purpose.[39] Even so, in spite of the awkwardness of the Commerce Clause, almost fifty years later the post-Civil War Field Court adopted Marshall's idea and judicially imposed a zone of immunity from state regulation and taxation.

This judicial activism spawned hundreds of decisions at the Supreme Court level alone and therefore it is a challenge to summarize the resulting law and practice in reasonable compass. In addition, the effort to isolate areas of interstate commerce from areas of non-interstate commerce runs head on into the fact that all commerce is interlinked; and a tax or regulation at one point will have effects at every other point. Consequently, the Court based its decisions on metaphysical distinctions between interstate and intrastate activities, rather than on the practical consequences of commerce.

The cases can be usefully grouped into periods that emphasize important shifts in the Court's doctrine. However, these shifts are only partly reflected in the statutory law and practice of the same period, for the decisions of one period continue to have important effects on law and practice long after they have been ignored or even repudiated by the Court. For this reason the Supreme Court's decisions in *Bank of Augusta* v. *Earle* (1839) and *Paul* v. *Virginia* (1869), decisions highly questionable under today's constitutional doctrines, go far to explain the structure of the modern statutory law of corporations, banking, and insurance regulation. Similarly, the statutory structure of state taxation today reflects Supreme Court decisions of the last third of the nineteenth century, even though those decisions have now been explicitly overruled.

The periods offered here are doctrinally defined. However, they also reflect shifts in the economic and political environment. For example, only in the 1870s did the maturing of railroad transportation technology convert interstate commerce in commodities into an important economic threat to local interest, and only then did

Regulation and the American Common Market / 23

the Court confront concerted state and local efforts to protect local markets by means of restricting interstate competition. And while it may have been reasonable in the nineteenth century to construe Congress's great commercial silence s as a preference for open markets, that inference became far less supportable in the twentieth century, when Congress not only asserted large taxing, wealth redistribution, and regulatory functions for itself, but also called on the states to perform similar roles. Matching grant programs after all, have to be matched.

The periods proposed for examination of the Supreme Court decisions are: (1) Marshall, 1790 to 1835; (2) Taney, 1835 to 1870; (3) Field, 1870 to 1937; (4) Stone, 1937 to 1976; and (5) Burger, 1976 to present. (The terms of the justices are not the same as the periods.)[40]

The Marshall period produced three Supreme Court decisions, all constitutional chestnuts which will not be restated here: *Gibbons v. Ogden*, 9 Wheat. 1 (1824); *Brown v. Maryland*, 12 Wheat. 419 (1827); and *Wilson v. The Black Bird Creek Marsh Co.*, 2 Pet. 245 (1829). The holdings of *Gibbons* and *Brown* were narrow, but Marshall used the occasion of the opinions to paint a broader picture of the implications of national union. *Gibbons*, which arose out of the same New York harbor commerce that had occasioned the New York-New Jersey conflict of 1787, was based on a generous reading of a federal licensing statute, presaging the role that preemption theory would play in this area. Dictum elaborated the theory of the negative Commerce Clause. *Brown* involved a discriminatory state tax on foreign imports that ran afoul of the prohibition on state duties without the consent of Congress, but Marshall did not hesitate to opine that the same principle would apply to trade between the states. In *Wilson*, the theory ran hard aground against the reality of congressional inaction. A private company had constructed a dam across a small navigable tributary to the Delaware River, pursuant to Delaware law, in order to reduce the tidal incursion on the adjacent lowlands. The defendants' sloop, as it passed up the creek, broke the dam. The owners of the dam sued for damages. A more complete blockage of commerce (albeit trivial commerce) is hard to imagine, but the absurdity of a holding that the states could not constitutionally act to improve the health and utility of their lowlands was apparent. John Marshall's opinion was short.

Taney was Jackson's chief justice, and he had figured importantly in the administration's campaign to rid the nation of the Bank of the United States. He personally rejected the negative Commerce Clause doctrine, and the paramount role of state power was affirmed

24 / Regulation, Federalism, and Interstate Commerce

repeatedly in this period. The leading case of the period was *Cooley* v. *Board of Warden's*, 12 How. 299 (1851), which upheld the application of Pennsylvania pilotage laws to ships entering or leaving the port of Philadelphia. The decision confined the negative Commerce Clause principle to matters that "are in their nature national, or admit only of one uniform system, or plan of regulation, may justly be said to be of such a nature as to require exclusive legislation by Congress."[41] Almost no state legislation was invalidated during this period, and the number of negative Commerce Clause cases remained small.

In *Bank of Augusta* v. *Earle*, 38 U.S. (13 Pet.) 517 (1839), Taney faced the question of the power of a corporation to do business outside its own state. The plaintiffs in the three companion cases were non-Alabama corporations that sued in federal court in Alabama on bills of exchange issued at Mobile. The defense set up was that under Alabama law, the plaintiffs were not empowered to buy and hold bills of exchange, and therefore they were not entitled to collect the amounts due. The circuit court upheld the defense. The Supreme Court reversed. Taney's opinion upheld both the right of the creditor corporation to collect, and the power of the state to keep it from doing business within its boundaries.

The disputes that surrounded the demise of the second Bank of the United States must have been in the justices' minds, for the Bank was a plaintiff in one of the companion cases. The Bank had found a second life as a Pennsylvania corporation, a privilege for which the Pennsylvania legislature had extracted no small price.[42] The issue now was whether it and other state banking corporations could provide interstate banking and financing services through a series of agent and contract relations.

The Taney opinion addressed two questions. First, can a corporation exercise powers not granted by its state of incorporation outside of that state? And second, did the law of Alabama prohibit the plaintiffs from buying bills of exchange in Alabama? The answer to the first question, which has had lasting importance for American law, was yes. The second answer, which was important at the time, was no.

Taney first denied that corporations were citizens within the meaning of the Privileges and Immunities Clause. He proceeded to characterize a corporation as an artificial entity that "can have no legal existence out of the boundaries of the sovereignty by which it is created. It exists only in contemplation of law, and by force of law; and where the law ceases to operate, and is no longer obligatory, the corporation can have no existence. It must dwell in the place of its creation, and cannot migrate to another sovereignty. . . . Every

Regulation and the American Common Market   /   25

power . . . of the description of which we are speaking, which a corporation excercises in another state, depends for its validity upon the laws of the sovereignty in which it is exercised; and a corporation can make no valid contract, without their sanction, express or implied.''[43]

Taney then turned to the question of whether the law of Alabama did or did not authorize the contracts at issue. He began with the international law doctrine of comity, arguing that it applied to foreign corporate activities within the states. ''The intimate union of these states, as members of the same great political family; the deep and vital interests which bind them so closely together; should lead us, in the absence of proof to the contrary, to presume a greater degree of comity, and friendship, and kindness towards one another, than we should be authorized to presume between foreign nations.''[44]

The argument that Alabama law forbade the activities of the plaintiffs was based on the Alabama banking policy of restrictive entry and state ownership, a policy enshrined in the state constitution. ''It is evidently the policy of Alabama,'' observed Taney, ''to restrict the power of the legislature in relation to bank charters, and to secure to the state a large portion of the profits of banking, in order to provide a public revenue, and also to make safe the debts which should be contracted by the banks.''[45] (The state had created seven banks. It owned five of them and two-fifths of the other two.) Taney would not infer a prohibition, even though interstate competition might reduce the profitability of Alabama banks. ''In another view of the subject, however, she [Alabama] may believe it to be her policy to extend the utmost liberality to the banks of other states in the expectation that it would produce a corresponding comity in other states towards the banks in which she is so much interested.''[46] If Alabama wished to exlcude the foreigners, its legislature would have to say so expressly.

When *Bank of Augusta* is put together with the decisions in *Swift v. Tyson*, 16 Pet. 1 (1842), and *Louisville R.R. Co. v. Letson*, 2 How. 497 (1844), a judicial program of voluntary commercial integration emerges. *Swift* held that in diversity cases, the federal courts would follow the general common law, particularly in commercial matters, unless the state had a statute providing a contrary rule. And in *Letson*, the Court held that a corporation could use the state of its incorporation to establish diversity jurisdiction, which would be available to that corporation everywhere outside its home state. Thus, while the federal courts recognized the paramount power of the states, they tendered to the states a system of uniform national commercial law, which the states were free to reject.

26 / Regulation, Federalism, and Interstate Commerce

It is fashionable and easy to criticize *Bank of Augusta* and *Swift*; indeed, they have caused endless confusion and difficulty in subsequent decisions. However, in their time, they were creative responses to a need for a national payments system. In these two cases, the Court honored the demands for state control that had figured so importantly in the debates over the Bank of the United States, and at the same time offered the states a common system of law by which to govern commercial transactions. The states had the power to reject that system, but they did not do so.[47]

The final decisions of the Taney period are *Woodruff* v. *Parham*, 75 U.S. (8 Wall.) 123 (1869), and *Paul* v. *Virginia*, 75 U.S. (8 Wall.) 168 (1869). *Woodruff* involved a nondiscriminatory sales tax placed by Alabama upon the sale of goods. The issue was whether this tax could be applied to out-of-state goods, still in their original package, that were sold in Alabama to residents. Marshall, in *Brown* v. *Maryland*, had said that it could not. The Taney Court explicitly rejected the dictum.

Paul v. *Virginia*, 75 U.S. (8 Wall.) 168 (1869), turned on the constitutionality of a Virginia statute that required foreign insurance companies to deposit a large security bond with the state as a condition of doing business in Virginia. The argument was made to the Court that the state had the right to take reasonable steps to make sure that foreign insurance companies, whose capital was located outside the state, would honor their insurance contracts.[48] The Court upheld the statute on more sweeping grounds. Mr. Justice Field, writing for the Court, first reiterated Taney's position in *Bank of Augusta*—that corporations were not subject to the Privileges and Immunities Clause. He then turned to the argument that the statute violated the negative Commerce Clause, and came to the surprising conclusion that insurance was not commerce. "These contracts are not articles of commerce in any proper meaning of the word. They are not commodities to be shipped or forwarded from one State to another, and then put for sale."[49]

The position was implicit in *Bank of Augusta* v. *Earle*. There, too, the argument was that an Alabama prohibition on bills of exchange would violate the negative Commerce Clause. "In the present state of the commercial world, bills of exchange are one of the great means of carrying on the commerce of the world. . . . [T]he legislature of Alabama has as much right to declare that no ship or vessel shall come into the ports of that state, which does not belong to one of her own citizens, and is not registered in some office established by a law of Alabama, as she has to prohibit any but her own citizens from dealing in exchange within her terri-

Regulation and the American Common Market / 27

tories."[50] Taney had ignored the question; and since he did not believe in the negative Commerce Clause, that was easy enough to do. But for Field, whose later decisions show him to be a strong adherent of the negative Commerce Clause, the issue could not be so easily ignored. By holding that corporations, bills of exchange, and insurance were not commerce the Court freed itself to deploy the negative Commerce Clause against the newer restraints on the movement of goods, without disrupting the state regulation of corporations, banking, and insurance that had developed dependent on *Bank of Augusta.*

Unlike so many changes in the law, the new era of reliance on the negative Commerce Clause dawned full blown. In *Low* v. *Austin*, 80 U.S. (13 Wall.) 29 (1872), the Court held that a California *ad valorem* personal property tax could not be applied to imported goods still in their original package. With respect to *Low*, *Brown* v. *Maryland* could have been easily confined to discriminatory taxes on imports, but the Court chose an expansive reading. And in the following *Case of the State Freight Tax*, 82 U.S. (15 Wall.) 232 (1873), the Court held unconstitutional a Pennsylvania tax imposed on all the common carriers of the state that was based on a flat charge per thousand pounds of freight carried.

The distinctive feature of this jurisprudence was an effort to carve out an area of interstate commerce that would be immune from state regulation while the rest of commerce would be free for unhindered state regulation. The purpose, reasonableness, or effects of the state legislations were not to count. The attempts of Congress to square its regulation over interstate commerce with state regulation over intrastate commerce caused no end of difficulty for the Court and the country. At times it appeared that there was commerce that did not fit either category. The distinction was less harmful when applied to the purposes of the negative Commerce Clause.

In *Low*, Field went out of his way to explain that "[t]here are provisions in the Constitution which prevent one State from discriminating injuriously against the products of other States, or the rights of their citizens, in the imposition of taxes, but where a State, except in such cases, has the power to tax, there is no authority in this court, nor in the United States, to control its action, however unreasonable or oppressive. The power of the State, except in such cases, is absolute and supreme."[51] When the Court did go beyond the form of the tax to examine its effects, as it did in *Robbins* v. *Shelby County Taxing District*, 120 U.S. 489 (1887), Field would dissent.

28 / Regulation, Federalism, and Interstate Commerce

Bizarre results were quickly apparent. In *State Tax on Railway Gross Receipts*, 82 U.S. (15 Wall.) 284 (1873), decided along with the *Case of the State Freight Tax*, the Court upheld (Field dissenting) a Pennsylvania tax of three-quarters of one percent on the gross receipts of a railway company, including that portion of the gross receipts derived from interstate shipments. The tax, said the Court, "is a tax upon the railroad company, measured in amount by the extent of its business, or the degree to which its franchise is exercised. . ."[52] The freight tax, on the other hand, was a tax on the freight, and thus on commerce itself. However, if one examines effects, the flat tax on freight per pound weighed more heavily on the short haul, largely intrastate traffic, while the gross receipts tax directly taxed that portion of the revenue derived from the out-of-state haul. (Of course the tax did not reach the intrastate portion of the inbound interstate haul.)

The negative Commerce Clause era produced some notable decisions. In *Welton* v. *Missouri*, 91 U.S. 275 (1976), the Court, in a Field opinion, struck down a Missouri statute that placed a special tax on persons who dealt in goods "which are not the growth, produce, or manufacture of this State, by going from place to place to sell the same."[53] The argument for the tax on peddlers was that the tax was imposed on the goods after they had left their original package, and hence was not a tax on interstate commerce. Field was equal to the task. "It is sufficient to hold now that the commercial power continues until the commodity has ceased to be the subject of discriminating legislation by reason of its foreign character."[54]

In *Robbins* v. *Shelby Taxing District*, 120 U.S. 489 (1887), the Court held unconstitutional a similar tax, imposed not on dealers in goods of foreign origin, but on "drummers and all persons not having a regular licensed house of business in the Taxing District." Chief Justice Waite wrote a long essay on the practical needs of out-of-state sellers, but the result was too much for Field's metaphysic and he dissented.

In the area of regulation, in *Hall* v. *DeCuir*, 95 U.S. 485 (1878), the Court held that a Louisiana reconstruction statute that prohibited passenger carriers from segregating passengers by race could not be applied to a passenger steamer on the Mississippi River. In *Wabash* v. *Illinois*, 118 U.S. 557 (1887), the Court held that Illinois could not regulate the relationship between rates for shipments from points within Illinois to New York, even though the difference in price was easily attributable to the portion of the carriage that was in the state. This decision is frequently cited as having disabled state regulation of interstate shipments and having occasioned the passage of the Interstate Commerce Act the following year. In *Leisy* v. *Hardin*, 135 U.S. 100 (1890), the Court overruled a Taney Court precedent and held that Iowa could not keep beer in the original keg out of the state. Congress quickly reversed the decision, and the Court acceded.

Two notable regulatory decisions came at the end of the Field period. In *Buck* v. *Kuykendall*, 267 U.S. 307 (1925), the Court held unconstitutional the application of a state statute that required a certificate of public convenience and necessity for a motor carrier to motor carriage between points inside and outside the state. And in *Baldwin* v. *G.A.F. Seelig, Inc.*, 294 U.S. 511 (1935), the Court held that New York could not exclude Vermont milk in pursuit of its regulatory program to raise the price of milk to its producers; the previous term, the Court had upheld the program in *Nebbia* v. *New York*, 291 U.S. 502 (1934). How New York was to hold the price of milk up in-state if its producers were not protected from interstate competition was not explained.

The next period is one of transition and instability in basic approach. The beginning is commonly traced to the dissenting opinion of Mr. Justice Stone in *DiSanto* v. *Pennsylvania*, 273 U.S. 34 (1927). In that case, the Court held a Pennsylvania statute that required a state license for the selling of steamship tickets to or from foreign countries to be an unconstitutional regulation of interstate commerce. In a dissenting opinion, Mr. Justice Brandeis argued that the activity was actually local, not interstate, and hence constitutional. Mr. Justice Stone briefly concurred in the dissent but argued that the approach of both the Court and the dissent was wrong. "[I]t seems clear," he wrote, "that those interferences [of the states] not deemed forbidden are to be sustained, not because the effect on commerce is nominally indirect, but because a consideration of all the facts and circumstances, such as the nature of the regulation, its function, the character of the business involved and the actual effect on the flow of commerce, lead to the conclusion that the regulation concerns interests peculiarly local and does not infringe the national interest in maintaining the freedom of commerce across state lines."[55] The question, in other words, is not whether the regulation or tax is or is not on interstate commerce. The question is whether, all things considered—including the national interest —the tax or regulation of commerce, interstate or not, is good or bad. This approach, of course, has a close kinship with the now discredited substantive due process of cases like *Lochner* v. *New York*, 198 U.S. 45 (1905). The Court abandoned substantive due process in the 1930s, but the method has lived on in Commerce Clause matters, explicitly justified on the grounds that failure of the state legislative body to represent the national interest justifies a more aggressive form of judicial review.

The approach was gradually but erratically accepted by the Court. In *Western Live Stock* v. *Bureau of Revenue*, 303 U.S. 250 (1938), the Court upheld a tax of two percent of the amounts received for advertising space in a magazine. The magazine was published in the state, but most of its advertising and most of its circulation was out of state. Stone's opinion pointed out that when judged by effect rather than by form, the prior decisions were inconsistent. "All of these taxes [that the Court has upheld as local] in one way or another add up to the expense of carrying on interstate commerce, and in that sense burden it; but they are not for that reason prohibited. On the other hand, local taxes, measured by gross receipts from interstate commerce, have often been pronounced unconstitutional."[56] Stone concluded: "[T]he tax assailed here finds support in reason, and in the practical needs of a taxing system which, under constitutional limitations, must accommodate itself to the double demand that interstate business shall pay its way, and that at the same time it shall not be burdened with cumulative exactions which are not similarly laid on local business."[57]

In the regulatory area, Stone wrote the opinion for the Court in *Southern Pacific Co.* v. *Arizona*, 325 U.S. 761 (1945), holding unconstitutional the application to interstate trains of a state statute that limited the length of trains. The statute was justified as local safety regulation under the *Cooley* exception to the negative Commerce Clause. Stone considered at length the issues of train and crossing safety and compliance cost. He found the statute wanting.

A new period began in 1976 when the Court, accepting that it had in fact embraced a new approach, began overruling the predecents set during the Field period. In *Michelin Tire Corp.* v. *Wages, Tax Comm'r*, 423 U.S. 276 (1976), the Court overruled *Low* v. *Austin* and held that an *ad valorem*, nondiscriminatory personal property tax could be imposed on goods still in their original package. In *Complete Auto Transit, Inc.* v. *Brady*, 430 U.S. 274 (1977), the Court overruled *Freeman* v. *Hewit*, 329 U.S. 249 (1946) (a case that rejected the Stone position and applied doctrine derived from the *State Tax on Railway Gross Receipts* decision) and held that a tax on the "privilege" of conducting interstate business was constitutional if it was nondiscriminatory. And in *Department of Revenue* v. *Association of Washington Stevedoring Co.*, 435 U.S. 734 (1978), the Court followed this principle to uphold application of a

Regulation and the American Common Market / 31

gross receipts tax to the business of Stevedoring, and again overruled precedents explicitly to the contrary. In the regulatory area, the Court held in *Hughes* v. *Oklahoma*, 441 U.S. 322 (1979), that an Oklahoma statute that prohibited the export of minnows from the state is unconstitutional. The Court overruled a line of decisions going back to *Geer* v. *Connecticut*, 161 U.S. 519 (1896) that held that the regulation of a state's game and other common property was not regulation of interstate commerce.

The rule that emerges is that a state can constitutionally tax or regulate all commerce within its jurisdiction (unless, of course, the regulation is contrary to federal statute) as long as its taxation or regulation does not discriminate between commerce wholly within that state and commerce between the state and other states. The discrimination inquiry is largely confined to an examination of the statute, but upon a sufficiently strong showing of discriminatory impact, the Court will look behind a formally neutral statute and evaluate the state interest versus the burden placed on interstate commerce. In the tax area, however, the Court considers the state interest in revenue so strong that any formally nondiscriminatory tax imposed by a state will be upheld without regard to the actual burdens placed on interstate, as opposed to intrastate, commerce.

This synthesis has two major implications for the future. On the one hand, states can assert regulatory and taxing jurisdiction more broadly, without fear that they will encounter constitutional limitations based upon the negative Commerce Clause. On the other hand, state regulatory activities previously characterized as local become subject to a reasonableness scrutiny under the Commerce Clause. Areas such as local zoning and building codes and local price and business controls become subject to judicial scrutiny from a national perspective. To suggest the potential reach of the argument, could it not now be argued that rent controls—an example of a currently re-surgent form of local regulation—are contrary to the national market because they reduce turnover and supply in the rental housing stock and impose particular hardship on those who must come into the jurisdiction to do business and hence must find housing? Rent control is a system by which the local jurisdiction can appropriate the rental stock for the use of its present residents and voters and eliminate the ability of outsiders to bid for its use through price.

The most interesting recent decisions of the Court are those cases that have grappled with this aspect of the new synethesis. A common theme of the cases or a refusal by the Court to base the decision on whether the activity is local, intrastate, or interstate; rather, the Court attempts to examine each regulation and balance the

32 / Regulation, Federalism, and Interstate Commerce

state purpose against the values of the national market. The Court frequently returns to the quotation from Mr. Justice Jackson that opens this paper. These recent decisions involve a variety of regulatory programs. They will be presented here chronologically.

In *Hughes* v. *Alexandria Scrap Corp.*, 426 U.S. 794 (1976), the Court considered a Maryland bounty program that was designed to speed the rate at which old and no longer usable cars went to scrap processors for destruction. The method chosen was to pay a bounty to processors for destroying the cars and thus increase the incentives for scrap dealers and others to bring the cars to the processors for destruction. The program was open to processors inside and outside of the state, and a substantial percentage of the cars on which bounty was paid were in fact processed by non-Maryland processors.

The Maryland legislature, of course, did not wish to spend Maryland funds to encourage the wrecks of other states on their way to the processing plant. Without some device to focus the bounty on wrecks and junk of Maryland origin, a sufficiently high bounty might in fact convert Maryland into a junk mecca, with disabled vehicles from throughout the east enjoying the benefits of the Maryland bounty. The means chosen was to insist that in order to be eligible for the bounty the car destroyed must have been a Maryland-titled vehicle. Title documentation was required to apply for the bounty.

The program described thus far might have been subject to challenge on the grounds that the payment of the bounty by Maryland disrupts interstate trade. The Maryland bounty effectively diverts the processing capacity from the wrecks of other states to Maryland-origin wrecks. This might set off a "bounty war" between the states, as they compete for the services of processors. This line of attack was not pursued, however, because it would threaten the validity of all local and state programs designed to subsidize or otherwise encourage local business at the expense of foreign competition. Throughout the long history of Commerce Clause litigation, state spending policies have not been attacked, presumably because they are considered to be local state decisions.

The feature of the bounty program that was attacked related to the procedures for receiving bounties on "hulks," which are defined as vehicles more than eight years old. The program was designed to encourage in particular the processing of older vehicles, but it was recognized that title documentation on such vehicles, perhaps long out of road use, would be difficult or impossible. Under the original

Regulation and the American Common Market / 33

program, the production of title documentation for hulks was excused. The statute was amended to excuse title documentation for in-state processors, but not for out-of-state processors.

It was this discrimination that was attacked by the plaintiff, a processor located in Virginia just across the Potomac River from Maryland. He complained that since the amendment of the statute, his business in interstate hulks—the bulk of the business under the bounty program—had dried up.

Mr. Justice Powell's opinion is significant because it did not take the line of justification that the program involved local environmental regulation and expenditure and was therefore beyond the scope of the Commerce Clause. Nor did the opinion uphold the in-state-versus-out-of-state classification as reasonable under the Commerce Clause because the Maryland legislature could have reasonably concluded that hulks processed at in-state processors were more likely to be true Maryland hulks—the ground explicitly used to uphold the statute against equal protection challenge. The basis for decision was more sweeping: "Nothing in the purposes animating the Commerce Clause forbids a State, in the absence of congressional action, from participating in the market and exercising the right to favor its own citizens over others."[58]

The sweep of this dictum is troubling. It is easy to understand that the Court did not wish to throw a pall over long-customary state programs designed to promote and advantage local producers. But the Court claimed to see no hint of local protectionism in the statute. The Court treated the statute as environmental in purpose. The application of a least restrictive means approach to that purpose might have resulted in invalidating the statute; at least it would have resulted in a more limited opinion. If the Court is serious about a commitment to a national market, it is difficult to justify subjecting taxing and regulatory policies to active judicial scrutiny while leaving spending programs completely unexamined.

The beginnings of *Exxon Corp.* v. *Governor of Maryland*, 437 U.S. 117 (1978), can be found in a statute passed by the state of Maryland that prohibited oil refiners from operating retail service stations in Maryland. Promulgation of the statute was spurred by a state determination that during the gasoline shortage of 1973, integrated refiners had favored their own outlets over independent dealers. Since such behavior was a rational response by the firms to the federal price controls then in effect, it was difficult to argue with the reasonableness of the finding. The justification for the statute was that it would eliminate an inherently unfair form of competition for the independent dealers.

34 / Regulation, Federalism, and Interstate Commerce

Again, the Court might have upheld the statute on the grounds that retail sales are local, or that forms of corporate organization are not commerce, as decided in *Bank of Augusta*—but it did not do so.

The plaintiffs—who included both major oil companies and independent companies such as "Red Head" and "Scot"—argued that vertical integration made them more efficient and they offered proof of the argument. Since all of Maryland's oil comes from outside the state, the effect of the statute was to raise the cost of interstate commerce. However, the Court upheld the statute on the grounds that it was not discriminatory. All refineries were prohibited from operating their own stations, and any interstate company that was not a refiner (such as Sears) was free to sell gasoline. "As indicated by the Court in *Hughes*, the Clause protects the interstate market, not particular interstate firms, from prohibiting or burdensome regulations. It may be true that the consuming public will be injured by the loss of the high-volume, low-priced stations operated by the independent refiners, but again that argument related to the wisdom of the statute, not to its burden on commerce."[59] To put the argument another way, if Maryland wants to raise the price of its gas, that is its problem, not the nation's.

In *City of Philadelphia* v. *New Jersey*, 437 U.S. 617 (1978), the Court held unconstitutional a New Jersey statute that prohibited the importation of solid or liquid waste for disposal in New Jersey without approval of the State Department of Environmental Protection. The state defended the statute under the local health regulation exception of *Cooley* v. *Board of Port Wardens*. The statute, the state argued, is like a quarantine regulation that requires entering passengers to undergo health inspection and be quarantined if they have or were exposed to certain diseases. The courts have repeatedly upheld such laws even though the states that established them did not at the same time require their own residents to be inspected and quarantined if they had the same condition or exposure. New Jersey argued that it would handle its own waste disposal problem as best it could, but before it took on the health burdens of foreign waste, it was entitled to impose reasonable protective conditions. The Court would not accept the argument. The discriminatory treatment of foreign waste invalidated the statute.

Closely tied to these decisions has been increased use of the Privileges and Immunities Clause.[60] From an early date, the clause has been confined to fundamental rights, although it has occasionally provided grounds for decision in the Commerce Clause

Regulation and the American Common Market / 35

context. In *Hicklin* v. *Orbeck*, 437 U.S. 518 (1978), the Court held unconstitutional under the Privileges and Immunities Clause a statute that required employers to prefer Alaska residents for jobs attributable to the production and distribution of oil from state lands. Very recently, the New York Court of Appeals relied on this decision to hold that New York cannot constitutionally exclude nonresidents from membership in its bar.[61]

In three recent cases the Court has addressed problems that arose from the need of the states to coordinate their regulatory and taxing activities.

In *Great Atlantic & Pacific Tea Co.* v. *Cottrell*, 424 U.S. 366 (1976), the Court held unconstitutional a Mississippi regulation that excluded Louisiana-processed milk solely because Louisiana had refused to accept milk processed and inspected in Mississippi. The Court has invalidated under the Commerce Clause milk inspection programs that unduly hamper interstate commerce, most notably in *Dean Milk Co.* v. *Madison*, 340 U.S. 349 (1964). But the Court has simply required the state to operate its own inspection program in a way that makes it possible for interstate milk to compete. It has not required the state to accept the foreign inspection system, which leads to the possibility of costly, multiple-inspection programs. Mississippi argued that the purpose of excluding the Louisiana milk was to put pressure on Louisiana to accept Mississippi-inspection, which Louisiana had withheld in bad faith. Without examining the grounds for Louisiana's action, the Court rejected the argument. "However available such methods in an international system of trade between wholly sovereign nation states, they may not constitutionally be employed by the States that constitute the common market created by the Framers of the Constitution."[62]

In *United States Steel Corp.* v. *Multistate Tax Comm'n*, 434 U.S. 452 (1978), the Court upheld the agreement among some twenty states that created the Multistate Tax Commission, against the argument that the agreement violated the Compact Clause because it had not been approved by Congress. The Commission had been formed in response to the growing imposition of state net income taxes and to the holding in *Northwestern States Portland Cement Co.* v. *Minnesota*, 358 U.S. 450 (1959), that out-of-state sellers were liable for the share of their profits attributable on their shipments into the taxing state. It was apparent that without interstate coordination the sum of the state taxes could easily be on a profits base well in excess of the total profits actually made by an interstate

36 / Regulation, Federalism, and Interstate Commerce

firm. The Court's construction of the Compact Clause was strained, clearly influenced by the Court's awareness of the value of coordination in this area and the failure of Congress to act on the problem.

In *Moorman Mfg. Co. v. Blair*, 98 Sup. Ct. 2340 (1978), the Court considered a challenge to Iowa's use of a single factor formula—sales—to apportion income to Iowa. The rest of the states, including Illinois, where Moorman's plant was located, use a three factor formula—sales, property and payroll. Moorman had only sales in Iowa and argued that the use of the two different formulas resulted in double taxation of its income by Iowa and Illinois. The Court received an amicus brief on behalf of fifteen distinguished economists that argued that the Iowa formula has an "anti-competitive effect that would seem to signify its unconstitutionality." The economists cautioned, "Courts should be ever mindful of the threat states can pose to the effective workings of a free and open marketplace."

The Court's problem was that there is no clear rationale for any apportionment formula for profit. The profit of a firm is the joint product of all the activities of the firm, attributable to all of them and to none of them. The problem with Iowa's formula for imposing corporate income taxes was that it varied from the formulas of the other forty-four states; however, if the Court held the Iowa formula unconstitutional, it would freeze into the Constitution the present choice of the forty-four, since no state could then constitutionally experiment with a different formula. The Court declined to follow the economists' lead.

THE CONSTITUTIONAL SYSTEM IN PRACTICE

In the American federal system, the states have had substantial regulatory and taxing autonomy—subject to regular review by the Court and to rare review by the Congress. This system raises a number of questions that must be addressed. How have the states used their authority? Has it been used to further the national interest, or in pursuit of narrow, local interests? In making this judgment, what standard is to be applied? The states have failed to meet a Pareto standard, but so has every other government. Under a comparative approach, one would attempt to assess the performance of the states in relation to the performance of other jurisdictions, such as national sovereigns acting within world markets. Another

Regulation and the American Common Market / 37

approach, pursued here, is to compare the performance of the states to that of the national government. The conclusion offered here is that when this comparison is made, the states appear to do relatively well. The large and important disruptions of the American common market have been both recent and imposed by the national government.

The States

The lack of a systematic body of scholarship on state economic regulation makes it impossible to offer any authoritative assessment of the performance of the states over time. This section draws on some of the available material to sketch the issues.

Louis Hartz's book, *Economic Policy and Democratic Thought: Pennsylvania, 1977-1980,*[63] is the leading study of state regulatory policy in the pre-Civil War period. It is generally cited for its conclusion—that during that period, Pennsylvania did not pursue a noninterventionist, *laissez-faire* economic policy. The issues Hartz discusses relate to state public works in the areas of canals and railroads; the chartering and regulation of corporations, particularly banks and railroads; the elimination of slavery and indentured servitude; the regulation of factory and mine working conditions; and liquor prohibition. The noncorporate enterprise of the period operated free of legislative restrictions on its activities.

At that time, the central and recurrent issue of economic policy in Pennsylvania was the construction and operation of a system of canals and then railroads. The state, mixed private-public corporations, and finally private corporations were enlisted to finance this task. Of course, the major commercial event of the period was New York's construction of the Erie Canal. New York, favored by a relatively level route west—from the Hudson River Valley along the Mohawk River Valley and across the state to Lake Erie at Buffalo— had succeeded in opening the whole West to its commerce. This commerce would naturally move through the port of New York, not Philadelphia. Philadelphia's commercial problems were compounded by the fact that its geography conspired to direct even the commerce of Pennsylvania to the south and west rather than through Philadelphia. Pennsylvania is crossed by several major ridges of the Appalchians, and the movement of her watercot ses is north and south. Running south across the eastern half of the state is the Susquehanna River, which, after passing through Harrisburg, flows on to the port of Baltimore. In the west, Pittsburgh had better access than Philadelphia to the state of New York—north on the

38 / Regulation, Federalism, and Interstate Commerce

Allegheny River—or to Baltimore, south on the Monagahelia River, and from there to the Potomac River. "In dark moments during the [eighteen] twenties," reports Hartz, "[Philadelphians] saw the approach of commercial isolation and decline, their own state split up among rival imperialisms—New York capturing the trade of the Easton area, Albany at the gates of Pittsburgh, Baltimore victorious in the Lancaster region."[64]

The public policy of Pennsylvania was designed to overcome the facts of her geography. Tax monies were used to support a system composed of canals and railroad that would link Philadelphia with Pittsburgh. This "main line" project, begun in 1826 and completed in 1835, was built and operated by the state. However, the tolls did not pay the state's interest expense. Futhermore, the Baltimore and Ohio Railroad, which was originally to have met the Ohio River at Pittsburgh, was forced to accept Parkersburgh, [West] Virginia. For a decade, Pennsylvania exploited her small Erie corner in order to block New York's rail connection to the West—the stretch connected by four different railroads with four different gauges. With the maturing of rail technology, the Pennsylvania Railroad Corporation became the instrument of the state's policy to offer a competitive route for east-west commerce. This accounts for Pennsylvania's monopoly railroad policy, in which the profitable parts of the system were used to subsidize the effort to overcome Pennsylvania's geographical limitations.

The effects of Pennsylvania's policies on interstate commerce were substantial. In the 1860s, Pittsburgh, though favorably located on the Allegheny River, downstream from the Appalachian oil deposits, was eclipsed as a refining center by Cleveland, in part because of unfavorable shipping rates to the East on the Pennsylvania.[65] Unlike Pittsburgh, Cleveland had two rail connections to the East—the Central system and the Erie—and thus it was able to obtain competitive rail rates. Pittsburgh responded by seeking a connection between Pittsburgh and the Baltimore and Ohio Railroad, an endeavor that was ultimately successful.[66]

The other feature of the law of the period that seems to have had a substantial effect on commerce was the legislative policy of special chartering. For instance, when the Second Bank of the United States came to the legislature for a state charter, one condition was that it subscribe $675,000 to state railroad stocks, and $139,000 to state turnpike companies. "Evidently all the hobbied and local schemes in the State," wrote William Graham Sumner, "clustered around this big carcass and fought with one another for slices of it."[67]

Nevertheless, it is clear that Pennsylvania's power to act was significantly constrained because competition from other states

Regulation and the American Common Market / 39

could tempt certain cities to deviate from a "Pennsylvania-first" policy. Pittsburgh, for instance, could always send goods down the Ohio to Parkersburgh, and from there east to Baltimore. Of interstate competition in banking, Hartz writes:

> The influx of varied currencies from adjoining states was always a primary factor conditioning the effectiveness of state policy, but in a purely competitive sense the foreign corporation factor had special implications there. Fear of a reliance upon outstate institutions, involving Pennsylvanians in all their weaknesses and none of their profits, was, especially during the early period, a strong consideration in the expansion of bank charter policy. In 1835 Biddle played heavily upon the state's anxiety to retain Philadelphia as the banking "seat" of the nation, and it has been argued that a controlling motive in the grant of a charter to the Second Bank was the appearance at that time of New York's plan for a great fifty-million dollar bank. In the insurance field the competitive idea was at least equally significant. Prior to 1812 incorporated marine insurance capital amounted to less than 8 per cent of the capital involved in Philadelphia's import-export trade, a situation which was blamed for heavy reliance upon British insurance offices "to whom we have, in fact paid a tax." Such dependency in time of loss was branded as unseemly and dangerous. Not only was this argument presented to expand insurance charter policy, but it accounted also for the maintenance throughout the entire period of statute restrictions on foreign corporation agents which were more stringent in the insurance field than in any other.[68]

George H. Miller's *Railroads and the Granger Laws*[69] is the authoritative study of the effort of the upper midwest states to control railroads in the 1870s. Miller shows that the most important force behind the Granger laws was commercial interests in the towns and cities whose position was impaired by the maturing of rail technology. Prior to the Civil War, the commerce of these states—Illinois, Iowa, Minnesota and Wisconsin—had moved down the Mississippi River Valley to the port of New Orleans. The river was closed during the Civil War, and after the war commerce began to move east by rail to the port of New York. During this process, established merchants at river transfer points such as Galena, Dubuque, and Peoria, found that they no longer had a stream of commerce to service. The state effort was to slow or stop this transition. The most notorious Granger law was the Potter Bill of Wisconsin, which imposed ceiling rates on Wisconsin's railroads on a per mile basis. The bill's purpose was to change the relative prices of the long haul versus the short haul in favor of the short haul and thus reduce the effects of the railroad's long-haul efficiency.

40 / Regulation, Federalism, and Interstate Commerce

Miller reports that these state schemes were almost immediately modified to accommodate the demands of the market. In 1871, Illinois passed a statute that compelled railroads to adjust their rates relative to the distance traveled.[70] In 1873, the state provided for commission regulation on reasonableness criteria in a statute "not particularly obnoxious to the railroads."[71] Iowa passed a law satisfactory to Dubuque in 1874;[72] it was repealed in 1878.[73] Minnesota's law of 1871 was replaced in 1874 with a law that followed the Illinois model; the 1874 law was repealed in 1875.[74] Wisconsin's Potter Law was passed in 1874[75] and repealed in 1876.[76]

Miller makes it clear that interstate commerce was instrumented in the political collapse of the protective program. The Illinois law of 1873 recognized "the impracticability of legislative regulation for a complex and constantly changing industry."[77] "The Iowa law remained in force for a period of four years, but the continuing decline of through rates after 1873 made the schedule of maximum rates obsolete soon after it was prepared. . . The percentage of trade stopping at the river remained relatively small."[78] Minnesota's law of 1874 was repealed in 1875 because "as a result of panic and depression of 1873 the railroads of Minnesota found themselves in desperate financial straits."[79] In Wisconsin, the Milwaukee Road could collect less on the short hauls only if it could charge more on its long haul to the port of Milwaukee, but it could not charge more on that haul if the Northwestern or Burlington Railroads then diverted its traffic to Chicago.

Ann Bowler and I have examined in detail a part of this episode— the ceiling placed by Illinois on the storage and transfer charges of grain elevators at the port of Chicago.[80] The elevators were the means by which grain was transferred from rail cars to lake vessels for shipment to the East Coast; from there it was exported to Europe. In *Munn* v. *Illinois*, 94 U.S. 113 (1877), the Court, relied on the local form of the contracts for its decision, and held that this regulation was not regulation of interstate commerce. It seems that a more serious impediment of interstate commerce could not be imagined, for if the legislature held down the price of this service, the service could no longer be offered in the optimum price-to-quality package. Our investigation showed, however, that the regulation was not such an impediment because the regulatory price was above the market price. It seems unlikely that Illinois would handicap its own transfer port when it faced competition from other ports and through traffic.

In the twentieth century, common carrier regulation imposed

by the state has impeded entry into transportation. Although the analogous federal regulation has received much more extensive study, it is clear that the state regulation has given existing operating rights substantial values. Because the interstate portions of this industry have been subject to federal regulation, the states have not faced strong competitive pressure against their regulation of strictly local traffic. I (along with Isaacson and Kasper) studied the regulation of taxicabs in Chicago and reported evidence of strong negative welfare effects.[81] Indeed, when the interstate railroads attempted to protect their transfer passengers in Chicago, the city interfered in a particularly clumsy way and was rebuked by the Supreme Court under the Interstate Commerce Clause.[82]

Regulation of "professions" and associated services is the most notable area in which twentieth century state regulatory activity has had significant negative welfare effects. An incredible array of activities have been drawn into these regulatory schemes, and the schemes have a strong local protection element. Benham's classic cross-sectional study showed dramatic positive price effects on eyeglasses in the most restrictive states.[83] Parshigian, in a recent study, concluded that this regulation has a large effect in reducing interstate mobility.[84] Even here, however, the picture is not unmixed. For professions such as accounting, law, and medicine, entrance requirements have been coordinated among the states, and national systems of professional education and training have developed. Many states recognize the professional credentials of other states.

The distribution utilities have been an important state regulatory responsibility. The federal government has left to the states significant authority over water, natural gas, telephone, and, until recently, electric utilities. In the nineteenth century, this authority was exercised on the local level, but with the movement of utility services outside of municipal limits and with the increase in some economies of scale, most states have adopted a state commission system of regulation. In the twentieth century, the firms have experienced significant growth and low capital costs while providing high levels of service. The Federal Communications Commission has recently challenged the traditional state regulatory policy that extends the telephone monopoly beyond the wire connection, but this development may reflect improvements in the technology as much as anything else.

State regulation of corporations by special charters was notoriously corrupt in the nineteenth century, but out of the competition that is implicit in state autonomy over corporations has evolved a quite

42 / Regulation, Federalism, and Interstate Commerce

serviceable and simple body of law for the operation and governance of corporations, both intrastate and interstate. State Blue Sky Laws appear to be an unjustified interference with the functioning of a national securities market, and the recent extension of state authority to the antitakeover area is troubling.

In regulation of banking, the states resisted interstate operation and the federal government followed this policy when it created national bank corporations in 1862. Bank enterprises are just now developing legal devices to support national operation.

Through the Commissioners on Uniform State Laws, the states have developed and enacted a system of national commercial laws, most notably the Uniform Commercial Code.

The Federal Government

In the nineteenth century, the major instrument of federal government economic policy was the tariff. However, the Constitution failed to check the desire of the North to use the tariff as means to benefit itself at the expense of the South. Although the Constitution required uniform tariffs, they could be uniform on goods that Northerners sold and Southerners bought. The tariff was a major grievance of the South Carolina Interposition Resolution of 1832, and it remained a grievance through the Civil War. The war itself resulted in a substantial increase in tariffs because of the need for federal revenue, and these tariffs were not reduced after the war. Taussig, in his classic study of American nineteenth century tariff policy (1905), showed that these tariffs could not be justified by the infant industry argument and that they were costly to consumers.[85]

National regulation of commerce is generally dated from the Interstate Commerce Act of 1887. Although the first statute was quite modest, Professor MacAvoy documented a positive influence on prices consistent with a negative welfare effect resulting from the act.[86] The regulation evolved, however, and by 1910 the Congress had effectively constrained price increases in the industry. The results were disastrous, and with the outbreak of World War I, it was considered necessary to nationalize the railroads and place them under army control in order to protect them from their regulator. The Transportation Act of 1920 ushered in an era of explicit federal cartelization of the railroad industry. Since that time, the federal government has consistently urged ever less competition and the industry has repeatedly experienced very serious operating problems (although the federal system of highway planning and construction

Regulation and the American Common Market / 43

funding is causally related to the railroad problem, it is generally regarded as a success.) Examples follow of assumption of jurisdiction by the federal government in various commercial areas.

The federal government assumed jurisdiction over interstate trucking in 1932 and pursued policies designed to substantially restrict competition.

The federal government assumed regulatory jurisdiction over aviation in 1935 and pursued policies designed to restrict competition. California pioneered a competitive approach, and the federal government has now changed its policies in this direction.

In the Jones Act, the federal government restricted interstate commerce by ship to American Flag vessels, making interstate shipment more expensive than international shipment.

The federal government assumed jurisdiction over telecommunications in the 1920s and 1930s and pursued policies designed to restrict competition, with some moderation in the last decade.

The federal government assumed regulatory jurisdiction over collective bargaining in 1935 and pursued policies designed to encourage union-negotiated labor contracts instead of individually negotiated contracts.

The federal government assumed jurisdiction over the interstate transportation of natural gas in 1935. Its early regulation followed the traditional utility model, but in 1954 the Supreme Court extended its jurisdiction to production and it began to pursue a price ceiling policy that disrupted the interstate market for natural gas. Ironically, in 1923, the Supreme Court had held that West Virginia could not, in a time of shortage, withhold its natural gas from Pennsylvania under the negative Commerce Clause. By the late 1960s, federal law barred interstate buyers from paying the market price for gas in Texas, and thus Texas had preferred access to its own gas because Texas suppliers could offer higher prices for intrastate gas. Congress responded to this situation by increasing the ambition and pervasiveness of the regulation of the industry. The regulation now attempts to impose different prices on different categories of users, favoring residences and disfavoring industry.[87]

The federal government assumed jurisdiction over interstate securities markets in 1934 and pursued policies designed to restrict competition, with some moderation in the last decade.

The federal government restricted the ability of corporations to escape state charter restrictions on interstate operations by means of the holding company device in the Public Utility Holding Company Act and the Bank Holding Company Act.

The federal government asserted systematic jurisdiction over

44 / Regulation, Federalism, and Interstate Commerce

agricultural markets in the 1930s and pursued policies designed to raise agricultural prices above world levels, to the detriment of the consuming states.

The Sherman Act has long been regarded as the crowning glory of the federal government's open markets policy. Modern scholarship of the actual enforcement of the act has concluded that it has had only modest significance, and that much of the enforcement has been anticompetitive.[88] Judicial construction of the act has tended to view contractual and firm restrictions on the movement of physical commodities as not furthering, but restricting commerce, a view with strange echoes of the doctrines of *Bank of Augusta* and *Paul v. Virginia.*

The federal government began a program designed to raise domestic petroleum prices in 1959, and in 1972 it asserted regulatory jurisdiction over the whole petroleum industry in order to hold down domestic prices.

Ironically, recent federal regulatory schemes have occasioned the first systematic barriers to trade between the states since the constitutional system began. The oil allocation system is organized on a state-by-state basis and federal law makes it illegal for petroleum products to flow from surplus states to deficit states. Under federal environmental regulation, a car approved for sale in California cannot be sold anywhere else, and vice versa. Section 7425(b) of the Clean Air Act authorizes a governor to prohibit a major fuel-burning stationary source "from using fuels other than locally or regionally available coal or coal derivatives to comply with implementation plan requirements." The powers conferred by this section have not yet been used.

The vast range of modern federal standard setting raises implicit issues of national trade patterns. The more the regulation shifts from performance standards that are calibrated for the purposes of the regulation to the imposition of direct standards, the more federal regulation dictates the course of commerce. Thus, federal clean air scrubbing standards have been designed to require cleaner emissions from low sulfur coal in order to partially preserve the comparative advantage of eastern as opposed to western coal, which has a low sulfur content.[89] The same issues have always arisen under the tariff laws. For instance, in the nineteenth century sugar industry, the adjustments in the tariff for various qualities of imported sugar differentially affected sugar refining firms.

State and local economic regulation has generally had a bad reputation. Numerous local jurisdictions are notoriously corrupt (although the federal government is losing its comparative purity

Regulation and the American Common Market / 45

in this area as its regulatory schemes become ever more ambitious and pervasive). Any student of regulation or administrative law recognizes that the states lack the indicia of quality operation that are commonly found in the federal government. Documentation is spotty, and studies, opinions, and reports are nonexistent or poorly reasoned. The professional qualifications and pay levels of state bureaucracies are generally inferior to those of the federal government. When one compares these resources to the complexity of some state regulatory responsibilities, they seem clearly inadequate. For instance, consider the problems the states face in operating a system of national corporate income taxation under the authority of *Northwestern States Portland Cement Co.* v. *Minnesota*, 358 U.S. 450 (1959). State taxing jurisdiction reaches most businesses that sell into the state. Profits must be fairly apportioned to those sales by every state that taxes. The decision was met with cries of business anguish. Congress passed a statute that slightly narrowed the decision's reach. Yet after a few years all was quiet. Less than half the states that have corporate profit taxes have even joined the MultiState Tax Commission.

It seems likely that much of such state regulation works not because of complex and sophisticated planning systems, but because of ongoing negotiations between the enforcement officers and the interstate businesses. The interstate businesses, armed with the reality of interstate competition, are able to work out with the enforcement authorities a host of accommodations that make the system workable. Such low-level, unreviewed, and invisible adjustments are contrary to our basic notions of good administrative procedure. It is not at all clear, however, that they are not very cost effective.

Occasionally there are opportunities to observe the state and federal processes operating side by side. One example is the area of cable television franchises, in which both the state and local governments asserted franchising authority, and the federal government asserted authority under the broadcasting title of the Federal Communications Act. The state and local regulation concentrated on local revenue, local politics, and in some cases, corruption. The federal process involved the most esoteric and fancy examination of the technological capacities and economic effects of cable, but in the end, its regulatory effect came down to a successful effort to slow the inroads of cable on the valuable preserves of the electromagnetic broadcasters. It is easy to conclude that the country was better off under the former rather than the latter regime.[90]

46 / Regulation, Federalism, and Interstate Commerce

THE COURT'S ROLE

The Court's doctrine suggests a way to determine whether the assertion of its review power under the negative Commerce Clause has helped or hindered freedom of interstate trade.[91] It has left corporations, insurance, and banking outside of the doctrine, while the commodity-producing and shipping industries fall within it. If the Court's role—or constitutional constraint—has important effects, then the strength of the common market should be greater in one area than the other.

The strongest case that can be made against the states and for the Court is in regulation of banking. There one sees enterprise organized explicitly along state lines. There are two ways to explain this phenomenon. One is that banks are a particularly attractive source of tax revenue, local government borrowing, and political favor. The persistence of the state boundary limitation is then explained by the strong interest of the state government in defending it. The alternative explanation is that for national commercial business, banks have been perfectly capable of competing nationwide without opening banking offices outside their home state. In this view, the state line restriction relates only to the local service side of the business; it is not a restraint on interstate commerce, or, at most, it is an unimportant restraint. Most states, of course, restrict not only the interstate expansion of banks, but also the in-state geographic expansion of banks, California being a notable exception.

In corporate law, the states have allowed Delaware to develop a system of flexible and responsive regulation and they have permitted Delaware corporations to roam among the states without substantial restraint.[92] This policy has been attacked, of course, as competition to the lowest standard, but the specific examples of "bad" Delaware law offered by the critics are weak.[93] The recent antitakeover statutes are a substantial departure from this pattern.

There is a vigorous national insurance market. New York functions as a lead state, and many other states pattern their regulatory actions after New York.

Conversely, the Court's assertion of the negative Commerce Clause doctrine seems often to be followed by national anticompetitive legislation. The *Wabash* decision was followed by the Interstate Commerce Act. *Baldwin* v. *Seelig* was followed by expanded national regulation of milksheds.[94]

The Court's modern balancing doctrine seems likely to have little importance. The methodological problems of substantive due process have not been solved, and the Court's results are likely to be

Regulation and the American Common Market / 47

confused, limited, and of small importance. A case like *Raymond Motor Transportation, Inc.* v. *Rice*, 434 U.S. 429 (1978), which held that Wisconsin cannot exclude "double" semi-trucks from Interstates 90 and 94 seems to rest more than anything else on the fact that Wisconsin considered the issue too unimportant to defend in the trial court. *Philadelphia* v. *New Jersey* may result only in costly and needlessly duplicative state regulation of local as well as interstate waste disposal. The *Alexandria Scrap* and *Exxon* decisions make it clear that a state bent on local protectionism will not need great ingenuity to evade the Court's doctrine.

Two desirable effects flow from the Court's participation in the regulatory process. First, the Court has occasionally given eloquent expression to the principle of national economic cooperation, and its advocacy of that principle may have had a small but positive political effect on the growth of the country. Second, the hidden presumption of preemption born in *Gibbons* v. *Ogden* has, over the years, checked what can be one of the most undesirable outcomes in a federal system—dual state and federal regulation of the same subject matter. An important recent example is *Sears, Roebuck & Co.* v. *Stiffel Co.*, 376 U.S. 225 (1964). In that case, the Court read into the copyright and patent laws federal preemption of product design. An even more recent example is *Douglas* v. *Seacoast Products, Inc.*, 431 U.S. 265 (1977), which, relying on the successor statute to the statute in *Gibbons*, held that the federal vessel licensing law preempted state regulation of fishing rights. Modern Congresses have become increasingly resistent to the Court's preemption activism. Most modern statutes contain sections that expressly limit their preemptive effect.

APPENDIX

Articles of Confederation, Article IV:

The better to secure and perpetuate mutual friendship and intercourse among the people of the different states in this union, the free inhabitants of each of these states, paupers, vagabonds and fugitives from justice excepted, shall be entitled to all privileges and immunities of free citizens in the several states; and the people of each State shall have free ingress and egress to and from any other State, and shall enjoy therein all the privileges of trade and commerce subject to the same duties, impositions, and restrictions, as the inhabitants thereof respectively; provided, that such restrictions shall not extend so far as to prevent the removal of property, imported into any State, to any other State of which the owner

48 / Regulation, Federalism, and Interstate Commerce

is an inhabitant; provided, also that no imposition, duties or restriction, shall be laid by any State on the property of the United States, or either of them.

Preamble to the Constitution:

WE, the People of the United States, in order to form a more perfect Union, establish Justice, insure domestic Tranquility, provide for the common Defence, promote the general Welfare, and secure the Blessings of Liberty to ourselves and our posterity, do ordain and establish this CONSTITUTION for the United States of America.

1. Article I, Section 8, cl. 1:

   The Congress shall have Power to lay and collect Taxes, Duties, Imposts and Excises, to pay the Debts and provide for the common Defence and general welfare of the United States; but all Duties, Imposts and Excises shall be uniform throughout the United States.

2. Article I, Section 8, cl. 3:

   The Congress shall have Power to regulate Commerce with foreign Nations, and among the several States, and with the Indian Tribes;

3. Article I, Section 8, cl. 4:

   The Congress shall have power to establish a uniform Rule of Naturalization, and uniform Laws on the subject of Bankruptcies throughout the United States;

4. Article I, Section 8, cl. 5:

   The Congress shall have power to coin Money, regulate the Value thereof, and of foreign Coin, and fix the Standard of Weights and Measures.

5. Article I, Section 8, cl. 7:

   The Congress shall have power to establish Post Offices and Post Roads;

6. Article I, Section 8, cl. 8:

   The Congress shall have power to promote the Progress of Science and useful Arts, by securing for limited Times to Authors and Inventors the exclusive Right to their respective Writings and Discoveries.

7. Article I, Section 9, cl. 5:

   No Tax or Duty shall be laid on Articles exported from any State.

8. Article I, Section 9, cl. 6:

   No Preference shall be given by any Regulation of Commerce or

Regulation and the American Common Market / 49

Revenue to the Ports of one State over those of another; nor shall Vessels bound to, or from, one State, be obliged to enter, clear or pay Duties in another.

9. Article I, Section 10:

No State shall enter into any treaty, alliance, or confederation; grant letters of marque and reprisal; coin money; emit bills of credit; make any thing but gold and silver coin a tender in payment of debts; pass any bill of attainder, *ex-post-facto* law, or law impairing the obligation of contracts; or grant any title of nobility.

No State shall, without the consent of Congress, lay any imposts or duties on imports or exports, except what may be absolutely necessary for executing its inspection laws; and the net proceeds of all duties and imposts, laid by any State on imports or exports, shall be for the use of the treasury of the United States, and all such laws shall be subject to the revision and control of the Congress. No State shall, without the consent of Congress, lay any duties of tonnage, keep troops, or ships of war, in time of peace, enter into any agreement or compact with another state, or with a foreign power, or engage in war, unless actually invaded, or in such imminent danger as will not admit of delay.

10. Article IV, Section 2:

The Citizens of each State shall be entitled to all Privileges and Immunities of Citizens in the several States.

11. Amendment XIV, Section 1, Sentence 2:

No State shall make or enforce any law which shall abridge the privileges or immunities of citizens of the United States; nor shall any State deprive any person of life, liberty, or property, without due process of law; nor deny to any person within its jurisdiction the equal protection of the laws.

12. Article XXI, Section 2:

The transportation or importation into any State, Territory, or possession of the United States for delivery or use therein of intoxicating liquors, in violation of the laws thereof, is hereby prohibited.

NOTES

1. H.P. Hood and Sons v. Dumond, 336 U.S. 525, 539 (1949).
2. Holmes, "Law and the Court," in *Collected Legal Papers* 291, 295-96 (1920).
3. Charles M. Tiebout, "A Pure Theory of Local Expenditures," 64 *Journal of Political Economics*, 416 (1956); G. Tulloch, "Federalism: Problems

50 / *Regulation, Federalism, and Interstate Commerce*

of Scale," 6 *Public Choice* 19 (1969); Wallace E. Oates, *Fiscal Federalism* (New York: Harcourt Brace Jovanovich 1972); Edwin S. Mills and Wallace E. Oates (eds.), *Fiscal Zoning and Land Use Controls* (Lexington, Mass.: Lexington Books, 1975); Albert Breton and Anthony Scott, *The Economic Constitution of Federal States* (Toronto: University of Toronto Press, 1978).

4. The effort and eventual failure of the progressive movement to use uniform legislation to overcome the effects of competition between the states is described in William Graebner, "Federalism in the Progressive Era: A Structural Interpretation of Reform," 44 *Journal of American History* 331 (1977).

5. The southern states also obtained a requirement in Article I, Section 8, cl. 1 that "all Duties, Imposts and Excises shall be uniform throughout the United States."

6. The South Carolina Nullification Resolution of 1832 complained of various acts "purporting to be acts laying duties, but in reality intended for the protection of domestic manufactures." See An Ordinance To Nullify Certain Acts of Congress of the United States, purporting to be Laws laying Duties and Imposts on the Importation of Foreign Commodities, Done in Convention at Columbia, November 24, 1832, in Massachusetts General Court, Committee on the Library, State Papers on Nullification 28 (1834, reprinted New York: DaCapo Press, 1970). Calhoun's argument for the unconstitutionality of the protective tariff can be found in John M. Anderson (ed.), *Calhoun: Basic Documents, A Speech on the Collection (Force) Bill,* February 15-16, 1833, at 136-137 (State College, Pa.: Bald Eagle Press, 1952).

7. See, e.g., Richard B. McKenzie, *Restrictions on Business Mobility: A Study in Political Rhetoric and Economic Reality* (Washington, D.C.: American Enterprise Institute, 1979).

8. *Federalist* No. 11 (Hamilton) (Modern Library edition, p. 68).

9. Farrand (ed.), The Records of the Federal Convention of 1787, III, 542 (Yale, 1937).

10. William W. Crosskey, *Politics and the Constitution in the History of the United States I,* 20 (Chicago, 1953).

11. Ernest J. Brown, "The Open Economy: Justice Frankfurter and the Position of the Judiciary," 67 *Yale Law Journal* 219, 223 (1957).

12. Davis, Hughes, and McDougall, *American Economic History* (Homewood, Ill.: Irwin, 1969), p. 7.

13. Douglass C. North, *Growth and Welfare in the American Past,* 2nd ed. (Englewood Cliffs, N.J.: Prentice-Hall, 1974), pp. 62-63.

14. The idea that the state of the nation under the Articles of Confederation was not notably unsatisfactory has received wide scholarly acceptance in this century. See Merrill Jensen, *The New Nation: A History of the United States During the Confederation 1781-1789* (1950) and Charles A. Beard, *An Economic Interpretation of the Constitution of the United States,* pp. 47-49 (1913, 1935 ed.). It is perhaps symptomatic of the unimportance of trade between the states that the general histories of the period do not directly address the question of what restraints, if any, were placed on it. There were serious conflicts between the states over western land claims because of the uncertain location of the western boundaries, see Jensen, pp. 330-37. The dispute between Pennsylvania and Connecticut settlers

Regulation and the American Common Market / 51

over the Wyoming Valley led to an attack upon the settlers by the Pennsylvania militia in 1782. *Id.*, p. 335. A general study of the economy in this period is Curtis P. Nettels, "The Emergence of a National Economy 1775-1815," Vol. II of *The Economic History of the United States* (New York: Holt, Rinehart & Winston, 1962).

15. *Federalist* No. 22 (Hamilton) (Modern Library ed., p. 132).
16. Allan Nevins, *The American States During and After the Revolution: 1775-1789* (New York: Macmillan, 1927), p. 555.
17. See Article IV in the appendix, page 47.
18. Discussed generally in Jensen, *supra* note 15, 400-407.
19. To Jay, May 8, 1975: "[T]he British Cabinet have conceived doubts, whether Congress have power to treat of commercial matters, and whether our States should not separately grant their full powers to a minister. I think it may be taken for granted, that the States will never think of sending separate ambassadors, or of authorizing directly those appointed by congress. The idea of thirteen plenipotentiaries meeting together in a congress at every court in Europe, each with a full power and distinct instructions from his State, presents to view such a picture of confusion, altercation, expense, and endless delay, as must convince every man of its impracticability. Neither is there less absurdity in supposing that all the states should unite in the separate election of the same man, since there is not, never was, and never will be, a citizen whom each State would separately prefer for conducting the negotiation. It is equally inconceivable that each State should separately send a full power and separate instructions to the ministers appointed by Congress. What a heterogeneous mass of papers, full of different objects, various views, and inconsistent and contradictory orders, must such a man pull out of his portefeuille, from time to time, to regulate his judgment and his conduct! He must be accountable, too, to thirteen different tribunals for his conduct; a situation in which no man would ever consent to stand, if it is possible, which I do not believe, that any State should ever wish for such a system. I suppose, too, that the Confederation has already settled all these points, and that Congress alone have authority to treat with foreign powers, and to appoint ambassadors and foreign ministers, and that the States have separately no power to do either."
20. Eg., to Jay, August 10, 1785: "These means [of preserving ourselves] can never be secured entirely, until Congress should be made supreme in foreign commerce."
21. To Jay, October 21, 1785.
22. Jensen, *supra* note 14, at 401-502. An amendment for perpetual power to regulate trade was proposed in 1785 by a committee of the Congress chaired by James Monroe, but it was never submitted to the states; *id.*, at 403-404.
23. *Federalist* No. 11 (Hamilton) (Modern Library ed., p. 66).
24. *Federalist* No. 7 (Hamilton) (Modern Library ed., p. 38).
25. Nevins, *supra* note 16, at 560.
26. William Frank Zornow, "Massachusetts Tariff Policies 1775-1789," 90 Essex Institute Historical Collections 194 (1954); "New York Tariff Policies 1775-1789," 37 *Proceedings of the New York State Historical Association* 40 (1956); "Tariff Policies in South Carolina 1775-1789," 55 *South Carolina Historical Magazine* 31 (1955); "The Tariff Policies of Virginia 1775-

52 / *Regulation, Federalism, and Interstate Commerce*

1789," 62 *Virginia Magazine of History* 306 (1954).
27. 37 *N.Y. Proceedings* 44.
28. Brown v. Maryland, 12 Wheat 419 (1827), holding goods still in the original package of importation immune from state taxation.
29. Not completely in Virginia, not until 1784 in South Carolina.
30. Nevins, *supra* note 16, at 561-562.
31. 37 *N.Y. Proceedings* 54-55.
32. The Federalism issues inherent in the national programs of the New Deal generated active scholarly interest in the issues discussed in this section. More recent constitutional scholarship has displayed little interest in the subject. The most ambitious and singular product of the "New Deal" scholarship was William Winslow Crosskey, *Politics and the Constitution in the History of the United States* (Chicago: University of Chicago Press, 1953). The synthetic ambition and meticulous detail of Crosskey's scholarship resulted in work completed after the issues had, in the view of men of practical affairs, long been settled. Other notable contributions of the period were Edward S. Corwin, *The Commerce Power versus States Rights* (Princeton, N.J.: Princeton University Press, 1936); Felix Frankfurter, *The Commerce Clause Under Marshall, Taney and Waite* (Chapel Hill: The University of North Carolina Press, 1937); F.D.G. Ribble, *State and National Power Over Commerce* (New York: Columbia University Press, 1937); and the essays on the Commerce Power collected in *Association of American Law Schools, 3 Selected Essays on Constitutional Law*, 26-361 (Chicago: The Foundation Press, 1938). Thomas Reed Powell pursued the subject with an elegance and balance that made it uniquely his. His valedictory is *Thomas Reed Powell, Vagaries and Varieties in Constitutional Interpretation* (New York: Columbia University Press, 1956).
33. The Fourteenth Amendment and the Twenty-first Amendment are also relevant. The text of these clauses is set out in the Appendix, pp. 48-49.
34. Wharton v. Wise, 153 U.S. 155 (1894).
35. The Council of State Governments, Interstate Compacts 1783-1977, pp. 29-30 (1977), lists 178 compacts now in force. The states have had available numerous other coordination devices, such as uniform laws, meetings and agreements of administrative officials from governor's conferences on down, professional organizations of enforcement officers, and so on. The Supreme Court has adopted a relatively narrow definition of the agreements between states that must be approved by Congress under the Compacts Clause. In United States Steel Corp. v. Multistate Tax Commission, 434 U.S. 452 (1978), the Court upheld the Multistate Tax Compact even though unapproved by Congress on the grounds that the clause is limited to agreements that enhance the political power of the member states in a way that encroaches on the supremacy of the United States.
36. The issues of the Bank of the United States was also linked to the question of the money standard. The Jacksonians advocated a specie standard and were opposed to the power of a central bank to create money substitutes. See Richard H. Timerlake, "The Specie Standard and Central Banking in the United States Before 1860," in A.W. Coats and Ross M. Robertson (eds.), *Essays in American Economic History* (London: Edward Arnold Ltd., 1969), p. 113.
37. The most elaborate expression of an activist Federalist vision is to be found in Hamilton's Report on Manufactures of 1791, *The Papers of*

Regulation and the American Common Market / 53

Alexander Hamilton (New York: Columbia University Press, 1966), p. 230.

38. See Albert S. Abel, "Commerce Regulation Before Gibbons v. Ogden: Interstate Transportation Facilities," 25 *North Carolina Law Review* 121 (1947).
39. Crosskey, *supra* note 10, at 352.
40. It has been customary to discuss the cases under the lawyer's implicit assumption of a fixed law into which all of the cases must be fit. Therefore, there is no critical tradition that attempt to identify periods of constitutional doctrine to which the periods here could be related.
41. 53 U.S. 319.
42. This episode is discussed in Louis Hartz, *Economic Policy and Democratic Thought: Pennsylvania, 1776-1860* (Cambridge: Harvard University Press, 1948), pp. 46-47. The first Bank of the United States was denied a charter in Pennsylvania. Stephen Girard purchased its office in Philadelphia, hired many of its former personnel, and operated as a private bank. Donald R. Adams, Jr., *Finance and Enterprise in Early America: A Study of Stephen Girard's Bank 1812-1831* (Philadelphia: University of Pennsylvania Press, 1978), pp. 13-20.
43. 38 U.S. 588-89.
44. 38 U.S. 590.
45. 38 U.S. 592.
46. 30 U.S. 594.
47. Morton Horowitz posits significant state resistance to negotiability overcome by the federal courts, and implies that the general commecial law of *Swift* overrode state law to the contrary. Morton J. Horowitz, *The Transformation of American Law 1780-1860* (Cambridge, Mass., 1977), pp. 225-226. He relies on Watson v. Tarpley, 59 U.S. (18 How.) 517 (1855). In that case, the Court refused to follow a Mississippi statute that limited the right to sue on a bill of exchange until maturity. The plaintiff had sued upon dishonor. The state statute regulated only the time of suit, not the validity of the contract. Although the opinion contains sweeping language, the Court viewed the statute as regulating access to the federal courts. See, 59 U.S. 521. Oates v. National Bank, 100 U.S. 239 (1879), also cited by Horowitz, expressly relied on the National Bank Act. *Id.* at 249-250.
48. 75 U.S. 176-177.
49. 75 U.S. 183.
50. 38 U.S. 531.
51. 80 U.S. 35.
52. 82 U.S. 294.
53. 91 U.S. 275.
54. 91 U.S. 282.
55. 273 U.S. 44.
56. 303 U.S. 255.
57. 303 U.S. 258.
58. 425 U.S. 810.
59. 437 U.S. 128.
60. See Gary J. Simson, "Discrimination Against Nonresidents and the Privileges and Immunities Clause of Article VI," 128 *University of Pennsylvania Law Review* 379 (1979).
61. Gordon v. Committee on Character and Fitness, 48 N.Y.2d 266, 397

54 / *Regulation, Federalism, and Interstate Commerce*

N.E.2d 1309 (1979). Gordon was an employee of an interstate corporate enterprise—Bell Telephone—who was transferred out of the state after he took the bar exam.

62. 424 U.S. 380.
63. Louis Hartz, *Economic Policy and Democratic Thought: Pennsylvania, 1776-1860* (Cambridge, Mass.: Harvard, 1948).
64. *Id.,* at 129.
65. Rolland H. Maybee, *Railroad Competition and the Oil Trade, 1855-1873* (Mt. Pleasant, Mich.: Extension Press of Central State Teachers College, 1940), pp. 232-238.
66. In 1871, *Id.* at 269.
67. Quoted in Hartz, *supra* note 63, at 47.
68. *Id.,* at 51.
69. George H. Miller, *Railroads and the Granger Laws* (Wisconsin, 1971).
70. *Id.,* at 86.
71. *Id.,* at 96.
72. *Id.,* at 114.
73. *Id.,* at 116.
74. *Id.,* at 137.
75. *Id.,* at 158.
76. *Id.,* at 160.
77. *Id.,* at 94.
78. *Id.,* at 115-116.
79. *Id.,* at 115.
80. Kitch & Bowler, "The Facts of Munn v. Illinois," 1978 *Supreme Court Review* 313.
81. Kitch, Isaacson & Kasper, "The Regulation of Taxicabs in Chicago," 14 *Journal of Law and Economics* 285 (1971). The principal evidence was the significant positive medallion price.
82. Railroad Transfer Service v. Chicago, 386 U.S. 351 (1967), Chicago v. Atchison, T.&S.F.R.Co., 357 U.S. 77 (1958).
83. Lee Benham, "The Effect of Advertising on the Price of Eyeglasses," 15 *Journal of Law and Economics* 337 (1972).
84. Peter Pashigian, "Occupational Licensing and the Interstate Mobility of Professionals," 22 *Journal of Law and Economics* 1 (1979).
85. F.W. Taussig, *The Tarriff History of the United States,* 6th ed. (New York: Putnam's, 1905).
86. Paul W. MacAvoy, *The Economic Effects of Regulation: The Trunk-Line Railroad Cartels and the Interstate Commerce Commission Before 1900* (Cambridge, Mass.: M.I.T., 1965).
87. See generally Edmund W. Kitch, "Regulation of the Field Market for Natural Gas By the Federal Power Commission," 11 *Journal of Law and Economics* 243 (1968).
88. William Baxter, in an extended effort to explore the politics of the act and its enforcement, was unable to identify any clear gainers or losers. See William Baxter, *The Political Economy of Antitrust, Paper Presented at Liberty Fund Conference October 26-28, 1979, Miami, Florida* (Lexington, Mass.: Lexington Books, forthcoming). The Clayton Act has prohibited mergers that would otherwise have occurred, but internal growth is a substitute for growth by merger in industries tending toward larger firm size and the failing business exception has permitted the mergers at a later point in time.

Regulation and the American Common Market / 55

89. See 44 Fed. Reg. 33580, 580-585 (June 11, 1979).

90. In the area of professional regulation, the Antitrust Division and the FTC have taken steps to reduce the harmful effects of state regulation. This bureaucratic, public-interest flank attack on these regimes may, however, represent only a short-run instability until the affected professional groups learn how to operate effectively in the new and unanticipated forum.

91. The exclusion of liquor from the Commerce Clause suggests another test less favorable to the states. The historical pattern of treating liquor differently from other commodities makes this experience difficult to generalize.

92. The leading examination and defense of the competitive law-making process that lies behind this development is Ralph Winter, *Government and the Corporation* (Washington, D.C.: American Enterprise Institute, 1978).

93. An important statement is William L. Cary, "Federalism and Corporate Law: Reflections Upon Delaware," 83 *Yale Law Journal* 663 (1974).

94. See Richard A. Ippolito and Robert T. Masson, "The Social Cost of Government Regulation of Milk," 21 *Journal of Law and Economics* 33, 36-37 (1978).

F
Public Choice and Federalism

[6]

FEDERAL DEFERENCE TO LOCAL REGULATORS AND THE ECONOMIC THEORY OF REGULATION: TOWARD A PUBLIC-CHOICE EXPLANATION OF FEDERALISM

*Jonathan R. Macey**

THE concept of federalism, which describes the complex relationship between the states and the federal government, is one of the most revered sacred cows on the American political scene. Conservatives and liberals alike extol the virtues of state autonomy whenever deference to the states happens to serve their political needs at a particular moment. Yet both groups are also quick to wield the power of the supremacy clause,[1] while citing vague platitudes about the need for uniformity among the states, whenever a single national rule in a particular area furthers their political interests.

The relationship between the ideal of federalism and the reality of the supremacy clause thus emerges as one of the most convenient of political expedients.[2] This Article seeks to place this relationship within the context of the economic theory of public choice.

Building on the earlier work of Professor George Stigler,[3] Professors Sam Peltzman[4] and Gary Becker[5] have specified the core characteristics of public-choice theory by developing what has come to be known as the "political-support-maximization" model, which has replaced the older cartel model as a tool for predicting political

---

* Professor of Law, Cornell University. I received helpful comments on earlier drafts of this Article that were presented at law school faculty workshops at the University of Chicago, Cornell University, New York Law School, and the University of Virginia. I received extremely useful advice and comments from Peter H. Aranson, Henry N. Butler, Lloyd R. Cohen, Richard A. Epstein, Clayton P. Gillette, Fred S. McChesney, Michael W. McConnell, Henry G. Manne, Roberta Romano, Robert E. Scott, Steven H. Shiffrin, Cass R. Sunstein, and Robert D. Tollison.

1 U.S. Const. art. VI, § 2.

2 See McConnell, Federalism: Evaluating the Founders' Design (Book Review), 54 U. Chi. L. Rev. 1484, 1488 (1987) ("[F]or most people . . . issues of federalism take second seat to particular substantive outcomes.").

3 Stigler, The Theory of Economic Regulation, 2 Bell J. Econ. & Mgmt. Sci. 3 (1971).

4 Peltzman, Toward a More General Theory of Regulation, 19 J.L. & Econ. 211 (1976).

5 Becker, A Theory of Competition Among Pressure Groups for Political Influence, 98 Q.J. Econ. 371 (1983).

behavior. The political-support-maximization model has been employed successfully to define regulatory action,[6] reversal of regulatory action,[7] and regulatory forbearance.[8]

As yet, however, the model provides no explanation of why federal lawmakers ever would *defer* to state regulators by allowing such local lawmakers to regulate in their stead. Given the federal government's broad authority under the supremacy clause to preempt local rules,[9] the political-support-maximization model would seem to predict that the federal government will always exercise its power to preempt local law—either to regulate or to forbear from regulating—in order to obtain for itself the political support associated with providing laws to interested political coalitions. But contrary to this prediction, we observe that the federal government willingly defers to local governments over a wide range of issues by allowing them to continue to supply laws.

Nor has Congress simply ceded regulatory authority over local issues to local governments and retained for itself exclusive authority to intervene in national affairs, as a public-interest defense of federalism would predict.[10] The federal government has, at times, taken a lively interest in regulating purely local matters, such as the responsibility of the states to provide funds for the education of handicapped children or the issuance of charters to banks that are unable to do business beyond the borders of the state in which their main office is located. Conversely, Congress has ceded to individual states the power to dictate what is, in effect, national policy in certain important areas. For example, Delaware's corporate law and South Dakota's law of usury both have truly national effects yet are promulgated at the state level.[11]

---

[6] See, e.g., Haddock & Macey, Regulation on Demand: A Private Interest Model with an Application to Insider Trading Regulation, 30 J.L. & Econ. 311 (1987).

[7] See, e.g., Jarrell, Change at the Exchange: The Causes and Effects of Deregulation, 27 J.L. & Econ. 273 (1984).

[8] See, e.g., McChesney, Rent Extraction and Rent Creation in the Economic Theory of Regulation, 16 J. Legal Stud. 101 (1987).

[9] See Van Alstyne, The Second Death of Federalism, 83 Mich. L. Rev. 1709 (1985); Nine for the Seesaw, The Economist, Mar. 2, 1985, at 21.

[10] McConnell, supra note 2, at 1494-96.

[11] Delaware's corporate laws have a national effect because they control the internal affairs of many major corporations whose principal business activities are located elsewhere. South Dakota's law of usury has a national effect because loans originated in South Dakota,

This Article seeks to show that deference to local regulators is in fact consistent with the political-support-maximization model that provides the theoretical underpinning of the economic theory of regulation. As will be seen, just as the political-support-maximizing solution for a particular issue may be for Congress to regulate in a specific area (or to prevent regulations from being implemented), for other issues Congress and administrative agencies will find that they can maximize political support by refraining from regulating—even when they *know* that regulators at the state level will step in and regulate in their stead.

While at first blush it may appear that this sort of regulatory deference permits local lawmakers to capture all of the gains associated with a particular regulatory enactment, this is not the case. The supremacy clause allows federal lawmakers to obtain political support in exchange simply for agreeing to permit local lawmakers to retain regulatory authority over certain issues. Current interpretations of the supremacy clause permit federal law to override state law not only in cases of actual conflict, such as when federal and state law provide different standards, but also where Congress is thought by the courts to have prohibited parallel state legislation by implication.[12] Thus, the supremacy clause is a considerable source of political rents for Congress because it allows Congress to obtain political support by permitting independent or concomitant state regulation at little or no political cost to itself.

This Article attempts to specify the conditions under which Congress will choose to delegate the responsibility for regulating to state governments. According to the theory presented here—and consistent with the political-support-maximization model of public-choice theory—Congress will delegate to local regulators only when the political support it obtains from deferring to the states is greater than the political support it obtains from regulating itself. Deference to local regulators is sometimes the strategy by which federal regulators maximize political support from interest groups. Deference to local regulators will also occur when legislating will cause Congress to *lose*

---

particularly purchases made with credit cards issued by South Dakota banks, are subject to South Dakota law.

[12] See J. Nowak, R. Rotunda & J. Young, Constitutional Law § 9.1 (3d ed. 1986). The supremacy clause also allows Congress expressly to prohibit state action. Id.

political support.[13]

The important point here is that deferring to state lawmakers does not deprive federal lawmakers of political support. But instead of receiving political support for regulating, they will receive political support for agreeing to allow local regulators to make local laws. Political support to members of Congress for deferring to state regulators may come from the relevant interest groups directly, or it may be channeled through a conduit such as the Conference of State Bank Supervisors or the National Governors Conference. In either case, the result will be the same: Congress receives political support in exchange for deferring to state lawmakers on a particular regulatory issue.

The theory here might be described as a "franchise theory of federalism." In an ordinary business franchise, the owner of a product, service, or technology, rather than market its own goods, often will choose to sell another firm the rights to market them under a franchise arrangement. Under certain circumstances firms find it in their interests to employ this sort of contractual arrangement.[14] This Article identifies three general situations in which Congress will "franchise" the right to regulate in a particular area to the states: (1) when a particular state has developed a body of regulation that comprises a valuable capital asset and federal regulation would dissipate the value of that asset; (2) when the political-support-maximizing outcome varies markedly from area to area due to the existence of spatial monopolies, variegated local political optima, and variations in voter preferences across regions; and (3) where Congress can avoid potentially damaging political opposition from special-interest groups by

---

[13] See infra notes 68-87 and accompanying text.

[14] See Brickley & Dark, The Choice of Organizational Form: The Case of Franchising, 18 J. Fin. Econ. 401 (1987); Caves & Murphy, Franchising: Firms, Markets, and Intangible Assets, 42 S. Econ. J. 572 (1976); Klein & Saft, The Law and Economics of Franchise Tying Contracts, 28 J.L. & Econ. 345, 349-54 (1985); Rubin, The Theory of the Firm and the Structure of the Franchise Contract, 21 J.L. & Econ. 223 (1987).

The use of the franchise metaphor is not to suggest that the concerns involved in Congress's decision whether to regulate exactly mimic those of a firm considering whether to become a franchisor. One important difference is that in the case of Congress, franchise fees (political support) are normally paid by the customer (interest groups) rather than by the franchisees (state regulators), although state legislators may in some circumstances pay for the right to regulate. The development of a comprehensive franchise theory of federalism is beyond the scope of this Article.

putting the responsibility for a particularly controversial issue on state and local governments.

Part I of this Article places the model presented here within the context of the general economic theory of regulation and explains why interest groups often find that federal law is superior to state law in providing them with wealth transfers. Part II elaborates the circumstances in which Congress maximizes its own political support by deferring regulation to local lawmakers.

I. LEGISLATIVE DEFERENCE AND THE ECONOMIC THEORY OF REGULATION

Under the economic theory of regulation, politicians can obtain payments (which may come in the form of honoraria, campaign contributions, indirect political support, and, of course, outright bribes) from interest groups in exchange for regulation.[15] The model posits that politicians maximize the aggregate political support that they receive from interest groups by supplying the legal rules that result in the highest net receipt of support.[16]

The first sort of interest-group activity observed by public-choice theorists was rent seeking. Politicians would supply rent-creating regulation to the groups best able to pay for it, sometimes by establishing cartels in particular industries,[17] but often in more subtle ways.[18] Later it was seen that exogenous shocks could alter an existing polit-

---

[15] See Berke, How Cash Is Given to Politicians' Interests, N.Y. Times, Dec. 10, 1989, § E, at 4; Easterbrook, What's Wrong With Congress?, The Atlantic, Dec. 1984, at 57, 70-72.

[16] More specifically, the model posits that legal rules are supplied to those groups that bid the most for them and that compensation is provided in the form of political support. Because particular aspects of much legislation, especially complicated legislation, affect some groups more than others, some groups will be more interested than others in specific aspects of a particular legislative package. The precise contours of the resulting law will reflect a political equilibrium representing the preferences of a variety of groups. See Peltzman, supra note 4, at 222-24.

In addition, the economic theory of regulation predicts that laws will tend to benefit small, cohesive special-interest groups at the expense of the general public. This result is due to two factors: (1) individuals lack sufficient incentives to promote laws that directly benefit the general public because of free-rider problems; and (2) interest groups have strong incentives to press for laws that transfer wealth from the general public to themselves. See Macey, Promoting Public-Regarding Legislation Through Statutory Interpretation: An Interest Group Model, 86 Colum. L. Rev. 223, 230-32 (1986).

[17] Stigler, supra note 3, at 5, 11-13.

[18] See Macey, Special Interest Groups Legislation and the Judicial Function: The Dilemma of Glass-Steagall, 33 Emory L.J. 1 (1984).

ical equilibrium, rendering a preexisting arrangement undesirable from the perspective of the regulated groups. In such instances, deregulation might become the political-support-maximizing strategy for a subsequent set of politicians. Where, for example, exogenous technical factors or general economic forces erode the rents associated with a particular activity, the demand for the regulatory regime supporting that activity may decline.[19] This diminution in demand ultimately may result in deregulation.[20]

In addition to extracting payments for regulating or for deregulating, politicians can obtain payments for agreeing not to regulate in a particular area. As Professor Fred McChesney has explained in an illuminating article, where private parties have created quasi-rents through capital investments that can be used only for particularized purposes, politicians can extract payments in exchange for promises to refrain from imposing regulations that would expropriate those investments.[21]

In a world of high information and transaction costs, the political-support-maximizing strategy is not always obvious to the politicians making the relevant decisions. Consequently, the period prior to legislative decisionmaking, which is often characterized by a series of hearings, fact findings, and related investigations, resembles a form of auction at which interest groups can express their preferences for particular regulatory configurations and signal their legislators about the intensity of these preferences. During this "bidding" process legislators discover which legislative strategy will allow them to obtain the most political support.

As presently understood, however, the economic theory of legislation does not explain why Congress would confer regulatory authority on state legislatures when it could easily legislate directly. Instead, the theory appears to imply that the federal government should supply all law, as deference to state regulators simply allows local lawmakers to capture for themselves the political support available for supplying regulation to rent-seeking constituents. It is not surpris-

---

[19] For an insightful discussion of the problem of durability of interest-group bargains, see Landes & Posner, The Independent Judiciary in an Interest-Group Perspective, 18 J.L. & Econ. 875 (1975).

[20] Jarrell, supra note 7; Macey & Haddock, Shirking at the SEC: The Failure of the National Market System, 1985 U. Ill. L. Rev. 315.

[21] McChesney, supra note 8, at 110-11.

ing that the economic theory of regulation does not specify a role for state law: For at least four reasons, obtaining a federal law will be the strategy of choice for most interest groups seeking to obtain wealth transfers.

The first factor that suggests that interest groups generally will prefer to obtain rents by invoking federal rather than state law involves transaction costs. It is simply less expensive to obtain passage of one federal statute than to obtain passage of fifty state statutes because a different state legislature must be lobbied in each state.[22] Even if interest groups would benefit marginally by having a myriad of local statutes, the benefits may not outweigh the transaction costs associated with obtaining passage of all of those statutes. Only when the benefits to interest groups of having a series of different local statutes are higher that the costs of obtaining such statutes would we expect to observe local statutes.

A related factor is that when statutes are passed at the state level, political support must still be provided to federal regulators to induce them to forbear from later preempting the field by enacting a subsequent law. In other words, the supremacy clause generally requires interest groups to pay twice to obtain a state law—once at the state level and once at the national level.[23] By contrast, where interest

---

[22] Butler & Macey, The Myth of Competition in the Dual Banking System, 73 Cornell L. Rev. 677, 709 (1988). Of course, interest groups are not forced to select between obtaining a single federal law on the one hand and 50 state laws on the other. An interest-group coalition can opt for "half a loaf" by obtaining the legislation it prefers in only a few states. At some point in the process, however, the cost of obtaining a single federal rule becomes lower than the cost of obtaining a multitude of state-law rules.

Furthermore, as Professor Saul Levmore has pointed out, at times interest groups that operate at the national level will press for a single nationwide rule in order to avoid problems of exploitation at the state level. Levmore, Interstate Exploitation and Judicial Intervention, 69 Va. L. Rev. 563 (1983). This situation will occur when the benefits of a particular rule are concentrated in one jurisdiction, but the costs are concentrated in other jurisdictions. For example, a given state may choose to impose an unusually harsh liability rule on manufacturers of a particular product if none of the manufacturers of that product are located in that state. In such a situation, the consumers will be more powerful politically than the producers at the state level. Nationally, however, the producers may dominate the political process.

[23] Even under the most expansive interpretations of the commerce clause, some aspects of state lawmaking authority are probably immune from federal preemption. For example, in Penry v. Lynaugh, 57 U.S.L.W. 4958 (U.S. June 26, 1989), the Court held that states possess the constitutional authority to permit the execution of retarded persons under certain circumstances. Congress has considered passing legislation to prohibit such executions, but it is not clear that Congress has such power over the states. It is clear, however, that Congress

groups are able to obtain federal legislation that preempts the field, they can avoid the necessity of making payoffs to local politicians.

A third reason interest groups may prefer national law to local law is that, from an interest group's perspective, federal law is often considered a higher quality product than state law. One reason for this belief is that federal bureaucrats and judges are perceived as more sophisticated than their state rivals and, consequentially, more able to develop innovative, responsive solutions to interest-group needs. Similarly, the fact that greater resources are available to federal regulators naturally implies that they will have more wealth to extend to interest-group supplicants than will local regulators. Finally, the deals made at the federal level are likely to be more durable than the deals made at the state level. This is because the full-time, professional politicians that dominate at the federal level have considerable reputational capital invested in the stability of the deals they make.[24] Moreover, because of its political independence, the federal judiciary represents a more reliable enforcement agency for interest-group bargains than generally exists at the local level.[25]

Finally, and perhaps most importantly, federal law is harder for adversely affected parties to avoid than is state law. Regulated entities often can shift assets or personnel to one state to avoid regulatory transfers imposed by another state. If, for example, one state imposes an onerous tax on firms or citizens within its borders, it would be relatively easy for parties who are adversely affected simply to relocate to another state. The wealth transfers effectuated at the national level, however, are likely to be harder to avoid than the wealth transfers effectuated at the local level. While exit can be used as a strategy for avoiding federal law, the costs of exiting to avoid federal law are generally much higher than the costs of exiting to avoid state law. For example, when individual states attempted to enact plant-closing laws, they found existing firms threatening to exit and new firms refusing to establish plants in such states. For this reason, plant-clos-

---

has the constitutional authority to intercede in an incredibly broad range of issues traditionally considered the province of state decisionmaking. The discussion in this Article pertains to these issues.

[24] Macey, Public Choice: The Theory of the Firm and the Theory of Market Exchange, 74 Cornell L. Rev. 43, 52-53 (1989).

[25] Landes & Posner, supra note 19, at 885-87.

ing laws proved almost wholly ineffective at the state level.[26] By contrast, the federal government was able to enact such laws far more successfully because the burden of relocating outside of the United States made the avoidance of the federal plant-closing laws inframarginal for most firms.[27] Thus, interest groups will favor federal law over state law because states face stiffer competition from one another than the federal government faces from other sovereign nations.[28] This stiffer competition is a manifestation of the fact that the groups or individuals harmed by interest-group wealth transfers can easily relocate to avoid the effects of such wealth transfer activity. As recent events in Eastern Europe have illustrated, the ability to exit poses severe constraints on the ability of interest groups to achieve their goals.

For all of these reasons, we observe interest groups exhibiting a strong preference for federal as opposed to state law in most areas. This preference enables federal regulators to reap political support by providing appropriate legislation. Yet we also observe federal regulators voluntarily deferring to local regulators in a variety of contexts. The economic theory of regulation is in need of some refinement in order to take account of this fact.

I wish to emphasize that such deference occurs despite the fact that federal legislators can obtain political support by providing favors directly to local constituents in certain situations. All members of Congress have sophisticated, well-staffed offices for the express purpose of delivering favors to local constituents. And, as the recent controversy over the closing of obsolete military bases has made clear, members of Congress do not view the provision of localized favors as outside the range of services they profitably can offer their constituents.[29] In addition, Professors Barry Weingast and William Marshall

---

[26] Macey, Externalities, Firm-Specific Capital Investments, and the Legal Treatment of Fundamental Corporate Changes, 1989 Duke L.J. 173, 195-96.

[27] Id. at 196-97.

[28] See R. McKenzie & G. Tullock, Modern Political Economy: An Introduction to Economics 398-400 (1978) (comparing the benefits of competition among governments with the advantages and disadvantages of centralization).

[29] Indeed, the need for legislators to deliver favors for their constituents back home, a commonplace observation in political science, explains the fact that logrolling is an effective political practice. See D. Mayhew, Congress: The Electoral Connection 31-33 (1974); Weingast & Marshall, The Industrial Organization of Congress; or, Why Legislatures, Like Firms, Are Not Organized as Markets, 96 J. Pol. Econ. 132 (1988).

recently have shown how the structure of the committee system within Congress can resolve certain contracting problems that exist among members of Congress, thereby enhancing the ability of legislators to provide discrete benefits to local constituencies.[30] Consistent with this analysis, a variety of empirical studies have demonstrated that members of particular congressional committees enjoy disproportionate success at obtaining local pork-barrel projects from legislation originating in their committees.[31]

The riddle here is that despite the fact that Congress possesses the power to preempt state law and the ability to use its lawmaking power to provide highly localized benefits to interested groups, it often chooses not to do so. The following Part explores the situations in which Congress will maximize political support by granting a regulatory "franchise" to local regulators.[32]

II. State Law as the Political-Support-Maximizing Solution

The above discussion of public-choice theory implies that when the political support that can be obtained from deference to local lawmakers is greater than the political support to be derived from direct federal regulation, we can expect federal regulators to defer to the states. At least three sets of conditions can be identified in which such deference will be the political-support-maximizing solution. The first is where interest groups have made an expropriable investment in

---

[30] Weingast & Marshall, supra note 29, at 144.

[31] See Macey, supra note 24, at 55 (summarizing the evidence).

[32] The above discussion also suggests the need for a minor modification of McChesney's powerful point about rent extraction. See text accompanying note 21. McChesney's model hypothesizes a world in which economic activities will not be regulated if Congress declines to regulate them. But if Congress simply declines to regulate without doing more, state governments can capture any available rents from regulating (or from declining to regulate) that otherwise would have gone to members of Congress. In other words, where the political-support-maximizing solution for federal regulators is to forbear from regulating, they must act affirmatively to prevent local governments from regulating. Congress can do this by passing specific enactments that do not change the state of the law, but that clearly supersede specific state laws. Congress also can act by expressing a desire to supersede local regulations or by passing a regulatory scheme under which local laws are invalid because they impermissibly interfere with the effectuation of congressional objectives. In addition, courts on occasion will invoke the so-called "dormant commerce clause" to invalidate state legislation that does not conflict with any federal statute, but that infringes upon interstate commerce. See J. Nowak, R. Rotunda & J. Young, supra note 12, § 9.3.

a particular set of local regulations. For example, over time local regulators may have developed particularized expertise in a specific subject area, or they may have developed a long-term contractual relationship with one or more interest groups through a pattern of repeat dealings. Where these conditions obtain, existing local regulation takes the form of an income-producing capital asset. Federal preemption in these areas would dissipate the value of this asset. Interest groups and local politicians therefore have an incentive to provide political support to Congress in exchange for Congress's agreement not to preempt these local regulations.

The second set of circumstances under which we are likely to observe federal deference to local regulators is where the political-support-maximizing solution for a particular regulatory issue differs markedly from jurisdiction to jurisdiction. Federal law is an unwieldy device for maximizing aggregate political support where there is a complex set of differing local political optima caused by local or spatial monopolies. In such circumstances, local regulators will be the best source for the complex matrix of differing regulatory schemes necessary to provide the diverse set of arrangements necessary to benefit the relevant groups.

A third set of conditions under which we will observe deference to state regulators is derived directly from Professor Morris Fiorina's earlier work on the delegation of legislative authority to administrative agencies.[33] As Fiorina pointed out, if Congress regulates in the form of a specific—that is, judicially enforceable—statute, members of Congress "engender[] the unalloyed approval of those benefited and the disapproval of those harmed."[34] Fiorina observed that delegating a decision to a regulatory agency has the advantage of permitting Congress to remove the blame for particularly controversial legislation from its own shoulders onto those of the relevant agency.

Fiorina's analysis can be extended from administrative agencies to include explicit or implicit delegations of legislative power to state governments. Indeed, Congress often can shift the blame for controversial enactments even more effectively by deferring to state legislators than by deferring to administrative agencies because Congress

---

[33] Fiorina, Legislative Choice of Regulatory Forms: Legal Process or Administrative Process?, 39 Pub. Choice 33 (1982).

[34] Aranson, Gellhorn & Robinson, A Theory of Legislative Delegatic 68 Cornell L. Rev. 1, 56 (1983) (describing Fiorina's conclusions).

often is considered at least partially accountable for the actions of the latter. By contrast, actions by state legislatures may bring excoriation on state legislators and cries for federal preemption, but will only rarely bring condemnation by Congress itself.[35]

The discussion that follows will elaborate on the conditions that will permit local law to dominate national law under an economic theory of regulation.

A. *The Protection of Asset-Specific Investments*

When an individual state creates a regulatory regime that accumulates particularized expertise, reputational value, or human capital in a specific subject area, that regulatory scheme represents a capital asset of that state. The beneficiaries of the state-law regulatory regime will be willing to pay to retain the current regulatory structure in the face of threatened federal intervention. Whenever existing, state-created rents on such assets are greater than the rents that can be created by federal regulation, the price the beneficiaries of the state regulation will pay Congress in return for retention of state control will be greater than the political support Congress could obtain by intervening directly. This situation represents a variation on McChesney's model of regulatory forbearance. Under McChesney's model, interest groups provide political support in return for an agreement to refrain from regulating. In this model, interest groups provide political support to retain an existing, alternative regulatory regime.

An example of this phenomenon involves the provision of corporate law by state legislatures. For years there has been a fierce debate about the efficacy of the jurisdictional competition for corporate charters that continues to rage among the states. One group contends that state law is preferable because competition among the states produces efficient corporate laws that maximize firm value and shareholder

---

[35] Congress will be particularly inclined to defer legislative authority to state legislatures rather than to administrative agencies whenever the relevant issues can be resolved by a discrete declaration of law, rather than by the ongoing series of interpretations that are the standard fare of administrative agencies. While ongoing regulation may present Congress with later opportunities to gain political support, simple, discrete matters do not. The abortion controversy thus presents a paradigmatic example of an issue that Congress will relegate to the states. See infra notes 72-87 and accompanying text.

wealth.[36] A competing group argues that federal law ought to pre-empt state law because competition among the states for corporate chartering revenues has led to an undesirable "race to the bottom" in which various states compete to provide the set of laws that best facilitate the transfer of wealth from shareholders to managers.[37]

But all states are not equal in the jurisdictional competition for corporate charters. One state, Delaware, has consistently led the field for the past fifty years.[38] Over forty percent of all companies listed on the New York Stock Exchange are chartered in Delaware,[39] and, even more significantly, eighty-two percent of all firms move to Delaware when they elect to reincorporate from the state in which they originally obtained their charter.[40]

Delaware's dominance in the market for corporate charters is not a consequence of a unique willingness to provide corporate laws that chartering firms find attractive. Many states have manifested an eagerness to do this in order to obtain a greater share of the significant revenues associated with granting state charters. Nor is Delaware's dominance a consequence of its greater technical expertise in promulgating a sophisticated and useful body of doctrine. Other states could easily replicate, or even improve upon, Delaware's body of doctrine.[41] Indeed, one cannot explain Delaware's dominance in the jurisdictional competition for corporate charters solely with reference to its distinctive corporate code because its corporate code is, in fact, not particularly remarkable or even distinguishable from that of other states.

---

[36] See, e.g., Easterbrook & Fischel, Voting in Corporate Law, 26 J.L. & Econ. 395 (1983); Winter, State Law, Shareholder Protection, and the Theory of the Corporation, 6 J. Legal Stud. 251 (1977).

[37] See, e.g., Louis K. Liggett Co. v. Lee, 288 U.S. 517, 559 (1933) (Brandeis, J., dissenting) (describing the competition among the states for corporate chartering revenues as a race "not of diligence but of laxity"); R. Nader, M. Green & J. Seligman, Taming the Giant Corporation (1976); Cary, Federalism and Corporate Law: Reflections Upon Delaware, 83 Yale L.J. 663, 666 (1974) (describing this competition as a "race for the bottom"); Jennings, Federalization of Corporation Law: Part Way or All the Way?, 31 Bus. Law. 991 (1976).

[38] Romano, Law as a Product: Some Pieces of the Incorporation Puzzle, 1 J.L. Econ. & Org. 225 (1985).

[39] See 1 N.Y. Stock Exchange Guide (CCH) 725-99 (1989).

[40] Romano, supra note 38, at 244.

[41] Nevada has attempted to duplicate Delaware's doctrine. See Macey & Miller, Toward an Interest-Group Theory of Delaware Corporate Law, 65 Tex. L. Rev. 469, 488 (1987). Recently, Pennsylvania also promulgated laws that appear to offer management a mcre attractive package.

Rather, Delaware dominates the jurisdictional competition for corporate charters because of the nature of that competitive process. Delaware is a small state. It obtains an extremely high proportion of its budget (sixteen percent) from franchise taxes on corporate chartering.[42] Delaware relies on these revenues more than other states because for other states, revenues from corporate chartering represent only a small portion of their total budget. In other words, the high percentage of Delaware's budget that is derived from chartering revenues represents a credible (bonded) promise that the state will not renege on its earlier promise to respond in consistent ways to new phenomena.[43] Delaware has been able to retain its dominance because it is able to offer a reliable promise that its corporation law will remain highly attractive to managers in the future.[44] Competing states are unable to match Delaware's promise of future performance because they cannot offer the same credible bond.

In exchange for the high percentage of state revenues derived from corporate chartering, Delaware also offers current and prospective charterers a highly specialized bar and a judiciary with particularized experience and expertise in corporate law.[45] Numerous attorneys, investment bankers, and corporate officers and directors both in and out of Delaware have made large investments of human capital that are specific to Delaware; hence, they have come to share Delaware's large stake in the preservation of its dominant position in the competition for corporate charters. These groups have learned the rules, practices, and traditions of the Delaware legislature and the philosophies of its judges, and they have familiarized themselves with the way the Delaware corporate code is likely to be interpreted.

In other words, the jurisdictional competition for corporate charters "is characterized by bilateral investment in assets that are specific to the chartering transaction, involving human capital on the firm side and the corporate legal system on the state side."[46] In sum, Delaware

---

[42] Romano, supra note 38, at 240-41.

[43] This theory of Delaware's dominance was first propounded by Professor Roberta Romano. See id. at 226.

[44] Id. at 226-27.

[45] See, e.g., Macey & Miller, supra note 41, at 488 (observing that "Delaware judges, corporate attorneys, and legislators are more knowledgeable about and have a greater interest in corporate law than do people with similar positions in other states"); Meyers, Showdown in Delaware: The Battle to Shape Takeover Law, Institutional Investor, Feb. 1989, at 64.

[46] Romano, supra note 38, at 226.

is committed to having a reliable and responsive system of corporate laws.

But the benefits of Delaware's dominant position in the competition for corporate charters are not randomly distributed. Rather, numerous interest groups, but particularly the Delaware corporate bar, benefit from Delaware's current dominant position.[47] Indeed, building on the earlier work of Professor Roberta Romano, Professor Geoffrey Miller and I have elsewhere shown that the precise contours of much of Delaware's corporate law can be explained by the fact that it effectively channels litigation into the state's courts.[48]

Thus, Delaware's dominant position in the market for corporate charters represents a valuable capital asset that generates revenues for Delaware corporations, corporate lawyers, investment bankers, and for the state itself. All of these groups have a large stake in seeing that Delaware retains its dominant position so that their specific capital investments will not be dissipated. These capital assets would be destroyed if the federal government enacted a pervasive system of federal corporate law that preempted the field. All of these groups, whatever their political disposition on issues of federalism generally or corporate governance in particular, have an incentive to work to avoid federal preemption. Thus, Congress can amass significant political support by refraining from preempting state law in this area. The fact that Congress has not enacted a national corporate law indicates that deference to the states is in fact its political-support-maximizing solution.

While public-choice theory thus offers an explanation for the persistence of state chartering, the phenomenon is wholly inconsistent with a public-interest view of federalism. Even the most ardent supporters of federalism recognize that national solutions are desirable in situations in which externalities exist, such as when a particular state can capture most of the benefits from regulating while bearing few of the costs associated with its regulatory regime.[49] But continued state regulation of corporate chartering permits one small state, Delaware, to enact laws that are truly national in focus. The consequences of these laws are felt nationally, while the benefits of the regulatory regime

---

[47] Macey & Miller, supra note 41, at 501-02.
[48] Id.
[49] See McConnell, supra note 2, at 1495.

accrue disproportionately to interest groups within Delaware.[50]

While other areas have not been studied in the same detail as Delaware's corporate law, it appears that the Delaware phenomenon is not unique. For example, Connecticut is well known for having developed specialized expertise in the provision of regulation for the insurance industry. To protect this asset, interest groups successfully have persuaded Congress not to displace state insurance regulation, despite the fact that there has been significant federal intervention in all other aspects of the financial services industry, particularly banking and securities.

Thus, when the Supreme Court reversed an 1868 decision[51] and held that states no longer had exclusive control of the insurance industry,[52] Congress responded by passing the McCarran-Ferguson Act less than a year later.[53] The McCarran-Ferguson Act specifically deferred regulatory authority over insurance to the states in order to "secure more adequate regulation" over the industry.[54] The McCarran-Ferguson Act, which has been described as a "sweeping" authorization by Congress of state regulation,[55] declared that the power to regulate the insurance industry would remain with the states and that no act of Congress should be interpreted as implicitly invalidating any state insurance regulation unless the congressional act specifically related to the business of insurance.[56]

---

50 See Macey & Miller, supra note 41, at 490-98.

51 Paul v. Virginia, 75 U.S. (8 Wall.) 168 (1868).

52 United States v. South-Eastern Underwriters Ass'n, 322 U.S. 533 (1944).

53 McCarran-Ferguson Act, ch. 20, 59 Stat. 33 (1945) (codified as amended at 15 U.S.C. §§ 1011-1015 (1988)).

54 H.R. Rep. No. 143, 79th Cong., 1st Sess. 4, *reprinted in* 1945 U.S. Code Cong. Serv. 670, 673.

55 L. Tribe, American Constitutional Law § 6-33, at 526 (2d ed. 1988).

56 15 U.S.C. § 1011 (1988):

> Congress hereby declares that the continued regulation and taxation by the several States of the business of insurance is in the public interest, and that silence on the part of the Congress shall not be construed to impose any barrier to the regulation or taxation of such business by the several States.

Exempting the insurance companies from the operation of the commerce clause turned out to be something of a mixed blessing for the insurance industry. As a consequence of the Act, states were able to impose taxes that discriminated against out-of-state insurance companies without fear that the taxes would be struck down as violative of the commerce clause. See Prudential Ins. Co. v. Benjamin, 328 U.S. 408 (1946) (upholding a South Carolina tax that charged a three percent premium on out-of-state insurance firms). The Supreme Court came to the rescue of the insurance industry almost 40 years later. See Metropolitan Life Ins. Co. v. Ward, 470 U.S. 869 (1985) (holding that an Alabama law imposing higher gross premiums on

The McCarran-Ferguson Act was paraded to the public as a bill to protect states' rights.[57] In fact, the bill was the product of the Association of Insurance Commissioners, which drafted a statute and presented it to Congress.[58] The bill proposed by the state insurance commissioners ultimately was accepted by Congress, although various proposals to exclude the insurance industry from the antitrust laws were rejected.[59]

Interestingly, the first significant incursion on the states' franchise to regulate the insurance industry has come in the area of products liability. Manufacturers persuaded Congress to pass the Product Liability Risk Retention Act of 1981[60] in order to "reduce the problem of the rising cost of product liability insurance by permitting product manufacturers to purchase insurance on a group basis."[61]

B. State Law as a Customized Response to Local Interest Groups

The fifty states that comprise the union differ dramatically in history, demography, economic orientation, and natural endowment. Consequently, it is not surprising that patterns of interest-group behavior differ significantly from state to state, and even from locality to locality. The political-support-maximizing equilibrium may require favoring a certain interest group in one state and a different interest group in another. The issue of gun control is a good example of this phenomenon. In general, states with largely urban populations tend to favor gun control while states with rural populations often prefer to provide citizens with broad rights to own and carry guns.

The implication of such variety is that the political-support-maximizing outcome for politicians in one state may not be the political-support-maximizing solution for politicians in another. And when interest-group preferences are aggregated, the political-support-maximizing solution at the national level may differ from many, perhaps most, of the local solutions. Inevitably, a national rule will impose

---

non-Alabama insurance companies would violate the equal protection clause if it were not related to a legitimate state interest).

[57] See 90 Cong. Rec. A4403 (1944) (statement of Sen. Hatch).

[58] Id. at A4403-07.

[59] See id. at A4405 (setting forth the proposals to exclude insurance industry from the antitrust laws, which proposals were not incorporated into the legislation as passed).

[60] Pub. L. No. 97-45, 95 Stat. 949 (codified as amended at 15 U.S.C. §§ 3901-3904 (1988)).

[61] H.R. Rep. No. 190, 97th Cong., 1st Sess. 4, *reprinted in* 1981 U.S. Code Cong. & Admin. News 1432, 1432.

high costs on some interest groups that have benefited from a conflicting local rule.[62] Interest groups that are likely to be disappointed by or indifferent to a national solution will pay to have matters resolved at the local level.

Of course, the transaction costs of obtaining individualized local rules likely will exceed the transaction costs associated with obtaining a single national rule. Only when the increase in political support that Congress can gain from deferring to the states outweighs, at the margin, the increase in transaction costs associated with promulgating a multitude of local rules will we expect to observe local instead of national rules.

Spatial monopolies such as those conferred by zoning laws represent the classic situation in which interest groups and politicians will prefer a myriad of local laws to a single federal rule.[63] A uniform zoning law passed at the national level would deprive innumerable local lawmakers of the ability to capture the rents associated with passing zoning laws and variances that favor local interest groups by providing them with spatial monopolies. Federal regulators can capture rents as well by agreeing to defer to such local lawmakers.

Furthermore, some of the factors that usually cause interest groups to favor federal laws over state laws are absent where the interest groups are seeking to protect spatial monopolies. First, while obtaining a single federal statute generally will be cheaper than obtaining *fifty* local laws, the costs of obtaining a single federal law generally will be greater than the costs of obtaining *one* local law. And one local law is all that is necessary to protect a spatial monopoly. Second, the cost of compensating federal lawmakers for declining to regulate spatial monopolies will probably be low because the cost of replicating this vast regulatory regime at the federal level is likely to be prohibitive, thus making it an unattractive prospect for federal

---

[62] See also Butler & Macey, supra note 22 (applying the theory presented here to the state and federal regulation of branch banking).

[63] A spatial monopoly is a monopoly that arises because one producer is able to locate at a sufficient distance from its competitors such that consumers must incur transaction costs to obtain goods produced by rivals. The producer can tack onto the competitive price of its goods an amount up to the amount of the transaction cost that the consumer would have to pay to do business elsewhere. Because different businesses are likely to dominate in different locales, the zoning law that provides the most political support for lawmakers in one jurisdiction is likely to differ markedly from that which provides the most political support for the lawmakers in another jurisdiction.

intervention. Finally, competition among states will not deter local lawmakers from exploiting spatial monopolies because, by definition, such locational advantages cannot be transported.

State laws regarding branch banking represent a particular type of "zoning" restriction and provide an instructive example of federal deference to state regulators to protect a variety of localized spatial monopolies.[64] States, with the aid of the federal government, have adopted a diverse panoply of laws designed to protect local banking cartels in order to maximize the political support received from banks. In some states these cartels are best protected by eliminating branch banking altogether. In other states, the political-support-maximizing solution has been to adopt home office protection statutes, which prohibit branching into the town or city where another bank maintains its home office. Other states prohibit banks from branching into counties that are not contiguous to the county in which the bank maintains its main office. Still others prohibit banks from branching into unincorporated areas of noncontiguous counties or into communities with less than a fixed number of residents. This farrago of laws is necessary to serve the needs of the variegated web of banking interests that exist within the states.

The predominant effect of these banking laws is local in nature. A single, uniform federal rule would be optimal from the perspective of some, but not all, local interest groups. By allowing local law to prevail, political-support-maximizing federal regulators can maximize the total sum of rents in the system.[65] Thus, state regulators survive to implement these sorts of laws, and federal regulators obtain payoffs for agreeing to defer to them.

At first blush, the analysis presented here appears to conform to the analysis contained in a public-interest model of federalism. A public-interest model would prescribe that local law should dominate whenever regulations have a purely local effect, while national law should dominate whenever regulations have a predominately national

---

[64] Butler & Macey, supra note 22, at 708.

[65] Obviously, payment problems and other contracting problems will hamper the ability of interest groups and politicians to forge agreements. See Macey, supra note 24, at 52-56 (discussing structural solutions to the contracting problem). In addition, as an empirical matter, it is very hard to link individual political payments by interest groups to specific promises by politicians. Clearly, however, the fact that such payments are made is strong evidence that interest groups believe they are receiving something in return.

effect.[66] The public-interest model, however, assumes that the full costs and benefits of a particular legal regime to the *public* is what motivates the local decisionmaker, while the model presented here focuses on the fact that interest groups have a strong incentive to press for local solutions to their regulatory problems.

Of course, over a wide range of issues, the outcomes predicted by the public-interest model will be identical to those predicted by the interest-group model when the political-support-maximizing solution varies widely from jurisdiction to jurisdiction. The crucial distinction lies in the *process* that leads to the predicted outcomes. The zoning hypothetical invoked above provides a useful illustration. A public-interest model would predict that zoning rules will be locally produced because virtually all of the costs and benefits of zoning ordinances are local. Local politicians, according to the public-interest model, enact the zoning ordinances that respond to "local conditions and tastes."[67] The public-choice model, on the other hand, predicts that zoning laws are passed because such laws benefit local special-interest groups by facilitating the creation of spatial monopolies. A striking example of this phenomenon are local zoning rules that prohibit liquor stores from locating too close together. Such rules, which are quite common, benefit existing liquor stores at the expense of new-comers. Similarly, zoning laws prescribing housing densities and imposing acreage restrictions on residential property also benefit local interests at the expense of outsiders.

C. Federal Deference as Risk Avoidance

In the spatial monopoly scenario illustrated above, federal legislators are able to reap political support by allowing interest groups to obtain customized local regulations from state regulators. Congress might also defer to the states in order to avoid the *loss* of political support on issues for which there is no clear national consensus. Just as passing the right kinds of laws can benefit lawmakers by enabling them to obtain political support, passing the wrong kinds of laws can result in a diminution of political support.[68] And, in a world of

---

[66] See McConnell, supra note 2, at 1492-1511.

[67] Id. at 1493.

[68] The same, of course, is true in the private sector. Just as good business decisions increase the wealth of decisionmakers in the private sector, bad business decisions are costly.

imperfect information, lawmakers will not always be certain of whether the political costs to them of passing a particular statute outweigh the benefits. As Professors Peter Aranson, Ernest Gellhorn, and Glen Robinson have observed, a politician "may not know what his constituents want, how regulation will affect them, and which affected [interest] group is stronger."[69]

Professor Fiorina and Kenneth Shepsle have observed that one strategy for maximizing political support under conditions of uncertainty is to delegate the matter to an administrative agency.[70] Another strategy will be to turn the matter to be regulated over to the states. Indeed, deferring a controversial regulatory matter to the states may insulate Congress from political fallout even more effectively than turning the matter over to an administrative agency. Congress is perceived as having more control over the actions of administrative agencies than of state legislatures; consequently, Congress is more likely to be held accountable for regulatory action taken by administrative agencies than it is for similar actions taken by states. In addition, Congress can justify virtually any decision to delegate a controversial policy matter to the states simply by uttering vague tributes to the virtues of federalism.

On the other hand, delegation to federal administrative agencies has certain advantages over delegations to the states. Specifically, in a complex area, such as establishing a comprehensive environmental policy, Congress can garner political support by passing a generalized statute containing vague platitudes about the virtues of a sound environment and then setting up a complex administrative agency that will respond to the interests of the regulated. The general public, which strongly favored the enactment of environmental safeguards, will find it too costly to monitor the agency's actions. Organized groups, by contrast, "will be unrelenting in their efforts to influence the day-to-day details of legislation's implementation."[71] Congress can thus engender political support (or at least avoid the loss of sup-

---

[69] Aranson, Gellhorn & Robinson, supra note 34, at 60.

[70] Professor Fiorina draws the connection between the formation of administrative agencies and legislative ambiguity most explicitly. See Fiorina, supra note 33, at 55-57; see also Shepsle, The Strategy of Ambiguity: Uncertainty and Electoral Competition, 66 Am. Pol. Sci. Rev. 555 (1972) (observing that the optimal political strategy for politicians often involves ambiguity); Aranson, Gellhorn & Robinson, supra note 34, at 33 (observing that Shepsle's strategy of ambiguity often involves the delegation of authority to an administrative agency).

[71] Lee, Politics, Ideology, and the Power of Public Choice, 74 Va. L. Rev. 191, 197 (1988).

port) from the general public through the initial delegation, while its subsequent administration provides opportunities to extract political support from interest groups disappointed with the original enactment. On the other hand, simple, discrete matters that can be easily understood and monitored by the public do not provide opportunities for interest groups to attempt to alter the legislation ex post by influencing the way the administrative agency interprets it. Thus, when a national political-support-maximizing course is not apparent, the issue will be delegated to the states.

Moreover, as with delegations to administrative agencies, Congress always can decide to regulate when and if interest-group political support galvanizes around a particular regulatory solution, thereby signaling Congress that it can intervene safely. Similarly, individual members of Congress also can obtain political support on matters traditionally settled by state law by acting as agents for powerful constituencies in their dealings with state legislators. In an era in which the federal government provides considerable funding of state-sponsored projects through direct grants and matching funds, state representatives have much to gain by appeasing Congress. Another strategy for garnering political support on matters traditionally relegated to state law is for federal regulators occasionally to threaten to regulate in these areas. Finally, individual members of Congress can obtain political support by acting entrepreneurially, identifying issues currently being regulated nationally and offering to sponsor legislation that would benefit interest groups by turning the issues over to local control.

The responsibility-shifting model described above appears to apply with great force to the abortion controversy. Unlike desegregation, which grudgingly was accepted as a way of life after the Supreme Court's decision in *Brown v. Board of Education*,[72] the issue of abortion has become increasingly controversial since the Supreme Court's decision in *Roe v. Wade*,[73] which invalidated state laws banning abortion. Emotions about the legality of abortion run extremely high, with groups on both sides of the debate expressing a willingness to confer or withdraw political support to particular candidates on the

---

[72] 347 U.S. 483 (1954).
[73] 410 U.S. 113 (1973).

basis of this single issue.[74]

Now, in the wake of *Webster v. Reproductive Health Services*,[75] Congress conceivably could preempt state action on the issue of abortion, either by making abortion legal or by preempting the field in some other way, perhaps by establishing an administrative agency with exclusive authority to promulgate rules and guidelines governing abortion.[76] Yet there is little doubt that Congress will refrain from stepping in and preempting the field. It is clear that *Webster v. Reproductive Health Services* leaves the abortion issue in the hands of the states, which now have almost exclusive responsibility for regulating in this area, despite the fact that Congress often regulates issues of far less notoriety or national significance.[77]

States are not being given the responsibility for regulating abortion because there is anything about the issue that suggests that states are a more appropriate or logical regulatory forum than the federal government. Clearly, a fetus in New York cannot be philosophically distinguished from a fetus in Alabama, any more than a New York woman can be said to possess a right to privacy or individual autonomy that differs from that of a woman in Alabama. Indeed, in an issue of similarly local concern, access to schooling for the handicapped, the federal government has taken an extremely active role, compelling states to provide appropriate educational opportunities for all students, including those in need of special education due to mental defects or retardation.

Rather, states are given the responsibility for regulating abortions because they provide a far safer forum from the perspective of

---

[74] See Apple, Limits on Abortion Seem Less Likely, N.Y. Times, Sept. 29, 1989, at A1, col. 1 (describing poll showing that "abortion remains one of the most divisive subjects in American life").

[75] 109 S. Ct. 3040 (1989). In *Webster*, the Supreme Court upheld a provision of a Missouri law that requires doctors to ascertain whether a fetus is viable by performing "such medical examinations and tests as are necessary to make a finding of the unborn child's gestational age, weight, and lung maturity" before performing an abortion on any woman believed to be 20 or more weeks pregnant. Id. at 3043.

[76] In 1983, for example, the so-called Hatch-Eagleton amendment to the Constitution, S.J. Res. 3, 98th Cong., 1st Sess., 129 Cong. Rec. S95 (daily ed. Jan. 26, 1983), which would have overturned *Roe v. Wade* and allowed Congress and the states to pass new laws restricting or prohibiting abortion, was defeated after vigorous debate. 129 Cong. Rec. S9310 (daily ed. June 28, 1983).

[77] Medoff, Constituencies, Ideology, and the Demand for Abortion Legislation, 60 Pub. Choice 185, 185 (1989).

national politicians than does the federal government. Unlike a complicated issue such as the environment, Congress cannot avoid the
political fallout associated with abortion by delegating the matter to
an administrative agency. The issue is too straightforward. As one
political commentator has observed, "[a]bortion is . . . a question of
conscience with two clear, opposing positions, there's hardly a hedge
to hide behind. Basically, you're on one side or the other."[78]

Opinions on the abortion issue vary widely among groups.[79]
Groups taking a strong position in favor of a woman's right to choose
to have an abortion include women of childbearing age in white collar
occupations, for whom the cost of having children is higher than for
other women,[80] and nonwhite women, who are "much more likely to
use abortion . . . than whites."[81] The group most vociferously
opposed to abortion, of course, is fundamentalist Christians, a group
that is "unified and adamant in its opposition to abortion."[82] In addition, a group that has been identified as the "passive poor,"[83] who are
older, Southern, and Democratic, are strongly opposed to abortion.
Forty-seven percent of this group "favor changing laws to make it

---

[78] Weisberg, Abortion Olympics, New Republic, Feb. 12, 1990, at 12.

[79] Netter, An Empirical Investigation of the Determinants of Congressional Voting on
Federal Financing of Abortions and the ERA, 14 J. Legal Stud. 245, 253 (1985).

[80] Kristin Luker cites the following argument as a "theme" among women who support the
right to abortion on demand:

> For women to achieve any kind of equality in the employment market requires
> acceptance by society that they are in control of their reproductive lives. . . . Legalized
> abortion . . . is certainly a factor in freeing women from the blanket accusation that
> they're going to be divided in their loyalty to their career because they're going to have
> children.

K. Luker, Abortion and the Politics of Motherhood 119 (1984); see also Mincer, Market
Prices, Opportunity Costs, and Income Effects, *in* Measurement in Economics: Studies in
Mathematical Economics and Econometrics in Memory of Yehuda Grunfeld 67, 75-79 (1963)
(finding an inverse relationship between earnings of women in white-collar occupations and
their "fertility rate").

[81] Medoff, supra note 77, at 187. Between 1973 and 1980, the abortion rate increased by
162% for nonwhite women but only by 106% for white women: By 1980 the abortion rate of
nonwhite women (56.8 per thousand) was more than double that of white women (24.3 per
thousand). Id. Thus, it is not surprising that "while abortion tends to be viewed as a women's
liberation issue, the civil rights movement (both black and Latin) has tended to support legal
abortion on the grounds that it is a social and civil rights issue." Id.

[82] Id. Although the Roman Catholic church officially opposes abortion, American
Catholics as individuals are split on the issue, thus nullifying the group's political impact with
respect to this issue. Id.

[83] See N. Ornstein, A. Kohut & L. McCarthy, The People, the Press, and Politics: The
Times Mirror Study of the American Electorate 17 (1988).

more difficult for a woman to get an abortion," and forty percent strongly identify themselves as "supporter[s] of the anti-abortion movement."[84]

It is important to distinguish an important, albeit subtle, difference between the political climate surrounding the abortion debate, which involves responsibility shifting, and that which surrounds an issue such as gun control, which involves differing local optima among various political subdivisions. The gun control issue is delegated to local governments because the political-support-maximizing solution varies dramatically across localities. It is not surprising that rural counties in Georgia support citizens' rights to bear arms, while Massachusetts's citizens support strict gun control measures.

But, as the recent gubernatorial elections in Florida, Virginia, and New Jersey illustrated, the political climate surrounding the abortion issue is clouded with uncertainty. Even at local levels there was uncertainty both about how prominent abortion would be as a political issue and about what the political-support-maximizing solution would be for particular politicians.[85] Perhaps the strongest indication of the ambiguity of the abortion issue was the extent to which candidates to elected office modified the tone or substance of their stance on the issue.[86] These modifications show that the politicians made erroneous predictions about the political-support-maximizing outcome and had to alter their positions to survive.

Many politicians predicted that the Court's departure from the principles espoused in *Roe v. Wade* would benefit the Republican Party, particularly in the South, where there appeared to be strong support for legal curbs on the right to obtain an abortion. Others, however, noted that interest groups supporting women's reproductive choice had not had any incentive to galvanize into an effective political coalition while *Roe* was still good law, but that such groups might

---

[84] Id. at 36.

[85] Apple, supra note 74, at A13, col. 1 (noting that "[a] less polarized, more ambiguous political situation has resulted, in which abortion sometimes counts a lot and sometimes does not, and in which it is sometimes hard to tell who is benefiting from the issue and who is not"); Pressman, Abortion Politics: U.S. Court Ruling Changes the Political Landscape, Cal. J., Oct. 1989, at 395, 396 (quoting a consultant to the California Assembly's Republican Caucus as saying that "both sides [of the abortion issue] would agree that we don't really know which side has the upper hand . . . . [I]t's fairly tight.").

[86] See Weisberg, supra note 78, at 14-15 (describing changes in stance on the abortion issue of various politicians).

emerge as an effective counter to the so-called right-to-life movement if significant changes were to occur in the legal landscape.[87]

Thus, unlike the situation with gun control, the abortion issue is clouded with uncertainty. Congress is able to avoid much of the political cost associated with this uncertainty by hiding behind the shield of "federalism." Local politicians are not. Gun control involves a situation in which the political-support-maximizing solution is far more clear to politicians in the individual states than it is at the national level. Abortion involves an issue in which uncertainty and risk exist at all levels of political life. Very few politicians can afford to take a stand on this issue without risking serious political repercussions. Thus, for Congress, the political-support-maximizing solution to the abortion issue is to shift the risk of error to the states.

III. CONCLUSION

This Article has identified three situations in which federal lawmakers will maximize political support for themselves by relegating regulatory authority to state officials. The first is where existing state law has created expropriable quasi-rents through the development of asset-specific investments whose continued value depends on the perpetuation of such laws. The second is when a single national rule, by permitting new entry, would deprive local interest groups of the advantage of an existing spatial monopoly. Finally, we have seen that federal lawmakers, who often must act under conditions of uncertainty, sometimes will wish to avoid the political fallout that accompanies particularly controversial decisions. Under these conditions, federal politicians will find that the best solution will be to relegate matters to state legislators. Thus, this Article has extended the economic theory of regulation to include an explanation of the gains available to federal officials from delegating regulatory matters to state and local officials. The ability to confer or withhold regulatory authority from state officials under the supremacy clause is a considerable source of rents at the national level.

---

[87] Apple, supra note 74, at A13, col. 1 (observing that "[i]n the last few years, the anti-abortion advocates tended to dominate the national debate, and their opponents were somewhat quiescent. But . . . [*Webster*] has awakened the defenders of abortion, and their voices have reached politicians.").

Many who have recognized the costs of public-sector activities in the United States have extolled the virtues of delegating such activities to state governments. I wish to emphasize in closing that nothing in the foregoing discussion is inconsistent with the traditional defense of a strong federalist system as a device for achieving a more efficient legal system by encouraging competition among the states. Rather, the point is that the supremacy clause, which permits Congress to trump the states whenever it sees fit, undermines much of the effect of jurisdictional competition among states in the provision of law.

From a public-choice perspective, the federalist system can only be viewed as a mechanism that provides a complement rather than a substitute for federal law as a mechanism by which interest groups can exchange political support for wealth transfers. Deferring regulatory matters to the state legislatures must take its place alongside the other strategies by which federal politicians can offer wealth transfers to interest groups in exchange for political support.

Part II
Fiscal Federalism and the
Optimal Structure of the Public Sector

A
Tests of the Tiebout Model

[7]

Micro Estimates of Public Spending Demand Functions and Tests of the Tiebout and Median-Voter Hypotheses

Edward M. Gramlich and Daniel L. Rubinfeld

University of Michigan

Responses to questions given to a random sample of Michigan households are used to estimate public spending demand functions. While income and price elasticities are similar to those obtained from aggregate data, positive income elasticities appear to arise because public services are distributed in a prorich manner. A relatively small variance in spending demands among urban and suburban communities in metropolitan areas with substantial public service variety suggests that the Tiebout mechanism works. This interpretation is supported by the fact that actual spending conforms substantially to desired levels in urban areas, but less so in rural areas with little public sector choice.

The existence of micro data on the demand for public goods makes it possible to test several hypotheses that have intrigued public finance economists. The first involves the estimation of parameters in public spending demand functions, specifically whether parameter estimates derived from the usual analyses of local government budgetary aggregates accurately reflect the demands that would be expressed by individual citizens. The second is Tiebout's (1956) now-classic idea that citizens with similar tastes for public goods will live together in

We have benefited from the comments of Theodore Bergstrom, David Bradford, Harvey Brazer, Paul Courant, Arthur Denzau, Martin Feldstein, Gerald Goldstein, Harvey Rosen, Perry Shapiro, Lawrence Summers, and an anonymous referee. We are also appreciative of the highly competent research assistance of Deborah Swift. Work on this project was supported by grants from the National Science Foundation and the Department of Housing and Urban Development.

[*Journal of Political Economy*. 1982, vol. 90, no. 3]

jurisdictions that can then supply these goods with relatively little economic inefficiency. The third is that whatever determines residential location, governments will supply the level of public goods desired by the median voter.

In this paper we use data from a micro survey on demands for public spending to test these hypotheses. The survey, taken by the University of Michigan's Institute for Social Research (ISR), includes 2,001 households in the state of Michigan, sampled randomly immediately after Michigan's 1978 tax-limitation vote. Most questions dealt with why voters voted for or against various tax-limitation amendments, but the survey was also designed to treat these more basic issues of public expenditure demand.[1] The strength of a survey such as this is that a relatively complete array of fiscal, demographic, voting, and attitudinal information is available for a random sample of the state population. These data as well as some direct questions about public sector demand allow one to test the underlying hypotheses. The weakness is that like all other survey data respondents do not have to act on the basis of their answers, and the results are therefore hypothetical.[2]

The first section of the paper gives the demand estimation results. We use standard utility-maximization procedures to derive public spending demand functions that, among other things, depend on both individual and community income. Results of the estimation of these equations to micro spending preferences data are used to try to resolve several issues in the applied public finance literature: the distribution of Buchanan fiscal residuals within a community, an apparent paradox between income-elasticity estimates from aggregated community data and polling data, and why the median-voter theorem works so well.

The next section of the paper tests the Tiebout hypothesis that location decisions permit public goods to be provided with a high degree of economic efficiency. One implication of this hypothesis is that households will group themselves according to their demand for public spending—all those desiring a large public sector will live together, as will all those desiring a small public sector. In statistical terms, the test is accomplished by observing whether the intracommunity variance of public goods demand is smaller than that for the whole statewide sample, either uncorrected or corrected (by regression) for the influence of important independent variables.

The third section goes on to see whether the fiscal taste grouping of

---

[1] The survey is described in Courant, Gramlich, and Rubinfeld (1980).

[2] See Converse (1975) for extensive discussions of the strengths and weaknesses of surveys such as this.

individuals is related to the actual level of public spending provided in the community. In part, this is a necessary complement to the Tiebout test, for if local government fiscal actions were unrelated to the tastes of voters, there would be no reason for individuals to group themselves in a Tiebout-like manner. But this test can even go beyond Tiebout and test the median-voter hypothesis of Hotelling (1929), Bowen (1943), Downs (1957), and others. Does public spending in the jurisdiction reflect the desires of the median voter (from our sample), or are actual spending totals systematically larger or smaller?

I. The Demand for Public Spending

We first develop demand functions for public spending in terms of the ith individual. Let this individual's utility be expressed in terms of the utility obtained from private goods, C_i, and public output, X_i, by

$$U_i = U_i(C_i, X_i). \tag{1}$$

Were all publicly provided goods pure public goods, X_i would be identical for all individuals residing in a community. If publicly provided goods deviate from this archetype, however, we might expect the provision of public goods to vary from individual to individual in the community. There are many ways to describe how it could vary from individual to individual. A convenient approximation first used by Denzau and Mackay (1976) is to let income be the conditioning variable:

$$X_i = (Y_i^{\alpha_1}/Y^*)(E/N), \text{ where } Y^* = \sum_i (Y_i^{\alpha_1}/N). \tag{2}$$

Here Y_i is the individual's income, E the real dollar expenditure on public services, and N the number of consumers of public services. The parameter α_1 reflects the distribution of public services. When $\alpha_1 = 0$, all individuals within the jurisdiction receive the identical level of services E/N. When $\alpha_1 > 0$, the distribution of services is positively related to income (prorich); and when $\alpha_1 < 0$, the distribution is negatively related to income (propoor). Note that, as given by (2), output X is measured in real dollars.

The next question involves the price of public goods. Assume that X is produced according to the Cobb-Douglas production function

$$X = L^{\alpha_3} K^{1-\alpha_3}. \tag{3}$$

The first-order conditions are that $W = \alpha_3 PX/L$ and $R = (1 - \alpha_3)PX/K$, where W is the real wage for public employees, P is the relative gross price for public goods, and R is the rental price of capital, assumed to be constant across jurisdictions. Solving the first-order expressions for L and K, substituting them into the production, and solving for P yields $P = \alpha_4 W^{\alpha_3}$, where α_4 is some constant.

The individual is then assumed to maximize utility subject to the usual budget constraint:

$$
\begin{aligned}
Y_i &= C_i + [(\alpha_4 W^{\alpha_3} H_i)/(V/N)](E/N) \\
&= C_i + [(\alpha_4 W^{\alpha_3} H_i)/(V/N)](Y^*/Y_i^{\alpha_1})X_i,
\end{aligned}
\tag{4}
$$

where H_i is the value of the individual's property and V is the community tax base. The tax price $(\alpha_4 W^{\alpha_3} H_i N/V)$ measures the price to the consumer of a dollar of real expenditure per capita of public spending. Note that (4) is written as if this price were a *marginal* tax price, so that fixed income tax revenues or fixed categorical or non-categorical grants will not affect it.

Maximizing (1) subject to (4) yields standard demand functions for private consumption C_i and for desired public services X_i. Writing the latter in multiplicative form, as is commonly done, and adding a random-error term to allow for omitted variables, we get

$$
X_i = e^{\beta_0 + \epsilon_i}(\alpha_4 H_i N/V)^{\beta_2} W^{\alpha_3 \beta_2} Y^{*\beta_2} Y_i^{(\beta_1 - \alpha_1 \beta_2)}.
\tag{5}
$$

The parameter β_1 is the individual's income elasticity of demand for public services and β_2 is the price elasticity. But since income terms are now in the price equation, the total elasticity with respect to individual income depends on both the income and price elasticity.

To this point we have not dealt with the congestion problem. To allow for the possibility that the publicly provided goods might be congested, or impure public goods, we modify a procedure employed by Borcherding and Deacon (1972) and Bergstrom and Goodman (1973). This involves rewriting (2) as

$$
X_i = (Y_i^{\alpha_1}/Y^*)(E/N^{\alpha_2}),
\tag{6}
$$

where α_2 is the crowding parameter estimated by the above authors. For α_2 equal to 0, public spending is a pure public good in the Samuelsonian sense (Samuelson 1954). Whatever the value of α_1, as α_2 increases the public goods become more and more crowded. Taking this perspective suggests that our coefficient α_1 may be thought of as an income-crowding parameter, just as α_2 is a population-crowding parameter. We might note, in addition, that more general formulations of the private-public nature of publicly provided goods—such as one allowing public goods to be distributed with house value and including various interaction terms—might also be imagined. However, these somewhat more general approaches were not found to be important in our empirical results, so we do not pursue them here.

We complete the model by accounting for some details of estimation. A first is that the dependent variable, per capita public spending, is actually measured in nominal terms, but we cannot observe a cross-sectional price index for public expenditures. Hence we multiply both sides of the expression by the gross price of public goods used above. A second approximation is to replace Y^* with $\overline{Y}^{\alpha_1}$, where $\overline{Y}$ is mean income in the community.[3] A third adjustment takes account of the fact that individual voters' utility will vary according to a vector of individual characteristics (Z_i) such as the number of children, political affiliation, and so forth. Making these adjustments, we have as our basic public goods demand equation

$$\ln (W^{\alpha_3} E/N) = \beta' + [\beta_1 - \alpha_1(1 + \beta_2)] \ln Y_i + \alpha_3(1 + \beta_2) \ln W$$
$$+ \beta_2 \ln (H_i N/V) + (\alpha_2 - 1) \ln N \qquad (7)$$
$$+ \alpha_1(1 + \beta_2) \ln \overline{Y} + \beta_3 Z_i + \epsilon_i,$$

where β' is a constant. Since the dependent variable here is the logarithm of per capita *money* public expenditures, the public wage elasticity is positive or negative as demand is inelastic or elastic. Otherwise the only nonstandard features in the equation are the crowding parameters, α_1 and α_2.

Estimating the Model

Equation (7) can be estimated with either macro or micro data. The usual approach of economists is to use macro data on the overall budgetary behavior of governments and make four additional assumptions: (*a*) The Z_i for individuals cannot be observed and are either assumed to be constant within the jurisdiction or approximated by mean or median values for the community. (*b*) Individual income is set at the median for the community, as if the median voter had median income and as if all other incomes in the community were irrelevant in determining public spending. (*c*) The tax-price term is replaced through a similar assumption. Within a community individual property values are assumed to equal the median residential

[3] This approximation is tantamount to assuming that X_i is distributed according to $(Y_i/\overline{Y})^{\alpha_1}$ in eq. (2). We use the form given only to highlight its adding-up features. Clearly our approximation is exact when α_1 equals either 0 or 1. To see what happens in other cases, we can consider varying assumptions about the income distribution. First, if income is uniformly distributed from 0 to maximum income B, the mean of $Y_i^{\alpha_1}$ equals $B^{\alpha_1}/(1 + \alpha_1)$, while (mean $Y)^{\alpha_1} = B^{\alpha_1}/2^{\alpha_1}$. It is clear that for α_1 in the range $(-.5, 1.5)$, $2^{\alpha_1} \approx (1 + \alpha_1)$. Second, we can assume a Pareto distribution, a two-parameter, nonsymmetric distribution of the form $f(Y) = rA^r/Y^{r+1}$ for A positive and r greater than or equal to two. In this case we calculate that the mean of Y^{α_1} is equal to $rA^{\alpha_1+1}/[r - (1 + \alpha_1)]$ while (mean $Y)^{\alpha_1} = A^{\alpha_1} r^{\alpha_1}/(r - 1)^{\alpha_1}$. The two are likely to be approximately equal for $A = 1$ and r large, not unreasonable possibilities.

value, and the community tax price is then usually expressed as the ratio of residential value to total value, as if owners of nonresidential property did not vote in local elections. (*d*) Grants from higher levels of government are introduced to the equation. Typically, just one grant term is added, but in fact several should be. Open-ended categorical grants should have their matching ratio used in the construction of tax prices. Close-ended noncategorical grants should be included in community income, unless there are so-called flypaper effects whereby a dollar of grant spending leads to more public spending than private income at the margin. And close-ended categorical grants should be entered as a separate linear term.[4]

For the sake of comparison, we first follow these conventions and estimate a macro relationship for the 83 counties of Michigan in 1977. The public wage is expressed as the starting salary for teachers and the tax price as the residential share of property values. Categorical and noncategorical grants are treated as separate logarithmic terms, and income is expressed either as county mean income (available in 1976) or as median income (available in 1970). The results are shown in table 1. The income elasticity (β_1) is slightly below that usually found in other studies and the tax-price elasticity (β_2) much below, and not always of the correct sign. The public wage coefficients always have incorrect signs. The crowding terms indicate that public goods are definitely not Samuelsonian, with community population an important determinant of services demand (α_2 is close to one), as is found by both previous studies using the term. In this form it is impossible to identify the α_1 coefficient and thereby tell whether community income is important in determining service demands.[5] Both categorical and noncategorical state and federal grants have fairly strong effects on community spending, much as is found in other studies.

Next we estimate (7) using micro data from our household survey. The dependent variable is derived from a sequence of questions that informed respondents of how local governments in Michigan spend tax dollars; then asked them whether they thought local spending and taxes in their jurisdiction were too large, too small, or about right; and then tried to elicit their preferred percentage change in all budgetary categories. It was stressed to respondents that if they desired a cutback in local spending the outcome would be the same percentage

---

[4] This is all spelled out in Gramlich (1977).

[5] We note that median income works better than mean income. This is a powerful finding because median income was only available for 1970, 7 years before the date of the dependent variable. It might satisfy Romer and Rosenthal's (1978) test of the median-voter hypothesis (median income should work better than any other income), but, as our later discussion will indicate, such an inference cannot be made unambiguously when community income is included in the equation.

TABLE 1

MACRO PUBLIC SPENDING EQUATIONS, 83 COUNTIES OF MICHIGAN, 1977

	Using Mean Income (1976)	Using Median Income (1970)
Independent variable:		
Constant	1.264	−.443
Income	.442 (3.2)	.531 (4.1)
Public wage	−.138 (1.0)	−.059 (.4)
Residential value/		
total value	−.058 (.9)	.010 (.2)
Population	.021 (1.1)	.010 (.5)
Categorical grants	.316 (7.6)	.320 (8.0)
Noncategorical grants	.187 (2.8)	.276 (4.0)
Fit statistics:		
R^2	.637	.663
SE	.115	.111
Parameter estimates:		
α_1	N.I.	N.I.
$\alpha_2 - 1$	.021 (1.1)	.010 (.5)
α_3	−.146* (1.1)	−.058* (.4)
β_1	.442 (3.2)	.531 (4.1)
β_2	−.058 (.9)	.010* (.2)

NOTE.—Dependent variable is per capita government spending; all variables in log form; absolute *t*-ratios in parentheses. N.I. = not identified.
* Incorrect sign.

cutback in all local spending and taxes.[6] Respondents' desired level of overall local spending, the dependent variable in the micro equations, was then overall per capita spending in the county multiplied by the adjustment factor. If the ith respondent desired a 5 percent cutback, we assumed that the desired spending level was 95 percent of actual local government spending in that county.[7]

The individual independent variables are also taken from our survey, from questions on individual income, tax payments, and from various demographic indicators. The same community variables that appear in the macro equations are also used in the micro equations.

The micro results are shown in table 2. These equations are fitted to

[6] The exact questions were: "Now considering just your local governments which spend mainly on schools, police, fire, parks, and sanitation services—would you favor an across-the-board increase in both local spending and taxes, a decrease in both local spending and taxes, or would you favor no change?" Those who favored a change were then asked: "How much of an increase (decrease) in *both* local spending and taxes would you favor: a 5 percent (increase/decrease), 10 percent, 15 percent, 20 percent (increase or decrease), or what?"

[7] In principle, it is possible to adjust only city spending to get the desired total for a voter. In practice, however, we had so much difficulty in allocating county spending to the various cities, some of which are big enough to have published data, some of which are not, that we simply spread all local spending in a county evenly across all people.

TABLE 2

MICRO PUBLIC SPENDING EQUATIONS,
1,125 MICHIGAN HOMEOWNER RESPONDENTS, 1978

	Adjusted by Respondent's Answer	Adjusted, with City Dummies	Not Adjusted, with City Dummies
Independent variable:			
Constant	.378	−1.24	−1.80
D, child in public school	.013 (1.7)	.011 (1.5)	−.003 (.7)
D, child in private school	.016 (1.2)	.015 (1.2)	−.005 (.7)
D, over 65	.015 (1.1)	.013 (1.1)	.005 (.8)
D, transfer recipient	.014 (.6)	.005 (.2)	−.002 (.2)
D, black	.010 (.7)	.039 (2.0)	.012 (1.2)
D, other nonwhite	−.048 (1.2)	−.046 (1.2)	−.017 (.8)
D, race not reported	.048 (.8)	.049 (.9)	−.007 (.3)
D, Republican	.001 (.1)	.004 (.5)	.006 (1.4)
D, independent	−.006 (.7)	−.004 (.4)	.005 (1.1)
D, party not reported	.052 (1.0)	.073 (1.5)	.008 (.3)
D, public employee	−.001 (.1)	−.001 (.1)	−.001 (.1)
D, nonresident public employee	.025 (1.5)	.023 (1.5)	.001 (.2)
D, expect real income up	.057 (2.9)	.048 (2.5)	.006 (.6)
D, expect no change real income	.044 (2.2)	.032 (1.7)	.003 (.3)
D, expect real income down	.011 (.6)	.002 (.1)	−.004 (.4)
D, Catholic	−.008 (1.0)	−.003 (.5)	−.003 (.9)
D, Jewish	.015 (.5)	.004 (.1)	.002 (.1)
D, religion not reported	−.020 (1.4)	−.023 (1.7)	−.006 (.9)
Individual income	.001 (.1)	.001 (.2)	.001 (.1)
House value/avg. house value	−.011 (2.2)	−.014 (2.7)	−.004 (1.4)
County income	.285 (5.5)	.347 (4.3)	.408 (9.7)
County public wage	.195 (3.4)	.358 (3.9)	.363 (7.7)
County population	.039 (6.7)	.033 (2.6)	.022 (3.3)
Categorical grants	.201 (15.4)	.178 (5.4)	.200 (11.8)
Noncategorical grants	.226 (11.1)	.265 (9.0)	.271 (17.9)
Fit statistics:			
R^2	.773	.792	.931
SE	.11	.11	.06
Parameter estimates:			
α_1	.288 (5.6)	.352 (4.4)	.410 (9.7)
$\alpha_2 - 1$	.039 (6.7)	.033 (2.6)	.022 (3.3)
α_3	.197 (3.6)	.363 (4.0)	.364 (7.7)
β_1	.286 (5.6)	.348 (4.3)	.409 (10.2)
β_2	−.011 (2.2)	−.014 (2.7)	−.004 (1.4)

NOTE.—Dependent variable is per capita government spending; continuous variables in log form; absolute *t*-ratios in parentheses.

the 1,125 respondents who answered the spending-demand questions, with renters omitted because of the difficulty in defining their tax payments and price.[8] Results are given only for the median-income variant, the one that fit best in table 1.

We have shown equations first using spending adjusted by our adjustment factor, then with community dummies included to test whether the dummies really measure individual city or county effects, and then with the dependent variable unadjusted by the answers to our hypothetical question to measure the importance of the adjustment. The independent variables also include a host of dummies (designated by D) to proxy the Z_i factors.

The results agree broadly with those of the macro equations, though there are some interesting differences. In all three equations the population-crowding coefficient α_2 is very close to one, indicating again that public expenditures are not for goods that are public in the Samuelsonian sense. Again the tax-price elasticity is very low, though now it is statistically significant in the first two equations.[9] The public wage coefficients are now of the correct sign, though still lower than they should be if public services have the distributive shares of most private outputs. Community income and grants have very strong and statistically significant effects in all equations, as they did before.

Taking together the Y_i and $\bar{Y}$ terms, the macro income elasticity of about .4 is confirmed in the micro regressions. But virtually all of the positive elasticity is due to *community* income, with individual family income having a coefficient that is very close to zero in all three equations. Our results do suggest a positive income elasticity of demand for public spending, but the increased demand is seen to come in a very special form. As higher-income individuals within a community are surveyed, they do not appear to have any greater taste for public spending. The apparent reason is that higher-income individuals already receive (or perceive that they receive) greater benefits from public spending than do lower-income individuals. Stated differently, if we contrast voters of the same income and tax prices residing in communities of different income but initially the same level of public spending, the voter in a high-income community, for a given level of private goods consumption, will perceive a lower level of public goods consumption and have a higher marginal rate of substitution and demand for public goods.

---

[8] We did some Box-Cox tests for functional form, comparing the fit of log-linear, log-log, linear, and semilog formulations of the model and found that the semilog version used gave a slightly better fit, although the substantive results were not much different. We report the log-log specifications because they are easier to interpret.

[9] We did not incorporate the federal income tax deductibility of the property tax with our measure of price. Had we done so our price elasticity estimate would have been slightly higher.

One other aspect of the individual-income term bears mentioning. A problem in inferring income elasticities from survey results is that only 1 year's income is recorded for respondents. If there were a large transitory component to income, the overall income elasticity would be understated in the micro results but not in the macro community results, because there transitory income deviations are pooled and averaged out. We have no fully satisfactory means of estimating permanent income for the micro equations, but we did try a question borrowed from other ISR surveys on whether the respondent expected real income gains or losses in the next 5 years. As can be seen from the two left-hand columns of table 2, this variable works quite well. Optimists and those who expect no decline want more public spending than those who expect a decline or did not answer the question (the null class). Hence a partial explanation for the low individual-income elasticity is a modified form of the permanent-income hypothesis. Other things equal, individuals who expect real-income growth will desire higher levels of government spending than those who do not.

Some Econometric Issues

Before trying to interpret these results, we take note of several possible econometric problems. One involves the level of information possessed by respondents. When they are poorly informed about the role that tax prices and benefit shares play in determining their utility levels, they might respond to questions as if income and prices did not matter in shaping their demand for public spending. There is no perfect way to control for the information possessed by respondents, but one imperfect way is to stratify the sample according to their education. If more educated respondents are also more informed, their absolute income and price elasticities should be greater than for those without much education. We have tested this hypothesis by simply running the model of table 2 for college-educated respondents, finding micro elasticities that were slightly greater than those given in table 2 but not enough to change the basic interpretation of the results.

A second possibility is that individuals may have differing income elasticities of demand for different budgetary items. Thus the individual-income coefficient might be low because a positive income elasticity of demand for education is canceling a negative income elasticity of demand for welfare. To pursue this issue, we used another sequence included in the survey that asks respondents whether they would like an increase, decrease, or no change in individual budgetary items. Unlike our overall expenditure-demand question, we did not try to measure quantitative preferred changes for these individual functional categories because such a task proved to be difficult in pretesting the questionnaire, and so we were not able to control for the county spending levels for each functional category. As a result, we have not obtained quantitative estimates of micro income and price elasticities. But we can say whether micro-income and tax-price variables are significant determinants of these functional spending desires. The suggestive findings for six functional categories are shown in table 3. We see that micro income does indeed have a positive and significant income elasticity for school spending and a negative and significant elasticity for welfare spending. The relative price elasticities are also significantly negative for schools, parks, and colleges. Hence the micro-income elasticity might have been higher if we had focused on more definable bundles, such as spending for public schools.

This test can be taken one step further. Since welfare benefits are constant throughout the state, the macro-income variable should have a zero coefficient. Including macro income in welfare regressions like those shown in table 3 does lead to this result. But since education benefits are likely to be distributed in a prorich manner, macro income there should, and does, take on a positive coefficient.[10]

Another issue of concern was the choice of unit to which public services are provided. Our tabulated results utilized per capita spending as the dependent variable, even though taxes are paid on a household basis. Since some public services such as education are provided to individuals, such an assumption seems reasonable. But other services are better viewed as household services, in which case per *family* spending might be a better choice for the dependent variable. When we made such an adjustment the price elasticity of demand remained essentially unchanged, but micro-income elasticity rose slightly and became significantly different from zero. Most of the other coefficients were not changed appreciably.

Finally, we were concerned about the correct specification of price in the demand equation. In particular, we attempted to account for the possibility that individuals responded to the reduced marginal tax price of public services created by the statewide property-tax credit program. However, the model with the circuit-breaker adjusted price fit more poorly than the model reported here, suggesting that individuals were not aware of and/or did not respond to the program. Alternatively, we tried a number of different price terms associated with varying assumptions about the impact of commercial and industrial property on tax price. Our model as specified implicitly assumes

[10] We do not present these education equations here, but a number of them are given in a paper by Bergstrom, Rubinfeld, and Shapiro (in press) on a related topic.

TABLE 3

MICRO DEMAND EQUATIONS FOR INDIVIDUAL BUDGET ITEMS, 1,125 MICHIGAN HOMEOWNER RESPONDENTS, 1978

Independent Variable	Schools	Welfare	Police & Fire	Roads	Parks	State Universities
Individual income	.108 (2.9)	-.123 (3.4)	-.032 (.8)	-.005 (.1)	.029 (.8)	.044 (1.1)
Residential value/ total value	-.137 (4.2)	.013 (.4)	-.060 (1.8)	-.040 (1.3)	-.060 (-1.8)	-.080 (2.5)
D, child in public school	.100 (3.2)	.010 (.3)	.080 (2.3)	-.030 (.9)	.030 (1.0)	.020 (.7)
D, black	.154 (4.7)	.207 (6.2)	.077 (.5)	.040 (1.3)	.080 (2.5)	.020 (.7)

NOTE.—Dependent variable = 1 if the individual desired an increase in the budget, 0 if no change, −1 if a decrease; all coefficients are standardized β coefficients; absolute t-ratios in parentheses. To save space, we have not presented results for the other independent variables appearing in table 2. None of the macro coefficients could be estimated very well because the dependent variable was not adjusted for county spending levels. The other macro variables that were statistically significant were schools: expect real income up, Jewish; welfare: transfer recipient, Republican, party other, public employee; police and fire: Jewish; roads: expect real income up, expect no change in real income; parks: transfer recipient, public employee; state universities: nonresident public employee, expect real income up, expect no change in real income.

547

that a commercial-industrial tax base reduces tax price, since tax revenues can be used to finance residential public services without encouraging firm outmigration. An alternative specification allowed for the perceived fiscal benefits of a commercial-industrial base to fall to zero (as suggested by Ladd [1975]). Since the price elasticity is small and not very significant, our results were essentially unchanged, but we did note a small worsening in goodness of fit when we used the Ladd assumption.

Interpreting the Results

In this section we digress slightly to show how this finding of a low micro-income elasticity and a high macro–community income elasticity, if true, bears on some current public finance questions.

The first question involves benefit share progressivity. The usual economist's view, to the extent that there is one, appears to be that the benefits of public services are *not* distributed in a prorich manner. The major proponents of this view have been Gillespie (1965), who finds a neutral distribution within communities, and Musgrave and Musgrave (1980), who indicated that state and local purchases, and education in particular, are distributed propoor. This implies that high-income individuals, with higher levels of consumption of private goods, should have a higher marginal rate of substitution for public services. It also implies that if tax shares depend on income, high-income individuals pay a higher fiscal residual (Buchanan 1950) and are more likely to emigrate from the community for fiscal reasons.

In this paper ·we find some negative evidence for both ideas. If public services are assumed to be normal goods and since high-income individuals do not have a higher marginal rate of substitution than do low-income individuals, these high-income individuals must be consuming more public services than low-income individuals; that is, the within-community distribution of public services must be pro-rich. The finding corresponds to the possibility noted by Denzau and Mackay (1976) for price-inelastic consumers. It also suggests that the fiscal incentive to migrate because of the presence of fiscal residuals may be overstated. If the income elasticity of property-tax payments within a community is approximately one (as is suggested by several studies and confirmed in our own data set), the benefit side elasticity of approximately .4 suggests that fiscal residuals may be only about half as dependent on income as would be the case if benefit distributions were independent of income. Clearly the impact of such residuals on the migration of high-income individuals from a community will also be smaller.

Since our results do seem to counter the conventional wisdom, at

least as espoused by Musgrave and Musgrave, a more careful examination of the current evidence about within-jurisdiction distributional benefits seems warranted. The evidence Musgrave and Musgrave present relates to education and to medical purchases, both of
which are financed in part at the state level. In addition, their analysis
is based on aggregate data and so does not pretend to control for
within-community spending patterns. Their conclusion about the
propoor pattern of medical expenditures seems consistent with our
knowledge about state and local public hospitals and health care.
However, the conclusion about education involves some strong assumptions and is controversial. To allocate benefits among income
groups, Musgrave and Musgrave simply examine the distribution of
students among households. As a result, the calculation does not take
into account quality differentials among neighborhood schools, nor
does it look at spending differences across communities. Finally, as
they acknowledge, their illustrative calculations are measured solely in
terms of expenditures made without taking into account the value at
which public services are assessed by the recipient of those services.
With a decreasing marginal utility of income, one would expect
higher-income individuals to pay more for education, so that their
calculation is likely to understate the benefits of education received by
those with higher incomes.

A more careful look at other studies by both political scientists and
economists leads us to a different view of the distributional impact of
local expenditures. When dealing with education, which makes up
roughly 57 percent of local budgets, Katzman (1968) examined variations in spending per pupil by neighborhood within several large
cities, as well as variations in factors that might affect school quality.
He found that the distribution of school quality was biased in favor of
upper-income areas. Levy, Meltsner, and Wildavsky (1974) found a
prorich allocation in Oakland, California, compensatory programs
notwithstanding. Other studies of education (Sexton 1961 [Detroit];
Berk and Hartman 1971 [Chicago]; Owen 1972; and Mandel 1974
[Detroit]) all lead to the same qualitative conclusion—a prorich distribution of educational spending within cities.

The evidence concerning other local public services is more spotty
and less conclusive. For police, Bloch (1974 [Washington]) found no
discernible pattern, while Weicher (1971 [Chicago]) found a strong
negative relationship between police expenditures and income up to
the $8,000–$9,000 range (middle income) but a positive relationship
past this point. For fire, Lineberry (1977) found a negative relationship, but his study uses as a measure of output distance from the fire
station, a measure that does not reflect expenditure differentials
across neighborhoods and does not take into account the fact that

citizen use of the system and the value of that use are likely to vary positively with income. For libraries, both Martin (1969 [Chicago]) and Levy et al. (1974) found a prorich distribution. However, for parks the studies are mixed, Gold (1974 [Detroit]) finding a negative relationship between income and benefits and the Community Council of Greater New York (1963) a positive relationship. Finally, for street repairs Antunes and Plumlee (1977 [Houston]) were inconclusive, as were Levy et al. (1974).

One can debate the quality and reliability of each of the studies cited. However, with education making up more than half the budget, and with the studies of most other budgetary items generally inconclusive, a net prorich distribution is at least a likely possibility.[11]

A related empirical issue involves differences between the economist's and noneconomist's views of the demand for public goods. The typical economist's view, based on macro–public goods equations of the sort estimated above in table 1, is that the income elasticity of demand is positive, usually about .6.[12] The usual noneconomist's view, based on polling individuals to find whether they want more, less, or the same amount of spending on public goods, is that implicit income elasticities are zero or sometimes even negative—income cannot explain deviations of desired from actual spending (see, e.g., ACIR 1979; Citrin 1979; or Clark and Ferguson 1981). Our results yield a simple resolution to the paradox. Both studies are right. As community incomes rise, the mean or median voter desires more public goods and public spending rises. But within a community, public services appear to be distributed in a prorich manner, implying that residual desires are uncorrelated with income.

A third idea that takes on a different interpretation is that of the Pareto optimality of the median-voter outcome, a topic dealt with first by Bowen (1943) and recently by Bergstrom (1979). Bowen established the idea that if the distribution of tastes is symmetric, so that the community's median-voter marginal rate of substitution (the result of majority rule) equals the mean marginal rate of substitution (the Pareto efficiency condition), the majority rule is Pareto efficient. Bergstrom argued that this could not be the case if public spending demand depended on income, because income is not distributed symmetrically. This led him to rescue the Bowen proposition through proportional income taxation and a symmetric distribution of "tastes."

[11] The only previous attempt to quantify these distributional results known to us appears in Inman and Rubinfeld (1979). Relying primarily on the studies mentioned above, they estimated a .25 weighted-average elasticity of expenditure benefits with respect to income. This elasticity of .25 is not too different from the .41 elasticity obtained from the survey analysis presented here.

[12] A long list of such studies is cited by Gramlich (1982).

Obviously, if our micro results are right, Bergstrom need not have worried about this problem—since public spending demand does not depend on income within a community, the Bowen majority-rule outcome could be Pareto efficient even without proportional income taxation.

A final point refers more directly to the median-voter proposition. Inman (1978) has shown that most of a sample of Long Island communities behaved "as if" the family with median income were the decisive voter in setting public expenditures. He argues that this finding confirms the median-voter hypothesis. While not necessarily denying that interpretation, the equations shown here offer an alternative possibility. Perhaps communities behave as if the median voter were decisive because of the importance of community median income in setting spending levels. Individual incomes are basically uncorrelated with spending desires, but as the median income in the community rises the community spends more.

II. The Tiebout Hypothesis

Another hotly debated issue in public finance is Tiebout's idea that voters group themselves with others having similar tastes so that public goods can be supplied efficiently. In principle there are many ways in which such an idea could be tested, but in practice the ways of testing the Tiebout hypothesis have been rather limited, and in many ways quite unsatisfactory.

Most attention has been directed at property-value changes, a tradition started by Oates (1969) and taken up by a number of authors, most recently Epple, Zelenitz, and Visscher (1978). The initial Oates article established that property values would be bid up in communities with low tax rates for a given bundle of public goods, or more public goods with a given tax rate. This suggested to Oates that there was a Tiebout-like *mechanism* at work. Economic agents were locating in communities with more favorable budgetary arrangements. Critics of this paper (Edel and Sclar 1974; Hamilton 1976) have argued that in a full Tiebout *equilibrium* property taxes should be simple benefit taxes, and if tax rates were shown to influence property values this would be proof that.the system was not in a full Tiebout equilibrium. Epple et al. took this argument farther and showed that Tiebout and non-Tiebout communities could only be distinguished by whether property taxes cause a deadweight loss and hence influence the demand for housing for nonmedian voter individuals (for the median voter the tax rate is determined simultaneously and the econometric test cannot be made). Moreover, they also showed that the property-value test becomes totally nonoperational

JOURNAL OF POLITICAL ECONOMY

whenever housing is supplied elastically or community boundaries are changeable.[13]

The data used here suggest a different, and perhaps less ambiguous, way to test the Tiebout hypothesis. If the hypothesis is true, two conditions must hold. (*a*) Citizens should have grouped themselves together with others with similar tastes for public goods, to eliminate many of the deadweight losses implicit in the communal supply of these goods. (*b*) The community must in fact supply this community-desired level of public goods. We concentrate on the first condition in this section and the second condition in the next section.

To test the first, we compare the variance of local spending demands within a community with those throughout the state. If there is Tiebout grouping, the within-community variance will be significantly smaller than the entire statewide sample variance.

There are in principle two ways to make the test. The first and most obvious would be simply to compare variances of spending demands within a community and throughout the whole state. The second would be to use regression equations, such as those given in table 2, to control for factors that might influence spending in all districts and then do the test on regression residuals. If, for example, public spending demands depend positively on community income, higher-income communities would be expected to have a smaller intracommunity variance than a statewide sample made up of residents of high- and low-income communities. In this case, the influence of income, and other factors, can be controlled for by the regression and the test made on just the residuals.

Both tests provide somewhat different kinds of information. The residual test asks whether individuals with similar unobservables, pre-

---

[13] A similar test has been devised by Reschovsky (1979). He used power-company data to examine the determinants of location for intracommunity movers and nonmovers, finding that movers were influenced by fiscal variables and nonmovers were not. The criticism would be the same as that directed at Oates: In a full Tiebout equilibrium where property taxes are benefit taxes, we would expect to find fiscal variables unimportant in explaining location. Hence the resident results could be consistent either with a full Tiebout equilibrium or with disequilibrium (as Reschovsky argues). By the same token, in a full equilibrium fiscal variables would affect moving decisions only if taxes were not benefit taxes; hence this finding confirms the Tiebout mechanism but not a Tiebout equilibrium. A different test is provided by Hamilton, Mills, and Puryear (1975). They view education as the primary public good and income as the primary determinant of spending, and attempt to estimate how much income segregation within communities (and thus public goods segregation) there is. They find some evidence that income varies less in suburban communities than in central city communities, and that in SMSAs with a large number of school districts there is less income variation than in those with fewer districts. They conclude that the data provide some mild support for the Tiebout hypothesis.

TABLE 4

TEST OF LOCATIONAL GROUPING HYPOTHESIS:
COMPARISON OF SPENDING DEMAND
VARIANCES AND RESIDUAL VARIANCES,
426 DETROIT METROPOLITAN AREA HOMEOWNERS

Location	Observations (N)	var (PE/N)	F(PE/N)	var (ε)	F(ε)
Wayne County:	201	. . .	. . .	. . .	. . .
Dearborn	21	3,889	8.17**	.005	2.42**
Dearborn Heights	13	26,406	1.20	.041	
Detroit	100	8,644	3.67**	.007	1.73**
Rest of Wayne	67	4,669	6.80**	.005	2.20**
Macomb County:	101	. . .	. . .	. . .	. . .
Roseville	10	880	36.09**	.001	9.31**
St. Clair Shores	10	495	64.17**	.001	10.08**
Sterling Heights	16	639	49.71**	.001	12.10**
Warren	25	7,327	4.33**	.023	.54
Rest of Macomb	40	3,058	10.39**	.007	1.66*
Oakland County:	124	. . .	. . .	. . .	. . .
Pontiac	13	23,104	1.37	.034	.36
Southfield	19	1,722	18.44**	.003	3.90**
Rest of Oakland	92	2,581	12.31**	.004	2.75**

Note.—Countywide expenditure and income data are as follows:

	PE/N	Y	PE/NY
Wayne	1,042	11,351	.092
Macomb	703	12,110	.058
Oakland	791	13,826	.057

* Significant at 5 percent level.
** Significant at 1 percent level.

sumably correlated with public sector demands, live together. The test using direct responses, however, looks at the effect of both observable and unobservable variables. Both tests are shown in tables 4 and 5.

Table 4 focuses on just the Detroit metropolitan area. Three counties—Wayne, Macomb, and Oakland—cover virtually all of the area within 30 miles of downtown Detroit and most of the area within 40 miles. Within this three-county area, it should be possible for all workers to find a residential area consisting of individuals with like tastes in public goods. Indeed, this appears to happen to an overwhelming degree, as is shown by both tests in table 4. The table shows spending demand variances, residual variances, and *F*-tests on each for the 426 respondents living in Wayne, Macomb, and Oakland counties, grouped by community when there are 10 or more respondents and by "rest of county" when not.[14] The countywide expenditure and income figures (in the note to the table) show that there is only a modest countywide dispersion in income (the low is 82 percent of the high) but a greater dispersion in the ratio of public expenditures to income (the low is 62 percent of the high). But what is remarkable about the table is the degree of grouping shown by the residuals. Using either F-test, in Wayne County 188 of the 201 (94 percent) respondents live in communities with an intracommunity variance of residual variance significantly smaller than the overall residual variance at the 1 percent level. In Macomb, all respondents do so using the straight variance test; 76 of the 101 respondents (75 percent) do so at the 5 percent level, and 36 of the 101 do so at the 1 percent level using the residual variance test. In Oakland, 111 of the 125 (90 percent) respondents do so at the 1 percent level for either test. Across all three counties 94 percent of the respondents are grouped together at the 1 percent level in the first test, and 79 percent of the respondents are grouped together at the 5 percent level and 88 percent of the respondents at the 1 percent level in the second. These calculations then indicate a very high degree of grouping by expenditure taste residuals in the three-county Detroit metropolitan area.[15]

A first check on this finding is to see whether it obtains in other medium-size communities in Michigan. In principle we would not expect there to be as much grouping in these other communities because there would not be as many fiscally independent jurisdictions to select from in a labor-market area. In fact, there is still a high degree of grouping, as is shown in table 5, which gives the identical information for the four areas with sufficient observations to make such a test. Using the straight variance test all respondents have grouped themselves together, but with the more stringent residual variance test only one-third of the sample observations are so grouped (at both the 5 and 1 percent levels).[16] At least for the residual test, the results are reasonably consistent with a Tiebout interpretation: In

[14] The test of whether two variances σ_1^2 and σ_2^2 are equal is provided by an F-test, since s_1^2/s_2^2 (the ratio of the estimated variances) is distributed as F with N_1 and N_2 the appropriate degrees of freedom. The test is valid only if the two χ^2 distributions associated with σ_1^2 and σ_2^2 are independent.

[15] The Detroit SMSA extends much farther out, including some counties with exterior borders almost 80 miles from downtown Detroit. We had relatively few observations from these other counties—St. Clair, Lapeer, Livingston, Washtenaw, and Monroe—in our sample, but had we included them in the test our conclusions would be tempered slightly because variances are greater in these outer counties. But still at least two-thirds of the sample observations would be grouped together in the 1 percent test and three-quarters in the 5 percent test.

[16] This percentage would be slightly higher were the next most populous city areas in the sample included (Bay City, Jackson, and Midland), but still not nearly as high as in the Detroit area.

TABLE 5

Test of Locational Grouping Hypothesis:
Comparison of Spending Demand
Variances and Residual Variances,
139 Non-Detroit Urban Michigan Homeowners

Location	Observations (N)	var (PE/N)	F(PE/N)	var (ε)	F(ε)
Flint SMSA:	35	. . .	. . .	. . .	. . .
Genessee County	15	4,692	6.77**	.008	1.53
Shiawassee County	20	722	43.99**	.003	3.56**
Grand Rapids SMSA	34	4,045	7.85**	.008	1.46
Lansing SMSA:	43	. . .	. . .	. . .	. . .
Lansing	25	7,310	5.35**	.018	0.68
Rest of Ingham	18	4,264	7.45**	.010	1.26
Kalamazoo SMSA	27	1,648	19.27**	.004	2.82**

** Significant at 1 percent level.

large metropolitan areas, there is quite extensive grouping; in smaller areas, there is some grouping.

III. The Median-Voter Hypothesis

The other aspect of the Tiebout hypothesis that can be evaluated with these data is the logically complementary one of whether the jurisdictions in question in fact supply the level of public goods desired by these grouped respondents. If they do not, there would not be much point in locating near others with similar tastes, for all voters would be forced to consume nonoptimal levels of public expenditures. Since we are now comparing actual with desired levels of public expenditures, this test generalizes to one involving the median-voter hypothesis: Do communities supply the levels of public expenditures desired by the median voter in their community?

For this we make two changes in the data. Since we are now concerned with correspondence between actual and desired expenditures, we analyze not the residuals in a public expenditure demand equation, as above, but the raw adjustment factors. The ith respondent desiring a 5 percent cutback is recorded as -5.

A second change enables us to run a straightforward test of the median-voter hypothesis. Instead of using homeowner respondents as the sample, we redefine the sample to include only voter respondents. Clearly renter voters should be added to the sample in testing the median-voter hypothesis. By the same token, for tests of the median-voter hypothesis, nonvoting homeowners should be dropped from the sample.

The results of this test are shown in table 6. Respondents are grouped into Detroit metropolitan area, other cities, and other nonurban areas, following the classifications used in tables 4 and 5. For all voters, the table indicates remarkable support for the median-voter hypothesis and also for the idea that voters group themselves because they gain the level of public spending they desire. In the Detroit area, two-thirds of the voters want no change in the level of public spending, and the mean desired level is less than 1 percent below the actual level. Since more than half of the voters favor no change, the median voter obviously favors no change. And in the right-hand column, only 19 percent of the voters favor a level of public spending much different from actual, defined here as a positive or negative change of more than 5 percent. Essentially the same results are obtained for other urban areas in the state: two-thirds of the voters favoring no change and only 19 percent wanting a big increase or decrease.

The results are not as striking for nonurban voters. The median-voter hypothesis still gains convincing support, in that 60 percent of the nonurban voters in the state favor no change in the overall level of public spending, while only 28 percent favor big increases or decreases. But while this supports the median-voter hypothesis, there is not quite as much satisfaction with the overall level of public spending. A slightly smaller proportion of the voters want no change than in urban areas and a slightly larger proportion want a large change. If it is true that the Tiebout mechanism should work less well in large nonurban counties where voters cannot relocate without changing jobs, there should in general be lower levels of satisfaction with government spending and these urban-rural differences would be plausible.

It is possible that with so many voters—two-thirds in urban areas and three-fifths in rural areas—opting for no change, respondents are displaying less dissatisfaction with the public sector than they truly feel. However, it is perhaps still meaningful that the same questioning procedure showed differences between urban and rural areas and that these differences do, if anything, support the Tiebout hypothesis.

IV. Implications

The presence of micro data on public spending demands at least in principle allows several tests to be made of propositions of long-standing interest in the field of applied public finance. For one thing,

TABLE 6

TESTING THE MEDIAN VOTER HYPOTHESIS: DIFFERENCE BETWEEN ACTUAL AND DESIRED SPENDING OF 858 MICHIGAN VOTERS

Place	Homeowner Respondents	Voter Respondents	Want Decrease	Want No Change	Want Increase	Mean Desired Change (%)	Want No Change (%)	Want Big Change* (%)
Detroit metropolitan area:	426	374	49	249	76	-.78	66.6	19.5
Dearborn	21	22	4	14	4	-.23	63.6	13.6
Dearborn Heights	13	11	2	8	1	-5.91	72.7	18.2
Detroit	100	106	12	61	33	-.82	57.5	21.7
Rest of Wayne	67	53	5	37	11	-.23	69.8	20.7
Roseville	10	6	1	5	0	-1.67	83.3	.0
St. Clair Shores	10	6	0	6	0	.00	100.0	.0
Sterling Heights	16	14	0	10	4	2.14	71.4	14.3
Warren	25	23	4	17	2	-1.39	73.9	13.0
Rest of Macomb	40	32	8	20	4	-2.81	62.5	28.1
Pontiac	13	12	2	4	6	3.75	33.3	50.0
Southfield	19	16	2	13	1	-1.81	81.3	12.5
Rest of Oakland	92	73	9	54	10	-.62	74.0	16.4
Other cities:	139	129	23	87	19	-1.10	67.4	18.6
Genessee City	15	15	1	10	4	.67	66.7	.0
Shiawasee City	20	15	3	10	2	-.33	66.7	20.0
Grand Rapids	34	33	9	21	3	-2.58	63.6	24.2
Lansing	25	20	3	13	4	-.25	65.0	25.0
Rest of Ingham	18	23	3	16	4	-.74	69.6	21.7
Kalamazoo	27	23	4	17	2	-1.74	73.9	13.0
Nonurban counties	417	355	78	215	62	-1.81	60.5	28.5

* Want spending changes (up or down) of more than 5 percent.

it appears that spending-demand equations fitted to micro data give approximately the same parameter estimates as those fitted to macro data, though the interpretation of these micro equations can be very different and very illuminating. Positive income elasticities of public spending demand appear to arise because public services are distributed in a prorich manner within communities, implying that, other things equal, residents of higher-income communities perceive that they receive lower levels of spending on public goods and want more. As a consequence, in any given community, there appears to be little difference between the marginal public spending demands of rich and poor respondents, just as public opinion polls suggest. At the same time, respondents who anticipate increases in their own real income do desire somewhat more public spending (or are willing to pay more taxes).

The existence of micro data also permits a different test of the Tiebout hypothesis. Controlling for all the independent variables in a statewide micro–spending demand equation, residuals from the set of observations in urban communities have a significantly smaller variance than in the whole sample in a very high percentage of the cases, indicating that at least in those urban communities there appears to be a high degree of grouping by public spending demands. The obvious explanation for this phenomenon is a Tiebout mechanism, whereby people locate in communities where others want and supply a menu of public goods similar to their own preferred level. This interpretation is supported by three other propositions that can also be established. Actual spending does conform to desired levels in these purportedly Tiebout-like communities, it does so less in rural communities where a Tiebout mechanism is unlikely to operate, and there appears to be less grouping by residuals in small urban labor market areas than in large areas.

References

Advisory Commission on Intergovernmental Relations (ACIR). *Changing Public Attitudes on Government and Taxes.* Washington: Government Printing Office, 1979.

Antunes, George E., and Plumlee, John P. "The Distribution of an Urban Public Service: Ethnicity, Socioeconomic Status, and Bureaucracy as Determinants of the Quality of Neighborhood Streets." *Urban Affairs Q.* 12 (March 1977): 313–32.

Bergstrom, Theodore C. "When Does Majority Rule Supply Public Goods Efficiently?" *Scandinavian J. Econ.* 81, no. 2 (1979): 216–26.

Bergstrom, Theodore C., and Goodman, Robert P. "Private Demands for Public Goods." *A.E.R.* 63 (June 1973): 280–96.

Bergstrom, Theodore C.; Rubinfeld, Daniel L.; and Shapiro, Perry. "Micro-based Estimates of Demand Functions for Local School Expenditures." *Econometrica* (in press).

Berk, R. A., and Hartman, A. "Race and District Differences in per Pupil Staffing Expenditures in Chicago Elementary Schools, 1970–71." Evanston, Ill.: Northwestern Univ., Center for Urban Affairs, June 1971.

Bloch, P. "Equality of Distribution of Police Services: A Case Study of Washington." Washington: Urban Inst., 1974.

Borcherding, Thomas E., and Deacon, Robert T. "The Demand for the Services of Non-federal Governments." *A.E.R.* 62 (December 1972): 891–901.

Bowen, Howard R. "The Interpretation of Voting in the Allocation of Economic Resources." *Q.J.E.* 58 (November 1943): 27–48.

Buchanan, James M. "Federalism and Fiscal Equity." *A.E.R.* 40 (September 1950): 583–99.

Citrin, J. "Do People Want Something for Nothing: Public Opinion on Taxes and Government Spending." *Nat. Tax J.* 32 (suppl.; June 1979): 113–39.

Clark, Terry N., and Ferguson, L. "The Middle Class: Policy Preferences and Political Involvement." Manuscript. Chicago: Univ. Chicago, Dept. Soc., 1981.

Community Council of Greater New York. "Comparative Recreation Needs and Services in New York Neighborhoods." New York: Community Council of Greater New York, 1963.

Converse, Philip E. "Public Opinion and Voting Behavior." In *Handbook of Political Science.* Vol. 4, *Nongovernmental Politics,* edited by Fred I. Greenstein and Nelson W. Polsby. Reading, Mass.: Addison-Wesley, 1975.

Courant, Paul N.; Gramlich, Edward M.; and Rubinfeld, Daniel L. "Why Voters Support Tax Limitation Amendments: The Michigan Case." *Nat. Tax J.* 33 (March 1980): 1–20.

Deacon, Robert T. "Private Choice and Collective Outcomes: Evidence from Public Sector Demand Analysis." *Nat. Tax J.* 30 (December 1977): 371–86.

Denzau, Arthur T., and Mackay, Robert J. "Benefit Shares and Majority Voting." *A.E.R.* 66 (March 1976): 69–76.

Downs, Anthony. *An Economic Theory of Democracy.* New York: Harper, 1957.

Edel, Matthew, and Sclar, Elliott. "Taxes, Spending, and Property Values: Supply Adjustment in a Tiebout-Oates Model." *J.P.E.* 82, no. 5 (September/October 1974): 941–54.

Epple, Dennis; Zelenitz, Allan; and Visscher, Michael. "A Search for Testable Implications of the Tiebout Hypothesis." *J.P.E.* 86, no. 3 (June 1978): 405–26.

Gillespie, W. Irwin. "Effect of Public Expenditures on the Distribution of Income." In *Essays in Fiscal Federalism,* edited by Richard A. Musgrave. Washington: Brookings, 1965.

Gold, Steven D. "The Distribution of Urban Government Services in Theory and Practice: The Case of Recreation in Detroit." *Public Finance Q.* 2 (January 1974): 107–30.

Gramlich, Edward M. "Intergovernmental Grants: A Review of the Empirical Literature." In *The Political Economy of Fiscal Federalism,* edited by Wallace E. Oates. Lexington, Mass.: Lexington, 1977.

———. "Models of Excessive Government Spending: Do the Facts Support the Theories?" In *Public Finance and Public Employment,* edited by Robert H. Haveman. Detroit: Wayne State Univ. Press, 1982.

Hamilton, Bruce W. "The Effects of Property Taxes and Local Public Spending on Property Values: A Theoretical Comment." *J.P.E.* 84, no. 3 (June 1976): 647–50.

Hamilton, Bruce W.; Mills, Edwin S.; and Puryear, David. "The Tiebout Hypothesis and Residential Income Segregation." In *Fiscal Zoning and Land*

Use Controls: The Economic Issues, edited by Edwin S. Mills and Wallace E. Oates. Lexington, Mass.: Heath, 1975.

Hotelling, Harold. "Stability in Competition." *Econ. J.* 39 (March 1929): 41–57.

Inman, Robert P. "Testing Political Economy's 'As If' Proposition: Is the Median Income Voter Really Decisive?" *Public Choice* 33, no. 4 (1978): 45–65.

Inman, Robert P., and Rubinfeld, Daniel L. "The Judicial Pursuit of Local Fiscal Equity." *Harvard Law Rev.* 92 (June 1979): 1662–1750.

Katzman, Martin T. "Distribution and Production in a Big City Elementary School System." *Yale Econ. Essays* 8 (Spring 1968): 201–56.

Ladd, Helen F. "Local Education Expenditures, Fiscal Capacity, and the Composition of the Property Tax Base." *Nat. Tax J.* 28 (June 1975): 145–58.

Levy, Frank; Meltsner, Arnold J.; and Wildavsky, Aaron. *Urban Outcomes: Schools, Streets, and Libraries.* Berkeley: Univ. California Press, 1974.

Lineberry, Robert L. *Equality and Urban Policy: The Distribution of Municipal Public Services.* Beverly Hills, Calif.: Sage, 1977.

Mandel, A. S. "The Allocation of Resources inside Urban and Suburban School Districts: Theory and Evidence." Ph.D. dissertation, Univ. Michigan, 1974.

Martin, Lowell A. *Library Response to Urban Change: A Study of the Chicago Public Library.* Chicago: American Library Assoc., 1969.

Musgrave, Richard A., and Musgrave, Peggy B. *Public Finance in Theory and Practice.* 3d ed. New York: McGraw-Hill, 1980.

Oates, Wallace E. "The Effects of Property Taxes and Local Public Spending on Property Values: An Empirical Study of Tax Capitalization and the Tiebout Hypothesis." *J.P.E.* 77, no. 6 (November/December 1969): 957–71.

Owen, John D. "The Distribution of Educational Resources in Large American Cities." *J. Human Resources* 7 (Winter 1972): 26–38.

Reschovsky, A. "Residential Choice and the Local Public Sector: An Alternative Test of the 'Tiebout Hypothesis.'" *J. Urban Econ.* 6 (October 1979): 501–20.

Romer, Thomas, and Rosenthal, Howard. "Political Resource Allocation, Controlled Agendas, and the Status Quo." *Public Choice* 33, no. 4 (1978): 27–43.

Samuelson, Paul A. "The Pure Theory of Public Expenditure." *Rev. Econ. and Statis.* 36 (November 1954): 387–89.

Sexton, Patricia C. *Education and Income: Inequalities of Opportunity in Our Public Schools.* New York: Viking, 1961.

Tiebout, Charles M. "A Pure Theory of Local Expenditures." *J.P.E.* 64, no. 5 (October 1956): 416–24.

Weicher, John C. "The Allocation of Police Protection by Income Class." *Urban Studies* 8 (October 1971): 207–20.

[8]

Assessing the Importance of Tiebout Sorting: Local Heterogeneity from 1850 to 1990

By Paul W. Rhode and Koleman S. Strumpf*

This paper argues that long-run trends in geographic segregation are inconsistent with models where residential choice depends solely on local public goods (the Tiebout hypothesis). We develop an extension of the Tiebout model that predicts as mobility costs fall, the heterogeneity across communities of individual public good preferences and of public good provision must (weakly) increase. Given the secular decline in mobility costs, these predictions can be evaluated using historical data. We find decreasing heterogeneity in policies and proxies for preferences across (i) a sample of U.S. municipalities (1870–1990); (ii) all Boston-area municipalities (1870–1990); and (iii) all U.S. counties (1850–1990). (JEL D7, H7, N3, R5)

In recent years there has been renewed emphasis on decentralized governance in many countries including the United States. A key rationale for this shift is the belief that local governments provide policies better suited to citizen preferences. This wisdom is grounded in the Charles Tiebout (1956) hypothesis which states that individuals will costlessly sort themselves across local communities according to their public good preferences. This simple theory is the workhorse of the local public finance literature and has been the subject of over one thousand economics and political science articles.

Tiebout sorting remains an active current research topic, with many recent papers taking a strict interpretation of the model. As examples, Dennis Epple and Holger Sieg (1999) and Epple et al. (2001) empirically model community choice as the product of costless sorting on housing prices and public good provisions. They estimate the underlying preference parameters under the maintained hypothesis of a Tiebout equilibrium. Other recent empirical papers have used the Tiebout framework to evaluate the effects of school competition (Epple et al., forthcoming), school choice (Caroline Hoxby, 2000), or to explain the number of local jurisdictions (Alberto Alesina et al., 2000). The theoretical local public economics literature also relies heavily on the Tiebout framework and often presumes that community selection is driven exclusively by public goods and taxes. Some prominent recent examples include Raquel Fernández and Richard Rogerson (1998), Hoxby (1999), and Thomas Nechyba (1999, 2000), who consider education quality/ spending; Jan Brueckner (2000), who analyzes local tax competition; Epple and Thomas Romer (1991), who investigate redistribution; Myrna Wooders (1999), who interprets Tiebout using cooperative game theory; Fernández and Rogerson (1997), who study the effects of zoning; and Nechyba (1997), Gerhard Glomm and Roger Lagunoff (1999), and Carlo Perroni and Kimberley Scharf (2001), who analyze generic local public goods.

* Rhode: Department of Economics, CB #3305, University of North Carolina, Chapel Hill, NC 27599, and National Bureau of Economic Research (e-mail: prhode@email. unc.edu); Strumpf: Department of Economics, CB #3305, University of North Carolina, Chapel Hill, NC 27599 (e-mail: cigar@email.unc.edu). We thank David Blau, Judith Blau, Dennis Epple, Claudia Goldin, Thomas Mroz, Felix Oberholzer, Wilbert van der Klaauw, participants at the 2000 AEA, 1999 NBER Development of the American Economy Summer Institute, 2001 Public Choice, and 2001 SSHA meetings, ZEI Workshop on Federalism and Decentralization, University of Chicago, Clemson University, University of Illinois Urbana-Champaign, University of Kentucky, University of Michigan, UNC-Duke, and Wharton School seminars, and two anonymous referees for comments and suggestions. This is a substantially revised version of an earlier paper, "A Historical Test of the Tiebout Hypothesis."

Local policies clearly matter for residential choice, but are they the dominant motive? Suggestive evidence to the contrary comes from the American/Annual Housing Survey (AHS), a longitudinal, nationally representative survey of over 50,000 homes begun in 1973. Among the AHS households who moved in the previous year, only 5 percent cited public services (including schooling) as their primary reason for moving. Roughly 50 percent said their move was primarily due to employment or family and friends, motivations excluded in the Tiebout model and the literature cited above.[1] These results indicate that non-Tiebout incentives are important and perhaps driving forces in residential decisions. If individuals select communities in large part due to employment or social interaction opportunities, then neighbors need not have homogeneous public good preferences and one of the central implications of the Tiebout model is violated.

This paper seeks to assess more formally the relevance of Tiebout sorting. Our strategy is to derive a more realistic version of the Tiebout hypothesis and empirically to test its implications. We first generalize the Tiebout model by relaxing the assumption of perfect mobility (no moving costs). We show in a general environment that as mobility costs fall, resident preference heterogeneity *across* communities should (weakly) increase. Under some standard assumptions on individual preferences, the variation of policies across communities will also increase. The empirical section begins by documenting the dramatic reduction in mobility costs over the last two centuries. This suggests that if Tiebout incentives are of first-order importance, then heterogeneity across communities will increase in the historical record.[2]

To evaluate this prediction, we consider: (i) a sample of U.S. municipalities over the 1870–1990 period; (ii) all municipalities in the Boston metropolitan area over the 1870–1990 period; and (iii) all counties in the United States over the 1850–1990 period. Almost all of our empirical results stand in opposition to the Tiebout prediction of increasing heterogeneity across communities.[3] Across the U.S. municipality sample, heterogeneity of local policy outcomes—total local taxes per capita and school taxes per capita—has declined significantly. The coefficient of variation for school taxes fell by two-thirds between 1880 and 1992. To test the comparative static prediction regarding preference heterogeneity, we consider proxies for public good preferences: race, age, and nativity, and over the 1970–1990 period, education, home ownership, and income. These proxies generally exhibit diminishing heterogeneity across our municipality sample. For example, the dissimilarity index for the black population share decreased from 0.72 to 0.57 between 1870 and 1990. We replicate our results using all municipalities in the Boston metropolitan area because some argue the Tiebout model should apply to small geographic regions. Even with a greater variety of preference proxies and policies including electoral outcomes and education spending, there is little evidence of increased stratification (except for racial composition, but there is no change in suburban heterogeneity and the city-suburb differences appear likely due to discrimination rather than local public goods).

---

[1] This result is quite robust. The motives behind moves are similar if we consider only within-metropolitan area moves; if we consider future moves by households who say their current local services are "so inadequate that they want to move"; or if we consider data reports from the Current Population Survey which includes migration data in 1945–1946, 1962–1963, 1974–1976, 1997–2000. All data sources and details on these calculations are contained in the Data Appendix, which is available at the authors' Web sites (www.unc.edu/~cigar/; www.unc.edu/~prhode/).

[2] An alternative cross-sectional test of the Tiebout prediction is to see if increases in mobility costs lead to reduced

stratification across communities. Using data for 65 large metropolitan areas in 1980 and 1990, we find higher commuting costs are associated with *greater* across-municipality heterogeneity (results available upon request). This is an important complement to our main results because it does not suffer from standard criticisms of long time series (e.g., changes in the aggregate preference distribution or in the nature and type of local public services).

[3] These results run counter to the conventional wisdom that greater sorting has occurred in the latter part of the twentieth century. We show that most contemporary segregation occurs between neighborhoods (as measured by Census tracts) within the same municipality. Such neighborhoods receive roughly the same level of local public services, and so such within-municipality stratification is difficult to explain with the Tiebout model.

We next consider county-level data. While some researchers consider counties too large to be considered communities, we show empirically that across-municipality heterogeneity is roughly equal to across-county heterogeneity plus a constant. This means that *trends* in across-county heterogeneity parallel trends in across-municipality heterogeneity. The advantage of using county-level data is that a wide range of variables is available for the full national population of counties. We assemble a vast data set comprising all of the counties in the United States (except Alaska) over the 1850–1990 period. Our results confirm the municipal-level analysis. The dispersion of local policy outcomes across counties has declined significantly since the late nineteenth century. The coefficient of variation for local per capita education spending fell from 0.66 in 1890 to 0.25 in 1992. A similar reduction in heterogeneity occurred in per capita taxes and revenues over the 1870–1992 period. We consider numerous proxies for public good preferences including religious affiliation. Almost every preference proxy exhibits diminishing heterogeneity across counties since 1850. Two of the more graphic examples are that the proportion of blacks living in black majority counties decreased from 48 percent in 1890 to 9 percent in 1990, and that the dissimilarity index of presidential vote shares decreased from 0.27 to 0.17 between 1892 and 1988. These patterns are not solely driven by changes in the South, by rural-urban migration, or by reduced salience of our preference proxies.

In total, these results suggest that Tiebout sorting has been historically overwhelmed by forces reducing across-community heterogeneity. (A referee has noted that a closer examination of the data indicates an even greater discrepancy between the historical record and the comparative static predictions of the generalized Tiebout model. Almost every heterogeneity series declines most strongly over the late nineteenth and early twentieth centuries when the reductions in transportation and communication costs appear most rapid.) These findings do not mean that Tiebout motives are irrelevant, but rather that they have not been the primary factor in long-run location decisions. This implies that any theoretical or empirical model that adopts a pure Tiebout framework, as is common in the literature, is misspecified. In more general models where nonpolicy factors influence residential choice, many implications of the Tiebout theory no longer hold (for example, it is not typically possible to rank communities according to public good demands).

It is important to contrast our approach with previous empirical tests of the Tiebout hypothesis. Most papers investigate the extent of heterogeneity within communities, the motives for household mobility, and the degree to which fiscal policies are capitalized into property value (see Keith Dowding et al., 1994).[4] These papers do not provide a basis for evaluating whether Tiebout incentives are of first-order importance. For example, when considering community composition it is unclear how large a deviation from perfect sorting is needed before concluding that non-Tiebout incentives dominate locational choices. Our comparative static approach provides a more meaningful assessment of Tiebout's importance because it implies a direction of change—to greater sorting—that is empirically refutable. We recognize that no single piece of evidence presented here is convincing by itself, but the absence of historical sorting trends among the dozen or so measures we analyze constitutes a serious challenge to the view that community choice is primarily driven by Tiebout incentives. Our work suggests that non-Tiebout motives must matter and that a more general approach is needed.[5]

Our empirical results are of independent interest because they contribute to two current literatures. First, they advance the segregation literature, which explores the spatial disper-

---

[4] An alternative Tiebout test considers whether greater population heterogeneity leads to increases in the number of local governments (see Ronald Fisher and Robert Wassmer, 1998, and the citations therein). But this literature is problematic because the empirical results are weak with many insignificant and wrong-signed parameters, the direction of causality is unclear, and the results are consistent with alternative sorting motives such as racism (see Jorge Martinez-Vazquez et al., 1997).

[5] Among the motives deserving more consideration are preferences for neighbors (e.g., racial discrimination or ethnic capital) and the role of employment (including commuting costs). Patrick Bayer (2000) improves upon the empirical literature by allowing residential choice to depend upon employment location and community racial composition.

sion of racial, religious, and ethnic groups. No other paper has explored segregation trends over such a long time period using such a wide variety of variables. Our analysis complements David Cutler et al. (1999), who study the segregation patterns of blacks in urban areas between 1890 and 1990. Our results are also consistent with and extend Michael Kremer (1997), who finds little change in across-tract heterogeneity in education over the 1960–1990 period. Second, our paper contributes to the growing literature on the efficiency implications of heterogeneity (e.g., Roland Benabou, 1996). Alesina and Eliana La Ferrara (2000) show that within-community heterogeneity empirically reduces participation in various social groups while Alesina et. al. (1999) find ethnic diversity decreases local provision of core public services like education. Claudia Goldin and Lawrence Katz (1999) find that variation in high school graduation rates across U.S. states at the beginning of the twentieth century was tied to the degree of religious heterogeneity. Our work provides new evidence on historical trends in several measures of community heterogeneity.

This paper is organized as follows. The next section extends the Tiebout model to include mobility costs and derives the theoretical prediction that the remainder of the paper tests: as mobility costs fall, heterogeneity across communities increases. Section II documents the long-run decline in selected measures of moving costs and Section III presents the empirical approach. Section IV investigates historical variation across municipalities in local policies and in population characteristics that proxy for public good preferences. Section V extends the analysis to the county level. The final section discusses implications of our analysis. A Data Appendix listing the sources used in our analysis is available at the authors' Web sites.

I. Adding Mobility Costs to the Tiebout Model

This section develops a model in which communities provide public goods and individuals, who belong to types characterized by their preferences for public goods, choose communities

subject to mobility costs.[6] As in the original Tiebout model, there is no property or employment, and communities cannot exclude individuals. We make no assumption about the initial distribution of types across communities.

Setup.—Consider a population of N individuals, indexed by i, distributed across C communities. Letting c_i be the community containing agent i, call $\mathbf{A} = (c_1, c_2, ..., c_i, ..., c_N)$ the *allocation* of the N individuals over the C communities. Each community c provides public goods, $\mathbf{G_c} \in \Gamma$ where Γ is a compact set. $\mathbf{G_c}$ can be a vector of local policies, each of which may be real valued (such as taxes and spending) or unordered and categorical (such as school curriculum contents).[7] Denote the set of community public goods as $\mathcal{G} = (\mathbf{G_1}, \mathbf{G_2}, ..., \mathbf{G_C})$.

We will assume that agents only care about $\mathbf{G_c}$ in their community.[8] Further assume that each agent belongs to a fixed type t characterized by the continuous utility function, $U_t(\mathbf{G_c})$. Let $\mathbf{G_t}$ be the unique ideal array $\mathbf{G_c} \in \Gamma$ for type t, and presume there are T types where $T \leq N$. In some of the results derived below, we will consider special assumptions with a scalar public good. In order of increasing restrictiveness they are:

ASSUMPTION 1: *Single-peaked preferences: $G_c \in \mathbb{R}$ and $U_t(G_c)$ is a twice-differentiable concave function in G_c, where $U_t''(G_c) < 0$,*

---

[6] Mobility costs have been added to other locational choice models. Some examples are William Carrington et al. (1996), David Wildasin and John Wilson (1996), Zvi Hercowitz and David Pines (1997), and John Kennan and James Walker (2000). These papers contain specific assumptions (such as treating government policy as fixed or presuming agents are identical) which preclude using them to generalize the Tiebout model.

[7] We implicitly have a bound on returns to scale in provision of government services. This is necessary to preclude formation of very large and heterogeneous communities, which is also an issue in the original Tiebout model (see Truman Bewley, 1981, for examples).

[8] That is, individuals only care about public good provision and not the characteristics of their neighbors. In principle, richer neighbors are more desirable because they contribute a greater tax share to the community budget constraint. The model implicitly rules out such income heterogeneity or presumes that only head taxes are possible.

1652   THE AMERICAN ECONOMIC REVIEW   DECEMBER 2003

$U'_t(G_c) > 0$ for $G_c < G_t$, $U'_t(G_c) < 0$ for $G_c > G_t$, and $U'_t(G_t) = 0$.[9]

ASSUMPTION 2: *Quadratic preferences:* $G_c \in \mathbb{R}$ and $U_{tc} = -(G_t - G_c)^2$.

Social Welfare.—Define the aggregate measure of social welfare for any allocation **A** and set of community public goods G as the sum of all agents' utility:

$$(1) \qquad W = \Sigma_c \Sigma_i U_{t_i}(\mathbf{G}_c).$$

The functional form of (1) is not essential and we discuss generalizations below.

Community Decisions.—Suppose that each community c chooses its policy $\mathbf{G}_c^*$ to maximize the sum of utilities of its current residents:

$$(2) \qquad \mathbf{G}_c^* = \underset{G_c \in \Gamma}{\text{argmax}} \ \Sigma_j U_{t_j}(\mathbf{G}_c).$$

Given our assumptions, $\mathbf{G}_c^*$ exists. Note that some of the communities, z, may be empty, implying $\mathbf{G}_z^* \in \varnothing$. The functional form of (2) is not essential for our analysis; what is important is that (2) has a parallel structure to (1).[10]

Individual Location Decisions and the Equilibrium Concept.—Assume that the agents can move in some sequential order, i.e., one individual at a time. This ordering may be deterministic or stochastic, as long as each agent's expected order in the sequence is finite. Refer to each agent's turn to move as her *location decision event*. When her decision event occurs, agent i can change communities at the cost of

m_i units of utility. This "mobility cost" may be individual specific.[11]

Assume that the mobility decisions are myopic. That is, each agent i takes the prevailing policies, G, as given (thereby ignoring how her move affects the communities' decisions or causes other individuals to move) and only considers migrating to the community currently yielding the highest utility for her type. In the migration decisions, assume each agent treats any empty community as setting policies equal to her ideal.

Definition of a myopic move: Under the *myopic movement rule,* agent i of type t_i moves from community d to community c at her location decision event if and only if:

$$(3) \qquad \mathbf{G}_c^* = \underset{G_e^* \in \mathcal{G}}{\text{argmax}} \ U_{t_i}(\mathbf{G}_e^*)$$

where e is a generic community; and

$$(4) \qquad U_{t_i}(\mathbf{G}_c^*) > U_{t_i}(\mathbf{G}_d^*) + m_i.$$

In equilibrium, no individual will move when her decision events occur.

Definition of an equilibrium: An *equilibrium* is an allocation **A** of individuals across communities such that no agent would choose to move at her location decision event given her mobility costs, m_i.

Results.—Tiebout's famous claim is that if mobility costs are zero and the number of communities C is at least as large as the number of types T, then individuals of each type will sort themselves into homogeneous communities providing their ideal public good bundle. It is easy to show the following proposition, which captures the Tiebout Hypothesis.

PROPOSITION 1: *If $C \geq T$ and policies are set via (2), then W is maximized when each community contains only one type.*

---

[9] Single-peaked preferences can be understood as an individual maximizing a utility function containing a public good and a private good subject to a budget constraint including a tax for the public good. See Thomas Romer and Howard Rosenthal (1977).

[10] (2) is used as a leading case. It is equivalent to majority rule with side payments in a world with transferable utility. See James Buchanan and Gordon Tullock (1962, pp. 190–92) for a rationalization of side payments and intuition about why they induce efficiency.

[11] We assume that mobility costs for individual i are constant across communities. The results below will not change if these costs vary with some measure of "distance."

Proposition 1 makes it clear that population heterogeneity within communities reduces welfare in the Tiebout model. This point can be further illustrated by the following example. Consider a model with quadratic preferences, Assumption 2. To maximize resident welfare via (2), a community c (with N_{tc} residents of type t, making a total of $N_c = \Sigma_t N_{tc}$) should set $G_c^* = \Sigma_t(N_{tc}/N_c)G_t$, the population-weighted mean of the ideal policies. Welfare per capita in community c, W_c/N_c, will then equal the negative of the population-weighted variance of the ideal policies:

$$(5) \quad W_c/N_c = -\Sigma_t(N_{tc}/N_c)(G_t - G_c^*)^2$$

$$= -\Sigma_t(N_{tc}/N_c)G_t^2 + (\Sigma_t(N_{tc}/N_c)G_t)^2.$$

Per capita welfare in community c would be maximized if its population were homogeneous. In this example, the degree of within-community heterogeneity can naturally be measured by the population-weighted variance. In the general case, appropriately measuring the degree of heterogeneity is more difficult. The important point is that in the Tiebout model *social welfare is positively related to increased sorting* (that is, lower within-community heterogeneity and higher across-community heterogeneity).[12]

By assuming that preferences satisfy the single-peaked condition Assumption 1 and that public good provisions are set via (2), we can show that sorting is a self-reinforcing "increasing returns" process. The movement of an individual of type s increases the attractiveness of the receiving community—and reduces the attractiveness of the sending community—for all type s agents. It has the opposite effects for some other types. (This is formally developed in the Appendix.) Even if other agents' mobility costs are fixed, the movement of a single agent can

have cascading effects, inducing the movement of others. In general, the dynamics can be quite complicated. The outcome depends upon the distribution of agents (their types and individual mobility costs) across communities and upon the specification of the sequential moving order (which may be stochastic). This complexity motivates the myopic moving rule, which supposes an agent does not try to solve through the general equilibrium implications of her move on the subsequent public good provisions or the movements of others.[13] An additional motivation is that in a large population, a single individual has a negligible direct effect on the provision of public goods.

Proposition 2 shows that any myopic move has a positive effect on social welfare and, as a consequence, any reduction in mobility costs has a nonnegative effect on social welfare. Notice that no special restrictions on individual preferences are needed for this result.

PROPOSITION 2: *When individual moves obey (3) and (4) and policies are set via (2),*

(a) *Any individual move strictly increases W (and does so by more than the mover's costs, m_i).*

(b) *If m_i falls, then individual i either stays or moves and if she moves, then W increases. The moving process yields a new equilibrium with a higher W.*

PROOF:

(a) Suppose that individual i moves from community d to c. The utility of three groups of agents will be affected. First, the net effect among residents of community d except i (k/i) is,

$$(6) \quad \Sigma_{k/i}[U_{t_k}(\mathbf{G}_{d/i}^*) - U_{t_k}(\mathbf{G}_d^*)] \geq 0$$

where the inequality follows from the definition of argmax in (2). The intuition is that a community cannot be made worse off by adjusting $\mathbf{G}$ to maximize the welfare of its

---

[12] In the above example, total welfare is $W = -\Sigma_t N_t(G_t - \chi)^2 + \Sigma_c N_c(G_c^* - \chi)^2$ where $\chi \equiv (\Sigma_t N_t G_t)/N$ is the aggregate population-weighted mean type/equilibrium policy. The first term is constant for all allocations of a given population and the second term measures across-community heterogeneity of types (the variance of the community mean types). A move from any allocation to perfect sorting increases W and, by the above expression, increases across-community heterogeneity.

[13] For a sense of the complexity of this process, see Ken Kollman et al. (1997).

1654   THE AMERICAN ECONOMIC REVIEW   DECEMBER 2003

current residents. The remaining residents of d (excluding i) are, by definition, at least as well off in aggregate under $\mathbf{G}_{d/i}^*$ as under $\mathbf{G}_d^*$. We call this the argmax argument.

Second, the net effect among the initial residents of community c (j/i) is,

(7) $\quad \Sigma_{j/i}[U_{t_j}(\mathbf{G}_{c+i}^*) - U_{t_j}(\mathbf{G}_c^*)] \leq 0$

where the inequality follows from the definition of argmax in (2). Finally, the effect on agent i has two components. From her myopic comparison of d and c,

(8) $\quad U_{t_i}(\mathbf{G}_c^*) - U_{t_i}(\mathbf{G}_d^*) - m_i > 0$

where the inequality follows from (3) and (4). The other component considers how her move will change G in c,

(9) $\quad U_{t_i}(\mathbf{G}_{c+i}^*) - U_{t_i}(\mathbf{G}_c^*)$.

But (7) + (9) equal,

(10) $\quad \Sigma_{j/i}[U_{t_j}(\mathbf{G}_{c+i}^*) - U_{t_j}(\mathbf{G}_c^*)]$

$\quad\quad + U_{t_i}(\mathbf{G}_{c+i}^*) - U_{t_i}(\mathbf{G}_c^*)$

$\quad\quad = \Sigma_j[U_{t_j}(\mathbf{G}_{c+i}^*) - U_{t_j}(\mathbf{G}_c^*)] \geq 0$

by definition of the argmax in (2). The intuition for (10) follows the argmax argument. In aggregate, the residents of c (including i) are at least as well off under $\mathbf{G}_{c+i}^*$ as under $\mathbf{G}_c^*$. The change in $\mathbf{G}_c$ may harm its initial residents, but the gain to i must more than offsets their losses; otherwise, $\mathbf{G}_{c+i}^*$ would not be selected by a community setting policies according to (2).

Thus the total effect (6) + (7) + (8) + (9) is positive. This implies that welfare net of moving costs, $W - m_i$, increases, and therefore, W increases.

(b) If agent i moves, this may induce others to migrate. By part (a), no matter how many moves occur, W increases. This process must end in a finite number of moves (that is, there exists an equilibrium) because

there are a finite number of possible allocations and each agent's expected order in the location decision sequence is finite. No allocation can reoccur because W is strictly increasing with each move. □

Three comments are in order:

(i) Proposition 2 also holds in a world of Leviathan governments where G is fixed. Here, (6), (7), and (9) are each zero, but (8) is positive by (3) and (4).

(ii) More generally, the basic results hold if the social welfare function (1) weakly reflects individual preferences (as in $W = F(U_1, U_2, \dots, U_N)$ with $F_i' \geq 0$), and in (2) each community maximizes its residents' welfare (as measured by this W).

(iii) The myopic moving rule, which implies that (8) is positive, plays a key role in Proposition 2. Suppose instead that individuals are forward looking and move if (8) + (9) is positive. If (8) is negative, then in principle (6) + (7) + (8) + (9) could be negative and the proposition does not hold (W may decrease).[14]

A further issue of interest is how a reduction in mobility costs affects the distribution of policy outcomes. Because it is difficult to define variation in multidimensional space, we focus on cases with scalar public goods.

OBSERVATION: *Under Assumption 1 with $C = T = 2$ or under Assumption 2, when local*

---

[14] In general, mobility inherently involves externalities, both positive and negative. Under the myopic movement rule, an individual moves only if the receiving community is *ex ante* preferable. This means that any move that benefits the individual also benefits society on net; that is, the benefits received by the mover and the other residents of the sending community exceed the costs imposed on existing residents of the receiving community. Under the nonmyopic rule, an individual may find moving beneficial simply because it makes the receiving community closer to her own tastes (*ex post*). This can impose costs on its existing residents that are greater than the benefits that mover and the other members of the sending community enjoy. Note that under either the myopic or nonmyopic rules, there may be socially beneficial moves that are not made when the private benefits fall short of the mobility costs.

policies are set via (2) then individual moves which obey (3) and (4) lead to increased variation of policy outcomes across communities.

A formal demonstration of the result is contained in the Appendix.[15] Consider first the case of single-peaked preferences, Assumption 1, when $C = T = 2$ holds. In this case, a community's policy will be the weighted average of the two types' ideal policies where the weight on a type's preference depends positively on its population share. Any myopic move will widen the difference in policies between the two communities by pushing the policy in the receiving (sending) community toward (away from) the mover's ideal G. Now consider the second case which assumes quadratic preferences, Assumption 2. Under (2) and Assumption 2, the policy in a given community is the mean of residents' ideal G's and the aggregate population-weighted mean policy is independent of the distribution of types across communities. Any move obeying (3) and (4) will widen the difference in policies between the sending and receiving communities, increasing the total population-weighted variance of policies.

To summarize, the theoretical model developed in this section extends the Tiebout framework to include mobility costs. Our results, while somewhat novel, are clearly in the spirit of Tiebout's argument. Mobility costs may prevent individuals from sorting into homogeneous communities of their own type—the allocation that maximizes social welfare. A reduction in mobility costs has a nonnegative effect on social welfare. This implies falling mobility costs increase heterogeneity across communities. We also find that sorting increases the variation of local policy outcomes under several variants of the model.[16]

---

[15] The observation also holds for generic preferences when the population is initially completely diffuse, implying policies are identical across communities. Moving to any level of greater sorting, the variation of policies across communities will be weakly greater, and in the fully sorted equilibrium, the variation will be strictly greater.

[16] Note that these results depend on the Tiebout assumption that residential choice is based only on public good provision. If individual resident decisions weigh factors (employment, proximity to family, amenities) not perfectly correlated with preferences over G_c, then reduced mobility

The remainder of the paper tests these predictions empirically.

II. Documenting Declining Mobility Costs

The conventional wisdom holds that mobility costs have fallen over time.[17] Yet constructing a comprehensive measure to document this "truism" is difficult. Anyone who has relocated knows that out-of-pocket expenditures represent only a fraction of the costs of moving. As human capital theory suggests, these costs include the lost work time—organizing before departure, traveling, and getting back up to speed at the destination. Given that real wages have generally risen, the value of this lost time would be increasing. However, several opposing forces more than offset this effect. Improvements in transportation and the increased similarity of regional cultures mean less time is now lost in the move. During the colonial period, the rigors of the transatlantic travel and the effects of exposure to a new disease environment were purportedly so severe that newly imported slaves and indentured servants required six months to two years to achieve positive levels of net output (David Galenson, 1996). Few migrants suffer such a loss today. The available evidence suggests that over the past one-and-one-half centuries, the reduction in direct travel time has more than offset the increase in the value of labor.[18] In addition, as is

---

costs need not induce greater Tiebout sorting. Indeed, given the policy rule (2), migration for non-Tiebout reasons may reduce the variation of G and dampen Tiebout incentives to migrate.

[17] To perform our comparative static exercise, an exogenous reduction in mobility costs is needed. While much of the transportation infrastructure (such as highways and airports) involves endogenously determined public goods, the reduction in transportation and communications costs was in large part a product of technological improvements (in steam and internal combustion engines, communications equipment, and production techniques).

[18] Between 1857 and 1999, the time required to travel between New York and Chicago has fallen from 2 days to less than 2 hours 40 minutes, or by a factor of 18; that for a trip between New York and Los Angeles has fallen from about 3.5 weeks to less than 8 hours, a factor of 75. The time for short-distance trips has also sharply decreased: the average automobile speed in 1970 is

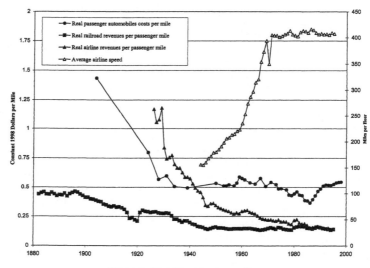

FIGURE 1. REAL TRANSPORTATION COSTS

argued below, communication improvements have reduced one of the key costs of moving, the lost contacts with one's friends and family in the home community.

There is clear evidence that physical moving costs have fallen over the last century. (In the interest of brevity, all sources are contained in the online Data Appendix.) The most obvious change is the spread of the personal automobile. In 1900, there was roughly one passenger car for every 10,000 Americans; today, the ratio is nearly one car for every two. This change was due in part to sharp reductions in the costs of owning and operating automobiles. The careful calculations of Hiram P. Maxim (1904), a leading engineer, showed driving costs in 1903 equaled 143.8 cents per mile in 1998 dollars. The American Automobile Association estimates that the full cost of driving the more reliable, comfortable cars of today averages 54.9 cents per mile. As the fragmentary data on automobile costs per mile (excluding finance charges) presented in Figure

1 indicate, most of this decline occurred before the Second World War. Also facilitating the spread of the personal car were massive investments in the nation's system of public roads, nearly doubling its mileage from 2.3 million in 1900 to almost 4 million today.[19] An important consequence of the spread of the automobile was to weaken the link between work and residence locations, potentially allowing greater Tiebout sorting.

Improvements in trains and airplanes have also significantly lowered mobility costs. As the series in Figure 1 reveal, the real cost of railroad service was about one-third as expensive in 1995 (13.4 cents per passenger mile) as it was in 1895 (37.4 cents). The real cost of air travel also fell sharply, with average airline revenues per passenger-mile dropping from about 108 cents in 1929 to 13.7 cents by 1995 (rough parity with

roughly 12 times the stage speed in 1840. Average real labor returns have increased between five- and sevenfold over the 1860–2000 period.

[19] This growth in mileage understates the true improvement in transportation access because most early roads were little more than dirt pathways. In 1904, for example, "surfaced" roads made up less than 7 percent of total mileage. The first coast-to-coast auto trip across North America, completed in 1903, purportedly took 65 days (http://www.nam.org/AboutMfg/timeline1901.html).

railroads). In addition, the speed of air travel nearly tripled since the early 1940's.

We also know that the real cost of moving household goods has fallen substantially. Circa 1995, the real rate per ton-mile for a private COD shipment by a household goods carrier averaged 57.8 cents, which is far less than the 88.1 cents charged a decade before. Tariff schedules filed with the Interstate Commerce Commission indicate that the real rate per ton-mile for a "modern" shipment was approximately 147 cents in 1936, implying costs have fallen by over 60 percent between 1936 and 1995.[20] The costs of local moves have declined as well. For example, when L. S. and Anna Shoen established the U-Haul Co. in 1945 at Ridgeway, WA, they charged $2 per day for a small trailer. Today renting such a trailer at I-5 Auto Sales near Ridgeway (or at many of the firm's other 15,000 retail locations) would cost $9.95 or about 40 percent less in real terms.

Long-run movements in communication costs reveal similar trends. This is important for several reasons. Lower communication costs improve information flows about other regions, reducing uncertainty. In addition, they allow migrants to maintain contacts with friends and family "back home." Finally, easier communication encourages more dispersed production activity, implying people are less tied to a particular community for employment reasons. Figure 2 shows the real costs of making three-minute daytime telephone calls from New York to Chicago and San Francisco have fallen almost continuously. To place a three-minute transcontinental call in January 1915 (when service first became available) cost $20.70 in current dollars, which was almost $314 in 1998 dollars. The real cost of such a call in 1995, even at ATT residential daytime rates, was less than *three-tenths of one percent* as high.[21]

These falling mobility costs have apparently set more Americans on the move. In 1940, about 11 percent of the American population (five years and older) had lived in a different county five years earlier. This fraction increased to 17 percent in 1970 and to 19 percent by 1990. Another useful measure of long-run mobility rates is the percentage of the native population residing in their state-of-birth. In 1870, almost 77 percent of the native population resided in their state-of-birth. Since 1900, the fraction has continuously fallen, with the most rapid rate of decline occurring during the 1940–1970 period. By 1990, only about two-thirds of the native population resided in their state-of-birth. Today's migration rates appear sufficiently high to allow the American population to achieve significant sorting across local jurisdictions according to policy preferences, if they so desired.[22]

III. Empirical Implementation

Given the secular decline of mobility costs, a natural test of the predictions of the generalized Tiebout model is to examine historical trends in the dispersion of local fiscal outcomes and in the sorting of population types across localities. While it is not clear how to define Tiebout's canonical community, the most natural definition is the municipality or the Census minor civil division (MCD). Unfortunately, electronic versions of comprehensive MCD-level data are not available before 1970. Instead we created a random 10-percent sample of counties and entered data for all MCDs in these counties for the earlier years.[23] We investigate heterogeneity

---

[20] It appears that the average weight of shipments has also risen. climbing from somewhat under two tons in the early period to three tons today, but this proportional increase is less than the fall in rates and is of course endogenous with respect to the price decrease. Over the 1994–1996 period, the average billed shipment weighed just under three tons (5,919 pounds) and traveled 1,261 miles.

[21] The reduction in postal rates, especially across country, was also notable. In 1860, during the Pony Express

period, it cost $10 to send a one-ounce letter between New York and San Francisco. By 1886, the cost fell to two cents in the currency of the day.

[22] Consider a population composed of two equally sized groups that are initially evenly distributed across two regions. If 4 percent of the population moved every year in accordance with Tiebout "voting with their feet" thinking, the regions would be completely segregated within 12.5 years.

[23] We cannot directly sample from the population of MCDs since there is no historically consistent listing of all municipalities. We entered information for years prior to 1970 where the Census tabulated MCD-level data. The years with coverage of all MCDs are: 1870 (demographics

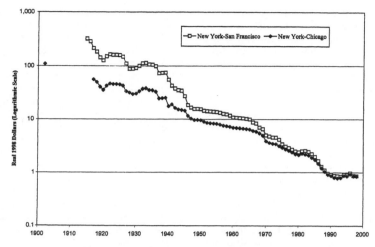

FIGURE 2. REAL COST OF A THREE-MINUTE PHONE CALL

trends across this MCD sample. Because some argue that Tiebout sorting only applies over limited geographic areas, we next extend the analysis to the full set of municipalities in the Boston metropolitan area.[24] Finally, we present additional results using the full set of U.S. counties. One potential complication is the growing number of municipalities and counties. This is mainly due to territorial division, which will lead to increases in our across-community heterogeneity measures even in the absence of individual movement (see Rhode and Strumpf, 2000, for details).[25]

The analysis investigates trends in across-community heterogeneity of policy variables and proxies for public good preferences. (De-

tails on the availability, precise definition, and sources for all variables are presented in the online Data Appendix.) Our local policy variables are per capita taxes and expenditures.[26] Taxes are a measure of the overall level of government activity; we consider both overall and school taxes. We also examine spending on education and protection (police and fire), the most prominent local services. For these policy variables, two heterogeneity measures are calculated, both of which increase with dispersion across governments and control for changes in mean levels. The first measure is the population-weighted coefficient of variation (CV), which is the ratio of the standard deviation to the mean,

$$(11) \qquad CV \equiv G^{-1}(\Sigma_j P_j (G_j - G)^2)^{0.5}$$

where G_j is per capita taxes/revenues/spending for government j, G is mean per capita taxes/revenues/spending for all governments,

---

only); 1880, 1890 (government finances only); 1930, 1940, and 1960 (demographics only). We have data for all years but 1940.

[24] We also explore more broadly whether sorting occurs over small geographic areas in the entire United States. Our analysis indicates that heterogeneity across adjacent communities has tended to remain flat over time. (The results are based on county-level data and are available upon request.)

[25] Because this is the direction of change that the Tiebout model predicts, finding empirical evidence of reduced sorting would be strong evidence against the model.

[26] Richard Ely (1888) contains a detailed discussion of the development and historical comparability of our taxation measures.

and P_j is the share of total population in government j. The second measure (DG) calculates the proportion of total taxes/revenues/spending in each year which would have to be reallocated across governments to yield a uniform per capita distribution (this is related to the dissimilarity index which is discussed below),

(12) $$DG \equiv \tfrac{1}{2} G^{-1} \Sigma_j P_j |G_j - G|.$$

Because preferences are not directly observable, we adopt the strategy of examining numerous characteristics that proxy for individual types.[27] For each characteristic, we partition the population into mutually exclusive and exhaustive categories. Our proxies are admittedly imperfect measures of the true types. But as an earlier version of the paper (Rhode and Strumpf, 2000) shows, even if the observable characteristics are noisy signals or available categories are too coarse, our measures of population heterogeneity remain informative.[28] This version also shows that the proxies retain their salience over time (in year-by-year regressions using the proxies to explain variation in local policy or election outcomes, the R-squared's do not trend down) and that the trends in heterogeneity across communities are not exclusively the result of the shift from a rural to urban society.

We consider the following proxies when available:

- *Race:* It is often observed that members of racial groups share economic interests and maintain strong common political affiliations. For example, the General Social Survey (GSS) reports 39.3 percent of blacks ($N = 1,864$) identify themselves as "Strong Democrats" while only 12.5 percent of whites ($N = 3,675$) do so.[29] There are also notable racial differences in the GSS over political ideology and attitudes towards government redistribution. We use the black population share to proxy for these beliefs.

- *Age categories:* The young population share (those between 5 and 20 years old) proxies for families with children; such households presumably prefer higher spending on local schools. The old population share (those at least 65 years old) is used, since the elderly should be less likely to favor education spending.[30] These variables should reflect life-cycle sorting.

- *Nativity:* The foreign-born represents another distinctive population with important ramifications for local politics (e.g., school curricula). Note that interpreting trends for the foreign-born share is complicated because immigrants may sort across communities for non-Tiebout motives, for example, to take advantage of social networks or ports of entry.

- *Party vote shares in presidential elections:* Individuals presumably vote for the party whose platform is closest to their own ideal policy, implying those voting for a particular party have similar preferences.[31]

---

[27] An ideal test of our model would involve construction of multidimensional measures of individual types (i.e., using the characteristics discussed below as inputs in a hedonic model of type). However, this would require detailed, individual-specific information about *all* persons living in a given local jurisdiction. Such data simply do not exist for the modern era.

[28] There is also evidence that several of our type measures are transmitted from parents to children. Thomas Piketty (1995) cites the extensive literature showing that political preferences have an important hereditary component even after controlling for income and social class. Frank Newport (1979) finds that in the mid-1970's over two-thirds of individuals maintain their childhood religion. Kremer (1997) shows there is a high rate of transmission of parental education to their children using the PSID (he also surveys work documenting the intergenerational transmission of many other characteristics considered here).

[29] The General Social Survey (1999) is a micro data set of individual attitudes collected over the 1972–1996 period.

[30] There is also some support from the GSS that age groups have distinct political beliefs. For example, while 5.8 percent of those aged 18–20 ($N = 1,181$) consider themselves "Strong Republicans," 16.8 percent of those aged 75 or older ($N = 2,311$) do. The GSS also indicates that similar age differences exist for the appropriate level of education spending.

[31] If all individuals in a community vote for the same party, the community is composed of like-minded residents and is sorted in the Tiebout fashion. If the residents split their votes, the community has not been sorted. It is important to notice that this measure only makes sense for elections over national office. This is because party platforms are strategically set with the objective typically being vote maximization. Even relatively homogeneous areas may split

- *Religion:* Individuals affiliated with a particular religion share their faith's set of beliefs, values, and cultural traditions and are, therefore, likely to have relatively similar policy preferences.[32] In the GSS, 26.5 percent of self-identified religious fundamentalists ($N = 162$) and 23.1 percent of evangelicals ($N = 208$) consider themselves to be "Strong Republicans" while only 4.5 percent of religious liberals ($N = 265$) do so. One of the advantages of using religious affiliation is that it allows a fine partition of the population: we can employ up to 27 denominational families.
- *Homeownership rates:* Homeowners are typically wealthier and have greater civic involvement in the community.[33]
- *Education:* Educational attainment is likely to be related to income, wealth, and attitudes toward government.[34] We use three groups: less than a high school degree, at least a high school degree but not a college degree, and a college degree or more.
- *Income:* This is the most natural measure of type. Unfortunately, the Census did not begin reporting data on local income *distribution* until 1949. Categorical information is available for both families and households (which include unattached individuals). The Census lists 14 income groups in 1949, 15 income groups in 1969, 17 income groups in 1979, and 25 groups in 1989.

To ensure robustness we employ several heterogeneity measures for our proxies. For variables with discrete types, the dissimilarity index and the Gini coefficient are used.[35] These measures, which are commonly used in the segregation literature, have three important properties. First, they vary between zero (when each type is equally represented in each community) and one (when the types are completely segregated). Thus a higher value indicates greater heterogeneity across communities. Second, they are normalized to control for the changing proportions of types in the aggregate population, implying they are unaffected if the groups grow at different rates nationally.[36] Third, the measures weight the communities by their population. In multiple (≥ 2) type comparisons, the dissimilarity index, D, and the Gini coefficient, GC, are defined as:

$$(13) \quad D \equiv \tfrac{1}{2}\Sigma_t\Sigma_j N_j |P_{tj} - P_t|/(N\Sigma_t P_t(1 - P_t))$$

$$(14) \quad GC \equiv \tfrac{1}{2}\Sigma_t\Sigma_k\Sigma_j N_k N_j |P_{tk} - P_{tj}|$$
$$\div (N^2\Sigma_t P_t(1 - P_t))$$

---

their vote on local offices because the local party platforms are likely to be quite similar. For national offices, however, parties are likely to set their platforms in a way to split the *national* vote. Individuals in a relatively homogeneous area are likely to have similar preferences over national parties, and so they will cast their votes for only one party.

[32] Based on the 1990 National Election Study, David Leege and Lyman Kellstedt (1993) show that affiliation with many of the denominational families used in our analysis are strong predictors of individual voting behavior and ideological preference. Laurence Iannaccone (1998) suggests that the link between religion and politics is largely limited to moral and social issues such as school prayer and abortion. However, he only focuses on evangelical-fundamentalist Protestants. Mark Noll (1990) also documents the historical link between religion and politics using largely nonquantitative analysis.

[33] See Robert Carroll and John Yinger (1994) and Denise DiPasquale and Edward Glaeser (1999).

[34] In the GSS, of those with less than a high school education ($N = 9,391$) 15.2 percent earn $25,000 or more and 25.4 percent think welfare benefits are too low. For those with only a high school degree ($N = 20,368$), the values are 40.5 percent and 17.6 percent; for those with a college degree or more ($N = 7,632$), the values are 63.2 percent and 16.7 percent.

[35] See Otis D. Duncan and Beverly Duncan (1955), Douglas Massey and Nancy Denton (1988), and Sean Reardon (1998). The dissimilarity index is the most widely used segregation measure. It shows the proportion of individuals who would have to change communities to create an evenly distributed population, expressed as a ratio of the number who would have to move if the types were completely segregated. The Gini coefficient generalizes the dissimilarity index. The main difference is that the Gini is sensitive to any change in the population distribution whereas the dissimilarity index is affected only by shifts in types between "surplus" and "deficit" communities.

[36] More formally, suppose that each group reproduces at a different rate and that the offspring live in the same community as the parents. If there are two groups, then both indices are invariant to the group growth rates (proof available upon request).

where N_j is the total population in community j, N is the total population, P_{tj} is the share of type t in the community j's population, and P_t is the share of type t in the total population.

We also employ entropy indices, which are additively separable and can be used to perform within- and between-region decompositions. Formally, let P_j be the share of the total population living in j. The community-level entropy index is,

$$(15) \qquad E \equiv 1 - \Sigma_j P_j H_j H^{-1}$$

where $H_j \equiv -\Sigma_t P_{tj} \log(P_{tj})$, $H \equiv -\Sigma_t P_t \log(P_t)$. If a type t is absent from community j, then by convention, $P_{tj} \log(P_{tj}) = 0$. The between- and within-region decomposition is,

$$(16)$$

$$E \equiv E_{Between} + E_{Within}$$

$$= (1 - \Sigma_R P_R H_R H^{-1})$$

$$+ \Sigma_R P_R H_R H^{-1}(1 - \Sigma_{j \in R} P_{jR} H_j H_R^{-1})$$

where R is the region; P_R is the share of the total population living in R; P_{jR} is the share of the region R's population living in j; P_{tR} is the share of type t in region R's population; and $H_R \equiv -\Sigma_t P_{tR} \log(P_{tR})$.

The heterogeneity measures for income are richer because the data is in ordered categories. The aggregate income distribution can be decomposed into within- and between-community components using the two additively-separable Theil measures,

$$(17) \qquad I_1 \equiv \mu^{-1} \Sigma_j P_j \Sigma_s P_{sj} \mu_{sj} \log(\mu_{sj}/\mu_j)$$

$$+ \mu^{-1} \Sigma_j P_j \mu_j \log(\mu_j/\mu)$$

$$(18)$$

$$I_2 \equiv \Sigma_j P_j \Sigma_s P_{sj} \log(\mu_j/\mu_{sj}) + \Sigma_j P_j \log(\mu/\mu_j)$$

where μ_j is the mean income, P_{sj} is now the proportion of individuals in income group s, μ_{sj} is the mean income of group s, all for community j, and μ is the aggregate mean income (Anthony F. Shorrocks, 1980). In the formulae, the first term

is the within-component and the second term is the between-component. To investigate within-community heterogeneity further, we also consider the Gini income coefficient and the CV. Because the available data is grouped in income ranges, both lower- and upper-bound Gini's are computed for each community j,

$$(19) \qquad GL_j \equiv (2\mu_j)^{-1} \Sigma_s \Sigma_t P_{sj} P_{tj} |\mu_{sj} - \mu_{tj}|$$

$$(20) \qquad GU_j \equiv GL_j + (\mu_j)^{-1} \Sigma_s P_{sj}^2(\mu_{sj} - a_{s-1})$$

$$\times (a_s - \mu_{sj})(a_s - a_{s-1})^{-1}$$

where a_s is the upper-income boundary for income group s (see Joseph Gastwirth, 1972).

IV. Trends in Heterogeneity Across Municipalities

A. National Sample of Municipalities

We first consider local policy outcomes for our national sample of municipalities (MCDs) and calculate our two heterogeneity measures, the coefficient of variation (CV) and the reallocation index (DG). Panel (a) of Table 1 presents heterogeneity trends for per capita taxes across municipalities over the 1880–1992 period. Dispersion between MCDs markedly *decreased* over the sample. The values in 1992 are roughly half of their 1880 values. Panel (b) shows the long-run reduction in dispersion of school district taxes is even more dramatic. While there has been a mild divergence in school district taxes between 1972 and 1992, the current dispersion levels are well below those prevailing a century ago. The remaining panels (c)–(e) have current operations spending data for the modern period, 1972–1992. There are small reductions in across-MCD heterogeneity for overall spending per capita. Dispersion also falls for the two most prominent local expenditure categories—protection (police plus fire) spending per capita, and school district education spending per pupil.[37]

---

[37] Given that samples are used, it is best not to read too much into these small reductions in the contemporary data. Still, the results suggest there is no trend towards greater spending heterogeneity.

TABLE 1—DISPERSION OF LOCAL POLICIES: ACROSS-MCD/SCHOOL DISTRICT AND ACROSS-COUNTY INDICES

| | (a) Municipal Per Capita Taxes | | | | | |
| | MCD (municipal)-level | | | Aggregated to county-level | | |
Year	N	CV	DG	N	CV	DG
1880	634	1.738	0.537	239	1.353	0.412
1890	968	1.321	0.349	268	0.793	0.307
1972	3,175	1.100	0.347	304	0.762	0.259
1982	3,196	0.864	0.311	305	0.703	0.224
1992	3,251	0.844	0.295	305	0.622	0.207

| | (b) School District Per Capita Taxes | | | | | |
| | School district-level | | | Aggregated to county-level | | |
Year	N	CV	DG	N	CV	DG
1880	634	2.093	0.796	239	0.759	0.313
1890	968	0.974	0.289	268	0.730	0.275
1972	1,352	0.573	0.216	275	0.504	0.202
1982	1,193	0.675	0.246	276	0.568	0.207
1992	1,221	0.696	0.264	276	0.571	0.218

| | (c) Total Spending (Current Operations) Per Capita | | | | | |
| | MCD (municipal)-level | | | Aggregated to county-level | | |
Year	N	CV	DG	N	CV	DG
1972	3,171	1.003	0.357	304	0.654	0.244
1982	3,177	0.847	0.304	305	0.503	0.192
1992	3,271	0.778	0.285	305	0.463	0.184

| | (d) Protection Spending (Current Operations) Per Capita | | | | | |
| | MCD (municipal)-level | | | Aggregated to county-level | | |
Year	N	CV	DG	N	CV	DG
1972	1,906	0.721	0.261	303	0.512	0.202
1982	2,257	0.603	0.229	305	0.470	0.188
1992	2,336	0.607	0.225	305	0.435	0.179

| | (e) Education Spending (Current Operations) Per Student Enrollment | | | | | |
| | School district-level | | | Aggregated to county-level | | |
Year	N	CV	DG	N	CV	DG
1972	1,346	0.253	0.091	275	0.232	0.085
1982	1,191	0.241	0.090	276	0.237	0.084
1992	1,225	0.217	0.080	276	0.220	0.077

Notes: The coefficient of variation, *CV*, is defined in equation (11) of Section III; the reallocation index, *DG*, is defined in equation (12). These values are based on a 1-in-10 sample of all municipalities, which is further described in the online Data Appendix. County-level taxes/spending are the sum of all municipal taxes/spending plus any county taxes/spending.

We next consider the available preference proxies: race, nativity, and age. To measure the dispersion of these proxies across municipalities we employ the dissimilarity index (*D*). Table 2 shows that heterogeneity across MCDs for each of the three public good proxies is lower in 1990 than in 1930, or where available in 1870. The dissimilarity index for

TABLE 2—DISPERSION OF PREFERENCE PROXIES: ACROSS-MCD AND ACROSS-COUNTY DISSIMILARITY INDICES

Year	Racial composition (black)			Nativity (foreign-born)		
	N	MCD-level	Aggregated to county-level	N	MCD-level	Aggregated to county-level
1870	2,071	0.724	0.697	2,071	0.559	0.511
1930	5,071	0.650	0.615	5,070	0.503	0.491
1960	3,798	0.510	0.477			
1970	3,020	0.528	0.499	3,039	0.476	0.447
1980	3,453	0.564	0.520	3,415	0.470	0.458
1990	3,456	0.572	0.525	3,456	0.482	0.465

Year	Young population			Old population		
	N	MCD-level	Aggregated to county-level	N	MCD-level	Aggregated to county-level
1930	5,071	0.106	0.087	5,071	0.182	0.161
1960	3,798	0.086	0.064	3,798	0.149	0.121
1970	3,275	0.073	0.045	3,275	0.169	0.136
1980	3,415	0.069	0.068	3,415	0.175	0.145
1990	3,456	0.073	0.054	3,456	0.176	0.147

Notes: The dissimilarity index is defined in equation (13) of Section III. The sample size (N) refers to the number of MCDs. Empty cells indicate missing data. These results are based on a 1-in-10 sample. Full details of the data as well as precise definition of the categories are in the online Data Appendix.

racial composition declines by a fifth between 1870 and 1990 while the index for nativity falls by a seventh over the same period. There is also a substantial reduction between 1930 and 1990 in the heterogeneity of the young population while there is a U-shaped pattern for the elderly population. The latter is particularly noteworthy because it runs counter to the tremendous growth of retirement communities in Florida and Arizona. Again the lesson from the preference proxy data is that any small increases in heterogeneity across MCDs over the recent decades should not mislead us; in general, the long-run historical trends indicate convergence.

These results are in conflict with the Tiebout prediction that greater across-community stratification should accompany reductions in mobility costs. The data indicate that as moving became easier municipalities actually become more similar in their residential composition and local policy outcomes. Indeed, the convergence between MCDs was strongest in the early period when the decline in mobility costs appears most rapid. These findings suggest some alternative incentives, working in direct opposition to Tiebout, have been dominating residential location choices.

Such long-run mobility trends have had important effects on community composition. Two pieces of evidence reveal that there is substantial population heterogeneity *within* contemporary municipalities. First, consider the entropy measure of racial heterogeneity across all Census tracts in the United States.[38] Given the entropy index is additively separable, this statistic can be decomposed into within- and between-MCD components. In 1980 the total entropy index of racial composition across all Census tracts is 0.546 ($N = 99,935$), whereas the within-MCD component is 0.253. This means the racial heterogeneity across tracts within a

[38] Census tracts are the smallest geographic unit with complete coverage of the United States in 1980 (the smaller Census block only covered MCDs with population exceeding 10,000). The Census considers tracts to be equivalent to neighborhoods. Full details on the definition and evolution of these units is presented in U.S. Bureau of the Census (1994), *Geographic Areas Reference Manual* (http://www.census.gov), while the data are discussed in the online Data Appendix.

1664 THE AMERICAN ECONOMIC REVIEW DECEMBER 2003

municipality is about equal to the heterogeneity across municipalities.[39] Second, we can decompose the national family income dispersion into Theil within- and between-MCD components. Using all MCDs in 1969 ($N = 34,842$), the total Theil$_1$ index is 0.265 while the within-MCD component is 0.229; in 1979 ($N = 34,809$), the total index is 0.250 while the within-component is 0.222; in 1989 ($N = 35,065$), the total index is 0.288 while the within-component is 0.243. This finding means that income heterogeneity within MCDs is quite high, contributing over four-fifths to the total dispersion. The Tiebout prediction of homogeneous communities appears to be a poor approximation for contemporary municipalities.

B. *Boston Metropolitan Area*

In addition to the national sample, we replicated and extended our analysis using the 92 municipalities in the Boston SMSA (1980 definition). This area provides an attractive test case for several reasons. Boston has been intensely studied and is often put forward as the archetype of the Tiebout model. Municipalities are the only important local government and directly provide all high-profile public services such as education and protection. There is also clear evidence of a secular decline in intra-Boston SMSA transportation costs.[40] The area has been fully incorporated with only minor border changes throughout the study period, so we can compare the same set of communities. Detailed data are available for the Boston area dating back to the late-nineteenth century. It is also possible to perform an event analysis and see whether changes in the policy environment, such as the introduction of property tax

limits in 1980 and of mandatory busing in Boston in 1974, are driving stratification patterns. Finally, as with many other metro areas there has been a dramatic shift of population from the city to the suburbs, with Boston's population share dropping from 40 to 20 percent between 1915 and 1990. This shift will itself lead to greater measured stratification.[41]

Figure 3 shows across-municipality heterogeneity trends for various political and demographic proxies for public good preferences over the 1855–1990 period. For one index, the black population share, there is greater sorting at the end of the period than at the beginning. This trend, which is consistent with Cutler et al.'s (1999) findings for a large number of cities over 1890–1990, fits the standard picture of "white flight" in response to the Great Migration of African-Americans to northern metro areas. But we should be careful not to generalize from this observation into a wholesale acceptance of the Tiebout model. First, as Cutler et al. (1999) note, the trend toward increased concentration reverses after 1970. Second, the rise was entirely due to city-suburb differences: Figure 3 also shows that segregation of blacks within the suburbs has changed little or if anything has declined, over the sample period. Moreover it is not clear that growing racial concentration within an urban area should be attributed to Tiebout sorting but rather could result from racism.[42] Consistent with this view, in 1950 and 1960 over two-thirds of the between-tract racial heterogeneity under the entropy measure is due to within-municipality dispersion (even excluding Boston, the within-municipality heterogeneity contribution is about

---

[39] While this result is partly driven by central cities, when the sample is restricted to MCDs with population less than 50,000 or to those with less than ten tracts the within-MCD component still contributes 20 percent of the total. It is worth noting that these figures likely understate within-MCD heterogeneity since the average MCD has only 3.25 tracts (53 percent of MCDs have only one tract meaning their within-component is calculated as zero).

[40] For example, see the discussion of the development of the Boston mass transit system in George Sanborn, *The Chronicle of the Boston Transit System* (http://www.mbta.com).

[41] All of our measures of heterogeneity across communities will increase under the following thought experiment: suppose the center city has a relatively heterogeneous population and is surrounded by more homogeneous, but distinctive suburbs. Then a representative set of city dwellers move to the suburbs in such a way that no municipality (including the central city) changes its population composition.

[42] Cutler et al. (1999) uses evidence from housing markets to stress the role of racial discrimination. Such a sorting mechanism will upset a Tiebout equilibrium, since attitudes concerning one's neighbor's race are not likely to coincide perfectly with public good preferences.

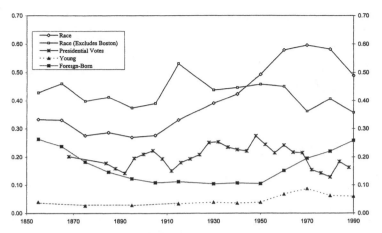

FIGURE 3. DEMOGRAPHIC HETEROGENEITY ACROSS MINOR CIVIL DIVISIONS
IN THE BOSTON SMSA (DISSIMILARITY INDEX)

Notes: Year (sample size): 1855 (79), 1865 (79), 1875 (88), 1885 (90), 1895 (91; 90 for Foreign-Born), 1905 (92), 1915 (92), 1930 (92), 1940 (92), 1950 (75), 1960 (83; 92 for Race), 1970 (91; 92 for Race), 1980 (92), 1990 (92). Presidential vote share is every four years (1868–1988) and includes 92 MCDs.

half).[43] A final reason not to leap from racial segregation trends to a wholesale acceptance of the Tiebout model is that none of the other preference proxies (vote shares, young, foreign-born) shows significant movement to greater sorting over the past century and a half. (Foreign-born heterogeneity did increase in the post-World War II period, but this represented a return to the levels of the 1855–1875 period.) Indeed, the party vote shares in presidential elections indicate reduced heterogeneity across Boston municipalities over the last 50 years.

The income data also reveal little sign of greater sorting. If individuals are becoming increasingly Tiebout sorted, then income inequality *within*-municipalities should fall and inequality *between*-municipalities should rise. Table 3 shows trends in household income heterogeneity over the

1949–1989 period. We first create two within-MCD measures by calculating a *CV* and Gini index for the income distribution in *each* MCD and then average the MCD values using by population weights. The data in the left panel show that the average within-MCD income heterogeneity has stayed roughly constant. This means the income distribution within each municipality has not changed much over the post-World War II period. The right panel examines trends in within- and between-MCD income heterogeneity using additively-separable Theil indices. These indices reveal the within- and between-components have changed little. Moreover, the between-component is quite small (less than a fifth of the within-component) which means almost all income heterogeneity is due to within-municipality diversity. Municipalities in the Boston area have strikingly similar income distributions and there has been little movement towards greater sorting over the last 50 years.

Nor is there evidence of increasing long-run heterogeneity of government policies across the MCDs of the Boston SMSA. Table 4 charts the trends in the key series over the 1906–1992 period. Although there has been a

---

[43] Again the idea is that tracts are neighborhoods. Under a racism model individuals have preferences over who they interact with, and so neighborhoods are greatly stratified. In the Tiebout model there should be no stratification across neighborhoods within a municipality since each neighborhood receives the same level of public services.

TABLE 3—HOUSEHOLD INCOME HETEROGENEITY WITHIN- AND BETWEEN-MCDs IN THE BOSTON SMSA

Year	N	Within-indices			Within-/between-decomposition			
		CV	GL	GU	$I_1 - W$	$I_1 - B$	$I_2 - W$	$I_2 - B$
1949	74	0.805	0.404	0.414	0.290	0.041	0.386	0.033
		(0.090)	(0.043)	(0.044)				
1979	92	0.788	0.394	0.398	0.261	0.041	0.316	0.039
		(0.106)	(0.039)	(0.039)				
1989	92	0.809	0.407	0.413	0.279	0.040	0.349	0.038
		(0.105)	(0.040)	(0.039)				

Notes: The coefficient of variation, *CV*, is defined in equation (11) of Section III. The Gini indices, *GL* and *GU*, are defined in equations (19) and (20), respectively. The Theil indices, I_1 and I_2 are defined in equations (17) and (18). The "*W*" is within-MCD, and "*B*" is between-MCD. The within-measures are population-weighted averages of each of the MCD indices. Standard deviations are reported in parentheses below the within-measures.

There is no electronic data available prior to 1979 for households. The results for households in 1979 and 1989 are similar if MCDs which are missing data in 1949 are omitted.

Results for families are not reported since there is no family-level data in the 1949 hardcopies (see the online Data Appendix for details). The family-level indices are quite similar to the household-level indices for 1979 and 1989.

To compute the indices, we need to know for each MCD the proportion of people in each income category and the mean income in each group. Because the latter is unavailable, the midpoint of each income interval was used as the mean. For the top-coded income group, a mean of 1.5 times the lower bound was used (several other values were considered and the results do not appear to be sensitive to this choice). For the Gini measures the upper and lower bound of each income interval is also needed. For the upper bound of the top-coded group, 20 times the lower bound was used (again the results are robust to using other values for the top-coded group).

small increase since the 1960's, the population-weighted *CV* of total government spending, measured by the per capita current operation budget, fell by a quarter between 1906 and 1992. We also investigate two major spending categories, protection and education, which typically comprise over one-half of total spending in these data. The *CV* for per capita protection spending fell by 30 percent over the past century. The *CV* for per capita education spending rose and then fell; the endpoint is roughly equal to the starting point.[44] These measures display considerable variability, but there is no observed long-run tendency for the policy *CV*s to rise as the model predicts. This finding reinforces the results for the national sample.

In conclusion, despite the urban flight from the heterogeneous central city, there is little evidence of increased sorting between municipalities in the Boston SMSA. The only measure giving clear evidence of growing concentration is racial composition between the city and suburbs, and this is likely due to racial discrimination rather than Tiebout sorting. In fact among the demographic variables we consider none ever exceeds the conventional standard of high heterogeneity (a dissimilarity index above 0.6). The population of the Boston SMSA appears to be far from the level of sorting that Tiebout would predict. Finally, changes in the dispersion of the spending variables or any of the preference proxies are not strongly linked to changes in the policy environment such as school busing in the 1970's or tax limits in the 1980's.

V. Trends in Heterogeneity Across Counties

We can gain a better understanding of trends in geographic heterogeneity by examining the more abundant county-level data. Empirically *trends* in across-county heterogeneity closely mirror trends in across-municipality

[44] There is a spike in education spending heterogeneity across MCDs in the 1960's which stems from Boston's relative reduction in education spending. Seymour Sacks (1972) documents that most urban school districts reduced spending relative to their suburban counterparts during this period. The elimination of the urban-suburban spending gap by the mid-1970's can likely be linked to costs associated with forced busing in Boston (see J. Brian Sheehan, 1984) and changes in the state school aid formula (see Steven Weiss, 1970).

TABLE 4—ACROSS-MCD CURRENT OPERATIONS SPENDING
IN THE BOSTON SMSA: COEFFICIENTS OF VARIATIONS (CV)

Year	N	G_{Total}	$G_{Protection}$	$G_{Education}$
1906	92	0.359	0.490	0.197
1913	92	0.297	0.402	0.218
1923	92	0.267	0.351	0.203
1932	92	0.281	0.346	0.181
1942	92	0.220	0.297	0.160
1955	92	0.236	0.350	0.190
1962	59	0.189	0.311	0.311
1967	59	0.216	0.281	0.356
1972	92	0.293	0.399	0.267
1977	92	0.242	0.365	0.177
1982	92	0.233	0.276	0.206
1987	92	0.243	0.334	0.187
1992	92	0.267	0.340	0.194

Notes: See the online Data Appendix for a list of sources
and definitions of these series. The coefficient of variation, CV, is defined in equation (11). All values are
population-weighted. In 1962 and 1967 there are no
values reported for the 33 municipalities which have
populations less than 10,000. The CV's in the remaining
years do not change significantly when these 33 municipalities are omitted (because the measure is population-
weighted and these are all small communities).

heterogeneity.[45] For example, Table 2 shows
that the racial dissimilarity index at the
county-level is approximately the MCD-level
index shifted down by a constant. Similar
parallels between MCD- and county-level
trends are evident for: (i) the other proxies in
Table 2; (ii) the tax and spending results in
Table 1;[46] (iii) all the proxies and local policy
outcomes using the full national set of MCDs
over 1970–1990 (results omitted); (iv) all the
variables from the Boston SMSA (see Rhode
and Strumpf, 2000).[47]

[45] We believe that Tiebout sorting should also apply to
counties. In Rhode and Strumpf (2000) we show that counties play an important role in providing local services and
that reduced sorting of type proxies occurs even in states
where counties have major fiscal responsibilities.
[46] Table 1 also indicates there is substantial within-
county heterogeneity in MCD/school district taxes or spending. However, the between-county differences are even
larger and typically on the order of two-thirds the overall
MCD dispersion.
[47] The Boston results are of interest since the counties of
Massachusetts have few fiscal responsibilities, and so there
is likely to be a divergence if subcounty Tiebout sorting is
the driving factor in residential choice.

A more formal demonstration employs the
MCD-level entropy index, which can be decomposed into within- and between-county
components. Table 5, which contains results
for a wide variety of preference proxies,
shows that the decline in overall heterogeneity between MCDs is almost entirely driven
by reductions in heterogeneity between counties. The within-county heterogeneity remains
roughly constant and small. For example, the
within-component contributes less than a fifth
to the racial composition index and less than
a third to the family income index. All these
results suggest that computing heterogeneity
trends across counties yields a reasonable approximation to heterogeneity trends between
MCDs, the more typical unit for Tiebout communities. We therefore consider the far more
abundant data for all U.S. counties over the
1850–1990 period.[48]

The available evidence reveals that the
variation in local policy outcomes across
counties fell dramatically over time. Perhaps
the most prominent category is education.
The top panel of Table 6 shows that the
dispersion across counties of per capita
spending (including all direct education expenditures within the county boundaries)
steadily falls by more than 50 percent between 1890 and 1992. The second set of local
policy outcomes includes real per capita taxes
and revenues. Due to data availability problems, we use four different variables: Tax_1,
taxes collected by counties; Tax_2, taxes collected by all local governments within the
county; Rev_1, revenues collected by counties;
and Rev_2, revenues collected by all local governments within the county.[49] The bottom
panel of Table 6 shows a sharp drop in dispersion across counties of all these variables
over the 1870–1992 period. Although there

[48] Whenever possible the sample includes all counties in
existence in a given year and the annual sample sizes are
presented in the tables and figures discussed below. Alaska
is omitted due to inconsistencies in its county codes.
[49] The main difference between taxes and revenues is
intergovernmental grants, which were typically small before
1945.

1668 THE AMERICAN ECONOMIC REVIEW DECEMBER 2003

TABLE 5—WITHIN-COUNTY/BETWEEN-COUNTY DECOMPOSITION OF THE MCD-LEVEL ENTROPY INDEX

		Racial composition (black)				Nativity (foreign-born)		
Year	N	MCD total	Within-county	Between-county	N	MCD total	Within-county	Between-county
1870	2,071	0.453	0.041	0.411	2,071	0.255	0.033	0.222
1930	5,071	0.374	0.051	0.323	5,070	0.207	0.011	0.196
1960	3,798	0.252	0.041	0.211				
1970	3,020	0.246	0.044	0.202	3,039	0.160	0.016	0.144
1980	3,453	0.274	0.044	0.230	3,415	0.166	0.010	0.156
1990	3,456	0.293	0.055	0.237	3,456	0.187	0.013	0.174

		Young population				Old population		
Year	N	MCD total	Within-county	Between-county	N	MCD total	Within-county	Between-county
1930	5,071	0.012	0.004	0.008	5,071	0.026	0.008	0.018
1960	3,798	0.008	0.002	0.005	3,798	0.026	0.008	0.018
1970	3,275	0.007	0.003	0.004	3,275	0.035	0.011	0.024
1980	3,415	0.007	0.003	0.004	3,415	0.034	0.010	0.024
1990	3,456	0.007	0.003	0.004	3,456	0.034	0.012	0.023

		Education				Homeowner occupation		
Year	N	MCD total	Within-county	Between-county	N	MCD total	Within-county	Between-county
1970	3,275	0.045	0.014	0.031				
1980	3,415	0.042	0.011	0.032	3,422	0.102	0.023	0.080
1990	3,455	0.047	0.011	0.033	3,456	0.098	0.029	0.070

		Family income: Theil_1-between				Family income: Theil_2-between		
Year	N	MCD total	Within-county	Between-county	N	MCD total	Within-county	Between-county
1969	3,275	0.029	0.007	0.022	3,275	0.028	0.007	0.021
1979	3,415	0.024	0.006	0.018	3,415	0.022	0.006	0.017
1989	3,456	0.037	0.011	0.025	3,456	0.034	0.010	0.024

Notes: The overall-, within-, and between-entropy terms are defined in equations (15) and (16) of Section III. Empty cells indicate missing data. These results are based on a 1-in-10 sample. Full details of the data as well as precise definition of the categories are in the online Data Appendix.

has been a slight increase in recent decades, the CV for Tax_2 fell by nearly one-half between 1870 and 1992. All of these results are robust to controlling for outliers, state fixed effects, and returns to scale in government services (see Rhode and Strumpf, 2000).

Heterogeneity across counties of the preference proxies remains flat or falls over the sample. Figure 4 plots the dissimilarity and Gini indices for presidential votes in elections between 1848 and 1988. (To register the importance of third parties, the figure also shows the two-party vote share.) There is a gradual downward trend, especially after 1892.[50] For example, the Gini trend line has a slope of

[50] The 1860 election was highly unusual because four major parties—Republicans, Democrats, Southern Democrats, and Constitutional Unionists—participated in the sectionally divided contest.

TABLE 6—DISPERSION OF LOCAL POLICIES ACROSS COUNTIES

Per Capita Education Spending

Year	N	CV	DG
1890	2,623	0.663	0.212
1932	3,084	0.487	0.183
1957	3,091	0.335	0.124
1962	3,103	0.302	0.116
1967	3,102	0.285	0.104
1972	3,106	0.297	0.109
1977	3,110	0.270	0.103
1982	3,110	0.251	0.087
1987	3,110	0.247	0.084
1992	3,112	0.249	0.089

Per Capita Taxes and Revenues

| Year | N | CV | | | | DG | | | |
		Tax_1	Tax_2	Rev_1	Rev_2	Tax_1	Tax_2	Rev_1	Rev_2
1870	2,098	1.179	0.933			0.349	0.338		
1880	2,302	0.878	0.889			0.282	0.327		
1890	1,308			1.015				0.364	
1902	2,679			0.745				0.297	
1913	2,902			0.868				0.338	
1922	3,024	0.695				0.255			
1932	3,083	0.677	0.473	0.640	0.463	0.248	0.191	0.234	0.187
1942	2,497	0.689		0.755		0.261		0.258	
1957	3,087				0.373				0.150
1962	3,093		0.464		0.346		0.192		0.139
1967	3,095		0.467		0.385		0.187		0.143
1972	3,097		0.485		0.419		0.197		0.159
1977	3,104		0.524		0.421		0.206		0.154
1982	3,103		0.503		0.363		0.183		0.134
1987	3,104		0.522		0.372		0.187		0.137
1992	3,104		0.497		0.350		0.182		0.129

Notes: The coefficient of variation, CV, is defined in equation (11) of Section III; the reallocation index, DG, is defined in equation (12).

For the top panel, the G variables involve education spending. For the bottom panel, the G's are taxes or revenues (G_1 = just county government G; G_2 = county + subcounty government G). Empty cells are due to missing data. See the online Data Appendix for further details about the data.

−0.010 per decade over the entire period, and of −0.014 from 1892 on (the index decreases from 0.38 to 0.24 between 1892 and 1988). The convergence of county election results is not due to the decline in importance of third parties and appears even after accounting for the Democratic party's loss of control of the South (see Rhode and Strumpf, 2000).

The heterogeneity across counties of the black population share declines more noticeably over the sample. Figure 5 shows the dissimilarity and Gini indices as well as the

fraction of blacks living in black majority counties. All series remain relatively flat from 1850 to 1890 and then begin falling. This reduction was quite dramatic: while 48.2 percent of blacks lived in black majority counties in 1890, only 9.0 percent did so in 1990. This pattern is consistent with the Great Migration of African-Americans from the South, where they were overrepresented (see Carrington et al., 1996). Nonetheless, excluding the South yields indices that are lower than the national series but follow exactly the same declining

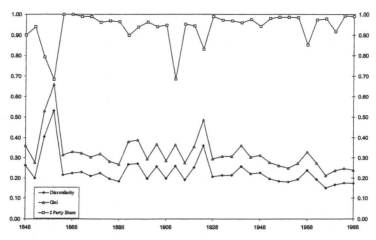

FIGURE. 4. HETEROGENEITY OF PRESIDENTIAL VOTE SHARES ACROSS U.S. COUNTIES

Note: Year (sample size): 1852 (1,551), 1860 (1,864), 1872 (2,177), 1880 (2,315), 1892 (2,667), 1900 (2,730), 1912 (2,970), 1920 (3,031), 1932 (3,091), 1940 (3,067), 1952 (3,097), 1960 (3,101), 1972 (3,105), 1980 (3,111), 1988 (3,113).

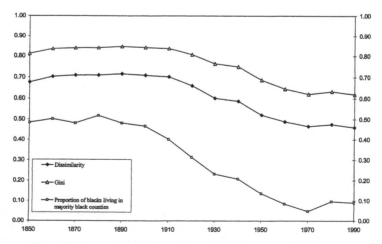

FIGURE 5. HETEROGENEITY IN BLACK POPULATION SHARE ACROSS U.S. COUNTIES

Note: Year (sample size): 1850 (1,596), 1860 (2,030), 1870 (2,185), 1880 (2,400), 1890 (2,743), 1900 (2,777), 1910 (2,950), 1920 (3,064), 1930 (3,100), 1940 (3,097), 1950 (3,100), 1960 (3,108), 1970 (3,111), 1980 (3,114), 1990 (3,116).

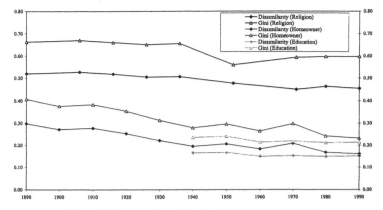

FIGURE 6. HETEROGENEITY OF RELIGION DENOMINATIONAL SHARES,
HOMEOWNERSHIP, AND EDUCATION ACROSS U.S. COUNTIES

Notes: Year (sample size with R denoting religious data): 1890 (2,753, R: 2,677), 1900 (2,825), 1906 (R: 2,767), 1910 (2,949), 1916 (R: 2,948), 1920 (3,064), 1926 (R: 3,064), 1930 (3,100), 1936 (R: 3,096), 1940 (3,097), 1950 (3,099), 1952 (R: 3,072), 1960 (3,103), 1970 (3,109), 1971 (R: 3,077), 1980 (2,753, R: 3,068), 1990 (3,110, R: 3,080). Unaffiliated and affiliates of minor denominations are excluded.

pattern.[51] Our investigation of county-level net migration patterns over the 1930–1980 period confirms these findings.[52]

The data on religious affiliation, displayed in Figure 6, reveal counties have become more alike over the past century. (The convergence is more apparent if one extrapolates back using data on church seating by denominations for the

1850–1890 period; see Rhode and Strumpf, 2000.) Figure 6 also shows the declining trends in heterogeneity across counties for homeownership and education levels. The homeownership indices each fall almost in half over the 1890–1990 period while the education indices decline slightly between 1940 and 1990.

Figure 7 presents county-level data for the age groups and the foreign-born. The heterogeneity indices for the young population share have no strong trend, though dispersion clearly falls in the post-World War II period. In this same period there is a slight growth in the heterogeneity of the old, but this is swamped by the reduction since 1850.[53] For the foreign-born share, there is a slight downward trend in across-county heterogeneity over the whole sample but a noticeable rise between 1960–1990 (which is due to the disproportionately rapid growth of Hispanic immigrants in

[51] Our results complement Cutler et al. (1999) who find that black urban segregation increased from 1890 to 1970 and then sharply declined. These contrasting results are likely due to the differences in the scope and level of spatial aggregation of the two analyses. They consider segregation within a city at the census-tract level whereas we are looking at all of the counties in the United States. Their analysis captures *within-city* heterogeneity while our data largely measures differences *across urban and rural areas.* So while the black rural-urban migration tended to reduce heterogeneity at the county level, it increased heterogeneity within cities if new black migrants tended to live in disproportionately black census tracts.

[52] In regressions both with and without controls for the South, black net migration rates have a negative and statistically significant relationship with the black population share (results omitted). That is, blacks disproportionately left counties where they were overrepresented. These results run counter not only to Tiebout sorting, but also to explanations for declined heterogeneity based on purely random movement.

[53] While there is no county-level data for the elderly between 1870 and 1920, we were able to compile a state-level time series over the period 1870–1970. The dissimilarity index computed from this data falls continuously, particularly during the period where we have no county data.

1672   THE AMERICAN ECONOMIC REVIEW   DECEMBER 2003

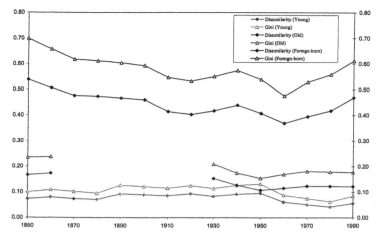

FIGURE 7. HETEROGENEITY OF FOREIGN-BORN, YOUNG, AND
OLD POPULATION SHARES ACROSS U.S. COUNTIES

Notes: Year (sample size): 1850 (1,607), 1860 (2,055), 1870 (2,230), 1880 (2,421), 1890
(2,780), 1900 (2,832), 1910 (2,955), 1920 (3,071), 1930 (3,102), 1940 (3,099), 1950 (3,102),
1960 (3,114), 1970 (3,112), 1980 (3,115), 1990 (3,117). There is no county-level data for the
old population share between 1870 and 1920. For foreign-born, 1850, 1860: includes entire
population; 1910–1930: white only; 1950: 21 years and over.

California, Texas, Florida, New Jersey, and
New York). Finally, Table 7 presents family
and household income inequality/heterogeneity
measures for 1949, 1969, 1979, and 1989. Paralleling the results for the Boston SMSA, within-
county heterogeneity has stayed roughly constant while the between-county component
is relatively small and declined between 1949
and 1979 before increasing slightly over the
1980's. Income groups have not become more
sorted.

These results reinforce and extend the MCD-
level analysis. There has been measurable convergence across counties in a wide range of
local policies and resident public good preferences over the last 150 years. These findings are
in conflict with the prediction of the generalized
Tiebout model since mobility costs have fallen
over this period.

VI. Conclusion

This paper evaluates the empirical relevance
of Tiebout sorting. Local public goods undoubt-

edly influence residential choice, but our evidence
indicates that other factors have overwhelmed
Tiebout sorting in the long run. The augmented
Tiebout model predicts greater heterogeneity
across communities in both resident preferences
and government policies as movement becomes
easier. Because of the secular decline in mobility costs, there should be a trend towards greater
stratification. However, we find little evidence
that the Tiebout mechanism played a dominant
role in sorting over the last 150 years. In fact a
wide variety of preference and policy variables
indicate that communities (as measured by municipalities and counties) have become more
alike.

These results provide an important challenge
for future local public economics research. We
need to determine which alternative motives
empirically explain long-run residential choices
and then incorporate them into our theoretical
models. Such revised models will likely have
implications that sharply contrast with those
from the Tiebout model. This calls into question
the literature that adopts a rigid Tiebout frame-

TABLE 7—INCOME HETEROGENEITY WITHIN- AND BETWEEN-COUNTIES

	Year	N	Within-indices			Within-/between-decomposition			
			CV	GL	GU	$I_1 - W$	$I_1 - B$	$I_2 - W$	$I_2 - B$
Families	1949	311	0.808	0.390	0.396	0.261	0.031	0.327	0.035
			(0.132)	(0.046)	(0.047)				
	1969	311	0.815	0.378	0.386	0.254	0.022	0.291	0.021
			(0.098)	(0.034)	(0.033)				
	1979	311	0.776	0.376	0.379	0.244	0.018	0.284	0.017
			(0.075)	(0.031)	(0.031)				
	1989	311	0.833	0.395	0.397	0.273	0.025	0.314	0.024
			(0.086)	(0.036)	(0.036)				
Households	1949	311	0.896	0.433	0.439	0.322	0.028	0.413	0.031
			(0.124)	(0.039)	(0.041)				
	1979	311	0.857	0.414	0.417	0.294	0.018	0.346	0.017
			(0.074)	(0.027)	(0.027)				
	1989	311	0.909	0.428	0.431	0.319	0.025	0.372	0.023
			(0.082)	(0.030)	(0.030)				

Notes: The coefficient of variation, CV, is defined in equation (11) of Section III. The Gini indices, GL and GU, are defined in equations (19) and (20), respectively. The Theil indices, I_1 and I_2 are defined in equations (17) and (18). The "W" is within-counties, and "B" is between-counties. The within-measures are population-weighted averages of each of the county indices. Standard deviations are reported in parentheses below the within-measures.

As described in the online Data Appendix, these values are based on a random, 1-in-10 sample. Household data for 1969 is not available in electronic form.

See Table 3 for additional comments.

work to explain community composition and mobility choices. To illustrate this, we conclude by briefly discussing two alternative models which are more consistent with the data.[54]

[54] One obvious candidate, the growing federal role in providing public services, cannot be the complete explanation for our data. Centralization limits the benefit of sorting, say, by providing some minimum bundle of public goods. While this is consistent with a reduction in the rate of sorting, it does not explain the unsorting we observe. Non-Tiebout incentives for residential choice are also needed: centralization increases the relative importance of these factors.

A second policy, zoning, also fails to explain the data. Bruce Hamilton (1975) argues that in the absence of zoning, poor individuals have incentives to move into high-income communities. This gives them access to the local public good at less than average cost, but also defeats the stratification that Tiebout predicts. With zoning, this poor-chasing-the-rich phenomenon could be avoided, say by imposing minimum lot sizes. Robert Nelson (1977) indicates zoning laws were almost entirely absent until the postwar period and they have grown in popularity over time. Hence the Tiebout model should be more appropriate today than in the past, and so the growth of zoning serves as an independent reason for a prediction of growing across-community heterogeneity.

A final and more promising candidate is growing local

First, suppose that individuals select communities based on employment opportunities as well as local public goods. This would hold if residents receive an exogenous, community-specific net wage (the wage differential could stem from commuting costs or community-specific labor demands which reflect the complementarity of different skill types in production). Such a model is consistent with the reduction in sorting documented in this paper if employment has dispersed or if the relative importance of local public goods has fallen over time (for example, because of growth in the central provision of public services). However, in this model communities cannot be ranked according to public good preferences which is the canonical Tiebout result invoked by a large

government competition. If some individuals are more desirable than others (say the rich), then in equilibrium communities adopt policies which are relatively favorable to these individuals (Nechyba, 1997, uses such an argument to explain the infrequency of local income taxes). This mechanism offsets Tiebout because it limits policy heterogeneity across communities and thus reduces incentives for individual sorting.

number of papers in the local public economics literature. This critique holds more generally within the class of models where some other non-Tiebout migration motive has grown in importance (see footnote 16).

Second, suppose we adopt the prevailing view in the empirical literature that Tiebout sorting occurs over a limited geographic area such as a metropolitan area. Under this model, Tiebout sorting within metro areas should increase because mobility costs have declined. This point can be reconciled with our finding

of declining national heterogeneity across communities only if the metro areas have become more similar (i.e., between-metro heterogeneity has declined). This should imply growing population diversity in the representative metro area. In fact, the average Herfindahl index of metro-area racial shares fell by over 10 percent between 1930 and 1990. But given moving costs and nonpublic goods motives for residential choice, this growing local diversity inhibits widespread conformity with the Tiebout model.

APPENDIX

This Appendix contains the example of sorting with single-peaked preferences, and proofs of cases where sorting is associated with increased policy variation.

EXAMPLE A: SORTING WITH SINGLE-PEAKED PREFERENCES

A preliminary: define the initial level of variable X as X^0 and the level after one agent of type s moves as X^1.

Suppose individual preferences satisfy Assumption 1 and communities set their policies according to (2). If an agent of type s moves from community d to c, then

(i) $|G_c^{*1} - G_s| \leq |G_c^{*0} - G_s|$ and $|G_d^{*1} - G_s| \geq |G_d^{*0} - G_s|$;

(ii) $U_s(G_c^{*1}) \geq U_s(G_c^{*0})$ and $U_s(G_d^{*1}) \leq U_s(G_d^{*0})$;

(iii) $U_t(G_c^{*1}) \geq U_t(G_c^{*0}) \ \forall \ t$ such that $\text{sign}(G_t - G_c^{*1}) = \text{sign}(G_s - G_c^{*1})$;

(iv) $U_t(G_c^{*1}) \leq U_t(G_c^{*0}) \ \forall \ t$ such that $\text{sign}(G_t - G_c^{*0}) = -\text{sign}(G_s - G_c^{*0})$;

(v) $U_t(G_d^{*1}) \leq U_t(G_d^{*0}) \ \forall \ t$ such that $\text{sign}(G_t - G_d^{*0}) = \text{sign}(G_s - G_d^{*0})$;

(vi) $U_t(G_d^{*1}) \geq U_t(G_d^{*0}) \ \forall \ t$ such that $\text{sign}(G_t - G_d^{*1}) = -\text{sign}(G_s - G_d^{*1})$.

To explain this example, we focus on the case for the receiving community because the case of the sending community is analogous. If public good provision is set by (2), the first-order condition $\Sigma_t N_{tc} U_t'(G_c^*) = 0$ must be satisfied, where N_{tc} is the number of type t in community c. If one more person of type s moves in, holding the other N_{tc} constant, the weight on the $U_s'(G_c^*)$ increases. Unless $U_s'(G_c^{*0}) = 0$, the community must move G_c^* closer to G_s to satisfy the new first-order condition. This increases the utility of type s and all types on the same side of G_c^* as s and reduces the utility of all types on the other side of G_c^{*0}. The inequalities are strict unless $U_s'(G_c^{*0}) = 0$.

PROOF OF THE OBSERVATION:

Examples B and C provide conditions under which *sorting is associated with increased variation of policy outcomes across communities.*

Example B: If preferences satisfy Assumption 1 and there are two communities and two types of individuals, then migration obeying (3) and (4) increases the differences between the communities' policies. Call the two communities c and d and the two types r and s, where $G_r < G_s$. Let N_i be the total population of type i and let N_{ic} be the number in community c. Given N_{rc} and N_{sc}, G_c^* will be set where $N_{rc}U_r'(G_c^*) = -N_{sc}U_s'(G_c^*)$. Note that $U_r'(G_c^*) < 0 < U_s'(G_c^*)$ and that $d[U_r'(G_c^*)/(-U_s'(G_c^*))]/dG_c^* < 0$. By the implicit function theorem, we can solve for $G_c^* = H[N_{rc}/N_{sc}]$ where $H' < 0$, $H[0] = G_s$ and $H[\infty] = G_r$. By a similar argument, $G_d^* = H[(N_r - N_{rc})/(N_s - N_{sc})]$. If $N_{rc}/N_{sc} > N_1/N_2$, then $G_r \leq G_c^* < G_d^* \leq G_s$. Community c will be the preferred community for type r and community d for type s. Migration obeying (3) and (4), which increases in N_{rc} and N_{sd}, causes greater segregation and widens the differences between the communities' policies: $d|G_d^* - G_c^*|/dN_{rc} > 0$ and $d|G_d^* - G_c^*|/dN_{sd} > 0$.

Example C: If preferences are quadratic as under Assumption 2, then any move obeying (3) and (4) increases the aggregate population-weighted variance of policies. Under (2) and Assumption 2, the policy in a given community is the mean of members' ideal policies and the aggregate population-weighted mean, χ, is independent of the distribution of types across communities. An agent i of type s will move from community d (initially with N_d^0 members) to community c (with N_c^0 members) if $(G_c^{*0} - G_s)^2 + m_i < (G_d^{*0} - G_s)^2$. Such a move will change the policy in community d from G_d^{*0} to $G_d^{*1} = (G_d^{*0}N_d^0 - G_s)/(N_d^0 - 1)$ and that in c from G_c^{*0} to $G_c^{*1} = (G_c^{*0}N_c^0 + G_s)/(N_c^0 + 1)$. Such a move will not affect the population-weighted mean of policies in c and d, i.e., $N_c^0 G_c^{*0} + N_d G_d^{*0} = (N_c^0 + 1)G_c^{*1} + (N_d^0 - 1)G_d^{*1}$. Nor will it change the aggregate mean or policies in communities other than c and d. But such a move does raise the population-weighted variances of policies:

$$\Sigma_e[N_e^1(G_e^{*1} - \chi)^2 - N_e^0(G_e^{*0} - \chi)^2]/N$$

$$= [(N_c^0 + 1)(G_c^{*1})^2 + (N_d^0 - 1)(G_d^{*1})^2 - N_c^0(G_c^{*0})^2 - N_d^0(G_d^{*0})^2]/N$$

$$= [(N_d^0/(N_d^0 - 1))(G_d^{*0} - G_s)^2 - (N_c^0/(N_c^0 + 1))(G_c^{*0} - G_s)^2]/N > 0$$

where the inequality follows from $(N_c^0/(N_c^0 + 1)) < 1 < (N_d^0/(N_d^0 - 1))$ and $(G_c^{*0} - G_s)^2 < (G_d^{*0} - G_s)^2$.

REFERENCES

Alesina, Alberto; Baqir, Reza and Easterly, William. "Public Goods and Ethnic Divisions." *Quarterly Journal of Economics*, November 1999, *114*(4), pp. 1243–84.

Alesina, Alberto; Baqir, Reza and Hoxby, Caroline. "Political Jurisdictions in Heterogeneous Communities." National Bureau of Economic Research (Cambridge, MA) Working Paper No. 7859, 2000.

Alesina, Alberto and La Ferrara, Eliana. "Participation in Heterogeneous Communities." *Quarterly Journal of Economics*, August 2000, *115*(3), pp. 847–904.

Bayer, Patrick. "Tiebout Sorting and Discrete Choices: A New Explanation for Socioeconomic Differences in the Consumption of

School Quality." Mimeo, Yale University, 2000.

Benabou, Roland. "Heterogeneity, Stratification, and Growth: Macroeconomic Implications of Community Structure and School Finance." *American Economic Review*, June 1996, *86*(3), pp. 584–609.

Bewley, Truman. "A Critique of Tiebout's Theory of Local Expenditures." *Econometrica*, May 1981, *49*(3), pp. 713–40.

Brueckner, Jan. "A Tiebout/Tax Competition Model." *Journal of Public Economics*, February 2000, *77*(2), pp. 285–306.

Buchanan, James and Tullock, Gordon. *The calculus of consent.* Ann Arbor, MI: University of Michigan Press, 1962.

Carrington, William; Detragiache, Enrica and Vishwanath, Tara. "Migration with Endogenous

Moving Costs." *American Economic Review*, September 1996, *86*(4), pp. 909–30.

Carroll, Robert and Yinger, John. "Is the Property Tax a Benefit Tax? The Case of Rental Housing." *National Tax Journal*, June 1994, *47*(2), pp. 295–316.

Cutler, David; Glaeser, Edward and Vigdor, Jacob. "The Rise and Decline of the American Ghetto." *Journal of Political Economy*, June 1999, *107*(3), pp. 455–506.

DiPasquale, Denise and Glaeser, Edward. "Incentives and Social Capital: Are Homeowners Better Citizens?" *Journal of Urban Economics*, March 1999, *45*(2), pp. 354–84.

Dowding, Keith; John, Peter and Biggs, Stephen. "Tiebout: A Survey of the Empirical Literature." *Urban Studies*, May 1994, *31*(4–5), pp. 767–97.

Duncan, Otis D. and Duncan, Beverly. "A Methodological Analysis of Segregation Indices." *American Sociological Review*, April 1955, *20*(2), pp. 210–17.

Ely, Richard. *Taxation in American states and cities*. New York: Thomas Crowell, 1888.

Epple, Dennis; Figlio, David and Romano, Richard. "Competition Between Private and Public Schools: Testing Stratification and Pricing Predictions." *Journal of Public Economics* (forthcoming).

Epple, Dennis and Romer, Thomas. "Mobility and Redistribution." *Journal of Political Economy*, August 1991, *99*(4), pp. 828–58.

Epple, Dennis; Romer, Thomas and Sieg, Holger. "Interjurisdictional Sorting and Majority Rule: An Empirical Analysis." *Econometrica*, August 2001, *69*(6), pp. 1437–66.

Epple, Dennis and Sieg, Holger. "Estimating Equilibrium Models of Local Jurisdictions." *Journal of Political Economy*, August 1999, *107*(4), pp. 645–81.

Fernández, Raquel and Rogerson, Richard. "Keeping People Out: Income Distribution, Zoning, and the Quality of Public Education." *International Economic Review*, February 1997, *38*(1), pp. 23–42.

_____. "Public Education and Income Distribution: A Dynamic Quantitative Evaluation of Education-Finance Reform." *American Economic Review*, September 1998, *88*(4), pp. 813–33.

Fisher, Ronald and Wassmer, Robert. "Economic Influences on the Structure of Local Govern-

ment in U.S. Metropolitan Areas." *Journal of Urban Economics*, May 1998, *43*(3), pp. 444–71.

Galenson, David. "Settlement and Growth of the American Colonies," in S. Engerman and R. Gallman, eds., *Cambridge economic history of the United States*, Vol. I. Cambridge: Cambridge University Press, 1996, pp. 135–207.

Gastwirth, Joseph. "The Estimation of the Lorenz Curve and the Gini Index." *Review of Economics and Statistics*, August 1972, *54*(3), pp. 306–16.

General Social Survey. *GSS 1972–1996 cumulative datafile*. Survey Documentation & Analysis Archive (http://csa.berkeley.edu:7502/ .1999).

Glomm, Gerhard and Lagunoff, Roger. "A Dynamic Tiebout Theory of Voluntary vs. Involuntary Provision of Public Goods." *Review of Economic Studies*, July 1999, *66*(3), pp. 659–77.

Goldin, Claudia and Katz, Lawrence. "Human Capital and Social Capital: The Rise of Secondary Schooling in America, 1910 to 1940." *Journal of Interdisciplinary History*, Spring 1999, *29*(4), pp. 683–723.

Hamilton, Bruce. "Zoning and Property Taxation in a System of Local Government." *Urban Studies*, June 1975, *12*(2), pp. 205–11.

Hercowitz, Zvi and Pines, David. "Migration Between Home Country and Diaspora: An Economic Analysis." *Journal of Public Economics*, July 1997, *65*(1), pp. 45–59.

Hoxby, Caroline. "The Productivity of Schools and Other Local Public Goods Producers." *Journal of Public Economics*, October 1999, *74*(1), pp. 1–30.

_____. "Does Competition Among Public Schools Benefit Students and Taxpayers?" *American Economic Review*, December 2000, *90*(5), pp. 1209–38.

Iannaccone, Laurence. "Introduction to the Economics of Religion." *Journal of Economic Literature*, September 1998, *36*(3), pp. 1465–95.

Kennan, John and Walker, James. "Geographical Wage Differentials, Welfare Benefits and Migration." Mimeo, University of Wisconsin, Madison, 2000.

Kollman, Ken; Miller, John and Page, Scott. "Political Institutions and Sorting in a Tiebout

Model." *American Economic Review*, December 1997, *87*(5), pp. 977–92.

Kremer, Michael. "How Much Does Sorting Increase Inequality?" *Quarterly Journal of Economics*, February 1997, *112*(1), pp. 115–39.

Leege, David and Kellstedt, Lyman, eds. *Rediscovering the religious factor in American politics*. Armonk, NY: M. E. Sharpe, 1993.

Martinez-Vazquez, Jorge; Rider, Mark and Walker, Mary. "Race and the Structure of School Districts in the United States." *Journal of Urban Economics*, March 1997, *41*(2), pp. 281–300.

Massey, Douglas and Denton, Nancy. "The Dimensions of Residential Segregation." *Social Forces*, December 1988, *67*(2), pp. 281–315.

Maxim, Hiram P. "Some Data on the Cost of Operating Automobiles for Commercial Purposes." *Scientific American*, Supplement No. 1479, May 7, 1904, pp. 23694–95.

Nechyba, Thomas. "Local Property and State Income Taxes: The Role of Interjurisdictional Competition and Collusion." *Journal of Political Economy*, April 1997, *105*(2), pp. 351–85.

_____. "School Finance Induced Migration and Stratification Patterns: The Impact of Private School Vouchers." *Journal of Public Economic Theory*, January 1999, *1*(1), pp. 5–50.

_____. "Mobility, Targeting, and Private-School Vouchers." *American Economic Review*, March 2000, *90*(1), pp. 130–46.

Nelson, Robert. *Zoning and property rights.* Cambridge, MA: MIT Press, 1977.

Newport, Frank. "The Religious Switcher in the United States." *American Sociological Review*, August 1979, *44*(4), pp. 528–52.

Noll, Mark, ed. *Religion and American politics: From the colonial period to the 1980s*. New York: Oxford University Press, 1990.

Perroni, Carlo and Scharf, Kimberley. "Tiebout with Politics: Capital Tax Competition and Constitutional Choices." *Review of Economic Studies*, January 2001, *68*(1), pp. 133–54.

Piketty, Thomas. "Social Mobility and Redistributive Politics." *Quarterly Journal of Economics*, August 1995, *110*(3), pp. 551–84.

Reardon, Sean. "Stata Module to Compute Multiple-Group Diversity and Segregation Indices." (http://ideas.uqam.ca/ideas/data/Softwares/bocbocodeS375001.html, 1998).

Rhode, Paul and Strumpf, Koleman. "A Historical Test of the Tiebout Hypothesis: Local Heterogeneity from 1850 to 1990." National Bureau of Economic Research (Cambridge, MA) Working Paper No. 7946, 2000.

Romer, Thomas and Rosenthal, Howard. "Bureaucrats Versus Voters: On the Political Economy of Resource Allocation by Direct Democracy." *Quarterly Journal of Economics*, November 1977, *93*(4), pp. 563–87.

Sacks, Seymour. *City schools/suburban schools: A history of fiscal conflict*. Syracuse, NY: Syracuse University Press, 1972.

Sanborn, George. *The chronicle of the Boston transit system* (http://www.mbta.com).

Sheehan, J. Brian. *The Boston school integration dispute: Social change and legal maneuvers*. New York: Columbia University Press, 1984.

Shorrocks, Anthony F. "The Class of Additively Decomposable Inequality Measures." *Econometrica*, April 1980, *48*(3), pp. 613–26.

Tiebout, Charles. "A Pure Theory of Local Expenditures." *Journal of Political Economy*, October 1956, *64*(5), pp. 416–24.

U.S. Bureau of the Census. *Geographic areas reference manual* (http://www.census.gov), 1994.

Weiss, Steven. *Existing disparities in public school finance and proposals for reform*. Federal Reserve Bank of Boston Research Report No. 46, 1970.

Wildasin, David and Wilson, John. "Imperfect Mobility and Local Government Behaviour in an Overlapping-Generations Model." *Journal of Public Economics*, May 1996, *60*(2), pp. 177–98.

Wooders, Myrna. "Multijurisdictional Economies, the Tiebout Hypothesis, and Sorting." *Proceedings of the National Academy of Sciences*, September 1999, *96*(19), pp. 10585–87.

B
Does Structure Matter?

[9]

Does Federalism Matter?
Political Choice in a Federal Republic

Susan Rose-Ackerman

Yale University

This paper builds upon some well-known facts about state government to generate new conclusions about social choice on the national level of a federal republic. Citizens vote against national laws that restrict their state's ability to export costs but support laws that reduce the costs imposed on them. Individuals may seek to extend the laws passed in some states to the entire nation or may oppose preemptive laws because they benefit from variety. Since these motivations are absent in a unitary system, national support for a law will depend upon whether a unitary or a federal structure prevails.

I. Introduction

This paper builds upon some well-known facts about state government to generate new conclusions about social choice on the national level of a federal republic. The central feature of state government behavior I shall exploit is the incentive each state has to improve its own position by imposing costs on the residents of other states. This search for local advantage takes many forms. On the one hand, states may impose taxes and regulations which are borne by out-of-state residents; on the other hand, they may try to attract investment from other states by providing tax breaks and special public services.[1]

This paper was presented at the Workshop on Analytical Urban Economics at Queen's University, Kingston, June 1978. I wish to thank Bruce Ackerman, the workshop participants, and the referee of this *Journal* for helpful comments.

[1] These incentives are stressed by Walker (1969, p. 890) and Posner (1977, chap. 26). McLure (1967) estimates that about one-quarter of all state taxes are exported. Externalities such as air and water pollution are emphasized by Breton (1965), Olson (1969), Tullock (1969), Rothenberg (1970), and Oates (1972). These authors discuss how a federal system can trade off interjurisdictional variety against the internalization of externalities through boundary definition, the assignment of functions to levels of government, and intergovernmental grants.

[*Journal of Political Economy*, 1981, vol. 89, no. 1]
© 1981 by The University of Chicago. 0022-3808/81/8901-0008$01.50

Whatever their particular character, these interstate spill-ins and spill-outs can alter the substance of national legislation. Citizens will vote against laws that restrict their state's ability to export costs but will support laws that reduce the costs imposed on them by their own and other states' choices. Since these strategic motivations are absent in a unitary system, national support for particular laws will depend upon whether a unitary or a federal structure prevails.

Despite its potential importance, the impact of federalism on the strategic position of voters has been largely ignored by social scientists. In his excellent review of the literature, for example, William Riker (1975) argues that federalism has no important influence on substantive national outcomes, suggesting that it does no more than delay the passage of national legislation opposed by a substantial minority of state legislatures.[2] Although Riker's conclusion is partly an empirical proposition, it is also based on an implicit model of how government systems behave. Riker argues (1975, pp. 155–56) that the underlying distribution of tastes in the population determines political outcomes. Since federalism per se has no impact on tastes, it will not, therefore, affect national political choices in the long run. The present paper challenges these theoretical underpinnings.

Since I am concerned not with an exhaustive taxonomy but with the relationship between political power and political structure, I concentrate on simple models. The system I discuss has only two "layers"—national and state.[3] States have fixed boundaries and cover the nation's entire geographical area so that every citizen lives in only one state. I will contrast the legislative choices of a unitary government with those of a "hierarchical" federal system where higher-level governments can always preempt the legislative choices of lower-level governments. If the superior government has taken no affirmative action, however, the statutes of inferior governments are binding.[4] I

[2] Riker (1975) proposes an imaginary experiment in which matched pairs of unitary and federal systems are examined to discover if there are important public policy differences. He hypothesizes that public policy within each pair will be "remarkably similar regardless of federalism" (p. 144). Furthermore, he argues that in the United States federalism delayed national regulation of business (p. 154) and helped perpetuate racist acts (pp. 154–56) but had no long-run impact on the character of national legislation.

[3] For an attempt to justify a three-layered system, see Ylvisaker (1959). With the exception of Wechsler (1963), Posner (1977), and Winter (1977), legal commentators have all but ignored the issues discussed in this paper and have instead concentrated on the relationship between state and federal courts. For a recent article in this tradition, see Cover and Aleinikoff (1977).

[4] This model should be contrasted with others which have a strict division of functions between high- and low-level governments. For example, see Wheare (1953, pp. 32–33). Recently, concern for a strict division of authority has given way to scholarship which recognizes the importance of interactions between levels of government. See, for example, Grodzins (1960, 1966) and Elazar (1962).

assume that both state and national governments are direct democracies where the only political actors are individuals and where all decisions are made by majority vote. Political issues are separable and well defined, and they appear to voters as simple dichotomous choices between maintenance of the status quo and a change.[5] The analysis concentrates on legislative choices. I do not discuss administrative or judicial issues or the possibility that the national government will seek to administer programs through state government agencies.

Section II shows that federalism "matters" in a political system where capital can move but people cannot. Section III considers the impact of permitting interstate migration of voters, and Section IV shows that federalism can matter even in the long run when states respond to the legislative choices of other states.

II. Federalism Does Matter

The major difference between a unitary system and a hierarchical federal structure is the characterization of the status quo. Let y = the status quo in a unitary system, and let x = a proposed, exogenously defined, legislative change. Suppose, for example, that in the status quo casino gambling is illegal. The federal government, however, proposes to make such gambling legal and to levy a tax on the profits.

In a hierarchical federal system, some states have passed legislation that is similar to x. Others have a status quo that is similar to y. Let us call the former x-type states and the latter y-type states. Continuing the example, x-type states permit casino gambling and levy a tax on earnings, while casino gambling is illegal in y-type states. Assume that if all states are x-type states, then the state laws taken together would have the same impact as x. Similarly, assume that if no states have passed the x-type law, the status quo is the same as in a unitary system. Thus, in my example the state gambling laws are duplicates of x and y, respectively. This assumption is not essential to the analysis, but it simplifies the exposition considerably.

Because of interstate spillovers of costs and benefits, individuals' preferences over x and y will not necessarily be the same as their preferences for alternative state legal regimes. In the gambling example, some people may favor a statewide gambling law and vote

---

[5] These assumptions permit me to look at the vote on a single issue and to avoid voting cycles in which majority rule does not produce a determinant outcome (Sen 1970, p. 38). The actual relationship between state statutes and federal law in the same area is, of course, considerably more complex. In reality, the relationship is seldom obvious and federal courts are frequently called upon to sort out the overlapping authority of state and federal statutes (see Tribe 1978, pp. 378–86).

against x at the national level. A state's residents gain when out-of-staters come to gamble and consume tourist services. The state would lose this advantage if gambling were legal in every state. In a unitary system, however, these same individuals might favor x over y since they would have no special advantage to protect.

A voter's preference for x over a system with a variety of state laws will often depend upon the number and location of x-type states. The economic advantages of permitting gambling in one's state of residence are larger the smaller the number of other states which also permit gambling. The benefits are also higher the more geographically distant are the other jurisdictions with legalized gambling. Let $g_i = z_i$ if state i has passed an x-type law, $g_i = w_i$ if state i is a y-type state, and let H = total number of states. Then, the status quo in a federal system is a vector $G = (g_1, \ldots, g_i, \ldots, g_H)$ where $g_i = z_i$ or w_i. Thus we can summarize the situation of those living in x-type states as $z(G)$ and the situation of those in y-type states as $w(G)$.

In this portion of the analysis, I assume that migration across state lines is impossible, so that the only way individuals can affect the legal regime under which they live is to vote for new state or federal laws. Capital, however, is free to move between jurisdictions. Given these assumptions, we can now compare the way voters with different preferences will cast their ballots in federal and unitary republics. Turning first to a unitary system, individual preferences can be straightforwardly translated in a social choice. Law x passes if and only if:

$$N(xRy) > N(yRx), \tag{1}$$

where R is the binary relation of "weak preference" ("at least as good as"). Then $N(aRb)$ is the number of people for whom aR_jb where R_j is the weak preference relation for individual j and R_j is reflexive, transitive, and complete.[6]

In a hierarchical federal system, under the assumption that only the current level of G is relevant, x passes at the national level if and only if:

$$N_1[xRz(G)] + N_2[xRw(G)] \geq N_1[z(G)Rx] + N_2[w(G)Rx], \tag{2}$$

where $N_1(aRb)$ is the number of people living in x-type states for whom aR_jb and $N_2(aRb)$ is the number of people living in y-type states for whom aR_jb.

Expressions (1) and (2) need not yield the same results. Individuals who would prefer x to y need not also prefer x to $z(G)$ or $w(G)$. If a

---

[6] In Sen's terminology (1970, p. 9), R_j is an ordering. The notation in (1) follows Sen (1970, p. 71).

TABLE 1

	$xRz(G)$	$z(G)Rx$	$xRw(G)$	$w(G)Rx$
xRy	A_1 (favor x)	A_3 (positive spill-ins to x types)	B_1 (favor x)	B_3 (positive spill-ins to y types)
yRx	A_2 (negative spill-ins to x types)	A_4 (oppose x)	B_2 (negative spill-ins to y types)	B_4 (oppose x)

state is able to export the costs of a program, then its citizens are likely to oppose preemptive federal laws even though they favor x-type legislation in their own state and would favor x over y in a unitary system. Similarly, if citizens can benefit from the legislative initiatives of other states then they may vote against x although they have xR_jy with a unitary government. The gambling example falls in the first category. Public health or pollution control laws in neighboring states may produce the second voting pattern. In fact, individual preferences may produce any of the possible rankings of $x, y,$ and $z(G)$ and $x,$ $y,$ and $w(G)$; and one can thus divide the population into groups depending upon their preferences and the states in which they live. For a given G, let $A(G)$ = set of people in x-type states and let $B(G)$ = everyone else.

People living in x-type states have $xRz(G)$ or $z(G)Rx$ or both. Those in set $B(G)$ have $xRw(G)$ or $w(G)Rx$ or both. In a unitary system voters have xRy or yRx or both. Table 1 is a matrix of the possible taste combinations. The entries in the matrix are the sets of people in each taste class. Thus $A(G) = A_1(G) \cup A_2(G) \cup A_3(G) \cup A_4(G)$ and $B(G) = B_1(G) \cup B_2(G) \cup B_3(G) \cup B_4(G)$.[7] In expression (1), $N(xRy) = N(A_1 \cup A_3 \cup B_1 \cup B_3)$. In expression (2), $N_1[xRz(G)] = N_1(A_1 \cup A_2)$ and $N_2[xRw(G)] = N_2(B_1 \cup B_2)$. Thus given G, the vote for x in a unitary system, $N(xRy)$, is greater than, equal to, or less than the vote in a hierarchical system, $N_1[xRz(G)] + N_2[xRw(G)]$, as:

$$N(A_3 \cup B_3) \gtreqless N(A_2 \cup B_2). \tag{3}$$

Expression (3) shows that federalism "matters." The size of the vote in favor of the national law may be higher or lower in a hierarchical federal system than in a unitary system. A law which passes in one system may be defeated in another. The practical importance of this result, however, depends upon whether sets A_3, B_3 and A_2, B_2 represent common preference configurations. Sets A_3 and B_3 include indi-

---

[7] The symbol $\cup$ stands for the union of sets, i.e., the set of people belonging to either set.

viduals who prefer x to y as the national law in a unitary system but who each favor conditions in their own states over x.[8] Sets A_2 and B_2 are the reverse of A_3 and B_3. They include individuals who would oppose x in a unitary system but favor preemptive legislation because it keeps them from losing at the expense of other citizens.

If sets A_2 and B_2 are large relative to sets A_3 and B_3, then a paradoxical result is possible. Although federalism is often justified as a way to preserve diversity and prevent the centralization of power, (3) implies that the existence of low-level governments may cause some voters to favor central control of an activity that they would otherwise have wanted unregulated. Without constitutional limits, a majority of citizens may be so unhappy with the mixture of independent state choices under federalism that they favor a more powerful central government than they would in a unitary system.

III.   Migration and the Vote for National Laws

When voters can move between jurisdictions in response to public policy changes, the vote for national preemptive laws will change. If migration is costless and if legal regimes are the only determinant of location, then, given G, national electoral support would fall in a hierarchical federal system. Voters are less likely to want national uniformity when they can move to congenial states.

Reality, of course, is somewhere between the extremes of a perfectly fixed population and a perfectly mobile one. Furthermore, different types of people have different moving costs, and the relation between these costs will help determine the political power of various groups at the state level. Thus, mobile groups may impose costs on immobile groups as a price for not leaving the state. Alternatively, undesirable groups may be induced to migrate by taxing or regulating them or by subsidizing their moving expenses. Variations in the cost of migration change the strategic environment. Those who can move cheaply have an advantage over those who cannot. Therefore, national decisions which require uniformity will be strongly supported by those who lose from the migration of others and opposed by those whose mobility permits them to gain at the expense of less mobile voters.

The possibility of migration has implications for national programs which seek to redistribute income from high-income to low-income families. Economic analyses of multiple government systems (e.g., Olson 1969; Oates 1972) conclude that interjurisdictional mobility

---

[8] It also, of course, includes those who are indifferent between any of these alternatives. Only people who are indifferent to all three alternatives are in both A_2 and A_3 or in both B_2 and B_3.

makes serious redistribution impossible at the state level. Progressive tax and spending policies must be carried out by preemptive laws at the national level. Interstate migration, however, also lowers the prospects for passage of national redistributive laws. If voters are mobile, support for a national preemptive law which redistributes income from the rich to the poor may be less than the support such legislation would obtain in a unitary system or in a federal system with no migration. Many who would support a particular progressive tax and spending program in a unitary system may oppose it in hierarchical federalism if the law preempts state "beggar-my-neighbor" laws which benefit these citizens. Selfishness will dominate altruism if the opportunity cost of altruism is too high.

IV. Does Federalism Matter in the Long Run?

The result in (3) applies when the number of x-type and y-type states is held constant (i.e., for a given G). One student of federalism (Riker 1975), however, argues that in the long run a federal system and a unitary one will converge to the same pattern of national laws. The view that federalism does not matter in the long run is based either on a hypothesis about how tastes change over time[9] or on a model that makes particular assumptions about the way votes change in response to new information and new circumstances (i.e., changes in G). The cases where federalism does not matter are contingent upon these assumptions. This section shows that it is possible to impose other plausible conditions on tastes, opportunities, and government structure and produce an equilibrium where x- and y-type states coexist in spite of majority support for x over y.

My analysis of state legislative choices challenges the idea that states are "lighthouses" that show the way to the federal government by enacting innovative laws. In my model, a law may spread to many states, not because it has been "tested" and found useful,[10] but rather

[9] Riker's argument turns on the overriding importance of individual tastes in determining political outcomes. He uses the example of white racism. "As long as whites strongly prefer racist institutions, one can expect institutions to be racist regardless of whether the country is federal or unitary. But when the preference for racist institutions weakens, then federalism helps racism by rendering difficult the enforcement of an anti-racist policy on the minority of white racists. So we can say that the beneficiaries of federalism get only marginal benefits on policy, but marginal or not, they are undoubtedly real" (1975, p. 156).

[10] See Walker (1969, 1971, 1973). By his choice of words, Walker appears to believe that early adopters of laws are progressive. He calls them "pioneers" (1969, p. 881). A glance at Walker's list of laws should warn anyone against this inference. Many involve the licensing of occupations such as barbers or real estate brokers. Others simply mandate the establishment of state agencies, many of which are required as a condition for receiving federal grants. For a different perspective on the same issue which emphasizes politicians' incentives to take risks, see Rose-Ackerman (1980).

because voters in y-type states want to avoid damage at the expense of others. Similarly, a national law may eventually pass in a federal system, not because a new initiative has been tested in the states, but rather because voters want to override the costs of spillovers and inconsistent laws.

Since a fully general analysis would be difficult to interpret, I concentrate on three special cases that capture the essential features of many actual situations. In these examples, I assume that tastes do not change over time, that voters have similar initial information, and that benefits that spill over to people in one group of states are costs to people in the other. In case 1, voters in x-type states receive positive spill-ins from out-of-state residents, and voters in y-type states bear costs. In case 2, voters in x-type states receive negative spill-ins from y-type states, and voters in y-type states benefit at the others' expense. Finally, in case 3, voters' beliefs in "states' rights" may conflict with their substantive position on other issues.

Case 1: Positive Spill-ins to x-Type States

Examples of case 1 are casino gambling or state-run lotteries in states where voters are concerned only with tax revenues and jobs. Taxes imposed on products sold to out-of-state consumers also fall into case 1. In these situations, A_2 and B_3 are empty sets.[11] Thus (3) becomes $N(A_3) \gtreqless N(B_2)$.

Since an x-type law leads to positive spill-ins, it is plausible to suppose that over time more and more states pass x-type laws (i.e., the set G changes). A few states institute lotteries, for example, and eventually many more follow their example. If this happens, people in set B now join set A. Many who favored a national lottery (i.e., those in B_1 and B_2) may now oppose it as a way of preserving their newly acquired positive spillovers (i.e., they move to A_3 and A_4, respectively).

As more states pass x-type laws, however, the level of net positive spillovers to each x-type state falls. In the case of casino gambling and lotteries, a state's consumers are less likely to gamble in other states if their own state has an x-type law.[12] In addition, negative spillovers to y-type states increase as more and more states export costs to them. The decline in net benefits and the increase in net costs as G changes

---

[11] Voters in A_2 favor preemption but oppose x in a unitary system. Voters in B_3 oppose preemption but favor policy x in a unitary system. Both of these preference patterns seem to be implausible if x-type states benefit at the expense of y-type states. This case would not hold if some people think that gambling brings costs (i.e., crowds, corruption).

[12] Similarly, tax incentives to encourage industry to locate in a jurisdiction provide few benefits to taxpayers if most states provide equivalent incentives. For an attempt to show the costs of interstate competition for business investment, see Jacobs (1979).

will raise the vote for a national preemptive law in individual x- and y-type states. Thus, a federal structure generates two influences that operate in opposite directions. A person whose state institutes a lottery is more likely to oppose federal preemption. However, as the number of states with lotteries increases, the benefits of multiplicity fall. If the first factor dominates the second, federalism will continue to matter even in the long run.

Case 2: Positive Spillovers to y-Type States

Examples of case 2 are minimum wage laws[13] or fair labor statutes that increase job opportunities in states without such laws and state pollution control laws where water and air cross state lines. Since in case 2 federalism permits y-type states to gain at the expense of x-type states, A_3 and B_2 are implausible preference patterns. Thus (3) becomes $N(B_3) \geqq N(A_2)$.

The majority of voters in x-type states have decided that, in spite of the costs, the law is worth having. Suppose that as time passes, voters in y-type states learn from the experience of those who have x-type (e.g., minimum wage) laws. If the benefits are greater than expected, then eventually more states pass minimum wage laws. People whose states enact such laws are now more likely to favor federal preemption. They no longer obtain the benefits of spillovers from other states, and they might like to prevent other states from benefiting at their expense. However, as the number of x-type states increases (G changes), the costs imposed on each x-type state fall and the benefits to each y-type state rise. This shift in costs and benefits should reduce support for a preemptive law in individual x- and y-type states. If the second (change in G) effect outweighs the first (change from B to A) effect, a national minimum wage law may not pass in a federal system even though many states have passed their own laws and $N(xRy) > N(yRx)$. Historical research, however, has stressed the cases where state initiatives led eventually to a federal statute,[14] leaving unanalyzed the many situations where the adoption of a law by many states has not been followed by a preemptive federal initiative.[15]

[13] Riker (1964, p. 146) uses the example of minimum wage laws that differ across states: "There is then much likelihood of capital flow from the high-wage localities to the low-wage localities for all those industries in which labor represents a high proportion of the cost. Aside from the imposition of a nationally uniform minimum wage, the only way that high-wage localities may counter this capital flow is by reducing the minimum wage level."

[14] See Fine (1956, pp. 353–85), who discusses the examples of antitrust laws, pure food and drug laws, protective labor legislation, social security, and welfare.

[15] Many of the laws studied by Walker (1969) have spread across many states but have never been adopted nationally. It is possible that some of these statutes might have majority support in a unitary system.

Case 3: States' Rights

In this case, some people put their belief in states' rights above their position on x (e.g., the abolition of slavery) and are in A_3 and B_3. Thus, no one favors imposing x on all states if they also oppose x in a unitary system (i.e., A_2 and B_2 are empty sets). Therefore, (3) becomes $N(A_3 \cup B_3) > 0$.

The vote for x in a federal system is certain to be less than the vote in a unitary system, and federalism may continue to matter so long as preferences remain constant.[16] Assume, however, that people with a substantive preference for x over y favor states' rights only if the results of independent state choices are not too far away from their position on x. Then, it is easy to tell a simple story where an unanticipated change leads to convergence of a federal and a unitary system. If the number of y-type states (e.g., slave states) increases exogenously, people who are opposed to slavery may now choose federal preemption over states' rights (i.e., some of those in A_3 and B_3 move to A_1 and B_1). Therefore, x may now pass at the national level. An exogenous change that seemed to favor y leads in fact to its repudiation by the nation. Thus, it may not be necessary to assume a growth in Northern antislavery sentiment to explain the evolution of pre–Civil War politics. As slavery spread across the South after the invention of the cotton gin, even people whose antipathy to slavery was constant might have supported a national policy of abolition if they thought that more and more states would permit slavery (i.e., they might shift from

---

[16] For symmetry, we could include a fourth case that appears to be of less empirical importance. In this final case, people believe in uniformity or in a strong central government and are willing to support a national law even when they would oppose the law in a unitary system. Thus, A_3 and B_3 are empty sets, (3) becomes $0 < N(A_2 \cup B_2)$, and the vote for x is always larger in a federal system than in a unitary system. If y is a status quo which permits the private market to operate with a minimum of government interference, then case 4 is illustrated by business managers who favor laissez-faire (yRx) but if faced with a mixture of differing state laws would rather have a uniform federal regulatory statute because it permits them to reduce costs. Employers who sell their products in many states often fit this preference pattern. They would rather not be regulated at all, but being regulated in some states is worse than a uniform national standard. For example, sellers of bottled mineral water are beginning to face a variety of labeling laws enacted by different states. According to *Business Week:* "Most bottlers say they would not oppose reasonable, uniform regulations. . . . Industry executives shudder at the prospect of trying to comply with rules that could vary widely among states" ("Mineral Water Could Drown in Regulation," *Business Week* [June 11, 1979]). State trucking regulations are sometimes inconsistent and costly for truckers. Thus, state regulations of the mudguards required on interstate trucks were inconsistent, and an Illinois law was overturned by the Supreme Court as interfering with interstate commerce (Bibb v. Navajo Freight Lines, Inc., 359 U.S. 520 [1959], discussed in Tribe [1978, p. 339]). Similarly, the Supreme Court ruled that Wisconsin's prohibition against twin trailers on interstate highways was an unconstitutional interference with interstate commerce ("Breaking a Bottleneck in Long-Haul Trucking," *Business Week* [March 7, 1978]).

162   JOURNAL OF POLITICAL ECONOMY

A_3 to A_1). When slavery looked as if it might expand into the western states, people who had favored a federal solution might begin to support abolition.[17]

V. Conclusions

Political economists have generally recognized that realistic political systems must include some interjurisdictional spillovers as a cost of providing citizens with a choice of public service levels. Intergovernmental grants may reduce these interjurisdictional costs (Breton 1965) but will not eliminate them. Because both the dispersion of tastes across the population and the level of externalities differ for different public services, some analysts have argued that a federal system is the best way to accommodate these conflicting tendencies (e.g., Oates 1972). In making this recommendation, however, these authors fail to make clear an important idealization inherent in their analysis. They assume that it is possible to assign functions unambiguously to levels of governments so that constitutional structure only has an impact on spillovers and on the position of minorities. In fact, it will often be impossible to assign responsibilities neatly to a particular political level. Indeed, this overlap is the characteristic feature of contemporary "cooperative" federalism. Given this fact, the present paper has shown that, when authority is divided, the choices of lower-level governments can have important consequences for the decisions of higher-level governments. Even when the central government has the power to preempt state and local laws, its democratic choices will depend upon the strategic position of citizens living under alternative state legal regimes. The essential difference between a hierarchical federalism and a unitary system is the difference in the status quo. This difference affects the vote on national legislation and the bargaining power of individuals. Individuals may vote against the extension of a state law to the nation as a whole even though they

[17] Potter (1976), in a history of the period from 1848 to 1861, stresses the difficult trade-offs faced by many people. He writes that "the problem for Americans, who, in the age of Lincoln, wanted slaves to be free was not simply that Southerners wanted the opposite, but that they themselves cherished a conflicting value: they wanted the Constitution, which protected slavery to be honored, and the Union, which was a fellowship with slaveholders to be preserved" (pp. 44–45). The Northern public "placed their antislavery feelings in a context of state action, accepting personal responsibility for slavery within their own particular states" (p. 46). In contrasting the position of Stephen Douglas in 1854 with that of his opponents, Potter shows how these trade-offs were resolved in different people. "Douglas was a vigorous believer in the democratic principle of local autonomy, but his opponents were equally vigorous believers in the moral primacy of freedom. . . . Douglas cared more about the Union than about the eradication of slavery and would never push the slavery issue to a point where it imposed too much strain upon the Union. Many antislavery men thought the Union hardly worth preserving so long as it had slavery in it" (pp. 172–73).

would favor the law in a system with only one government. They may wish to extend a state law to all citizens although they would oppose the law in a unitary system.

The analysis suggests a promising area for future empirical research. Congressional votes on particular issues might be associated with existing state laws,[18] and the timing of federal passage of laws in several areas could be related to the patterns of state adoptions of similar laws. Empirical work is also needed on specific policy areas. For example, one might study the impact of local power over schools on state and federal education policy or see how federal efforts to reduce poverty have been conditioned by prior state and local efforts.

My discussion of federalism also suggests that, at the point of constitutional choice, people are more likely to support a federal system with strong lower-level governments, the fewer the strategic possibilities open to individual states. Strong low-level governments will be attractive if people are grouped geographically by their taste for public services and if it is difficult to impose costs on other jurisdictions. This implies that many people would support constitutional constraints on state governments that limit the states' strategic behavior while retaining many of the benefits of variety and experimentation. I would also expect that, if interjurisdictional migration is possible, then those who favor aid to currently disadvantaged groups at the expense of mobile capital and labor resources will favor a strong central government.[19] It is a commonplace in economic analyses of federalism to note that low-level governments cannot carry out redistributive policies (e.g., Oates 1972). My point, however, goes beyond this conclusion to the observation that if states try to gain at the expense of other states, then interstate redistribution can occur that bears little relation to anyone's notion of social justice and may end up making all households worse off. The end result depends upon each state's strategic position, that is, its ability to export taxes and import benefits.

References

Breton, Albert. "A Theory of Government Grants." *Canadian J. Econ. and Polit. Sci.* 31 (May 1965): 175–87.

[18] McLure (1967, p. 72), in a study of the export of state taxes, recognizes that "states with the largest export rates can be expected to favor state or local assumption of governmental activities while those with low export rates might reasonably favor federal action."

[19] Thus, Dye (1973, p. 62) writes that "urban interests, low-income groups, blacks, ethnic groups and labor organizations frequently turn to the national government for help. States' rights arguments have little appeal to those groups, which are important in the national electorate, but do not constitute majorities in the large number of sparsely settled states."

Cover, Robert M., and Aleinikoff, T. Alexander. "Dialectical Federalism: Habeas Corpus and the Court." *Yale Law J.* 86 (May 1977): 1035–1102.

Dye, Thomas R. *Politics in States and Communities.* 2d ed. Englewood Cliffs, N.J.: Prentice-Hall, 1973.

Elazar, Daniel J. *The American Partnership: Intergovernmental Co-operation in the Nineteenth-Century United States.* Chicago: Univ. Chicago Press, 1962.

Fine, Sidney. *Laissez Faire and the General-Welfare State.* Ann Arbor: Univ. Michigan Press, 1956.

Grodzins, Morton. "The Federal System." In *President's Commission on National Goals for Americans.* Englewood Cliffs, N.J.: Prentice-Hall, 1960.

———. *The American System: A New View of Government in the United States*, edited by Daniel J. Elazar. Chicago: Rand McNally, 1966.

Jacobs, Jerry. "Bidding for Business: Corporate Auctions and the 50 Disunited States." Mimeographed. Washington: Public Interest Res. Group, August 1979.

McLure, Charles E., Jr. "The Interstate Exporting of State and Local Taxes: Estimates for 1962." *National Tax J.* 20 (March 1967): 49–77.

Oates, Wallace E. *Fiscal Federalism.* New York: Harcourt Brace Jovanovich, 1972.

Olson, Mancur, Jr. "The Principle of 'Fiscal Equivalence': The Division of Responsibilities among Different Levels of Government." *A.E.R. Papers and Proc.* 59 (May 1969): 479–87.

Posner, Richard A. *Economic Analysis of Law.* 2d ed. Boston: Little, Brown, 1977.

Potter, David M. *The Impending Crisis, 1848–1861.* New York: Harper & Row, 1976.

Riker, William H. *Federalism: Origin, Operation, Significance.* Boston: Little, Brown, 1964.

———. "Federalism." In *Handbook of Political Science.* Vol. 5, *Governmental Institutions and Processes*, edited by Fred I. Greenstein and Nelson W. Polsby. Reading, Mass.: Addison-Wesley, 1975.

Rose-Ackerman, Susan. "Risktaking and Reelection: Does Federalism Promote Innovation?" *J. Legal Studies* 9 (June 1980): 593–616.

Rothenberg, Jerome. "Local Decentralization and the Theory of Optimal Government." In *The Analysis of Public Output*, edited by Julius Margolis. New York: Columbia Univ. Press (for Nat. Bur. Econ. Res.), 1970.

Sen, Amartya K. *Collective Choice and Social Welfare.* San Francisco: Holden Day, 1970.

Tribe, Laurence H. *American Constitutional Law.* Mineola, N.Y.: Foundation Press, 1978.

Tullock, Gordon. "Federalism: Problems of Scale." *Public Choice* 6 (Spring 1969): 19–29.

Walker, Jack L. "The Diffusion of Innovations among the American States." *American Polit. Sci. Rev.* 63 (September 1969): 880–99.

———. "Innovation in State Politics." In *Politics in the American States: A Comparative Analysis*, 2d ed., edited by Herbert Jacob and Kenneth N. Vines. Boston: Little, Brown, 1971.

———. "Comment: Problems in Research on the Diffusion of Policy Innovations." *American Polit. Sci. Rev.* 67 (December 1973): 1186–91.

Wechsler, Herbert. "Political Safeguards of Federalism." In *Selected Essays on Constitutional Law 1938–1962*, edited by Edward L. Barrett, Jr., et al. St. Paul, Minn.: West Publishing (for Assoc. American Law Schools), 1963.

Wheare, Kenneth C. *Federal Government.* 3d ed. London: Oxford Univ. Press, 1953.

Winter, Ralph K., Jr. "State Law, Shareholder Protection, and the Theory of the Corporation." *J. Legal Studies* 6 (June 1977): 251–92.

Ylvisaker, Paul. "Some Criteria for a 'Proper' Areal Division of Governmental Powers." In *Area and Power: A Theory of Local Government*, edited by Arthur Maass. Glencoe, Ill.: Free Press, 1959.

[10]

The Implications of Competition among Jurisdictions: Does Tiebout Need Politics?

Dennis Epple and Allan Zelenitz

Carnegie-Mellon University

The paper investigates whether competition among local jurisdictions is, by itself, sufficient to ensure efficient provision of local public goods. Jurisdictions have fixed boundaries, and each has an entrenched government with the power to tax and supply the public good. Residents can move costlessly among jurisdictions. It is shown that competition among numerous jurisdictions is not sufficient to guarantee public sector efficiency. Though residents can "vote with their feet," land is immobile. Hence, governments can usurp some land rents for their own ends. Increasing the number of jurisdictions limits but cannot completely eliminate the ability to exercise discretionary governmental power.

I. Introduction

Governments are alleged to be too big, inefficiently operated, and unresponsive to the public. The assumption that government activities are undertaken to serve the public has fallen into disrepute.[1] Instead, positive analyses of public activities increasingly take the governmental objective to be that of satisfying a bureaucratic goal such as expenditure maximization or maximization of the utility of the head of the government agency.[2] Such objectives have been assumed to characterize local as well as national governments.[3] Indeed, the idea

We would like to thank the participants in the Political Economy Workshop at the University of Pennsylvania, the Microeconomics Workshop at the University of Virginia, the Public Choice Workshop at Virginia Polytechnic Institute, and an anonymous referee for helpful comments. We thank Robert Inman for his comments and for suggesting the title for the paper.

[1] See, e.g., Downs (1957) and Stigler (1971) for seminal arguments.

[2] See Posner 1974; Tullock 1974; and Niskanen 1975.

[3] See Wagner and Weber 1975.

[*Journal of Political Economy*, 1981, vol. 89, no. 6]

© 1981 by The University of Chicago. 0022-3808/81/8906-0002$01.50

that local governments may pursue various goals is implicit in analyses of local fiscal variables which assume that the values of these variables are dependent on or influenced by the process of collective choice; the characteristics of the decisive voter(s) as well as the nature and institutional form of local governments are presumed to matter.[4]

At the national level, it is often argued that competition via the electoral process leaves the bureaucrat considerable latitude because voters have limited incentive to learn about candidates or to vote their preferences. At the local level, however, it has been argued that competition among jurisdictions restricts a bureaucrat's ability to pursue policies which do not reflect the residents' desires. In fact, Tiebout (1956) argued that jurisdictional competition would guarantee the same efficiency in the provision of local public goods that competition among firms assures in private goods markets. Tiebout's argument thus appears to imply that the ballot box is unnecessary, that efficient provision of local public services will arise because residents can vote with their feet. If, in fact, jurisdictional competition leads to efficient local goods provision, then analyses of the political choice process would appear to be applicable primarily in those cases in which the relevant set of jurisdictions is small.

In a recent article, Courant, Gramlich, and Rubinfeld (1979) study the choice of fiscal variables by a local government that has been captured by its bureaucracy. Their analysis, which focuses upon decision making in a single jurisdiction, investigates the extent to which the ability of residents to leave the jurisdiction limits the power of its bureaucracy. Their paper provides an interesting analysis of the trade-off faced by a public employees' union in a single jurisdiction whose residents are mobile.

Our analysis focuses on the equilibrium among jurisdictions. We seek to determine how changing the number of jurisdictions (i.e., changing the degree of competition among jurisdictions) constrains tax and expenditure policies of individual governments. We posit alternative assumptions about governmental objectives to examine the consequences of jurisdictional competition.[5]

In particular, we question whether competition among a large number of jurisdictions forces governments to implement policies that are in the best interests of their residents. To answer this question, we deliberately consider a rather extreme version of government

---

[4] See Barr and Davis 1966; Borcherding and Deacon 1972; Bergstrom and Goodman 1973; Denzau and Mackay 1976; Inman 1978; and Romer and Rosenthal 1978.

[5] Courant and Rubinfeld (1978) explore benefit measurement issues in a model with equilibrium among jurisdictions. However, neither jurisdictional competition nor an investigation of implications of alternative governmental objectives is the focus of their paper.

entrenchment. The government (the mayor, the bureaucracy, or however defined) in each jurisdiction is assumed to choose a tax rate and level of government spending to maximize government profit. The government is limited in its choice of tax instruments by a constitution over which it has no control, but there is no political mechanism by which residents can affect the tax rate or the level of government spending. Residents can, however, move freely among jurisdictions. *We do not claim that local governments actually maximize profits; we do not wish to argue that local governments are entrenched and unresponsive to their electorates. Resident voters, via intrajurisdictional processes, may indeed restrain governmental behavior to be in accord with their own desires. Without denying this possibility, this paper addresses the question of whether interjurisdictional competition can, in itself, accomplish the same end.* Although increasing the number of jurisdictions reduces each government's ability to levy taxes in excess of expenditures, we demonstrate that competition among jurisdictions, even with very many jurisdictions, is not sufficient to prevent individual governments from pursuing policies which are not in the interests of their residents. We thus demonstrate that the right of citizens to choose among many communities cannot completely eliminate governmental monopoly power; that is, competition among governments is not equivalent to competition among firms. A further implication is that the political choice process can matter.

The above results are established in a model in which every government seeks to maximize governmental profit and in which each jurisdiction is equivalent in size and location. Once this result has been established, it is natural to ask whether governments in different jurisdictions can coexist while pursuing different objectives. This question is answered affirmatively even when the number of jurisdictions is very large. In answering this question, we shed additional light on the "capitalization hypothesis" and further clarify the interpretation of tests of the Tiebout hypothesis. Finally, we explain what would happen if all jurisdictions were not homogeneous in size or locational desirability or both. One of the implications is that the presence of a large number of jurisdictions in one portion of the metropolitan area, say, the suburbs, limits the monopoly power of jurisdictions in that portion of the metropolitan area but has little effect on the monopoly power of jurisdictions in other portions of the metropolitan area, say, the central city.

In the section which follows, the model is introduced and some comparative statics are derived for use in the subsequent sections. In Section III, governments are assumed to maximize profits, and the implications of jurisdictional competition are examined. The consequences of jurisdictional competition when objectives differ among governments are examined in Section IV. In Section V we investigate the case in which jurisdictions of differing size occupy differing portions of the metropolitan area. A summary and conclusions are presented in Section VI.

II. Equilibrium with Multiple Jurisdictions[6]

In a metropolitan area with homogeneous individuals each of whom can freely choose the jurisdiction in which he wishes to reside, no jurisdiction can unilaterally create a level of well-being for its residents different from that available to residents of the remaining jurisdictions (assuming more than one). If, for instance, one jurisdiction chooses a fiscal package (i.e., tax rate and level of government services) which residents find relatively unattractive, they will respond by moving to other jurisdictions. As a result of this movement, housing prices adjust to compensate for differences in the desirability of fiscal packages. In this section, we will set forth more exactly the implications of this assumption that individuals can choose their residential location. The primary purpose of this section is to derive properties of the equilibrium. These properties are used in the analyses in subsequent sections. The analyses in this and the following section are kept relatively simple by the assumption that all jurisdictions are alike both in terms of their natural physical amenities and in terms of their fiscal variables.

Consider, therefore, a metropolitan area with a fixed total land area, $\bar{L}$, in which there are J jurisdictions.[7] The land area is divided equally among the jurisdictions, so that each has a fixed boundary encompassing land area $L = \bar{L}/J$. Housing is produced by competitive firms in the jurisdiction from land and nonland factors via a constant-returns neoclassical production function. The price of nonland factors is assumed fixed and uniform throughout the metropolitan area. The housing-supply function in the jth jurisdiction can then be written as:[8]

$$H^j_s = Lh^j_s(P^j_H), \tag{1}$$

---

[6] In this and subsequent sections of the paper, we assume an equilibrium exists and we investigate the properties of the equilibrium.

[7] In Sec. V we show that our results are not changed qualitatively if it is assumed that additional land is available at the urban fringe.

[8] The housing-supply function is obtained by assuming that housing producers choose the ratio of nonland to land inputs to maximize profits. The production function is assumed to exhibit constant returns to scale. The ratio of nonland to land inputs will be an increasing function of the price of housing, and it follows that the amount of housing supplied per unit of land will increase as the price of housing increases.

where P_H^j is the price of housing in the jth jurisdiction and h_s^j is the supply function of housing per unit of land.

The jurisdiction supplies G^j units of a local public good; each resident is assumed to receive an equal nonshared amount. The good is produced with constant returns to scale from nonland factors, and its unit cost will be taken as unity. Thus, the total cost of the good is proportional to the number of residents. The jurisdiction finances this good by assessment of a flat rate property tax, t^j, on the market value of housing in the jurisdiction. Determination of the levels of G^j and t^j will be discussed in the following sections.

There are $\bar{N}$ identical individuals in the metropolitan area and N^j in the jth jurisdiction. Each individual has a utility function over government services, housing, and numeraire goods (B), $U(G, h, B)$, and faces the budget constraint, $I = P_H h(1 + t) + B$. Individuals in each jurisdiction choose housing quantity to maximize utility, taking G^j and t^j as given. Let $V[G^j, P_H^j(1 + t^j)]$ denote the indirect utility function that results. That is,

$$V[G^j, P_H^j(1 + t^j)] = \max_{h_d^j} U[G^j, h_d^j, I - P_H^j h_d^j(1 + t^j)]. \tag{2}$$

The demand function for housing by an individual in jurisdiction j, given the decision to live in jurisdiction j, that results from this maximization is:

$$h_d^j = h_d^j[G^j, P_H^j(1 + t^j)]. \tag{3}$$

Note that h_d expresses housing demanded per person, unlike h_s, which expresses housing supplied per unit of land.

Each individual is free to move among jurisdictions, and his locational choice is that which maximizes his utility. In equilibrium, no individual has an incentive to move. Thus, utility must be the same in all jurisdictions:

$$V[G^i, P_H^i(1 + t^i)] = V[G^j, P_H^j(1 + t^j)]. \tag{4}$$

All N^j individuals in each jurisdiction must be housed, so

$$N^j h_d^j = L h_s^j, \tag{5}$$

and all individuals in the metropolitan area must live in some jurisdiction,

$$\bar{N} = \sum_{j=1}^{J} N^j. \tag{6}$$

Conditions (5) and (6) can be combined to yield:

$$\bar{N} = \sum_{j=1}^{J} \frac{L h_s^j}{h_d^j} = L \sum_{j=1}^{J} \frac{h_s^j}{h_d^j}. \tag{7}$$

We will assume that the government of each jurisdiction, whatever its objective, adopts a Cournot-Nash strategy, choosing its G^j and t^j treating all other jurisdictions' choices of G and t as parameters (i.e., no attempt will be made to investigate strategies in which one government attempts to determine how changes in its tax rate or service level will affect the choice of tax rates or service levels in other jurisdictions). In the remainder of this section, we derive the comparative static response of P_H^j and N^j in each jurisdiction when t^k and G^k are varied in any one jurisdiction. For notational convenience, we will denote jurisdiction 1 (i.e., $k = 1$) as the jurisdiction whose tax and spending levels are perturbed.[9]

If jurisdiction 1 differentially changes its tax rate while no other fiscal parameter is altered, individuals would move into or out of jurisdiction 1 and out of or into the remaining $J - 1$ jurisdictions. Changes in housing prices will ensure that equilibrium, as described by conditions (4) and (7), is restored. Consequently, totally differentiating (4) and (7), we obtain the response of prices to a change in t^1:

$$-U_B^1 h_d^1 (1 + t^1) dP_H^1 + U_B^j h_d^j (1 + t^j) dP_H^j = U_B^1 h_d^1 P_H^1 dt^1, \, j \neq 1. \tag{8a}$$ [10]

$$L \sum_{j=1}^{J} \frac{\partial (h_s^j / h_d^j)}{\partial P_H^j} dP_H^j = -L \frac{\partial (h_s^1 / h_d^1)}{\partial t^1} dt^1. \tag{8b}$$

In order to simplify notation, for each jurisdiction, let η^j represent the elasticity of housing demand with respect to the gross-of-tax price

---

[9] Technically, this model is not "closed" for two reasons. First, land has a positive price in all jurisdictions and the return on land wealth has not been included as income to consumers. Second, if the government obtains tax revenue in excess of expenditures, the profit should be counted as income to some agent. Formally incorporating these elements requires dealing with wealth effects—which are a nuisance and do not shed any light on the issues of interest to us. The return on land wealth could be incorporated in one of two ways. Title to land could be created with each consumer-resident endowed with shares valued at $1/N$th of the aggregate value of the land in the metropolitan area. This would not change our analysis or our results in any essential respect. Alternatively, the utility function of consumers could be assumed to display a constant marginal utility of the numeraire commodity, i.e., to be of the form $U = W(G,h) + B$. With this utility function, variations in wealth arising either from changes in land value or from profits in the government sector would not affect the equilibrium in the market for housing within or across jurisdictions. The fact that wealth effects can be introduced in these ways without affecting our qualitative results reinforces our assertion that they can be assumed away. While closing the model by one or more of the devices mentioned above may be an appealing formalism, the added complexity adds cumbersome detail without in any way illuminating the issues being addressed.

[10] In obtaining (8a) from (4), we have made use of eq. (2). Note that (4) and (2) together imply that the direct utility function evaluated at the optimum choice of housing must be equal across jurisdictions. Hence we simply use the envelope theorem, that residents' housing demand optimally adjusts to the new gross-of-tax price of housing, $P_H(1 + t)$, in each community.

of housing ($\eta < 0$), let θ^j represent the elasticity of housing supply with respect to the net-of-tax price of housing ($\theta > 0$), and let γ^j represent the elasticity of housing demand with respect to government services. In addition, let δ^j represent the functionally determined density of population.

Since in this section all governments are assumed to behave identically and adopt the same strategy and all governments and residents are identical, we assume that all governments will adopt the same G and t in equilibrium. Thus, when t^1 is perturbed, $dP_H^2 = \ldots = dP_H^j$, and the levels of all endogenous variables are the same in all jurisdictions. Using these conditions and the elasticities and ratio defined above, we may rewrite equations (8) as:[11]

$$\frac{dP_H^1}{dt^1} = \frac{P_H[\eta - (J-1)(\theta - \eta)]}{J(1+t)(\theta - \eta)} < 0, \qquad (9a)$$

$$\frac{dP_H^j}{dt^1} = \frac{P_H\theta}{J(1+t)(\theta - \eta)} > 0, \qquad j = 2, \ldots, J. \qquad (9b)$$

It is apparent from (9a) that an increase in the number of jurisdictions increases the sensitivity of P_H^1 to changes in t^1; that is, as J increases, dP_H^1/dt^1 becomes more negative, and in the limit as $J \to \infty$ it approaches $-P_H/(1+t)$. This implies that in the limit the derivative of the gross-of-tax price, $d[P_H^1(1+t^1)]/dt^1$, approaches zero, so that any change in t^1 is fully offset by a change in P_H^1. As the number of jurisdictions becomes large, the price in other jurisdictions is unaffected by changes in t^1, as is seen by taking the limit of (9b) as $J \to \infty$.

Under our simplifying assumption of identical governments and residents, the comparative static effects on housing prices caused by a change in G^1 can be derived in the same manner as the effects caused by changes in t^1. These comparative statics are:

$$\frac{dP_H^1}{dG^1} = \frac{(J-1)U_G}{JU_Bh_d(1+t)} + \frac{\gamma P_H}{JG(\theta - \eta)}; \qquad (10a)$$

$$\frac{dP_H^j}{dG^1} = -\frac{U_G}{JU_Bh_d(1+t)} + \frac{\gamma P_H}{JG(\theta - \eta)}. \qquad (10b)$$

The first term in (10a) reflects the increase in housing prices arising because jurisdiction 1 becomes more desirable to consumers as G^1 rises, so that more consumers wish to enter. The second term indicates the effect of the complementarity ($\gamma > 0$) or substitutability ($\gamma < 0$) of government services and housing. If they are complementary, an increase in G^1 causes an increase in housing demand *per*

[11] Detailed enumeration of the steps in deriving these results and results in subsequent sections is available on request.

consumer—which in turn causes P_H^1 to be bidden up.[12] The terms in (10b) are interpreted similarly.

As the number of jurisdictions increases, equation (10b) indicates that the effects of changes in G^1 on prices in other jurisdictions go to zero. As $J \to \infty$, equation (10a) shows that any rise in G^1 will be offset by a rise in P_H^1 to keep the consumer-resident's utility constant.

The effects of changes in t^1 and G^1 on the population in jurisdiction 1, N^1, are derived by differentiation of (5) and by use of the results in (9) and (10). Performing the necessary differentiation and substitutions yields:

$$\frac{dN^1}{dt^1} = \frac{-(J-1)N^1\theta}{J(1+t)} < 0, \tag{11a}$$

$$\frac{dN^1}{dG^1} = N^1\left[\frac{-\gamma}{G} + \frac{\gamma}{JG} + \frac{(J-1)U_G(\dot{\theta} - \eta)}{JU_BP_Hh_d(1+t)}\right]. \tag{11b}$$

These results are easily summarized. An increase in the tax rate causes a decline in the jurisdiction's population because the fall in the equilibrium net-of-tax price (see [9a]) causes a reduction in housing supply. By contrast, a rise in government services makes the jurisdiction more attractive. As a consequence, the population of the jurisdiction will rise, except in the case where complementarity of housing and government services causes an increase in per capita housing demand large enough to offset the decline in per capita demand that results from the price increase exhibited in (10a).

It should be emphasized that the comparative static results derived above do not depend on any particular objective function for the jurisdictions. They simply characterize an equilibrium in which identical jurisdictions pursue identical Cournot-Nash strategies. They can thus be used to investigate governmental objectives such as maximization of property values, the utility of the median voter, government expenditure, or "government profit."

III. Profit-maximizing Government

In this section we assume that each jurisdiction is controlled by a monopolist whose objective is to maximize governmental profit, defined here as the excess of tax revenue over government expenditure. We will neither defend nor deny the realism of this governmental objective; this choice of extreme objective is simply a convenient vehicle for determining whether jurisdictional competition can

---

[12] In their study of incidence, Polinsky and Rubinfeld (1978, p. 257) find that this complementarity or substitutability is one factor determining how a change in government services affects land prices and other variables.

eliminate the power of local governments to adopt policies which are
not in the best interests of their residents. In practice, voting by
residents might prevent such exercise of monopoly power. However,
our purpose is to determine whether competition among jurisdictions
is by itself sufficient to prevent the exercise of governmental power.
Hence, we deliberately assume that the monopolist can set G and t
without electoral approval.

Profit to the government of the representative jurisdiction is:[13]

$$\pi = tP_H(t, G)H_s[P_H(t,G)] - N(t,G)G. \tag{12}$$

Superscripts have been dropped since all jurisdictions are identical.

Differentiating (12) and using (1) and the comparative static properties of the functions $P_H(t,G)$ and $N(t,G)$, we can write the first-order
conditions for profit maximization as:

$$\frac{\partial \pi}{\partial t} = L\left\{\frac{P_H h_s}{(1+t)}\left[1 - t\theta + \frac{t\theta(1+\theta)}{J(\theta - \eta)}\right] + \frac{G\delta(J-1)\theta}{J(1+t)}\right\} = 0. \tag{13a}$$

$$\frac{\partial \pi}{\partial G} = L\left\{\left[\frac{U_G(J-1)\delta}{U_B JP_H h_d(1+t)} + \frac{\gamma\delta}{JG(\theta - \eta)}\right]\right.$$
$$\left.\left[tP_H h_d(1+\theta) - G(\theta - \eta)\right] + (\gamma - 1)\right\} = 0. \tag{13b}$$

Canceling L, taking limits as $J \rightarrow \infty$, and rearranging the above, we
obtain:

$$tP_H h_d = G + \frac{P_H h_d}{\theta}, \tag{14a}$$

$$\frac{U_G}{U_B}\left[1 + \frac{G\eta}{P_H h_d(1+t)}\right] = 1 - \gamma. \tag{14b}$$

From (14b) it is apparent that the marginal rate of substitution of
government services for numeraire goods departs from the ratio of
relative prices (which equals one). However, because of the distortion
that arises from the property tax on housing, even a welfare-
maximizing government would choose a level of public good supply
such that the marginal rate of substitution does not equal the price
ratio.

From (14a), it is clear, unlike the Cournot result when the number
of firms is increased, that government monopoly profits are positive
even when the number of jurisdictions is large. Tax revenue per
capita, $tP_H h_d$, exceeds government spending per capita, G, by a posi-

---

[13] We assume that the government does not consume housing.

tive amount, related to the value of housing per capita, $P_H h_d$, and to the housing-supply elasticity, θ. Thus competition among governments encompassed by fixed boundaries is not sufficient to eliminate those governments' monopoly power.

For an intuitive understanding of why jurisdictional competition does not eliminate governmental power, consider the following simplified version of the model. Suppose consumers get no utility from government services. Obviously, then, the bureaucratic monopolist will set $G = 0$. The condition determining the profit-maximizing value of t is then (13a) with $G = 0$. Suppose further that θ and η are constant over the relevant range. Then (13a) can be solved for t to yield:

$$t = \frac{J(\theta - \eta)}{\theta[J(\theta - \eta) - 1 - \theta]}. \qquad (15)$$

Taking the limit of (15) as $\eta \rightarrow -\infty$, it is seen that:

$$\lim_{\eta \to -\infty} t = \frac{1}{\theta}. \qquad (16)$$

Thus, when housing demand is perfectly elastic, the profit-maximizing tax rate is determined solely by the elasticity of housing supply independent of the number of jurisdictions. With perfectly elastic housing demand, the price of housing is exogenous, but bureaucratic monopolists can still profit by sharing in the rents of the landowners whose land is confined to some given jurisdiction. Alternatively, suppose that housing is in perfectly elastic supply. Then, from (15):

$$\lim_{\theta \to \infty} t = \begin{cases} \dfrac{-1}{\eta + 1} & \text{if } J = 1 \\ 0 & \text{if } J > 1. \end{cases} \qquad (17)$$

With only one jurisdiction, the bureaucratic monopolist can exploit the housing-demand elasticity. If there is more than one jurisdiction, housing can be expanded indefinitely at constant cost in each jurisdiction, and the individual jurisdictions are unable to exploit the elasticity of the demand curve.

Next, consider the effects of an increase in the number of jurisdictions in (15):

$$\lim_{J \to \infty} t = \frac{1}{\theta}. \qquad (18)$$

Comparing (16) and (18), we see that the effect of having very many jurisdictions is similar to the effect of having an infinitely elastic housing demand. Competition among jurisdictions prevents a bureaucratic monopolist from exploiting the demand elasticity but not the supply elasticity.

Finally, differentiating t with respect to J in (15) reveals that

$$\frac{dt}{dJ} = -\frac{(\theta - \eta)(1 + \theta)}{\theta[J(\theta - \eta) - (1 + \theta)]^2} < 0. \tag{19}$$

An increase in the number of jurisdictions does monotonically decrease the tax rate.

While these results are surprising, they are easily explained. The government of each jurisdiction is given the exclusive right to tax the property in that jurisdiction. Since boundaries are fixed, a landowner cannot move his land to another jurisdiction by a redefinition of boundaries. Fixity of boundaries prevents the tax on land from being competed away. Jurisdictions compete for residents, and competition among a large number of jurisdictions prevents exploitation of the elasticity of housing demand. Jurisdictions in our model here do not compete for land; consequently, the existence of a large number of jurisdictions does not prevent exploitation of the elasticity of housing supply.

Although the tax exploits only the elasticity of supply when there are many jurisdictions, one should not conclude that the tax merely redistributes wealth from landowners to bureaucrats. The tax reduces the unit price of housing received by suppliers, thereby reducing the supply of housing relative to the no-tax equilibrium. As a result, the gross-of-tax price of housing must be higher and per capita housing consumption lower than in the no-tax equilibrium. The only exception would be if housing supply were perfectly inelastic. For this case, the tax would not affect housing production or consumption.

Our results can be illustrated geometrically if we consider a simplified version of the model in which G is fixed at zero for all jurisdictions. Each curve in the right-hand portion of figure 1 shows combinations of net-of-tax housing prices and tax rates that generate the same gross-of-tax price and hence the same level of utility. The further to the northeast, the lower is the utility level. Let V^0 represent the highest utility attainable, that level which would occur if $t = t^0 = 0$ in all jurisdictions and competitive market forces determined a net-of-tax price of P_H^0. The housing market is depicted in the left-hand diagram. Recall that the housing-supply function per unit of land, h_s, is independent of the number of jurisdictions and of the tax rate. The housing-demand function per unit of land is a product of the housing demand per person, $h_d[P_H(1 + t), \bar{G}]$, and the population density, δ. Hence each jurisdiction exhibits the same housing price, P_H^0, and the same population density, δ^0. The zero tax equilibrium in the housing market is shown as point Z.

Now consider the situation in which all governments set the same positive tax rate, t^1. We show that this lowers utility and results in a

1208   JOURNAL OF POLITICAL ECONOMY

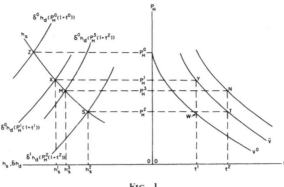

FIG. 1

net-of-tax price lower than P_H^0. If the net-of-tax price were to decline sufficiently to reestablish the original utility level, at point W, the housing-demand function would be unaltered at $\delta^0 h_d[P_H^0(1 + t^0)]$. But with the resulting lower net-of-tax price and an unaltered demand, there would be a housing shortage. With a tax rate of t^1, the housing market could clear only if the net-of-tax price rose above the level at point W. This requires an increase in the gross-of-tax price, hence a decrease in utility below the V^0 level. If P_H did not fall, the housing-demand curve (not shown) would shift downward since $P_H^0(1 + t^1) > P_H^0(1 + t^0)$ and δ is unchanged at δ^0. This would create a housing surplus. Thus, the housing market will clear only if P_H falls below P_H^0, say, to P_H^1. Consequently, a feasible equilibrium with tax rate t^1 is shown as point X in the housing market and as point Y in the utility space. Finally, the tax base per unit of land, with $t = t^1$, is found as the area $OP_H^1 X h_s^1$.

Now, suppose the points X and Y represent the equilibrium when there are many jurisdictions. We illustrate why it would not be in the interest of any of these jurisdictions to unilaterally depart from this equilibrium. We then illustrate why it would be in the interest of a monopoly jurisdiction to choose a higher tax rate.

Suppose a competitive jurisdiction, say jurisdiction 1, were to uni-laterally choose a tax rate, say, $t^2 > t^1$.[14] Given residential mobility, the utility level cannot differ across jurisdictions. Thus, the gross-of-tax price in jurisdiction 1, $P_H^2(1 + t^2)$, would equal $P_H^1(1 + t^1)$, which implies $P_H^2 < P_H^1$. Consequently, fewer housing units would be supplied in jurisdiction 1. To restore equilibrium in the housing

---

[14] We assume in the diagrammatic exposition that competition among jurisdictions does not force all jurisdictions to offer the same tax-service package. This issue is investigated in Sec. IV.

market, it would be necessary for some residents to move to other jurisdictions, lowering the population density in jurisdiction 1, say, to $\delta^1 < \delta^0$. The new hypothetical equilibrium for jurisdiction 1 is illustrated by points S and T. Since it contains but a small fraction of the area's land and population, migration out of jurisdiction 1 would have no effect on the remaining jurisdictions. Thus, the hypothetical equilibrium for the remaining jurisdictions remains at points X and Y.

By increasing its tax rate, jurisdiction 1 decreases its tax base per unit of land to $OP_H^2 Sh_s^2$. Should the percentage decline in the tax base be greater than the percentage increase in the tax rate (as suggested by fig. 1), it would not be in the jurisdiction's interest to increase its tax rate. Similarly, were any one jurisdiction to reduce its tax rate below t^2, the resulting increase in the tax base would be more than offset by the decline in the tax rate. Consequently, points X and Y describe the equilibrium for competitive jurisdictions, because there are no incentives for any of the economic agents, governments, residents, or housing suppliers to alter their behavior. Note that, in equilibrium, there are tax revenues collected by each jurisdiction, even when $\bar{G} = 0$; jurisdictional competition is not sufficient to eliminate government profit.

Note that any jurisdiction's incentive to change its tax rate, and hence the equilibrium tax rate, depends on the elasticity of the h_s function. The lower is this elasticity, the greater is the incentive to raise the tax rate. This result can be indicated by considering the case in which h_s is completely inelastic; in particular, assume that h_s rises vertically through point X. If any jurisdiction were to increase its tax rate, any decline in housing demand would not cause a loss of housing units; hence the jurisdiction's tax revenue would increase as long as the percentage increase in the tax rate, $\Delta t/t$, is greater than the percentage decline in the net-of-tax price, $\Delta P_H/P_H$. Since gross-of-tax price is constant, $(P_H - \Delta P_H)(1 + t + \Delta t) = P_H(1 + t)$, and consequently $\Delta P_H/P_H = \Delta t/(1 + t + \Delta t) < \Delta t/t$. A similar incentive to increase t would face each jurisdiction, and t would be continuously forced higher. By altering the supply curve through point X, we can easily show that the incentive to raise t decreases with an increase in the supply elasticity and that a sufficient increase in elasticity creates an incentive to lower the competitive equilibrium tax rate.

Next, suppose that the metropolitan area has but one monopoly jurisdiction. Also assume that the tax rate was initially set at t^1 and that the housing market and utility configurations were initially described by points X and Y. If the monopolist were to choose a higher tax rate, such as t^2, this would increase the tax revenue per unit of land, unlike the situation for the single competitive jurisdiction, because residents cannot escape the monopolist by moving to other jurisdictions. Population density throughout the monopolist's jurisdiction would be unchanged at δ^0. An increase in the tax rate to t^2 has two effects. First, assuming momentarily that the net-of-tax price is unchanged at P_H^1, the per capita demand for housing declines, since $P_H^1(1 + t^2) > P_H^1(1 + t^1)$. But with population density fixed at δ^0, this implies an excess supply of housing. Consequently, the second effect is that the net-of-tax price must fall, say to P_H^3. The resulting situation is depicted as points M and N. Note, though, that the decline in the monopolist's tax base per unit of land, to $OP_H^3Mh_s^3$, is substantially smaller than the decline previously indicated for a competitive jurisdiction contemplating the same tax rate increase. Thus, the monopoly jurisdiction would find it profitable to increase its tax rate, even though a competitive jurisdiction would not. Assuming tax revenue changes monotonically with the number of jurisdictions, it follows that tax revenue per unit of land, hence total tax revenue, is inversely related to the number of jurisdictions. With G fixed, government profit is also inversely related to the number of jurisdictions.

IV. Differing Objectives among Governments

As we indicated in the Introduction, data for local jurisdictions have been used extensively for empirical studies of models of government. The implicit presumption of these studies is that competition among jurisdictions does not prevent different governments from pursuing different goals or prevent them from offering different tax and service packages. In this section, we demonstrate that this presumption is correct. In so doing, we provide a theoretical justification for viewing local jurisdictions as natural laboratories for studying models of government. At the same time, we demonstrate that interdependence among local jurisdictions should not be ignored when such studies are conducted. Finally, results in this section make it clear that our result in the preceding section, that competition does not prevent governmental exercise of monopoly power, is not an artifact of our assumption of homogeneous governmental objectives.

As in the preceding section, we assume that an equilibrium exists, and we characterize the properties of that equilibrium as the number of jurisdictions becomes large. It is first necessary to derive the comparative static properties of an equilibrium in which tax and service packages differ across jurisdictions. Conditions (1) through (7) still obtain. The comparative static responses of prices in all jurisdictions to a change in the tax rate in an arbitrarily chosen jurisdiction can be derived from equations (8). There are J equations in (8) from which the J expressions $\partial P_H^j / \partial t^1$ can be derived. The derivation differs from that employed in Section II only in that jurisdictions are not assumed to adopt identical tax-service packages in equilibrium. By similarly perturbing G in some arbitrarily chosen jurisdiction, say, 1, we can derive the J expressions for $\partial P_H^j / \partial G^1$. Thus, just as in Section II, comparative static responses of price in each jurisdiction to changes in its own fiscal variables and to changes in other jurisdictions' tax rates and service levels can be derived.

By investigating the limiting properties of these comparative statics, we find that, when the number of jurisdictions in a particular subarea becomes very large, the level of utility of residents of any of these jurisdictions is invariant to its choice of tax rate or level of government services. The amount of land in any of these jurisdictions is very small relative to both the total land area and to the land area of jurisdictions having the same amenity level. Consequently, the number of residents migrating into or out of any one of these jurisdictions in response to a change in its tax rate or level of government services is too small to affect the price of housing elsewhere. Hence, utility does not change elsewhere. Rather, the migration induces an adjustment of the housing price within the jurisdiction and that adjustment ensures that the level of utility within the jurisdiction continues to equal the utility level available elsewhere. By contrast, if a jurisdiction has a nonnegligible share of the land in the metropolitan area, migration induced by a change in its fiscal variables is sufficient to change housing prices and utility in all jurisdictions.

While an individual government cannot affect the equilibrium level of utility of its residents when the number of jurisdictions is large, tax rates and service levels are not similarly constrained. Whether changes in these variables are desirable depends upon the government objectives pursued, but it is clear that local governments have latitude in choosing these variables. Put differently, the "market" for local public goods does not force the government to act as a "tax rate taker."[15] This is illustrated in figure 1. Suppose that there are a large number of jurisdictions each of which occupies a small fraction of the land in the metropolitan area. Let $\bar{V}$ be the level of utility realized in equilibrium in all jurisdictions. Consider two of these jurisdictions and assume, for simplicity of illustration, that both offer the same level of government services, $\bar{G}$. The jurisdictions offer differing tax rates, t^1 and t^2, but residents of both jurisdictions enjoy the same level of utility, $\bar{V}$ (shown by the equilibrium points Y and T), and the same

---

[15] Each of the many jurisdictions faces the constraints as described by $(dP_H^j / dt^1) = (dP_H^j / dG^1) = 0$ and by eqq. (1), (2), and (4). If one, and perhaps only one, of these jurisdictions should be a profit-maximizing jurisdiction, as defined in the previous section, it is relatively easy to show that such a jurisdiction would choose its fiscal variables such that conditions (14) are attained. Hence, choice of t and G by profit maximization is not inconsistent with jurisdictional competition.

gross-of-tax price as all other residents of the metropolitan area. In this equilibrium, jurisdiction 2 has a higher tax rate, a lower net-of-tax price, and a smaller population than jurisdiction 1.

By holding the tax rate constant, jurisdictions offering different levels of government services can be illustrated by a diagram similar to that in figure 1. The diagram would differ only in that G would replace t on the right-hand quadrant, and indifference curves would slope upward. Jurisdictions offering high levels of G would attract more residents than jurisdictions offering low levels of G. As a result, the price of housing would be higher in jurisdictions offering higher levels of government services. Competition will require that utility be the same in all jurisdictions, but equality of utility across jurisdictions does not require equality of tax rates or equality of levels of government services.

The finding that, in equilibrium, utility of residents of a jurisdiction is independent of its government's fiscal decisions is a startling result, one which highlights an important conceptual distinction between residents of a jurisdiction and its landowners. For residents who rent housing, the choices of tax rate and government spending level are matters of complete indifference in equilibrium. Housing prices will adjust to maintain their equilibrium utility level. By contrast, the wealth of landowners is directly affected by the choice of tax rates and level of government service. A resident landowner would clearly support a governmental objective of property value maximization. Such an objective would maximize the wealth of the resident as landowner, and, given his mobility, it would not diminish his utility as a consumer of government services and housing.

The results in this section also have implications for tests of the Tiebout hypothesis. In proposing his test of the Tiebout hypothesis, Oates (1969) argued that differences in tax rates or in the level of public services provided would be capitalized in housing prices. Edel and Sclar (1974) argued precisely the opposite—that in a long-run Tiebout equilibrium, tax rates and government spending levels would be uncorrelated with housing prices. In the model developed here, Oates's interpretation is clearly correct. In equilibrium, differences in tax rates and levels of government services will result in differences in housing prices across jurisdictions. This result does not depend on the existence of a large number of jurisdictions, nor does it depend on the objectives being pursued by individual governments.[16]

---

[16] It does, however, depend on the assumption that governments do not directly intervene into housing markets (e.g., via zoning) to induce individuals to consume more housing than they would otherwise choose. See Epple (1980) for further discussion of this issue.

The test proposed by Oates may be interpreted as a test of equilibrium condition (4). In equilibrium, with homogeneous residents, the maximum utility level individuals can achieve will be the same everywhere. Denote this utility level $\bar{V}$. Setting $V[G^i, P_H^i(1 + t^i)] = \bar{V}$ and solving for P_H^i, we obtain an equation of the form estimated by Oates:

$$P_H^i = \frac{f(\bar{V}, G^i)}{(1 + t^i)}. \qquad (20)$$

In any given equilibrium, $\bar{V}$ is the same across jurisdictions, and hence it is impounded in the constant term in a regression equation. To empirically test this equation, it is necessary that one have observations on at least two jurisdictions. However, the equation holds regardless of the number of jurisdictions. The above result and results in our previous paper (Epple, Zelenitz, and Visscher 1978) indicate the crucial role of assumptions about movability of jurisdictional boundaries. In our earlier paper, we argued that housing prices must necessarily be equal across jurisdictional boundaries when boundaries can be costlessly redrawn. By that argument, the hypothesis of Edel and Sclar is correct, but Oates's hypothesis is correct when boundaries are fixed exogenously.[17]

When the number of jurisdictions is large, changes by any one jurisdiction have no effect on $\bar{V}$. Thus, when the number of jurisdictions is large, differentiation of (20) provides equations that correctly indicate the marginal change in the net-of-tax price of housing which will compensate residents when their jurisdiction changes its tax rate or service level. When the number of jurisdictions is small, a change by any one jurisdiction affects $\bar{V}$. In that case, the appropriate expression for the price derivatives cannot be deduced from equation (20), and, as a result, the compensating alteration in housing price caused by a change in tax rate or service level cannot be deduced from (20).

V. Jurisdictions Differentiated by Size and Location

In preceding sections we considered models in which land at all locations is identical and jurisdictions are identical in size. In this

---

[17] Note again that the test proposed by Oates is a test of equilibrium condition (4). If individuals are costlessly mobile among jurisdictions, if individuals have full information concerning jurisdictions' alternative fiscal environments, and if jurisdictions do not restrict residents' consumption bundles, then, as Oates clearly saw, equilibrium condition (4) obtains. This is not, however, a test of Tiebout's hypothesis. The latter is a normative statement, concerning the achievement of an amount of the public good, G, which maximizes individuals' utilities. As is clear from the analysis in the paper, there is no assurance that the utility-maximizing level of G is attained for any individual.

section we generalize the model to permit jurisdictions to differ in both size and degree of desirability. We argue that our preceding results concerning competition hold when jurisdictions are differentiated by desirability of location. We also discuss how the presence of a large number of small jurisdictions in one part of the metropolitan area affects the monopoly power of a large jurisdiction in the same metropolitan area. Finally, we discuss the effects of permitting new jurisdictions to form at the urban fringe.

Since the method of analysis required here is similar to that employed in previous sections, our discussion is presented without benefit of explicit mathematical argument or proof. Technical details are available on request.

To investigate the effects of differentiation of locations, we assume that the total land area $\bar{L}$ is divided into K subareas or locations indexed by k. Each subarea has amenity (or accessibility) in amount A_k. Variable A is assumed to enter the utility function directly. This specification permits investigation of the effects of varying either the number of jurisdictions at each location or the number of distinct locations.

Equilibrium conditions analogous to (2) through (7) continue to apply. Differences are that amenity level now appears in the utility and demand functions. In addition, supply and demand for housing must be equilibrated at each location. Comparative static results are derived by the same procedure used to obtain equations (9), (10), and (11), and governmental objectives are studied using the approach employed in Sections III and IV.

The implications of increasing the number of jurisdictions offering a given amenity level are found to be similar to those derived in Section III. The presence of a large number of small jurisdictions offering the same amenity level prevents any one of these jurisdictions from exploiting the elasticity of housing demand but not the elasticity of housing supply. The profit-maximizing tax rate for these jurisdictions converges to the inverse of the housing-supply elasticity, a result analogous to that in (18). Tax revenue per unit of land will be higher in locations with a high A_K because the price of housing will be higher at such locations. This is a consequence of the equilibrium condition requiring utility to be constant across jurisdictions.

The presence of a large number of small jurisdictions in one part of the metropolitan area, however, does not prevent a large jurisdiction in another part of the metropolitan area from exploiting both the elasticity of housing demand and supply—a result analogous to that in (15).

To interpret these results, think of two locations in a metropolitan region, one the central city and the other the suburban area. The above results imply that a large number of jurisdictions in the suburban region are sufficient to prevent individual suburbs from exploiting the elasticity of housing demand. But the relatively large proportion of metropolitan land area occupied by the central city enables its bureaucratic monopolist to exploit the elasticity of housing demand, even if there are a large number of jurisdictions in the suburban region.

Instead of hypothesizing an increase in the number of jurisdictions offering a given amenity level, we might argue that each jurisdiction encompasses land with unique attributes. The implications of increasing the number of distinct jurisdictions occupying a fixed land area are found to be the same as those derived in Section III. The presence of a large number of small jurisdictions, even if each offers a unique amenity, is sufficient to prevent any jurisdiction from exploiting the elasticity of housing demand but not the elasticity of housing supply.

Finally, it might be argued that our results in Section III arise because we assumed a fixed amount of land available for urban use. This conjecture is incorrect. To demonstrate this point, suppose that locations are indexed in order of decreasing desirability, so that jurisdiction K has the lowest amenity level of the existing jurisdictions. Land with amenity level A_{K+1} may then be thought of as the urban fringe, which we assume to be in perfectly elastic supply. With these assumptions, the utility that can be achieved by choosing land with amenity level A_{K+1} is constant at, say, $\bar{U}$.

There are two possible equilibria. All individuals may find the existing K jurisdictions more attractive than the urban fringe. In that case, the urban fringe is uninhabited and all results are unchanged. Alternatively, some individuals may live on the urban fringe. Since all individuals must achieve the same level of utility in equilibrium, the utility level throughout the metropolitan area is $\bar{U}$. However, as demonstrated in Sections III and IV, an entrenched government that must provide its residents an exogenously specified level of utility can still profit by exploiting the elasticity of housing supply. The existence of jurisdictions at the extensive margin does not eliminate land rents in inframarginal jurisdictions, nor does it prevent the taxation of those rents. Therefore, regardless of which outcome occurs, jurisdictional competition, even when residents can relocate on the urban fringe, cannot prevent an entrenched government from exercising monopoly power.

In summary, by the introduction of heterogeneous urban locations, we demonstrate new results and establish that the results of Sections III and IV hold in a much more general setting. Whether the focus be on one urbanized area in isolation or on all urbanized areas within a nation, whenever rents exist, jurisdictional competition does not prevent an entrenched government from expropriating part of those rents.

VI. Conclusions

The major finding of this paper is that competition among many local jurisdictions is not sufficient to prevent local governments from exercising monopoly power. While we have derived this finding in a model in which government revenues are raised via property taxes, the result also follows if communities are empowered to levy a sales tax (i.e., a tax on the numeraire commodity), an income tax, or a combination of these three taxes.[18]

The feature of our model that is primarily responsible for this result is the assumption of fixed jurisdictional boundaries.[19] A government given taxing powers in a jurisdiction with fixed boundaries can exploit the immobility of land and share in the rents accruing to that land. Mobility of residents across a large number of jurisdictions can prevent individual governments from exploiting the elasticity of housing demand but not the elasticity of housing supply.

These results vindicate researchers seeking to develop a positive political theory of local government behavior. Jurisdictional competition does not predetermine the outcome; Tiebout does need politics. On the other hand, these results highlight the importance of considering the economic as well as the political environment of local governments. As shown in Section IV, competition among a large number of jurisdictions establishes constraints on the choices made by individual governments. Such constraints should not be ignored in modeling decision making by local governments.

References

Barr, James L., and Davis, Otto A. "An Elementary Political and Economic Theory of the Expenditures of Local Governments." *Southern Econ. J.* 33 (October 1966): 149–65.

Bergstrom, Theodore C., and Goodman, Robert P. "Private Demands for Public Goods." *A.E.R.* 63 (June 1973): 280–96.

Borcherding, Thomas E., and Deacon, Robert T. "The Demand for the

---

[18] See, e.g., Courant's (1977) investigation of the incidence and excess burden of taxes on mobile capital, where the tax rate may be heterogeneous across jurisdictions. He is able to demonstrate that landlords as a class bear at least all of the excess burden of the system of taxes, but he finds that the effects, locality by locality, are not easily characterized.

[19] This is also the feature in Courant et al. (1979) which leads to their conclusions regarding the power of public employees.

Services of Non-Federal Governments." *A.E.R.* 62 (December 1972): 891–901.

Courant, Paul N. "A General Equilibrium Model of Heterogeneous Local Property Taxes." *J. Public Econ.* 8, no. 3 (December 1977): 313–27.

Courant, Paul N.; Gramlich, Edward M.; and Rubinfeld, Daniel L. "Public Employee Market Power and the Level of Government Spending." *A.E.R.* 69, no. 5 (December 1979): 806–17.

Courant, Paul N., and Rubinfeld, Daniel L. "On the Measurement of Benefits in an Urban Context: Some General Equilibrium Issues." *J. Urban Econ.* 5, no. 3 (July 1978): 346–56.

Denzau, Arthur T., and Mackay, Robert J. "Benefit Shares and Majority Voting." *A.E.R.* 66, no. 1 (March 1976): 69–76.

Downs, Anthony. *An Economic Theory of Democracy.* New York: Harper, 1957.

Edel, Matthew, and Sclar, Elliott. "Taxes, Spending, and Property Values: Supply Adjustment in a Tiebout-Oates Model." *J.P.E.* 82, no. 5 (September/October 1974): 941–54.

Epple, Dennis. "What Do Tests of Tax Capitalization Test?" Working Paper, Carnegie-Mellon Univ., Graduate School Indus. Admin., September 1980.

Epple, Dennis; Zelenitz, Allan; and Visscher, Michael. "A Search for Testable Implications of the Tiebout Hypothesis." *J.P.E.* 86, no. 3 (June 1978): 405–25.

Inman, Robert P. "Testing Political Economy's 'As If' Proposition: Is the Median Income Voter Really Decisive?" *Public Choice* 33, no. 4 (1978): 45–65.

Niskanen, William A. "Bureaucrats and Politicians." *J. Law and Econ.* 18, no. 3 (December 1975): 617–43.

Oates, Wallace E. "The Effects of Property Taxes and Local Public Spending on Property Values: An Empirical Study of Tax Capitalization and the Tiebout Hypothesis." *J.P.E.* 77, no. 6 (November/December 1969): 957–71.

Polinsky, A. Mitchell, and Rubinfeld, Daniel L. "The Long-Run Effects of a Residential Property Tax and Local Public Services." *J. Urban Econ.* 5 (1978): 241–62.

Posner, Richard A. "Theories of Economic Regulation." *Bell J. Econ. and Management Sci.* 5, no. 2 (Autumn 1974): 335–58.

Romer, Thomas, and Rosenthal, Howard. "Political Resource Allocation, Controlled Agendas, and the Status Quo." *Public Choice* 33, no. 4 (1978): 27–43.

Stigler, George J. "The Theory of Economic Regulation." *Bell J. Econ. and Management Sci.* 2, no. 1 (Spring 1971): 3–21.

Tiebout, Charles M. "A Pure Theory of Local Expenditures." *J.P.E.* 64, no. 5 (October 1956): 416–24.

Tullock, Gordon R. "Dynamic Hypothesis on Bureaucracy." *Public Choice* 19, no. 2 (Fall 1974): 127–31.

Wagner, Richard E., and Weber, Warren E. "Competition, Monopoly, and the Organization of Government in Metropolitan Areas." *J. Law and Econ.* 18, no. 3 (December 1975): 661–84.

C
Vertical and Horizontal Competition

[11]

A retrospective overview

The whole of Part II focuses on *inter*governmental competition. The analysis it proposes extends that of Part I, which was exclusively concerned with *intra*governmental competition, by concentrating on the interaction of governments with one another. To simplify, the four chapters of which Part II is constituted take the relationship of centers of power within each government as given. The analysis extends that of Part I, but it also builds on it by making use of the same model of demand as that proposed in Chapter 2. It assumes that all governments maximize expected consent. All that is needed to use the model of demand is, therefore, a small change in the notation of equations (2.7) to (2.10), which the reader can easily provide.

To proceed, I must first dispose of a semantic issue. Our habit of thinking of governments as monolithic institutions is so engrained that we do not appear to possess in ordinary discourse words that would make it easy to distinguish between the entire apparatus of government on the one hand and the multiplicity of units that constitute the whole on the other. We lack a distinction such as that between industry and firms that plays such an important role in the microeconomic analysis of market supply. Among commonly used expressions, the one that corresponds most to that of industry is *public sector,* but this term contains too many elements that belong to demand to be completely satisfactory. I therefore propose to adhere throughout to the conventions of calling the apparatus of state in its entirety the *governmental system;* the component units I simply call *governments*. In addition, as already indicated, Part II and Part III disregard the various centers of power that make up individual governments. Keep in mind, however, that whenever the word *government* is used, it is as a contraction for the entire constellation of centers of power that make up governments.

Having dealt with this first problem of vocabulary, let me immediately remark that modern democratic governmental systems, even those of unitary states, are all multilevel systems. That statement continues to be true even if we insist in recognizing as jurisdictional levels only those at which political decisionmakers are popularly elected. France, Italy, and Spain, for example, which are often used to illustrate what the typical unitary state looks like, each has four levels of elected governments. Britain, outside London and its six

181

182   **Governmental systems**

other metropolitan conurbations,[1] also has four tiers of elected governments.[2] I have not been able to find among contemporary democracies a single example of a governmental system in which there are fewer than three jurisdictional levels (see, however, footnote 2). Furthermore, if we do not require that political decisionmakers be elected, the number of levels becomes larger mostly but not exclusively because of the importance of special authorities and special district governments – in France, *syndicats,* and in Italy, *consorzi* – that can have the responsibility for such powers or functions as schools, fire protection, police, public transportation, water, sewerage, libraries, hospitals, and cemeteries.

A theory of governmental systems that would embody a theory of federalism as a special case is still lacking. The best discussions – those that reflect at least some of the ongoing research – continue to line up, in ad hoc fashion, decentralization theorems, models of the assignment of powers, of interjurisdictional spillovers, and of intergovernmental grants, propositions related to vertical fiscal imbalance and dependence, and hypotheses about optimum jurisdictional size, fiscal mobility, and real estate markets, without, to all appearances, being wary of the fact that in the absence of a unified and complete theory it is not possible to check if these fragmentary and disparate exercises are theoretically apposite, empirically meaningful, or relevant to policy. To develop a tolerably complete and unified theory of governmental systems, it is essential to focus the analysis on the nature and attributes of intergovernmental competition.

To establish that proposition, the remainder of this chapter provides a brief overview of the literature that is concerned with the relationships that governments that are located at different jurisdictional levels on the one hand and those that inhabit the same level on the other, entertain with each other[3] – on

1. Birmingham, Leeds, Liverpool, Manchester, Newcastle, and Sheffield.
2. Prior to 1986, the year that Prime Minister Thatcher's government suppressed the Greater London Council and the six Metropolitan county governments, these seven areas had three levels of elected governments. Since 1986, London and the other six metropolitan areas have had only two.
3. I do not review early work – that by Alexis de Tocqueville (1835, 1840), James (Lord) Bryce (1888), Henry Sidgwick (1919), Johannes Popitz (1927), Harold Laski (1939), Albert Dicey (1962), and Kenneth Wheare (1963) – which, in one way or the other, is concerned mostly with vertical relationships, that is, with the assignment of powers among orders of government. (Some of that literature is examined in Breton, 1990.) I also neglect the more quantitative work of Alan Peacock and Jack Wiseman (1961), Frederic Pryor (1968), David Davies (1970), Wallace Oates (1978) and Werner Pommerehne (1977). [Much of that research has been well surveyed by my colleague Richard Bird (1979, 1986)]. I neglect all that work because I restrict my investigation to studies directly formulated in terms of, or easily converted into, the methodology of optimization and equilibrium comparative statics. I must add that for heuristic reasons, I review the literature on vertical fiscal imbalance and intergovernmental grants – a part of the writings on vertical relationships – not in this, but in the next chapter.

what I call vertical and horizontal relationships.[4] Both types of relationships have been extensively studied, though, as will become apparent, the problems to which they give rise have been satisfactorily resolved for neither. In what follows, I note some of the difficulties that scholars have encountered and have so far not been able to overcome. In the process, I sketch an approach based on intergovernmental competition that I believe must be adopted to model both vertical and horizontal relationships.

7.1. More definitions

It is essential to make clear at the outset a few more of the semantic conventions to which I adhere throughout the discussion in Part II. The literature on vertical relationships in governmental systems has made and continues to make abundant use of the concept of *centralization* (and of decentralization). Richard Bird (1979, 1986), more forcefully than others, has warned that the concept is difficult to use and often misleading. However, in practical applications, it is sometimes possible, as recent work by Anthony Scott (1991) demonstrates, to do away with it altogether. For that reason but also because it plays such a large role in the literature I will be reviewing and because it simplifies theoretical discussions, I will use it. Later in the analysis, I also make use of the concept of *concentration* introduced in the literature by Alan Peacock and Jack Wiseman (1961). I will distinguish between expenditure concentration and revenue concentration. *Expenditure concentration* can be defined as the central government's share of total expenditures on goods and services (appropriately defined, see Chapter 1, Section 1.1) incurred by all the governments of a given governmental system. This index (or metric) may sometimes be biased. For example, if the expenditures of central and local governments fall and those of provincial or state governments rise, the expenditure concentration index could decline, but the "real" degree of concentration could easily have risen. For that reason, it may be necessary in certain circumstances to use a definition based on a vector of the ratios of the expenditures of governments located at each of all the jurisdictional levels of the governmental system to the total expenditures of all the governments of the system. *Revenue concentration* is defined in a similar way. In what follows, I use the simpler scalar definitions of expenditure and revenue concentration.

I also distinguish between powers and functions. The first is a constitutional or legal concept that I use in conjunction with the notion of centralization. The second is associated with the activities, tasks, and processes that lead to

---

4. Jack Walker (1969) was the first, to my knowledge, to distinguish *analytically* between horizontal and vertical intergovernmental relations. As I note in Chapter 9, he was also the first to identify these relations as competitive – he used the word "emulation" (p. 890) to describe the phenomenon. Finally, he also addressed the question of the stability of the outcomes resulting from horizontal competition (p. 890). No mean achievement.

184   **Governmental systems**

the supply and "financing" of goods and services by governments. I use it in conjunction with the concepts of expenditure and revenue concentration.

7.2.   Vertical competition

In the fiscal federalism literature – the literature concerned with multitier governmental systems – the problem of centralization has two dimensions: one that relates to the division of powers among orders of government and another that pertains to the number and to the morphology of the jurisdictions that make up governmental systems and, therefore, to the structure of these systems. It is in general possible either to take the structure as given and to seek to discover an equilibrium assignment or alternatively to take the division of powers as given and to establish what the equilibrium structure looks like. One problem is the *dual* of the other.[5] For that reason it is possible to deal with only one dimension of the centralization problem without loss of generality. I focus on the one that has received most attention: the assignment or division of powers.

In the literature to which I am restricting myself, the earlier models were all based on the implicit assumption of a strict equivalence between an assignment of powers and an assignment of functions or responsibilities for the supply of particular goods and services. To put it differently, it was tacitly assumed that publicly supplied (i.e., government-supplied) goods and services could be aggregated into unambiguous classes, which were then treated as powers. The assumption led many students of federalism [for example, Oates (1972), Musgrave and Musgrave (1984), and Rubinfeld (1987)] to formulate the assignment problems as pertaining to the allocation, redistribution, and stabilization powers without, however, indicating the return passage to real-world assignments as these are embodied in, say, constitutional documents or actual practices.

However, when the assignment problem was formulated in terms of goods and services (functions), first by Breton (1965), then by Mancur Olson (1969), and finally by Oates (1972), the goods and services were invariably assumed to be *pure* Samuelsonian (1954) public goods, with the additional supposition that their "spans" varied from good to good, thus generating a more or less perfect hierarchy of goods.[6] These were then identified as local

5. This is easily seen in simple cases like that of "optimal currency areas" (Mundell, 1961). That problem can be resolved either by assigning the power over currency to a given jurisdictional level or by redesigning the frontiers of the area.

6. The span of a pure public good is the word introduced by Breton and Scott (1978) to reflect the number of persons who benefit (equally since the good is a pure public good) from the good. If the seeding of a cloud generates rain over the city of Kingston, then the span of the public good that we may call weather modification is equal to the population of Kingston (including visitors, if any). The span of a private good is accordingly equal to one person. The definition is easily adjusted to the case of nonprivate, or impure, public goods.

or municipal, metropolitan, regional, provincial, or national goods, depending on their spans. Because spans and spatial jurisdictional domains – the exogenously given structures of governmental systems – would not in general match each other (that is, map perfectly into each other), interjurisdictional spillovers were to be expected. As a consequence, the problem of the assignment of functions came to be defined as one in the efficient management of spillover flows, more or less as in the Welfare Economics conception of the State suggested by William Baumol (1969).

To illustrate, in Breton (1965) efficient management meant that the chosen assignment would minimize interjurisdictional spillovers. The remaining flows – which would obviously be larger, the more severely constrained was the minimization – would then be internalized by a system of intergovernmental Pigovian (1920) grants designed and administered by the central government. One year exactly after the publication of Breton's (1965) paper and years before the appearance of the Olson (1969) and Oates (1972) variations, Jack Weldon (1966), in a paper that went considerably beyond the assignment problem, showed that the approach itself was fundamentally flawed. His argument was simple and, for those who read it, effective. He argued that if central governments could correctly calculate the exact size of the grants needed to internalize the spillovers, all functions should be assigned to it. If, in other words, central governments could perform the difficult task of estimating all marginal spillover flows and designing the appropriate grants program, a division of functions was not only unnecessary but wasteful. The ideal governmental system was a single-tier unitary state. One should add that beyond the Weldon critique, the Breton–Olson–Oates approach suffers from another crippling defect in that it contains no body that can produce or institute the desired division of functions, except an *omniscient* central government or *omniscient* planner.

This is a convenient place to mention two other attempts to solve the assignment problem. One, of venerable vintage, can be called the *principle of responsiveness;* the other, of more recent birth, is the *principle of subsidiarity* and is very much part of current debates in Europe, where it was invented [for a good discussion, see Subtil (1990)]. Responsiveness is not modeled. Instead, it is assumed that governments that are lower in the hierarchy of governmental systems are closer to the people and ipso facto more responsive to the preferences of citizens than governments higher up in the structure (see, for example, Tullock, 1969, p. 21, and Rosen, 1985, p. 511). Because responsiveness is assumed to be a virtue, the principle simply states that a power or function (no distinction is made between the two in these discussions) should be assigned to a jurisdictional level higher in the hierarchy only if governments at lower levels cannot technically discharge the responsibilities associated with the power or function. Analysis of the technical capacity of junior governments to discharge responsibilities rapidly leads to discussion of inter-

186   **Governmental systems**

jurisdictional spillovers (see, for example, Rosen, 1985, pp. 511–12; and Rubinfeld, 1987, p. 631) and to issues not unlike those encountered in the Breton–Olson–Oates approach.

The problem with the principle of responsiveness is not, however, principally related to spillovers but extends to the basic intractability of the notion of responsiveness itself. Suppose, for example, that all governments are in some sense equally responsive to the preferences of citizens. Suppose also that the preferences of the citizens are more homogeneous at lower levels in the hierarchy of governmental systems. Then, if governments are equally misinformed about the preferences of their citizens, preferences will not be as well satisfied at higher jurisdictional levels as at lower ones, even though by construction governments are equally responsive, simply because there is more variability in the distribution of preferences in higher jurisdictions and, as a consequence, more information is needed by senior governments to provide goods and services in volumes that generate the same level of utility loss as that generated by junior governments. Only in a system in which everyone has the same preferences for all goods and services can the principle of responsiveness be unambiguously applied. In such a system, however, the Weldon critique applies with even more force. If all citizens have the same preferences, it makes no difference how powers or functions are assigned; furthermore, if there are costs to decentralization – even small ones – the best assignment is full centralization.

The principle of subsidiarity is essentially the same as that of responsiveness, except that responsiveness per se is not explicitly considered. The principle then reduces to the statement that a power or function should not be assigned to a jurisdictional level higher up in the hierarchy of governmental systems if the responsibilities it embodies can be discharged equally well or better by governments at lower levels. Because the notion of responsiveness is absent from the formulation, an appropriate notion of spillovers, defined by reference to the preferences of citizens, is also lacking. However, it is difficult to resist the view that when the principle is eventually fleshed out, some "technical" analog to spillovers, possibly defined by a central authority, will find its way into the analysis. Subsidiarity, like responsiveness, would then become vulnerable to the Weldon critique.

Confronted with these failures, Breton and Scott (1978) proposed a theory of the assignment of powers (not of functions) inspired by the Coasian (1960) revolution then in full swing, which suggested that the problem of externalities (spillovers) was better understood and disposed of by shifting both analytical and practical emphasis from the externalities themselves to the transaction costs of internalizing them. Breton and Scott's decision to adopt that line of analysis was to a considerable extent influenced by Gordon Tullock's (1969) seminal paper on federalism.

A retrospective overview 187

The basic mechanics of Ronald Coase's approach is very simple. Suppose that a negative externality inflicts a utility loss on a victim. A Coasian victim, as distinguished from a Pigovian victim, is not passive in that he or she does not expect a benevolent government to tax the source and thus internalize the externality. Instead, the victim, prompted by the loss of welfare (or money) caused by the externality and on the assumption that the source is not liable for damages, initiates negotiations with that source, negotiations that induce it, against receipt of a "bribe" or payment, to reduce the volume of the externality to the point at which the marginal damages inflicted on the victim are equal to the marginal benefits received by the source. The Coasian calculus is, however, very much a function of the size of transaction costs and, properly construed, concentrates on the effects of transaction costs (see, for example, Shavell, 1987). Breton and Scott adopted more or less the same perspective. They identified four different kinds of transaction or organization costs – mobility, signaling, administration, and coordination – which, they argued, vary as the degree of centralization or as the assignment of powers varies. They then showed that if these *ceteris paribus* cost functions satisfied certain restrictions, the minimization of the cost functions would yield an equilibrium assignment of powers. By the properties of the dual, this minimization also yields an equilibrium number of jurisdictional levels and an equilibrium number of jurisdictions per level – in other words, an equilibrium organization of government systems.

That would seem to have put an end to the matter. Breton and Scott seem to have achieved two goals: (1) the formulation of a model of the division of genuine constitutional powers as distinguished from a model of the assignment of goods and services or functions; and (2) the development of a model that did not appear to be vulnerable to the Weldon critique. Some commentators, such as Gérard Bélanger (1985), faulted the model's usefulness on the ground that the organization cost functions were difficult to measure. Although acknowledging the criticism, one must also recognize, first, that measurement problems are pervasive in the social sciences generally without being seen as insuperable barriers and, second, that the measurement problems of the Breton–Scott model are, it would appear safe to assert, no more serious than those of the Breton–Olson–Oates model or of other spillover approaches.

Immediately after the publication of *The Economic Constitution of Federal States*, John Dales, a friend and colleague at the University of Toronto, commented verbally that the Breton–Scott model had not altogether met the Weldon critique. Indeed, instead of omniscient central governments that marred the assignment models of the 1960s and early 1970s, it was omniscient constituent assemblies that, in its explicit canonical form, the model used to perform the minimization exercises that were now the stumbling

188   **Governmental systems**

block. Whatever progress may have been achieved by the Breton–Scott model, the Dales critique correctly asserted that the final equilibrium assignment was the product, as are final equilibria in conventional Welfare Economics, of a *deus ex machina*. It is true that the Breton and Scott monograph contains an institutional model of the assignment of powers, but that model has two main weaknesses. First, although recognizing that the mode of operation of constituent assemblies is different in federal and in unitary states, little by way of explicit modeling of the different bargaining and other interaction processes is provided in the book and certainly nothing that can tell us whether the equilibrium of the canonical model will be even approximately approached institutionally. Second, the analysis uses a model of bureaucracy borrowed from William Niskanen (1971), in which one of the parties involved is completely passive – an assumption Breton and Wintrobe (1982) have shown to be irrational (see also Chapter 6 of this book). It is interesting to note in this context that in their second book, which was squarely focused on constituent assemblies, Breton and Scott (1980) abandoned any attempt at explaining real-world assignments and climbed on board the normative wagon – a standard cop-out that is always a sign that the positive or descriptive apparatus is seriously defective.

How then can the Weldon and Dales critiques be met? How is it possible to obtain a division of powers that would minimize organization costs but that would dispense with omniscient decisionmakers? The idea that made it possible for me to answer this question was born of discussions of the papers presented at a Villa Colombella Seminar on federalism. Following that seminar, in what was to become my "Supplementary (or "Minority") Report" to the *Report of the Royal Commission on the Economic Union and Development Prospects for Canada* (1985), I tried to extend some of the ideas that nourished these discussions and to organize them around the notion of competitive federalism or, as I would now call it, around the idea of competitive governmental systems. (That Report and the papers presented at the Seminar were subsequently published as a Special Issue of the *European Journal of Political Economy,* Breton, 1987).

The idea that competition is ever present in governmental systems is not new. It provides the background to Alfred Marshall's (1890, Appendix G) discussion of local government finance; it is the implicit but inexorable driving force in the enormous literature on tax harmonization (see, for example, Shoup, 1967; Thirsk, 1980; Bird, 1984, 1986, Chapter 7; and McCready, 1991); it is explicit in formal models of tax competition (see, for example, Mintz and Tulkens, 1986); it underlies the Breton–Scott (1978, pp. 85–7) analysis of minimum and national standards in federal states. And in some renditions of Tiebout's (1956) theory of local public goods, competition spurred by political mobility regulates the behavior of junior governments.

A retrospective overview

In all that literature, the focus is, however, restricted (as it is in my own Report, 1985) to horizontal competition. An exception is the work on tax harmonization, but that work, being almost single-mindedly preoccupied with the nitty-gritty of harmonization, has little if anything to say about competition. None of this is an accident. It is easy to rationalize horizontal competition; the mobility of consuming households, labor, capital, and/or technology among jurisdictions is sufficient to motivate its existence. But there is no mobility among orders of government. What could drive governments located on different jurisdictional tiers to compete with one another? And what would they be competing over?

Answers to these questions were provided by Salmon (1987a) at the 1984 Villa Colombella Seminar referred to earlier and in a later (1987b) elaboration and extension. Salmon uses the economic theory of rank-order tournaments, initially proposed by Edward Lazear and Sherwin Rosen (1981) and refined by many others, to develop a mechanism to explain why governments are motivated to compete across tiers as well as within tiers. Greatly simplified, the *Salmon mechanism,* as I will call it, can be summarized as follows: Citizens use the information they acquire about the supply performance of one or more benchmark governments to appraise and evaluate the supply performance of their own governments. Opposition parties, therefore, have ready-made platforms, based on the same information as that of their citizens, from which to challenge incumbent governments. The latters' response is a manifestation of competition between them and the benchmark governments. For example, a citizen observes the performance of governments at tier i as it pertains to the supply of, say, road maintenance, education, research incentives, broadcasting, police protection, or health care, and compares that performance with the performance of governments at tier j. Because the citizen can influence government by granting or withholding consent, the governments at tiers i and j are induced to compete in supplying whatever is the object of comparison. (I look at the Salmon mechanism again in Chapter 9, Section 9.1, Subsection ii.)

In passing from the Breton–Scott organization cost model to that of competitive governmental systems based on the Salmon mechanism, I have also moved from focusing on powers to concentrating, as the early models did, on the divisions of functions (goods and services). I have not, however, returned to the initial position, because omniscient decisionmakers have been replaced by the blind force of competition. To mark this transition, I henceforth use the word *concentration* when analyzing the division of functions or supply responsibilities.

For more than 100 years, the debates on the principles that (should?) govern the assignment of powers – debates that have always been importantly influenced by jurists – have been based on the tacit assumption that the

190   **Governmental systems**

distribution of the supply flows of goods and services between orders of government is effectively determined by the constitutionally or legally specified assignment of powers. A model of vertical competition requires that this assumption be reversed. I therefore propose that we assume that the division of powers and, hence, the degree of centralization be determined by the jurisdictional distribution of supply flows and, therefore, by the degrees of expenditure and revenue concentration, and not the other way around.

To look at the matter from a different perspective, competition will force governments to specialize in the supply of the goods and services in which each is relatively most efficient and will thus help to determine the equilibrium degree of expenditure and revenue concentration. All kinds of forces have an impact on the extent of intergovernmental specialization in the supply of goods and services. These are analyzed in Chapter 8, where a model of the way they interact to generate an equilibrium governmental system is also suggested.

Replacing the assumption that constitutions and constituent assemblies, constitutional experts and judges determine the extent of specialization by an assumption that says it is competition that accomplishes that task does not mean, of course, that constitutionally entrenched assignments are irrelevant. Their role must, however, now be conceived as constraints on the competition that orders the relationship of governments engaged in the production and provision of goods and services and, therefore, on the evolution of the equilibrium degree of revenue and expenditure concentration.

An illustration of how entrenched assignments can constrain competition is useful. Suppose that a particular power – let us call it P_i – has been assigned to the provincial or state order of government sometime in the past either by a formal body that met for that purpose or by a court's interpretation of a past assignment. Governments at the provincial or state level, therefore, have the constitutional or legal authority to supply goods and services $g_{ki} = g_{1i}, \ldots,$ g_{ni} given that $g_{ki} \in P_i$. Suppose now that as a consequence of an external disturbance, relative efficiencies change and the central government finds itself in a position to out-compete provincial or state governments in supplying the entirety or a subset of g_{ki}. Over time, the constitutional or legal assignment of powers will formally be altered or the old assignment will be given a new interpretation by the courts. This new assignment will then again – in a second period, as it were – act as a constraint regulating the competition that pits governments against one another in their efforts to cater to the demands of citizens. Chapter 8, Section 8.3, looks at this process in more detail.

7.3.   Horizontal competition

That horizontal intergovernmental relations are competitive has been widely recognized. As mentioned earlier, it has been acknowledged indirectly by those who have been preoccupied with problems of tax harmonization and, one should add, by those – often political scientists – who have been concerned with what is known as "cooperative federalism" or, as I would call it, with "cooperative governmental systems" [see, for example, Elazar (1991) and Kincaid (1991) and the literature they cite]. Acknowledgment has been indirect because this literature has for the most part been particularly interested in the ways and means of squelching or controlling competition. That intergovernmental relations are competitive has also been accepted by those who assume that the mobility of citizens *qua* consuming persons or households, that of human, physical, and financial capital, and that of technology are the main driving forces generating equilibrium outcomes in the supply of goods and services, in the location of people, in housing prices, and so on, and in understanding equilibrium displacements.

As we shall discover in the next chapter (Section 8.2, Subsection ii), an equilibrium division of functions and powers among orders of governments must accord pride of place to *coordination costs* and, therefore, to tax harmonization and to other forms of "cooperation." The question at this point does not pertain to coordination costs but to the mobility of persons as a driving competitive force. In many models of intergovernmental competition based on political mobility, it is not clear, the elegance and mathematical sophistication of the models notwithstanding, how political mobility is revealed and how it stimulates competition. I do not have in mind Dieter Bös's (1983) stricture in his commentary on Roger Gordon's (1983) model of the assignment of taxation powers. Bös decries the "typical attitude of United States economists" who, in his view, "over-stress . . . the importance of migration" (p. 46) presumably even for the United States but certainly for other societies. Within the conventional paradigm, it is always possible to reply to Bös that mobility is not apparent – appears not to exist – because governments adjust the volume of goods and services they supply and/or the taxprices they charge for these goods and services so rapidly that citizens who would otherwise be moving are induced to stay put. Governmental systems of the real world, the conventional paradigm would be saying, are always in equilibrium.

The point I wish to make eventually rejoins Bös's point, but it has a different origin. It pertains to what we may call the "dilemma of mobility." I have noted earlier that all democratic governmental systems (*pace* Thatcher's Britain) are constituted of three or more – sometimes many more – jurisdictional tiers. How, then, does a citizen who lives in a three-tier system and who wishes to consume the bundle of goods and services provided by Fairfax, but does not want to consume those supplied by Virginia, choc where to reside? The problem could be simplified if there were other Fairfaxes in surrounding provinces or states, but it need not be completely resolved. Suppose that all the desired Fairfaxes outside of Virginia happen to be located in desirable Canadian provinces but that our individual is totally averse to the bundle of

192   Governmental systems

goods and services offered by Canada. What is this citizen then to do? Stay put in Fairfax, Virginia, U.S.A., as Bös believes generally happens?

The point, to summarize, is not that there is no political mobility of persons but that that mobility is in general so analytically intractable that it cannot be the unique reed on which to hang a theory of competition in governmental systems. It may in practice sometimes be the case that the goods and services provided by governments at all jurisdictional levels, except those at one particular tier, are nearly indistinguishable from one another or if they are distinguishable, that the intensity of preferences for these goods and services – the marginal rate of substitution between them and a numéraire – is so low compared to that for one good or service offered by the governments at the particular jurisdictional tier that an n-tier (n ≥ 3) governmental system behaves as a two-tier system. To illustrate, suppose that education is offered by governments at a particular jurisdictional level, that in the preference ordering of parents with school-age children education dominates by a wide margin all the other goods and services (parks, sewerage, public libraries, police protection, fire protection, etc.) provided by all other governments or that the variance in the distribution of quality is seen by parents to be much greater for education than for other goods and services supplied. Then such a governmental system, even if n-tier (n ≥ 3), would behave as a two-tier structure. In such a context, competition will exist at the level offering education, but it will be absent elsewhere in the system. I return to this *Tiebout mechanism* in Chapter 9, Section 9.1, Subsection i).

It is important to mention that because they have no preference for goods and services and because they are fungible, "the dilemma of mobility" does not affect capital and technology. As a consequence, the mobility of capital and technology – their responsiveness to differential incitations – will motivate horizontal competition among the governments of a given governmental system. If, however, competition is only weakly motivated by the obligation to respond and cater to the preferences of citizens and is strongly motivated by the imperatives of capital and technology mobility, a theory of the organization of governmental systems based on competition as its ordering principle would have only a limited explanatory power. This is why the Salmon mechanism – which is capable of motivating both vertical and horizontal competition – is of such primordial importance.

Competition can be beneficial only if it is governed by rules that we may call "rules of competition," if these rules are policed and enforced, and if infractions are penalized. I am not concerned at the moment with the rules themselves – those pertaining to barriers to mobility, to tax exporting, to conspiracies, and so on – but with the particular problems posed by the necessity that the rules be enacted and enforced. (For a discussion of some rules, see Chapter 9, Section 9.4, Subsection ii). At least since the days of *The*

Federalist (1787–8), it has been known that in any governmental system the policing and enforcement functions in respect of the rules of horizontal competition had to be the responsibility of the central government, which in respect of these activities could be called a *monitor*.[7] The need for monitors of horizontal competition and some of the instruments they make use of in stabilizing that type of competition are discussed in Chapter 9, Section 9.4, Subsections i and ii.

Assigning the responsibility for monitoring horizontal competition to central governments creates a difficulty in that these governments are also engaged in (vertical) competition with the junior governments of their respective governmental systems. The problem takes a particular configuration in federal states because in these states the divided powers are constitutionally "owned" by the jurisdictional levels to which they have been assigned. To appreciate this point, it is enlightening to recall that the Founding Fathers of the American Constitution, gathered in Philadelphia in the summer of 1787, had no great difficulty in agreeing on a division of powers.[8] After all, all the governmental systems they knew had divided powers. It was not the division of powers that posed a problem; it was their ownership. The Founding Fathers were aware that the confederal arrangement of 1778 was falling apart and, without much hesitation, decided that it could not be repaired, in flagrant violation of their "terms of reference." However, they had an horror of unitary states, which were then identified with European monarchical governments in general and in particular with the government of George III, the enemy in the recently fought War of Independence. They were therefore led to discard two obvious forms of ownership. The only alternative left was divided ownership.

The problem the Founding Fathers saw with divided ownership – to a degree the problem that nourished their aversion to unitary states – was that the central government, in devising, policing, and enforcing the rules governing horizontal competition, would have some freedom to do so in a way that could benefit itself when competing (vertically) with the junior governments. It is in resolving this problem while holding to divided ownership of powers – a task that was long and arduous and at which they nearly failed – that the

7. It is not easy to give a name to that role of central governments. In *The Federalist* (1787–8), Alexander Hamilton used the words "umpire," "common judge" (p. 35), and "discretionary superintendence" (p. 91) to identify what I call a monitor. Umpire is also used by Donald Smiley and Ronald Watts (1985) but in a more restrictive sense than by Hamilton. William Riker (1975) characterizes the role of central governments vis-à-vis the provincial or state governments by the verbs "control," "discipline," and "force." Like *The Federalist*, he refers to the reverse relationship as one of obedience (p. 108). I have opted for "monitor" and "monitoring" because they seem to me to be more neutral and, hence, less misleading.

8. The Fathers of the Canadian Constitution, meeting in Charlottetown in 1864, had no great problem, either, in agreeing on a division of powers.

194   **Governmental systems**

Fathers of the American Constitution invented federalism or what *The Feder-alist* called a "compound republic."

Their solution was to insert into the institutional apparatus of the central government features that would make it difficult – impossible, they hoped – for that government to alter the de jure and/or the de facto responsibility for the supply of goods and services by altering the rules of competition. The main solution of 1787 was the invention of a Senate in which state representa-tion would be equal irrespective of size, would be appointed by the States, and would be an essential legislative component of the whole structure. Other institutions – for example, the Electoral College – were also tending in the same direction. How a senate achieves that end is discussed in Chapter 9, Section 9.4, Subsection iii, where other instruments that can be applied to the pursuit of the same end are also considered.

7.4.   Conclusion

This chapter had two objectives. First, to argue that the evolution of doctrines on governmental systems has through some process of natural selection been tending toward theories and models in which intergovernmental competition is the central organizing principle; and, second, to raise in a preliminary way some of the major problems that a theory of competitive governmental sys-tems must address. As already indicated, the next chapter proposes a model in which vertical competition, constrained by technological and institutional factors, leads actual and potential governments to specialize, in part or com-pletely (think of "special" authorities, say), in the supply of certain goods and services and in the process to divide the overall supply of goods and services – the functions – and ultimately the powers, among themselves. As the chapter will make clear, the division of functions on the one hand and of powers on the other is therefore a consequence of vertical competition constrained by technological and institutional factors, among which the costs of coordination play a central role. In addition, the specialization inherent in the division of functions implies that transfers of funds between governments at different jurisdictional tiers play a fundamental role in any concentration and centraliz-ation equilibria. These equilibria in turn have to be enforced. The chapter also argues that the cost of enforcing intergovernmental contracts has an influence on the division of functions. Finally, the constraining role of the constitu-tionally entrenched division of powers is analyzed.

In Chapter 9, after a more detailed discussion of the Tiebout and Salmon mechanisms, I provide empirical evidence of the existence and properties of horizontal competition among governments. On the basis of that evidence as well as of *a priori* arguments, I suggest that intergovernmental competition – both horizontal and vertical – may often generate unstable outcomes, from

A retrospective overview   195

which I conclude to the need for third-party enforcers of what I call the "rules of competition." I suggest, following *The Federalist* (1787–8), that that role is played by *central governments*. I also examine some of the instruments used for that purpose. Finally, in Chapter 10, the analysis of Chapter 9 is brought to bear on the problems of intergovernmental competition at the international level.

The organization of governmental systems

The topics that naturally fall within the domain of this chapter – the topics of the subdiscipline of Public Finance (or Public Economics) known as Fiscal Federalism – are not only numerous, but each one is interesting and challenging in its own right. Fiscal Federalism wrestles with the question of why functions, powers, or both are divided among levels of government and examines how that division is (or should be) determined at a point in time and how it changes over time.[1] Discussions of expenditure, regulatory, redistribution, stabilization, and taxation responsibilities flow naturally into the analysis of harmonization in respect of all these powers. Problems related to vertical fiscal imbalance as reflected in intergovernmental grants also receive a great deal of attention. The attention given to fiscal imbalance and grants is not an accident. As will become apparent, all problems of Fiscal Federalism can be discussed in a model of fiscal imbalance and intergovernmental flow of funds.

The work done over the past forty years or so by a large number of economists has taught us much. However, conventional Fiscal Federalism still lacks a consistent unified treatment. Too many propositions are exclusively normative, or more exactly nominal, that is, they lack any descriptive or real-world basis. Too many are based on the premise that agents who are assumed to be rational – among them governmental decisionmakers – systematically misallocate resources and cause inefficiencies. Too many cannot be applied to governmental systems made up of three or more jurisdictional tiers – virtually all existing systems. And too many, if they are not inconsistent with one another, must live separate lives because bridges that would help us go from one to the other do not exist.

It will help give concreteness to these criticisms, as well as serve as an

---

1. As I emphasized in Chapter 7, all democratic governmental systems – except that of the United Kingdom since Prime Minister Thatcher's reform of metropolitan governments – have three or more jurisdictional levels. Many of these are not federal under any definition of the word. However, because many of the principles that govern the assignment of powers in a theory of competitive governmental systems apply to both federal and unitary states, the lack of rigor in the definition of the word *federal* is of small consequence. That is not the case, however, in standard discussions based on some presumed technical properties of public goods. The point will become clearer as we proceed.

introduction to my own analysis of the organization of governmental systems, if I begin with a discussion of the state of the art in regard to fiscal imbalance – a topic, as I have already noted, that occupies a central position in any theory of the organization of governmental systems and especially in one that rests on the hypothesis that intergovernmental relations are competitive. The literature and the models are well known. I will therefore do no more in the next section than provide a brief outline of the models that have the widest circulation, and I will offer also in that section a critical assessment of these models. In Section 8.2, I suggest an alternative approach that emphasizes how competition constrained by technology, as well as by coordination and contractual enforcement costs, determines an equilibrium division of functions. Section 8.3 examines the relation between functions and powers and looks at the influence of constitutional entrenchments on the division of functions. Section 8.4 reexamines the Wicksellian Connection and Section 8.5 concludes the chapter.

8.1.   The standard explanation

The existence of vertical fiscal imbalance – the mismatch of own revenues and expenditures of governments located at various jurisdictional tiers – and the consequent flow of funds among governments are often (sometimes implicitly or tacitly) assumed to be given or, technically speaking, to be exogenous. When this assumption is made, analysis of necessity concentrates on the *effects* of the imbalance and of the intergovernmental money flows. Exogeneity is a way of disregarding origin or motivation and of focusing on consequences on the tacit assumption that effects are unrelated in any way to origin or motivation. I note three effects on which the standard view of fiscal imbalance has concentrated. A first line of analysis has focused on the distortions in the spending priorities of recipient jurisdictions. The first, and still among the best, model is Scott (1952); see also Wilde (1971) and Gramlich (1977). A second has stressed the incentive to fiscal irresponsibility on the part of the same governments that results from the separation of expenditure and taxation decisions, which the money flows imply (see, for example, Hicks, 1978, and Walsh, 1991, 1992). And a third has underlined the promotion of fiscal illusion in citizens and the encouragement to bureaucratic manipulation, which also are caused by the separation of revenue and spending decisions (see, for example, Courant, Gramlich, and Rubinfeld, 1979; Romer and Rosenthal, 1980; and Winer 1983). Words like distortion, irresponsibility, illusion, and manipulation, if they do not automatically speak of intrinsic evil, do not signal much that should be encouraged and nurtured, either. Whenever those who focus on the effects of vertical fiscal imbalance and on the money flows among governments choose to jettison the exogeneity assumption – not systematically but as a prelude to sagacious *obiter dicta* – they almost invariably decry vertical imbalance and the consequent flows of intergovernmental funds.

The limit of the exogeneity assumption has been widely recognized, however, and this has led to the formulation of a variety of models aimed at explaining why vertical imbalance and intergovernmental flows of funds exist in all multitier governmental systems. One group of explanations derives from Welfare Economics and Keynesian macroeconomics or from Musgrave's (1959) translation of these traditions into the allocation (efficiency), redistribution (equity), and stabilization functions and branches of governments. The efficiency argument rests on the assumption or observation that there are uneven spillover flows among jurisdictions that are consequent on the supply of goods and services by "junior" governments and that in the absence of what are in effect Pigovian subsidies, these spillovers lead to nonoptimal provisions of goods and services (see Breton, 1965, and Oates, 1972).

The equity argument has two strands. According to one of them, if the level of income in a jurisdiction is so low that its government cannot match the "fiscal residuum" (Buchanan, 1950) ruling in other jurisdictions without provoking destabilizing mobility, central governments, which are necessarily less affected by this type of mobility because of the spatial dimension of their jurisdiction, should equalize fiscal residuums by using income redistributive intergovernmental transfers.[2] The second strand is based on the assumption or the fact that fiscal capacities, needs, or both differ among jurisdictions and that these differences call for some form of equalization payments from governments situated at one jurisdictional level to those at another level.

Straddling the standard efficiency and equity arguments just outlined and, in a way, intersecting both is the argument advanced by Frank Flatters, Vernon Henderson, and Peter Mieszkowski (1974) and extended by Robin Boadway and Flatters (1982a, 1982b) that if junior governments provide goods and services whose span (for a definition, see Chapter 7, footnote 6) is less than national – namely, goods and services that are private, congestible, or both – and if per capita residence-based public revenues are larger in some jurisdictions than in others because of, let us say, an uneven endowment of taxable marketable natural resources, intergovernmental transfers should be used to eliminate inefficient mobility among jurisdictions. The central government should tax the jurisdictions that are rich in natural resources and transfer the proceeds to those that are poor, thus permitting both to adopt taxation and expenditure patterns that eliminate the interjurisdictional mobility of labor that would otherwise occur. These efficiency grants would, incidentally, also contribute to an equalitarian equity objective because they lead to transfers from rich to poor jurisdictions.

2. A fiscal residuum is the difference between the utility that a citizen attaches to the goods and services provided by governments and the utility that attaches to the private goods and services that that citizen sacrifices when paying taxes.

In their monograph on the division of powers and the assignment of these powers to governments at different jurisdictional tiers, Breton and Scott (1978) argued that it was very unlikely that the minimization of organizational costs – the cost of public administration and of intergovernmental coordination on the one hand and the cost of signaling preferences and of mobility incurred by citizens to insure that their preferences are attended to on the other – would lead to an assignment of powers that would guarantee to all governments revenues and expenditures that in equilibrium would match one another. A cost-minimizing constituent assembly or a social welfare maximizing ethical observer or planner would have to create a degree of vertical imbalance and a corresponding flow of funds among governments to insure that the organization of the governmental system economizes on the use of scarce resources.

For the sake of completeness, let me note that stabilization of overall economic activity may call for cyclical budgetary imbalance at the national level, but as a matter of logic, it precludes a corresponding converse imbalance at other jurisdictional levels. It is, therefore, not related to the problem of vertical imbalance and will not, as a consequence, further retain my attention in this chapter.[3]

I begin my criticism of the foregoing explanations of vertical fiscal imbalance and of the derived intergovernmental money flows by remarking that even if these two phenomena are features of all democratic federal systems of government, they are also attributes of democratic unitary states, all of which – the word *unitary* notwithstanding – are multitier governmental systems. Vertical imbalance is, therefore, not a reflection of a constitutionally entrenched division of powers that is too costly to change, either because of rigidities in the amending formula or because of a lack of sufficient consent among decisionmakers. In unitary states the power to alter the division of powers is unambiguously nested in central governments – that is why they are called unitary – so that interjurisdictional spillovers can be easily removed by reassigning the provision of the goods and services that cause the externalities to governments higher up in the system, thus eliminating in one swoop the need for intergovernmental transfers and the concomitant vertical fiscal imbalance.[4]

Moreover, as Breton and Angela Fraschini (1992) have documented, some unitary states, such as France and Spain, have for a decade or so been doing

3. The argument that macroeconomic stabilization of the Keynesian variety calls for permanently larger revenues than expenditures at the national level and therefore for vertical imbalance is logically untenable. For a good discussion, see Walsh (1992).

4. From a strictly legal point of view, states are said to be unitary when *all* legislation emanates from the central government. When junior governments make decisions, as they in fact do, say, on tax rates, this is deemed not to be legislation but administration. In view of the highly nominalistic and arbitrary character of this legal conception of the state, I pay no further attention to it and consider the setting of tax rates as legislation.

exactly the opposite. Their central governments have significantly reduced the degree of expenditure concentration in their respective governmental systems. We should therefore conclude, if we adhere to the Welfare Economics credo, that they have willfully created interjurisdictional spillovers that demand intergovernmental transfers that cause vertical imbalance and, one should no doubt add, that foster distortions, irresponsibility, illusion, and manipulation. Such long-term, all-pervasive irrationality on the part of central governments cannot be presumed. It is imperative that we ask why interjurisdictional spillovers exist or, even more to the point, why they appear to be created by the multiplication of jurisdictional tiers.

The Breton–Scott (1978) model of assignment of powers can be easily adapted and used to answer such a question. The argument would be developed along the following lines. A constituent assembly in attempting to minimize organizational costs – the costs of administration and intergovernmental coordination as well as the costs of gauging the preferences of citizens, not the costs of producing and supplying goods and services – would sometimes elongate the governmental system by adding jurisdictional tiers and would increase vertical fiscal imbalance by assigning expenditure responsibilities to these new tiers, while maintaining all revenue responsibilities at the national level, because that would economize on organizational resources. That line of reasoning is not only attractive, it is also correct. The problem with it is that the postulated constituent assembly – like the planners and ethical observers who maximize social welfare functions and the decisionmakers who operate behind veils of ignorance – does not have any empirical or institutional counterpart. As already noted and will be argued, it is possible to dispense with the notion of a constituent assembly by adopting a theory of competitive governmental systems. That theory also allows us to examine a second criticism of the explanation of vertical imbalance erected on the presence of interjurisdictional spillovers. For that purpose, I immediately provide a brief preliminary sketch of that theory.

Assume, then, that there are at least two levels of government in a particular governmental system and that all the governments of the system – let me call them central and provincial or state, whether they be the governments of federal or of unitary states – provide goods and services to citizens from whom they raise revenues to pay for these supplies. Assume further that governments at various jurisdictional tiers compete with one another. Competition will force each one of these governments to specialize in the supply of the goods and services in which each is relatively efficient, that is, in the supply of the goods and services each can provide at taxprices that other governments cannot match.

It is difficult to predict with any degree of precision what the long-term equilibrium will be. For example, it could be that the goods and services

The organization of governmental systems   201

whose benefit spans exceed the territory of a particular government, but are within the territory of the whole governmental system, will be supplied by the central government or by one or more coalitions of provincial or state governments. By this means, supply taxprices are brought to their competitive levels in the same way that in competitive markets economies of scale external to firms but internal to the industry are internalized and the supply of goods and services made to reflect the opportunity cost of resources. In addition to the goods and services they provide to all citizens, central governments could also supply – in total or in part – some goods and services in provinces or states or even in local jurisdictions, because they are more efficient than the junior governments in doing so. Another possibility is that a coalition made up of the central government and of some subset of provincial or state governments could together supply certain goods and services, with the remainder provided severally. In all these cases and in others like them, vertical imbalance and intergovernmental transfers may exist because the efficient (competitive) assignment of expenditures and revenue responsibilities differ, but they are not generated by interjurisdictional spillovers.

The foregoing should not be read to imply that in competitive governmental systems all externalities are always internalized. There are costs to the formation of coalitions. Coalitions may degenerate into conspiracies, barriers to entry may exist, and so on. Still, the presumption cannot be that provincial or state governments will deal with spillovers only if they are paid to do so by a perfectly informed and disinterested higher-level planner. On the contrary, the presumption must be that competition will force them to act and, as the script says, force them to act in the right way.

To summarize, the efficiency argument for vertical imbalance and intergovernmental transfers derived from Welfare Economics is based on three assumptions: first, an exogenously given or institutionally vacuous division of powers; second, the existence of interjurisdictional spillovers consequent on that division of powers; and third, the absence of intergovernmental competition. The way I have stated it, the third assumption is too vague. It is not only that competition is ruled out in the Welfare Economics paradigm but that either cooperation or a master–servant relationship between the central and provincial or state governments is required. The senior government, after having estimated the size of the externalities – more precisely, the size of the marginal damages (and/or of the marginal benefits) generated by the spillovers – must raise, in the most neutral way possible, the revenues required to deal with them, and enter into an agreement with the provinces or states that will permit an implementation of the decision to internalize the spillovers. In unitary states, because master–servant rules may obtain, the agreement may reflect instructions of senior governments. In federal states, the agreement must presumably be cooperative because the central government generally

202   **Governmental systems**

cannot impose its decisions on provincial or state governments (see, however, Section 8.2, Subsection iii). The third assumption, therefore, speaks of instructions from above or of cooperation. Welfare Economics begets autocracy or cooperation, at least as long as the division of powers begets spillovers.

These comments on competition and cooperation bring me to what may be called the "Queen's model" of vertical imbalance and transfers (both Henderson and Mieszkowski were at Queen's University when working on the problem, and Boadway and Flatters still are). This particular explanation is based on the view, explicitly acknowledged by some of its originators (Boadway and Flatters (1982b, p. 6), that from an economic perspective the ideal form of government – that is, the one that is most conducive to efficiency and equity – is the single-tier unitary state (which, as already noted, does not exist anywhere). It is a simple matter to go from that view to the argument that in real-world governmental systems, any specific advantage that improves the relative efficiency of a junior government in supplying goods and services and that thus makes it more competitive should be suppressed by taxing the advantage away and by transferring the proceeds to less-well-endowed jurisdictions. The resulting vertical imbalance and flow of funds will inhibit the mobility of labor that the advantage, left untaxed, would have provoked. The argument can be put in different words: The supply of goods and services and their taxprices should be exactly the same in multitier as in a single-tier system of government, and the role of intergovernmental transfers is to insure that this result will obtain.

In the Queen's model, vertical imbalance and intergovernmental transfers, though they extinguish intergovernmental competition, are not overtly motivated by that objective. They have a different purpose: to recapture (capture?) the efficiency and equity properties of markets and of *single-tier unitary states*. Intergovernmental competition is not needed for this goal nor is cooperation. In this case, Welfare Economics begets only itself. In addition, if intergovernmental competition leads to efficiency in governmental systems, the Queen's model of vertical imbalances and of transfers, by sacrificing that competition to achieve efficiency in labor markets, can make society worse off than it would otherwise be.

The income redistribution argument for vertical fiscal imbalance and intergovernmental transfers that derives from Welfare Economics can be sustained only if it is assumed that "donor" governments suffer from systematic chronic irrationality. Why? Because, as will be argued in the next chapter (Section 9.5, Subsection ii, c), intergovernmental transfers are not an efficient instrument for redistributing income in comparison to interpersonal transfers, namely, transfers from persons to persons mediated by governments or other agencies. However, as also argued in the next chapter, it is better not to assume that governments are irrational but to suppose instead that intergovernmental transfers are not used for the purpose of redistributing income among persons but for that of stabilizing horizontal intergovernmental competition. In this last case, Welfare Economics begets nothing.

8.2. An alternative explanation

To be sure that it is not an exogenously given, constitutionally entrenched division of powers that creates vertical imbalance and intergovernmental transfers, I disallow this kind of entrenchment. I also exclude all divisions of powers that are imposed by constituent assemblies of any kind or by the central governments of multitier unitary states. I assume that there are no barriers, legal or otherwise, to the emergence of any division of functions called forth by the competition of governments engaged in producing and supplying goods and services to the citizens of a particular country. (I look at some of these barriers in Section 8.3.) To understand what happens under these circumstances, we must begin by taking note of the fact that intergovernmental competition will drive governments to seek to improve their productive capacity through a division of functions among levels of government. They will strive to increase their overall productivity by specializing, in most instances only partially but in some cases, as when special authorities are created, completely.

It is correct to say that to a degree the relative efficiency or comparative advantage of governments – including that of special authorities – as suppliers of particular goods and services is acquired through specialization. We shall shortly discover that a powerful incentive to specialize derives from specific characteristics of production and supply technologies that help to determine the behavior of the average cost curves of tasks and activities associated with the production of goods and services.

If the productivity of individual governmental units is a *ceteris paribus* function of the extent to which these units are specialized, the productivity of governmental systems in their entirety depends on other factors as well, among which the most important are the costs of coordinating the various production tasks and activities undertaken by governmental units whenever coordination is called for and the costs of contractual enforcement. In other words, there are limits set by coordination and contractual enforcement costs to the advantages that can be garnered through specialization.

The discussion of the remainder of this section is organized as follows: First, I examine the influence of technology (as the volume of output varies) on the division of functions – on the extent of specialization – and illustrate by looking at two functions: an expenditure and regulatory function and a revenue function. Then in Subsection ii I examine the origin, nature, and effects of coordination costs. In Subsection iii I analyze the problems posed by the fact that agreements – contracts – have to be enforced. And finally in Subsection iv I note other factors that can affect the division of functions among orders of government. Subsections ii and iv, but especially Subsection ii, repeat and extend the analysis of coordination and administration costs already accorded a central place in Breton and Scott's (1978) *The Economic Constitution of Federal States*.

i.   *Technology*

More than forty years ago, on the implicit assumption that the costs of market transactions as well as those of intrafirm transactions were given, Stigler (1951) proposed an elaboration of Adam Smith's (1776, p. 17) famous proposition "that the division of labor is limited by the extent of the market" or that the division of functions among firms and industries is determined by the volume of output.[5] Stigler's model begins with the fact that there is a large number of separate activities or tasks associated with the transformation of a raw material into a finished product. For example, wheat has to be grown, harvested, graded, stored, and milled; the flour, mixed with other ingredients, must be kneaded and baked; the bread must be stored, its qualities advertised; and credit possibly extended to buyers – to name only a fraction among the most obvious of all the tasks associated with what we call the making of bread. How are these activities or processes divided among firms and industries?

To answer this question, Stigler focused on a particular firm and assumed that the average cost curves of some of the activities needed to produce its output were U-shaped, that others rise, and still others fall throughout for relevant rates of flow of output. When the size of the market is small, that firm will have to assume responsibility for activities subject to continuously increasing and continuously decreasing returns (in addition, of course, to those that display increasing and then decreasing returns). It will have to do this even though the tasks that are subject to continuously increasing and decreasing costs are being operated at inefficient rates, because without the output associated with these processes, the product could not be produced. However, as the size of the product market grows, the firm will "seek to delegate decreasing and increasing cost functions [activities] to independent (auxiliary) industries" (Stigler, 1987, p. 172). As the size of the market grows, total unit costs will be reduced if the processes that display continuously increasing and continuously decreasing average costs are delegated or contracted out to other firms – if the original firm specializes. In the case of the activities characterized by decreasing costs, the adopting firms will be able to exploit the economies of scale

5. The assumption is explicit in Stigler (1966, Chapter 9, and 1987, Chapter 10).

The organization of governmental systems   205

inherent in the production technologies of these processes by meeting the demand of the firm that is delegating or contracting out and of the other firms that the expanded market has made possible. As the size of the product market continues to expand, the markets for the delegated activities will also increase and become more competitive. In the case of increasing cost processes, the original firms may produce a part of their needed input in-house and delegate or contract out for the remainder of what they need.

In effect, what is happening as a result of the expansion of the product market is an alteration in the relative efficiency or comparative advantage of firms in exploiting the economies and diseconomies of scale associated with certain activities or tasks. As the size of the market increases, the original firm will find that it will be able to compete more effectively in selling its output if it buys some inputs from another firm that can produce them at lower costs than it can itself achieve. Expansion in the size of the market, together with economies and diseconomies of scale, help explain (with other factors analyzed later) the degree of vertical integration of activities and tasks and the degree of vertical "disintegration" [Stigler's (1951, p. 135) word] of others – or, what is the same, the extent of specialization.

I suggest that the division of functions in the sort of governmental system I am, for the moment, postulating is determined in a similar fashion. To see this at its simplest, focus first on a particular expenditure and regulatory function or more precisely on the set of activities and tasks – the set of goods and services – associated with a particular function. I will concentrate on a labor policy function, though I could as easily have chosen to illustrate with functions related to, say, environmental policy, agricultural policy, housing policy, urban policy, educational policy, cultural policy, economic and development policy, defense policy, or welfare policy. In the case of labor policy, the number of tasks and activities that make up the policy is almost limitless. Among them, one finds training, labor exchanges, job security, compensation for injuries, mediation of labor strife, redress against discrimination, unemployment insurance, occupational licensing, and many others.

It is not unreasonable to suppose that the average cost curves associated with the production and delivery of some of these goods and services – with some of these tasks and activities – are U-shaped, that others rise, and that still others fall throughout for relevant rates of production. If that is the case, exactly the same forces modeled by Stigler will be at work and will lead to the vertical integration of some functions and the vertical disintegration of others, that is, to some degree of specialization and a division of functions among jurisdictional levels.

I will be more explicit by looking at a second function, namely, the revenue policy function. Conventional Public Finance discussions of tax administration and tax collection distinguish between enforcement and compliance. The first identifies a governmental activity, whereas the second pertains to the behavior of taxpayers which, one need not add, will affect enforcement. Revenue policy contains more than the tax-collection activities relating to enforcement and compliance, but for the purpose of the present exercise, it is not necessary to be concerned with the other tasks (such as selecting and defining tax bases, setting tax rates and tax brackets when appropriate, choosing exemption and credit levels, and so on).

The tasks and activities associated with the enforcement of tax laws and tax codes include the assessment of tax returns, the selection of samples of returns, the auditing of taxpayers, the prosecution of delinquents, and so on. All these activities require "large" setup expenses on personnel, computers, storage, training, and so on. The setup costs and the learning by doing associated with on-the-job training imply decreasing unit costs as volume expands [see Alchian (1959) and Arrow (1962)]. Average cost curves of that type in turn mean that gains can be realized by delegating tax collection to one or more governments at higher jurisdictional levels.

Compliance relates to tax avoidance and to tax evasion.[6] The volume of avoidance and evasion depends on factors such as the height of tax rates, economies of scale in avoidance, and evasion technologies (Scharf, 1992), "public morality" (Schwartz and Orleans, 1967; Vogel, 1974; Spicer and Lundstedt, 1976), fiscal coordination or harmonization (see Section 8.2, Subsection ii), and others.[7] In what follows, I hold these variables constant – except for coordination, which I examine in the next subsection – and focus on the effect of the number of governments at given jurisdictional levels (on the effect of revenue concentration), on avoidance and evasion.[8] First, it is easier to avoid and evade paying taxes the greater the interjurisdictional mobility of tax bases, the greater the difficulty of appraising their sizes, and the greater the ease of obtaining favorable alterations in bases and rates through political influence. Second, the strength of these factors varies from tax base

6. A literature on optimal evasion (not avoidance), based on the assumption of exogenous governments, that is, of governments that are outside the economy and above economic agents, exists (see, for example, Allingham and Sandmo, 1972; Srinivasan, 1973; and Sandmo, 1981). There is also a related empirical literature on underground economies (for a good survey, see Pommerehne and Frey, 1981). It is not clear how one should read the literature on optimal evasion once governments are endogenized and the sharp distinction between avoidance (legal) and evasion (illegal) no longer permitted (see Chapter 2, footnote 11).
7. For a survey of the literature and for new estimates of all collection costs with an emphasis on compliance costs, see Vaillancourt (1989), and also Vaillancourt and Hébert (1990). The evidence, such as it is, appears consistent with the view that unit costs fall as the size of jurisdictions increases.
8. Recall, from Chapter 7, Section 7.1, that revenue concentration can be defined, as a first approximation, to be the share of revenue collected by the central government level to total revenue collected by all governments of a governmental system.

to tax base. In what follows, I will demonstrate that these variables are related to the number of jurisdictions or governments at any jurisdictional level.

If capital is mobile, its interjurisdictional mobility will increase as the number of jurisdictions increases. As a consequence, when there are more jurisdictions it is easier for anyone to reside in a high-benefit jurisdiction and to invest in one in which tax rates on capital income are low. If jurisdictions are numerous and small enough and if labor income is taxed at source, it is easier to avoid and evade taxes by living in a high-benefit area and working in a low-tax one and easier also to purchase goods and services that are taxed at lower rates outside the jurisdiction of residence.[9] Finally, a large number of jurisdictions increases the incidence of multijurisdiction enterprises and therefore increases the capacity to shift profits among jurisdictions through the use of transfer pricing.

When the number of jurisdictions is large, the number of taxpayers who will earn income and other taxable benefits in a multiplicity of jurisdictions will be larger, thus complicating the reporting problem, that is, the problem of ascertaining the size and location of the tax bases. That too will make avoidance and evasion easier. There is finally the matter of political pressure. To the extent that the effectiveness of these pressures depends on interpersonal relations, we expect that the larger the number of jurisdictions and therefore the smaller their size, the stronger the interpersonal relations. That will also facilitate avoidance and evasion.

The burden of the foregoing discussion is that, *ceteris paribus,* an increase in the degree of revenue concentration will reduce the volume of tax avoidance and evasion and increase the amount of revenues collected. That happens because an increase in revenue concentration means that revenue collection moves to higher jurisdictional tiers where by definition the number of jurisdictions is smaller. Because the mobility of tax bases, the cost of ascertaining their size, and the responsiveness of governments to political pressure are less at higher levels of jurisdiction, more senior governments are relatively more efficient, *ceteris paribus,* than more junior ones at controlling tax avoidance and evasion and therefore at collecting revenues.

We must therefore conclude that the functions and tasks associated with the enforcement and compliance aspects of the revenue policy function possess average cost curves characterized by economies of scale. We should then in turn expect – factors so far not considered held constant – that governments, driven by competition and desirous as a consequence to reap all possible gains, will delegate tax collection to a government higher up in the hierarchy of governmental systems.

9. It is interesting that when tax bases are interjurisdictionally mobile, an increase in detection probabilities or penalty rates by one government will lead to *more,* not to less, evasion as the optimum tax evasion models, cited in footnote 6, conclude.

Before moving on to the analysis of coordination costs, there are two issues that the foregoing discussion already allows us to address. The first is suggested by the literature. Should revenue concentration be analyzed, as I have done, as a manifestation of competition operating to exploit the advantages offered by technology or, following Brennan and Buchanan (1983), as a manifestation of cartelization and monopoly? Brennan and Buchanan conceive of a situation in which lower-level governments "*cede* their powers to tax to a higher level of government in return for an appropriate share in the total revenue: the whole intergovernmental grant/revenue-sharing structure can then be treated as a means of sharing the profits from political cartelization" (1983, p. 62, emphasis added). As a consequence of the reassignment of the power to tax, the higher-level government then becomes a monopolist; lower-level governments will therefore no longer engage in beneficial tax competition.

It is sometimes difficult to decide whether a particular phenomenon is a reflection of competition or of monopoly. Take the celebrated cases of resale price maintenance and exclusive territories, which for a long time were taken to be *prima facie* evidence of monopoly in the marketplace but are now seen as consistent with, nay, called for by competition [see, for example, Klein and Murphy (1988)]. Stigler (1951, p. 133) recognized that the delegated decreasing cost process would make the receiving firm – the delegatee – at least temporarily into a monopolist. He also noted, however, that it would be a monopoly facing very elastic demands because it could not charge a price for its output higher than the average cost of that output to the firm ceding it. Lower-level governments are in the same kind of relationship with the higher-level monopoly ones.

As the language used by Brennan and Buchanan (1983) makes clear, the monopoly of central governments is not achieved by force or capture but by cession or delegation from junior governments. In such a model, as distinguished from that of Brennan and Jonathan Pincus (1990) – to which I return later – the lower-level governments are implicitly identified, in my view correctly, as the principals and the central governments as agents in principal–agent relationships. That kind of model is not consistent with cartelization and monopoly, except of the most fragile variety and of a variety that brings about a more efficient allocation of resources (however, see Section 8.2, Subsection iv).

The second issue pertains to the divisions of functions themselves. These divisions will have two characteristics. First, these divisions are not likely to be neat airtight assignments such as those called for by "classical federalism" à la Wheare (1963). Instead, we should expect governments at different jurisdictional levels to be involved in different activities and tasks – in supplying different goods and services – associated with particular functions such as police protection, road construction, international affairs, financial regulation, administration of justice, and health, in addition to those listed earlier and, of course, many others. Under the postulated circumstances, concurrency – joint occupation of functions though not, one should stress, of activities, tasks, and processes – is the rule. This is why the Salmon mechanism (for a discussion, see Chapter 7, Section 7.2 and Chapter 9, Section 9.1) is capable of motivating vertical competition.

In addition, it is important to keep in mind, first, that even if governments at different tiers supply different goods and services, that does *not* mean that all governments at a particular tier supply a given good or service. Some jurisdictions may be too small or too large to accommodate efficient technologies, and then the activities and tasks of which this is true will be assigned higher up or lower down as circumstances warrant. Second, if all processes and tasks associated with a function are characterized by economies of scale – as was the case for the activities of the revenue policy function examined earlier – all the activities and therefore the whole function will be assigned to central governments. On the other hand, if all tasks are characterized by increasing costs, all the activities and processes and therefore the whole function will be assigned to governments at a junior level of jurisdiction. The prevalence of concurrency would seem to indicate that these instances are not widespread. (On the question of overlap and duplication, see Appendix F.) The second characteristic of divisions of functions that follows from the foregoing analysis is that only by accident will revenue concentration be equal to expenditure concentration, so that vertical imbalance and the consequent intergovernmental flow of funds are features of virtually all governmental systems. I am now, however, running slightly ahead of my story. I must turn my attention immediately to the effect of coordination costs on the foregoing results.

ii.   *Coordination costs*

The division of revenue and expenditure functions (including regulatory and redistribution functions) may exceed or fall short of what competition and technology alone would call for because of the presence of other factors that also impinge on the division of functions. One of these factors, already placed in center stage by Breton and Scott (1978), is coordination costs. Three problems related to these costs need to be examined: One pertains to their origin; a second to their nature; and a third to the way they influence technical outcomes.

a. Origin: Breton and Scott (1978), still laboring under the dominion of models of the assignment of functions based on intergovernmental spillovers

210   **Governmental systems**

– virtually all the economic models (as distinguished from the constitutional models) that had preceded their own – placed the origin of coordination and hence of coordination costs solely on spillovers, neighborhood effects, and beggar-thy-neighbor policies. Examples of these external effects are easy to come by. The development of a community center in a jurisdiction, because it would provide to young people interesting things to do, could reduce the incidence of crime in that jurisdiction *and* in a neighboring one that would then become the beneficiary of the spillover. But unless the two jurisdictions coordinate their efforts, the center will not be built if its costs exceed its benefits to the first jurisdiction in isolation. The unilateral erection of trade barriers between two provinces or states is a way of dumping local unemployment from one jurisdiction to the other. By judiciously selecting and tailoring tax bases, it is possible for a government to export a part of the burden of its taxes to the citizens of other jurisdictions. These are examples of external effects that can be addressed through coordination – that is, by expending money, time, and effort on formulating jointly acceptable solutions to the problems they pose. There can be no doubt that spillovers and neighborhood effects can create a genuine need for coordination.

In addition, coordination may be required by the existence of complementarities among activities, tasks, and processes – among the goods and services supplied – pertaining to a function or even across functions. For example, among the activities defining the labor policy function discussed earlier, training, ease of moving, information about market conditions (vacancies), and unemployment insurance may all be complementary with one another and also with activities and tasks associated with such other functions as housing, education (schooling), arts and culture, and so on. Complementarities can be upstream or downstream, that is, they can be found among activities that would on strictly technological grounds have to be assigned higher up or lower down than when coordination costs are taken into account.

In the absence of careful empirical work, it is not possible to say whether externalities or complementarities are a more important incitation to coordination, but on the basis of no more than admittedly casual evidence, I would not be surprised to learn that the second is far more important than the first.

b. Nature: There are many instances of successful coordination among the units of governmental systems – for example, the portability of pension plans, the transferability of unemployment and health insurance claims, the integration of police services in matters such as traffic violations and other offenses, the sharing of information on economic trends and crops, and so on. No doubt there are just as many, possibly more, cases of failure to coordinate. It would therefore be possible by looking at all or at a subset of these events, to acquire a solid idea concerning the nature and properties of coordination costs – the

The organization of governmental systems   211

costs that allow or impede coordination.[10] That would be a major undertaking and certainly one beyond the scope of this volume. Consequently, my aim will be more modest. At a conceptual level, I will seek to assemble some of the more important elements that can explain why coordination in the area of taxation – tax harmonization – is sometimes successful and sometimes not. I leave to the reader the task of similar exercises in other areas.

Notwithstanding the existence of a considerable, though largely prescriptive, literature on the subject, tax harmonization and, more important, the cost of tax harmonization, remain poorly understood phenomena. For example, it is often tacitly assumed that the costs of adopting common definitions for variables such as income, tax brackets, deductions, exemptions, and credits are high and, therefore, that the standardization that makes it easy for junior governments, in Cliff Walsh's (1991, p. 11) words, to "piggy-back" on the tax system of the senior government difficult to achieve. Still, the marginal cost to central governments of administering special provisions in the income tax forms for each province or state is not likely to be large – depending on nothing more than a little extra complexity in computer programs and a few additional clerks and tax auditors – so that central governments could easily administer a separate rate for every deduction, credit, or special provision by simply mailing different forms to people, depending on their province or state of origin.

Tax harmonization is costly because (1) it is the product of an exercise in coming to an agreement and as such, it absorbs scarce resources; (2) it constrains junior governments by reducing or even suppressing their autonomy to exploit monopolistic or quasi-monopolistic advantages and/or to overcome idiosyncratic disadvantages; and (3) it inhibits the capacity of junior governments to compete with other governments located at the same jurisdictional level.[11]

The costs of harmonization depend on the number of jurisdictions that have to be party to an agreement to make that agreement worthwhile. These costs will increase, possibly more than proportionally, as numbers increase. Harmonization costs will also depend on precedents, on conventions derived from historical compromises, and on the distance initially separating the contracting parties. Loss of autonomy will be small – possibly nil – for a jurisdiction that possesses no natural advantage that could be exploited or no natural disadvantage that could be surmounted by adopting tax measures that departed from those incorporated in a tax harmonization agreement. But if a jurisdiction possesses a real monopolistic advantage it could exploit or a

10. For an excellent analysis of coordination between Canada's central and provincial governments in three different policy areas, see Simeon (1972).
11. The advantages are of the same kind as those that give substance to the theory of optimum tariffs (see, among many discussions, Johnson, 1953–4).

212   **Governmental systems**

specific disadvantage it could void by special tax measures, the loss in autonomy caused by tax harmonization could be a significant cost. The ability to
compete – which depends on a host of factors including, as Stanley Winer
(1992, p. 359) pointedly reminds us, on the ability to fine-tune tax bases,
credits, deductions, exemptions, and other provisions of the tax code – will
be reduced by tax harmonization. That could impose much heavier costs on
some jurisdictions than on others. The need to compete and, therefore, the
cost of tax harmonization may also be less in the presence of efficient regional
development policies implemented by senior governments.

The decision to harmonize and the degree of tax harmonization will, as a
consequence, be the outcome of a balancing of the discounted marginal benefits
of specialization (consequent on the division of the revenue function) against
the marginal costs of tax harmonization. Countries and jurisdictions in which
the expected benefits from the economies of scale in tax collection are large
may still rationally shun tax harmonization completely if the number of jurisdictions that have to coordinate is large and the costs of lost autonomy and the
hindrance to competition are significant. These countries and jurisdictions will
be characterized by a relatively low degree of revenue concentration. At the
other end of the spectrum, countries and jurisdictions in which the number of
governments is small and none of which has significant unique advantages or
disadvantages or a specific capacity to compete may still harmonize even if
benefits of specialization are small. In these countries and jurisdictions the
degree of revenue concentration will be relatively high.

These considerations provide a rationale, even in the presence of significant
economies of scale in tax collection, for the absence of tax collection agreements between Washington and the American states such as those that exist
between Ottawa and the Canadian provinces. It also allows us to understand
the decision of the governments of Alberta, Ontario, and Quebec to collect
their own corporation income taxes and, in part (for the rest of the explanation, see Section 8.2, Subsection iii), for the decision of the government of
Quebec to withdraw from the Tax Collection Agreements in respect of the
personal income tax.[12]

c. Effects: In their discussion of coordination costs, Breton and Scott (1978)
defend the hypothesis that as these costs increase, functions – activities and
tasks – will move upward in the tier hierarchy of governmental systems to
economize on the resources that coordination absorbs. Conversely, as coordination costs fall, functions will travel downward, thus reducing the degree

12. In the opinion of Strick (1985, p. 93) and in that of Musgrave, Musgrave, and Bird (1987,
    p. 381), whom I quote, Alberta, Ontario, and Quebec "tend to consider them [the corporate
    tax rate differentials] a major factor [in locations decisions] and therefore engage in low-rate
    competition to attract capital."

of concentration (in the language of their book, the degree of centralization) of governmental systems.

That proposition, however, is true only if it is assumed that the technologies that support the activities and processes associated with functions are all characterized by constant returns to scale or long-term constant unit costs of production and supply. If we assume instead that functions, activities, and tasks are characterized by economies of large scale, low coordination costs will be associated with high concentration. In the case of revenue collection, for example, it appears that the tax collection technologies display significant economies of scale. Assuming this to be the case, high coordination costs would prevent the exploitation of these economies and lead to a lower degree of revenue concentration than technological considerations alone would have dictated. Consider another case. Suppose that the production technologies of the activities and tasks associated with the housing policy function are all characterized by significant diseconomies of scale calling for a low degree of concentration of the function. High coordination costs in respect of the function's various activities and tasks would call, on grounds of efficiency, for a higher degree of concentration than technology alone would.

The general conclusion must therefore be as follows:

1. In the presence of constant average costs of producing activities and tasks, low coordination costs call for low concentration, and high coordination costs for high concentration – the traditional result.
2. In the presence of increasing unit costs of production, low coordination costs require low, possibly lower, concentration, and high coordination costs demand higher concentration, than technology alone would call for.
3. In the presence of decreasing average costs of production, low (high) coordination costs call for more (less) concentration than technology alone does.

iii.   Contractual enforcement costs

To proceed, I assume that the equilibrium outcome of the workings of competition constrained by technology and coordination costs is a governmental system in which there is more concentration in revenue collection than in the provision of goods and services, which conventional treatment identifies, not always felicitously, with the expenditure, regulatory, and redistribution functions. For the sake of completeness, I should mention that a high level of revenue concentration can be achieved in one of two ways but that one dominates the other. First, lower-level – local and provincial or state – governments can delegate all or part of the revenue collection function to a more

214   **Governmental systems**

senior government and, through this choice, give rise to a governmental
system characterized by vertical imbalance and intergovernmental flows of
funds from the top to the bottom. Or, second, they may decide to create their
own tax collection agency. If economies of scale in tax collection are at all
significant, the first alternative will always be chosen because the second,
though it leads to the exploitation of some economies of scale, leads to an
exploitation that is necessarily less than that which is possible when the
collection of the senior government's revenue is also part of the package.

Lower-level governments will delegate the revenue collection function to a
more senior government to be able to deliver goods and services to their
citizens at lower unit costs and, through the consequent reduction in (marginal) taxprices, to minimize the utility losses inflicted on these same citizens.
That will be possible only if senior (sometimes federal and sometimes provincial or state) and junior (sometimes provincial or state and sometimes local)
governments can enter into contractual agreements that make it possible for
the first to guarantee that taxes will be efficiently collected and efficiently
transferred to the second. If an enforceable contract cannot be drawn up, the
competition that is calling for a greater degree of revenue concentration than
of expenditure concentration will not be allowed to yield its beneficial effects.

To understand the nature of contractual relations between senior and junior
governments and in particular the nature of the contractual enforcement problem in the presence of vertical fiscal imbalance, it is important to be aware
that this imbalance can be accommodated in one or both of two ways. First,
the senior government can act as a revenue collection agency for the junior
governments, much in the way the central government in Canada, through the
Tax Collection Agreements, does for the provinces (except Quebec) in respect
of the personal income tax. I will henceforth call the sums thus collected by
senior governments and returned to junior governments, *remittances*. Second,
the senior government can raise revenues that it delivers to the junior governments as conditional transfers. I will call these second sums *revenue payments*. [13]

Intergovernmental contracts relating to vertical fiscal imbalance and to the
resulting flow of funds between governments are both necessarily incomplete
and implicit contracts. A complete contract would specify all relevant contingencies over the life of the contract, foresee a course of action for each of
these contingencies, deny the signatories the possibility of renegotiation so as
not to deprive the original agreement of its credibility, and provide for each
contingency, before the contract is signed, a mechanism for dispute settlement
that is satisfactory to all parties. Most contracts are, given these requirements,

13. This chapter is not concerned with the intergovernmental transfers, which are sometimes used
    to stabilize horizontal intergovernmental competition and which I call "stabilizing grants."
    These are discussed in Chapter 9, Section 9.4, Subsection ii, c.

incomplete. If incomplete contracts are supplemented with unarticulated and generally shared expectations and understandings, they are said to be *implicit*.

In regard to intergovernmental flows of funds, the idea that relations between governments have characteristics that place them (the relations) in the category of incomplete and implicit contracts is not new. It can be traced back at least to the work of Martin McGuire (1975, 1979) and to that of Ernst Zampelli (1986). Recently, Brennan and Pincus (1990) have argued that contracts regulating grants from central to provincial or state governments contain tacit "provisos, riders, or contingencies" (p. 129) and that, as a consequence, all grants are conditional. The tacit provisos, riders, or contingencies imply that in the conventional framework of analysis, all grants have substitution as well as income effects. Brennan and Pincus in effect tell us that donors are not disinterested or neutral in regard to the sums they grant. They do not tell us, however, why these donors are concerned and interested in the behavior of recipients. Brennan and Pincus, like McGuire and Zampelli, though they allude to or make use of the concept of implicit contracts, do not use the rich economic theory that has developed in respect of these contracts.

In the present context, namely, the one in which senior governments are, as it were, hired by junior governments to collect their revenues, incomplete and implicit contracts have two particularly important facets. First, even if junior governments (the principals) through monitoring can observe, say, a degree of shirking in tax collection by the senior government (their agent), they cannot demonstrate to a third party (a court, say) that the senior government has indeed breached the contract and caused them damages – the contract is said to be nonverifiable. Incompleteness and implicitness also mean, and that is the second crucial facet of these contracts, that reverse cheating is possible: Principals can breach contracts just as well as agents can. Specifically, junior governments can renege on contractual undertakings as much as senior governments can.

If, as is dictated by the fact of nonverifiability, enforcement by third parties is not possible and if trust is ruled out on the ground that intergovernmental relations are too fickle for trust to form the basis of long-term enforcement, contractual relations will be possible only if contracts are self-enforcing. Self-enforcement requires that both principals (in the case under analysis, junior governments, namely, provincial or state or municipal governments) and agents (central or provincial or state governments) can credibly commit to perform the tasks specified in the implicit incomplete contractual agreement. Put differently, each must be seen by the other as having something to lose from the termination of the contract consequent on nonperformance.

From theory (for example, Klein, Crawford, and Alchian, 1978; Klein and Leffler, 1981; and Williamson, 1975, 1985) we know that if junior governments choose to rely on a self-enforcing contract, they must be able to create a

216   **Governmental systems**

valuable stream of (political) quasi-rents and deliver that stream to the senior government. The capital loss that the principals can then impose on the agent by extinguishing that stream will be sufficient to induce the agent to perform as long as the present value of the delivered stream exceeds the present value of the advantages of nonperformance. Can junior governments create such streams of quasi-rents? The answer to this question is "yes." A demonstration of the affirmation requires, however, that we distinguish between remittances and revenue payments.

In the case of remittances – the sums returned by the senior to the junior governments on the basis of some revenue collection agreement – the quasi-rents are created, as already argued, by the exploitation of economies of scale consequent on the greater ability of senior governments to control tax avoidance and evasion than that of junior governments. Note that the flow of quasi-rents accruing to senior governments will be greater, the larger the fraction of their own tax revenues that junior governments delegate for collection to the senior government. Indeed, given the economies of scale, the unit cost of tax funds *to the senior government* will diminish as that fraction increases.

In delegating tax collection to senior governments, junior governments create a stream of quasi-rents that *can* benefit those senior governments. It *will* do so, however, only if a particular condition is satisfied. To appreciate what that condition is, consider what would happen, in an admittedly extreme case, if the factors discussed in the last two subsections called for a division of functions that demanded that the tax revenues of the entire governmental system had to be raised by senior governments and that all of them had to be spent by the junior governments. The only expense of senior governments under these circumstances would be remittances to the junior governments. As a consequence, the value of low-cost tax funds to senior governments would be zero and so would the value of the stream of quasi-rents. Only if senior governments provide some goods and services to citizens can they themselves benefit from the low unit cost of tax funds. These benefits will rise as the volume of goods and services supplied increases, or to put it differently, the value of the stream of political quasi-rents increases as expenditures concentration also increases.

More generally, if the factors governing the division of functions call for a low degree of expenditure concentration and if there are economies of scale in tax collection that can technically be exploited, the required volume of remittances may be so large and the value of the stream of political quasi-rents accruing to the senior government consequently so low that that stream will be unable to insure performance on the part of that government. To guarantee performance – to control shirking, negligence, and other forms of inefficient behavior in tax collection – the volume of remittances will have to be reduced below what would be possible in a world in which the cost of insuring

The organization of governmental systems

performance was zero. The inherent conflict between the benefits of a high degree of revenue concentration and the benefits of a low degree of expenditure concentration implies that there are limits in the extent to which remittances can be used to create a stream of valuable political quasi-rents that can be delivered to senior governments to insure performance.

The volume of remittances will therefore be determined by two factors: (1) the cost of tax harmonization; and (2) the value of reductions in the unit cost of tax revenues to senior governments. If, for example, the expenditures of senior governments on own-goods and own-services decline significantly so that low-cost tax funds generate only a limited stream of quasi-rents and if the costs of harmonization increase, senior and junior governments may not be able to enter into contractual arrangements in respect of remittances that would permit much exploitation of the economies of scale in tax collection.

Does that limit on the volume of remittances imply that relevant economies of scale in tax collection cannot be exploited, or that the degree of expenditure concentration has to be greater, or both, than that called for by the division of functions reflecting the relative efficiencies or comparative advantage of competing governments as reflected in production technologies? The answer is "no." All economies of scale in tax collection can be exploited, and the optimal division of functions can be achieved by making use of what I have earlier called revenue payments. These transfers permit the exploitation or, if remittances already exist, the further exploitation of economies of scale in tax collection, and they allow junior governments to spend the sums transferred on the goods and services that they produce and deliver relatively efficiently.

The revenue payments must be conditional, and the conditions have to be specified in terms of particular goods and services supplied. Why? Remember that the problem remains one of insuring that senior governments find it in their own interest to abide by the terms of an incomplete contract and act as efficient tax collectors for the junior governments. That can happen only if the revenue payments create a sufficiently large stream of political quasi-rents for senior governments that they will not want to risk losing it through nonperformance. These conditions will in the first instance, therefore, attach the revenue payments to goods and services that are in high demand and for which demand is relatively easy to estimate, thus reducing the utility losses resulting from supply. Typically, these goods and services will be educational services, health and hospital care, vocational and other forms of training, transportation services, care of the blind and of other disabled persons, and so on. As times and circumstances change, the demand for goods and services may change, the volume demanded may become more difficult to appraise, or both – thus increasing the chances of providing quantities and qualities that differ more markedly from those desired – and the conditions that attach to the revenue payments will also change.

218   **Governmental systems**

Two complementary points should be made. First, the conditions that attach
to the transfers are willed by the junior governments; these are the governments that wish to create the stream of political quasi-rents for the benefit of
the senior government. Second, senior governments will as a rule have a say
in the formulation of the conditions and will monitor how well the conditions
are adhered to, simply because the conditions are the factors that cause the
stream of quasi-rents accruing to them to be created. The available evidence
indicates that the conditions are, indeed, negotiated as suggested earlier [see
for example, Bella (1979), Chernick (1979), and Strick (1971)].

Two other problems must be addressed to complete the analysis. The foregoing discussion tells us that junior governments are capable of creating a
stream of political quasi-rents to induce senior governments to exploit the
relevant economies of scale in tax collection and to pay the sums collected to
junior governments either as remittances or as revenue payments. That discussion did not, however, tell us why senior governments could expect the junior
governments to adhere to their side of the contract. It did not tell us why
senior governments should expect the junior governments to continue to deliver the stream of quasi-rents they are capable of creating if circumstances
change in such a way that it becomes advantageous for them not to deliver. It
does not tell us, either, why junior governments would be efficient suppliers
of the goods and services to which the conditions of the revenue payments
attach. Both problems are easily dealt with. I consider them in turn.

Junior governments must not only be able to create a stream of political
quasi-rents for the benefit of the senior governments; they must also be able to
make a credible commitment that they will continue to deliver that stream as
long as senior governments perform, that is, do not shirk on tax collection.
Such a commitment is possible for both remittances and revenue payments if
the costs to the junior governments of raising their own revenues – of forgo-
ing the economies of scale in tax collection – exceed the sums that have to be
paid to senior governments for the collection service *plus* the costs, expressed
in comparable monetary units, of creating the political quasi-rents.

We must recognize that the costs of contracting or, more precisely, the costs
of contractual enforcement may be so high that the division of functions called
for by competition constrained by technology and coordination costs may not
be possible. In other words, if the supply price of tax collection or the costs of
creating a stream of (political) quasi-rents are "high," it may not be possible to
achieve the division of functions called for by the unit costs of producing and
supplying activities and tasks on the one hand and the cost of coordinating
these activities and tasks on the other. For example, in some federations at
certain times, because of widespread negative feelings vis-à-vis the senior
government in one or more junior units, the costs of creating a flow of

The organization of governmental systems   219

political quasi-rents to the benefit of that senior government are so high that these units will choose to forgo the benefits of an optimal division of functions. That, I suggest, is what led the government of the province of Quebec as early as 1947 to seek and to gain control of the personal and corporate tax fields and to continue to stay out of the collection agreements. In general, such decisions inflict losses on the whole governmental system – the supply price of goods and services is higher for all – but the losses are larger for the unit or units that choose to collect their own taxes.

Turning to the second problem, that of the efficient performance of junior governments in supplying the goods and services to which the conditions of revenue payments apply, it is sufficient to recognize that if the stream of political quasi-rents is appropriately divided between the senior and junior governments or, put differently, if the conditions that attach to the revenue payments generate large enough political quasi-rents for both levels of government, junior governments will have an incentive to perform efficiently. To see why, consider what would happen if the whole stream of quasi-rents accrued to the senior government. Under such circumstances, the junior governments would have no incentive to perform, that is, to be efficient providers of the goods and services financed by the revenue payments. An appropriate division of the political surpluses is needed to deal with the reverse cheating problem.

The conventional model of intergovernmental grants based on the assumption that the origin of grants is exogenous to the analysis makes a prediction that has been tested empirically by a number of scholars [the classic paper is Gramlich (1977); see also, for a good survey of the empirical literature, Fisher (1982)]. The prediction is the following: If $X is received by a junior government in the form of an unconditional transfer, a fraction of $X will be spent on the goods and services supplied by that junior government. The rest will serve to reduce taxes and thus lead to an increase in private- or market-supplied goods and services bought by citizens, as long as privately and publicly provided goods are normal goods. When tested, the evidence indicated that if not all of $X, at least a larger fraction than expected is spent by junior governments and, as a consequence, little, relative to what should have been expected, takes the form of tax reductions. Edward Gramlich (1977) called the anomaly the "flypaper effect," a colorful expression designed to describe the fact that money appears to stick where it hits.

This chapter does not deal with unconditional grants proper, that is, with stabilizing transfers, which I will later associate with equalization payments and revenue-sharing. But because of the position taken by Bird and Jack Mintz (1992, pp. 22–3) and others [see Musgrave, Musgrave, and Bird (1987, p. 512)] that, in Canada at least, "so-called conditional grants programs (such as grants for education) actually have few conditions attached to them," I must consider the various views taken with respect to the flypaper effect and state what the model proposed here implies about this effect.[14]

Early explanations of the flypaper effect appealed to fiscal illusion and to bureaucratic empire building. More recently – in recognition, no doubt, of the inherent weakness of explanations based on assumptions of irrationality and inefficient behavior – analysts have been arguing that whatever the legal and formal terms in which grant programs are embodied, there are always, often only very implicit, provisos that effectively transform all grants into matching conditional grants. In the more recent framework of analysis, all grants – whether formally unconditional or whether effectively untied as is the case, except for corner solutions, with specific-purpose grants – have substitution effects, so that it is not necessary to appeal to a flypaper effect to explain why money sticks where it hits.

More recently still, Brennan and Pincus (1991), building on an earlier analysis of Fisher (1982), have argued that because the citizens of governmental systems are citizens of both junior and senior jurisdictions and, *a fortiori*, are taxpayers and consumers of the goods and services at the two levels, intergovernmental grants have no net income effects whatsoever, only substitution effects. The positive income effect enjoyed by individuals in their role as citizens of a grant-receiving junior jurisdiction is canceled by the negative income effect suffered by those same individuals as citizens of the grant-paying senior jurisdiction. Redistributional effects may exist, but overall the positive and negative income effects will cancel each other out to yield a zero net income effect. Brennan and Pincus (1991, p. 2) claim that the conventional model of intergovernmental grants is really a model of international aid, not one of federal aid.

The difficulty with the first "new" explanation of intergovernmental money flows – that based on implicit adjustments by recipients à la McGuire or on implicit provisos by donors à la Brennan and Pincus – is that it provides no rationale for these flows (grants are exogenously determined), and it assumes that decisionmakers are always and exclusively senior governments. In the McGuire (1975, 1979) and Zampelli (1986) explanation, the junior governments, unhappy to be victims of particular grant programs they do not like, seek redress by disguised manipulations of the terms of the contract, and hapless senior governments do nothing about it. In the Brennan and Pincus

14. The view of Brennan and Pincus (1990) that (in Australia at least) unconditional grants always have implicit conditions attached to them seems in contradiction with the position of Bird and Mintz (1992) that (in Canada at least) conditional grants are really unconditional. I suspect that the contradiction is superficial and will dissolve once an appropriate model of intergovernmental money flows is accepted.

The organization of governmental systems 221

(1990) earlier explanation, senior governments, unwilling to give funds without attaching strings to them, covertly tie conditions to the grant. Why senior governments would act that way is unclear; the easiest explanation is that they behave like empire-building leviathans. If so, the presumption must be that the outcome is socially inefficient.

In Brennan and Pincus's (1991) most recent attempt, the existence of intergovernmental grants derives from the preferences of median voters and from the assumption that the excess burden of federal tax funds is smaller than the excess burden of provincial or state tax funds. The explanation for the existence of unconditional grants rests on the assumption that there is a unique median voter – the same at the federal and provincial or state levels of government – who, through grants, economizes on the cost of tax revenues. These grants are therefore efficient. For matching grants, two different median voters are needed – one at each jurisdictional tier. It is assumed that the median voter at the senior level makes the grant. The resulting expenditure level and tax mix are inefficient. This most recent attempt appears to be headed in the direction of producing results not much different from those of conventional models, except that the income effect has been removed.

The model suggested in this chapter is based on an accepted theory of incomplete and implicit contracts, which rests on the assumption that all agents are rational and that resources are used efficiently by them. It does away with the assumption that intergovernmental relations, at least as regards intergovernmental flows of funds, are necessarily master–servant relations. It does not assume that intergovernmental flows of funds are Pigovian subsidies aimed at interjurisdictional spillovers – a plus in a world in which that policy instrument is rarely if ever used; but it does not assume that Pigovian subsidies could not be used to deal with interjurisdictional spillovers. It is able to explain why the degree of expenditure and revenue concentration varies between governmental systems and from period to period. It is able to explain why revenue and expenditure concentration usually differ and, therefore, why vertical fiscal imbalance and the accompanying flows of funds exist. It can explain why transfers from senior to junior governments are often conditional and efficient.[15] It is consistent with the observed fact that governmental systems are sometimes lengthened and sometimes contracted (Breton and Fraschini, 1992). It can explain why the degree of tax harmonization varies from time to time and from context to context. Finally, it establishes naturally that the flypaper effect is not an anomaly of the real world, only an anomaly of a particular theoretical *weltanschauung*.

---

15. I have not analyzed the case when tax funds flow from junior to senior governments, but the model can be adapted to that case relatively easily.

222   **Governmental systems**

iv.   Caveats

Many other factors no doubt help to determine the division of functions
between orders of government. Most, I believe, are insignificant, but two
deserve to be mentioned: (1) information costs and (2) conspiracies or collusive arrangements.

a. Information costs: Governments, whatever the location they occupy in
governmental systems, can inflict utility losses on their citizens by providing
goods and services in quantities (and qualities) that differ from those that at
given taxprices and incomes are desired. Scholars have examined a number of
factors that are taken to be structural components of governmental systems
and that are presumed to induce utility losses. Among them is the "bundling"
of goods and services, that is, the provision in a single package of a number of
goods and services. Yoram Barzel (1969) has shown that bundling can impose
utility losses on citizens.

It has been suggested (Borcherding and Deacon, 1972) that the goods and
services supplied by junior governments are more in the nature of (technical)
private goods, whereas those provided by senior governments are more like
Samuelsonian (1954) public goods. It has also been suggested that populations sort themselves by preferences – or by traits such as language, upbring-
ing, customs, and religions that mold preferences – in such a way that preferences tend to be more homogeneous at lower than at higher tiers of governmental systems. Finally, Tullock (1969) has argued that bundling increases as
both the number of goods and services *and* the number of persons to whom
they are supplied increases. It then follows, as a matter of definition, that
there will be more bundling at higher than at lower jurisdictional levels.

These arguments would seem to imply that in addition to coordination and
contractual enforcement costs, the division of functions would also be constrained by the greater ability of governments at lower jurisdictional tiers to
unbundle supply, that is, to provide citizens with goods and services in quantities and qualities that better match what they desire. A function, which on
the basis of economies of scale alone – and disregarding coordination and
contractual enforcement costs – would have to be assigned to a more senior
jurisdictional tier would, as a consequence, be located with more junior
governments.

Notwithstanding the importance of this line of reasoning in the literature, I
believe that it is seriously flawed. In Chapter 2, I have argued that governments impose utility losses on citizens because they lack information about
demand functions. As the reader will recall, the reasoning is simple. With
perfect information about demand functions, governments can always alter
taxprices or find goods and services that are either substitutes for or comple-

ments to those that have the character of (technical) public goods and to those that are bundled and, by fine-tuning supply, reduce everyone's utility losses to zero.

To defend the traditional line of reasoning, it is therefore essential to be able to argue that more junior governments can acquire information about demand functions at lower costs than can governments located higher up in the system. That may be the case. Casual observation, however, points to economies of scale in polling, canvassing, and consulting and to economies of size in interest groups or demand lobbies that convey information on the preferences of their members (see Chapter 2, Section 2.3). Furthermore, cliques, family compacts, and other cabals that filter information to governments may be easier to create at more junior levels. Given these possibilities, it is prudent to assume that information costs do not vary systematically with jurisdictional level and have as a consequence no systematic effect on the degree of expenditure and revenue concentration, that is, on the division of functions.

b. Collusion: I have discussed collusion and conspiracies in Chapter 3, Section 3.3 and again in Chapter 5, Section 5.3. I have nothing new to add on the phenomenon here, except to say that collusion may, indeed, exist and when it does, it will affect the resulting division of functions. Although acknowledging the possibility of collusion, I hold to the view that it is better to analyze the division of functions in a model in which competition is sometimes marred by conspiracies than in one in which collusion is the rule, except for brief flashes of competition.

8.3.   The constitutional factor

Although it is not possible to assume, for reasons that have already been suggested, that the formal division of powers determines the distribution of functions, we must recognize that together with other constitutional provisions it does sometimes constrain – John Whyte's (1985) words are "condition . . . , restrict . . . or frustrate . . . " (p. 29) – changes that may be required in the assignment of functions. I do no more in what follows than indicate in broad terms how constitutions and formal divisions of powers constrain what is mandated by competition and technology adjusted for coordination and contractual enforcement costs.

I start with the assumption that in the beginning, before the appearance of any constitution and of any division of powers, competition between governments produces a distribution of functions between jurisdictional levels, resulting in an equilibrium degree of revenue and expenditure concentration. During this initial period, we can presume that rules exist to insure that competitive outcomes are enforced, but there is no formal division of powers to

224   Governmental systems

restrict or frustrate the workings of competition. I now assume that in a second period the country we are looking at is given to constitutional experts who, after having deciphered the distribution of functions reflected in the equilibrium degree of revenue and expenditure concentration and in the flows of remittances and revenue payments determined during the initial period, codify all of this in a constitution. As a consequence, they are thereafter known as the Fathers (and/or Mothers) of the Governmental System or simply as the Founding Fathers (and/or Mothers).

Why do the Fathers (and/or Mothers) translate a degree of expenditure and revenue concentration – a division of functions – into a degree of centralization – a constitutional division of powers? They do so to define and fix a pattern of ownership of functions by, as it were, converting functions into powers. As we shall have occasion to ascertain once more in the next chapter (Section 9.4), there are three fundamental patterns of ownership of functions, and each is associated with a particular form of governmental systems, to wit confederalism, unitarianism, and federalism. In the first, all powers are owned by the junior governments, even if some functions have been assigned to senior governments. In the second, all powers are owned by senior governments, even if functions are assigned to junior ones. And, in the third, the ownership of powers is divided among orders of government, though at any one moment some of the functions embodied in a particular central government power may have been assigned to junior governments, or vice versa.

The patterns of ownership and assignments – the division of powers and functions – are especially important when exogenous disturbances require changes in one or in both. Change always reflects the influence of history, political culture, prejudice, interests, and last but not least, political power. These various factors are, however, necessarily channeled or work themselves through one or the other pattern of ownership. Specifically, decisions pertaining to changes in assignment are unilateral in confederal and unitary states, but they are bilateral and more often multilateral in federal states. One should, therefore, expect that the biases imparted by history, political culture, and prejudice and the distorting influence of interests and power to be less in federal than in confederal and unitary states. It is not the division of functions among orders of government or intergovernmental competition that accounts for the superiority of federalism over confederalism and unitarianism, since functions are divided and competition exists in all governmental systems. It is in the pattern of ownership of powers and in the procedures (based on the equality of all participants) used to alter that pattern of ownership that one finds the fundamental superiority of the federal form of government. These procedures serve as a protection against abuse of power, trespass, legerde-

The organization of governmental systems   225

main, and unilateral abrogation of agreements, which, even if they are not illegal may not be efficient.

Assume that in a third period there is an exogenous disturbance that leads to a change in the equilibrium degree of concentration established in the initial period. Should we expect this change to produce a corresponding change in the degree of constitutional centralization? The answer depends on the nature of the disturbance. Suppose, to illustrate, that the constitution drafted during the second period entrenches the power over education in provinces or states. An exogenous shock that called for an increase in expenditures on that function might or might not call for a change in the division of powers. If the increase in expenditures was large, the need for more revenues could lead to a further concentration of revenue collection and to a larger flow of revenue payments to the provinces or states, requiring adjustments that could be accommodated within the framework of the constitution of the second period. However, if the greater concentration of revenue collection cannot be achieved because the formal constitutional division of powers raises the costs of coordination, of contractual enforcement, or of both, then the formal assignment of powers will be altered.

Changes can be effected in many ways – through formal amendments of the constitution, through judicial reinterpretation based on jurisprudence, or through negotiations between the various units of governmental systems. In federal governmental systems, formal constitutional amendments are difficult to achieve and are, as a consequence, little used. They are, however, a preferred instrument for change in unitary states because constitutional amendments are often no more than changes in the legislation of central governments. In federal states, the assignment of powers – their division as well as the functions they embody – is continuously tested in the courts, so that judicial review and reinterpretation are important instruments to alter constitutions. These instruments are not as widely used and for obvious reasons in unitary states. Negotiations over powers (and other related matters) have been identified by some students of federalism [for example Friedrich (1968)] as being central to an understanding of how federal governmental systems work. These writers distinguish between the structure of governmental systems – the degree of concentration and of centralization – and what they call "the process of federalism," and they claim that we should focus on the latter in analyzing federal states. One reason for the claim is that structure, it is argued, can explain little of what we observe in intergovernmental relations. Another is that those federal structures – the former Soviet Union, for example – in which process has been suppressed are not federal states in any meaningful sense [for a good discussion of the matter, see Elazar (1987)]. One need not accept fully the conception of governmental systems advocated by that school

226   **Governmental systems**

of thought to recognize that process plays an important role in federal systems in moving ownership patterns from one configuration to another and that it is less salient in confederal and unitary states.

8.4.   The Wicksellian Connection remembered

The forces described in Part I that foster and tighten Wicksellian Connections operate in the same way in governmental systems as they do in single governmental units. The only reason for recalling the Wicksellian Connection in this chapter is the long and solidly held conviction of many Public Finance economists that vertical fiscal imbalance and the intergovernmental flows of funds that it necessarily implies breaks the connection between revenues and expenditures and leads to fiscal illusion, bureaucratic manipulation, and waste (see Section 8.1 for some references to the relevant literature). In view of the assumption strongly held by mainstream Public Finance that there is no relationship between revenues and expenditures except an accounting one, in the budget making of single isolated governments, that position is somewhat mysterious.

The purpose of Part I was to establish that a Wicksellian Connection between taxprices and quantities demanded is forged by intragovernmental competition. Must that conclusion be rejected when the analysis moves from single governments to governmental systems? The foregoing discussion has made it clear that vertical fiscal imbalance under competitive conditions does not lead to an undoing or unfastening of the Wicksellian Connection built earlier. Indeed, how could a division of functions and of powers that minimizes the real resource cost of supplying goods and services through specialization, the coordination costs of harmonizing spillover flows and complementarities, and the contractual enforcement costs of insuring efficient performance destroy Wicksell–Lindahl efficiency? On the contrary, we should expect intergovernmental competition to reinforce the results of intragovernmental competition and to generate an overall allocation of resources in which utility losses are even smaller than they would be in single-tier unitary states.

It is true that collusion and conspiracies among governments can lead to insufficient or to excessive specialization. It is also true that what I have called the "constitutional factor" can lead to the same outcomes. However, given that multilateral negotiations between equals, litigation involving equals, and constitutional amendments accepted by equals will generate changes in the formal constitutional division of powers that more faithfully track alterations in expenditure and revenue concentration – in the division of supply responsibilities – in federal than in confederal and unitary governmental systems, we should expect the constitutional factor to be less an obstacle to efficient adjustments in the first than in the second types of governmental systems. We should expect patterns of ownership of powers in federal, more than in confederal and unitary states, to accommodate smoothly the modifications in the division of functions that are needed and thus insure the minimization of all costs – production, delivery, coordination, and contractual enforcement – called for by competition. Under these circumstances, we expect the Wicksellian Connection to be such that utility losses are small in all governmental systems but especially in federal systems. We expect intergovernmental competition in all types of governmental systems but especially in federal states to lead to the revelation of the citizenry's true demand functions for government-supplied goods and services.

The reader will recall that in Chapter 4 we established a presumption that utility losses would be smaller in parliamentary than in congressional systems of government. This presumption combined with the foregoing discussion implies that it is in federal parliamentary systems of government that utility losses are the smallest and the Wicksellian Connection the tightest – a conclusion that I myself would have rejected only a few years ago (Breton, 1985).

8.5.   Conclusion

After a review of earlier work, this chapter has proposed a model of the causes and consequences of vertical fiscal imbalance in governmental systems in which vertical competition exists. In that model, governments specialize in the production and supply of certain goods and services. Specialization in turn calls for coordination; it also leads to vertical imbalance and to the necessity of intergovernmental flows of funds. These can be effected only if self-enforcing contracts can be "signed," because the necessarily implicit and incomplete nature of contracts among governments precludes third-party enforcement. The self-enforcing contracts provide an explanation for conditional grants and for other characteristics of intergovernmental relations. The model suggested also implies that it is specialization in response to the obligation to minimize production, coordination, and contractual enforcement costs forced on governments by competition that determines the formal constitutional division of powers and not the other way around. Finally, it is argued that contrary to a prevalent belief, the Wicksellian Connection is not weaker but stronger in governmental systems than in isolated governments and that that proposition is especially true for federal systems of government.

References

Alchian, Armen, "Cost and Outputs," in Paul A. Baran, Tibor Scitovsky, and Edward S. Shaw, eds., *The Allocation of Economic Resources* (Stanford: Standford University Press, 1959), 23–40.

Allingham, Michael G., and Agnar Sandmo, "Income Tax Evasion: A Theoretical Analysis," *Journal of Public Economics* (Vol. 1, No. 3/4, November 1972), 323–38.

Arrow, Kenneth J., "The Economic Implications of Learning by Doing," *Review of Economic Studies* (Vol. 29, No. 3, June 1962), 155–73.

Barzel, Yoram, "Two Propositions on the Optimum Level of Producing Collective Goods," *Public Choice* (Vol. 6, Spring 1969), 31–7.

Baumol, William J., *Welfare Economics and the Theory of the State*, Second Edition (Cambridge, MA: Harvard University Press, 1969; First Edition, 1952).

Bélanger, Gérard, "The Division of Powers in a Federal System: A Review of the Economic Literature, with Applications to Canada," in Richard Simeon, ed., *Division of Powers and Public Policy* (Toronto: University of Toronto Press, 1985), 1–27.

Bella, Leslie, "The Provincial Role in the Canadian Welfare State: The Influence of Provincial Social Policy Initiatives on the Design of the Canada Assistance Plan," *Canadian Public Administration* (Vol. 22, No. 3, Fall 1979), 439–52.

Bird, Richard M., *Financing Canadian Government: A Quantitative Overview* (Toronto: Canadian Tax Foundation, 1979).

"Tax Harmonization and Federal Finance: A Perspective on Recent Canadian Discussion," *Canadian Public Policy* (Vol. 10, No. 3, September 1984), 253–66.

Federal Finance in Comparative Perspective (Toronto: Canadian Tax Foundation, 1986).

Bird, Richard M., and Jack M. Mintz, "Introduction," in Bird and Mintz, eds., *Taxation To 2000 and Beyond* (Toronto: Canadian Tax Foundation, 1992), 1–28.

Boadway, Robin, and Frank Flatters, "Efficiency and Equalization Payments in a Federal System of Government: A Synthesis and Extension of Recent Results," *Canadian Journal of Economics* (Vol. 15, No. 4, November 1982a), 613–33.

Equalization in a Federal State: An Economic Analysis (Ottawa: Supply and Services Canada, 1982b).

Borcherding, Thomas E., and Robert T. Deacon, "The Demand for the Services of Non-Federal Governments," *American Economic Review* (Vol. 62, No. 5, December, 1972), 891–901.

Bös, Dieter, "Commentary of Roger Gordon's 'An Optimal Taxation Approach to Fiscal Federalism,'" in Charles E. McLure, Jr., ed., *Tax Assignment in Federal Countries* (Canberra: Centre for Research on Federal Financial Relations, Australian National University, 1983), 43–7.

Brennan, Geoffrey, and James M. Buchanan, "Normative Tax Theory for a Federal Polity: Some Public Choice Preliminaries," in Charles E. McLure Jr., ed., *Tax Assignment in Federal Countries* (Canberra: Centre for Research on Federal Financial Relations, Australian National University, 1983), 52–65.

Brennan, Geoffrey, and Jonathan Pincus, "An Implicit Contract Theory of Intergovernmental Grants," *Publius: The Journal of Federalism* (Vol. 20, No. 4, Fall 1990), 129–44.

"A Minimalist Model of Federal Grants," (Typescript 1991).

Breton, Albert, "A Theory of Government Grants," *Canadian Journal of Economics and Political Science* (Vol. 31, No. 2, May 1965), 175–87.

"Supplementary Report," in *Report* of the (Macdonald) *Royal Commission on the Economic Union and Development Prospects for Canada* (Ottawa: Supply and Services, 1985). Reprinted as "Towards a Theory of Competitive Federalism," *European Journal of Political Economy* (Vol. 3, Nos. 1–2, 1987), 263–329.

Centralization, Decentralization and Intergovernmental Competition. The 1989 Kenneth R. MacGregor Lecture (Kingston: Queen's University, Institute of Intergovernmental Relations, 1990).

Breton, Albert, and Angela Fraschini, "Free-riding and Intergovernmental Grants," *Kyklos* (Vol. 45, No. 3, 1992), 347–62.

Breton, Albert, and Anthony Scott, *The Economic Constitution of Federal States* (Toronto: University of Toronto Press, 1978).

The Design of Federations (Montreal: Institute for Research on Public Policy, 1980).

Breton, Albert, and Ronald Wintrobe, *The Logic of Bureaucratic Conduct. An Analysis of Competition, Exchange, and Efficiency in Private and Public Organizations* (New York: Cambridge University Press, 1982).

Bryce, James, *The American Commonwealth* (New York: Macmillan, 1888/1911).

Buchanan, James M., "Federalism and Fiscal Equity," *American Economic Review* (Vol. 40, No. 4, September 1950), 583–99. Reprinted in Richard A. Musgrave and Carl S. Shoup, eds., *Readings in the Economics of Taxation* (Homewood: Irwin, 1959), 93–103.

Chernick, Howard A., "An Economic Model of the Distribution of Project Grants," in Peter M. Mieszkowski and William H. Oaklands, eds., *Fiscal Federalism and Grants-in-Aid* (Washington: The Urban Institute, 1979), 81–103.

Coase, Ronald H., "The Problem of Social Cost," *Journal of Law and Economics* (Vol. 3, October 1960), 1–44.

Courant, Paul N., Edward M. Gramlich, and Daniel L. Rubinfeld, "The Stimulative Effects of Intergovernmental Grants: Or Why Money Sticks Where It Hits," in Peter M. Mieszkowski and William H. Oakland, eds., *Fiscal Federalism and Grants-In-Aid,* (Washington: The Urban Institute, 1979), 5–21.

Davies, David G., "The Concentration Process and the Growing Importance of Noncentral Governments in Federal States," *Public Policy* (Vol. 18, Fall 1970), 649–57.

Dicey, Albert, *Introduction to the Study of the Law of the Constitution*, Tenth Edition (New York: St. Martin's Press, 1962).

Elazar, Daniel J., *Exploring Federalism* (Tuscaloosa: University of Alabama Press, 1987).

"Cooperative Federalism," in Daphne A. Kenyon, and John Kincaid, eds., *Competition Among States and Local Governments* (Washington: Urban Institute, 1991), 65–86.

Fisher, Ronald C., "Income and Grant Effects on Local Expenditure: The Flypaper Effect and Other Difficulties," *Journal of Urban Economics* (Vol. 12, No. 3, November 1982), 324–45.

Flatters, Frank R., J. Vernon Henderson, and Peter M. Mieszkowski, "Public Goods, Efficiency, and Regional Fiscal Equalization," *Journal of Public Economics* (Vol. 3, No. 2, May 1974), 99–112.

Friedrich, Carl J., *Trends of Federalism in Theory and Practice* (New York: Praeger, 1968).

Gordon, Roger H., "An Optimal Taxation Approach to Fiscal Federalism," in Charles E. McLure, Jr., ed., *Tax Assignment in Federal Countries* (Canberra: Centre for Research on Federal Financial Relations, Australian National University, 1983), 26–42.

Gramlich, Edward M., "Intergovernmental Grants: A Review of the Empirical Literature," in Wallace E. Oates, ed., *The Political Economy of Fiscal Federalism* (Lexington: D. C. Heath, 1977), 219–39.

Hicks, Ursula, K., *Federalism: Failure and Success* (London: Macmillan, 1978).

Johnson, Harry G., "Optimum Tariffs and Retaliation," *Review of Economic Studies,* (Vol. 21, No. 2, 1953–4), 142–53. Reprinted in Johnson, ed., *International Trade and Economic Growth* (Cambridge, MA: Harvard University Press, 1958), 31–55.

Kincaid, John, 'The Competitive Challenge to Cooperative Federalism: A Theory of Federal Democracy," in Daphne A. Kenyon and John Kincaid, eds., *Competition Among States and Local Governments* (Washington: The Urban Institute Press, 1991), 87–114.

Klein, Benjamin, Robert G. Crawford, and Armen A. Alchian, "Vertical Integration, Appropriable Rents, and the Competitive Contracting Process," *Journal of Law and Economics* (Vol. 21, No. 2, October 1978), 297–326.

Klein, Benjamin, and Keith B. Leffler, "The Role of Market Forces in Assuring Contractual Performance," *Journal of Political Economy* (Vol. 89, No. 4, August, 1981), 615–41.

Klein, Benjamin, and Kevin M. Murphy, "Vertical Restraints as Contract Enforcement Mechanisms," *Journal of Law and Economics* (Vol. 31, No. 2, October 1988), 265–97.

Laski, Harold J., "The Obsolescence of Federalism," *The New Republic* (Vol. 98, May 1939), 367–69. Reprinted in Ashner N. Christensen and Evron M. Kirkpatrick, eds., *The People, Politics, and the Politician: Readings in American Government* (New York: Holt, 1941), 111–17.

Lazear, Edward P., and Sherwin Rosen, "Rank-Order Tournaments as Optimum Labor Contracts," *Journal of Political Economy* (Vol. 89, No. 5, October 1981), 841–64.

Marshall, Alfred, *Principles of Economics*, Eighth Edition (New York: Macmillan, 1890/1952).

McCready, Douglas J., *Tax Harmonization in Canada, 1991* (Mimeo., 1991).

McGuire, Martin C., "An Econometric Model of Federal Grants and Local Fiscal Response," in Wallace E. Oates, ed., *Financing the New Federalism* (Baltimore: John Hopkins University Press, 1975), 115–38.

"The Analysis of Federal Grants into Price and Income Components," in Peter M. Mieszkowski and William H. Oakland, eds., *Fiscal Federalism and Grants-in-Aid* (Washington: The Urban Institute, 1979), 31–50.

Mintz, Jack, and Henry Tulkens, "Commodity Tax Competition Between Member States of a Federation: Equilibrium and Efficiency," *Journal of Public Economics* (Vol. 29, No. 2, March 1986), 133–72.

Mundell, Robert A., "A Theory of Optimum Currency Areas," *American Economic Review* (Vol. 51, No. 4, September 1961), 657–65.

Musgrave, Richard A., *The Theory of Public Finance* (New York: McGraw-Hill, 1959).

Musgrave, Richard A., and Peggy B. Musgrave, *Public Finance in Theory and Practice*, Fourth Edition (New York: McGraw Hill, 1984).

Musgrave, Richard A., Peggy B. Musgrave, and Richard M. Bird, *Public Finance in Theory and Practice*, First Canadian Edition (Toronto: McGraw-Hill Ryerson, 1987).

Niskanen, William A., Jr., *Bureaucracy and Representative Government* (Chicago: Aldine-Atherton, 1971).

Oates, Wallace E., *Fiscal Federalism* (New York: Harcourt Brace Jovanovich, 1972).

"The Changing Structure of Intergovernmental Fiscal Relations," in Horst C. Recktenwald, ed., *Secular Trends of the Public Sector* (Paris: Cujas, 1978), 151–60.

Olson, Mancur, Jr., "The Principle of Fiscal Equivalence," *American Economic Review* (Vol. 59, No. 2, May 1969), 479–87.

Peacock, Alan T., and Jack Wiseman (assisted by Jindrich Veverka), *The Growth of Public Expenditure in the United Kingdom* (Princeton: NBER and Princeton University Press, 1961; reissued with a new Introduction by Allen and Unwin, 1967).

Pigou, Arthur C., *The Economics of Welfare* (London: Macmillan, 1920/1951).

Pommerehne, Werner W., "Quantitative Aspects of Federalism: A Study of Six Countries," in Wallace E. Oates, ed., *The Political Economy of Fiscal Federalism* (Lexington: Heath, 1977), 275–346.

Pommerehne, Werner W., and Bruno S. Frey, "Les modes d'évaluation de l'économie occulte," *Futuribles* (Vol. 50, décembre 1981), 3–32.

Popitz, Johannes, "Der Finanzausgleich," in *Handbuch der Finanzwissenchaft* (Tübingen, 1927).

Pryor, Frederic L., *Public Expenditures in Communist and Capitalist Nations* (London: Allen and Unwin, 1968).

Riker, William H., "Federalism," in Fred I. Greenstein and Nelson W. Polsky, eds., *Handbook of Political Science: Government Institutions and Processes*, Vol. 5 (Memlo Park: Addison-Wesley, 1975), 93–172.

Romer, Thomas, and Howard Rosenthal, "An Institutional Theory of the Effect of Intergovernmental Grants," *National Tax Journal* (Vol. 33, No. 4, December 1980), 451–8.

Rosen, Harvey S., *Public Finance* (Homewood: Irwin, 1985).

Rubinfeld, Daniel L., "The Economics of the Local Public Sector," in Alan J. Auerbach and Martin Feldstein, eds., *Handbook of Public Economics*, Vol. II (Amsterdam: North-Holland, 1987), 571–645.

Salmon, Pierre, "The Logic of Pressure Groups and the Structure of the Public Sector," in Albert Breton, Gianluigi Galeotti, Pierre Salmon, and Ronald Wintrobe, eds., *Villa Colombella Papers on Federalism, European Journal of Political Economy* (Vol. 3, Nos. 1 & 2, 1987a), 55–86.

"Decentralization as an Incentive Scheme," *Oxford Review of Economic Policy* (Vol. 3, No. 2, Summer 1987b), 24–43.

Samuelson, Paul A., "The Pure Theory of Public Expenditure," *Review of Economics and Statistics* (Vol. 36, No. 4, November, 1954), 387–9. Reprinted in Joseph E. Stiglitz, ed., *The Collected Scientific Papers of Paul A. Samuelson*, Vol. II (Cambridge, MA: M.I.T. Press, 1966), 1223–5.

Sandmo, Agnar, "Income Tax Evasions, Labour Supply, and the Equity-Efficiency Tradeoff," *Journal of Public Economics* (Vol. 16, No. 3, December 1981), 265–88.

Scharf, Kimberley Ann, "Optimal Commodity Taxation with Increasing Returns-to-Scale Evasion Technologies" (University of Warwick, Discussion Paper 9433, 1992).

Schwartz, Richard D., and Sonya Orleans, "On Legal Sanctions," *University of Chicago Law Review* (Vol. 34, No. 2, Winter 1967), 274–300.

Scott, Anthony D., "The Evaluation of Federal Grants," *Economica* N.S. (Vol. 19, November 1952), 377–94.

"Piecemeal Decentralization: The Environment", in Robin W. Boadway, Thomas J. Courchene and Douglas D. Purvis, eds., *Economic Dimensions of Constitutional Change* (Kingston: John Deutsch Institute, 1991), 273–97.

Shavell, Steven, *Economic Analysis of Accident Law* (Cambridge, MA: Harvard University Press, 1987).

Shoup, Carl S., *Fiscal Harmonization in Common Markets*, Vols. I and II (New York: Columbia University Press, 1967).

Sidgwick, Henry, *The Elements of Politics* (London: Macmillan, 1919).

Simeon, Richard, *Federal-Provincial Diplomacy. The Making of Recent Policy in Canada* (Toronto: University of Toronto Press, 1972).

Smiley, Donald V., and Ronald L. Watts, *Intrastate Federalism in Canada* (Toronto: University of Toronto Press, 1985).

Smith, Adam, *An Inquiry into the Nature and Causes of the Wealth of Nations* (New York: Random House, 1776/1937).

Spicer, M. W., and S. B. Lundstedt, "Understanding Tax Evasion," *Public Finance/Finances publiques* (Vol. 31, No. 2, 1976), 295–305.

Srinivasan, T. N., "Tax Evasion: A Model," *Journal of Public Economics* (Vol. 2, No. 4, November 1973), 339–46.

Stigler, George J., "The Division of Labor Is Limited by the Extent of the Market," *Journal of Political Economy* (Vol. 59, No. 3, June 1951), 185–93. Reprinted in Stigler, ed., *The Organization of Industry* (Chicago: University of Chicago Press, 1968), 129–41.

The Theory of Price, Third Edition (New York: MacMillan, 1966).

The Theory of Price, Fourth Edition (New York: Macmillan, 1987).

Strick, John C., "Conditional Grants and Provincial Government Budgeting," *Canadian Public Administration* (Vol. 14, No. 2, Summer 1971), 217–35.

Canadian Public Finance, Third Edition (Toronto: Holt, Rinehart and Winston of Canada, 1985).

Subtil, Marie-Pierre, "Un casse-tête: la répartition des compétences entre la Communauté et les Etats membres," *Le Monde* (Vendredi, le 22 juin 1990), 7.

Thirsk, Wayne R., "Tax Harmonization and Its Importance in the Canadian Federation," in Richard M. Bird, ed., *Fiscal Dimension of Canadian Federalism* (Toronto: Canadian Tax Foundation, 1980), 118–42.

Tiebout, Charles M., "A Pure Theory of Local Expenditures," *Journal of Political Economy* (Vol. 64, No. 5, October 1956), 416–24.

de Tocqueville, Alexis, *Democracy in America*. Translated by George Lawrence (Garden City: Harper & Row, Anchor Books, 1835, 1840/1969).

Tullock, Gordon, "Federalism: Problems of Scale," *Public Choice* (Vol. 6, Spring, 1969), 19–29.

Vaillancourt, François, *The Administrative and Compliance Costs of the Personal Income Tax and Payroll Tax System in Canada, 1986* (Toronto: Canadian Tax Foundation, 1989).

Vaillancourt, François, et Martine Hébert, "Les déclarations d'impôts personnels des Québécois pour l'année 1985: qui les complète et à quel coût?" *L'actualité économique, Revue d'analyse économique* (Vol. 66, No. 2, Juin 1990), 242–59.

Vogel, Joachim, "Taxation and Public Opinion in Sweden: An Interpretation of Recent Survey Data," *National Tax Journal* (Vol. 27, No. 4, December 1974), 499–513.

Walker, Jack L., "The Diffusion of Innovations Among the American States," *American Political Science Review* (Vol. 63, No. 3, September 1969), 880–99.

Walsh, Cliff, *Reform of Commonwealth-State Relations – "No Representation Without Taxation,"* (Canberra: Federalism Research Centre, Australian National University, Discussion Paper No. 2, 1991).

Fiscal Accountability, Vertical Fiscal Imbalance and Macroeconomic Management in Federal Fiscal Systems (Canberra: Federalism Research Centre, Australian National University, Discussion Paper No. 7, 1992).

Weldon, Jack C., "Public Goods (and Federalism)," *Canadian Journal of Economics and Political Science* (Vol. 32, No. 2, May 1966), 230–8.

Wheare, Kenneth C., *Federal Government*, Fourth Edition (London: Oxford University Press, 1963).

Whyte, John D., "Constitutional Aspects of Economic Development Policy," in Richard Simeon, ed., *Division of Powers and Public Policy* (Toronto: University of Toronto Press, 1985), 29–69.

Wilde, James A., "Grants-In-Aid: The Analytics of Design and Response," *National Tax Journal* (Vol. 24, No. 2, 1971), 143–55.

Williamson, Oliver E., *Markets and Hierarchies: Analysis and Antitrust Implications. A Study in the Economics of Internal Organization* (New York: Macmillan, 1975).

The Economic Institutions of Capitalism: Firms, Markets, Relational Contracting (New York: Free Press, 1985).

Winer, Stanley, L., "Some Evidence on the Effect of the Separation of Spending and Taxing Decisions," *Journal of Political Economy* (Vol. 91, No. 1, February 1983), 126–40.

"Taxation and Federalism in a Changing World," in Richard M. Bird and Jack M. Mintz, eds., *Taxation to 2000 and Beyond* (Toronto: Canadian Tax Foundation, 1992), 343–69.

Zampelli, Ernst M., "Resource Fungibility, The Flypaper Effect, and the Expenditure Impact of Grants-in-Aid," *Review of Economics and Statistics* (Vol. 68, No. 1, February 1986), 33–40.

D
Federalism, Development
and Self-Enforcing Federalism

[12]

JLEO, V11 N1 **1**

The Economic Role of Political Institutions: Market-Preserving Federalism and Economic Development

Barry R. Weingast
Stanford University

Thriving markets require not only an appropriately designed economic system, but a secure political foundation that limits the ability of the state to confiscate wealth. This requires a form of *limited government*, that is, political institutions that credibly commit the state to honor economic and political rights. This article studies how limited government arose in the developed West, focusing on the critical role of federalism for protecting markets in both England and the United States. Federalism proved fundamental to the impressive economic rise of England in the 18th century and the United States in the 19th and early 20th centuries. The article also shows that federalism underpins the spectacular economic growth in China over the past 15 years.

Introduction

The fundamental political dilemma of an economic system is this: A government strong enough to protect property rights and enforce contracts is also strong enough to confiscate the wealth of its citizens. Thriving markets require not only the appropriate system of property rights and a law of contracts, but a secure political foundation that limits the ability of the state to confiscate wealth. Far from obvious, however, are the circumstances that produce a political system that plays one role instead of the other.

This dilemma is readily apparent for the case of economic reform in Eastern Europe and the former Soviet Union. Economists focus on providing for the broad outlines of a market system, that is, on "getting prices right." Unfortu-

---

The author is a senior fellow of the Hoover Institution and professor, Department of Political Science, at Stanford University. He gratefully acknowledges Annelise Anderson, Robert Bates, Peter Bernholz, Peter Boettke, Thomas Gilligan, Victor Goldberg, Avner Greif, Nina Halpern, Gabriella Montinola, Douglass North, Richard Posner, Yingyi Qian, Douglas Rivers, Hilton Root, Kenny Schultz, Urs Schweizer, Kenneth Shepsle, Susan Shirk, Dorothy Solinger, Pablo Spiller, Scott Thomas, George Tsebelis, Oliver Williamson, and Christine Wong for helpful conversations and Paulina Favela for editorial assistance. This article was prepared under a cooperative agreement between the Institution for Policy Reform (IPR) and the Agency for International Development (AID), Cooperative Agreement No. PDC-0095-A-00-1126-00. Views expressed here are those of the author and not necessarily those of IPR or AID.

2   The Journal of Law, Economics, & Organization, V11 N1

nately, the economists' focus ignores politics and the possibility that political forces might intervene in the future to halt the development of a market system or to redistribute a large portion of the wealth thus created. Not only do political forces hold the potential to destroy a fragile, nascent economic system, but their prospect deters the economic activity necessary for economic growth. As economists have long realized, the absence of secure protection for the reward to effort deters investment and, hence, economic development (Eggertson, 1990; North, 1981, 1990; Olson, 1982; Williamson, 1994).

The fundamental political dilemma forces us to ask what form of political system is required so that a viable, private market economy is a stable policy choice of that political system? The answer concerns the design of political institutions that *credibly commit* the state to preserving markets, that is, to limits on the future political discretion with respect to the economy that are in the interests of political officials to observe (Levy and Spiller, 1994; North, 1993; Weingast, 1994a, 1994b; Williamson, 1994). The central component of a credible commitment to limited government is that these limits must be self-enforcing. For limits on government to be sustained, political officials must have an incentive to abide by them. This implies that designers of economic reform must pay attention not only to the reform's content but to how the future exercise of political discretion might alter that policy.

In the language of the new institutional economics, providing a secure and predictable political foundation for the markets requires a form of *governance structure* (Williamson, 1985, 1994; Weingast, 1993b).[1] To understand the political foundations of markets, we must begin with the *constitution*, conceived here as the set of institutions governing political decision-making—that is, the institutions or rules governing how policy choices are made, especially among alternative specifications of the economic system. All societies possess a constitution in this sense, whether or not they possess an explicit document called "the constitution."[2] For example, Roeder (1993) describes the operation of the working constitution of the former Soviet Union, as opposed to its nominal, written constitution. Understanding the relationships between constitutional provisions and economic performance requires development of a new *positive theory of constitutionalism* that seeks to explain how constitutional limits work and why some constraints prove binding in practice.[3]

---

1. Notice that this logic directly parallels that in the theory of the firm. Williamson (1985: 48-49), for example, argues that when transactions are subject to ex post problems, wise bargaining parties will attempt to mitigate these problems ex ante by creating a *governance structure*. See Milgrom and Roberts (1992) for a recent and comprehensive statement of the theory.

2. Nor does this require that the constitution contain provisions supporting democracy, representation, or secure political and private rights for individuals, though most Western constitutions do so. Constitutions in the developed West are thus an important special case of constitutions. In contrast to the more general range of constitutions, those in the West possess a range of additional (and generally thought to be desirable) attributes.

3. Recent work includes Hardin (1989), North and Weingast (1989), Ordeshook (1993), Ordeshook and Schwartz (1994), Przeworski (1990), Riker (1982), and Weingast (1994a); see also

One of the central limits of the literature is that few scholars actually provide a complete analysis of any mechanism purported to provide such credible commitments (an important exception is Levy and Spiller, 1994). We remain remarkably ignorant about how constitutions affect credible commitments to secure economic rights and, more generally, limited government.

To learn something about how constitutions credibly commit a state to markets, this article considers how such commitments were provided in the developing West over the past few centuries. Because many of the crucial questions facing today's developing states were once faced by developed nations, considerable insight can be provided about today's problems by studying similar problems as they arose in the past. Although today's circumstances differ substantially from those of earlier eras, important lessons about the political foundations of markets can still be learned.

For this purpose, I focus on federalism, an important mechanism underpinning development in many nations. For most of the last 300 years, the richest nation in the world has had a federal structure: the Netherlands from the late 16th through mid-17th century, England from the late 17th or early 18th through the mid-19th century, and the United States from the late 19th century until the late 20th century. A specific form of federalism, here called *market-preserving federalism*, limited the degree to which each of these country's political systems could encroach upon its markets.

The economic consequences of market-preserving federalism are well-known: Federalism restricts economic policymaking via limits on the discretion of the government (Tiebout, 1956; Oates, 1972). Less well understood is the central problem of this article: how a system of federalism provides for its own survival. If federalism has strong, binding effects, what makes its restrictions self-enforcing? Specifically, what prevents interest groups and distributional coalitions, limited in their influence over lower-level governments, from pressing the central government to break the restrictions of federalism and intervene in the economy (Riker, 1964)? The answer cannot be simply a written rule, for rules can be changed, avoided, or ignored. To survive, federalism requires self-enforcing restrictions, ones that make it in the interests of national political actors to honor them. The purpose of this article is to show how these mechanisms work in three contexts where federalism has underpinned rapid economic development: England during the 18th century, the United States during the 19th century, and modern China. In so doing, the article provides some general principles of a society's constitutional order that are necessary to provide secure political foundations for markets.

The article is divided into three parts. Part 1 contains two sections that focus on the effects of federalism and puts these in a political perspective. Section 1.1 describes the political theory of market-preserving federalism, and Section 1.2 discusses its role in the economic development of England and the United

---

Elster (1991), Hammond and Miller (1989), North (1981, 1990). Much of Brennan and Buchanan's (1984) work is also included, though much of it is also normative in character.

4 The Journal of Law, Economics, & Organization, V11 N1

States. Part 2 focuses on the deeper question of what made federalism and its restrictions credible. Section 2.1 analyzes how federalism was sustained in England, and Section 2.2 does so for the United States. Part 3 turns to contemporary settings of economic reform in the former communist states, focusing on economic reform in China. My conclusions follow.

1. The Effects of Federalism

1.1 A Political Theory of Federalism

The essence of federalism is that it provides a sustainable system of political decentralization. Although the political theory of federalism has a long history, it is useful to start with Riker.[4] In his seminal work on the political theory of federalism, Riker (1964: 11) defines a political system as federal if it has two characteristics: (F1) a *hierarchy* of governments, that is, at least "two levels of governments rule the same land and people," each with a *delineated scope of authority* so that each level of government is autonomous in its own, well-defined sphere of political authority; and (F2) the *autonomy* of each government is institutionalized in a manner that makes federalism's restrictions self-enforcing.

In what follows, I focus on a subset of federal systems called *market-preserving federalism* (see also McKinnon, 1994; and Montinola, Qian, and Weingast, 1995). A federal system is market-preserving if it has three additional characteristics: (F3) subnational governments have primary regulatory *responsibility over the economy*; (F4) a *common market* is ensured, preventing the lower governments from using their regulatory authority to erect trade barriers against the goods and services from other political units; and (F5) the lower governments face a *hard budget constraint*, that is, they have neither the ability to print money nor access to unlimited credit. This condition is not met if the central government bails out the lower one whenever the latter faces fiscal problems (McKinnon, 1994).

Each of these characteristics plays an important part in federalism's market-preserving role. The first is clearly a defining characteristic establishing minimal or necessary conditions for a federal system. But it alone is not sufficient. The reason is that federal systems are not generally sustainable if they depend solely on the discretion of the highest political authority, because that delegation of power can always be reversed. As Riker observes, a central problem for federal systems is that the highest or central government may *overawe* the lower units. A sustainable system of federalism therefore must prevent the central government's ability to overawe the lower governments, as condition two requires.

The first two characteristics define a viable system of federalism, but they say nothing about the authority over economic issues. To have market-preserving

---

4. This section draws on the work of Aranson (1991), McKinnon (1994), Oates (1972), Riker (1964), and Tiebout (1956). See also Elazar (1987), Friedrich (1968), Hayek (1939), and Wheare (1953). Although most of the latter discuss many of the conditions that follow, sometimes implicitly, all omit the critical third condition about self-enforcement.

economic effects, federalism must also have the third, fourth, and fifth characteristics. The central government's authority to make economic policy must be
limited; this authority must be in the hands of the lower political units. Moreover, the local governments must face hard budget constraint. This constraint
induces proper fiscal management (McKinnon, 1994). Were lower governments bailed out of fiscal problems, either by the central government or via
access to printing money, they would have far less reason to worry about the
fiscal consequences of their decisions.

Notice that some states will call themselves federal although they fail to meet
the above five criteria, while others may not call themselves federal but do meet
the criteria. Thus, as Williamson (1994) observes, there is a distinction between
de facto and de jure federalism. This suggests that traditional approaches to
federalism are based on formal or legal distinctions that are irrelevant for the
questions studied here. In what follows, we study states that meet the above
five criteria without regard to whether they call themselves federal.

1.1.1 Economic Consequences of Market-Preserving Federalism. The econo-
mic consequences of market-preserving federalism, explored by Hayek (1939,
1960) and made famous by Tiebout (1956), are sufficiently well-known that
they need be described only briefly here.[5] The first and perhaps best studied effect is the induced competition among lower units of the federal structure. The
restrictions on the central government's regulatory power combine with competition among lower jurisdictions to imply that no government has monopoly
control over economic regulation. As long as capital and labor are mobile,
market-preserving federalism constrains the lower units in their attempts to
place political limits on economic activity, because resources will move to
other jurisdictions.

The literature on the economic effects of federalism yields two principal
conclusions about public policy choice. First, political competition implies
that jurisdictions must compete for capital, labor, and economic activity by
offering menus of public policies (e.g., levels of taxation, security of private
rights, social amenities, and public goods). Economic actors make location
decisions based in part on those menus. In combination, the choices of local
jurisdictions and economic actors yield a diversity of public goods, with some
jurisdictions providing lower taxes and a lower level of public goods and others
providing higher taxes and a higher level of public goods.[6]

Second, competition implies that only those restrictions that citizens are
willing to pay for will survive. Were a jurisdiction to respond to political
pressure by attempting to cartelize an industry, the mobility of labor implies
that it will relocate in more compatible jurisdictions. If a jurisdiction attempts
to confiscate the wealth of an industry, the mobility of capital implies that firms

---

5. For recent results and surveys of this literature, see Aranson (1991), Casella and Frey (1992),
Inman (1987), McKinnon (1994), Oates (1972), Rubinfeld (1987), and Scotchmer (1994).

6. Here too, qualifications to the general results have appeared; see Aranson (1991), Inman
(1987), and Scotchmer (1994).

6   The Journal of Law, Economics, & Organization, V11 N1

will relocate. The mobility of resources thus raises the economic costs to those jurisdictions that might establish certain policies, and they will do so only if the political benefits are worth these and other costs.

Federalism thus greatly diminishes the level and pervasiveness of economic rent-seeking and the formation of distributional coalitions. Competition among the lower units limits the success from rent-seeking. Because such regulation qua rent-seeking can only be local, it provides firms outside that locale with a competition advantage over those being regulated. Nonetheless, when, in a given locale, individuals' willingness to pay is sufficient, local governments will provide a specific array of goods and services.

1.1.2 Sustaining Market-preserving Federalism.   A principal feature of the economic analysis of federalism is that it takes federalism's division of political authority as given.   In political terms, the economic analysis of federalism ignores how Riker's second characteristic F(2) is achieved. Although I postpone until Part 2 the discussion of how it is achieved in practice, the previous discussion demonstrates why it is necessary.

The beneficial economic consequences of federalism result from the political decentralization of economic authority that induces competition among the lower political units. Were the structure of political authority solely at the discretion of the central authorities, the beneficial effect could not be realized, because they would respond to the interests' appeals for intervention in precisely the same manner as if there were no federalism. Without a mechanism to prevent this action by the central level, market-preserving federalism would be neither sustainable nor market-preserving. Something must provide durability to the limits on the central government's authority to regulate directly, to usurp that authority, or simply to remove its earlier grant of that authority to the lower levels. In short, federalism's restrictions must be self-enforcing.

1.2 Market-preserving Federalism in Practice

This section surveys two systems characterized by market-preserving federalism: 18th-century England and the 19th-century United States.[7]

1.2.1 Federalism in England.   Though the British do not use the label *federalism*, by the criteria given above, 18th-century England was a de facto federal system.[8] First, the national and local governments were important and distinct sources of political authority. Second, by the beginning of the 18th century, the

---

7. Though what follows focuses only on Anglo-American cases, similar arguments can be made for the role of federalism in the economic rise of Switzerland and Germany.

8. The reason England was not a de jure system of federalism is that 18th-century England did not possess political jurisdictions such as states, cantons, or *länder* that are associated with governments typically labeled as federal. Nonetheless, despite the absence of states or *länder*, 18th-century England fits the five criteria given above. As we show below, various local governments had considerable political and economic freedom over the economy.

national government was limited in its ability to regulate the domestic economy (though international trade was heavily controlled). The constitutional changes during the 17th century abolished, greatly restricted, or granted jointly to Parliament and the Crown many of the powers used by the deposed Stuart kings. Throughout the Stuarts' reign, rent-seeking activity was prevalent (Ekelund and Tollison, 1981), and many of these constitutional changes were aimed at preventing it.

From the standpoint of this article, England's market-preserving federal structure proved critical to the industrial revolution. The importance of the induced competition among localities is revealed by its effects on the pattern of local economic controls. In nearly all the established commercial centers of England, production was controlled via local regulatory laws. Various industries and professions, for example, were governed by guilds, whose regulatory controls attempted to limit competition, pricing, entry, and training. These constraints handicapped potential entrants, including those attempting to devise new forms of economic activity or to promote significant innovation for existing activities.

Two interrelated aspects of the industrial revolution concern us. First, economic historians emphasize that one of the central factors underlying the industrial revolution was the absence of enforcement of these restrictions (see, e.g., Mokyr, 1988). Second, that absence was neither uniform nor accidental (see Hartwell, 1971; and esp. North, 1981: chap. 12). And it is important from our perspective that the absence of restrictions reflected local political policy choices. As is well-known, industrialization did not proceed in the established commercial centers, but instead in the north. One of the foremost scholars of the industrial revolution, T. S. Ashton, concluded that the absence of regulatory restrictions was decisive for location decisions:

> It is beyond doubt that employers often transferred their activities from corporate towns in order to escape from restrictions imposed by privileged groups of workers, or from municipal regulations as to labour ... [T]he movement of industry was rarely induced by the prospect of lower wages in the new area. (Ashton, 1955: 94)

Trying to evade local economic restrictions, many of the new entrepreneurs who were so critical to the industrial revolution located in areas traditionally outside the commercial orbit.

Root's (1994) comparison of England and France reveals an important difference in the legal response to the locational decisions of new enterprises. In England, Parliament and many local Justices of the Peace (JPs) refused to extend guild restrictions and jurisdiction to the countryside. Typically selected from the local gentry, JPs were unpaid and owed only nominal allegiance to the crown, particularly after the Glorious Revolution (1688–89). Local JPs cared far more about local prosperity—often their own—than about implementing policies for the benefit of those outside their jurisdiction. "By contrast, the French royal courts supported the claims of French guilds to regulate rural production,"

8   The Journal of Law, Economics, & Organization, V11 N1

thus hindering rather than fostering industrial development in France (Root, in press: chap. 5).[9]

Two aspects of England's market-preserving federalism fostered economic growth during the industrial revolution. First, limits on the national government's authority to regulate economic activity prevented it from responding to efforts by the established economic interests to provide national controls that would have effectively prevented many of the new industrial activities.[10] Second, the induced political competition among local jurisdictions implied that some localities were willing to take on the extra burdens in exchange for the prospect of generating new forms of economic activity, local employment, and taxes. The absence of local political freedom would have significantly hindered the industrial revolution. Federalism thus provided a necessary and decisive *political* foundation for England's industrial revolution.

1.2.2 Federalism in the United States.   At its inception, the United States Constitution granted the states the power to provide their citizens with various forms of public goods. The historical record shows that they took advantage of these powers in different ways (Handlin and Handlin, 1947; Hartz, 1948; Hughes, 1977). The Constitution also allowed states to respond to interest groups and distributional coalitions, but limited the reach of each state's policies to its own territory. Federalism provided strong limits on the degree to which these coalitions could impose uniform national regulations.

The commerce clause provided one of the Constitution's central pillars in its protection of markets (for a discussion of this issue, see Aranson, 1991).[11] This clause prevented states from regulating interstate markets and from erecting various forms of trade barriers. It also limited federal regulation to problems truly national in scope, an authority not exercised via direct intervention in domestic markets for the first 100 years of the Constitution. As Hayek (1960: chap. 12) observed, federalism thus proved the solution to the dilemma of how to limit the states' protectionist activities without providing the national government with too much power.

The consequence was one of the largest common markets in the world, one with strong protection of property rights and an absence of economic regulation. The constitutional limits on state and federal governments provided the critical political foundation for the enormous expansion of the economy during the 19th century. By mid-century, the pattern of interregional trade had transformed the

---

9. These conclusions are shared by a range of scholars. Landes (1969: 18–19), for example, emphasizes that "a crucial element in the rise of industrial capitalism [was] the spread of commercial manufacture from the towns to the countryside . . . [Yet] the very unevenness of this development . . . is testimony to the fierce and successful opposition it encountered from privileged interests in the towns."

10. Indeed, the Stuarts' inclination toward this form of regulation, paralleling similar inclinations in absolutist France, underpinned one group of the domestic opposition to them during the Civil War in the 1640s and the Glorious Revolution in the late 1680s.

11. The commerce clause was by no means the sole clause designed for this purpose; another example is the privileges and immunities clause.

nation from one of largely self-sufficient farmers at the time of the Constitution to one of striking regional—and international—economic specialization (North, 1961; Fogel, 1989). The growth in national wealth reflected this pattern of specialization.

In broad outline, the South specialized in the production of cotton and other exports. During the early part of the century, strong and growing international demand for cotton helped fuel American economic growth (North, 1961; Lee and Passell, 1979). The Northeast specialized in providing commercial services, for example, transporting cotton to European markets. It also provided insurance, marketing, and other financial services attending the growth and delivery of these exports. The Northwest, largely self-sufficient at first, increasingly came to specialize in growing food. These crops were shipped south along the water routes and, increasingly, east via canals and railroads. On the eve of the Civil War, a large portion of Midwestern farmers were specialists in international markets, producing grain bound for Europe (Bogue, 1963; Fogel, 1989). Except for the interruption of the Civil War (including its lasting deleterious effects on the South), this process of growth and specialization continued throughout the century. By century's end, the United States was the richest nation in the world.

The relatively unregulated aspect of the thriving markets of the 19th century is so taken for granted by modern economic historians that it is not analyzed in any detail (see, e.g., Lee and Passell, 1979; or Fogel, 1989: Part 1; an important exception is Temin, 1991). Neoclassical economics, taking property rights as given, accepts secure economic rights in the 19th century without analysis. And yet the absence of federal intervention to alter markets and property rights was neither inevitable nor due to lack of demand. Just as today we observe a host of displaced economic interests providing political support for intervention to halt or reverse the changes accompanying economic growth, so too did groups in the 19th century. Thus commercial agents along the traditional water transportation routes fought the growth of the railroads. Cattle producers in upstate New York sought relief from cheaper producers farther west. Nascent manufacturers in the Northeast fought cheap land policy at the federal level because lower prices increased immigration rates. Although the reasons varied from case to case, these interests were by and large unsuccessful in their attempts to gain beneficial legislation.[12]

The absence of debilitating regulatory intervention critically depended on the common market's secure political foundation limiting the ability of state and federal governments to respond to distributional coalitions. For well over a century, domestic, interregional markets were not only unregulated but *protected from regulation* by the Constitution's constraints. As emphasized above, federalism was central to these constraints.

---

12. See Miller (1971) on the railroads and Passell and Schmundt (1971) on Northeastern interests and immigration policy. More generally, see Chandler's (1977) systematic study of industrial change in the second half of the 19th century.

10   The Journal of Law, Economics, & Organization, V11 N1

2. Credible Commitment to Federalism

Part 2 discusses the principal constitutional mechanisms that underpinned federalism in England and the United States, focusing on what made federalism self-enforcing.

2.1 Self-Enforcing Market-preserving Federalism and the Rule of Law in 17th- and 18th-Century England

The task of this section is twofold: to develop a model of a constitutional consensus about the limits on governmental action and to apply it to help explain the absence of economic intervention in 18th-century England.

The question we study concerns the limits on sovereign or state power. Why are institutional constraints on government observed? In particular, given the omnipresent temptations to avoid, break, ignore, or end-run these restrictions, what preserves limited government? One approach concerns the notion of *legitimacy*: A regime finds it difficult to violate provisions of a constitution that its citizens feel are legitimate. Although promising, this approach is fraught with problems: What determines when a constitution is legitimate? Can this notion be operationalized so that it is not tautological? And how does legitimacy translate into the preservation of a specific constraint on government?

The purpose of this section is to develop an approach to the problem of legitimacy in a way that answers these questions.[13] To make sense of this concept, we begin with individual citizens. To avoid tautology, we root legitimacy in individual citizens, not in the society. We assume that each citizen holds a specific view about the appropriate bounds on governmental action.

Defined in this way, the problem of legitimacy creates two enormous social problems. The first arises because in and of itself, nothing brings citizens to a uniform view. Indeed, economic, political, and social differences work to differentiate their notions of what actions are legitimate. In the language of game theory, the problematic nature of citizen agreement on the appropriate bounds of government creates a *coordination* problem.

The second problem concerns the relationship between a citizen's views about the appropriate bounds on government and what happens when those bounds are violated. Put simply, even if all the citizens agree on the appropriate bounds of government, what keeps the government from ignoring those bounds?

The importance of these two problems arises because they hold the key to the success of limited government. Constraints can be policed only when citizens react in concert against the government's violations. Success requires the conjunction of two aspects of citizen behavior: First, citizens must react to violations by punishing the government; and second, they must hold sufficiently similar views about the appropriate bounds on government that they react in concert when the government oversteps those bounds. In the language of game theory, we are searching for an equilibrium to a game in which the government has the opportunity to violate constraints but chooses not to do so.

---

13. What follows summarizes the model and results presented in Weingast (1994b).

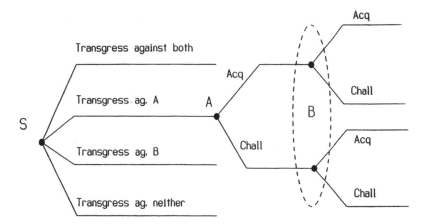

Figure 1. The sovereign-constituency transgression game.   (Acq = to acquiesce to a transgression, Chall = to challenge it).

The model is based on two assumptions about the relationship between a sovereign and his or her citizens. First, a necessary condition for an individual citizen to support the sovereign is that the sovereign not transgress that citizen's rights. Second, remaining in power requires that the sovereign retain a sufficient degree of support among the citizenry. Without the necessary support, the sovereign loses power.

2.1.1 The Model.   We suppose there is a single sovereign, S, and two groups of citizens, A and B. The groups of citizens have different views about the legitimate boundaries of the state and hence what actions by the sovereign are considered a fundamental violation of their rights. In this game, the sovereign needs the support of at least one of the two groups in order to retain power.

The sequence of actions in this game is shown in Figure 1. S moves first and may choose to attempt to transgress against both A and B, against A alone, against B alone, or against neither. After S moves, A and B move simultaneously.[14] Each may choose to acquiesce or to challenge the sovereign. Challenging is costly; moreover, each may challenge even if the sovereign has not transgressed. If both A and B challenge, the sovereign is deposed and any transgression attempted by the sovereign is rebuffed. If only one group of citizens challenges S, the challenge fails and any transgression attempt by S succeeds. Of course, if both A and B acquiesce, any attempted transgression succeeds.

---

14. The simultaneous move between A and B is represented in Figure 1 as follows: A moves first, followed by B, and the dashed ellipse or "information set" around B's two nodes indicates that B does not know A's decision when choosing his own move.

12 The Journal of Law, Economics, & Organization, V11 N1

Table 1. Payoffs for the Sovereign-Constituency Transgression Game

Sovereign's Move	Induced Subgame Between A and B (Payoffs: S, A, B)

Transgress against both

		B	
		Acq	Chall
A	Acq	(5, 1, 1)	(5, 1, 0)
	Chall	(5, 0, 1)	(0, 3, 3)

Transgress against A

		B	
		Acq	Chall
A	Acq	(3, 1, 4)	(3, 1, 3)
	Chall	(3, 0, 1)	(0, 3, 3)

Transgress against B

		B	
		Acq	Chall
A	Acq	(3, 4, 1)	(3, 4, 0)
	Chall	(3, 3, 1)	(0, 3, 3)

Transgress against neither

		B	
		Acq	Chall
A	Acq	(1, 4, 4)	(1, 4, 3)
	Chall	(1, 3, 4)	(0, 3, 3)

Power is valuable to the sovereign, who receives 1 if he retains power. Successful transgressions are also valuable to the sovereign and are worth 2 each. A transgression against either group costs that group 3, reflecting the fact that there are economic costs associated with transgressions—for example, a loss of wealth. Challenging costs each challenger 1, regardless whether the challenge is successful.

The payoffs from this game are given in Table 1. Outcomes and payoffs are determined by the strategy combinations chosen by the three players. If S attempts to transgress against both A and B and both acquiesce, the transgression succeeds and the payoffs are: 5 to S, 1 to A, and 1 to B. If S attempts to transgress against both A and B and both challenge, the transgression fails and S loses power, resulting in payoffs of 0, 3, 3. The Pareto optimal outcome for society occurs when no transgressions or challenges are attempted (the parties obtain 1, 4, and 4, respectively).

Although more complicated than the standard Prisoners' Dilemma, the structure of this game resembles it. This holds because responding to transgressions is costly to each citizen group. Consider the set of incentives facing the citizens if S attempts to transgress against B. B prefers that both challenge. Notice, however, that A has a dominant strategy: no matter what strategy B plays, A prefers to acquiesce. Knowing this, B will acquiesce.

This structure of interaction allows the sovereign to transgress some citizens' rights and survive.[15] In the one-shot game, there are three pure strategy equi-

15. Throughout this analysis we use the concept of subgame perfection as an equilibrium concept, defined as follows. A *strategy* is a specification of the action a player will take at every branch

libria, and the Pareto optimal strategy combination with no transgressions is not among them. Which equilibrium occurs depends in part on the reaction functions of the citizens' groups to a transgression. The worst outcome for the citizens—where the sovereign transgresses against both—is an equilibrium. This occurs if citizens acquiesce whenever they are the target of a transgression. Acting alone and taking the behavior of the others as given, each citizen group can only increase its costs by challenging; it cannot change the outcome.

On the other hand, A and B might both play a different strategy, namely that they challenge S if and only if both are the targets of a transgression. In this case, there are two equilibria, depending on which citizen group S chooses as a target. Suppose that S chooses to target B in every period and that A and B respond as just suggested. Then S has no incentive to deviate: transgressing against both leads to being deposed; transgressing against A instead of B is no better; and transgressing against neither leaves the sovereign worse off. Furthermore, neither citizen group has an incentive to deviate. For A, this conclusion is obvious. For B, it follows because B can do no better. Given that B alone is the target, and thus that A will not challenge, challenging will not change the outcome but will increase B's costs. Hence B is better off acquiescing if it alone is the target.

The situation is more complicated when this game is repeated, that is, when the interaction between the sovereign and citizens is ongoing. Given the structure of payoffs, the "folk theorem" applies, implying that virtually any outcome can be sustained as an equilibrium of the repeated game (Fudenberg and Maskin, 1986). In particular, any of the equilibria of the one-shot game is an equilibrium of the repeated game. The existence of multiple equilibria is a problem for prediction, an issue we return to below.

The folk theorem implies that the Pareto optimal outcome can be sustained. The key to this result, as with the one-shot game, concerns the behavior of each citizen group when the sovereign attempts to transgress against the other. The difference is that repetition provides the opportunity for citizens not only to punish the sovereign, but to punish one another. The Pareto optimal outcome is supported by both groups challenging the sovereign when the sovereign attempts to transgress against either. The reason why that behavior can be supported under repeat play is that, as in the repeated Prisoners' Dilemma, the players can use "trigger" strategies to punish one another for failure to cooperate. If, for example, A fails to challenge the sovereign when the sovereign attempts to transgress against B, then B can retaliate by failing in the future to challenge the sovereign whenever the sovereign attempts to transgress against A. This behavior by B allows the sovereign to transgress successfully against A.

B's trigger strategy provides A with the following strategy choice. It can acquiesce today, avoiding the cost of 1, and then face losing 3 in all future periods; or it can challenge today, costing 1 but maintaining 3 in all future

---

of the game tree. An *equilibrium* is a set of strategy combinations in which no player has an incentive to deviate given the strategies of others. The equilibrium is *subgame perfect* if it remains an equilibrium when restricted to every subgame.

14   The Journal of Law, Economics, & Organization, V11 N1

periods. Clearly, when A does not discount the future too heavily, it will prefer
the latter, so that B's threat strategy induces A to challenge the sovereign when
the latter attempts to transgress against B alone.

Unfortunately, the Pareto optimal outcome is not the only equilibrium. Although that equilibrium is normatively attractive, it will not inevitably occur.
The game might instead yield any of the three equilibria of the one-shot game,
allowing successful transgressions against some or all citizens. In particular,
the sovereign may transgress the rights of some citizens while retaining the
support of others.

So far, we have taken the definition of a transgression as given, ignoring the
content of the underlying views of individuals about these transgressions. The
most natural way to interpret a transgression in the model is as an act directed
against a group of citizens—for example, an attempt to confiscate their wealth.
Another subtler way to think about a transgression is to disassociate it from the
target. For many citizens, the importance of a transgression lies in its nature,
regardless of who is the target. This view of transgressions implies that citizens
have a duty to challenge the sovereign when the latter attempts a transgression,
regardless of the target. This view still allows for a diversity of opinion over
what acts constitute transgressions. The question then becomes, given this
interpretation of transgressions and citizen duty, what combinations of beliefs
about the nature of transgressions can be supported in equilibrium?

Given the second interpretation of a transgression, one way to think about
the problem of multiple equilibria is that the question of which equilibrium
will occur depends on the diversity of beliefs about transgressions and about
citizen duties when the sovereign attempts to transgress against other citizens.
Indeed, as Ferejohn (1990) argues, in the context of multiple equilibria, we
can suggest which equilibrium will result if we know the pattern of beliefs in
a society.

In the present context, Ferejohn's argument implies the following. Suppose there is a diversity of preferences over outcomes, especially if citizens'
economic circumstances differ considerably—some might be wealthy elites,
others successful commercial agents or economic entrepreneurs, others farmers who own their land, still others peasants who work land they do not own.
Under these circumstances, the nature of citizen views about the appropriate
role of the state and what actions constitute a transgression are likely to differ
widely. Because there is no automatic mechanism to produce a consensus on
these issues, the most natural equilibrium of the game is the asymmetric one.
Put another way, the diversity of preferences impedes the development of the
Pareto optimal equilibrium, making it more likely that the game will result in
one of the asymmetric equilibria in which the sovereign transgresses the rights
of some and retains the support of others.

Ferejohn's argument also implies that, for those issues over which citizens
agree about the nature of a transgression, the Pareto optimal outcome can be
supported. When the state of agreement in society is large, producing something
approaching a consensus, a sovereign who attempts to transgress against citizens
cannot survive.

Summary and Implications.   The model shows that it is costly for the citizens to police the sovereign or government. Policing limits on the state requires that citizens be willing to bear this cost when the state violates them. Yet if citizen beliefs about the appropriate limits on the state differ considerably, it is difficult for them to react in concert to state actions.   Indeed, this diversity allows the sovereign to form a coalition with one group of citizens against another, allowing the sovereign to transgress boundaries considered fundamental by other citizens.

This approach models the problem of policing a state or sovereign as a coordination problem. In this context, a constitution serves as a coordinating device, helping citizens to coordinate their strategy choices so that they can react in concert and police state behavior.[16] An appropriately chosen set of public rules embodied in a constitution can serve as a coordination device because it provides each citizen with a similar way of judging and reacting to state action. Of course, the availability of such a mechanism in principle does not tell us under what circumstances it may be used in practice. This approach demonstrates that a central step in the creation of limited government is that citizens or their representatives construct a mechanism that solves the coordination problem.

2.1.2 Application of the Model to the Glorious Revolution.   This model has con-siderable implications for the constitutional changes following the Glorious Revolution in England and the rise of a national consensus about the appro-priate boundaries of the state. Two aspects of market-preserving federalism allowed the industrial revolution to take place outside the traditional commer-cial areas: decentralized regulatory authority, which allowed local variation in economic controls; and the absence of national regulatory authority to extend economic controls to cover those areas that did not have them. A range of elements contributed to this result. The most important from our standpoint was the strengthening of the rule of law at the end of the 17th century, whereby a consensus emerged opposing national economic intervention.[17]

The 17th century saw considerable political turmoil. Within a decade of the accession of the Stuarts in 1603, problems emerged between the sovereign and many of his citizens. The century included a civil war and the beheading of the king (1640s), a restoration of the monarchy (1660), and the Glorious Revolution (1688–89), which deposed the last of the Stuart kings, James II, in favor of William and Mary.

Throughout the century, the citizenry was deeply divided over the role of the sovereign, the appropriate limits on state behavior, and the benefits of var-

---

16. This point is made generally by Hardin (1989).

17. Other aspects include: first, among all states in early modern Europe, England had the strongest tradition of private property rights; second, after the Glorious Revolution, Parliament counterbalanced the Crown, by and large opposing national economic intervention.

16 The Journal of Law, Economics, & Organization, V11 N1

ious public policies. By century's end, two political coalitions had emerged, called Tories and Whigs. Whigs were more focused on commercial activities, favored secure property rights, advocated low and stable taxes on economic activity, and took an activist profile in international relations to promote and defend their economic claims around the world. They also sought explicit limits on the sovereign's behavior. Tories, on the other hand, cared much less about commercial activity, wanted a limited international presence, and preferred low and stable taxes on land, their primary source of wealth. They also strongly supported the Church of England and opposed explicit limits on the Crown.[18]

During the reign of the late Stuarts (from the Restoration to the Glorious Revolution) and especially by the mid-1670s, the Tories supported the Crown while the Whigs opposed it. Moreover, the late Stuarts transgressed significant rights of the Whigs while retaining the support of the Tories. The most important sovereign transgression concerned the campaign to "pack the constituencies." In the early 1680s, the Crown began to disenfranchise the major sources of Whig opposition. The strategy proved a huge success.[19]

Although the events that occurred next are straightforward in outline, the explanation for them has been debated for more than 300 years. First, the initiator of the campaign to disenfranchise the Whigs, Charles II, died and was succeeded by his brother, James II. Second, for a variety of reasons, there was considerable suspicion between James and his supporters. Not long after taking power, James became embroiled in a dispute with the Tories and reacted by attempting to disenfranchise them. Although this attempt nearly succeeded, it ended in dismal failure. The result was a political nation united against James II, forcing him to flee.

The Glorious Revolution was more than a simple coup, however, for it also resulted in significant constitutional changes. James's behavior convinced the Tories that explicit limits on the sovereign and the state were required. Although the two coalitions disagreed about the content and role of these limits, they agreed not only that limits were necessary, but so too was a consensus about those limits (Schwoerer, 1981). The result was the Revolution Settlement passed by Parliament in early 1689. From our standpoint, the key is the Bill of Rights, a set of two lists. The first identified those actions of the previous sovereign that constituted fundamental violations of citizens' rights. The second listed activities that the sovereign could no longer undertake. Although sovereign power would wax and wane over the next century, the limits established in the Revolution Settlement were, by and large, adhered to.

---

18. "It is an oversimplification to see the Whigs as the party of business and the Tories of seigneurial power.... But one can safely contrast emphasis on commerce as a point in the Whig profile, and emphasis on agriculture as a point in the Tory one. So, too, the Whigs tended to internationalism ... while the Tory was inward-looking and protectionist" (Carswell, 1973: 40–41).

19. Jones (1972: 47) reports that of the 104 formerly Whig strongholds rechartered between 1681 and 1685, only one returned a Whig to the next parliament in 1685.

2.1.3 Sustaining Market-preserving Federalism in England.   These events are readily interpreted in terms of the model above. Before the Revolution, citizens fundamentally disagreed about what actions they considered violations of their rights. Marked divisions in 17th-century England prevented the formation of a shared system of beliefs about critical matters such as the role of the state, the limit of sovereign power, citizen duty, and the appropriate definition of economic and political rights. The diversity of beliefs allowed the Crown to transgress rights held as fundamental by the Whigs as long as the Tories were willing to acquiesce. This described the situation from at least the mid-1670s through the mid-1680s. This pattern of transgression was seemingly stable, reflecting the nature of the asymmetric equilibrium of the game.

James's move against his own constituents broke this pattern, losing him the support required to retain power. Not only was he removed from power, but his actions caused a wholesale and speedy revision in opinions and beliefs about fundamental issues. This change led to the construction of a new consensus that provided a clearer definition of the legitimate actions of the state and of citizen duty.

These changes reflect an attempt to construct a coordinating device. Constitutional innovations, such as the Revolution Settlement and its Declaration of Rights, were designed, in part, to define what actions constituted a fundamental transgression. The new consensus was critical to preventing further transgressions. According to Jones (1972: 318):

> The thirteen points in the Declaration were not just statements of the true nature of the law of the constitution, they were also intended to provide a guideline for the future conduct of government, so that any departure from legality would be instantly signalled, and remedial action could be taken.

This is precisely the mechanism modeled above. Because the new boundaries were both explicit and consensual, they fundamentally changed the interaction between the citizenry and the new sovereign. For many of the central political issues of the era, a single set of limits on sovereign behavior had been negotiated by leaders of the opposing parties. This process resulted in a set of shared beliefs about what constituted a fundamental transgression by the state and about what citizens should do in the face of these transgressions. These shared beliefs implied that citizens would react in concert against any future sovereign transgression, thus ensuring that their political and economic rights were more secure.[20]

But how did this new coordinating mechanism translate into protection for federalism in England? Given the distinct hierarchy in English government, the main question as to whether post–Glorious Revolution England had market-preserving federalism concerns the limits on national regulatory authority.

---

20. Reflecting the achievement of coordination, the American Justice Bradley, writing in the late 19th century, observed that a constitutional violation "would produce a revolution in an hour" (J. Bradley's dissent in the *Slaughter House Cases*, 1873).

18   The Journal of Law, Economics, & Organization, V11 N1

After the Glorious Revolution, citizens more closely guarded local power, authority, and autonomy. Because violating local political liberty had been the principal factor in the campaign to pack the constituencies—and hence in the Revolution—citizens throughout England were wary of national interference with their authority. As Miller (1992: 53) suggests:

> The right, in most towns, to practice a particular trade or take part in municipal government was confined to a comparatively restricted group of craftsmen and traders possessing the "freedom" of their town or craft guild which gave them rights denied to other citizens. Municipal and other corporations (including colleges and universities) had been granted (usually by the Crown) the right to a measure of control over their own affairs: here "freedom" meant immunity from outside intervention.

Local political freedom thus emerged as part of the constitutional consensus at the end of the 17th century.[21]

By way of summary, national interference with local power during the campaign to pack the constituencies produced a consensus that protection of local power against national interference was essential to the maintenance of individual liberty and security. The consensus was embodied in the Revolution Settlement, an important addition to the English constitution. This explicit agreement served as a coordinating device necessary to establish the equilibrium in which citizens react in concert to violations of the limits on governmental action.

Though the Glorious Revolution was largely backward looking, in the sense that its limits were intended to prevent transgressions by the sovereign, it had important—if unintended—forward effects on the economy. By strengthening local power and limiting the ability of the national government to intervene in the economy, the new English constitutional system provided for market-preserving federalism. This in turn proved a critical political component of industrial revolution, for it allowed local governments to ignore, avoid, or repeal the regulatory restrictions on the local economy that economic historians have emphasized were crucial to the success of the new entrepreneurs and enterprises.

2.2 The Durability of Federalism in the United States

The United States had market-preserving federalism from the inception of the Constitution through the mid-1930s.[22] During this period, what made market-preserving federalism durable—that is, what prevented the federal government

---

21. An additional element limited national authority to regulate: the elevation of the common law courts as the protector and promoter of private property rights. This effectively removed many decisions about property rights from national politics. One of the central consequences of the Glorious Revolution was also to establish an "independent" judiciary much less subject to political manipulation.

22. What follows draws on Weingast (1993a, 1994a).

from overawing the states? The immediate answer—that the Constitution prevented it—begs the question, for it ignores the issues of constitutional interpretation and constitutional adherence.

At the most fundamental level, the answer to the question is that not only did the Constitution proscribe intervention, but the vast majority of Americans favored this outcome. A national consensus supported the limited role of the federal government. Because this view was so widely held, all the major parties before the 1930s championed it (first, the Federalists and Jeffersonians, then the Democrats and Whigs, and finally the Democrats and Republicans).[23] National parties not only promoted the view of a limited federal role, but created and maintained a series of institutional mechanisms designed to provide a credible commitment to limited federal government.

To see how the consensus translated into the mechanisms of Constitutional durability, consider the problem during the second party system, roughly 1828 through the early 1850s. During this time, the nation was divided into free and slave states. This division had a critical influence on American history, notably, on the interpretation of the Constitution, the three major antebellum political crises, and the Civil War and Reconstruction.[24]

Most citizens were deeply suspicious of the national government because of its potential to impose policies favored by other regions or interests. Early in the 19th century, before the rise of an integrated, interregional economy, the solution was simply for both North and South to agree to limit the federal government's authority, thus limiting the ability of either region to impose its will on the other. Although the partisan debate involved the role of the federal government in the economy, the range of involvement was relatively circumscribed, limited to such issues as tariffs and internal improvements.

The "balance rule," or the equal representation of the North and the South in the Senate, served as the principal institution providing durability to the agreement between the regions. The balance rule afforded each region a veto over national policymaking. As I argue at length elsewhere, this institution had a profound effect on national politics (Weingast, 1994a; see also Roback, 1994). The main implication for present purposes is that the set of concurrent vetoes prevented national policies that were considered especially inimical by either region. The balance rule's double veto thus provided the political foundations for the preservation of a slave economy in the South, a free one in the North, and a limited national government.

As the economy became interregional, however, many policy questions were no longer so easily disaggregated. For example, should growth of interregional

---

23. The one possible exception to this unanimity was the Republican party on the issue of slavery and the rights of the freedmen. These policies emerged only within the context of the Civil War. A version of the view that follows applies to the bulk of the policies they devised and implemented during their period of political hegemony (1860–1932).

24. Other political divisions were also important, but in what follows we concentrate on the former. For a discussion of the interaction of slavery and other issues during the period of the second party system, see Weingast (1994a).

20 The Journal of Law, Economics, & Organization, V11 N1

trade be subsidized by federal support for roads, canals, and, later, railroads? Should national and agrarian expansion be encouraged via low prices for federal land on the frontier? At about the same time, the Missouri crisis (1818–20) convinced Southerners that the national government's authority might be used against their "property" and their "institutions"—that is, against slavery (Carpenter, 1930).

In the late 1820s and early 1830s, the Jacksonian Democrats tried to form a political coalition to retain national political power. In responding to the political questions noted above, they articulated a set of policy goals consistent with limited federal government and a constitutional jurisprudence of states' rights to underpin these limits. The Jacksonian appeal was built on a set of principles that provided considerable security for slaveholders, helping this party secure majority support in the South and in the nation. This approach held considerable appeal to Southerners seeking to forestall any precedent for expanding the scope of national authority. But it also appealed to many Northerners, particularly throughout the old Northwest and among laborers and farmers in the East.

The Democrats' approach allowed them to dominate national elections and hence to control national policy.[25] Their successes depended on more than mere campaign promises and reputation. Indeed, the Jacksonians added a series of political institutions to provide their officials with incentives to implement and adhere to their policies. Three instances of institutions and practices are worth noting. First, the Democrats articulated a constitutional jurisprudence of states' rights, avoiding any precedents for increased national authority. As their Supreme Court appointments reflected these views, they led to compatible constitutional decisions. Second, as part of their appeal to Southerners, they adopted the two-thirds rule for nominating candidates to the presidency (Potter, 1976; Weingast, 1994a). This granted Southerners a veto over their party's presidential candidate, assuring them considerable influence not only over their party's candidate but—as the Democrats held the presidency in three-fourths of the Congresses between 1828 and 1860—over the presidents as well. Third, they were willing to maintain the balance rule at the national level, assuring the South a veto over national policy via its equal representation in the Senate. Expansion and imperialism were rationalized by "manifest destiny." Given the centrality of slavery to the South, significant slippage between promise and implementation would clearly ruin the party's ability to compete in that region and thus, as all knew, its ability to maintain its majority position.

This argument shows how the Constitution and allied institutions provided the principal mechanisms of political decentralization inherent in federalism during the second party system. Because the majority party in the nation favored that position, it was able to maintain strong limits on national government both

---

25. During the 16 Congresses between the elections of Jackson and Lincoln, the Democrats held all three national institutions in 9 of 16 Congresses, whereas the Whigs held all three only once. The Jacksonians also dominated Supreme Court appointments. From 1828 to 1860, 11 justices were appointed under united Democratic control, 2 under divided control, and none under Whig or Republican control (see Weingast, 1994a).

as official policy and as constitutional law. The majority party in the nation proved instrumental in translating a broad, national consensus for limited federal government into a series of institutions making those limits credible.

The argument in this section exhibits strong parallels with the approach developed in Section 2.1. Underlying the limited role of the federal government was a national consensus that this was appropriate. Although no sovereign was relevant for the United States, a parallel problem existed between the two groups of citizens: each worried that the other might come to dominate the national government, allowing it to use national power for its own regional purposes. Because the problem was symmetric, both sides agreed to limits on national authority as a means of limiting the ability of the other to dominate. This agreement, in turn, required a combination of institutions and attitudes to succeed. The institutions ranged from federalism and the commerce clause discussed above, to the various attempts to provide regional balance in the Senate. These institutions, in turn, fundamentally rested on the attitudes and preferences of citizens, requiring that the vast majority in the nation believe these agreements were appropriate. Problems emerged only at the end of the second party system when a new party, the Republicans, proved no longer willing to maintain these institutions, notably, the balance rule (Weingast, 1994a).

3. Implications for Economic Reform
3.1 Federalism Chinese-style: Economic Growth in Modern China

The contrast between the success of economic reform in southern China and the troubled path of reform in the former Soviet Union and its satellites not only is striking but appears to reflect the lessons of this article.[26] Beginning in the late 1970s, China embarked on economic reform. As one of Asia's fastest-growing economies in the past 15 years, it has had remarkable success, especially in the south.

A range of factors has contributed to China's economic success relative to the former Soviet Union. These factors include, for example, the proximity of South China to foreign capital, notably family wealth of those who had previously fled the communists to Hong Kong or Taiwan; the relatively limited initial scope of economic reform, perhaps including its focus on agriculture while ignoring the large-scale public enterprises; in contrast to the former Soviet Union, China's relatively shorter experience with communism, its leaders' more pragmatic and less ideological pursuit of socialist economic principles, and a far less interdependent economy. Moreover, in contrast to the republics and satellites of the former Soviet Union, which inherited a nge of economic and fiscal problems from their former regimes, China initiated the reforms from a position of relatively strong fiscal health.

All of these factors contributed to China's success. And yet these and related factors provide an inadequate understanding of that success. A central though

---

26. These ideas are pursued at greater length in Montinola, Qian, and Weingast (1995) and Qian and Weingast (1995).

Economics of Federalism I

22   The Journal of Law, Economics, & Organization, V11 N1

underemphasized factor of China's economic reform is that it was initiated with political reform. As applied to China, the term *political reform* usually refers to democratization. Democratization is clearly a central task of political reform, one of sufficient value that it receives special attention. Yet it reflects only one aspect of politics and political reform. In what follows, I use the term in its broader sense (see Montinola, Qian, and Weingast, 1995).

As part of the effort to pursue economic reform, the Chinese central authorities instituted a form of political decentralization that limited their own power. This decentralization produced a form of market-preserving federalism. This federalism, Chinese-style, differs considerably from Western-style federalism—for example, in having no connection to individual rights and political freedoms. Nonetheless, China's political system approximates the five necessary characteristics of market-preserving federalism identified above.[27]

Critical to China's economic success, the new decentralization affords local governments considerable discretion over economic policy. In many areas, officials have used this authority to create markets and entrepreneurial enterprises, and it is these areas that are experiencing the most significant growth. The economic effects of the decentralization have been felt in the growing entrepreneurialism found at the local level and the growing participation of these enterprises in international markets (Byrd and Lin, 1990; Montinola, Qian, and Weingast, 1995; Nee, 1992; Oi, 1992; Qian and Xu, 1993; Walder, 1992).

Underpinning this success was the central government's seeming toleration of the loss of political control over local economic policy-making. This has had two effects. First, it has lowered the influence and importance of the relevant ministries of the central government and hence of central planning. Second, the incentives of local political officials changed dramatically. With the growing success of economic reform, local revenues came to depend on the economic health of the local economy, not on political allegiance to the central government or conformity to a central plan. Parallelling the incentives facing the English justices of the peace during the industrial revolution, decentralization in China provided many local political officials with the incentives to create an economic and political environment that fosters economic growth. In both 18th-century England and modern China, prospering economic enterprises provide an expanding local resource base, aligning the interests of local officials with local economic success.

The loss of central government influence and control over local officials provides the answer to why the critical second condition of market-preserving federalism holds. The process by which the decentralization was initiated sheds considerable light on how durable limits on government are established. Decentralization was established by decree, and, initially, it had no special durability. Nonetheless, the degree of support among the central authorities,

---

27. One notable exception is the presence of internal trade barriers. The economic costs of these provisions are unknown. Most of China's growth has occurred in the areas with the fewest barriers to the rise of an export economy.

notably Deng Xiaoping, led to a range of experiments, emphasizing aspects that could be changed in the short run and that did not leave long-term investments vulnerable. As these proved successful and the central government did not revoke them, they were expanded and imitated. As the process continued, local incentives gradually changed from those promoting allegiance and control by the central authorities to those reflecting local economic prosperity. Thus the durability of the reforms did not arise all at once but grew as the degree of economic success increased.

The central government's loss of control over local officials directly limits its ability to intervene adversely in these new markets. Short of using the army— still under national control and therefore potentially a factor in the future—the central government no longer appears able to reverse its political, and hence economic, reform efforts.

The Chinese government's failed effort to halt or reverse economic reform after Tiananmen Square suggests the durability of the political reforms. At that time, the conservatives gained the most political, ideological, and military power. If ever they had sufficient power for a reversal of reform, that was it. Moreover, economic woes of inflation and corruption in 1988 and the following political backlash after the Tiananmen Square incident in 1989 also put economic reform on hold. An austerity program was implemented between 1989 and 1991 to cool down the so-called "overheated" economy. In 1990, there were even discussions among conservatives about the possibility of recollectivization of agriculture.

Several events combined to undo the central government's attempted reversal. First, many areas of the economy began to decline, raising fears of unemployment and vast new fiscal commitments for the central government without a concomitant expansion of fiscal resources. Second, as part of the government's campaign, it attempted to promote the large, state-owned enterprises. This effort not only failed to produce results but had significant, negative fiscal consequences. Third, the economic retrenchment was resisted by local officials from the areas experiencing the highest economic growth, officials who had no interest in seeing the retrenchment succeed. Li Peng, the conservative premier, failed in his attempt to recentralize investment and financial powers from the provinces. The governor of Guangdong refused, and many other governors followed suit (Shirk, 1993).

This incident emphasizes the striking new power of local governments, power not held during most of the communist era.[28] The abandonment of retrenchment revealed that the government was unwilling to pay the price of reversing the reforms. This, in turn, reduced the political uncertainty about the durability of the reforms.[29] The new decentralization limited the discretion of the central

---

28. In contrast, on several previous occasions when the economy faced difficulties (for example, in 1962, and as recently as 1981), Chen Yun, an advocate of central planning, successfully compelled the provincial governments to "help the central government overcome the difficulties"—that is, to turn over more revenue to the central budget.

29. Growth rates since the abandonment have, if anything, been higher than before the retrench-

24   The Journal of Law, Economics, & Organization, V11 N1

government, adding an important degree of durability to the reforms. Barring extreme events, the reforms have become a central component of modern China.

A number of important qualifications to China's economic success must be raised. First, China's strategy for economic reform has put off dealing with the extensive and growing problem of the state enterprises, including their large subsidies (see Wong, 1991). Second, the decentralization of power has not been uniform, explaining in part why reform has varied across regions. Third, critical national public goods remain underprovided. The common market is inadequately secured, and considerable internal trade barriers remain across regions, including barriers to labor migration. In some areas, local officials have taken advantage of political decentralization to protect local enterprises, raising complaints about rising "dukedom economies." Considerable problems also arise from the lack of centralized control over the monetary system, resulting in softness of budget constraints and in inflation. Fourth, a large number of tasks of economic reform emphasized by economists have yet to be tackled (e.g., a law of commerce or credit). The mechanisms for enforcing long-term agreements with sources of foreign capital remain underdeveloped. Finally, given the aging octogenarians underpinning the central government's reform effort, uncertainty over political succession implies a degree of political risk. Considerable uncertainty remains about the possibility of an antireform backlash, and hence about the course of Chinese reform.

4. Conclusions

The main lesson of this analysis for contemporary development and economic reform is a variant on the now commonplace observation that the benevolent attitude of the government cannot be taken for granted:[30] Markets require protection and thus a government strong enough to resist responding to the inevitable political forces advocating encroachments on markets for private gain. The fundamental political dilemma of an economic system is that a state strong enough to protect private markets is strong enough to confiscate the wealth of its citizens. The dilemma implies that understanding economic growth requires attention to the question of what guides the state down the former path. As North (1993: 11–12) argues:

> Throughout most of history and in much of the present world, institutions have not provided the credible commitment necessary for the develop-

---

ment. The *Economist*, for example, reports that they have been over 20 percent per year in some areas. This is consistent with the view that removing a degree of political risk increased expected economic returns, thus enhancing the willingness of entrepreneurs and investors to undertake actions promoting growth. Similarly, since early 1992, Hong Kong has felt a new optimism. The increasing ties of Hong Kong's economy to that of South China are one factor contributing to the durability of Hong Kong's economy. Unfortunately, as recent events remind us, it is not the only factor.

30. On the limits of assuming a benevolent government in the developing context, see, among others, Campos and Root (1994), Ekelund and Tollison (1981), Krueger (1992), Levy and Spiller (1994), North (1981, 1990), North and Weingast (1989), Przeworski (1990), Root (in press), Weingast (1994a, 1994b), and Williamson (1994).

ment of low cost transacting in capital and other markets. There is, therefore, little evidence to support the view (apparently implicitly held by many economists doctoring the ailing economies of central and eastern Europe) that the necessary institutions will be the automatic outcome of getting the prices right through elimination of price and exchange controls.

Put simply, the political foundations of markets are as essential to their success as the details and specification of the market itself. This conclusion implies that markets and limited government are complementary aspects of economic development and reform; each enhances the value of the other. Political development must therefore take place simultaneously with economic development.

Limited government, in turn, requires that restrictions on the government be self-enforcing. Although this claim is made regularly in the literature, few analyses have shown how constitutions actually accomplish this difficult task in practice. The possibility of beneficial limits on government is not realized automatically. This observation forces us to ask what makes those limits credible—that is, what makes them binding on political actors? To address this question, I have examined here how England and the United States grappled with these problems in the past and how China is grappling with them in the present. Although a range of considerations is important, I have focused on the institution of market-preserving federalism, a central factor in the economic development of all three.

Several facets of federalism account for its success in England and the United States. First, federalism provided the political basis for the common market. Second, the prohibitions against the national government's exercise of economic regulation greatly reduced the government's political responsiveness to interest groups. In a growing economy, this limited the ability of economic interests, potentially displaced by economic change, to use political means to constrain or prevent their competitors' success. Third, the prohibitions on internal trade barriers allowed entrepreneurs, new enterprises, and new economic activities to emerge in new areas that could outcompete interests in older areas. In England, these factors provided the political foundation for the success of the industrial revolution. In the United States, they fostered first regional and then international specialization, underpinning American economic growth.[31] By creating credible restrictions on governmental policy choice, federalism provided the basis for the rule of law and hence the political underpinnings of economic freedom.

Yet what made these restrictions credible? What made them binding in practice? Though the details differ considerably, both cases reveal that federalism's success in practice relied on a mix of formal and informal constraints. As North

---

31. As Casella and Frey (1992: 640) argue: "If private economic decisions are influenced by public goods, . . . as we expect them to be, then markets and institutions should develop together."

26   The Journal of Law, Economics, & Organization, V11 N1

(1993) emphasizes, it is not only the institutions of society that help provide for secure rights, but a mix of institutions and complementary informal norms that constrain the behavior of the players at numerous margins. It is this mix of formal institutions and informal norms that I now wish to stress, for the first two points received considerable emphasis above.

The critical feature for England and the United States is that the success of constitutional constraints promoting the rule of law depended on the emergence of a social consensus about the appropriate limits of the state. Holding the state to prescribed limits does not depend on a constraint being explicit, nor does it require that it might have been agreed on at some time in the past. Limited government instead depends on how citizens react to a potential violation of that constraint. The ultimate sanction on a government is the withdrawal of support by a sufficient portion of its citizens so that the government cannot survive.

The failure of this form of citizen reaction allows a host of constitutional violations in Latin America and other parts of the third world (see, e.g., Montinola's 1994 discussion of Marcos's rejection of the Philippine Constitution). Notice, in contrast, the reaction to President Franklin Roosevelt's famous court-packing scheme. Although it was proposed at a time of unprecedented political support for Roosevelt and the New Deal, and although it was designed to benefit his constituents, it was deemed illegitimate by a sufficient number of his supporters that its future was highly questionable.[32]

For both England and the United States, the decentralization of political authority implied by market-preserving federalism was the product of a historical process resulting in a strong consensus supporting these limits. The English state's failure to respect citizen rights in the late 17th century led not only to the Glorious Revolution but to a new consensus about the appropriate limits on the national government's authority. Constructed through negotiations in Parliament among the leaders of the various factions in society, the consensus over limits was embodied in a new set of constitutional arrangements, including increased reliance on the common-law courts rather than royal discretion, increased security of property rights, and concern for the maintenance of local political authority, especially in matters of economic control and regulation. These arrangements at once created the political decentralization necessary to support market-preserving federalism and the national consensus to provide it with durability.

During the first 150 years of the United States, the foundations of market-preserving federalism rested on the fact that the vast majority of the population consistently favored policies and parties limiting the federal government and protecting economic rights. The two breakdowns of this consensus underscore its role and importance. The first concerned the role of the federal government with respect to slavery and resulted in a civil war. The second—and

---

32. Roosevelt did not pursue this scheme for several reasons, most notably that the Supreme Court itself reversed direction in early 1937. For a recent review, see Gely and Spiller (1992).

permanent—breakdown occurred during the Great Depression. At that time, a new political majority emerged. The new majority not only resulted in expansion of the national government beyond the traditional limits of the Constitution, but engineered a reinterpretation of the principal constitutional constraints underpinning market-preserving federalism. Within five years, the latter were removed.

The discussion of economic reform in China also emphasizes the importance of the economic role of political institutions. Because the problems faced by China and Russia are very different, strong conclusions cannot be drawn from a brief comparison between them. Nonetheless, it is striking to note not only the enormous difference in the approaches to reform, but their relative degrees of success. The former Soviet Union, and later Russia, concentrated on reform of its economic system, retaining strong discretionary powers for the government. No attempt was made to establish limited government or to tie the government's hands with respect to future economic policy (Boettke, 1993; Litwack, 1991; Williamson, 1994). Although there has been some attempt to institute political rights and democracy, these limits on the government do not yet extend to economic rights or the basic structure of the economic system. As Ordeshook and Schwartz (1994) emphasize, all rights in Russia—personal, property, and democratic—remain highly insecure because of the liberal clauses in the Russian Constitution that allow the government to suspend these rights when they prove inconvenient.

In contrast, China began with a political reform in which the central authorities, although not completely binding their own hands, made it much harder to use those hands. The central government limited itself by transferring power to local authorities in a way that would be difficult—and that recently proved difficult—to retake. This transfer, in turn, set the stage for a series of economic transformations across much of China. For local governments, political freedom and political protection from the central state combined with economic opportunities to provide strong incentives to foster and protect markets. The results are remarkable. Moreover, the economic effects of local political freedom in China exhibits some striking parallels with those in 18th-century England. In both cases, local political officials had strong incentives to foster local prosperity, underpinning the rise of new and very successful firms.

For the emerging democracies of Eastern Europe and the former Soviet Union, this analysis suggests that economic and political institutions should be redesigned simultaneously. In particular, these institutions need to be consistent with one another. What economic incentives are implied by the degree of discretion afforded the government under the political institutions? Are they compatible with secure property rights and the development of the rule of law?

The three cases of federalism studied here do not constitute a test of the theory, for they were not randomly selected. Putting the theory at risk requires a more systematic investigation of market-preserving federalism, attempting to test whether states characterized by its provisions reveal appreciably more economic development than those not so characterized. Although such a test is beyond the scope of this study, we do mention that other instances of de jure

28   The Journal of Law, Economics, & Organization, V11 N1

federalism, but not market-preserving federalism, appear to have fared much more poorly than the cases studied here. Argentina, Brazil, and India are all de jure federal systems but not market-preserving federal systems. In all of these countries, the political authority of the national government compromises the independence of local political authority. On the critical dimension of economic performance, none of these states has experienced economic development that parallels the cases studied here.

In sum, I have argued that securing the political foundations of markets must be accomplished at the same time and is equal in importance to the development of markets and "getting prices right." The historical evidence presented above supports this position (see also North, 1981, 1993). The discussion of reform in China further suggests that limited government appears to be an important component of economic reform. It emphasizes the critical *economic* role for *political* institutions—to provide the appropriate foundations for economic policy-making and a secure system of economic and political rights.

References

Aranson, Peter. 1991. "Federalism: Doctrine Against Balance," manuscript, Emory University.

Ashton, T. S. 1955. *An Economic History of England: The 18th Century*. London: Methuen.

Boettke, Peter J. 1993. *Why Perestroika Failed: The Politics and Economics of Socialist Transformation*. London: Routledge.

Bogue, Allan. 1963. *From Prairie to Corn Belt: Farming on the Illinois and Iowa Prairies in the Nineteenth Century*. Chicago: University of Chicago Press.

Brennan, Geoffrey, and James M. Buchanan. 1984. *Reason of the Rules*. New York: Cambridge University Press.

Brewer, John. 1989. *The Sinews of Power*. New York: Alfred A. Knopf.

Byrd, W., and Q. Lin, eds. 1990. *China's Rural Industry: Structure, Development and Reform*. New York: Oxford University Press.

Campos, Edgardo, and Hilton Root. 1994. "Beyond the Asian Miracles," manuscript, Hoover, Institution, Stanford University.

Carpenter, Jesse T. 1990 [1930]. *The South as a Conscious Minority, 1789–1861*. Columbia: University of South Carolina Press.

Carswell, John. 1973. *From Revolution to Revolution: England 1688–1776*. New York: Scribner's.

Casella, Alessandra, and Bruno Frey. 1992. "Federalism and Clubs: Towards an Economic Theory of Overlapping Political Jurisdictions," in *European Economic Review*, Papers and Proceedings.

Chandler, Alfred D. 1977. *The Visible Hand*. Cambridge: Harvard University Press.

Eggertsson, Thrainn. 1990. *Economic Behavior and Institutions*. New York: Cambridge University Press.

Ekelund, Robert, and Robert Tollison. 1981. *Mercantilism as a Rent-Seeking Society*. College Station: Texas A&M Press.

Elazar, Daniel J. 1987. *Exploring Federalism*. Tuscaloosa: University of Alabama Press.

Elster, Jon. 1991. "Constitutionalism in Eastern Europe: An Introduction," 58 *University of Chicago Law Review* 447–82.

Ferejohn, John. 1990. "Rationality and Interpretation: Parliamentary Elections in Early Stuart England," manuscript, Hoover Institution, Stanford University.

Fogel, Robert W. 1989. *Without Consent or Contract: The Rise and Fall of American Slavery*. New York: Norton.

Friedrich, Carl J. 1968. *Trends of Federalism in Theory and Practice*. New York: Praeger.

Fudenberg, Drew, and Eric Maskin. 1986. "Folk Theorems in Repeated Games with Discounting and Incomplete Information," 54 *Econometrica* 553–54.

Gely, Raphael, and Pablo T. Spiller. 1992. "The Political Economy of Supreme Court Constitutional Decisions: The Case of Roosevelt's Court Packing Plan," 12 *International Review of Law and Economics* 45–67.

Hammond, Tom and Gary Miller. 1989. "Stability and Efficiency in a Separation-of-Powers Constitutional System," in B. Grofman and D. Wittman, eds., *The Federalist Papers and the New Institutionalism*. New York: Agathon Press.

Handlin, Oscar, and Mary Handlin. 1947. *Commonwealth: A study of the Role of Government in the American Economy, Massachusetts, 1774–1861*. New York: New York University Press.

Hardin, Russell. 1989. "Why a Constitution?" in B. Grofman and D. Wittman, eds., *The Federalist Papers and the New Institutionalism*. New York: Agathon Press.

Hartwell, R. M. 1971. *The Industrial Revolution and Economic Growth*. London: Methuen.

Hartz, Louis. 1948. *Economic Policy and Democratic Thought: Pennsylvania, 1776-1860*. Cambridge, Mass.: Harvard University Press.

Hayek, Friedrich. 1939. "The Economic Conditions of Interstate Federalism," reprinted in F. Hayek, *Individualism and the Economic Order* (chap. 12). Chicago: University of Chicago Press, 1948.

———. 1960. *Constitution of Liberty*. Chicago: University of Chicago Press.

Holmes, Stephen. 1988. "Precommitment and the Paradox of Democracy," in J. Elster and R. Slagstad, eds., *Constitutionalism and Democracy*. New York: Cambridge University Press.

Hughes, Jonathan. 1977. *The Governmental Habit*. New York: Basic.

Inman, Robert P. 1987. "Markets, Government, and the 'New' Political Economy," in A. J. Auerbach and M. Feldstein, eds., *Handbook of Public Finance*, vol. 2. Amsterdam: North-Holland.

Jones, J. R. 1972. *The Revolution of 1688 in England*. New York: W. W. Norton.

Krueger, Anne. 1992. *Economic Policy Reform in Developing Countries*. Oxford: Blackwell.

Landes, David S. 1969. *The Unbound Prometheus: Technological Change and Industrial Development in Western Europe from 1750 to the Present*. Cambridge: Cambridge University Press.

Lee, Susan Previant, and Peter Passell. 1979. *A New Economic View of American History*. New York: W. W. Norton.

Levy, Brian, and Pablo T. Spiller. 1994. "The Institutional Foundations of Regulatory Commitment: A Comparative Analysis of Telecommunications Regulation," The World Bank.

Litwack, John M. 1991. "Legality and Market Reform in Soviet-type Economies," 5 *Journal of Economic Perspectives* 77–89.

McKinnon, Ronald I. 1994. "Market-Preserving Fiscal Federalism," unpublished manuscript, Department of Economics, Stanford University.

Milgrom, Paul, and John Roberts. 1992. *Economics, Organization, and Management*. Englewood Cliffs, N.J.: Prentice Hall.

Miller, George. 1971. *Railroads and the Granger Laws*. Madison: University of Wisconsin Press.

Miller, John. 1992. "Crown, Parliament, and People," in J. R. Jones, ed., *Liberty Secured?* Stanford: Stanford University Press.

Moe, Terry. 1990. "The Politics of Structural Choice: Toward a Theory of Public Bureaucracy." in O. E. Williamson, ed., *Organization Theory: From Chester Barnard to the Present and Beyond*. New York: Oxford University Press.

Mokyr, Joel. 1988. "The Industrial Revolution and the New Economic History." in J. Mokyr, ed., *The Economics of the Industrial Revolution*. Totowa, N.J.: Rowman and Allanheld.

Montinola, Gabriella. 1994. "Institutional Foundations of Crony Capitalism: The Rise and Fall of the Marcos Regime in the Philippines," manuscript, Department of Political Science, Stanford University.

———, Yingyi Qian, and Barry R. Weingast. 1995. "Federalism, Chinese Style: The Political Basis for Economic Success in China," 48 *World Politics* (forthcoming).

Nee, Victor. 1992. "Explaining the Transitions from State Socialism," unpublished manuscript, Cornell University.

North, Douglass C. 1961. *The Economic Growth of the United States: 1790–1860*. New York: W. W. Norton.

———. 1981. *Structure and Change in Economic History*. New York: W. W. Norton.

———. 1990. *Institutions, Institutional Change, and Economic Performance*. New York:

30   The Journal of Law, Economics, & Organization, V11 N1

Cambridge University Press.

_____. 1993. "Institutions and Credible Commitment," 149 *Journal of Institutional and Theoretical Economics* 11–23.

_____, and Barry R. Weingast. 1989. "Constitutions and Credible Commitments: The Evolution of the Institutions of Public Choice in 17th Century England," *Journal of Economic History* 000–000.

Oates, Wallace. 1972. *Fiscal Federalism*. New York: Harcourt Brace Jovanovich.

Oi, Jean C. 1992. "Fiscal Reform and the Economic Foundations of Local State Corporatism in China." 45 *World Politics* 99–126.

Olson, Mancur. 1982. *The Rise and Decline of Nations*. New Haven, Conn.: Yale University Press.

Ordeshook, Peter. 1993. "Constitutional Stability," 3 *Constitutional Political Economy* 137–75.

_____, and Thomas Schwartz. 1994. "Institutions and Incentives: The Prospects for Russian Democracy," unpublished manuscript, California Institute of Technology.

Passell, Peter, and Maria Schmundt. 1971. "Pre-Civil War Land Policy and the Growth of Manufacturing," 9 *Explorations in Economic History* 000–000.

Potter, David M. 1976. *The Impending Crisis: 1848–1861* (edited and completed by Don E. Fehrenbacher). New York: Harper and Row.

Przeworski, Adam. 1990. *Democracy and the Market*. New York: Cambridge University Press.

Qian, Y., and C. Xu. 1993. "Why China's Economic Reforms Differ: The M-Form Hierarchy and Entry/Expansion of the Non-State Sector," 1 *The Economics of Transition* 135–170.

Qian, Yingyi, and Barry R. Weingast. 1995. "Institutions, State Activism, and the Role of Government in Economic Development," in Masahiko Aoki and Hyung-Ki Kim, eds., *The Role of Government in East Asian Economies: Rent Creation, Coordination, and Institutional Development*. New York: Oxford University Press (forthcoming).

Riker, William H. 1964. *Federalism: Origin, Operation, and Significance*. Boston: Little Brown.

_____. 1982. *Liberalism Against Populism*. San Francisco: W. H. Freeman.

Roback, Jennifer. 1994. "An Imaginary Negro in an Impossible Place," unpublished manuscript, George Mason University.

Roeder, Philip G. 1993. *Red Sunset: The Failure of Soviet Politics*. Princeton, N.J.: Princeton University Press.

Root, Hilton L. *The Fountain of Privilege: Institutional Innovation and Social Choices in Old Regime France and England*. Berkeley: University of California Press, in press.

Rubinfeld, Daniel. 1987. "Economics of the Local Public Sector," in A. J. Auerbach and M. Feldstein, eds., *Handbook of Public Economics* vol. 2. New York: Elsevier.

Schwoerer, Lois. 1981. *The Declaration of Rights, 1689*. Baltimore, Md.: Johns Hopkins University Press.

Scotchmer, Suzanne. 1994. "Public Goods and the Invisible Hand," in J. Quigley and E. Smolensky, eds., *Modern Public Finance*. Cambridge: Harvard University Press.

Shirk, Susan. 1993. *The Political Logic of Economic Reform in China*. Berkeley: University of California Press.

Taylor, George R. 1951. *The Transportation Revolution: 1815–1860*. New York: Holt, Rinehart, and Winston.

Temin, Peter. 1991. "Free Land and Federalism: A Synoptic View of American Economic Development," 21 *Journal of Interdisciplinary History* 371–89.

Tiebout, Charles. 1956. "A Pure Theory of Local Expenditures," 64 *Journal of Political Economy* 416–24.

Walder, Andrew G. 1992. "Markets and Political Change in Rural China: A Property Rights Analysis," unpublished manuscript, Harvard University.

Weingast, Barry R. 1993a. "The Political Foundations of Antebellum American Economic Growth." Paper presented at the annual meetings of the Economic History Association, Tucson, Ariz.

_____. 1993b. "Constitutions as Governance Structures: The Political Foundations of Secure Markets," 149 *Journal of Institutional and Theoretical Economics* 286–311.

_____. 1994a. "Institutions and Political Commitment: A New Political Economy of the American Civil War Era," unpublished manuscript, Hoover Institution, Stanford University.

_____. 1994b. "The Political Foundations of Democracy and the Rule of Law," unpublished manuscript, Hoover Institution, Stanford University.

Wheare, K. C. 1953. *Federal Government.* London: Oxford University Press.

Williamson, Oliver. 1985. *The Economic Institutions of Capitalism.* New York: Free Press.

Williamson, Oliver. 1994. "The Institutions and Governance of Economic Development and Reform." unpublished manuscript, University of California, Berkeley.

Wong, Christine P. W. 1991. "Central-Local Relations in an Era of Fiscal Decline: The Paradox of Fiscal Decentralization in Post-Mao China," 128 *The China Quarterly* 691–715.

E
Cooperative Federalism

[13]

Journal of Economic Perspectives—Volume 11, Number 4—Fall 1997—Pages 43–64

Rethinking Federalism

Robert P. Inman and Daniel L. Rubinfeld

F ederalism is a founding political principle of the U.S. Constitution and one of our country's recent intellectual exports. In Europe, the former Soviet Union, South Africa, and elsewhere, the view that effective government will involve a well-chosen mix of local and central governmental decision-making is now accepted. Federalism questions—how many local and state governments there should be, how they will be represented in the central government, and how policy responsibilities should be allocated between the central government and the lower tiers—are once again a central research concern of constitutional lawyers, political scientists, and economists alike.[1]

America's federalism debates were initially resolved by the U.S. Constitution. The resolution of the tension over which levels of government should do what has evolved during the past two centuries: from a period of "dualism" (1790–1860) in which states and the central government had comparable responsibilities; through an early period of "centralizing federalism" (1860–1933) in which the still modest federal responsibilities grew; through a later time of "cooperative federalism" (1933–1964), which marked a substantial growth in social programs arising out of the Depression; and finally to a period of "creative federalism" since 1964 in which

---

[1] For a presentation of our views on the current debates in federalism, see Inman and Rubinfeld (1996b, 1997). For other perspectives on current research on federalism, see Bednar and Eskridge (1994) on constitutional issues; Bermann (1994) on subsidiarity and the European Union; Bird, Ebel, and Wallich (1995) on federalist issues in the former Soviet Union; Ahmad and McLure (1996) on federalism in the new South Africa; and Rivlin (1992) on a federalism approach to leading U.S. policy issues.

■ *Robert P. Inman is Professor of Finance and Economics, Wharton School, University of Pennsylvania, Philadelphia, Pennsylvania, and Research Associate, National Bureau of Economic Research, Cambridge, Massachusetts. Daniel L. Rubinfeld is Robert L. Bridges Professor of Law and Professor of Economics, University of California, Berkeley, California.*

the federal government has taken a direct and active role in the problems of state and local governments (Scheiber, 1969).

This most recent period of creative federalism was spurred in part by Walter Heller and Joseph Pechman's call in the 1960s for general revenue sharing from the federal government to the states. Heller and Pechman feared that progressive federal taxation would lead to growing federal budget surpluses and a "fiscal drag" on the economy; their solution was to share these surpluses with the more fiscally needy state and local sector (Heller, 1966; Perloff and Nathan, 1968). What proved particularly "creative" about the period of creative federalism, however, were the arguments for additional federal grants-in-aid offered by state and local government officials and their elected Washington colleagues (Beer, 1972). From 1962 to 1976, the number of separate federal grants programs to state and local governments increased from 160 in 1962 to 412 by 1976 (ACIR, 1978, pp. 25, 32), and the amount of money allocated by these programs over this time rose from $42 billion to $169 billion (in 1996 dollars). From 1976 to 1996, total federal grants to state and local governments has risen an additional $46 billion to $215 billion (in 1996 dollars), a real growth rate for that time of about 1.2 percent per annum (Council of Economic Advisers, Economic Report of the President, 1997, Table B-83). This expansion of centrally financed grants-in-aid drives a significant fiscal wedge between the costs and benefits of financing state and local governments.[2]

There are currently a number of efforts to check the drift toward centralization in the U.S. fiscal structure and reallocate funding responsibilities for redistributive services from Washington to state capitols. Of course, the current initiatives are not new; many of them date back to the "new federalism" espoused during Reagan's first term. It is too early to tell, but it is possible that these current reforms will mark the beginning of a new period in U.S. federalism. If so, this newest federalism period is likely to be built on an intellectual foundation that reflects recent work in public economics, law and economics, and political economy. In what follows, we sketch out our view of the principles that could form that foundation.

Three Principles of Federalism

Three alternative principles, or models, of federalism can be identified in contemporary debates. In considering the implications of these principles, it is helpful to bear in mind that those who value a federal system typically do so for some mix of three reasons: it encourages an *efficient* allocation of national resources; it fosters *political participation* and a sense of the democratic community; and it helps to protect basic *liberties and freedoms*. The means for implementing these three objectives

---

[2] Quigley and Rubinfeld (1996) offer an empirical overview of the changing system of intergovernmental grants. Inman (1988) has estimated that this fiscal wedge between those paying the costs of public services and those receiving the benefits created by federal grants has resulted in a "Harberger triangle" of allocative inefficiency equal to about $.17 per dollar of federal aid distributed.

involve decisions about the institutions of federalism: the number of lower-tier governments, their representation in the central government, and the assignment of policy responsibilities between the vertical tiers of government.

Economic Federalism

The principle of economic federalism prefers the most decentralized structure of government capable of internalizing all economic externalities, subject to the constitutional constraint that all central government policies be decided by an elected or appointed "central planner."

This view elevates the goal of economic efficiency to the highest priority; only if two federal structures are equally efficient in the allocation of resources do other goals of federalism—political participation or the protection of individual rights—come into consideration. Oates's (1972) classic *Fiscal Federalism* still provides the most complete description of economic federalism; essentially, the central government is assigned responsibility for those public activities distinguished by significant externalities involving spatially dispersed populations, while local governments have responsibility for those public activities for which such spillovers are limited or absent. Decentralization to small jurisdictions is justified because, as Oates (1994, p. 130) put it more recently, "The tailoring of outputs to local circumstances will, in general, produce higher levels of well-being than a centralized decision to provide some uniform level of output across all jurisdictions . . ."

The appropriate number of local (or lower-tier) governments is specified so that all economies of scale in the provision of public services to households are just exhausted.[3] When public services are pure public goods for which the marginal cost of adding another user will be zero (national defense, basic research), or when there are inefficiencies arising from externalities across jurisdictions, then under economic federalism the central government will be assigned responsibility for those services. However, for public services that become congested as more households use the service—that is, to accommodate additional households at current service levels, additional public facilities must be provided—then relatively small communities are more likely to provide the service efficiently. When the average cost per user of providing a given level of a "congestible" government service just equals the marginal cost of adding one more user, then the community has reached its efficient size. Important public services such as education, police and fire protection, sanitation, recreation, and even public health can be produced efficiently by relatively small communities, perhaps as small as 10,000 households.[4]

---

[3] This statement assumes that there are sufficient number of each "preference type" of household to achieve the efficient level of public goods provisions. If there are too few households of a particular type then one must balance allocative efficiency—satisfying demands—against technical efficiency—reaching the minimal efficient scale for the community.

[4] On education, see Hanushek (1986); on police services, see Craig (1987); on fire services, see Duncombe and Yinger (1993); on parks and recreation, see Edwards (1990); on sanitation, see Gonzalez, Means, and Mehay (1993). For services where efficient production will require larger user populations, small communities can band together to form purchasing cooperatives, although writing contracts for such cooperatives is a subtle matter; see Williamson (1976). State governments often sanction such "contracts" when allowing local governments to form special districts.

Tiebout (1956) presented the first systematic argument as to how a decentralized federal structure could be used to achieve economic efficiency in the provision of public services; Bewley (1981) made Tiebout's insights precise. In the Tiebout economy, most public services are assumed to be congestible and efficiently provided by small communities. Thus, lower-tier governments are given significant policy responsibilities. Households are assumed to be freely mobile; they shop among local jurisdictions for that community which offers their preferred package of services, taxes, and regulations. In this institutional structure, if any jurisdiction were to provide public services inefficiently, households would move to another jurisdiction that was more efficient. It is this variety and the pressure it imposes on the unfavored communities and states which Justice Brandeis most likely had in mind when advocating local and state governments as "laboratories" for the design of public policies.[5] However, when there are significant intercommunity interdependencies (like pure public goods or spillovers), Tiebout's competition among small governments may result in economically inefficient public policies. Potential examples of such inefficiencies include low income assistance (Gramlich, 1985), regulation (Oates and Schwab, 1986), and local income and business taxes (Inman and Rubinfeld, 1996a). The principle of economic federalism assigns the central government the task of correcting such misallocations.

The structure of central government decision-making under economic federalism is relatively simple. A single central planner is elected and charged with providing public goods and correcting intercommunity spillovers. The planner can rely on the voting mechanism to reveal voter (presumably, the median voter) preferences or perhaps apply more sophisticated revelation mechanisms such as auctions (Grossman and Helpman, 1994) or demand-revealing processes (Laffont, 1987).

The central government can provide public goods and correct spillovers in either of two ways: provide the good directly or mandate outcomes (a "quantity" control),[6] or subsidize or tax the local governments to provide the efficient levels of the activity on their own (a "price" control). Central governments currently use both approaches. In the United States, national defense, old-age social security, and environmental protection are directly provided or mandated by the central government, while low-income assistance, interstate highways, and basic research are largely managed through central government price subsidies or matching grants to state and local agencies or nonprofit organizations.

Which of the two approaches—quantity controls or price subsidies—is to be

---

[5] "It is one of the happy incidents of the federal system that a single courageous state may, if its citizens choose, serve as a laboratory; and try novel social and economic experiments without risk to the rest of the country." Justice Brandeis (dissenting) in *New State Ice Co. v. Liebman* 285 U.S. 262, 311 (1932).

[6] The choice between direct provision and mandates is primarily a distribution issue. Mandates allocate the costs of the national policy to the local jurisdiction, while direct provision or lump-sum grants allocate the costs to taxpayers nationally. The recent U.S. Supreme Court decision in *Printz v. U.S.* (1997 U.S. Lexis 4044 [June 27, 1997]) overturned the federal unfunded mandate that state governments provide background checks on future gun owners in part for this distributional reason.

preferred by the central government depends upon the particular economic circumstances of the public good or intercommunity spillover. Direct provision of the public good or mandates by the central government will be preferred when the social marginal benefit curve of the good or corrected spillover is relatively inelastic and the social marginal cost curve is relatively elastic (Weitzman, 1974; Inman, 1982). Lump-sum grants targeted to a particular service can also be used in this case; if tightly monitored, targeted lump-sum grants are functionally equivalent to direct provision.

Untargeted lump-sum grants may also have a role to play in the efficient federal economy. For example, to ensure the efficient location of private sector workers across fiscally competitive jurisdictions, lump-sum transfers from the residents of the fiscally favored community to the residents in the fiscally disadvantaged locality may be needed (Boadway and Flatters, 1982; Myers, 1990). Further, if local tax administration is inadequate, it may make sense for central government to collect tax revenues for, and then transfer grants revenues to, state and local governments. To avoid the moral hazard of having local governments view such transfers as "blank checks" from the central government, the amount of such grants should be firmly tied to a publicly reviewed and locally decided tax rate. There are even circumstances where efficiency requires a grant *from* local government *to* the central government. Boadway and Keen (1996) present an analysis with tax interdependencies, in which tax decisions by local government increase the marginal cost of raising central government revenues. In this case, a grant from local governments to the center internalizes the costs that those governments impose on the central government. Finally, intergovernmental transfers can be used to improve the equity performance of the local public sector. For example, a state may decide that school districts should receive a certain amount of money depending directly on the rate at which they tax themselves—not on the tax base. This "tax base equalization aid" would involve transfers from districts with high tax bases to those with lower bases (LeGrand, 1975). The case for such transfers is strengthened if certain local public services such as education are considered "merit wants" (Musgrave, 1987); categorical matching grants can be designed to increase their provision (Inman and Rubinfeld, 1979).

For most economists, the principle of economic federalism, with its recommended institutions of competitive decentralized local governments and a strong central government to provide pure public goods and control intercommunity externalities, essentially defines what federalism is about. However, the principle has had only mixed success as a guide to economic policy. Its strength has been to articulate how fiscal competition among decentralized local governments can ensure the efficient provision of congestible public services; several recent studies offer empirical support for the proposition that competitive local governments do provide citizens the public services they want at the lowest cost (Brueckner, 1982; Bergstrom, Roberts, Rubinfeld, and Shapiro, 1988; Gramlich and Rubinfeld, 1982; Rubinfeld, 1987). The primary weakness of the principle of economic federalism has been to advocate the central government as the only institution best able to provide pure public goods and correct interjurisdictional externalities. With our growing understanding of how central government policies are decided, the deference of economic federalism to a strong central government may be excessive. For example, there often appears to be little connection between actual interjurisdictional spillovers and the size or structure of federal grants received (Oates, 1994; Inman, 1988). Alternative principles of federalism, ones which explicitly recognize the potential failings of central government policy-making, should be considered too.

Cooperative Federalism

The principle of cooperative federalism is to prefer the most decentralized structure of government capable of internalizing all economic externalities, subject to the constitutional constraint that all central government policies are agreed to unanimously by the elected representatives from each of the lower-tier governments.

The insights of cooperative federalism spring from the law and economics literature. Like economic federalism, cooperative federalism embraces the goal of economic efficiency as its central objective and advocates the use of lower-tier governments to provide congestible public services. However, cooperative federalism is much less optimistic as to the ability of a central government alone to resolve the intercommunity inefficiencies which might arise. Thus, the principle of cooperative federalism requires all central government policies to be unanimously approved by the elected representatives from each of the lower-tier governments. Since central government political agreements will be achieved through bargaining between all affected parties, any central government policies which are unanimously approved will likely be Pareto-improving. These agreements can take place directly within a central legislative body (Wittman, 1989) or through intergovernmental agreements between subsets of local governments which are then approved by the central government or by some agreed-upon neutral party, like an appointed court (Ellickson, 1979).

Agreements between lower-tier governments will require those who are harmed by the fiscal policy of some other jurisdiction to "compensate" the residents inside that jurisdiction for removing the offending policy.[7] As Coase (1960) and others have pointed out, when there are sufficient benefits to the outside residents from removing a harmful policy, then compensation can be paid to inside residents so that all residents—outside and inside—are better off. In practice, such compensation would be paid through an intercommunity agreement in which jurisdictions raise taxes and pay compensation to their neighboring governments,

---

[7] This specification of the interstate bargaining assigns the "property rights" to public policy to the government passing the policy. The alternative is to assign property rights to the affected governments; in this case, governments would have veto power over the actions of others. Each assignment has its problems when information is less than perfect, raising the possibility of extortion. Most constitutions assign the property rights to policy to the governments passing the laws.

which in turn return those funds to groups initially favored by the inefficient policy.[8] Thus, cooperative federalism views the primary function of the central government as encouraging and enforcing interjurisdictional contracts to provide pure public goods and to correct the failings of lower-tier fiscal competition.

There a number of reasons, however, that cause us to be skeptical that interjurisdictional Coasian bargains can be effective. Arguably the most important source of bargaining failure is the inability of the parties to agree how the economic surplus generated by the bargaining process should be divided (Cooter, 1982), since this may well involve irreconcilable ideas of fairness (Hoffman and Spitzer, 1985; Sutton, 1987). Furthermore, Coasian bargainers may make poor estimates of each other's threat point or miscalculate the chances that the other party will accept a compromise offer, thus taking a hard line that prevents agreement. Unless costs and benefits are common knowledge, all sides are likely to seek strategic advantage by concealing information (Myerson and Satterthwaite, 1983). Jurisdictions being asked to change may overstate the compensation they require for changing. Finally, if many governments are adversely affected by one state's public policy, the affected jurisdictions may have a difficult time determining how much each is willing to pay, since each individual jurisdiction will face a free-rider incentive to understate how it is affected and what it would pay, hoping that the other jurisdictions will bear the costs of the change. Strategic interplay becomes ever more complicated as the number of bargaining jurisdictions increases beyond two or the bargain is one of many (Mailath and Postlewaite, 1990).

Enforceability of agreements can also be a problem. In principle, intergovernmental agreements are legally enforceable (Ellickson, 1979), but in practice, when the violating party is a state or local government, the central government's only recourse may be military action. When the ultimate enforcement mechanism becomes so costly, all sides face incentives to renege on prior agreements.[9] When jurisdictions are tempted to renege, there is less incentive to reach agreements in the first place.

How well has cooperative federalism done in providing public goods or controlling intercommunity externalities? The overall record has not been impressive. Even agreements among few jurisdictions often fail to achieve fully efficient outcomes (Coates and Munger, 1995), and U.S. states often engage in non-cooperative behavior when significant benefits might arise from cooperation (Kolstad and Wolak, 1983). In fact, the limitations of cooperative federalism were evident from our nation's beginning. The U.S. Constitution was largely a response to the inability of

---

[8] One important application of this Coasian approach to intercommunity externalities is found in the work of Myers (1990) and Krelove (1992), who argue central government grants-in-aid are not necessary to correct misallocations arising from excessive, fiscally-induced relocations. Rather, the "over-populated" community has an incentive to pay the residents of the "under-populated" community not to relocate, and a Coasian agreement to this effect can be written between the two communities to correct the market failure. No central government aid is needed.

[9] This point was well-appreciated by Hamilton in his critique of the Articles of Confederation in *Federalist* 15: "The consequences of this (The Articles of Confederation) is, that though in theory their resolutions concerning those objects are laws, constitutionally binding on the members of the Union, yet in practice they are mere recommendations, which the States observe or disregard at their option."

the Articles of Confederation to achieve agreement among the states for financing the defense of the newly independent colonies (Rakove, 1989). As a consequence, Article I, Section 8 of our Constitution explicitly allocates the task of providing that defense to the new national Congress. Nationally provided social insurance, the other major expenditure activity of the U.S. central government, arose too from a failure of U.S. states to cooperatively respond to growing unemployment. During the Great Depression, rather than working together to provide a common level of social insurance, the states chose instead to act alone to keep as many of their current jobs as possible through low taxes and low unemployment assistance (Patterson, 1969, ch. 2 and 3), a problem which still exists today (Helms, 1985; Feldstein and Vaillant, 1994). Under Roosevelt's New Deal, the national government decided to fund some insurance systems directly (the Social Security Act of 1935) and to use matching grants to encourage states to take on the task of providing income assistance for the indigent elderly, the blind, and mothers with dependent children (Patterson, 1969, p. 88; Wallis, 1984).

Finally, the macro-management of the economy, perhaps government's single most important regulatory activity, can also be viewed as the response of the central government to a failure of Coasian bargaining among the states. Individual states do have some power to use fiscal policy to stimulate their economies (Gramlich, 1987; Inman and Rubinfeld, 1994), but the fact that most states are small, open economies severely limits their ability to implement effective aggregate demand fiscal policies. Only an agreement among the many states to coordinate their fiscal policies will work. The struggle in Europe to form a viable monetary union illustrates how difficult such agreements on appropriate macroeconomic policies can be.

To be completely clear, our point here is not that the levels of central government defense spending, social insurance, or macroeconomic stability have always been optimal; rather, it is that if the nation had waited for states to agree unanimously on such policies, economic outcomes would almost surely have been far worse. Our reading of the historical and contemporary evidence does not provide much support for the claim that lower-tier governments can solve their important collective action problems on their own through unanimous Coasian agreements. If economic federalism seems too biased in favor of centralization, cooperative federalism seems to bias the fiscal constitution too far in the other direction.

Democratic (Majority-Rule) Federalism

The principle of democratic (or majority-rule) federalism is to prefer the most decentralized structure of government capable of internalizing all economic externalities, subject to the constitutional constraint that all central government policies are agreed to by a simple (51 percent) majority of elected representatives from lower-tier governments.

Like the principles of economic and cooperative federalism, democratic federalism also embraces the use of lower-tier governments to provide congestible public services, and again, the number of lower-tier governments is determined by the technology of public services. With regard to its views on the economic performance of the central government, however, democratic federalism stands between economic federalism and cooperative federalism. Unlike economic federalism, it does not implicitly assume that the central government will provide public goods and regulate interjurisdictional spillovers efficiently. In contrast to cooperative federalism, only majority-rule—not unanimity—is required to make a decision. Of course, there is no guarantee that policies chosen by a majority-rule legislature will be efficient either. Democratic federalism seeks to balance the potential efficiency gains of greater centralization in a world of local spillovers and pure public goods against the inefficiencies which might arise when a democratic central legislature sets policies (Tullock, 1969; Inman and Rubinfeld, 1996b). Considering this trade-off requires a specification of the federal institutions of government. What is the extent of local representation in the central legislature? Should there be an independently elected executive with veto powers? How should policy responsibilities be assigned to the different tiers of government?

In thinking about how the institutions of a democratic central government might be specified, it is useful to contrast two commonly used approaches to legislative decision-making. The first assigns agenda-setting powers to a small subset of members, say the speaker of the house or a key legislative committee. Other members in the legislature then simply vote—up or down—on the items in the approved agenda. Most likely, policies will be approved by a bare majority—a minimal winning coalition—in this strong agenda-setter legislature (Baron and Ferejohn, 1989). A second strategy shares agenda-setting powers among all members, giving each legislator a right to select a most preferred policy in that policy area most germane to the legislator's constituents. This second approach to legislative decision-making involves each legislator deferring to the preferred policies of all other legislators, provided the other legislators defer to the legislator's own policy requests (Weingast, 1979; Niou and Ordeshook, 1985; Weingast and Marshall, 1988). The guiding norm here is one of deference—"You scratch my back, I'll scratch yours"—and it typically results in legislative proposals which are approved nearly unanimously. For this reason such legislatures are often called "universalistic."

There are reasons to believe that minimum winning coalition legislatures may be more economically efficient than universalistic legislatures (Inman and Fitts, 1990). But this alternative environment will not arise unless the representatives themselves prefer to do business in a minimum winning coalition environment. A single legislator choosing between the closed rules of a bare majority, minimal-winning-coalition legislature or the more open rules of a universalistic legislature managed by a norm of deference will typically favor the more open rules. With closed rules, you must belong to a winning coalition to have your constituent's projects approved; without strong political parties or additional side-deals, the probability of being in that coalition is at best 50:50. In constituent-based politics, it may be better to have the sure slice of a smaller pie under universalism, than run the risk of no slice at all under minimal-winning-coalition politics.

Universalistic legislatures operating under a norm of deference run a significant risk that their chosen policies will be economically inefficient. The essential problem is that each legislator chooses a program that will disproportionately benefit their own constituency, with the costs paid by residents of all jurisdictions. Because of this cross-subsidy, each legislator has an incentive to ask for too much of their own preferred good or regulation (Weingast, Shepsle, and Johnsen, 1981; Persson and Tabellini, 1994). The subsidy becomes larger, and the potential inefficiencies greater, the greater is legislative representation, or equivalently, the smaller are the legislative jurisdictions relative to the nation as a whole. The legislative norm of deference allows these inefficiencies to stand, not just for one jurisdiction but for all jurisdictions represented in the legislature. Inman (1988) and Inman and Fitts (1990) offer some tentative evidence on the magnitude of the allocative inefficiencies created by such a legislature.

What can be done to strike a more appropriate balance between the gains of centralized assignment and the costs of this assignment when the legislature is inefficient? One set of options is to reform the central government's legislative process in ways that would discourage an inefficient universalistic legislature, perhaps by strengthening the hand of political parties over members' decisions (Aldrich, 1995) or by increasing executive powers (Fitts and Inman, 1992).

Alternatively, one might adjust the institutions of federalism. For example, if given the legislative process and size of the legislature, the assignment of policy responsibility to the central government is less efficient than retaining those responsibilities at the local level, even with associated spillovers, then constitutional assignment can reallocate the activity to the lower tiers of government. In effect, this is what President Reagan sought to achieve through the informal influence of his presidency with his 1982 budget and his "new federalism" reforms. However, since the Reagan reforms asked the central legislature to surrender influence over spending, it is perhaps not surprising these efforts did not survive his presidency.[10]

Another institution of federalism that can be adjusted is the extent of representation of local governments to the national legislature. Does every community have direct representation or does the constitution combine communities, with groups of local jurisdictions electing one representative? If the central government's legislature operates under a norm of deference, economic inefficiencies are likely to be greater the larger the legislature and the smaller the unit of represen-

---

[10] Formal constitutional assignment of functions to lower-tier governments might also be tried, but such constraints, when effective, are often quite "heavy-handed." Either the assignment excludes everything from the central level or, if exceptions are written, potentially nothing. Recent efforts to write an effective, but flexible, federal balanced budget amendment is a case in point. The current Rehnquist Supreme Court is struggling to find a more nuanced interpretation of assignment in our Constitution. Since *Garcia v. San Antonio Metropolitan Transit Authority* (469 U.S. 528 [1985]), the Court has abandoned trying to define assignment by governmental function. In *United States v. Lopez* (115 S. Ct. 1624 [1995]) the Court embraced a process approach to evaluating congressional actions which affects states. The Court now requires national laws to explicitly state a national interest (for example, interstate commerce) being rationally served by the legislation. This does not seem a particularly high hurdle. Inman and Rubinfeld (1997) suggest another approach to raising the bar using a Federalism Impact Statement (or "FIST").

tation; so for efficiency, smaller legislatures and larger units of representation may be preferred (Inman and Fitts, 1990; Gilligan and Matsusaka, 1995). The efficient legislature is unlikely to be very small, however. Legislatures serve as bargaining halls and help to reveal preferences. A small legislature puts all the burden for preference revelation on the candidate election, losing the potential efficiency gains which come with face-to-face deal-making. Setting the size of the efficient legislature requires us to balance the gains from having more voices heard against the risk that too many bargainers means only inefficient or unstable deals are done (Buchanan and Tullock, 1962, ch. 7).[11]

Which Principle of Federalism Should One Choose?

Constitutions establish the rules for collective decision-making. The unique contribution of a *federal* constitution is to allow for multiple tiers of governments, each with a domain of policy responsibilities. Federal constitutions must specify the number of lower-tier governments, the representation of those governments to the central government, and the assignment of policy responsibilities between the upper and lower tiers.

For economic efficiency, all three principles of federalism embrace the logic of the Tiebout model and the use of lower-tier governments to provide congestible public services. It is in the specification of central government representation and in the assignment of pure public goods and spillovers to the central government that the three principles of federalism may disagree. Economic federalism has all local governments select one central government representative—a "president-planner"—and then assigns all pure public goods and spillovers as central responsibilities. It is the job of the president-planner to set and administer central government policies efficiently, presumably guided by principles of efficient (second-best) public finance.[12] Cooperative federalism gives each local government one representative to the central government and then allows those representatives to fashion Coasian agreements to improve the welfare of their citizens. Agreements may involve all local governments—for example, an agreement to enforce agreements—or only a subset of governments. Cooperative federalism assigns all public goods and spillovers locally, unless local governments voluntarily agree to centralize. Democratic federalism jointly decides representation and assignment as part of an effort to balance the efficiency gains of central government provision

---

[11] Although Buchanan and Tullock's (1962) classic *Calculus of Consent* does not discuss federalism explicitly, they do advocate an approach to constitution-writing much like that suggested by democratic federalism (p. 112): "As we have suggested, the costs of reaching agreement, of bargaining, are, from a 'social' point of view, wasteful. One means of reducing these costs is to organize collective activity in the smallest units consistent with the extent of the externality that the collectivization is designed to eliminate."

[12] The president-planner's objective may, or may not, correspond to an ethically appealing social welfare function, but whatever the objective, the president-planner can be assumed to pursue it with the most efficient use of the policy instruments available. For a discussion of how such a president-planner might be chosen and set policies in a democracy, see Besley and Coate (1997).

against the inefficiencies which might arise when central legislatures decide what that level of provision should be (Inman and Rubinfeld, 1996b). Large legislatures will do a good job representing preferences of all citizens but may foster inefficiently large ("universalistic") budgets. Small legislatures are less representative but the budgeting may be less prone to excessive spending.

However one evaluates the economic efficiency performance of federal constitutions, it must be recognized that the federal institutions chosen will have important implications for political participation and the protection of individual rights and liberties, two other constitutional values central to past and current federalism debates. James Madison's arguments in Federalist 10 for a strong but highly representative central government as the best protector of individual rights helped to define the representation and assignment outcomes in our Constitution. Current concerns in the European Union over political participation and the Union's "democratic deficit" may have a similar effect by elevating the European Parliament to greater institutional importance in the new EU's constitution (Garrett and Tsebelis, 1996).

Finally, there are good reasons to think that efficiency, participation, and the protection of individual rights may at times conflict, and that setting the institutions of the federal constitution will require hard choices. For example, a strong central government built on the principles of economic federalism or democratic federalism with a small legislature is likely to be the relatively more efficient federal structure for the provision of public goods and spillovers. However, such a structure may shortchange the valued goal of political participation which is typically best served by giving small local governments stronger central government representation and more policy responsibilities (Frug, 1980; Inman and Rubinfeld, 1997). Individual rights might also be threatened by a strongly centralized federal constitution, Madison's arguments not withstanding. Legal scholars concerned with the protection of individual political rights (McConnell, 1987; Rapaczynski, 1986) have strongly criticized from a rights perspective the Supreme Court's recent *Garcia* decision giving the central government carte blanche for setting public policies,[13] while Easterbrook (1983) and Weingast (1995) both argue forcefully for decentralized policy assignments as the best means for protecting individual property rights. Those charged with selecting a principle of federalism must understand and then balance these potentially important tradeoffs between economic efficiency, political participation, and individual liberties.

---

[13] After years of frustration in trying to establish a workable assignment principle based upon the Tenth Amendment, the Supreme Court in *Garcia v. San Antonio Metropolitan Transit Authority* (469 U.S. 528 [1985]) gave the task of deciding the allocation of federal and state policy responsibilities to the central government, arguing that state representation in the U.S. Senate would adequately protect state policy interests. Two more recent Supreme Court decisions have placed some modest limits of what Washington can do. In *United States v. Lopez* (115 S. Ct. 1624 [1995]) the Court required Congress to make explicit the connection between national regulations of state activities and a national objective, while in *New York v. United States* (505 U.S. 144 [1992]) and more recently in *Printz v. U.S.* (1997 U.S. Lexis 4044 [June 27, 1997]), the Court overturned the use of unfunded mandates on the states.

Welfare Reform: Budget Cutting or A New Federalism?

The U.S. Constitution is a broadly representative but centralized federal constitution. In response to Madison's concerns that the new democracy be representative of all the people, the Constitution requires representation of the populace in the House of Representatives and equal voices for all the states in the Senate. To avoid the collective action problems inherent in the Articles of Confederation, the Constitution through the Tenth Amendment assigns all policy powers to the majority-rule central government. Ultimately, this representative central government will decide which tier of government will set America's economic policies.

We may be at the start of a quiet revolution in Washington's view of how to assign policies. In summer 1996, President Clinton signed the Personal Responsibility and Work Opportunities Reconciliation Act of 1996, known more generally as the Welfare Reform Act of 1996. The act has two primary objectives: 1) to reduce welfare roles by providing families currently on welfare with the means and the incentives to seek work; and 2) to end welfare's 60-year status as a nationally funded entitlement.[14] Of central interest to us here is the second objective, since it potentially represents a significant shift in the responsibilities of different levels of government for the provision of low income assistance, and how Washington may wish to manage our federal relations generally.

The Welfare Reform Act of 1996 has two potentially important consequences for federal-state relations in the provision of low-income assistance; it saves the federal government money and it breaks the federal-to-state-to-recipient entitlement for low income assistance. Prior to the passage of the Welfare Reform Act, the federal government shared directly in the financing of states' decisions for welfare through an open-ended matching grant for aid to families with dependent children (AFDC), for job training (JOBS), and for aid for homeless children (Emergency Assistance). If the state spent more on welfare, the federal government shared in that expenditure at the federally set matching rate. The Welfare Reform Act replaced these matching aid programs with a single block grant called Temporary Assistance for Needy Families (hereafter TANF). TANF breaks the direct call of states and their low income households on additional central government dollars. Importantly, this shift from matching to block grants was not necessary to achieve the budgetary savings of the Welfare Reform Act. Of the $54 billion that welfare reform will save over the next six fiscal years, $46 billion will come from provisions which deny Social Security Income (SSI) supplements and food stamps to legal immigrants (U.S. House Committee on Ways and Means, 1996, p. 1332). The savings from the consolidation of AFDC, JOBS, and Emergency Assistance into the TANF block grant equals only $7.8 billion over six years. To put it another way, the

---

[14] For an analysis in this journal of the possible success of the Welfare Reform Act in reaching its first goal, encouraging work by current welfare recipients, see Blank (1997).

same level of savings in federal spending from TANF could have been achieved with an (approximate) 8 percent cut in federal matching rates, say from .50 to .46 for rich states and from .78 to .72 for poor states.[15]

These cost figures, together with much political rhetoric, suggest that the real fiscal target of the Welfare Reform Act of 1996 was not lower federal spending, but the federal-state relationship for how poverty dollars are budgeted. Since its inception during the Depression, AFDC had guaranteed each eligible individual (originally children only, but later mothers were included) a state-determined stipend with state spending supported by an open-ended matching grant from the federal government. Federal standards for a minimum level of the stipend and funding through a federal, open-ended matching grant guaranteed at least minimal AFDC payments to all eligible households. Higher state spending is allowed and the federal government will match that spending. Originally, the federal government matched state spending at a uniform rate of $1 of federal money for each $2 of state spending, implying a federal "matching rate" of .33. Subsequent reforms have raised federal matching rates to .50 ($1 federal for each state $1) for the very richest states and to .78 for the poorest states ($3.50 federal for each state $1). The welfare reform ends this federal guarantee of fiscal support for state spending by consolidating AFDC, JOBS, and Emergency Assistance into the TANF block grant. Replacing welfare matching aid with the TANF block grant frees the federal budget from the welfare entitlement and makes states responsible for the full cost of each additional dollar spent on low income assistance.

Further, the Welfare Reform Act of 1996 gives states wide latitude to determine program eligibility and benefits, and largely removes federal government regulations for low income assistance. TANF dollars can be reallocated away from direct income support to programs which promote job training, child care, prevention of teen pregnancy, and marriage. Given these alternative uses of the TANF block grant, TANF monies are likely to be highly fungible out of direct income support, if that is what a state's politics prefers.[16] The only requirements imposed on the

---

[15] This is only approximate, because a cut in the federal matching rate for state spending will reduce the states' own spending and thus have "second-order" effects further reducing total federal outlays. These second-order effects would be small. Craig and Inman (1986) estimate the price elasticity of own state spending with respect to changes in the federal matching rate to equal .12; thus an 8 percent reduction in the matching rate will reduce state spending by less than 1 percent.

[16] Legally, a state will be free to reallocate those dollars over 80 percent of the state's TANF allocation, as the Welfare Reform Act of 1996 requires that 80 percent of the TANF allocation be spent on approved welfare-related activities. Once the 80 percent target is met, TANF monies may be allocated to other state activities outside the welfare budget, including general tax relief. However, state and local governments are very clever in labelling programs to circumvent federal regulations—one Pennsylvania high school district reclassified fourth year AP Spanish as a bilingual language program to qualify for federal low-income education aid—so that the Welfare Reform Act's maintenance of effort regulation may prove only a weak constraint. If so, state welfare spending will become fully fungible and each additional dollar spent on welfare will imply an opportunity cost to the state of $1. Finally, TANF funding may diminish in importance over time. While generous in the near-term, TANF funding is not indexed and there is only modest protection if welfare roles rise during a deep recession. WRA 96 establishes a contingency fund with $2 billion in reserves to be allocated through TANF when a recession occurs. The fund is

Robert P. Inman and Daniel L. Rubinfeld   57

states are those which restrict the size of the state welfare roles. TANF funds cannot be used to support assistance for families whose members have received assistance for five or more years, although states can exempt 20 percent of their caseload from this requirement. Adults receiving TANF funds must "engage in work" within two years; states may choose a shorter grace period. By 1997, 25 percent of single parents receiving TANF funds (50 percent of two-parent families) must be engaged in work for at least 20 hours per week; by 2002, 50 percent of single parents (90 percent of two-parent families) must be working, although states retain some flexibility in de-fining "work."

What will happen to low-income assistance now that fiscal responsibility has been moved back to the states? Only tentative predictions can be drawn from the numerous studies of state financing of AFDC spending. Two offsetting incentives are at work. First, the Welfare Reform Act of 1996 eliminates AFDC's matching rates for additional state spending, which raises the effective price (the net of matching aid price) of an additional dollar of low-income assistance for a state from $(1 - \text{matching rate})$ to 1; poor states will see the effective price of an additional dollar of poverty assistance rise from .22 $(= 1 - .78)$ to 1, while richer states will see their prices rise from .5 $(= 1 - .5)$ to 1.[17] Even though most studies estimate modest price elasticities of demand for welfare spending, ranging from $-.02$ to $-.50$ (Ribar and Wilhelm, 1996), having the effective price of welfare increase by 354 percent (for poor states) or 100 percent (for rich states) implies potentially large conse-quences. For example, a price elasticity of $-.20$ would imply nearly a 70 percent cut in spending in poor states and a 20 percent reduction in richer states.

On the other side, although the welfare reform removes the price incentive for state welfare spending, it substitutes a block grant of a nearly equal dollar amount. Direct estimates of the elasticity of welfare spending to lump-sum grants range from .01 to .30, with lower estimates corresponding to more "fungible" grants-in-aid (Craig and Inman, 1986; Inman, 1979). Using these estimates we expect the TANF block grant equal to the state's current loss in matching aid to increase welfare spending in poor states from 4 percent (for a block grant elasticity of .01) to perhaps as much as 30 percent (for a block grant elasticity of .30) and from 2 percent (.01 block grant elasticity) to 20 percent (.30 block grant elasticity) in rich states.[18]

Combining these effects, a price elasticity of $-.20$ implies a decline of welfare spending in the poor states from 40 to 66 percent (that is, a drop of 70 percent from the price effect and an increase of either 4 or 30 percent from the TANF

---

modest, however; the $2 billion reserve would have covered only about one-third of the increase in AFDC spending which occurred during the mild 1991–92 recession; see Blank (1997, p. 175).

[17] The precise specification of the price of welfare spending is a bit more involved, depending on which political economy model and policy interactions are being estimated. For a useful review of the various price specifications for state welfare spending, see Chernick (1996).

[18] The above-estimated percentage changes following a TANF block grant are based upon these grants elasticities and the average welfare spending and grants levels reported in Craig and Inman (1986). The larger effects for poorer states reflect the fact that they will receive a larger percentage increase in block grant aid from the new TANF grant.

block grant) and a fall in the rich states from 0 to 18 percent (a 20 percent decline from the price effect plus either a 2 or 20 percent increase from the TANF grant effect). The larger declines occur when federal welfare aid is highly fungible from welfare spending into other areas of the state budget. It remains to be seen how much of a decline, if any, will finally occur. That there are "maintenance of effort" provisions in the Welfare Reform Act, requiring that 80 percent of TANF grants be spent on welfare-related programs, suggests that at least a majority in Congress is concerned that declines may be significant.[19]

Of the three principles of federalism specified above, the principle of cooperative federalism seems to us to provide the strongest rationale for the federalism reforms undertaken by the Welfare Reform Act of 1996. For example, the principle of economic federalism, aimed as it is at internalizing all relevant externalities, would advocate either full and direct central government provision or the use of matching aid as the most economically efficient ways of adjusting for fiscal spillovers between jurisdictions. When providing low-income assistance, there are two sets of spillovers to be internalized, those on the cost side and those on the benefit side. On the benefit side, Boadway and Wildasin (1984) emphasize that residents of one state may derive benefits from the provision of low income assistance in another state. On the cost side, Gramlich (1985) emphasizes that mobile taxpayers and mobile poor drive up the costs to states of providing a dollar of benefits to their own poor residents, since higher taxes and benefits may drive away the residential or business tax base while attracting additional poor. For both reasons, the private marginal cost to a state of providing $1 in additional welfare benefits will be larger than the social marginal cost. If grants are used, the matching rate should be set to internalize for state politicians these two types of spillovers.[20]

---

[19] Even so, we remain skeptical that this maintenance of effort provision alone will have much effect in preventing states from allocating resources away from poor households *if* such reallocations are the politically preferred allocation. Central government rules on state budget allocations are typically very difficult to enforce.

[20] One can offer a back-of-the-envelope calculation that the recent matching rates used in AFDC were reasonable adjustments for expected spillovers. The appropriate formula for a matching rate that corrects for spillovers is: $m = (1 - 1/\rho\phi)$, where m is the matching rate, ρ is the factor (presumably greater than 1) by which one must multiply the private marginal benefit received from a change in welfare benefits to account for the benefits felt by those in other jurisdictions, and ϕ (also presumably greater than 1) is the factor by which one must multiply the costs for a state of changing welfare benefits to make up for the cost spillovers incurred by scaring off or attracting businesses and the poor. Helms (1985) estimates the elasticity of state incomes to a tax-financed increase in welfare benefits to be about .1 and Blank (1988) estimates the elasticity of welfare immigration to an increase in benefits to also be about .1. These two effects have an additive impact, so that the private cost to a state of providing an extra $1 of social assistance will be about 20 percent higher than the $1 social cost, or about $1.20; thus ϕ can be taken to equal 1.2. On the benefit side, if we assume that if one state spends an extra $1 on benefits, it raises the utility of each of the other 49 states by an average of 2 cents, then the social marginal benefit of having one state spend an additional $1 will be nearly $2 (the $1 spent plus a spillover of 49 × 2 cents). Thus, ρ equals about 2. Using these estimates of ϕ and ρ, the matching rate formula implies an efficient welfare matching rate to control spillovers of .58, close to AFDC's average matching rate before the welfare reforms.

The more general conclusion that matching rates are an appropriate policy is not very sensitive to

The principle of democratic federalism also will support the continuation of direct central government provision or matching aid, again to internalize interstate spillovers from welfare, though this principle might well advocate reductions in direct support or matching rates if the evidence points to inefficient current policies because of political logrolling. After all, welfare spending subsidizes poor families. In this light, the politics of these subsidies should be no different than the politics of all subsidies: tax deductions for charitable giving, farm price supports, tariffs, or low cost loans to cities, states, and non-profit institutions. For some evidence that welfare has been part of this wider subsidy logroll, see Ferejohn (1983). While lower matching rates might be justified by the principle of democratic federalism, the continued presence of cost and benefit spillovers when states provide welfare still recommends direct central government provision or a targeted matching rate greater than zero.

Nor can the fiscal reforms in the Welfare Reform Act of 1996 be well-explained by a shift towards greater concern for the competing constitutional values of political participation and the protection of individual liberties. Though one might justify the back-to-work welfare reforms from a principle of personal liberty, it is hard to see how the fiscal reforms replacing matching aid with a fungible block grant enhances personal freedoms. Nor is overall political participation likely to be greatly affected by the reforms. On one side, increasing state discretion over welfare policies does take an important step towards local control of policies, which should enhance participation. However, setting the matching rate at zero significantly raises the cost to the middle class voters of including lower-income families in any budget coalition. This may well reduce overall participation in deciding state fiscal choices. Finally, as long as efficiency is still a valued social objective and the central government is allowed to set policies, then matching aid, not fungible block grants, is the better policy.

The principle of cooperative federalism seems to account best for all the major fiscal reform features of the Welfare Reform Act of 1996. Cooperative federalism advocates the decentralization of policy to the lower tiers of government with the federal government's role limited to encouraging efficient agreements between jurisdictions. The Welfare Reform Act seems to do just that. First, states, not cities or counties, are chosen by the act as the appropriate unit of government to receive the new welfare responsibilities. This assignment recognizes the significant mobility of lower income families and tax base within metropolitan areas (Inman, 1992) as well as the possibility of significant benefit spillovers between local governments (Pauly, 1973). States are generally the right unit of government to internalize such metropolitan-wide spillovers from welfare policies. Further, the Welfare Reform Act

---

the numbers chosen for ρ and ϕ. If the benefit of spending \$1 in one state raises utility by only half a cent in 49 other states, and the cost spillover parameter is 1.1, a still significant matching rate of .27— almost the matching rate when AFDC was first approved in 1935—is justified. As state economies become more open, as they surely have over the past 60 years, then the spillover parameters ϕ and ρ will increase and the efficient AFDC matching rate will rise as well, as it has over the past 60 years.

directly removes a possible interstate spillover from welfare policy by allowing states to impose residency requirements for the receipt of benefits, although this provision seems sure to be challenged in court. In short, the Welfare Reform Act seems designed to assign welfare responsibility to those lower-tier governments (states) which internalize as many welfare externalities as possible. For any welfare spillovers that might remain, the act grants states wide latitude to set welfare policies, discretion which should facilitate interstate agreements. Finally, and perhaps most decisively for the view favoring cooperative federalism as the rationale for welfare reform, the act drops matching grants in favor of fungible block grants, thereby removing an important impediment to efficient bargaining between states.[21]

Seen in the light of our three principles of federalism, the recent fiscal reforms in welfare policy appear to be a significant institutional experiment with an alternate paradigm of federalism, one which emphasizes the ability of states, not the central government, to handle cross-jurisdiction spillovers. If the experiment proves successful, then other central government policies like Medicaid (another entitlement poverty program), environmental and business regulation, infrastructure spending, and perhaps even Social Security and Medicare may become candidates for fiscal decentralization too.

Conclusion

Rethinking federalism means rethinking the terms under which sovereign citizens or states join together to form a "more perfect union." Whether one is struggling to form a political union for the first time (European Union, South Africa, Russia), deciding to break away from an existing union (Quebec), or to reform a stable one (United States), decisions must be made along each of the institutional dimensions which define the federal constitution: the number of lower-tier governments, their representation to the central legislature, and the assignment of policy responsibilities between the center and lower tiers. Whatever federal constitution is selected will have important implications for the valued goals of government: economic efficiency, political participation, protection of rights.

Most countries will want to mix and match their federal institutions, depending on how they view the performance and weigh the goals of government. For example, for economic efficiency, lower-tier governments might best be assigned responsibility for congestible public services; both economic theory and the available evidence seem to support this allocation. For the problems of pure public goods and interjurisdictional spillovers, the principle of economic federalism recommends that these goods be assigned to the central government. However, the prin-

---

[21] As first noted by Buchanan and Stubblebine (1962), central government using taxes or subsidies alone to internalize spillovers alters the marginal incentives of agents who are bargaining, leading to an inefficient, post-bargain allocation. In other words, Pigovian taxes without compensation is a substitute for, not a complement to, the Coasian bargain.

Robert P. Inman and Daniel L. Rubinfeld 61

ciples of cooperative federalism and democratic federalism are less clear on the point. The ability of central governments to provide pure public goods efficiently may depend crucially on how representatives are selected for the national legislature. Locally chosen representatives may place parochial interests above the collective interest in efficient public goods provision. Cooperative federalism argues for assigning pure public goods and spillovers to the local level, much as the new welfare reforms have done; cooperative federalism counts on the ability of interjurisdictional bargaining to allocate such goods better. The principle of democratic federalism retains central government assignment for pure public goods and spillovers but argues for a more rough and ready representation of local interests at the national level, like recommending nationally elected representatives to a majority-rule national legislature. Finally, other goals for government will be considered too, such as political participation and protection of individual rights. These important constitutional values might favor extensive local representation in the national legislature, even allowing for the potentially significant efficiency costs imposed by a large constituent-based legislature, or they might favor many local governments and the local assignment of public goods and spillovers, even recognizing the possibly large inefficiencies imposed by spillovers left unresolved because of incomplete interjurisdictional bargains.

As we rethink federalism, we must recognize—as did our Founding Fathers—that the selection of the institutions of federalism necessarily carries with it a balancing of these competing social goals of economic efficiency, political participation, and the protection of individual rights and liberties.

■ *We would like to acknowledge with thanks the financial support by the National Science Foundation (Inman) and the Fisher Center for Real Estate and Urban Economics (Rubinfeld). We must also mention the financial and intellectual support of the Center for Advanced Study in the Behavioral Sciences (SES-9022192), which provided us with a unique opportunity to begin our own rethinking about federalism. Thanks too to Richard Bird, Steve Coate, Brad De Long, Michael Fitts, Geoffrey Garrett, Alan Krueger, Wallace Oates, Eric Posner, Harvey Rosen, Timothy Taylor (particularly), and Michael Wiseman for their helpful comments on an earlier draft.*

References

ACIR (Advisory Commission on Intergovernmental Relations), *Categorical Grants: Their Role and Design*, A-52, Washington, D.C.: U.S. Government Printing Office, 1978.

Ahmad, Junaid and Charles McLure, "Federalism in the New South Africa," Paper Presented at the International Seminar on Public Economics (ISPE) Conference on "Fiscal Policy in Emerging Federations," Nashville, Tennessee, August 26–28, 1996.

Aldrich, John, *Why Parties? The Origin and Transformation of Party Politics in America.* Chicago: University of Chicago Press, 1995.

Baron, David, and John Ferejohn, "Bargaining in Legislatures," *American Political Science Review,* 1989, *83,* 1181–1206.

Bednar, Jena and William Eskridge, Jr., "Steadying the Court's Unsteady Path: A Theory of Judicial Enforcement of Federalism," *Southern California Law Review,* 1995, *68,* 1447–91.

Beer, Samuel, "The Adoption of General Revenue-Sharing: A Case Study in Public Sector Politics," *Public Policy,* 1972, *24,* 127–95.

Bergstrom, Theodore, Judith Roberts, Daniel L. Rubinfeld, and Perry Shapiro, "A Test for Efficiency in the Supply of Public Education," *Journal of Public Economics,* 1988, *35,* 289–308.

Bermann, George A., "Taking Subsidiarity Seriously: Federalism in the European Community and the United States," *Columbia Law Review,* 1994, *94,* 331–456.

Besley, Timothy and Stephen Coate, "An Economic Model of Representative Government," *Quarterly Journal of Economics,* 1997, *112,* 85–114.

Bewley, Truman, "A Critique of Tiebout's Theory of Local Public Expenditures," *Econometrica,* 1981, *49,* 713–39.

Bird, Richard, Robert Ebel, and Christine Wallich, *Decentralization of the Socialist State: Intergovernmental Finance in Transition Economies.* Washington, D.C.: The World Bank, 1995.

Blank, Rebecca, "The Effect of Welfare and Wage Levels on the Location Decisions of Female-Headed Households," *Journal of Urban Economics,* 1988, *24,* 186–211.

Blank, Rebecca, "Policy Watch: The 1996 Welfare Reform," *Journal of Economic Perspectives,* 1997, *11,* 169–77.

Boadway, Robin W., and Frank Flatters, "Efficiency and Equalisation Payments in a Federal System of Government: A Synthesis and Extension of Recent Results," *Canadian Journal of Economics,* 1982, *15,* 613–33.

Boadway, Robin W, and Robert P. Keen, "Efficiency and the Fiscal Gap in Federal Systems," Paper Presented at the International Seminar on Public Economics (ISPE) Conference on "Fiscal Policy in Emerging Federations," Nashville, Tennessee, USA, August 26–28, 1996.

Boadway, Robin and David E. Wildasin, *Public Sector Economics.* Boston: Little Brown, 1984.

Brueckner, Jan, "A Test for Allocative Efficiency in the Local Public Sector," *Journal of Public Economics,* 1982, *11,* 223–45.

Buchanan, James and W. Craig Stubblebine, "Externality," *Economica,* 1962, *29,* 371–84.

Buchanan, James and Gordon Tullock, *Calculus of Consent.* Ann Arbor: University of Michigan Press, 1962.

Chernick, Howard, "Fiscal Effects of Block Grants for the Needy: A Review of the Evidence," Department of Economics, Hunter College and Graduate Center, CUNY, Revised, 1996.

Coase, Ronald, "The Problem of Social Cost," *Journal of Law and Economics,* 1960, *3,* 1–44.

Coates, Dennis and Michael Munger, "Strategizing in Small Group Decision-Making: Host State Identification for Radioactive Waste Disposal Among Eight Southern States," *Public Choice,* 1995, *82,* 1–15.

Cooter, Robert, "The Cost of Coase," *Journal of Legal Studies,* 1982, *11,* 1–33.

Council of Economic Advisors, Economic Report of the President, 1997.

Craig, Steven, "The Impact of Congestion on Local Public Good Production," *Journal of Public Economics,* 1987, *32,* 331–53.

Craig, Steven G, and Robert P. Inman, "Education, Welfare, and the New Federalism: State Budgeting in a Federalist Public Economy," in H. Rosen, ed., *Studies in State and Local Public Finance.* Chicago: Chicago University Press, 1986.

Duncombe, William and John Yinger, "An Analysis of Returns to Scale in Public Production, with an Application to Fire Protection," *Journal of Public Economics,* 1993, *52,* 49–72.

Easterbrook, Frank, "Antitrust and the Economics of Federalism," *Journal of Law and Economics,* 1983, *26,* 23–50.

Edwards, John Y., "Congestion Function Specification and the 'Publicness' of Local Public Goods," *Journal of Urban Economics,* 1990, *27,* 80–96.

Ellickson, Robert, "Public Property Rights: Vicarious Intergovernmental Rights and Liabilities as a Technique for Correcting Intergovernmental Spillovers," in D. L. Rubinfeld (ed.) *Essays on the Law and Economics of Local Governments.* Washington, D.C.: Urban Institute, 1979.

Feldstein, Martin and M. Vaillant, "Can State Taxes Redistribute Income?" National Bureau of Economic Research, Working Paper no. 4785, 1994.

Ferejohn, John, "Congress and Redistribution," in A. Schick (ed.) *Making Economic Policy in Congress.* Washington, D.C.: AEI, 1983, 131–57.

Fitts, Michael and Robert P. Inman, "Controlling Congress: Presidential Influence in Domestic Fiscal Policy," *Georgetown Law Journal,* 1992, *80,* 1737–85.

Frug, Gerald, "The City as a Legal Concept," *Harvard Law Review,* 1980, *93,* 1059–1154.

Garrett, Geoffrey and George Tsebelis, "An

Institutional Critique of Intergovernmentalism," *International Organization*, 1996, *50*, 269–99.

Gilligan, Thomas and John Matsusaka, "Deviations for Constituent Interests: The Role of Legislative Structure and Political Parties in the States," *Economic Inquiry*, 1995, *33*, 383–401.

Gonzales, R. A., T. S. Means, and Steven L. Mehay, "Empirical Test of the Samuelsonian Publicness Parameter: Has the Right Hypothesis Been Tested?" *Public Choice*, 1993, *77*, 523–34.

Gramlich, Edward M., "Reforming U.S. Fiscal Arrangements," in J. M. Quigley and D. L. Rubinfeld, eds., *American Domestic Priorities*. Berkeley, U. of California Press, 1985.

Gramlich, Edward M., "Subnational Fiscal Policy," *Perspectives on Local Public Finance and Public Policy*, 1987, *3*, 3–27.

Gramlich, Edward and Daniel L. Rubinfeld, "Micro-estimates of Public Spending Demand Functions and Tests of the Tiebout and Median Voter Hypotheses," *Journal of Political Economy*, 1982, *90*, 536–60.

Grossman, Gene and Elhanan Helpman, "Protection for Sale," *American Economic Review*, 1994, *84*, 833–50.

Hanushek, Eric, "The Economics of Schooling: Production and Efficiency in the Public Schools," *Journal of Economic Literature*, 1986, *24*, 1141–77.

Heller, Walter, *New Dimensions of Political Economy*. Cambridge: Harvard University Press, 1966.

Helms, L. Jay, "The Effect of State and Local Taxes on Economic Growth: A Time Series-Cross Section Approach," *Review of Economics and Statistics*, 1985, *67*, 574–82.

Hoffman, Elizabeth and Matthew Spitzer, "Entitlements, Rights, and Fairness: An Experimental Examination of Subjects' Concepts of Distributive Justice," *Journal of Legal Studies*, 1985, *14*, 259–97.

Inman, Robert P., "The Fiscal Performance of Local Governments: An Interpretative Review," in P. Mieszkowski and M. Straszheim (eds.) *Current Issues in Urban Economics*. Baltimore: Johns Hopkins University Press, 1979, 270–321.

Inman, Robert P., "The Economic Case for Limits to Government," *American Economic Association Papers and Proceedings*, 1982, *72*, 176–83.

Inman, Robert P., "Federal Assistance and Local Services in the United States: The Evolution of a New Federalist Fiscal Order," in H. Rosen, ed., *Fiscal Federalism*. Chicago, University of Chicago Press, 1988, 33–74.

Inman, Robert P., "Can Philadelphia Escape its Fiscal Crisis with a Tax Increase?" *Business Review of the Federal Reserve Bank of Philadelphia*, September-October 1992, pp. 5–20.

Inman, Robert P. and Michael A. Fitts, "Political Institutions and Fiscal Policy: Evidence from the U.S. Historical Record," *Journal of Law, Economics and Organization*, 1990, *6* (Special Issue), pp. 79–132.

Inman, Robert P. and Daniel L. Rubinfeld, "The Judicial Pursuit of Local Fiscal Equity," *Harvard Law Review*, 1979, *92*, 1662–1750.

Inman, Robert P. and Daniel L. Rubinfeld, "Can We Decentralize Our Unemployment Policies: Evidence from the United States," draft, 1994.

Inman, Robert P. and Daniel L. Rubinfeld, "Designing Tax Policies in Federalist Economies: An Overview," *Journal of Public Economics*, 1996a, *60*, 307–34.

Inman, Robert P. and Daniel L. Rubinfeld, "The Political Economy of Federalism," in Dennis Mueller, ed., *Perspectives on Public Choice*. New York: Cambridge University Press, 1996b.

Inman, Robert P. and Daniel L. Rubinfeld, "Making Sense of the Antitrust State Action Doctrine: Resolving the Tension between Political Participation and Economic Efficiency," *Texas Law Review*, 1997, *75*, 1203–99.

Krelove, Russell, "Efficient Tax Exporting," *Canadian Journal of Economics*, 1992, *25*, 145–55.

Kolstad, Charles and Frank Wolak, "Competition in Interregional Taxation: The Case of Western Coal," *Journal of Political Economy*, 1983, *91*, 443–60.

Laffont, Jean-Jacques, "Incentives and the Allocation of Public Goods," in A. J. Auerbach and M. Feldstein (eds.), *Handbook of Public Economics II*. New York: Elsevier Science Publishers, 1987.

LeGrand, Julian, "Fiscal Equity and Central Government Grants to Local Authorities," *Economic Journal*, 1975, *85*, 531–47.

Mailath, George and Andrew Postlewaite, "Asymmetric Information Bargaining Problems with Many Agents," *Review of Economic Studies*, 1990, *57*, 351–67.

McConnell, Michael, "Federalism: Evaluating the Founders' Design," *University of Chicago Law Review*, 1987, *54*, 1484–1512.

Musgrave, Richard A., "Merit Goods," in J. Eatwell, M. Milgate, and P. Newman, *The New Palgrave: A Dictionary of Economics*. 1987, *3*, 452–53.

Myers, Gordon, "Optimality, Free Mobility, and Regional Authority in a Federation," *Journal of Public Economics*, 1990, *43*, 107–21.

Myerson, Roger and M. Satterthwaite, "Efficient Mechanisms for Bilateral Trading," *Journal of Economic Theory*, 1983, *29*, 265–81.

Niou, Emerson, and Peter Ordeshook, "Universalism in Congress," *American Journal of Political Science*, 1985, *29*, 246–58.

Oates, Wallace, *Fiscal Federalism.* New York: Harcourt, Brace, Jovanovich, 1972.

Oates, Wallace, "Federalism and Government Finance," in J. M. Quigley and E. Smolensky, eds., *Modern Public Finance.* Cambridge: Harvard University Press, 1994.

Oates, Wallace and Robert Schwab, "Economic Competition among Jurisdictions: Efficiency Enhancing or Distortion Inducing?" *Journal of Public Economics*, 1986, *35*, 333–54.

Patterson, James, *The New Deal and the States.* Princeton, N.J.: Princeton University Press, 1969.

Persson, Torsten and Guido Tabellini, "Does Centralization Increase the Size of Government?" *European Economic Review*, 1994, *28*, 765–73.

Pauly, Mark, "Income Distribution as a Local Public Good," *Journal of Public Economics*, 1973, *2*, 35–58.

Perloff, Harvey S. and Richard P. Nathan, eds. *Revenue Sharing and the City.* Baltimore: Johns Hopkins Press, 1968.

Quigley, John M. and Daniel L. Rubinfeld, "Federalism and Reductions in the Federal Budget," *National Tax Journal*, 1996, *49*, 289–302.

Rakove, John, "The Phases of American Federalism," in M. Tushnet (ed.), *Comparative Constitutional Federalism: Europe and America.* New York: Greenwood Press, 1989, 1–19.

Rapaczynski, Andrzej, "From Sovereign to Process: The Jurisprudence of Federalism After Garcia," *Supreme Court Review*, 1985, 341–419.

Ribar, David and Mark Wilhelm, "The Demand for Welfare Generosity," Department of Economics, George Washington University, Department of Economics, 1996.

Rivlin, Alice, *Reviving the American Dream.* Washington, D.C.: The Brookings Institution, 1992.

Rubinfeld, Daniel L., "The Economics of the Public Sector", in A. J. Auerbach, and M. Feldstein (eds.), *Handbook of Public Economics II.* New York: Elsevier Science Publishers, 1987.

Scheiber, Harry, "The Condition of American Federalism: An Historian's View," Subcommittee on Intergovernmental Relations to the Committee on Governmental Operations, U.S. Senate, October 15, 1969.

Sutton, John, "Bargaining Experiments," *European Economic Review*, 1987, *31*, 272–84.

Tiebout, Charles, "A Pure Theory of Local Expenditures," *Journal of Political Economy*, 1956, *64*, 416–24.

Tullock, Gordon, "Federalism: Problems of Scale," *Public Choice*, 1969, *6*, 19–29.

U.S. House of Representatives, Committee on Ways and Means, *1996 Green Book: Background Material and Data on Programs Within Jurisdiction of the Committee on Ways and Means.* Washington, D.C.: U.S. Government Printing Office, 1996.

Wallis, John, "The Birth of the Old Federalism: Financing the New Deal: 1932–1940," *Journal of Economic History*, 1984, *44*, 139–59.

Weingast, Barry, "A Rational Choice Perspective on Congressional Norms," *American Journal of Political Science*, 1979, *23*, 245–62.

Weingast, Barry, "The Economic Role of Political Institutions: Market-Preserving Federalism and Economic Development," *The Journal of Law, Economics, and Organization*, 1995, *11*:11, 1–31.

Weingast, Barry and William Marshall, "The Industrial Organization of Congress," *Journal of Political Economy*, 1988, *96*, 132–63.

Weingast, Barry, Kenneth Shepsle, and C. Johnsen, "The Political Economy of Benefits and Costs: A Neoclassical Approach to Distributive Politics," *Journal of Political Economy*, 1981, *89*, 642–64.

Weitzman, Martin, "Prices vs. Quantities," *Review of Economic Studies*, 1974, *41*, 477–91.

Wittman, Donald, "Why Democracies Produce Efficient Results," *Journal of Political Economy*, 1989, *97*, 1395–1424.

F
Optimal Taxation and Fiscal Instruments and Intergovernmental Grants

[14]

ELSEVIER

Journal of Public Economics 60 (1996) 307–334

JOURNAL OF
PUBLIC
ECONOMICS

Designing tax policy in federalist economies: An overview

Robert P. Inman[a,b,*], Daniel L. Rubinfeld[c]

[a]*Finance Department, Wharton School, University of Pennsylvania, Philadelphia, PA 19104-6367, USA*
[b]*NBER, Cambridge, MA 02138, USA*
[c]*University of California, Berkeley, CA 94720, USA*

Abstract

The emerging economic federations of the European Union, Russia, and South Africa, along with the established federations in Australia, Canada, and the United States, confront the task of designing the institutions for federal fiscal policy. This paper reviews the literature on the design of tax policy in federalist economies. We conclude that taxation by lower level governments can lead to significant economic inefficiencies and inequities. The usual 'assignment' view of federalism recommends central government policies – for example, resident-based taxation or grants-in-aid – to correct these failures. These recommendations assume that the central government will act as a benevolent social planner. The 'political economy' view of federalism suggests that this assumption is in error and that additional federalist institutions must be considered. Alternative legislative structures and constitutional rules are considered.

Keywords: Fiscal federalism; Political economy; Tax assignment; Tax competition

JEL classification: H21; H71; H77; R51

1. Introduction

Current constitutional efforts to construct a new Russian federation, the emergence of a more open and economically integrated Europe through the

* Corresponding author.

308   *R.P. Inman, D.L. Rubinfeld / Journal of Public Economics 60 (1996) 307–334*

European Union, the drafting of a democratic constitution for South Africa, and more generally, a widespread disaffection with central government policy-making as 'the' solution to all economic inefficiencies and inequities, raise anew a longstanding question in public finance: How do we allocate responsibilities for economic policy among alternative levels of government? An important component of this federalist research agenda, and the focus of this review, is the allocation of taxing powers among the various levels of government.

Section 2 organizes, and hopefully clarifies, the new theoretical and empirical results on the design of tax systems for federalist public economies. When read separately, the many papers in this literature may seem to give conflicting advice. When taken together, however, the studies offer a consistent agenda for the design of a welfare-maximizing tax policy. Whether this agenda becomes social policy is another question, however. Section 3 argues that in one plausible model of democratic decision-making the efficient tax structure of Section 2 will be difficult to sustain. This important result extends the research agenda for the design of tax policy in federalist public economies. In addition to the design of tax policy, one must also consider the design of political institutions to implement the policy agenda. We suggest informal legislative structures using strong political parties and executive veto powers and formal constitutional rules assigning taxes and setting the number of states in the federation as possible institutional reforms. Section 4 provides a concluding comment.

2. Tax assignment in federalist economies: the economic arguments

In an elegant paper entitled 'An optimal taxation approach to fiscal federalism', Gordon (1983) clarifies what is required for the efficient and equitable performance of taxation in a two-tier – local and central – federalist public economy. His analysis, and our extensions of his model here to a richer political economic specification, provide the conceptual framework – the 'skeleton' – for organizing the body of the new theoretical and empirical literature on taxation in federalist economies.

2.1. Coordinated and decentralized tax policies

In the Gordon analysis, the federalist public economy consists of K non-overlapping 'state' jurisdictions and one central government. Residents reside in only one state, but they may purchase final goods and services and sell their factor inputs anywhere in the national economy.[1] Each citizen i owns factor inputs, denoted individually as x_{fk}^{il} for the amount of the fth factor sold in the kth state by the ith person residing in the lth state[2]. Factor f receives a pre-tax return of v_{fk} depending upon the state in which it is employed. Each citizen i buys goods and services, denoted as y_{jk}^{il} for the jth good bought in the kth state by the ith person residing in the lth state. Good or service j sells for a pre-tax price of p_{jk} depending on the state in which it is purchased.

State governments and the central government also hire factor inputs to produce public goods and services. The factor inputs are denoted b_{fk} for the aggregate amount of the fth factor hired by the kth state government. For simplicity, only state governments produce public goods. The central government could produce a public good in this model; it would do so within the boundaries of one or more of the states using the inputs b_{fk}. Since our focus is on the design of tax policy in federalist economies, we shall assume that each b_{fk} – and thus the level of public facilities – is exogenously given in each state.[3]

State k meets its revenue needs to finance its expenditures on factor inputs – $R_k = \Sigma_f b_{fk} \cdot v_{fk}$ – by using taxes on factors and on goods and services. State taxes may be resident-based or source-based. *Resident-based* taxes (also known as *destination-based* taxes) tax factors based on the owners' residence and tax goods and services by the consumers' residence. *Source-based* taxes (also known as *origin-based* taxes) tax factors where they are employed and tax goods and services where they are purchased. Source-based taxes are typically easier to administer and, for this reason, are often the more common form of lower government taxation. We shall consider, initially, the design of state taxation assuming source-based taxation only.[4]

Source-based state tax rates on factors are per-unit taxes levied at the uniform rate t_{fk} on factor f employed in state k. Factors of production therefore earn an after-tax return or wage of $w_{fk} = v_{fk} - t_{fk}$. Consumers of goods and services in state k pay a per-unit tax s_{jk} and face after-tax prices $q_{jk} = p_{jk} + s_{jk}$. Total tax revenues in state k will be

[1] 'States', as presented here, can be viewed as US states, Canadian provinces, German lander, European nations in the new European Union, the participating provinces and republics of the new Russian federation, or the provinces in the new Republic of South Africa. The analysis can be extended to a three-tier federalist economy.

[2] The notation is admittedly burdensome and we have tried whenever possible to match that used by Gordon (1983).

[3] This restrictive assumption precludes a feedback from tax policy to spending policy. Other studies of competitive tax policy have studied this interaction specifically; see footnote 7.

[4] Subsection 2.3 comments on how the results change with resident-based taxation.

310   R.P. Inman, D.L. Rubinfeld / Journal of Public Economics 60 (1996) 307–334

$$T_k = \sum_f x_{fk}^{**} \cdot t_{fk} + \sum_j y_{jk}^{**} \cdot s_{jk} + \sum_f b_{fk} \cdot t_{fk} \, .$$

The first asterisk represents the aggregation over all i persons residing in state l and the second asterisk represents the aggregation over all l states; thus, x_{fk}^{**} is the national use of factor f in state k. Similarly, y_{jk}^{**} is the national consumption of good j in state k. Note also that factors used in the public sector are taxed. Importantly, with source-based taxation, non-resident factor incomes and non-resident consumption can be taxed. State k is required to balance its budget. Thus, $R_k = T_k$, or

$$\sum_f b_{fk} \cdot v_{fk} = \sum_f x_{fk}^{**} \cdot t_{fk} + \sum_j y_{jk}^{**} \cdot s_{jk} + \sum_f b_{fk} \cdot t_{fk} \, ,$$

or

$$\sum_f x_{fk}^{**} \cdot t_{fk} + \sum_j y_{jk}^{**} \cdot s_{jk} - \sum_f b_{fk} \cdot w_{fk} \equiv 0 \, .$$

The social policy objective is to select the levels of each tax instrument in each state, t_{fk} and s_{jk}, so as to maximize society's aggregate social welfare function defined as

$$W = \sum_i \omega^i \sum_k n^{ik} V^{ik} \{ q_{**}, w_{**}, c^k(q_{**}, w_{**}); E^{ik}, b_{*k} \} \, , \tag{1}$$

where ω^i is the social welfare weight for people of type i, n^{ik} is the number of people of type i living in state k, and $V^{ik}(\cdot)$ is the indirect utility of the ith person in the kth state. Utility in turn depends upon the vectors of after-tax prices for commodities (q_{**}) and factors (w_{**}), a congestion parameter c^k unique to state k, which itself depends upon prices (since prices determine the location of residents and factors), and exogenous factor endowments (E^{ik}) and the vector of exogenous public sector facilities (b_{*k}) provided in state k.

The chosen tax rates must be sufficient to pay for the exogenously given public sector factor inputs, specified by the aggregate budget constraint:

$$\sum_k \left[\sum_f x_{fk}^{**} \cdot t_{fk} + \sum_j y_{jk}^{**} \cdot s_{jk} - \sum_f b_{fk} \cdot w_{fk} \right] \equiv 0 \, . \tag{2}$$

This specification of the budget constraint allows for cross-state redistribution of tax revenues; excessive revenues can be raised in one state to cover shortfalls in another via centrally administered grants-in-aid.

The central planner's policy instruments are the tax rates t_{fk} and s_{jk}, some of which may be less than zero if grants exceed taxation. The rates t_{fk} and s_{jk} are chosen to maximize Eq. (1) subject to the revenue constraint in Eq. (2). Table 1 summarizes the first-order conditions which must be satisfied if the central planner is to maximize social welfare; Gordon (1983, appendix)

R.P. Inman, D.L. Rubinfeld / Journal of Public Economics 60 (1996) 307–334   311

Table 1
Taxation of outputs and inputs in a federalist economy

Direct (1)	Distribution (2)	Congestion (3)	Tax Revenue (4)	Public costs (5)	Terms of trade (6)
	Centralized planning				

For $\tau_{jl} = s_{jl}$
$(\mu - \theta) y_{jl}^{**}$
For $\tau_{jl} = t_{jl}$
$(\mu - \theta) x_{jl}^{**}$

$$+ \sum_k \sum_i \left\{ d\theta^{ik} \frac{\partial I^{ik}}{\partial \tau_{jl}} \right\} + \sum_k \frac{\partial C^k}{\partial \tau_{jl}} + \mu \sum_k \frac{\partial T^k}{\partial \tau_{jl}} - \mu \sum_k \frac{\partial R^k}{\partial \tau_{jl}} + \theta \sum_k \frac{\partial \Pi^k}{\partial \tau_{jl}} = 0$$

Decentralized competition

For $\tau_{jl} = s_{jl}$
$\{\mu^l - \theta^l (\Sigma_{i \in P} \, n^{il} y_{jl}^{il} / y_{jl}^{**})\} y_{jl}^{**}$
For $\tau_{jl} = t_{jl}^{**}$
$\{\mu^l - \theta^l (\Sigma_{i \in P} \, n^{il} x_{jl}^{il} / x_{jl}^{**})\} x_{jl}^{**}$

$$+ \sum_{i \in P} \left\{ d\theta^{il} \frac{\partial I^{il}}{\partial \tau_{jl}} \right\} + \frac{\partial C^l}{\partial \tau_{jl}} + \mu^l \frac{\partial T^l}{\partial \tau_{jl}} - \mu^l \frac{\partial R^l}{\partial \tau_{jl}} + \theta^l \frac{\partial \Pi^l}{\partial \tau_{jl}} = 0$$

presents the derivation. There are six distinct effects on social welfare because of changes in state tax rates.

Term (1) *The Direct Revenue Effect*: Small changes in either the per-unit state tax rate on consumption – denoted by the rate $\tau_{jl} = s_{jl}$ – or the per-unit state tax rate on a factor – denoted by the rate $\tau_{jl} = t_{jl}$ – will raise revenues of y_{jl}^{**} and x_{jl}^{**}, respectively, in state l and improve social welfare by $(\mu - \theta) y_{jl}^{**}$ and by $(\mu - \theta) x_{jl}^{**}$, respectively. The additional revenue of y_{jl}^{**} and x_{jl}^{**} creates a social marginal benefit of μ dollars when allocated to the public sector and imposes a social marginal burden of θ when taken from the private economy.[5] When social marginal benefits exceed social marginal costs ($\mu > \theta$), then increasing a state tax rate adds to social welfare.

Term (2) *The Distributional Effect*: Changes in state taxes may change factor and commodity prices throughout the economy and thus the real incomes (I^{ik}) of citizens. The resulting changes in income are weighted by $d\theta^{ik}$, the difference between the social marginal utility of a private dollar given to each citizen and the social value of that dollar when given to the economy's 'average' citizen: $d\theta^{ik} = \omega^i \alpha^{ik} - \theta$, where ω^i is the social welfare weight for people of type i, α^{ik} is the private marginal utility of income for

---

[5] Formally, μ is the value of the Lagrange multiplier for the aggregate revenue constraint in Eq. (2); μ measures the gain in social welfare when an additional dollar of public revenues are raised. Formally, $\theta = \Sigma_k \Sigma_i [(n^{ik} \omega^i \alpha^{ik} / N)]$, where α^{ik} is the private marginal utility of income for the ith person in the kth state and N is the total population in all states; θ can be interpreted as the socially weighted value of a dollar to the average citizen in the entire economy when that dollar remains in the private economy for the consumption of goods and services.

312   *R.P. Inman, D.L. Rubinfeld / Journal of Public Economics 60 (1996) 307–334*

the ith person in the kth state, and θ is the social value of that dollar given to the average citizen in society. For lower income households and households in more congested states, $d\theta^{ik} > 0$ is likely, while for upper income households and households in less congested states, $d\theta^{ik} < 0$. Thus, changes in state taxes that increase factor returns and reduce commodity prices for lower income households and households in more congested states will be favored by the distribution effect.

Term (3) *The Congestion Effect*: Increases in one state's tax may drive businesses and households from that state to other states. The state that loses businesses and residents may now have less crowded streets, less polluted air, and easier access to public facilities. Those citizens who remain are better off. Residents of the states that receive migrant firms and households will experience increased congestion, and suffer a decline in welfare. In state k,

$$\partial C^k / \partial \tau_{jl} = \sum_i n^{ik} \omega^i (\partial V^{ik} / \partial c^k)(\partial c^k / \partial \tau_{jl}),$$

where C^k is total congestion.

Term (4) *The Indirect Revenue Effect*: Increases in a state tax rate alter private sector consumption and factor use. These changes, when multiplied by existing tax rates, mean an additional, but indirect, change in public revenues. The social value of an extra dollar of public revenues, μ, is then multiplied by this indirect change in revenues to define the net effect on social welfare. The indirect effect on tax revenues in state k is

$$\partial T^k / \partial \tau_{jl} = \sum_k \left[\sum_f (\partial x_{fk}^{**} / \partial \tau_{jl}) \cdot t_{fk} + \sum_r (\partial y_{rk}^{**} / \partial \tau_{jl}) \cdot s_{rk} \right].$$

Term (5) *The Indirect Public Cost Effect*: As factor prices change with changes in state tax rates, governments must pay the new factor prices. These factor price changes provide a windfall gain (if costs fall) or a windfall loss (if costs rise), which is evaluated at the social value of a public dollar, μ. The indirect effect on public sector costs in state k (R^k) is

$$\partial R^k / \partial \tau_{jl} = \sum_k \left[\sum_f (\partial w_{fk} / \partial \tau_{jl}) \cdot b_{fk} \right].$$

Term (6) *The Terms of Trade Effect*: State tax rates may alter aggregate pre-tax incomes earned in communities, when rates change pre-tax prices on goods sold by firms and pre-tax prices on factors hired. These aggregate income changes are evaluated at the average social marginal utility of private income, θ. However, when aggregated over all private firms in this competitive economy this term must equal zero, as firms earn zero excess profits before and after tax rate changes. What remains in the competitive

R.P. Inman, D.L. Rubinfeld / Journal of Public Economics 60 (1996) 307–334   313

economy is a terms of trade effect for the exogenous public factors employed in producing public services:

$$\partial \Pi^k / \partial \tau_{jl} = \theta \sum_k \left[\sum_f (\partial w_{fk} / \partial \tau_{jl}) \cdot b_{fk} \right].$$

Against this standard of a fully planned federalist economy stands the actual performance of the decentralized federalist public economy. In this economy, households and factors are mobile across jurisdictions, and state governments are allowed to set their own tax rates, constrained only by the requirements that states balance their budgets and satisfy the re-election demands of local constituents. The budget constraint for a typical state l requires that

$$\sum_f x_{fl}^{**} \cdot t_{fl} + \sum_j y_{jl}^{**} \cdot s_{jl} - \sum_f b_{fl} \cdot w_{fl} \equiv 0. \tag{3}$$

State politics demands that the state l's political objective function be maximized:

$$\mathscr{P}^l = \sum_i \rho^{il} n^{il} V^{il} \{ q_{**}, w_{**}, c^l(q_{**}, w_{**}); E^{il}, b_{\cdot l} \}, \tag{4}$$

where ρ^{il} is the political weight for group i in state l's politics.[6] In the simplest case of median voter politics, $\rho^{il} = 1$ for the median voter and all other political weights are zero. More complicated coalition politics may involve several non-zero values of ρ^{il}; see Hettich and Winer (1988).

Maximizing the political objective function $\mathscr{P}^l$ subject to state l's budget constraint defines state l's preferred tax rates. The state is only allowed to optimize over its own tax rates, however: $\tau_{jl} = s_{jl}$ for taxes on factors employed in state l and $\tau_{jl} = t_{jl}$ for goods consumed in state l. In Gordon (1983, p. 577) each state is assumed myopic when setting its preferred tax rates, taking as given all other states' tax rates and ignoring the effects of its own tax policies on the relocation of people across jurisdictions.[7] We assume that an equilibrium in this competitive federalist economy exists; see Mintz

---

[6] Gordon (1983, p. 577) assumes all states weight each household type identically in the state objective function – that is, $\rho^{il} = \rho^i$ across all l. As Gordon acknowledges, such an assumption removes variation in local politics from consideration in federalist policy.

[7] Gordon does allow for mobile households and the equal utility constraint when solving the central planner's problem (see Gordon, 1983, appendix), but he ignores the constraint when solving the decentralized game of inter-jurisdictional fiscal competition. Introducing this constraint into a model of inter-jurisdictional fiscal competition can have significant consequences for the conclusions; see Krelove (1992b) and Myers (1990) and the discussion below in sub-section 2.4.

314   *R.P. Inman, D.L. Rubinfeld / Journal of Public Economics 60 (1996) 307–334*

and Tulkens (1986) and Kanbur and Keen (1993).[8] If so, the first-order conditions of Table 1 for the decentralized competitive economy define each state's locally preferred tax rates.

In this decentralized economy each individual state's optimizing strategy ignores the allocative consequences of its own tax rate on neighboring states and on residents outside its decisive political coalition ($\rho^{il} \equiv 0$). A comparison of the first-order conditions in Table 1 reveals that this competitive fiscal economy is unlikely to achieve the optimal, centrally planned structure of state tax rates. Tax exportation (Term 1), politically determined distribution policies (Term 2), 'not-in-my-backyard' or NIMBY congestion effects (Term 3), competitive tax spillovers on revenues (Term 4) and public goods costs (Term 5), and 'beggar-thy-neighbor' income effects (Term 6), are all potential sources of tax inefficiency or inequity in decentralized federalist economies.

Term 1 reveals a tax subsidy effect in the decentralized case. Here μ^l is the marginal value of a dollar to the politically decisive coalition in state l while θ^l is the marginal cost of a dollar raised from the members of that decisive coalition. Importantly, the decisive coalition of P residents pays only a fraction $-(\sum_{i \in P} n^{il} y_{jl}^{il} / y_{jl}^{**})$ for a tax on good j consumed in state l and $(\sum_{i \in P} n^{il} x_{jl}^{il} / x_{jl}^{**})$ for a tax on factor j employed in state l – of the marginal burdens associated with each dollar of revenues raised. This implicit subsidy from non-residents and the politically disenfranchised to members of the decisive coalition is known as 'tax exporting'. The subsidy is likely to encourage the inefficient over-use of the subsidized tax; see Arnott and Grieson (1981) generally, McLure and Mieszkowski (1983) for an application to natural resource taxation, and Mintz and Tulkens (1996) for an application to capital taxation.

Competitive state taxation may also lead to vertical tax inequities (Term 2). Politics within a state create a regressive bias to local tax structures when factors are mobile. In particular, mobile, upper income households may threaten to exit any state unless local taxes approximate benefit taxation. The threat of exit acts as a constraint on within-state redistribution.

State taxes can also be used to discourage the location of unpleasant congestion activities, where the taxing state ignores the congestion effects of such taxes on the welfare of residents in other states (Term 3). Such 'not-in-my-backyard' or NIMBY taxation can lead to the over-taxation of socially beneficial, but locally noxious activities.

The indirect effects of state l's taxation can have significant effects on the budgets of other states that state l ignores; compare Terms 4 and Terms 5.

---

[8] Wildasin (1988) has shown that competitive outcomes can be different if states compete via public goods provision rather than tax rates. Tax rate competition turns out to be the dominant strategy for competitive states, however; see Wildasin (1991).

R.P. Inman, D.L. Rubinfeld / Journal of Public Economics 60 (1996) 307–334   315

Here the welfare benefits of taxation in state l are likely to flow outside the taxing state to non-residents. As state l raises its taxes on goods or factors, consumption and factors in that state may migrate outside the state. This migration raises tax revenues (Term 4) and lowers the costs of buying public sector inputs (Term 5) in the other, recipient states. Capital taxation is the usual example; see Wilson (1986), Wildasin (1989), and Gordon (1992). This positive revenue windfall for the rest of the nation is ignored by the decisive coalition in state l when setting the state's tax policy. Thus, taxes with mobile tax bases will typically be underutilized in competitive federalist economies.[9]

Finally, the terms of trade effects (Term 6) of state taxation can be important. Typically, this means very low tax rates – perhaps even subsidies – for mobile inputs that raise factor returns to the state's decisive coalition and that lower the prices of the goods that the members of the coalition consume. These 'beggar-thy-neighbor' fiscal incentives for valued private inputs are typically socially inefficient; see Oates and Schwab (1988).

One decentralized federalist economy will satisfy the conditions for a socially optimal allocation, however. This is the Tiebout (1956) economy. The Tiebout economy's use of a residential head tax or its equivalent (see Hamilton, 1975) to pay for public facilities ensures that there will be no tax spillovers. Terms 2–6 in Table 1 are zero for this tax. Residential head taxes also prevent cross-community tax exporting. Since households are freely mobile and states are elastically supplied, there can be no within-community tax-exporting. Thus, the direct effects of taxation in the decentralized case (Term 1) no longer involve tax subsidies. Finally, interstate competition for residents ensures that the marginal benefits (μ') of a dollar of revenue must equal its marginal cost (θ') in each state. Otherwise, residents will exit. A competitive Tiebout economy therefore achieves tax efficiency.

2.2. Are tax inefficiencies and inequities economically important?

The prospects for tax inefficiencies and inequities in a system of decentralized public finance turn fundamentally upon the mobility of consumption and factors of production across state borders. Are either or both mobile across borders? The empirical evidence says *yes*. Geographic and social

[9] In this paper, we are concerned with the influence of tax competition on the optimal structure of taxation, and thus hold fixed the level of government spending. Here tax competition leads to too little use of the tax with positive spillovers. Other papers in the tax competition literature – e.g. Zodrow and Mieszkowski (1986) or Wilson (1986) – allow for only one tax, but permit endogenous government spending. In those models, tax competition leads to too little taxation, which translates into too little spending relative to the social optimum. The two class of models are exploring different consequences of the same problem.

316   *R.P. Inman, D.L. Rubinfeld / Journal of Public Economics 60 (1996) 307–334*

impediments to relocation appear to give way, even to modest economic incentives.

Empirical analysis shows that cross-border shopping is common and elastic with respect to even small consumption tax differentials – see, for example, Wales (1968). This sensitivity of consumption with respect to tax rates is likely to increase with the spread of video and mail-order shopping. Further, the evidence both for the United States (Gyourko and Tracy, 1989, and Tretz et al., 1993) and Canada (Day, 1992) makes clear that labor is mobile even across large regions – states and provinces – in response to tax-related changes in local goods prices and real wages. Finally, though the evidence on the sensitivity of capital's mobility in response to tax rates is somewhat less decisive, recent studies with improved measures of tax rates find that capital does relocate to tax-favored locations, both within a given country (see Papke, 1991, and Bartik, 1991, ch. 2, for a survey), and internationally (Baxter and Crucini, 1993).

With mobile consumption and factors, decentralized tax inefficiencies and inequities are possible. Are they economically important? The answer turns crucially on the tax involved.

For consumption taxes, tax exporting (Term 1) is significant. Internationally, OPEC nations have historically earned significant rents from implicitly taxing exported oil; other international cartels have taxed copper and bauxite; see Pindyck (1978). Even when the cartel breaks down, but there are only a few producers, taxing exports can still mean significant fiscal transfers from non-residents to the taxing states; see, for example, Kolstad and Wolak's (1983, 1985) studies of the US market for Western Coal. Tax-exporting of consumption taxes from the politically decisive coalition to the disenfranchised within a city or state also occurs. Studies of state and local government fiscal choice show that the decisive median voter enjoys a transfer from the taxation of the housing stock of other residents leading to increased taxation of housing as the value of the housing stock increase; see Rubinfeld (1987).

In contrast, tax exporting (Term 1) is likely to be less important for factor taxes. When capital and labor owned by non-residents are mobile, it will be very difficult to export capital and labor taxes to non-residents. For evidence that labor taxation induces work relocations in open economies, see Grieson (1980), Inman (1992), and Feldstein and Vaillant (1994). For evidence that capital taxation induces capital mobility in open economies, see Papke (1991) and Feldstein (1994). In the case of capital taxation, there may be some shifting after capital is in place; see Ladd's (1975) study of local residential taxation of commercial–industrial property. In the long run, however, exporting of factor taxation will be limited to locally fixed factors of production such as land and natural resources.

A bias towards regressive tax structures in decentralized public economies

(Term 2) is well documented. To retain mobile middle and upper income households, cities resort to regressive taxes whose burdens fall on the less mobile poor and elderly; see Inman and Rubinfeld (1979) for a review of the US city evidence. Inman (1989) found that large US cities adjusted local tax structures by increasing the locally regressive property tax and reducing the locally proportional sales tax in response to central government efforts in the 1986 Tax Reform Act to make the overall burden of local and state taxation less regressive. Chernick (1992) and Metcalf (1993) studying states' responses to the federal efforts in the 1986 Tax Reform to improve state tax equity also found a return to a regressive bias in state taxation. For further evidence that the large US states are constrained in their efforts to redistribute income across households because of labor mobility, see Feldstein and Vaillant (1994).

'Not-in-my-backyard', or NIMBY, taxation (Term 3) is common in the United States, seen most often as an absolute prohibition (infinite tax) on the location of the noxious activity.[10] Communities that do accept noxious waste activities typically charge processing fees that exceed the long-run average costs of safely handling and storing waste.

Tax spillovers (Terms 4 and 5) and terms-of-trade effects (Term 6) are not likely to be a serious problem for consumption taxes, with one possible exception. When only a few states supply a good (e.g. beach vacations) then a tax on that good may affect the demand for goods (surfboards) and services (mountain vacations) supplied by firms in other states.

Tax spillovers and terms-of-trade effects are important for factor taxes, however. Wassmer (1993) documents the extensive use of tax subsidies in US metropolitan areas. Computable general equilibrium (CGE) tax models for regional economies have shown tax spillovers with factor taxation to be very important. Kimbell and Harrison (1984) and Jones and Whalley (1988, table 7) show for plausible parameterizations of a federalist economy that tax increases on capital in one state or province will lead to an economically significant relocation of capital and subsequent changes in factor and goods prices in the other regions.[11] The CGE models of Morgan and Mutti show that such price effects can translate into significant out-of-state revenue effects (Term 4) and significant within-state terms-of-trade income gains (Term 6). In Mutti et al. (1989, tables 3 and 4) a 1% increase in a region's tax on business capital leads to a significant outmigration of regional capital,

---

[10] See 'Coping in the age of NIMBY', *New York Times*, Sunday, 10 June, 1988, Section 3, p. 1.

[11] In Kimbell and Harrison (1984) an increase in the tax rate on the value of capital from 0.05 to 0.20 increases prices throughout the economy from 9% in the taxing state to 4% outside the taxing state. Jones and Whalley (1988) compute the income-equivalent welfare effects on all provinces in Canada of lowering one region's taxes (Ontario); again, the effects are economically significant.

318	*R.P. Inman, D.L. Rubinfeld / Journal of Public Economics 60 (1996) 307–334*

which raises capital tax revenues elsewhere in the US regional economy. In Morgan et al. (1989, table 4) US regions that can unilaterally substitute a lump-sum tax for their existing taxes on the income of mobile labor – rates ranging from 0.034 to 0.056 – and mobile capital – rates ranging from 0.04 to 0.53 – can increase regional residents' incomes by 6–10%.[12] Finally, Helms' (1985) econometric study of state income growth using a sample of 48 US states reaches similar conclusions as the CGE simulations. In Helm's work a 2.33% increase in the property tax used to finance redistributive services reduces state incomes by 1.5% in the long run.

Current empirical evidence lends support to the conclusion that tax exporting, regressivity, NIMBY taxation, tax spillovers, and beggar-thy-neighbor tax competition are each important in decentralized public economies. To correct the resulting tax inefficiencies and inequities, central government fiscal policies may be in order.

2.3. Designing central government policies

Given the potential importance of tax inefficiencies and inequities in decentralized public economies, it is natural to turn to central government policies for remedies. Policies should be designed so that fiscally competitive state governments will internalize all relevant fiscal externalities when selecting state tax rates. Two alternative central government policy strategies are considered here: the regulation of state tax bases[13] or the use of grants-in-aid as fiscal incentives to alter state tax choices.

(1) *Regulation*. A central government regulatory policy, which requires all state taxes to be resident-based – or destination – taxes, rather than source-

[12] While such tax spillover and terms-of-trade effects are hard to ignore, it should be noted that all CGE estimates were derived in federalist economies with only a few states or regions. Most theoretical models of fiscal competition suggest that the magnitude of spillovers in individual states declines as the number of competing states increases. When many states absorb the exit of consumption or factors from the taxing state, the effects on each of the absorbing economies will tend to zero. It would be instructive to know how sensitive the CGE results of significant spillovers are to increasing the number of competing states.

[13] An alternative 'tax harmonization' strategy, not considered here, is to regulate state tax rates at a common rate. Harmonization has been discussed extensively with respect to the European Union. The formal economic analysis of harmonization has been limited to the case of single taxes, however; either commodity taxes in Keen (1987), de Crombrugghe and Tulkens (1990), and Kanbur and Keen (1993), or capital taxes in Giovannini (1989). While a regulated increase in tax rates above the competitive outcomes is typically shown to be pareto improving, fully harmonized (or uniform) rates are not preferred; see Giovannini (1989) and Kanbur and Keen (1993). No studies have yet considered the harmonization of individual state tax rates when states have access to several taxes, the general case under review here. We conjecture, however, that in this general case, tax rate harmonization may be attractive when tax spillovers (Term 4) or beggar-thy-neighbor tax competition (Term 6) lead to inefficiently too low rates of taxation on a particular good or factor (e.g. capital).

R.P. Inman, D.L. Rubinfeld / Journal of Public Economics 60 (1996) 307–334   319

based – or origin – taxation, moves a significant way towards tax efficiency in decentralized public economies. With resident-based taxation, factors and consumption can only be taxed by the state of residence of the owner or consumer.

With a complete resident-based tax system, the tax inefficiencies from tax exporting in the decentralized competitive economy (Term 1 inefficiencies) are curtailed. Here, the decisive coalition's share of local taxation becomes

$$\left(\sum_l \sum_{i \in P} n^{il} y_{jl}^{il} / y_{j\bullet}^{*l} \right)$$

for a tax on good j consumed everywhere by the residents of state *l*, and

$$\left(\sum_l \sum_{i \in P} n^{il} x_{jl}^{il} / x_{j\bullet}^{*l} \right)$$

for a tax on factor *j* employed everywhere by the residents of state *l*, where $y_{j\bullet}^{*l}$ and $x_{j\bullet}^{*l}$ (aggregate consumption (employment) of the *j*th good (factor) in all (*) states by all (*) residents in the *l*th state) is the state's aggregate tax base with complete resident-based taxes. Resident-based taxation removes the implicit tax subsidy from non-residents. Further, in the case where all residents of state *l* are part of the decisive political coalition, then

$$\sum_l \sum_{i \in P} n^{il} y_{jl}^{il} = \sum_l \sum_i n^{il} y_{jl}^{il} = y_{j\bullet}^{*l} \, ,$$

and similarly so for factor taxation. Now all tax exporting is removed. Thus, the subsidized incentive to overuse a state tax – the problem with source-based taxation – is controlled with resident-based taxation. NIMBY tax competition (Term 3 inefficiencies) are also constrained with resident-based taxation; taxing noxious factors of production is precluded unless owned by residents. Further, tax competition (Terms 4 and 5 inefficiencies) or beggar-thy-neighbor tax competition (Term 6) are also likely to be curtailed with resident-based taxation since mobile capital, the most likely factor affected by tax competition and/or tax subsidies, is uniformly taxed across locations under the residency principle.

The administration of a complete resident-based tax system may be difficult, however. It requires the central government to trace all out-of-state transactions. For consumption taxes, this requires either full border controls or the honest reporting of out-of-state consumption. This seems likely only for those goods that require registration with the resident's home state – for example, autos. Taxation of factors of production using resident-based taxes seems more promising, but again, only if the central government can successfully monitor transactions. Tax policies that allow states to 'piggy-back' a state-chosen tax rate onto a central government wage or capital income tax are administratively feasible and seem the most promising

320　　R.P. Inman, D.L. Rubinfeld / Journal of Public Economics 60 (1996) 307–334

approach to resident-based taxation. Piggy-backing on to a national personal income tax is straightforward and currently done by several US states. Giovannini and Hines (1991) outline how such a tax system might work for the more difficult case of capital taxation.[14]

What a resident-based tax system does not resolve is the regressive bias (Term 2) of local taxation. Additional regulatory instruments are required. For example, in the United States, requiring the full market value assessment of property would remove regressive assessment bias and be a significant step towards a proportional local property tax; see Inman and Rubinfeld (1979). More generally, the central government could regulate the rate structures as well as the tax base of local taxation. This is most easily accomplished by limiting state and local taxation to 'piggy-backing' on the central tax structure. Here, the state selects a uniform tax rate, which is simply added to the residents' central government tax rate.

(2) *Grants-in-aid*. When resident-based taxation is not administratively or politically feasible – as may well be the case in newly emerging federalist economies – then centrally allocated grants-in-aid may be used to overcome the inefficiencies and inequities of decentralized taxation. For example, the propensity to overuse taxes that permit significant tax exportation (Term 1 inefficiencies) can be controlled by a central government that taxes the exported good at the point of production (a source-based tax) and shares the proceeds via grants-in-aid, which are allocatively neutral; equal lump-sum grants per person across all states is one alternative. If states retain the right to use source-based taxation, then equalizing grants giving more aid to the relatively tax-poor states and 'taxing' (negative aid) the relatively tax-rich states will be needed; see Boadway and Flatters (1982). In effect, such aid formulae centralize source-based taxation.

Tax inequities (Term 2) can also be controlled by grants-in-aid. When the cause of the inequity is a local political basis against low income residents, then a central government grant to governments that penalizes the use of regressive taxes (e.g. consumption taxes on necessities such as housing) and subsidizes the use of progressive taxes (e.g. factor taxes on residents' capital

---

[14] If a complete resident-based system is too difficult to administer, then a partial resident-based tax might still be considered, in which taxation is based on residents' earnings and consumption only within their home states. In this case, the relevant aggregate tax base is y_{jl}^{*l} and x_{jl}^{*l} (aggregate consumption (employment) of the jth good (factor) in the lth state by all ($*$) residents in the lth state). Of course, there will be strong incentives to shelter income and consumption by working, investing, and living outside one's state of legal residence. A partial residence-based tax system will solve the problem of tax exportation, but it is likely to significantly constrain the ability of small states, or states with limited natural economic advantages, to raise revenues. If legal residents can still use state services – e.g. free public schools or universities for their children – then a budget imbalance may result.

income) might be favored. Such incentives were included as part of the US General Revenue Sharing Program; see Reischauer (1975).[15]

Central government grants policies can also be used to mute the adverse congestion effects (Term 3 inefficiencies) from the relocation of economic activity. Taxes in one state may drive consumers and factors to another, reducing benefits there from common property resources (public facilities, air quality, roadways). The central government can correct this inefficiency either by charging the relocating consumers or factors directly for the congestion they create through a location-specific central government tax, or by taxing the decisive coalition in the original state through a 'negative' grant equal to the aggregate costs of the tax-induced congestion imposed upon its neighboring states;[16] see Wildasin (1985).

To control the adverse effects of tax competition, the revenue and cost-saving fiscal benefits (Term 4 and 5 inefficiencies) created for neighboring states from a state's taxation of mobile consumption and factors should be rewarded by central government grants-in-aid. This can be done through the imposition of a source-based central government tax on the mobile good or factor, which in turn finances a locationally neutral grants-in-aid; see Wildasin (1989) and, more generally, Krelove (1992a). Rivlin (1992, ch. 8) gives such policies a central place in her plan to revive the fiscal role of US states.

Finally, state tax policies designed to enhance local private incomes (Term 6 inefficiencies) through beggar-thy-neighbor fiscal incentives for factor and consumption relocations are likely to lead to state tax rates that are inefficiently too low relative to the planned tax allocation. Low state taxes on capital and on tourist and convention centers are two examples. As with tax competition, the grants solution is for the central government to tax the 'attractive' factor or good at its source and to then redistribute the proceeds in a locationally neutral fashion to the states.

Both the regulation of the tax base and the payment of grants-in-aid can be used by the central government to correct the tax inefficiencies and inequities in decentralized federalist economies. From an economic perspec-

---

[15] The current US federal tax code provides a subsidy to state taxation of housing and income; the Tax Reform Act of 1986 recently dropped its subsidy of sales taxation. The rate of subsidy is the taxpayer's federal income tax rate and is limited to only those who itemize their deductions; typically, middle and upper income households. By the arguments here, middle and upper income households are the appropriate target group, for they constitute the likely decisive coalition in state politics. Because of the likely regressive bias when localities assess property for taxation, tax equity requires that the subsidy should be limited to just income taxation, however.

[16] See, for example, 'Grants stir interest in nuclear waste site', *New York Times*, Thursday, 9 January 1992, p. A10.

322   R.P. Inman, D.L. Rubinfeld / Journal of Public Economics 60 (1996) 307–334

tive, the choice of one strategy over the other ultimately turns on the transactions costs of administering the policies. The regulatory strategy of resident-based taxation requires the central government to trace economic transactions to individual taxpayers. This will require a developed system of personal income and consumption records by the central government. Less expensive perhaps – particularly so for developing economies – would be the administration of grants-in-aid strategies. The grants strategy requires centrally collected source-based taxes on firms and then grants payments to state and local governments. In developing countries, accounting records may be more complete and enforcement problems less severe for firms and governments than for households.

2.4. Are central government policies really needed?

Recent papers by Krelove (1992b) and Myers (1990) (hereafter KM) raise a provocative challenge to the prevailing view articulated above that central government intervention is required to achieve tax efficiency in decentralized federalist economies.[17] In a decentralized public goods economy with competing regions, each with access to a non-resident tax base, an efficient tax (and expenditure) policy will result *if* each region's government: (i) is allowed to use a tax on land rents (or rents from another fixed factor), (ii) sets those tax rates to maximize residents' welfare, and (iii) explicitly recognizes that resident welfare must equal that offered to the resident in competitive, neighboring regions. In this federalist economy, no central government policy intervention is needed.

How does the federalist economy in KM differ from that in Gordon? Three assumptions are crucial. First, in the KM economy all households have identical preferences and endowments. Gordon allows for household preferences and endowments to differ. Second, local taxes in the KM economy are limited to head taxes (the resident-based tax) and taxes on rents (the source-based tax), which are assumed sufficient to pay for public

---

[17] Krelove's and Myers' papers are addressing the same substantive issue of designing financing systems for local public goods when labor is mobile between competing localities. Krelove's analysis describes the problem as one of 'tax exporting', where a portion of a region's tax falls upon non-resident landowners, while Myers' describes the same problem as one of 'fiscal externalities'. Krelove's shows that under appropriate assumptions (see above) 'tax exporting' is not a problem at all; in fact, tax exporting is necessary for fiscal efficiency. Using the same assumptions, Myers shows that locally chosen intergovernmental transfers financed by local taxes will also achieve the efficient financing of local public goods. A comparison of Myers' locally financed grants and Krelove's taxation of non-residents reveals that the two policy instruments are identical. Thus, while the two papers seem to be addressing two separate problems, they in fact address the same question with the same model and the same policy instrument. They reach the same important, and provocative, conclusion: under conditions (i)–(iii) listed below, central governments are not needed for efficient local finance.

goods expenditures. In contrast, Gordon also allows for taxes on goods with elastic demands and on factors with elastic supplies. Third, and most crucially, KM's local governments explicitly recognize that mobile residents in their locality cannot be made better off than residents in other communities through local fiscal policy. Gordon's local governments, however, behave myopically and assume local residents' welfare can be improved at their neighbors' expense.

Were the KM model to simply assume identical households and to limit taxation to local head taxes we would be in a Tiebout public goods economy. Taxation, public goods provision, and the economic location of factors of production would be efficient and (by assumption) fair. Problems arise, however, because KM allow their local governments to use a tax on rents of a fixed factor and the rent-earning assets are owned in part by non-residents. The source-based taxation of rents leads to tax-exporting and thus a potential incentive to overuse this tax – what we have called Term 1 inefficiencies.[18]

KM's key additional assumption that local governments explicitly consider the effects of their fiscal decisions on relative household welfare across localities solves, perhaps surprisingly, the problem of Term 1 inefficiencies. When localities explicitly consider the effects of their fiscal decisions on relative household welfare, they introduce an additional constraint into their local decision to tax; namely, that household utilities are equalized across all citizens in all communities, or, more formally, that $V^{\cdot l} = V^{\cdot k}$ for the identical households in localities l and k. Intuitively, to see why the equal utility constraint removes Term 1 inefficiencies, note that a \$1 increase in rental taxation to fund public goods in community l initially costs residents an amount equal to their share of the ownership of the fixed factor – n^l/N in the simple case. They receive a tax-exporting subsidy of $1 - (n^l/N)$ dollars, which increases their utility by $[1 - (n^l/N)]\alpha$, where α is the private marginal utility of income. The equal utility constraint, however, cannot let this small advantage stand for the citizens in community l. The government in community l takes this fact into account when setting taxes on rents. Entry of new workers will bid down wages in l until the utility of residents in l falls by exactly $[1 - (n^l/N)]\alpha$; that is, until wages fall by the amount of the tax-exporting subsidy of $[1 - (n^l/N)]$. The true marginal cost of raising this last \$1 of rental taxation to the residents of community l is therefore n^l/N in

---

[18] Note that by assuming identical households, the KM model rules out Term 2 inequities. The only mobile factor of production is labor and, since all market goods are free of externalities and all government goods are purely public, labor imposes no congestion costs when it relocates; thus, there can be no Term 3 inefficiencies. Finally, KM rule out taxes on the income of the mobile factors of production or on consumption; thus, there can be no Terms 4, 5, or 6 inefficiencies. Tax exporting is, therefore, the only inefficiency at issue in the KM model.

324   R.P. Inman, D.L. Rubinfeld / Journal of Public Economics 60 (1996) 307–334

direct tax costs plus $[1 - (n^l/N)]$ in reduced wages or $1 – and local governments know this! There is no incorrectly perceived tax-exporting to non-residents, and thus the efficient level of rental taxation obtains.[19] This is a striking conclusion, particularly in light of the discussion in Section 3 that central governments may themselves be inefficient when attempting to correct the failures of the local public economy.

We need to assess how close real federalist economies come to meeting the assumptions of the KM economy. Certainly, allowing local governments to consider the equilibrium effects of household relocations on resident welfare seems a reasonable extension of the Gordon model of local fiscal behavior, though one should test the empirical validity of this assumption against the alternative hypothesis of myopic local jurisdictions. If local politicians have short planning horizons, much depends on how quickly outsiders relocate into tax-exporting jurisdictions. More troubling is the restriction in the KM model to consider only identical households. Limiting the analysis to a single representative agent does more than just rule out (Term 2) tax inequities. It also means that when each local government considers the equal utility constraint $(V^{\cdot l} = V^{\cdot k})$, it does so for only one, politically decisive, type of resident. But if there are multiple types as in the Gordon economy, one community might consider only the welfare of residents of type $i = 1$, while another community considers only the welfare of residents of type $i = 2$, etc. The KM equilibrium will not, in general, be efficient in this case. Only if local governments (politically) weigh all consumer types identically when making local fiscal choices $(\rho^{il} = \rho^{ik}$ for all l and $k)$ will the KM conclusion remain; Krelove (1992b, p. 154). This seems unlikely. Finally, important to the KM conclusion is their assumption limiting local taxation to head taxes and rental taxes. In public goods economies, where all important factors of production including land are in elastic supply, there will be no rents to tax. Without rental taxation, head taxes must fully finance local public goods. This is, of course, the Tiebout economy. If head taxes prove infeasible, the burden of financing local public goods must then fall on consumption and factor taxes. This is Gordon's

---

[19] See Krelove (1992b). Rather than the local labor market, Myers (1990) uses intergovernmental transfers to ensure efficient use of local taxation of the economy-wide asset. Intuitively, the taxing jurisdiction realizes that residents outside the jurisdiction will move into the area and depress wages unless they receive a transfer sufficient to discourage their entry. This will require a transfer of $[1 - (n^1/N)]$ dollars, the advantage of relocation. Residents inside the taxing jurisdiction raise the $[1 - (n^1/N)]$ through the local head tax. In the end, $1 of rental taxation costs the residents of the taxing jurisdiction n^1/N in rental tax costs plus $[1 - (n^1/N)]$ in head taxes to pay for the inter-governmental grant or a total of $1. Again, inefficient tax exporting is avoided.

R.P. Inman, D.L. Rubinfeld / Journal of Public Economics 60 (1996) 307–334   325

economy, and local tax inefficiencies and inequities return; see Burbidge and Myers (1994).

While an important caveat to the need for policy interventions into the local public economy, the Krelove and Myers economy is not sufficiently general for us to put the potential need for central government fiscal regulations and grants aside.

3. The political economy of implementing central policies

While regulatory or fiscal policy instruments are available to the central government to correct the failures of decentralized taxation, there remains the political issue of whether the central government itself will select socially preferred policies. In federalist economies, central government legislatures are typically composed of representatives elected from the federation's states or provinces with a mandate to represent the preferences and concerns of their state constituents. Central government policies result when a majority of the elected representatives approve a policy.

Before any policy decisions are made, however, the elected legislature must resolve majority-rule democracy's major defect: the propensity to cycle from one policy outcome to another. When no winning coalition is capable of holding its majority against small policy variations offered by a losing minority, then either no decision will be made or final policy outcomes will be randomly chosen or manipulated by an agenda-setter. Legislatures have adopted a variety of procedures for overcoming this instability and its consequences, from formal rules of who can offer proposals to informal norms of voting behavior.

One model of legislative choice specifies an informal norm for legislators' voting to control cycling.[20] The norm, first specified formally by Weingast (1979) and Niou and Ordeshook (1985), is a norm of deference. Under this norm, individual legislators or coalitions are allowed to propose their preferred policies. Those policies will be approved, *if* that legislator or coalition approves, or defers to, similar proposals by all other members of the legislature. This norm – popularly characterized as, 'You scratch my back, and I'll scratch yours' – typically leads to proposals receiving universal

---

[20] While there is growing evidence that the model presented here is a good description of legislative decision-making in the US Congress – see Weingast and Marshall (1988) – it is certainly not the only model of legislative politics that overcomes cycling. Shepsle (1979) and Baron and Ferejohn (1989) have presented alternative models using formal legislative rules to ensure stable policy outcomes. Becker (1983) and Wittman (1989) present a model of legislative choice based on Coasian bargains between represented interest groups.

326   *R.P. Inman, D.L. Rubinfeld / Journal of Public Economics 60 (1996) 307–334*

support.[21] Such legislatures are often called 'universalistic' for this reason.[22] Once adapted, the norm is a stable Nash equilibrium; no member of the legislature has an incentive to deviate if all others adhere to the norm.

Universalistic legislatures operating under a norm of deference run a significant risk that the resulting fiscal policies will be economically inefficient, however. Central government funding of state-specific expenditures creates an implicit subsidy from non-residents to residents of the state receiving the centrally funded expenditure. Residents in the recipient state have an incentive to over-spend on the now centrally subsidized service. Adherence to the norm of deference protects these inefficiencies.

Fig. 1 illustrates the allocative consequences of central government funding of state-specific spending as, for example, might occur with central government grants to correct state tax inefficiencies and inequities. The downward sloping $mb_k(g^k)$ schedule measures the marginal benefit to the winning political – perhaps median – coalition in state k of a state-specific expenditure of g^k. The downward sloping $MB(g^k)$ schedule measures the aggregate social marginal benefits in improved tax efficiency or equity from the grant of g^k. The horizontal curve $p_k(g^k)$ measures the marginal social costs of providing the grant of size g^k, while the lower curve $\phi_k p_k(g^k)$ measures the share (ϕ_k) of those costs borne by the winning coalition in state k. In the very simple case where all state residents are in the decisive coalition and each state has an equal share of the national tax base, $\phi_k = 1/K$, where K is the number of states in the federation. If the decisive coalition is smaller than the state's full population, then $\phi_k < 1/K$. Typically, ϕ_k is small and the decisive coalition pays only a fraction of the total costs of central government expenditures allocated to their state.

Social efficiency requires $MB(g^k) = p_k(g^k)$, or the allocation g^{ke}. However, a legislature operating under a norm of deference will provide g^{ku} in each state, where $mb_k(g^k) = \phi_k p_k(g^k)$. The efficiency of these allocations

---

[21] The intuition of why the norm of deference is individually preferred to simple majority-rule legislatures is straightforward. Without the norm, each legislator can expect his state to pay for a little more than half of the legislature's average project, since all states share in the costs of each legislator's project and one more than half of all the states receive projects. Further, each legislator can expect his state to be given a project, on average, a little more than half the time. Thus, expected net benefits from simple majority rule will be a little more than $0.5 \times$ [State project benefits – Average project costs]. When the legislature operates under a norm of deference and all projects are accepted with certainty, then expected net benefits will be simply [State project benefits – Average project costs]. If state benefits exceed average project costs, then the norm of deference will be preferred; see Weingast (1979).

[22] For some evidence that the US Congress is, in fact, universalistic, see Collie (1988). There are now growing indications that the voting for representatives to the newly empowered European Parliament is also being driven by local, rather than Union-wide, economic concerns; see 'European issues are few as Europe votes', *International Herald Tribune*, 10 June 1994, p. 1.

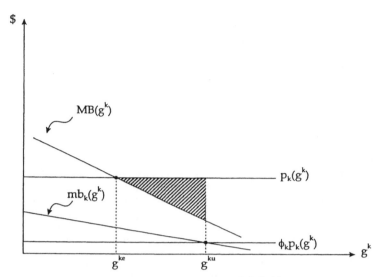

Fig. 1. State allocations from universalistic legislatures.

depends upon the distribution of citizen demands relative to the distribution of tax burdens. Since the decisive coalition's share of state benefits from g^k spending is likely to be much larger than their share of the national cost of funding g^k, an over-provision of a state-specific good seems the most likely outcome – that is, $g^{ku} > g^{ke}$ as shown in Fig. 1.[23] The shaded area in Fig. 1 measures the inefficiency in the provision of g^k when that good is over-provided.

Inman (1988) provides evidence that this has, in fact, been the outcome of US grants policies. In an econometric analysis of US grants policies over the

---

[23] Define the relationship between the social marginal benefit and the decisive coalition's marginal benefit by the proportional relationship: $\Psi_k MB(g^k) \equiv mb_k(g^k)$. Note that $\Psi_k MB(g^k) \equiv mb_k(g^k)$ by construction, and $mb_k(g^k) = \phi_k p_k(g^k)$ by the political process. Thus, $\Psi_k MB(g^k) \equiv mb_k(g^k) = \phi_k p_k(g^k)$ or $(\Psi_k/\phi_k)MB(g^k) = p_k(g^k)$. The demand share parameter for the decisive coalition, Ψ_k, is defined by the distribution of citizens' demands for the state expenditure (grant), while the cost share parameter for the decisive coalition, ϕ_k, is defined by central government's tax rates and the distribution of the tax base. Public goods are over-provided $(MB(g^k) < p_k(g^k))$, efficiently provided $(MB(g^k) = p_k(g^k))$, or under-provided $(MB(g^k) > p_k(g^k))$ as $(\Psi_k/\phi_k) > 1$, $= 1$, or < 1 – that is, as the decisive coalition's share (Ψ_k) of national benefits exceeds, equals, or is less than their share (ϕ_k) of national costs. The likely case – shown in Fig. 1 – is for the decisive coalition's share of benefits to exceed their share of costs when state-specific spending is financed by national taxation.

328   *R.P. Inman, D.L. Rubinfeld / Journal of Public Economics 60 (1996) 307–334*

past thirty years, Inman finds that the structure of direct US grants to states does little to control tax spillovers on the margin, nor does it provide appreciably greater assistance to low income or resource-poor states. Further, national subsidies have not typically provided tax relief from local source-based state taxation. Grants revenues are spent either on state public goods or provide relief for resident-based taxes. Finally, Inman's econometric estimates of US grants spending under the assumption of a universalistic central legislature predicts values of $g^{ke} = \$120$ per capita and $g^{ku} = \$179$ per capita for a typical US state; see Fig. 1. The shaded area of inefficiency is estimated to equal $18 per capita or approximately $0.10 for each dollar of aid distributed.[24]

Might central government regulation of source-based state taxation fare better? If central government legislatures operate under a norm of deference, there are good reasons to be skeptical. Citizens in individual states benefit when their states are allowed access to the tax base of non-residents through source-based taxation. Just as individual states push to inefficiently expand state-specific grants from the national tax base, so, too, might they seek to expand source-based taxation so as to maximize transfers from non-residents. Under a norm of deference, states that benefit from source-based taxation (e.g. mineral-rich states) will ask, and be given, the right to use such taxes. The decision to grant source-based taxes is identical to the decision to offer any other nationally-financed, state-specific public good. Fig. 1 therefore applies, and inefficiencies, namely a move to source-based taxation, can result. It is instructive that each of the three prominent federalist democracies – Australia, Canada, and the United States – allow states access to source-based taxation.

We conclude that central governments run by universalistic legislatures are not likely to manage efficiently the tax failures that arise within a decentralized federalist public economy. In these legislatures, the same economic incentives that lead states to adopt inefficient tax policies in the decentralized public economy may well lead their elected representatives to adopt inefficient central government policies to correct those tax failings. What can be done?

Two strategies are available, one legislative and the other constitutional. The legislative strategy is to replace the norm of deference with an alternative decision-making structure less susceptible to local interests when

---

[24] Wildasin (1989) provides a more encouraging view of one aspect of the US grants program for state taxation. He estimates that the efficient rate of subsidy for capital taxation when capital is mobile ranges from 0.17 to 0.40 depending on the degree of capital mobility. US firms are allowed to deduct state taxes when calculating their taxable income for federal corporate taxation. The current tax rate on corporate income is 0.34. Deductible state taxes on capital income are, therefore, subsidized at a marginal rate of 0.34, within Wildasin's range of efficient capital tax subsidies.

R.P. Inman, D.L. Rubinfeld / Journal of Public Economics 60 (1996) 307–334 329

setting national policies. Strong political parties with the ability to replace legislators who do not conform to party positions is one alternative. Such parties may internalize the tax costs of public spending to all party members, not just to the legislators from the one state or province receiving the allocation. This raises the relevant tax share in Fig. 1 to a 'party' tax share $\phi_p > \phi_k$. The likely consequence is a decline in inefficient over-spending on localized goods; Inman's (1988) study of US grants policy estimates that strong political parties (evident through the late 1960s) would have reduced grants spending by 24% from the universalistic level of $179 per capita found in the late 1970s.[25] A second legislative strategy is to strengthen the hand of a nationally elected executive – for example, giving that executive veto powers over inefficient grants. Inman's (1988) analysis of US grants policy shows that President Reagan's use of the executive veto threat was successful in trimming inefficient national grants to state and local governments by 15–22% in real terms over the 1980s.[26]

Two constitutional strategies are also available to constrain central government tendencies to adopt inefficient policies towards lower-tier tax financing. The first, and most promising, is to constitutionally assign only resident-based taxation to the lower tiers of government, allocating all source-based taxation to the central government. The most likely assigned tax is a resident-based income tax, administered centrally through locally decided rates 'piggy-backed' on to the national income tax. To the extent that resident-based taxation does not fully ensure local tax efficiency or fairness, central government grants remain a useful policy tool. The risk of inefficient grants design and local over-spending within universalistic central legislatures also remains, however. The propensity to over-spend within universalistic legislatures can be constrained by a second constitutional strategy: limiting the number of states in the federalist hierarchy. Fewer

---

[25] A decline in grants spending is clearly the outcome when the grant benefits only the resident of the recipient state. However, strong political parties may be able to redesign local grants so that they achieve their true social objectives of controlling tax exporting and internalizing tax spillovers. If so, then the decisive national party's marginal benefit curve from spending on g^k lies above the local marginal benefit curve – $mb_p(g^k) > mb_k(g^k)$ – reflecting the wider social benefits of the redesigned grant to state k. While tax costs of grants spending in state k are higher as $\phi_p > \phi_k$, so, too, is the marginal benefit curve as $mb_p(g^k) > mb_k(g^k)$. With efficiently designed grants, grants spending in state k may actually increase. The important point, however, is that this added grants spending is for targeted grants affecting wider social goals, not just per capita transfers to state k. Economic efficiency is improved thereby.

[26] The newly adopted South African Constitution allows for both strategies, first by requiring proportional representation to the national parliament from a national election for parties, and then by giving the President control over a Financial and Fiscal Commission with powers to review all national grants policies. It remains to be seen whether strong political parties and a strong Financial and Fiscal Commission will actually emerge to control domestic grants spending.

330   *R.P. Inman, D.L. Rubinfeld / Journal of Public Economics 60 (1996) 307–334*

states may lead to more inclusive tax shares – ϕ_k rises – that reduce g^{ku} in Fig. 1. Limiting the number of states also leads to fewer constituent districts claiming inefficient grants from the central government.[27]

4. Fiscal institutions and fiscal efficiency in federalist economies

Our theoretical understanding of competitive tax policies and the growing empirical evidence strongly suggest that at least for local government source-based taxation, fiscal inefficiencies and inequities are likely in federalist public economies. Tax exportation, competitive tax spillovers, and NIMBY and beggar-thy-neighbor tax competition may each lead to an inefficient mix of state taxes. Within-state politics when tax bases are mobile may lead to tax inequities. After identifying the problems, current tax theory also suggests possible solutions.

Requiring states to use only resident-based taxation goes a long way towards solving the problems of tax exportation and tax competition. Central government taxation of natural resources and mobile capital at source coupled with locationally neutral grants-in-aid is an alternative policy option to limit the inefficiencies from tax exportation, tax spillovers, and tax competition. Such grants can also be designed to correct within-state tax inequities and to control congestion, or NIMBY, tax inefficiencies.

While policies exist that can correct the potential inefficiencies and inequities of a decentralized tax system, those policies must be approved by a central government. In one political economy model of central government policy-making – a model that seems to describe US congressional behavior – political approval of efficient central government reforms seems unlikely. In representative universalistic legislatures, the same economic incentives that leads states to export their local tax burdens lead them to retain source-based taxation and to over-use a central government grants policy.

This review stresses the importance both of informal, less permanent, legislative structures and formal, more permanent, constitutional constraints to improve the central government's allocation of federalist tax policies. Decentralized legislatures controlled by local political interests will not

---

[27] There are costs to fewer states in the federalist structure, however. Fewer states means greater heterogeneity of demands for state-specific public goods financed by state taxes. This may lead to within-state inefficiencies in the provision of state-specific public goods; see Rubinfeld (1987). We have abstracted from this issue here by fixing the level of public goods spending within each state. A more general specification of the constitutional design in federalist economies would balance the gains of increased national efficiency on the financing side against the costs of increased within-state inefficiencies on the spending side; see Inman and Rubinfeld (1996).

R.P. Inman, D.L. Rubinfeld / Journal of Public Economics 60 (1996) 307–334   331

approve central government policies capable of constraining those local interests. Strong political parties and strong executives elected by a national constituency are needed if national interests in efficient federalist tax policies are to result. Constitutional constraints also have a role to play. Most promising is to assign resident-based taxation as the only constitutionally allowed state and local tax. State and local governments would be permitted to 'piggy-back' a local rate on to a nationally administered tax such as personal income tax. Source-based taxation would be limited to the central government. A cruder, but potentially still useful, constitutional constraint is to limit the number of states or provinces in the Union. Fewer states mitigates against the potential inefficiencies of representative universalistic legislatures; of course, fewer states may also mean state fiscal policies that are less responsive to the heterogeneity of citizen demands for local public goods.

An obvious but not generally acknowledged lesson emerges from this review: good tax policy in a federalist public economy will require local and central political institutions capable of first approving, and then maintaining, such policies. Recent theoretical and empirical research on the effects of taxes in decentralized economies provides the guidelines needed to fashion an efficient and fair federalist tax structure. A deeper understanding of exactly how governments set fiscal policy in federalist economies – at both the state and central levels – seems an important next step in our research agenda. Only with this understanding can we be confident that good economic advice will become good economic policy.

Acknowledgements

This research was begun while the authors were Fellows at the Center for Advanced Study in the Behavioral Sciences, Stanford, CA. We very much appreciate the support of the Center (NSF Grant, SES-9022192) and the Smith Richardson Foundation. The comments of the participants at the August 1993 ISPE conference on The Political Economy of Tax Policy are much appreciated, particularly those of our discussants, Friedrich Schneider and Sijbren Cnossen. Two referees provided helpful comments on earlier drafts.

References

Arnott, R. and R. Grieson, 1981, Optimal fiscal policy for a state or local government, Journal of Urban Economics 9, 23–48.

Baron, D. and J. Ferejohn, 1989, Bargaining in legislatures, American Political Science Review 83, 1182–1206.

Bartik, T., 1991, Who benefits from state and local economic developmental policies?, Upjohn Institute, Kalamazoo, MI.

Baxter, M. and M. Crucini, 1993, Explaining saving-investment correlations, American Economic Review 83, 416–436.

Becker, G., 1983, A theory of competition among pressure groups for political influence, Quarterly Journal of Economics 98, 371–400.

Boadway, R. and F. Flatters, 1982, Efficiency and equlization payments in a federal system of government: A synthesis and extension of recent results, Canadian Journal of Economics 15, 613–633.

Burbridge, J.B. and G.M. Myers, 1994, Population mobility and capital taxation, Regional Science and Urban Economics 24, 441–459.

Chernick, H., 1992, A model of the distributional incidence of state and local taxes, Public Finance Quarterly 20, 572–585.

Collie, M.P, 1988, Universalism and the parties in the United States House of Representatives, American Journal of Political Science 32, 865–883.

de Crombrugghe, A. and H. Tulkens, 1990, On Pareto improving commodity tax changes under fiscal competition, Journal of Public Economics 41, 335–350.

Day, K., 1992, Interprovincial migration and local public goods, Canadian Journal of Economics 92, 123–144.

Feldstein, M., 1994, Tax policy and international capital flows, Bernhard Harms Prize Lecture, Kiel, Germany.

Feldstein, M. and M. Vaillant, 1994, Can state taxes redistribute income? NBER Working Paper 4785, Cambridge, MA.

Giovannini, A., 1989, National tax systems vs. the European capital market, Economic Policy 4, 346–385.

Giovannini, A. and J. Hines, 1991, Capital flight and tax competition: Are there viable solutions to both problems?, in A. Giovannini and C. Mayer, eds., European financial integration (Cambridge University Press, Cambridge).

Gordon, R, 1983, An optimal taxation approach to fiscal federalism, Quarterly Journal of Econoics 95, 567–586.

Gordon, R., 1992, Can capital income taxes survive in open economies?, Journal of Finance 47, 1159–1180.

Grieson, R., 1980, Theoretical analysis and empirical measurement of the effects of the Philadelphia income tax, Journal of Urban Economics 8, 123–137.

Gyourko, J. and J. Tracy, 1989, The importance of local fiscal conditions in analyzing local labor markets, Journal of Political Economy 97, 1200–1231.

Hamilton, B., 1975, Zoning and property taxation in a system of local governments, Urban Studies 12, 205–211.

Helms, L.J., 1985, The effect of state and local taxes on economic growth: A time series–cross section approach, The Review of Economic and Statistics 67, 574–582.

Hettich, W. and S. Winer, 1988, Economic and political foundations of tax structure, American Economic Review 78, 701–712.

Inman, R., 1988, Federal assistance and local services in the United States: The evolution of a new federalist fiscal order, in: H. Rosen, ed., Fiscal federalism (University of Chicago Press, Chicago, IL) 33–74.

Inman, R., 1989, The local decision to tax: Evidence form large U.S. cities, Regional Science and Urban Economics 19, 455–491.

Inman, R., 1992, Can Philadelphia escape its fiscal crisis with another tax increase?, Business Review, Federal Reserve Bank of Philadephia, September–October, 5–20.

R.P. Inman, D.L. Rubinfeld / Journal of Public Economics 60 (1996) 307–334 333

Inman, R. and D. Rubinfeld, 1979, The judicial pursuit of local fiscal equity, Harvard Law Review, 92, 1662–1750.

Inman, R. and D. Rubinfeld, 1996, The political economy of federalism, in: D. Mueller, ed., Perspectives on public choice (Basil Blackwell, New York).

Jones, R. and J. Whalley, 1988, Regional effects of taxes in Canada: An applied general equilibrium approach, Journal of Public Economics 37, 1–28.

Kanbur, R. and M. Keen, 1993, Jeux sans frontieres: Tax competition and the tax coordination when countries differ in size, American Economic Review 83, 877–892.

Keen, M., 1987, Welfare effects of commodity tax harmonization, Journal of Public Economics 33, 107–114.

Kimbell, L. and G. Harrison, 1984, General equilibrium analysis of regional fiscal incidence, in: H. Scarf and J. Shoven, eds., Applied general equilibrium analysis (Cambridge University Press, Cambridge) 275–313.

Kolstad, C. and F. Wolak, 1983, Competition in interregional taxation: The case of Western Coal, Journal of Political Economy 91, 443–460.

Kolstad, C. and F. Wolak, 1985, Strategy and market structure in Western Coal taxation, The Review of Economics and Statistics 67, 239–249.

Krelove, R., 1992a, Competitive tax theory in open economies: Constrained inefficiency and a Pigovian remedy, Journal of Public Economics 48, 361–375.

Krelove, R., 1992b, Efficient tax exporting, Canadian Journal of Economics 25, 145–155.

Ladd, H., 1975, Local education, fiscal capacity, and the composition of the property tax base, National Tax Journal 28, 145–158.

McLure, C. and P. Miezkowski, 1983, Fiscal federalism and the taxation of natural resources, (Lexington Books, Lexington, MA).

Metcalf, G., 1993, Tax exporting, federal deductability, and state tax structure, Journal of Policy Analysis and Management 12, 109–126.

Mintz, J. and H. Tulkens, 1986, Commodity tax competition between member states of a federation: Equilibrium and efficiency, Journal of Public Economics 29, 133–172.

Mintz, J. and H. Tulkens, 1996, Optimality properties of alternative systems of taxation of foreign capital income, Journal of Public Economcis 60.

Morgan, W., J. Mutti and M. Partridge, 1989, A regional general equilibrium model of the United States: Tax effects on factor movements and regional production, Review of Economics and Statistics 71, 626–635.

Mutti, J., W. Morgan and M. Partridge, 1989, The incidence of regional taxes in a general equilibrium framework, Journal of Public Economics 39, 83–107.

Myers, G., 1990, Optimality, free mobility, and the regional authority in a federation, Journal of Public Economics 43, 107–121.

Niou, E.M.S. and P.C. Ordeshook, 1985, Universalism in Congress, American Journal of Political Science 29, 246–259.

Oates, W. and R. Schwab, 1988, Economic competition among jurisdictions: Efficiency enhancing or distortion inducing?, Journal of Public Economics 35, 333–354.

Papke, L., 1991, Interstate business tax differential and new firm location: Evidence from panel data, Journal of Public Economics 45, 47–68.

Pindyck, R., 1978, Gains to producers from the cartelization of exhaustible resources, Review of Economics and Statistics 60, 238–251.

Reischauer, R., 1975, General revenue sharing – the program's incentives, in: W. Oates, ed., Financing the new federalism, (Johns Hopkins University Press, Baltimore, MD) 40–87.

Rivlin, A., 1992, Reviving the American dream (The Brookings Institution, Washington, DC).

Rubinfeld, D., 1987, The economics of the local public sector, in: A.J. Auerbach and M.S. Feldstein, Handbook of public economics, vol. II (North-Holland, Amsterdam).

Shepsle, K., 1979, Institutional arrangements and equilibrium in multidimensional voting models, American Journal of Political Science 28, 27–59.

Tiebout, C., 1956, A pure theory of local government expenditures, Journal of Political Economy 60, 415–424.

Tretz, G., D.S. Rickman, G.L. Hunt and M.J. Greenwood, 1993, The dynamics of U.S. internal migration, Review of Economics and Statistics 75, 209–214.

Wales, T., 1968, Distilled spirits and interstate consumption effects, American Economic Review 68, 853–863.

Wassmer, R., 1993, The use and abuse of economic development incentives in a metropolitan area, Proceedings of the National Tax Association 46, 146–157.

Weingast, B., 1979, A rational perspective on congressional norms, American Journal of Political Science 23, 245–262.

Weingast, B. and W. Marshall, 1988, The industrial organization of Congress: or why legislatures, like firms, are not organized like markets, Journal of Political Economy 96, 132–163.

Wildasin, D., 1985, Urban public finance (Harwood, New York).

Wildain, D., 1988, Nash equilibria in models of fiscal competition, Journal of Public Economics 35, 229–240.

Wildasin, D., 1989, Interjurisdictional capital mobility: Fiscal externality and a corrective subsidy, Journal of Urban Economics 25, 193–212.

Wildasin, D., 1991, Some rudimentary 'doupolity' theory, Regional Science and Urban Economics 21, 393–421.

Wilson, J.D., 1986, A theory of inter-regional tax competition, Journal of Urban Economics 19, 296–315.

Wittman, D., 1989, Why democracies produce efficient results, Journal of Political Economy 97, 1395–1424.

Zodrow, G. and P. Mieszkowski, 1986, Pigou, Tiebout property taxation and the underprovision of local public goods, Journal of Urban Economics 19, 356–370.

G
Leviathan and the Size of Government

[15]

Open economy, federalism, and taxing authority

> It is better to keep the wolf out of the fold, than to trust to drawing his teeth and claws after he shall have entered.
>
> Thomas Jefferson, *Notes on Virginia: The Writings of Thomas Jefferson*, p. 165

Implicit in all of the analysis of earlier chapters has been the assumption that the polity and the economy are perfect mappings of each other with respect to geography, membership, and the extent of trade and resource allocation. That is, we have assumed the economy to be closed: neither trade nor migration extend the economy beyond the boundaries of the political unit. Consequently, all fiscal activities are carried out exclusively within the polity.

In this chapter we propose to relax the closed economy/closed polity assumption. We shall do so in two stages, the first of which contains two parts. In Section 9.1, we allow the economy to be open to trade; hence, citizens may buy and sell goods from citizens of other polities–economies. In that section, however, we continue to assume that migration across governmental boundaries does not occur. The model is the relatively familiar one of a small, independent, national state whose citizens trade in an international market but who remain resident within the small state. In Section 9.2, this model is modified to allow for interunit migration. The analysis of this section provides a bridge between the first and second stages of the analysis of this chapter. In the remaining sections, we examine the prospect of deliberate constitutional partitioning of the political power (and hence of the taxing power) within the confines of a larger and more inclusive political jurisdiction, within which internal trade and migration are unrestricted. Federalism is a means of constraining Leviathan constitutionally; hence, it becomes a topic of some importance in the framework of our analysis.

168

9.1. Toward a tax constitution for Leviathan in an open economy with trade but without migration

The analysis of this section is obviously related to that which has been developed by international and public-finance economists under the rubrics of "optimal tariffs" and "tax exportation." As before, however, the difference between our discussion and that of the orthodox literature lies in our concentration on the constitutional calculus of the potential taxpayer under Leviathan-like assumptions about the workings of the political process. A Leviathan government, interested solely in maximizing net revenue surplus for its own purposes, need not make any significant distinction between citizens and foreigners. This distinction is, however, quite crucial to the potential taxpayer, in his determination of the range and extent of taxing powers granted to government. The reason is straightforward: to the extent that government can be assigned taxing powers that impose costs on foreigners rather than on citizens, resources both for the provision of public goods and for the generation of Leviathan's net surplus are not drawn directly from the private incomes of citizens.

Recall our simple algebraic formulation, in which Leviathan's maximand, S, is determined by the difference between revenues, R, and G, the amount that it must spend on providing public goods:

$$S = R - G \tag{1}$$

If, as we previously postulated, government must spend a fixed share, α, on G, we get

$$S = (1 - \alpha)R \tag{2}$$

If R can be increased without any increase in domestic taxation, it follows that G can be increased without cost, no matter how small the value of α may be. Of course, it remains true that the citizen-taxpayer would prefer α to be as large as possible and will take appropriate constitutional steps to increase its value whenever possible. But for a given α, the citizen-taxpayer will rationally attempt to raise maximal taxes from foreigners.

The potentiality for shifting the burden of taxes from citizens to foreigners depends on the degree to which domestic demand and supply may be separated from foreign demand and supply and upon the relative elasticities of the relevant demand and supply functions. In considering possible tax bases that might be assigned to government, the individual would favor those for which foreign demand

170   The power to tax

looms large relative to domestic demand, and for which domestic supply is relatively elastic. Hotel rooms in Bermuda offer an example. At a constitutional level, the Bermuda government might be assigned the authority to levy taxes on hotel rooms with the assurance that only a relatively small part of the cost will fall on Bermuda citizens. In such a case, there need be little or no concern about the size of the aggregate revenue potential in relation to some globally efficient level of public goods and services. At essentially zero cost, the ideally desired level of public goods provision for local citizens may be very high indeed.

The domestic supply elasticity of the possible tax bases is, however, of critical importance. If domestic supply is available at sharply increasing costs, or if supply is such as to ensure that prices embody large elements of economic rents, any attempt to export tax burdens to foreigners may fail. Regardless of demand elasticities, the potential taxpayer (who will also be potential supplier of the taxed good and, hence, a potential rent recipient) may not want to allow government to have access to a tax base characterized by low supply elasticity.

The conclusions above relate to taxes on domestically produced goods and services, on exports, broadly considered. The same sort of analysis may, of course, be applied to imports, with the obverse relationships being relevant. If foreign supply to the domestic market is relatively inelastic whereas domestic demand is relatively elastic, the levy of a tax on such a good would be borne largely if not exclusively by foreign citizens rather than those who are resident of the tax-levying jurisdiction. Burden shifting by means of taxes on imports may not be an important instrument for exploitation by a small country, however, since foreign supplies of most goods, to that country, may be highly elastic. On the other hand, when large countries are considered, the whole problem of possible retaliation among a small number of trading countries must be incorporated into the analysis.

Detailed consideration of various possible cases need not be worked out here. It should be clear that the constitutional assignment problem in an open economy involves a set of different prospects from those that are relevant to the closed economy setting. With precisely the same model of political process, and with the same preferences for publicly provided goods and services, an individual in an open economy will select a differing range and mix of taxing powers to be allowed to government. He will allow Leviathan access to tax bases that promise a higher potential revenue yield than would be true in a closed economy, and he will tend to choose different bases in accordance with the export-potential criteria sketched out above.

The "prisoners' dilemma" aspects of tax competition among separate states cannot substantially modify these general results. The individual, at the constitutional choice stage when initial taxing authority is assignable to government, may recognize that if different governments try to export tax burdens to citizens beyond their jurisdictions the net result, for citizens of all jurisdictions, may be harmful. It would be better, for everyone, if each government should be constrained so that no tax burden exportation could exist. But the individual is not placed in a position, even conceptually, to choose "the tax constitution for the world." At best, he can partially constrain the taxing powers of his own national state by constitutional means. In such a choice setting, the individual must consider tax exportation prospects, regardless of the dilemma created by a world regime of mutual retaliation. If he fails to do so, if he selects domestic tax rules on some Kantian-like principle of generalization, he must reckon on being exploited fiscally by the taxing powers assigned to governments other than his own and over which he has no control. The individual will find himself, and his fellow nationals, paying the ultimate costs of public goods and services enjoyed by citizens of other states and also financing the surpluses of the Leviathan rulers of those governments. At the same time, citizens of other countries will be escaping possible payments for at least some share of domestically supplied public goods and some share in the financing of the home-grown Leviathan's surplus. In a world of dog eat dog, the dog that does not eat gets eaten.

9.2. Tax rules in an open economy with trade and migration

The economic interdependence among persons in different political jurisdictions changes dramatically when trade in final goods is supplemented by the prospects of resource mobility across governmental boundaries. If persons are free not only to engage in trade but also to shift capital and labor resources in response to differential economic signals, the economy becomes genuinely international, even if political units remain separate. It should be evident that the constitutional choice problem concerning the initial grant of taxing authority becomes different in this setting from that faced in either the closed economy/closed polity model of earlier chapters or the open economy-with-trade model examined above.

172   The power to tax

Freedom of trade and migration among separate governmental units acts as a substitute for overt fiscal constraints. In this sense, free trade and migration parallel in effect some of the Wicksell-like procedural rules examined in Chapter 8. By contrast with the latter, however, the indirect controls over Leviathan exercised by free international economic exchange seem closer to the realm of the institutionally politically feasible, at least in Western nations, than do the required procedural departures from majoritarian electoral processes.

The limiting case of free trade and migration is the idealized Tiebout world.[1] Assume a world of competing governments, each one of which supplies some public goods to its citizens, public goods whose benefits do not spill over beyond the boundaries of the individual polity. Each "national" government is, we assume, modeled as a revenue-seeking, surplus-maximizing Leviathan. Migration across governmental boundaries is, however, also assumed to be costless. Further, let us assume that persons are motivated exclusively by the economic returns available to them. No persons exhibit personal preferences as to jurisdiction of residence, and no persons earn locational rents. In this extreme case, there is no surplus available for potential exploitation by any potential Leviathan in the resource equilibrium generated by the voluntary decisions of persons in the whole international economy. Each governmental unit, regardless of its motivations to maximize net revenue surplus, will find it necessary to offer public goods in the efficient quantities desired and to finance these goods efficiently. In this limiting case, freedom of trade and migration will render any overt fiscal constraints unnecessary.

Once we depart ever so slightly from this extremely restrictive model, however, the idealized Tiebout process will not fully substitute for constitutional tax rules or limits, even if we continue to allow for costless migration.[2] If locational rents accrue to persons in particular places of residence or occupation and/or if personal preferences as among the separate locations are known to exist, a potential surplus for governmental exploitation becomes available. Interestingly, the governmental jurisdiction that is most "favorably situated" in terms of the generation of locational rents, on the production or the utility side of the individual's choice calculus, opens up the prospect for the relatively greater degree of fiscal exploitation. Those governmental jurisdictions that are "pedestrian" in the sense that they offer no locational rents at all, in utility or in production (they have neither sunny beaches nor oil beneath the rocks), may remain immune from the fiscal inroads of Leviathan.[3]

Open economy, federalism, and taxing authority   173

At the constitutional stage of consideration, the individual who looks upon his jurisdiction as possessing, actually or potentially, the capacity to generate locational rents, may seek to impose overt constraints on the taxing power. But even in such cases, the effectiveness of freedom of trade and migration in serving as a substitute for such direct constraints should not be overlooked. On the other hand, unless free trade and free migration are themselves constitutionally guaranteed, the indirect limits that these controls might impose on the fiscal proclivities of Leviathan cannot be predicted to operate. Nor is an individual, at some initial constitutional stage, likely to prefer open migration on a one-way basis. That is, the individual may not want to ensure that migrants from other jurisdictions can freely enter into his own unless reciprocal guarantees of free outmigration and immigration into other jurisdictions are also offered. These latter guarantees cannot, of course, emerge in the constitution making for a single jurisdiction. Further, even in a world where such guarantees might emerge from some multinational convention, predicted disparities in income and wealth levels among persons of separate jurisdictions may make free migration undesirable for members of particular jurisdictions. The protection against the fiscal exploitation of Leviathan that the opening up of governmental boundaries offers may not outweigh the predicted costs in locational rents destroyed by such action.

For the foregoing and other considerations, the full substitutability of trade and migration for explicit constraints on governmental fiscal authority does not seem likely to characterize the constitutional calculus. Although he might well recognize the relationships here, the person who has an option at the constitutional stage would presumably select some constraint on governmental taxing power even in a world that is predicted to be characterized as truly international or interjurisdictional.

9.3. Federalism as a component of a fiscal constitution

The analysis of Section 9.2 provides a useful introduction to that of federalism. In the earlier analysis, we adopted a model that contained a large number of political jurisdictions, each one of which defined the "range of publicness" for the goods and services to be supplied governmentally, but all of which were contained within a suprajurisdictional economy, characterized by open migration and free trade among persons in all the governmental units. Here we introduce a different model. We define the inclusive jurisdictional–political

174   The power to tax

boundary to be coincident in both membership and territory with that
of the economy. In this respect, we are back to the implicit closed
economy/closed polity models of earlier chapters. There are no
"independent nations" to be considered; there is only one political
community. We want, however, to examine the prospect of using
federalization of the political structure as an indirect means of imposing constraints on the potential fiscal exploitation of Leviathan. It may
be possible that an explicit constitutional decision to decentralize and
hence to disperse political authority may effectively substitute for
overt fiscal limits. In conducting this discussion, we wish to contrast
both the approach and the results with the reigning orthodoxy in the
economic theory of fiscal federalism. We begin, therefore, with a brief
descriptive statement of the main elements of that theory.

The conventional theory of fiscal federalism. In what might be called the
conventional or orthodox "economic theory" of federalism, the various functions of government are assigned to different levels (central,
state or provincial, local) in accordance with the spatial properties of
the public-goods externalities embodied in the carrying out of these
functions.[4] In terms of the efficiency norm of the economist, this
theory places or specifies for any particular public good or service a
lower bound on the size of the political (or administrative) jurisdiction
that should be assigned powers to finance and supply that good or
service. In this framework, assignments to jurisdictions of smaller size
(below such a boundary limit) would generate interunit spillovers.
Efficiency in the overall organization of public-goods financing and
supply, therefore, seems to dictate "merger" into "optimal-sized"
units.

Note, however, that this argument does not establish any case for
federalism per se, because there are no logical grounds against
assigning functions to jurisdictions larger or more extensive than the
lower bound determined by the appropriate ranges of publicness.
There would seem to be no reason why strictly localized public goods
should not be provided by supralocal governmental units, which
might, of course, decentralize administratively as the relevant externality limits dictate. In other words, the conventional theory offers no
basis for deriving an *upper bound* on the size of political jurisdictions.
There is no analysis that demonstrates the superiority of a genuinely
federal political structure over a unitary structure, with the latter
administratively decentralized.

This result is not, in itself, surprising when we recognize that the
"economic theory" of federalism is no different from standard

Open economy, federalism, and taxing authority   175

normative economics in its implicit assumptions about politics. The normative advice proffered by the theory is presumably directed toward the benevolent despotism that will implement the efficiency criteria. No support can be generated for a politically divided governmental structure until the prospects for nonidealized despotism are acknowledged. Once government comes to be modeled either as a complex interaction process akin to that analyzed in standard public choice or, as in this book, in terms of Leviathan-like behavior, an argument for a genuinely federal structure can be developed. Further, the normative theory that emerges can be as "economic" as the conventional one. The individual, at the initial stage of constitutional deliberation, may find it "efficient" to decentralize and to disperse the effective taxing power as between the central and the subordinate units of government.

The central government and protective-state functions. Let us continue to model government in Leviathan terms. Whether central, provincial, or local, we assume that government will try to maximize net surplus within the set of internal and external constraints that it confronts. The question to be examined is whether or not explicit constitutional decentralization and dispersal of fiscal authority can provide effective substitutes, in whole or in part, for direct controls over the taxing power.

We must first take account of the initial leap out of Hobbesian anarchy, the primal establishment of government as the enforcer of individual rights and contracts, sometimes called the minimal or the protective state.[5] The protective functions will almost necessarily be assigned to the governmental unit that is coincident in area and membership with the area of the potential economic interdependence. Political subdivision into fully sovereign national units will create prospects for internal conflict, quite apart from internal barriers to trade and migration.[6] If protective-state functions are assigned to the central government, with no constraints on the taxing power, the individual will predict Leviathan provision of protective state services (internal security, enforcement of rights and contracts, and external defense) but that taxes will be imposed so as to maximize the net surplus over and above the costs of supplying such services. Since the size of the potential tax base (income and wealth in the economy) is clearly dependent on the size and quality of the protective-state services offered, government may well be in the position discussed in Chapter 7. (See, particularly, Figure 7.2, and related discussion.) At the constitutional stage, the individual will

176   The power to tax

clearly seek to restrict the central government's power to tax while leaving it with sufficient authority to finance the desired level of protective-state services. This objective may be accomplished by assigning to the central government a relatively narrow revenue potential through an appropriate base-rate restriction, one that directly relates revenue potential to the services provided.[7]

Productive-state functions: "national" public goods, costless migration, no locational rents. Our concern is not primarily with the financing of protective-state functions assignable to the central government. It is, instead, centered on the possible extension of central government competence beyond such limits with the corresponding extension of taxing power. For purposes of analysis in this and succeeding subsections, we assume that the central government carries out its protective-state functions satisfactorily. It guarantees rights of property and contract, protects against external threats, and ensures free internal trade and migration within its boundaries. It finances these activities by some appropriately limited taxing power, one that restricts the central government's possible exploitation of taxpayers within relatively narrow bounds.

We shall develop our argument in a series of models, arrayed in some rough order of increasing complexity (and realism). In the first three models discussed below, we shall make the extreme assumption that migration is costless. There are no moving costs, and no one has personal preferences as to location within the inclusive territory. Further, there are no locational rents to be earned anywhere in the economy.

In the first case, let us assume now that there is a single public good potentially desired by citizens, a good that is technologically nonexcludable throughout the whole "national" territory. Further, we assume complete nonrivalry in consumption. The good is ideally Samuelsonian. (No such good may exist, but the polar case is useful for expository purposes.)

From the precepts of the orthodox theory of fiscal federalism, the financing and provision of such a "national" public good under these conditions should be assigned to the central government rather than to subordinate units of less-than-optimal size for the function. In the latter assignment, interunit spillovers emerge to generate inefficiency, and total supply of the good will tend to be suboptimal. What emerges from the Leviathan perspective?

Assignment of the "national" public good to central government fiscal authority will require constitutional constraints both to ensure that revenues will be expended on provision of the good and that

Open economy, federalism, and taxing authority   177

there will be limits on total revenue collections. Some such constraints could surely be constructed, in accordance with the norms emergent from the analyses of earlier chapters, and as we have already assumed to be present with respect to protective-state services. Nonetheless, as the analyses have also suggested, the constraints that might be imposed will accomplish these purposes only within certain tolerance limits, and cannot be expected to ensure "efficiency" in any narrowly defined sense. Government could, in other words, be expected to secure some net surplus, a surplus that represents net efficiency loss to taxpayers.

The problem to be posed is one in comparative institutional analysis. It would be possible, at the constitutional stage, to assign the financing and provision of the "national" public good to subordinate units rather than to the central government, despite the "national" range of both nonexcludability and nonrivalry. The predicted results of such a *federal* assignment may then be compared with centralized assignment.

Under the extreme conditions postulated, the equilibrium solution under the federal assignment will be zero taxation along with zero provision of the public good. Any attempt on the part of any single subordinate unit of government, under Leviathan motivation, to levy taxes, even for the provision of the good, will result in total and immediate outmigration to the remaining jurisdictions in the economy. There will be no tax or fiscal exploitation in this solution. But the net efficiency loss will be measured by the potential difference between the benefits of the public good and its costs. There is no way of determining a priori whether these efficiency losses will be greater than, equal to, or less than those that are to be expected under centralized assignment. For our purposes, it suffices to demonstrate that the federal assignment *may* involve lower efficiency loss than the equivalent assignment of the function to the central government authority. The mobility constraint that prohibits local governments from exploiting citizens is tantamount to a constitutional rule that restricts the domain of public spending in such a way as to prohibit provision of the public good.

Productive-state functions: costless migration, no locational rents, complete "national" jointness efficiency but with provincial excludability. The efficiency argument for federal assignment increases dramatically if we drop the nonexcludability assumption from the model considered above while leaving all other assumptions of the model invariant. Let us continue to assume that the "range of publicness" defined in terms of costs of provision over numbers is genuinely "national." We assume

178   The power to tax

now, however, that subordinate units of government may, without undue cost, effectively exclude noncitizens from enjoying the public-goods benefits from localized provision.

In this model, by contrast with that examined above, any single unit of government can tax-finance and supply the public good without motivating mass outmigration from its boundaries to other units within the inclusive territory. To the extent that taxes are imposed so as to leave citizens with more surplus than they could obtain in competing jurisdictions, individuals will be motivated to remain in the fiscally responsive jurisdiction.

The equilibrium solution in this model will involve the concentration of all members of the inclusive jurisdiction into only *one* of the subordinate governmental units. This concentration will be necessary to exploit fully the jointness efficiency aspects of the public good. The single government that remains fiscally viable, however, will, in the extreme conditions postulated, be unable to secure any net fiscal surplus. Taxes will be levied on citizens strictly in terms of their relative public-goods evaluations; all taxes will tend to approximate Lindahl prices. Any attempted departure from this pattern of taxation will immediately set up the potentiality for a competing government to offer better terms to everyone; immediate mass outmigration from the unit that tries to undertake any fiscal exploitation will result.

In this model, therefore, there is a clear efficiency gain in adopting the *federal* rather than the centralized assignment for the public good, even though the range of publicness defined in the jointness sense remains "national." There are no efficiency losses in the federal solution, whereas, as earlier indicated, there may be efficiency losses in the centralized solution stemming from the failure of taxing constraints to eliminate all Leviathan surplus prospects. Note that the federal assignment secures the reduction of predicted efficiency loss to zero without the introduction of any overt fiscal constraints on the authority of the local governmental units. The fiscal discipline that is forced upon these units in the solution emerges from the mobility of resources across subordinate governmental boundaries within the inclusive territorial jurisdiction. These units of government cannot spend revenues for other purposes than public-goods provision, and they cannot tax in any arbitrary way so that net surplus may be generated.

Production-state functions: costless migration, no locational rents, localized public goods. If we now modify the model by relaxing the assumption concerning the range of publicness, and allow for local-governmental

Open economy, federalism, and taxing authority   179

limits on the jointness efficiency in public-goods provision, we are back in the idealized Tiebout world discussed earlier in this chapter. Elaboration at this point is unnecessary. The equilibrium solution differs from that immediately above in that, with localized public goods, population will not be concentrated in single units but will instead be dispersed among separate units, with each unit producing an efficient level of public goods, and with each unit imposing essentially Lindahl tax prices. As in the earlier case, the solution will be fully efficient. A federal assignment is dictated, both from our Leviathan set of assumptions about government and from the set of assumptions that characterize the orthodox theory of fiscal federalism.

Locational value, costs of mobility, and localized Leviathans. The models introduced to this point in our discussion of federalism are grossly unrealistic in their assumptions about locational value and costs of mobility. They should be considered to be preliminary to more realistic models that incorporate locational preferences of taxpayers, locational rents earned by economic resources, and positive costs of moving as between locations. Once any or all of these elements are allowed for in the distribution of people and resources throughout the territory of an economy, the efficacy of the indirect constraint in reducing or eliminating fiscal exploitation by subnational units of government is decreased. If a person, for any reason, simply prefers to live in X rather than in Y, within an inclusive jurisdiction containing both X and Y, he becomes vulnerable to some fiscal exploitation by the government of X, even if it remains in "competition" for people and resources with the government of Y.

The existence of locational value implies that local governments should not be allowed unconstrained taxing power, as might have been implied by some of the extreme models when this value was assumed away. Acknowledgement of the existence of positive locational value does not, however, directionally modify the argument for federal assignment of functions sketched out in the simpler models given above. To the extent that the indirect mobility constraint is operative at all, subordinate governments will be limited in their fiscal powers in comparison with centralized government powers.

Toward an "optimal" federal structure. The argument for a constitutional-stage federal assignment of functions, with accompanying taxing powers, under certain conditions may be accepted, and the suggested modification of the "range of publicness" mappings im-

180   The power to tax

plicit in orthodox analysis may be rejected. But we have not, to this point, offered a definitive set of suggestions concerning "optimality" in the design of a federalized structure itself, given our Leviathan assumptions about political process. How small or how large should competing subordinate units of government be? How many subordinate units should be contained within the inclusive protective-state jurisdiction?

There are at least four elements that need to be considered as relevant to any answer to this question: costs of mobility, potentiality for collusion, ranges of publicness, and economies of scale in administrative organization.

The costs of moving presumably increase with geographical distance. "Costs of moving" include here not only actual costs of shifting among locations, but, also, subjective or psychological costs involved in shifts among locations along scales of preference. (A person may be relatively indifferent as between Broward and Dade County in Florida. She may place a high value on Florida over any other state.) Empirical evidence confirms the simple analytical results here; persons tend to shift among jurisdictions more readily if these jurisdictions are geographically close one to another. From this fact it follows that the potential for fiscal exploitation varies inversely with the number of competing governmental units in the inclusive territory. This element, taken alone, implies the efficacy of a large number of subordinate governmental units.

A second element also points toward the desirability of a multiplicity of jurisdictions. For reasons equivalent to those familiar in oligopoly theory, the potentiality for collusion among separate units varies inversely with the number of units. If there are only a small number of nominally competitive governments, collusion among them with respect to their mutual exercise of their assigned taxing powers may be easy to organize and to enforce. On the other hand, the costs of organizing and enforcing collusive agreements increase disproportionately as the number of competitors increases.

The "range of publicness" or "economies of scale in consumption" element offsets the first two elements, at least to some degree and for some functions. As the orthodox analysis suggests, the equivalence mappings between the size of political jurisdictions and the range of publicness is of relevance, if not necessarily of dominating importance. It is worth noting as an analytic footnote in this connection that it is the nonexcludability characteristic of public goods rather than the economies of scale in consumption as such that is the more crucial limit on the capacities of decentralization.

A final element involves the costs of administration and organization, which tend to point in the direction of a smaller number of units and toward a combination of functional authorities within single units. There is economic content in the familiar argument for fiscal consolidation among localized jurisdictions. What is often neglected in discussions of consolidation, however, is the offsetting potential for fiscal exploitation, a potential that only emerges when something other than the benevolent despotism model of government informs the analysis.

A normative theory of the "optimal" federal structure would have to incorporate each of the elements noted, along with other relevant considerations, among which would be the locational fixity of productive resources, the homogeneity of the population, and the predicted efficacy of explicit constitutional constraints on central-government and local-government taxing powers. Our purpose here is not to offer such a "theory," even in the form of a few highly abstracted models. Our purpose is the much more limited one of suggesting a rationale for introducing a dispersal of fiscal authority among differing levels of government as a means of controlling Leviathan's overall fiscal appetites.

9.4. An alternative theory of government grants

The orthodox theory of fiscal federalism includes as one of its parts a theory of intergovernmental grants. The traditional justification for such grants can take three forms: first, certain functions of government allocated to lower levels may generate interjurisdictional spillovers, which can be internalized only by payments between jurisdictions, or appropriate transfers from higher levels of government; second, economies of scale in the administration of taxation may be obtained if central (or higher level) governments are responsible both for revenue raising and for disbursing funds to lower-level jurisdictions for expenditure; or third, interregional disparities in income (or possibly population) may be seen to require interregional redistribution on more-or-less standard "equity" grounds, by higher-level governments.

As elsewhere in this book, we set aside this third possible justification as lying outside the domain of the current discussion. The other two arguments are, however, of a type that would make them relevant to the constitutional calculus of the typical voter-taxpayer as we have posited it. In principle, they are arguments that ought to bear weight, but like other aspects of the economic theory of federalism, they

182   The power to tax

presume a model of government as the benevolent despot – far removed from our own.

The Leviathan model does, however, readily enough generate a theory of "government grants," with both positive and normative aspects. Within a constitutionally designed federal structure, we would predict that there would be constant pressures by competitive lower-level governments to secure institutional rearrangements that would moderate competitive pressures. One obvious such arrangement would be one that established a uniform tax system across all jurisdictions: this would remove one major element of the competitive government process. And the logical body to administer any such agreement is the higher level of government. In return for an appropriate share of the additional revenue, the central government would act as an enforcer of the agreement between lower-level governments, doling out financial penalties to those jurisdictions which attempted to breach the agreement. Appropriate "fiscal effort" would become an important criterion for determining the share of total revenue that went to each lower-level government: if some state/province levied a low rate of tax in relation to some revenue instrument over which it retained jurisdiction, other states would need to be able to penalize it by means of its grant appropriation by the central government.

With revenue-raising powers thus reassigned to the central government, we would expect both some pro rata return of revenues to state governments and some remaining "special" grants to particular states. The reason for these latter "redistributions" in this model lies in the presence of differential locational rents among states. Those states where locational rents are high, and which could therefore charge higher taxes in the genuinely competitive setting, would no doubt expect a larger share of total revenues per capita in the cartelized case where the central government organizes revenue collection. Correspondingly, in those states where locational rents are lowest, we would expect states to obtain a lower per capita share of total revenue. Additionally, since any lower-level government unit can effectively break the cartel by remitting taxes and attempting to attract extra resident/taxpayers thereby, one might expect that some proportion of the additional tax proceeds from cartelization would be shared on a more-or-less equal-share basis. In this sense, we ought to expect small states to obtain a larger per capita share than large states. There are, then, clear empirical implications here that could be tested to determine the extent to which this explanation of revenue sharing and the structure of grants is an acceptable one. In this connection, there is one observation that deserves mention. With conventional explanations/justifications of intergovernmental grants, one would expect that a considerable amount of intergovernmental transfer could and would occur bilaterally between governments at the same level: interjurisdictional spillovers, for example, would seem to be most appropriately handled in this way. With our alternative theory of the central government as monitor of a cartel among lower levels of government, simple bilateral negotiation between particular jurisdictions would be almost useless since it increases monopoly power only modestly, and we would expect it to be a rare phenomenon. In practice, of course, it is: in very few federations do we observe any significant transfer of funds between jurisdictions at the same level – virtually everything is channeled through the higher level of government.

The normative implications of our alternative theory are clear. Revenue sharing is undesirable, because it subverts the primary purpose of federalism, which is to create competition between jurisdictions. Each jurisdiction must have responsibility for raising its own revenue and should be precluded from entering into explicit agreements with other jurisdictions on the determination of uniform rates. This conclusion is, of course, congruent with the one that emerges from more familiar models of public choice; in a setting where electoral choices are constraining, it is desirable to have expenditure and revenue decisions determined at the same jurisdictional level. The Leviathan construction, however, arrives at similar conclusions from a quite different route.

9.5. A tax constitution for a federal state

It is interesting to consider here the nexus between the structural constraints imposed by an internally competitive federal polity discussed in this chapter and the explicit revenue limits that have been our concern in earlier chapters. To do so, we pose the question: How will (or how should) the power to tax be allocated among jurisdictions? The answer to this question seems clear. Recognizing that mobility will constrain governments at lower levels more severely than governments at higher levels, the citizen will, in making his constitutional determinations, be forced to rely more heavily on fiscal constraints at those higher levels. Assignment of taxing powers to jurisdictions should reflect this. At the lowest level of government, access to even minimally distorting taxes (such as head taxes, or possibly property taxes) may be appropriate, because the discipline of

184   The power to tax

mobility restricts the capacity of government to exploit those tax instruments to the fullest. Equally, at the central level, since there will be little discipline exerted by the possibility of mobility, tax limitations of the sort discussed in earlier chapters remain crucial. Therefore, we would expect that, at this level, the taxpayer-citizen would select tax instruments with limited revenue potential (excises on specific items, perhaps), and otherwise choose fiscal rules designed to limit central government spending.

The tax recommendations that are derived here are, of course, somewhat at variance with practice: central governments have access to broad-based instruments with enormous revenue potential, whereas in many cases more localized governments have much more modest revenue instruments, though the property tax – widely a local government revenue instrument – does have substantial revenue potential. The fact that the property tax is not in practice levied at revenue-maximizing levels is perhaps a casual test of the severity of the mobility constraint.

9.6. Conclusions

The predicted intergovernmental competition for fiscal resources and the predicted mobility response of persons and resources to the exercise of governmental fiscal authority provide the relationship between the open economy and the federal political structure and, hence, the basis for this chapter's organization. The constitutional-level choice facing the individual in a potentially open economy/open polity is significantly different from that faced in a closed system. Intergovernmental competition for fiscal resources and interjurisdictional mobility of persons in pursuit of "fiscal gains" can offer partial or possibly complete substitutes for explicit fiscal constraints on the taxing power. In prospect rather than retrospect, however, the individual cannot constitutionally ensure that his economy/polity will remain open to trade and/or migration with differing national entities. Critical dependence on "openness" of the economy seems, therefore, unlikely to characterize the rational constitutional choice of an individual.

The substitutability between intergovernmental competition for fiscal resources and explicit constitutional constraints on governmental taxing power become important, however, even in a closed economy/closed polity setting, once the possibility of federalization is introduced. Since the constitutional rules are, in this setting, presumed to remain binding, the individual may choose to rely on the

Open economy, federalism, and taxing authority   185

indirect mobility constraints guaranteed by dispersed political–fiscal power in partial substitution for the more direct constraints that would otherwise have to be imposed. Protective-state functions would, presumably, be assigned to the central government, along with some appropriately restricted powers to tax sufficient to finance these functions. Beyond this minimal limit, however, the intergovernmental competition that a genuinely federal structure offers may be constitutionally "efficient," regardless of the more familiar considerations of interunit spillovers examined in the orthodox theory of fiscal federalism.

The normative "theory of federalism" that emerges from our analysis differs sharply from the orthodoxy which places primary emphasis on the spatial properties of public goods. These properties become only one of several elements worthy of consideration in a constitutional choice among alternative functional assignments. And as our analysis has indicated, federalization may be efficient even when the desired public goods are estimated to be "national" in the polar Samuelsonian sense. Our emphasis is on federal assignment as a means of ensuring that individuals have available options as among the separate taxing-spending jurisdictions, and on the effect that the potential exercise of these options has on the total fiscal exploitation in the system.

In much modern policy discussion, local governments are allegedly "starved" for funds. Our analysis suggests that this situation is perhaps dictated by the competitive setting within which such governments find themselves, and, indeed, the analysis implies that this situation may well be efficient in the constitutional sense. Total government intrusion into the economy should be smaller, *ceteris paribus*, the greater the extent to which taxes and expenditures are decentralized, the more homogeneous are the separate units, the smaller the jurisdictions, and the lower the net locational rents.

Possibilities for collusion among separate governmental units, either explicitly organized and enforced by the units themselves or mandated by the central government, must be included in the "other things equal." When the central government collects and administers taxes on behalf of the subordinate units, the effect is identical to explicit collusion on the part of these units. Local units should tax and spend independently. But the point here is not the traditional one to the effect that jurisdictions should be responsible for both the tax and expenditure decisions in order to ensure some proper balancing of the two sides of the account, as driven by some cost benefit/public choice model of electoral choice. Our point is the quite different one

186   The power to tax

to the effect that tax *competition* among separate units rather than tax collusion is an objective to be sought in its own right. The argument is of course, obvious when the parallel is drawn with the monopoly–competition relationship in economic theory. But notions that are obvious in one area are often neglected elsewhere, and restatement of the familiar from one setting becomes a challenge to orthodoxy in another. The modified vision of federalism that emerges here suggests, once again, the critical relationship between the normative evaluation of institutions and the political model that is employed in positive analysis.

Chapter 9. Open economy, federalism, and taxing authority

1. Charles M. Tiebout, "A Pure Theory of Local Government Expenditures," *Journal of Political Economy,* 60 (October 1956), 415–24.

2. David Friedman has analyzed a regime of competitive revenue-maximizing nations, with costless migration, but with attractiveness related to population density. See his "A Competitive Model of Exploitative Taxation" (Mimeographed, Virginia Polytechnic Institute and State University, August 1979). See also Dennis Epple and Allan Zelenitz, "Competition among Jurisdictions and the Monopoly Power of Governments" (Working Paper, Graduate School of Industrial Administration, Carnegie-Mellon University, March 1979).

3. Does Hong Kong offer a real-world example? Interestingly, we observe little or no fiscal exploitation of Hong Kong citizens by the Hong Kong government.

4. For a clear example, see Albert Breton, "A Theory of Government Grants," *Canadian Journal of Economics and Political Science,* 31 (May 1965), 175–87. But also see Gordon Tullock, "Federalism: Problems of Scale," *Public Choice,* 6 (Spring 1969), 19–29; Mancur Olson, "The Principle of 'Fiscal Equivalence,'" *American Economic Review,* 59 (May 1969), 479–87; Albert Breton and Anthony Scott, *The Economic Constitution of Federal States* (Toronto: University of Toronto Press, 1978); Richard A. Musgrave, "Approaches to a Fiscal Theory of Political Federalism," in National Bureau of Economic Research, *Public Finances: Needs, Sources, and Utilization* (Princeton, N.J.: Princeton University Press, 1961), pp. 97–122; and Charles M. Tiebout, "An Economic Theory of Fiscal Decentralization," in *Public Finances: Needs, Sources, and Utilization,* pp. 79–96.

5. For further discussion, see James M. Buchanan, *The Limits of Liberty* (Chicago: University of Chicago Press, 1975). Also, see Robert Nozick, *Anarchy, State, and Utopia* (New York: Basic Books, 1974).

6. Historically, of course, federalized political structures have emerged from some coordination between previously independent units rather than from the deliberative dispersal of political power at a constitutional stage of decision. For our purposes, however, the conceptualization of the latter model of origination of federalisms is more helpful analytically.

7. Earl Thompson has implied that protective-state services are directly related to "coveted wealth." From his argument a case can be made for allowing a central government to tax nonhuman wealth, presumably with designated rate limits. See Earl Thompson, "Taxation and National Defense," *Journal of Political Economy,* 82 (July/August 1974), 755–82. Thompson derives his theory from the predicate that governments are totally efficient and entirely constrained to produce results desired by the electorate. Our alternative model of public choice generates a quite different normative evaluation of the wealth tax. (See Chapter 5.)

[16]

Reviving Leviathan: Fiscal Federalism and the Growth of Government

Jonathan Rodden

Abstract   This article revisits the influential "Leviathan" hypothesis, which posits that tax competition limits the growth of government spending in decentralized countries. I use panel data to examine the effect of fiscal decentralization over time within countries, attempting to distinguish between decentralization that is funded by intergovernmental transfers and local taxation. First, I explore the logic whereby decentralization should restrict government spending if state and local governments have wide-ranging authority to set the tax base and rate, especially on mobile assets. In countries where this is most clearly the case, decentralization is associated with smaller government. Second, consistent with theoretical arguments drawn from welfare economics and positive political economy, I show that governments grow faster as they fund a greater portion of public expenditures through intergovernmental transfers.

For good or ill, fiscal decentralization is commonly thought to restrict the growth of government spending. Just as tax competition in an era of globalization is believed to place constraints on the revenue-raising capacity of governments, interjurisdictional competition within decentralized countries is believed to hamper government's ability to tax. For those who see government as a revenue-hungry beast, this is a welcome muzzle. For others, fiscal decentralization creates a worrisome "race to the bottom" that favors capital over labor and prevents governments from providing important collective goods. Pushing the normative and ideological questions aside, this article seeks to determine whether there is a link between decentralization and smaller government. At first glance the proposition seems doubtful: throughout the era of globalization and fiscal decentralization in the latter part of the twentieth century, public sectors have grown faster than private sectors around the world. On average, government expenditures accounted

The author wishes to thank Jim Alt, Jeff Frieden, Michael Hiscox, Per Pettersson-Lindbom, Antonio Rangel, Karen Remmer, Susan Rose-Ackerman, Anwar Shah, Ken Shepsle, Romain Wacziarg, Barry Weingast, Erik Wibbels, Justin Wolfers, and seminar participants at Harvard, Stanford, Texas A&M, the University of Washington, and the World Bank for helpful comments.

International Organization 57, Fall 2003, pp. 695–729
© 2003 by The IO Foundation.   DOI: 10.1017/S0020818303574021

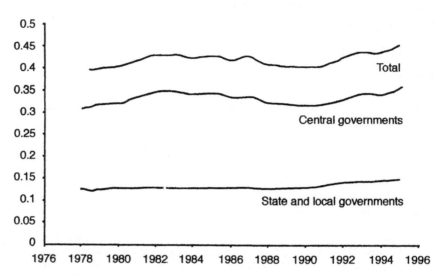

FIGURE 1. *Government expenditure as share of GDP: Average for 29 countries*

for around 39 percent of gross domestic product (GDP) in 1978, while by 1995 the average had increased to more than 45 percent for a sample of twenty-nine countries. (See Figure 1.)[1] The growth has been particularly pronounced in the 1990s.

Political scientists and economists have long sought to explain cross-national variation in levels and changes in government expenditure, often with mixed success. Although the academic literature focuses almost exclusively on central governments, the growth of state and local public sectors has been more pronounced in relative terms. This article directs attention to the balance of taxing and spending authority between central and subnational governments. In doing so, it returns to one of the oldest, and perhaps least successful, explanations of fiscal scale with a new perspective and new data. With their famous "Leviathan" hypothesis, Geoffrey Brennan and James Buchanan posit that "total government intrusion into the economy should be smaller, ceteris paribus, the greater the extent to which taxes and expenditures are decentralized."[2] Depicting government as a revenue-maximizing Leviathan, Brennan and Buchanan argue that as long as some individuals and firms are mobile, fiscal decentralization forces governments to engage in tax competition, thus destroying Leviathan's monopoly on taxation and bringing

---

1. The data set used to create Figure 1 is introduced below. The twenty-nine countries are those for which a full time series from 1978 to 1995 was available (with the exception of a small number of missing observations that were interpolated to create the chart).
2. Brennan and Buchanan 1980, 15.

government spending closer to the preferences of citizens. This argument dove-tails with other less cynical suppositions that decentralization helps resolve an in-herent agency problem between citizens and government.

This hypothesis was the subject of several empirical analyses in the 1980s. Though fiscal decentralization has been linked to lower government spending in some U.S., Canadian, and Swiss case studies,[3] cross-national studies have been unable to demonstrate the hypothesized relationship.[4] Indeed Wallace Oates has declared Leviathan a "mythical beast."[5] More recently, Ernesto Stein demon-strates that fiscal decentralization is actually associated with larger government in Latin America.[6]

However, this article argues that existing cross-national studies are insufficient to dispel the myth of Leviathan for two reasons. First of all, they employ cross-section averages or single-year snapshots. Thus they shed little light on the dy-namic nature of decentralization and the growth of government—both of which are processes that unfold over time. Governance in many countries around the world is undergoing a major transformation since the 1980s. Cross-national empirical analysis demonstrates that a pronounced trend toward fiscal decentral-ization is linked with transitions to democracy—especially in large, formerly cen-tralized countries.[7] Using the same group of twenty-nine countries as Figure 1, Figure 2 shows that average state and local expenditure as a share of the total government sector has jumped from around 20 percent in 1987 to 32 percent in 1995. Thus it may be inappropriate to conduct empirical analysis as if all coun-tries have reached a long-term equilibrium.

Second, until very recently, insufficient attention has been given to the precise institutional incentives created by different forms of decentralization. Above all, if decentralization is to have a constraining effect on the growth of government, it must occur on both the expenditure and revenue sides. In the vast majority of countries, however, increased state and local expenditures are funded primarily by grants, shared revenues, or other sources that are controlled and regulated by the center. Expenditure decentralization without corresponding local tax powers will not engender the tax competition that drives the Leviathan model, nor will it strengthen the agency relationship between local citizens and their representatives.

On the contrary, decentralization funded by "common pool" resources such as grants and revenue-sharing might have the opposite effect. By breaking the link between taxes and benefits, mere expenditure decentralization might turn the pub-lic sector's resources into a common pool that competing local governments will attempt to overfish. Depending on whether funded by local or common pool

---

3. For example, Marlow 1988; Joulfaian and Marlow 1990; Grossman 1989; and Feld, Kirch-gässner, and Schaltegger 2003.

4. For an exhaustive literature review, see Feld, Kirchgässner, and Schaltegger 2003.

5. Oates 1985.

6. Stein 1999.

7. See Panizza 1999; and Garrett and Rodden 2003.

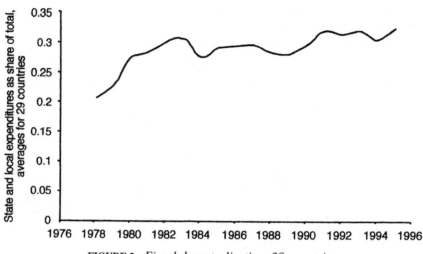

FIGURE 2. *Fiscal decentralization, 29 countries*

resources, decentralization might either retard or intensify the growth of government. Thus meaningful cross-national analysis requires data on transfers, revenue-sharing, and local taxation that have heretofore not been examined.

This article reexamines the link between decentralization and the growth of government by addressing each of these problems. First, rather than concentrating exclusively on cross-country variation, I use panel data from a large group of countries spanning the years from 1978 to 1997 and use an error-correction setup to distinguish between transitory and long-term effects. Second, while expenditure decentralization is rather easy to measure across countries, subnational revenue autonomy is often swept under the rug in empirical research because it is conceptually complex and difficult to capture with cross-national data. As a corrective, I use a new data set that aims to pinpoint different aspects of subnational revenue autonomy.

The analysis demonstrates quite clearly that the effect of decentralization on government size is conditioned by the nature of fiscal federalism. Other things equal, decentralization (a relative shift in revenue from the center to the subnational governments), when funded by common pool resources, is associated with faster growth in overall government spending. In contrast, though the result relies on a smaller sample, decentralization that is funded by autonomous local taxation is associated with slower government growth.

The rest of this article proceeds as follows. The next section reviews and expands on existing theories linking decentralization and the size of government. The following section introduces the data set and empirical approach and then estimates a basic model exploring the conditional effects of decentralization on government size for a large sample of countries. The next section takes a closer look at the role of intergovernmental transfers by conducting separate analyses of central and subnational expenditures. While the global data set is useful for distinguishing between budgetary grants and various forms of "own-source" subnational revenue, it is poorly suited to examine state and local tax autonomy. The following section takes up this task with a smaller data set composed of countries from the Organization of Economic Cooperation and Development (OECD). The final section concludes and points out avenues for further research.

Decentralization and Government Spending

Perspectives on the Size of Government

A good deal of variation across countries in the size of government can be explained by examining the demands of citizens for public spending, which are to a large extent shaped by demographic and geopolitical factors. For instance, countries with a large portion of the society above or below the working age might have larger governments. According to popular interpretations of "Wagner's Law," the income elasticity of demand for government output is greater than unity, which leads to an increasing government share of total output as the economy expands. Additionally, the distribution of income before taxes and transfers within a country might shape the strength of demands for redistribution.[8] Another literature examines the role of international trade and demands for government spending.[9]

Most models of government spending in the public finance tradition ignore the problem of preference aggregation—government is by assumption a benevolent despot that implements socially optimal policies.[10] An alternative body of research in political economy examines government size as reflecting the optimal policy of the median voter. From either analytical perspective, government spending is viewed as ultimately "responsive" to underlying exogenous preferences. Yet another perspective views government spending as inherently "excessive,"[11] taking seriously the problem that demands by citizens for public spending are satisfied through an agency relationship that is fraught with difficulties. By no means does governmental policy necessarily represent the ideal point of the median voter. First of all, officials might abuse the natural information asymmetry between rulers and ruled and line their own pockets, leading to a larger public sector than

---

8. See, for example, Meltzer and Richard 1981; and Bolton and Roland 1997.

9. Cameron 1978 argues that small, open economies are more likely to develop strong labor movements and left-wing parties, and in turn these political conditions have been conducive to the growth of the public economy. Alternatively, Rodrik 1998 argues that increasing trade interdependence heightens insecurity, which in turn strengthens demands for public sector risk-sharing.

10. The classic text is Musgrave 1959.

11. A distinction between "responsive" and "excessive" explanations for the growth of government spending was made by Buchanan 1977. The distinction is explored empirically in the U.S. politics literature. See, for example, Berry and Lowry 1987.

citizens would prefer. This has been the concern of the vast public choice literature on "rent-seeking," which departs from traditional public finance models and derives its analytical insights from assuming that governments maximize "perks" or "rents" that are at odds with the interests of voters.[12]

Second, in the institutional political economy literature, politicians are viewed as primarily interested in reelection rather than rents or social welfare. Their electoral incentives, combined with the constraints of legislative institutions, might lead them to tax and spend more (or less) than the median voter would prefer. An important literature in this vein examines the possibility that representatives will seek to externalize the costs of government expenditures in their jurisdiction onto citizens of others, turning public revenue into a common pool that is quickly overfished.[13] As a consequence of the incongruence between spending and taxation that arises when geographically targeted expenditures are funded with general taxation, representatives misperceive the costs of spending and demand an "excessive" amount, because they take into account all of the benefits but only consider the share of taxes that falls on their constituents. This might lead to spending that exceeds the socially optimal amount. According to Buchanan and Wagner,[14] a further problem is that voters do not fully understand the relationship between current deficits and future taxes—they simply reward spending and punish taxation. Politicians with electoral motivations face incentives to take advantage of their "fiscally illuded" voters with excessive deficit-financed spending, especially in election years.

In a more recent literature, Persson and Tabellini argue that majoritarian—as opposed to proportional—elections increase competition between parties by focusing it in some key marginal districts, which leads to policies favoring targeted redistribution at the expense of broad public goods and social insurance programs.[15] They also argue that presidential regimes encourage more intense competition than parliamentary regimes, which leads to fewer rents, less redistribution, and smaller government in the former.[16]

Such institutional arguments hold constant demands for expenditure—as determined by demographics, economic growth, trade, and so on—and examine the role of institutional incentives structuring the agency relationship between citizens and politicians. One common thread in these arguments is the notion that institutions can strengthen or undermine the ability of citizens to discipline government's "natural" tendency toward excess. If one assumes that the natural tendency of government is to overspend, improved oversight should lead to smaller

---

12. An engaging debate between these perspectives is presented in Buchanan and Musgrave 1999.
13. See Buchanan 1977; and Weingast, Shepsle, and Johnsen 1981.
14. Buchanan and Wagner 1977.
15. Persson and Tabellini 2000, chaps. 8–9. Milesi-Ferretti, Perotti, and Rostagno 2001 derive rather similar predictions from a model focusing on how electoral institutions affect voters' strategic delegation.
16. Persson and Tabellini 2000, chap. 10. Empirical support is provided in Persson and Tabellini 2002.

government. But in more recent literature, institutions affect the size of government in ways that do not require rent-seeking assumptions. Institutions might systematically provide career-oriented politicians with incentives to overfish the common revenue pool, or to favor one group over another—rural over urban dwellers, residents of marginal or "swing" districts, the middle class, or perhaps capital over labor. In this view, institutions that favor voters with strong preferences for public goods or redistribution should be associated with larger government.

Decentralization as a Constraint on Leviathan

Each of these intellectual traditions has posited a link between fiscal decentralization and the size of the public sector. First, to the extent that fiscal decentralization brings government "closer to the people" and facilitates a better match between local preferences and local policies, it may enhance the information available to voters about government activities and put them in a better position to sanction poor performance or rent-seeking, perhaps even clarifying the tax-benefit link and reducing the problem of fiscal illusion.[17] Besley and Case argue that "benchmark competition" allows voters in adjacent jurisdictions to compare directly tax prices paid and public goods received, assessing whether decentralized governments are wasting or stealing resources.[18] If one assumes that a component of tax revenue is always stolen or wasted, having a more efficient jurisdiction next door might put limits on the size of that component.

However, such argument linking decentralization and enhanced accountability require hefty assumptions about the quality of the local democratic process and the information available to voters. Under plausible conditions, decentralization is just as likely to lead to capture by local interest groups and increased corruption.[19] Moreover, given the limited resources that citizens have to invest in monitoring the fiscal activities of government, it is plausible that they are better equipped to monitor only one level of government—the central government—and any decentralization of spending or taxing authority will undercut monitoring.[20] Taking a different perspective, Wallace Oates questions the link between better monitoring and smaller government, pointing out that if decentralization enhances oversight of government, voters might actually demand more spending, knowing that less of it will be dissipated in rents.[21] In short, the arguments asserting a relationship between decentralization, improved accountability, and smaller government are driven by rather strong assumptions about the preferences of voters and politicians. Moreover, the logic of each of these arguments requires not only the

17. For a welfare economics perspective, see Oates 1972. For a public choice perspective, see Buchanan 1995.
18. Besley and Case 1995.
19. See Bardhan and Mookherjee 2000; Rodden and Rose-Ackerman 1997; and Treisman 2001.
20. Franzese 2001.
21. Oates 1985 gives credit to John Wallis for formulating this argument.

decentralization of expenditure authority but also tax authority. A stronger tax-benefit link, clearer information, stronger incentives for monitoring, and benchmark competition will not arise if taxation remains centralized.

In addition to strengthening monitoring, tax decentralization might help resolve the common pool problem. Consider a "fiscally centralized" system where local public goods are funded through general taxation and allocated in a central legislature featuring district-based representation. In the basic common pool setup, each district decides on the supply of public goods, and the centralized tax rate is residually determined. The common pool problem arises because each district internalizes the benefit of its public goods but internalizes only a fraction of the social marginal cost of higher taxes. Spending should be lower in an alternative decentralized scenario in which all public goods must be funded at the district level by local taxes. However, the existence of the common pool problem in practice depends a great deal on the specifics of legislative organization[22] and can be rather easily circumvented by determining the size of the budget before addressing allocation, or by delegating authority to a strong finance minister or president.[23] The presence of a legislative common pool problem is very difficult to pinpoint using cross-national data, so it is difficult to identify the countries in which fiscal decentralization might solve it.

The literature on tax competition—which spans the perspective of public choice, public finance, and institutional political economy—provides the most unambiguous link between fiscal decentralization and smaller government. Brennan and Buchanan made the argument that under decentralization, government's quest for rents and revenue is undermined by the need for jurisdictions to compete with one another for mobile sources of revenue.[24] A much earlier version of this argument was made by Friedrich von Hayek, who laid out a vision of "interstate federalism" in which "the methods of raising revenue would be somewhat restricted for the individual states. Not only would the greater mobility between the states make it necessary to avoid all sorts of taxation that would drive capital or labor elsewhere, but there would also be considerable difficulties with many kinds of indirect taxation."[25] In this "excessive government" public choice perspective, tax competition reduces rents and, hence, a smaller public sector enhances overall welfare.

A similar connection between tax competition and smaller government has also been established in public economics models with benevolent despots in an opti-

---

22. Inman and Rubinfeld 1997 contrast "minimum winning coalition" legislatures and "universalistic" legislatures. The latter are more likely to demonstrate the common pool problem. Moreover, weak or fragmented coalition governments may find it difficult to withstand spending pressure, as in Rattsø 2000. A less political model is presented by Persson and Tabellini 1994, in which subnational governments bribe the central government to provide them with a larger share of common resources.

23. See Von Hagen 1998.

24. Brennan and Buchanan 1980.

25. Hayek 1939, 270; 1948, 260. This argument has recently been extended to explain commitments to the preservation of markets. See, for example, Weingast 1995.

mal taxation framework.[26] But this perspective often views the result as pushing public spending away from the social optimum rather than toward it. Tax competition is viewed as a problem to be solved with central government intervention. Not surprisingly, the debate has taken an ideological tone, often turning into arguments about the appropriateness of radically different optimistic and cynical assumptions about the motivations of politicians.

However, one need not make blunt assumptions about benevolent or malevolent politicians to derive a link between tax competition and small government. The same result can be obtained by adopting an institutional political economy perspective and analyzing a conflict between owners of relatively mobile and less mobile assets. Specifically, decentralized capital taxation implies not only a shift in the burden of taxation toward owners of immobile assets, but under very plausible conditions it also implies smaller government.

Consider a closed, centralized country with n identical districts, where each district consists of individuals divided into cleavages based on the relative mobility of the assets from which they receive their income (labor versus capital, land owners versus renters, farmers versus light manufacturing). Also assume that these moving costs are exogenous and that—especially plausible for labor and capital—the owners of relatively immobile assets outnumber the owners of mobile assets (by the same margin within each district and in the country as a whole). In this centralized system, the level of spending on public goods, G^c, is determined by the national median voter—an owner of relatively immobile assets—and distributed to the districts according to population. In this scenario, the national median voter will choose to externalize as much of the fiscal burden as possible onto owners of more mobile assets. In the extreme case, the tax rate on mobile assets is set at the revenue-maximizing rate at the top of the Laffer curve, T_m^c, while the rate on immobile assets, T_i^c, is set at zero. Ignoring deficit finance, the level of public expenditure is

$$G^c = M(T_m^c) + I(T_i^c) \tag{1}$$

where M is the value of mobile assets and I is the value of immobile assets. Because T_i^c is zero, public expenditures are simply equal to $M(T_m^c)$.

Contrast this with a decentralized setting in which the same districts are independent jurisdictions who set their own tax rates and choose their own levels of spending. Spending in the decentralized system, G^d, is a summation of the level chosen by each individual jurisdiction. The median voter within each jurisdiction still prefers to externalize the same portion of the fiscal burden onto owners of mobile assets, but the latter are now free to shop around for jurisdictions that can offer them a lower tax rate. Unless the jurisdictions can form a cartel, in the

---

26. For example, see Zodrow and Mieszkowski 1986; and Wilson 1986. For a literature review, see Wilson 1999.

presence of fiscal competition it will be impossible for any jurisdiction to charge T_m^c. The less mobile within each jurisdiction must compete with those in other jurisdictions for mobile individuals and firms to tax, and T_m^d falls to the equilibrium value in the intergovernmental marketplace. Especially when the relevant distinction is between capital and labor, labor will be forced to lower capital taxation to preserve jobs. The only way to maintain the same level of public spending as in the centralized scenario is for each jurisdiction to raise T_i to the point where $I(T_i^d) = M(T_m^c - T_m^d)$. Stripped of the power to externalize the funding of public goods onto the mobile, owners of immobile assets must now choose only the level they can afford by taxing themselves. If they choose to make up the full difference, decentralization would merely entail a shift in the tax burden from the mobile to the immobile. In the more likely event that the immobile majority demands higher levels of expenditure in the centralized scenario (where the tax burden falls on concentrated owners of mobile capital), tax decentralization implies that expenditures fall below the level that the median voter would select in a world where the exit power of the mobile minority is limited.[27]

In sum, whether one travels the roads of welfare economics, public choice, or institutional political economy, one arrives at the same hypothesis, though with radically different normative interpretations: other things equal, decentralized taxation—in particular capital taxation—restricts the size of government. Though decentralized taxation might reduce agency costs as well, the simplest and most compelling logic involves limitations on the taxation of mobile capital.

Decentralization as a Boon for Leviathan

The intergovernmental tax competition literature resonates with theories of globalization and public spending. A familiar logic holds that as countries open capital markets and compete for foreign investment, governments are forced to reduce capital taxation and ultimately either shift the burden of taxation onto the immobile or reduce public expenditures. Even if the median (presumably immobile) voter prefers higher expenditures in a world of perceived increasing economic insecurity and governments are primarily interested in making voters happy, the constraints of competing for mobile capital may force government expenditures below this ideal point.

There is a very important difference, however, between global tax competition and fiscal decentralization within countries—the presence of a central government "Leviathan." No system of fiscal federalism is anarchic. Even in the most decentralized fiscal systems, such as Canada and the United States, the activities of the

---

27. Again, the empirical prediction is clear, but the normative implication is not. Persson and Tabellini 2000, chap. 6, provide a more complete dynamic model of distributive battles between capital and labor in the context of mobility with a similar result. They point out that even though equilibrium expenditure is pushed below the ideal point of the median voter, tax competition might nevertheless be socially desirable because it lends credibility to a policy of nonconfiscatory capital taxes. Without tax competition, the government cannot commit ex ante not to over-tax capital after it has accumulated.

central government are interdependent with those of the subnational governments. In more centralized systems, such as the United Kingdom or Norway, governments regulate virtually every aspect of local taxation, expenditure, and borrowing. In all systems of fiscal federalism, subnational governments are agents not only of local citizens, but also—and in some cases much more so—agents of the central government. The vision of unconstrained tax decentralization in the simple decentralization scenario above is unrealistic. In addition to direct regulation, central governments alter the incentives of subnational governments through intergovernmental grants.

Such grants can affect the link between fiscal decentralization and the size of government in several ways. First of all, in the traditional public economics literature on fiscal federalism, grants are made by benevolent central governments primarily to internalize externalities and solve coordination problems. Under the reasonable assumption that a shift toward greater local government resources and autonomy leads to increased interjurisdictional externalities and coordination problems, the demand for corrective intergovernmental transfers will increase. Decentralization funded through grants might also be associated with a larger public sector if something exogenous, such as a baby boom or terrorist threat, increases the demand for local public goods, such as primary education or emergency preparedness, which in many countries are funded through general taxes that are transferred to states, towns, or districts. In fact, the global trend toward fiscal decentralization has occurred almost exclusively through increased grants and shared revenues rather than the devolution of tax authority. In newly decentralizing developing countries, this fact is shaped in part by the challenges of developing effective systems of local tax administration in the context of poverty, regional inequality, and administrative underdevelopment.

It is relatively clear from public economic theory that increased grants should be associated with increased subnational expenditures. In a model that focuses on the indifference of the median voter between spending income on public and private goods, Bradford and Oates posit that the effect of a grant can be equivalent to that of a reduction in taxes to individual taxpayers.[28] When grants go up, the median voter will demand some increase in the consumption of private goods. However, unless one makes the extreme assumption that the income elasticity of demand for public goods is zero, increased grants should have a positive effect on spending by local governments. Moreover, a massive empirical literature spanning many decentralized countries shows not only that increased grants have positive effects on local expenditures, but in contrast to the "equivalence theorem," very little if any of the windfall is absorbed by tax reductions. Though the underlying logic is poorly understood, the "flypaper effect"—the observation that money "sticks where it hits"—is one of the most enduring empirical results in public economics.[29]

---

28. Bradford and Oates 1971.
29. For a review of theoretical and empirical studies, see Hines and Thaler 1995.

Existing literature provides much less insight into what happens to the budget of the central government when it increases grants. Do increased intergovernmental transfers supplement or replace existing central government expenditures? The latter is possible but seems unlikely. For instance, if an increase in grants is motivated by demands to solve an interjurisdictional externality problem or respond to rising demands for local public goods, there is no compelling reason to believe that demands for other forms of central government expenditure will wane. In short, though somewhat ambiguous, one might expect that other things equal, increasing reliance on intergovernmental grants will be correlated with larger government purely from a welfare economics perspective, without the introduction of rent-seeking and electoral motivations.

But the adoption of a public choice or institutional political economy perspective makes the case much stronger. In practice, intergovernmental grants are not distributed by benevolent central planners, but rather by strategic politicians. Political incentives might create a distributive logic in grant programs that puts upward pressure on the size of government. Governments will not compete if they do not tax, or if fiscal equalization schemes guarantee them a flow of revenue that undermines their incentives to exert tax effort.[30] In fact, some public choice scholars view intergovernmental grants as cartel-like collusion among subnational governments to avoid the discipline of tax competition.[31] Alternatively, revenue-sharing and transfer schemes might originate as attempts by less mobile groups, such as farmers and laborers, to exert voice at the center to avoid the deleterious (for them) effects of tax competition. Contrary to the simple scenario described above, even in the most decentralized countries, the central government reserves the right to tax mobile capital. This gives the "losers" from tax competition a chance to mobilize at the central level. If the power to set tax rates on mobile capital is devolved to lower-level governments, immobile asset owners might attempt to raise the federal tax rates on mobile capital to make up for the difference between $M(T_m^c)$ and $M(T_m^d)$, distributing these revenues through grants or revenue-sharing programs.

Second, returning to arguments about agency and monitoring, decentralization might actually distort information and weaken oversight if funded by intergovernmental grants rather than local tax effort. The involvement of two or three levels of government in funding, legislating, and implementing the same policies makes it difficult for voters to identify and punish waste and rent-seeking. Moreover, the center-local agency relationship is laden with adverse selection problems, because local governments have incentives to exaggerate costs and distort information when reporting to the center to receive larger transfers. Decentralization funded by increased transfers might muddle rather than clarify the link between taxes and benefits, which increases the likelihood of fiscal illusion. In addition to the problems

---

30. Careaga and Weingast 2000 refer to this as the "fiscal law of 1 over n" in which revenue-sharing programs undermine incentives for fiscal effort among recipient governments.
31. See Grossman 1989; and Grossman and West 1994.

of complexity and opacity, intergovernmental grants create the appearance that local public expenditures are funded by nonresidents, causing voters to demand an excessive amount.[32] In this context, legislators face strong incentives to over-fish the common revenue pool as described above, leading to larger government if the budget process and organization of the legislature do not place firm limits on overall expenditures. Rather than ameliorating the common pool problem, decentralization funded by increased transfers might exacerbate it.

The problem is only compounded if local governments have access to independent borrowing, in which case the fiscal illusion associated with intergovernmental transfers can soften the local budget constraint and create an intergovernmental moral hazard problem. For a variety of reasons, central governments might find it difficult to commit to a policy of ignoring self-induced subnational fiscal crises, especially when these threaten to undermine the stability of the banking system, the macroeconomy, and the country's credit rating, not to mention the government's re-election chances.[33] Heavy dependence on intergovernmental transfers increases the likelihood that central government officials will be held politically responsible for local service reductions or defaults. If local tax autonomy is limited and subnational governments are dependent on a large and increasing flow of finance from the common revenue pool to fund public expenditures, voters and creditors are likely to perceive an implicit bailout guarantee.[34] This encourages local governments to borrow aggressively rather than adjust in the face of revenue shortfalls, attempting to externalize the costs of adjustment onto other jurisdictions. If cofinancing obligations undermine the center's commitment to ignore subnational fiscal woes, the long-term result will be higher expenditures at every level of government.

Though the normative implications diverge widely, one can derive the same empirical prediction from public economics, public choice, or institutional political economy: decentralization funded by intergovernmental grants from the common revenue pool will be associated with higher overall government spending.

The Conditional Effect of Fiscal Decentralization on the Growth of Government

Depending on the precise nature of political and fiscal incentive structures, fiscal decentralization might lead either to a smaller or larger public sector. Some variant of the "Leviathan" hypothesis should hold if a shift toward greater local government expenditure as a share of the total public sector is driven by a shift toward greater local tax autonomy. More precisely, decentralization should lead to smaller government if it explicitly shifts taxation—especially of mobile assets—from the

32. For an overview of concepts and measurements of fiscal illusion and a literature review, see Oates 1991. For a theoretical application to intergovernmental grants in particular, see Oates 1979.
33. See Rodden, Eskeland, and Litvack 2003.
34. See Rodden 2002, 2003; and Eichengreen and Von Hagen 1996.

center to the subnational governments without a corresponding increase in central government taxation. On the other hand, the common pool hypothesis holds that if decentralization is funded by intergovernmental transfers or revenue-sharing schemes, it will be associated with a larger public sector.

Previous Studies

In the first study to use cross-national evidence to assess the Leviathan hypothesis, no distinction was made between the Leviathan and common pool hypotheses, and the measures of decentralization were quite simple—subnational revenue and expenditure shares of the total public sector.[35] While Wallace Oates found no significant relationship, more recent work by Ernesto Stein and his associates finds a significant positive relationship between decentralization (measured in a similar way) and the size of government.[36] They introduce intergovernmental grants into their analysis and find that, consistent with the common pool hypothesis, this relationship is compounded by dependence on intergovernmental transfers. Moreover, the Stein study demonstrates the advantage of using a small data set with cross-section averages; it allows one to focus on specific aspects of the intergovernmental system—such as the procedures through which grants are formulated and distributed—that might help shed further light on the common resource problem.

However, this empirical approach does not allow for the possibility that the relationship between decentralization and government spending might be reversed in those countries where decentralized spending is funded primarily by local taxes. In other words, it only tests a version of the common pool hypothesis and ignores the Leviathan hypothesis, though the two are not mutually exclusive. Thus in the analysis that follows, I attempt to improve on previous attempts to distinguish between decentralization that is funded by grants and "own-source" local revenue.

Perhaps the most serious disadvantage of previous empirical approaches has been the exclusive reliance on cross-section rather than diachronic variation.[37] A more convincing test of the relevant hypotheses would examine both cross-national and within-country changes in the nature of fiscal decentralization that might speed, retard, or perhaps even reverse the growth of the public sector. Thus in the analysis that follows, I use a data set composed of yearly observations from the period from 1978–97 for forty-four countries—all of the countries and years for which sufficient time-series data are available, along with smaller subsamples. These include countries from every continent and level of development. Descriptive statistics and further details about the dataset are provided in the Appendix.

35. Oates 1985.
36. See Inter-American Development Bank 1997; and Stein 1999.
37. For a critique of cross-country regressions on government size without a time-series component, see Berry and Lowery 1987.

Dependent Variables

The dependent variable for the regressions presented below is a measure of total public-sector expenditure as a percent of GDP. This is calculated for each country-year by taking the sum of expenditures of the central, state, and local governments from the IMF Government Finance Statistics (GFS)[38] and dividing by GDP (from the IMF's International Finance Statistics).[39] The regressions in the next section also examine central and subnational expenditure shares of GDP separately.

Main Independent Variables

For the purposes of this article, total government revenue can be broken down into three types:

- *Central revenue*: Revenue that is raised and spent by the central government.

- *Grants*: Revenue that is raised by the central government and transferred to lower-level governments.

- *Own-source subnational*: Revenue that is raised and retained by lower-level governments themselves.

Fiscal decentralization is defined as a decline in central revenue relative to grants and "own-source" subnational revenue. While critically important, the distinction between grants and "own-source" revenue is often difficult to make in practice. Fortunately, the GFS distinguishes between "grants" and various forms of "own-source" subnational revenue (local taxes, user fees, interest income, and so on). However, the residual category of "own-source" revenue is not necessarily a proxy for tax autonomy, because it fails to distinguish between tax revenues that are legislated and collected locally and those that accrue to the subnational governments automatically through revenue-sharing schemes. As a result, "own-source" revenue measured with the GFS may not be ideal for a cross-country analysis of public spending, because it does not fully capture the directness of the tax-benefit link or the likelihood of tax competition, both of which may be undermined by revenue-sharing programs or central regulation of local tax rates or bases.

Nevertheless, the distinction is important, and these data are quite valuable for the analysis of changes over time within countries. The GFS classification "grants" refers to explicit intergovernmental transfers that appear in the yearly budget but exclude recurring automatic distributions of shared taxes. Th s the grants reported

---

38. To avoid double-counting intergovernmental transfers (in the expenditures of the center and again at subnational levels), grants are subtracted out.

39. Surprisingly, all of the existing papers on globalization and the size of the public sector only measure central government spending (for example, Rodrik 1998; Garrett 2001; and Quinn 1997). The measures used in these studies are virtually identical to the central government component of the variable used here (correlation .97), but these studies severely underestima e the size of the public sector in the United States, Canada, Switzerland, and several other highly decentralized countries.

by the GFS reflect the subnational revenue flows that are most subject to central government discretion—arguably the type of transfer that is most likely to create a common resource dilemma or encourage bailout expectations. Hence grants to lower-level governments, taken as a percent of total public sector revenue at all levels of government (center + state + local), are a useful source of variation over time within countries to test the common pool hypothesis. This variable captures the effect of a shift in the balance of revenue from the center to the subnational governments that is funded by budgetary grants. The second independent variable, "own-source" subnational revenue as a share of total revenue, captures the effect of a relative shift that is funded by taxes, user fees, revenue-sharing, and other types of revenue. Taken together, these two variables capture the effects of two different types of fiscal decentralization.[40]

Estimation Technique

To assess properly the effects of different types of decentralization on the size of government, it may be important to distinguish between short-term and long-term dynamics. The arguments relating decentralization to the size of government are best understood as pertaining to long-term equilibria. A variety of factors might cause a transitory one-year increase in subnational revenue as a share of the total without altering any of the incentives discussed above. Rather, to shed light on the long-term "moving equilibrium," an error-correction model (ECM) is attractive. By estimating changes in the dependent variable and including both changes and lags of the independent variables, it is possible to distinguish between short-term or transitory effects of different types of decentralization, and the effects of a long-term moving equilibrium level. The error-correction version of the basic model can be expressed as follows:

$$\Delta LOG\ GOVERNMENT\ SIZE_{it}$$

$$= \beta_0 + \beta_1\ LOG\ GOVERNMENT\ SIZE_{it-1}$$

$$+\ \beta_2\ \Delta LOG\ GRANTS/TOTAL\ REVENUE_{it}$$

$$+\ \beta_3 LOG\ GRANTS/TOTALREVENUE_{it-1}$$

$$+\ \beta_4\ \Delta LOG\ OWN\text{-}SOURCE\ SUBNAT.REV./TOTAL\ REVENUE_{it}$$

$$+\ \beta_5\ LOG\ OWN\text{-}SOURCE\ SUBNAT.REV./TOTAL\ REVENUE_{it-1}$$

$$+\ \Sigma CONTROLS + \Sigma COUNTRY\ DUMMIES + \varepsilon \qquad (2)$$

---

40. In a preliminary set of regressions (not reported), I confirm the finding of Oates 1985 that when measured simply as subnational expenditures or revenues as a share of the total, decentralization has no significant effect on government size.

The coefficients of interest are β_3 and β_5, which estimate long-term effects.[41]

Im-Peseran-Shin and Levin-Lin tests for unit roots lead to the conclusion that the two decentralization variables are stationary. Total public expenditure as a share of GDP exhibits a pronounced upward trend, but tests conclude that the first differences used as the dependent variable are stationary.

It is important to include fixed country effects for several reasons. First of all, even with a large and carefully selected matrix of control variables, it is likely that without the country dummies, the analysis would suffer from substantial bias owing to omitted variables that help determine long-term cross-country differences in levels of public expenditure. Moreover, I have argued that the GFS distinction between grants and "own-source" revenue is more useful within countries over time than across countries, so it is prudent to focus on long-term within-country changes with a fixed-effects model.[42]

There is considerable debate about the appropriate estimation technique for such a model. The results presented below are from models that use the panel-corrected standard errors to deal with heteroskedasticity. However, the presence of the lagged level of the dependent variable can bias the fixed-effects ordinary least squares (OLS) estimator even if the error term is not correlated over time. In panels where the time-series dimension is long, this bias may not be severe. The data set used in this section does cover a reasonable number of years (1978–97), but in order to include as many countries as possible (including some in Sub-Saharan Africa and Central and Eastern Europe, for whom data were available only for shorter periods), the panels are unbalanced and include a smaller number of years for some countries. Thus I have explored (1) subsamples that allow for balanced panels and a long time-series dimension, and (2) a variety of alternative estimation techniques—described below—but each yields very similar results to the results reported in the tables.

Control Variables

The models presented below include a matrix of control variables suggested by the existing literature on the growth and size of government. For most of these variables as well, it is useful to examine separately the effects of first differences and lagged levels. First, I include several variables that might affect the demand for public expenditures. To take account of government attempts to smooth tax rates over time or conduct counter-cyclical policy in the short-term, or the possibility of the long-run "Wagner's law" effect, I include both changes and lagged levels of real GDP per capita (purchasing power parity in international dollars).[43] Demands for welfare spending might be driven by demographics, so I include

41. Logarithmic transformations of the fiscal variables are used because they improve the fit of the model and facilitate interpretation of coefficients.

42. In addition, a Hausman test rejects the random effects estimator, and the country dummies are jointly significant.

43. Taken from *Penn World Tables*. Data set available at ⟨http://pwt.econ.upenn.edu⟩. Accessed 7 July 2003.

changes and lagged levels of population and the "dependency ratio"—the portion of the society above or below the working age.[44] Country size (square kilometers) is included in some of the regressions as well. To control for the arguments discussed above about trade and capital account openness, I use changes and lagged levels of trade/GDP ratios to capture the international integration of national goods and services markets. In addition, capital account openness is a dummy variable from the IMF's annual Exchange Arrangements and Exchange Restrictions describing whether countries impose significant restrictions on capital account transactions (coded as "0") or not ("1" = open).

Next, I include variables that control for the effects of institutions. Demands for redistribution may be harder to ignore in more democratic countries, but, on the other hand, it is plausible that citizens have better control over rent-seeking politicians in democracies. To deal with these possibilities, I include changes and lagged levels of Gurr's 20-point scale of democracy (taken from the Polity 98 Data Set). In addition, there is a large literature linking divided government (in presidential systems) and fragmented governing coalitions (in parliamentary systems) to "wars of attrition" and budget deficits.[45] The implications of such political fragmentation for fiscal scale are less clear, but it seems plausible that "wars of attrition" in systems with large debt levels create a status quo bias in expenditures. A measure of executive and legislative fragmentation that bridges the parliamentary-presidential divide by incorporating both institutional and partisan veto players is included in the World Bank's Database of Political Institutions (DPI).[46] If the effect of political fragmentation on expenditures is through slowed adjustment, this variable should be interacted with the lagged debt level. Because debt data are unavailable for many countries, the central government's lagged deficit/GDP ratio is used instead. To control for the possibility of electoral spending cycles, I include a dummy variable for federal executive election years, also taken from the DPI. Next, given the arguments of Persson and Tabellini about presidential versus parliamentary regimes, I include a variable from the DPI that takes the value zero for presidential systems, one for systems with assembly-elected presidents, and two for parliamentary systems. Finally, to control for the effect of government partisanship, I include a variable, also from the DPI, that takes the value −1 when the executive is controlled by the left, 0 for the center, and 1 for the right.[47]

44. Taken from *World Development Indicators* 2000.
45. See Alesina and Drazen 1998; and Roubini and Sachs 1989.
46. The variable, called "CHECKS2A" is the sum of 1 for the president and 1 for each legislative chamber in presidential systems. Legislative chambers are not counted if elections are noncompetitive, or if list proportional representation (PR) is used and the president controls more than 50 percent of the body. For parliamentary systems, it is the sum of 1 for the prime minister and 1 for each coalition party. The number is reduced by 1 if closed lists are used and the prime minister is in the coalition. For noncompetitive elections, the number of coalition parties is reduced to zero. Finally, the index is augmented by 1 for every veto player whose left-right orientation is closer to the opposition's than to the average of the rest of the government.
47. All of the models presented below were also estimated with a full matrix of year dummies, but these were never jointly significant, nor did they affect the substance of significance of the results.

TABLE 1. *Estimates of changes in the size of government*

	Model 1: sample with five-year cutoff		Model 2: smaller balanced panel sample	
Dependent variable				
Δ LOG TOTAL EXPENDITURE/GDP				
Independent variables				
Δ LOG GRANTS/TOTAL REVENUE	0.007	(0.030)	0.049	(0.030)*
LOG GRANTS/TOTAL REVENUE$_{t-1}$	0.033	(0.015)**	0.047	(0.015)***
Δ LOG "OWN-SOURCE" SUBNATIONAL REVENUE/				
TOTAL REVENUE	0.032	(0.043)	−0.012	(0.033)
LOG "OWN-SOURCE" SUBNATIONAL REVENUE/				
TOTAL REVENUE$_{t-1}$	−0.086	(0.028)***	−0.073	(0.029)***
Control variables				
Δ LOG GDP PER CAPITA	−0.346	(0.118)***	−0.595	(0.144)***
LOG GDP PER CAPITA$_{t-1}$	0.025	(0.073)	−0.012	(0.074)
Δ LOG POPULATION	−1.345	(1.182)	−2.133	(1.441)
LOG POPULATION$_{t-1}$	−0.067	(0.115)	0.121	(0.104)
Δ DEPENDENCY RATIO	0.662	(0.947)	2.048	(1.201)*
DEPENDENCY RATIO$_{t-1}$	0.215	(0.192)	0.490	(0.186)***
Δ TRADE/GDP	0.023	(0.115)	0.057	(0.088)
TRADE/GDP$_{t-1}$	0.004	(0.059)	0.020	(0.075)
OPENNESS	0.036	(0.018)**	0.068	(0.017)***
Δ DEMOCRACY	−0.008	(0.005)	−0.003	(0.006)
DEMOCRACY$_{t-1}$	−0.001	(0.005)	−0.007	(0.006)
CENTRAL GOVT. SURPLUS$_{t-1}$	−0.907	(0.425)**	−0.769	(0.298)***
VETO PLAYERS	0.005	(0.004)	0.005	(0.004)
VETO PLAYERS × CENT. GOVT. SURPLUS$_{t-1}$	0.126	(0.072)*	0.151	(0.073)**
EXECUTIVE ELECTION YEAR	−0.001	(0.023)	0.034	(0.019)*
SYSTEM (pres/parl)	0.020	(0.022)	−0.024	(0.035)
PARTISANSHIP OF EXECUTIVE	−0.008	(0.007)	−0.002	(0.005)
LOG TOTAL EXPENDITURE/GDP$_{t-1}$	−0.432	(0.087)***	−0.372	(0.075)***
Constant	0.420	(2.196)	−1.924	(1.232)
Observations	514		310	
Number of countries	44		24	
R^2	0.45		0.39	

Note: Panel-corrected standard errors in parentheses. Fixed effects models, coefficients for country dummies not shown.
***$p < .01$, **$p < .05$, *$p < .1$.

Results

Table 1 presents two sets of results. Model (1) uses an unbalanced panel of all countries for which at least five time-series observations were possible. This group

---

Following the arguments of Easterly and Levine 1997, models were also estimated that controlled for ethnic fractionalization (as measured in the *Atlas Narodov Mira* 1964 and presented in Taylor and Hudson 1972). This variable was unavailable for several countries and the data are of questionable quality. In any case, the inclusion of this variable for a smaller sample did not affect any of the results.

includes forty-four countries with 503 total observations with an average of twelve years per country. Model (2) uses the best possible complete balanced panels, which includes twenty-five countries from 1980 to 1993.

The results are consistent with the "common pool" hypothesis. Other things equal, the predicted effect of a long-term 10 percent increase in grants as a share of total government revenue (for example, going from 10 percent—the mean value for the entire data set—to 11 percent) is somewhere between a 0.03 and 0.05 percent increase in the growth of the public sector. This result withstands a number of robustness checks and alternative estimation techniques. In fact, a relaxation of the five-year time-series cutoff allows for the inclusion of 600 observations from fifty-nine countries, which also yields similar results. Similar or even more pronounced results were found no matter what criteria were used for the inclusion of cases, and the result is not affected by dropping countries or even entire regions.[48] Finally, because of the potential bias associated with including the lagged level of the dependent variable in a fixed effects model, similar models were estimated using the Praise-Winsten transformation, as well as the generalized method of moments (GMM) estimator derived by Arellano and Bond, again yielding very similar coefficients and standard errors.

The negative coefficient on lagged "own-source" revenue (as a share of total revenue) is intriguing but difficult to interpret. It would appear that other things equal, a relative shift in resources away from the central government—if funded by sources other than budgetary grants—actually curbs the growth of government. This variable is not an acceptable proxy for the type of decentralization implied by the Leviathan literature, but the result invites the more refined analysis pursued below.[49]

A Closer Look at Grants

Fiscal decentralization, when funded by intergovernmental transfers from the central government, is associated with increasing overall public expenditures. Thus far it is unclear, however, whether this is driven by expenditures at the sub-

48. Separate effects were also estimated for federal and unitary countries, and the coefficients are quite similar for both.

49. The coefficients for most of the control variables behave as expected. The negative short-term coefficient for GDP per capita would seem to indicate counter-cyclical expenditure policy or smoothing. Because GDP is the denominator in the dependent variable, this suggests that expenditure growth lags behind the growth of the private sector during short-term booms and exceeds the growth of the private sector during short-term downturns. Larger countries demonstrate faster-growing government spending. The dependency ratio is a good predictor of government spending in the smaller sample but not the larger sample, which includes more non-OECD countries. Open capital accounts are associated with faster government growth. The conditional coefficients involving veto players tell a surprising story. When lagged deficits are large, increasing the number of veto players has a slight negative effect on government growth, but the effect becomes positive for a lagged surplus. Finally, election years are associated with higher expenditures in the smaller sample.

national level, the central level, or both. This section examines central and subnational expenditures separately. Rather than examining grants and "own-source" local revenues as portions of total revenues as before, here they are entered as shares of GDP to facilitate direct comparisons of their stimulative effects on expenditures at each level:

$$\Delta GOVERNMENT\ SIZE_{it} = \beta_0 + \beta_1\,\Delta GOVERNMENT\ SIZE_{it-1}$$
$$+ \beta_2\,\Delta GRANTS/GDP_{it}$$
$$+ \beta_3\,\Delta LOG\ GDP\ PER\ CAPITA_{it}$$
$$+ \Sigma PANEL\ DUMMIES + \varepsilon \qquad (3)$$

where government size is either SUBNATIONAL EXPENDITURE/GDP (model 3) or (CENTRAL GOVERNMENT EXPENDITURES-GRANTS)/GDP (model 4) in country i at year t. Borrowing from the empirical literature on the flypaper effect, the primary goal is to estimate the effect of changes in grants on changes in expenditures to obtain the marginal effect of a one-unit increase in grants on expenditures.[50] The basic question of this section is whether increased grants substitute or complement other forms of subnational revenue or central government expenditure.

First of all, when a subnational government receives an increase in grants, what portion of the increase goes to increased expenditures versus decreased local taxation? This is the key empirical question of the flypaper literature. For the regression in which SUBNATIONAL EXPENDITURE/GDP is the dependent variable (model 3), it is not necessary in three-tiered systems to combine the state and municipal sectors as above. Rather, because subnational rather than total expenditures are being estimated, the state and municipal sectors in such systems can be entered as separate panels, providing a greater number of observations.

Model (3) in Table 2 affords a simple estimation of the flypaper effect using each state and local sector used in Model 1 above.[51] The coefficient for Δ GRANTS/ GDP is close to unity. A one-unit increase in grants is associated with a 0.97 unit increase in expenditures by subnational governments. In the literature on the flypaper effect, this is at the upper end of the spectrum of findings for block grants.[52] Aggregate data for entire state or municipal sectors are quite blunt, and the grant programs around the world vary widely from specific-purpose matching grants to

50. Though similar results with a slightly better fit can be obtained using logarithmic transformations of the fiscal variables, here the interpretation of the coefficients is more intuitive using the raw data.

51. The overall fit and results of models (4) and (5) are unaffected by the inclusion of the control variables included in models (1) to (3).

52. Endogeneity likely biases the results of flypaper models using OLS. Above all, expenditures will affect grants in countries using matching grants. An alternative is the GMM estimator derived by Arellano and Bond 1991. This approach uses first differences and instrumental variable estimation, where the instruments are the lagged explanatory variables and lagged dependent variable (in differences). This approach yields a coefficient of 0.93. Using a range of different samples and estimation techniques, 0.93 was the lowest coefficient obtained, and the highest was slightly over 1.

TABLE 2. *Estimates of changes in the size of subnational and central government, disaggregated analysis*

	Model 3		Model 4	
Dependent variable	Δ SUBNATIONAL EXPENDITURE/GDP		Δ NON-GRANT CENTRAL GOVT. EXPENDITURE/GDP	
Independent variables				
Δ GRANTS/GDP	0.975	(0.074)***	0.537	(0.314)*
Δ LOG GDP PER CAPITA	0.002	(0.002)	−0.063	(0.044)
Δ DEPENDENT VARIABLE$_{t-1}$	−0.053	(0.073)	−0.122	(0.154)
Constant	0.0003	(0.003)	0.017	(0.024)
Observations	597		507	
Number of panels	53		44	
R^2	0.41		0.07	

Note: Panel-corrected standard errors in parentheses. Estimates for fixed unit effects not reported.
***$p < .01$, **$p < .05$, *$p < .1$.

open-ended block grants—but these results suggest that as an empirical phenomenon the flypaper effect is quite universal. Subnational governments appear to spend virtually all of the grants they receive from higher-level governments.

The next question is whether, when central governments increase their expenditures on grants to subnational governments, there is a corresponding decrease in direct (nongrant) central government expenditures. Model (4) uses the same independent variables as model (2) but examines the central government's expenditures (net of grants) instead.[53] If increased grants merely substitute for forms of expenditure that were formerly provided directly by the center, the coefficient would be negative. The results presented in Table 2 show that the coefficient is actually positive (though only significant at the 10 percent level)—increasing transfers are associated with increases in other forms of expenditure as well.

In short, this section has added precision to the relationship between grants and the growth of government demonstrated in the previous section. Increased grants to subnational governments appear to supplement rather than replace existing central government expenditure programs, while virtually the entire increase is spent by the recipient government.

A Closer Look at Tax Autonomy

The negative effect of "own-source" revenue decentralization on the growth of government discussed above is interesting, but it must not be construed as support

---

53. Similar to models (1) to (2), the subnational variables are once again state-local aggregations in three-tiered systems.

for the Leviathan hypothesis. While the GFS measure is a good start (and the only available cross-national time-series data), it drastically overestimates local revenue autonomy in cases where "own-source" subnational revenue is merely the output of a revenue-sharing scheme or where the tax rate and/or base are set by the central government. Fortunately, a recent report published by the OECD has undertaken the first systematic cross-national examination of subnational tax autonomy.[54] Although the OECD report only covers a small number of countries and does not examine changes over time, it contains valuable new information from which it is possible to calculate the share of total tax revenue for which subnational governments not only collect revenue, but also set the base and rate themselves.[55] The OECD study reveals that some local government sectors, such as the Danish municipalities and counties—although they raise a good deal of revenue—do not determine the bases and rates. Thus the value of this variable for Denmark is zero. At the other end of the spectrum, 30 percent of tax revenue in Canada is legislated and collected by the provinces and local governments. (See the descriptive statistics in the Appendix). Tax competition, and hence the Leviathan hypothesis, is much more plausible in countries such as Canada than in countries such as Denmark.

Because the OECD researchers collected their data in the early 1990s, it is useful to plot the tax autonomy index against the average size of government from 1985 to 1995. One of the key lessons of the OECD study is immediately clear in Figure 3: full tax decentralization is more unusual than commonly thought. The three developed, highly decentralized federations—Canada, Switzerland, and the United States—are in a class by themselves and their public sectors are among the smallest in the sample. By contrast, although welfare expenditures and even revenue collection are quite decentralized in the Scandinavian countries, either the tax rates, the determination of the base, or both are tightly regulated by the center.[56]

Perhaps the ideal empirical test of the Leviathan hypothesis would be a "natural experiment" in which some countries radically decentralize tax authority over time. In fact, Spain and Belgium may provide such an opportunity in the years ahead. But as a second-best approach, though the degrees of freedom are low, the tax autonomy index is a poor proxy for actual tax competition, and there are limits to what can be learned from cross-section averages, it is useful to estimate a simple regression on cross-section averages to examine the long-term effect of fiscal decentralization that features autonomous subnational taxation. The tax autonomy variable can be used in an interactive specification to examine the long-term effects of decentralization on the size of government at various levels of tax autonomy:

54. OECD 1999.
55. The OECD study does not include the United States and Canada. For these cases, I applied the OECD methodology to data collected from country sources.
56. Note that the index looks very different if the focus is solely on autonomy over rates. For instance, Swedish local governments do have wide-ranging autonomy over rates.

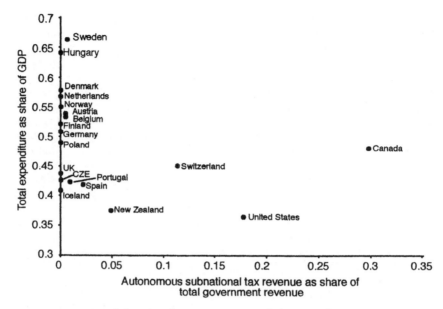

FIGURE 3. *Subnational tax autonomy and the size of government*

LOG AVE. GOVERNMENT SIZE$_i$

$\quad = \beta_0 + \beta_1 LOG\ AVE.\ AUTONOMOUS\ TAXES/SUBNAT.REVENUE_i$

$\quad + \beta_2 LOG\ AVE.\ SUBNAT.\ REVENUE/TOTAL\ REVENUE_i$

$\quad + \beta_3 LOG\ AVE.\ AUTONOMOUS\ TAXES/TOTAL\ REVENUE_i$

$\quad + \Sigma CONTROLS + \varepsilon$ (4)

The second term is the long-term (1985–95) average level of total government revenues accruing to subnational governments—the decentralization variable used in most previous studies using cross-country averages. The first term measures autonomous subnational taxation as a share of subnational revenue, and the third term (displayed in its raw form in Figure 3) is the multiplicative interaction of the first two. This setup allows for the calculation of conditional fiscal decentralization effects at different levels of subnational tax autonomy. The regression is presented in Table 3, and the conditional coefficients are plotted in Figure 4.

TABLE 3. *Estimates of long-term average size of government (1985–95), OECD sample*

Dependent variable	Model 5	
LOG TOTAL GOVERNMENT SPENDING/GDP		
Independent variables		
LOG AUTONOMOUS SUBNATIONAL TAX REVENUE/SUBNATIONAL REVENUE	0.48	(0.46)
LOG SUBNATIONAL REVENUE/TOTAL REVENUE	0.57	(0.11)***
LOG AUTONOMOUS SUBNATIONAL TAX REVENUE/TOTAL REVENUE	−2.93	(0.96)**
Control variables		
LOG GDP PER CAPITA	−0.22	(0.17)
LOG POPULATION	0.01	(0.02)
AREA (log square km)	0.09	(0.03)**
DEPENDENCY RATIO	1.10	(0.85)
TRADE/GDP	1.16	(0.18)***
WESTERN EUROPE DUMMY	−0.36	(0.11)**
EASTERN EUROPE DUMMY	−0.18	(0.15)
Constant	−0.10	(1.43)
Number of countries	18	
R^2	0.93	

Note: Model 5 is an ordinary least squares (OLS) "between effects" model. Standard errors in parentheses.
***$p < .01$, **$p < .05$, *$p < .1$.

In spite of the small number of observations, the variables of interest are highly significant. The R^2 is 0.93, while for the same model without the fiscal federalism variables it is 0.61.[57] In Figure 4, the horizontal axis represents the share of subnational revenue that is raised through autonomous local taxation, while the vertical axis represents conditional coefficients for the estimated effect of revenue decentralization on the long-term average size of government. The bold line is the conditional effect and the gray lines represent the 95 percent confidence interval. At the far left, decentralization is driven exclusively by revenue sources that the subnational governments do not directly control (grants, shared revenue, or centrally regulated taxes). This type of decentralization has a significant positive relationship with the average size of government. Figure 4 indicates that the majority of the OECD cases fall in this range. Moving to the right, decentralization has a smaller positive estimated effect on the size of government as subnational governments gain tax autonomy, and the coefficient is reversed when we reach the range of Switzerland, the United States, New Zealand, and Canada. Obviously the neg-

57. Only the control variables that approached statistical significance are included, along with region dummies.

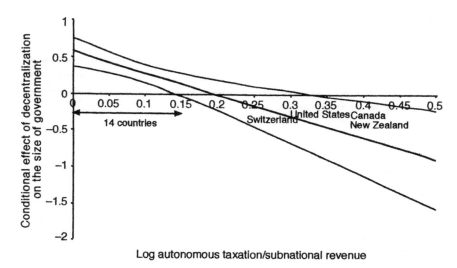

FIGURE 4. *The conditional effect of decentralization on the size of government* *(model 5, cross-country averages)*

ative conditional coefficients should be interpreted with caution, because they are based on such a small number of cases (as indicated by the widening confidence bands), but the results are similar if influential cases or even pairs of cases are dropped.

As a third-best approach, though the variable taken from the OECD study does not exhibit time-series variation, it is reasonable to assume that tax autonomy is relatively stable over time[58] and estimate an ECM model similar to models (1) and (2) using the smaller OECD data set, interacting the tax autonomy variable with the "own-source" decentralization variable to differentiate between the effects of "own-source" decentralization in countries with and without substantial tax autonomy.

Model (6), presented in Table 4, takes a simple approach. Given the skew in the tax autonomy data (see Figure 3), it makes sense to divide the countries into two discreet groups. Canada, the United States, Switzerland, and New Zealand can be classified as having high subnational tax autonomy and the others as low. Model (6) simply replicates model (1) but interacts the "own-source" decentralization variables with dummies for "high" and "low" tax autonomy. Controlling for grants (which demonstrate a similar positive effect on total expenditures as in larger sam-

---

58. The coverage does not include recent reforms in Spain and Belgium.

TABLE 4. *Estimates of changes in total government expenditure as share of GDP, OECD sample*

	Model 6		Model 7	
Dependent variable Δ LOG TOTAL EXPENDITURE/GDP				
Independent variables				
Δ LOG GRANTS/TOTAL REVENUE	0.024	(0.014)*	0.025	(0.018)
LOG GRANTS/TOTAL REVENUE$_{t-1}$	0.027	(0.008)***	0.015	(0.006)***
Δ LOG "OWN-SOURCE" SUBNATIONAL REVENUE/ TOTAL REVENUE × HIGH TAX AUTONOMY	−0.270	(0.196)		
LOG "OWN-SOURCE" SUBNATIONAL REVENUE/ TOTAL REVENUE$_{t-1}$ × HIGH TAX AUTONOMY	−0.188	(0.078)***		
Δ LOG "OWN-SOURCE" SUBNATIONAL REVENUE/ TOTAL REVENUE × LOW TAX AUTONOMY	0.038	(0.015)***		
LOG "OWN-SOURCE" SUBNATIONAL REVENUE/ TOTAL REVENUE$_{t-1}$ × LOW TAX AUTONOMY	0.015	(0.017)		
Δ LOG "OWN-SOURCE" SUBNATIONAL REVENUE/ TOTAL REVENUE			0.043	(0.017)***
LOG "OWN-SOURCE" SUBNATIONAL REVENUE/ TOTAL REVENUE$_{t-1}$			0.026	(0.013)**
LOG AUTONOMOUS SUBNATIONAL TAX REVENUE/ "OWN-SOURCE" SUBNATIONAL REVENUE			0.126	(0.087)
LOG AUTONOMOUS SUBNATIONAL TAX REVENUE/ TOTAL REVENUE			−0.690	(0.293)**
Control variables				
Δ LOG GDP PER CAPITA	−0.958	(0.103)***	−1.000	(0.096)***
LOG GDP PER CAPITA$_{t-1}$	−0.040	(0.057)	−0.022	(0.037)
Δ LOG POPULATION	−1.038	(1.664)	−0.214	(1.371)
LOG POPULATION$_{t-1}$	0.126	(0.155)	0.002	(0.006)
AREA (log square km)			0.007	(0.005)
Δ DEPENDENCY RATIO	−0.662	(1.020)	−0.363	(0.894)
DEPENDENCY RATIO$_{t-1}$	−0.072	(0.225)	0.041	(0.102)
Δ TRADE/GDP	0.083	(0.071)	0.122	(0.066)*
TRADE/GDP$_{t-1}$	−0.002	(0.062)	0.064	(0.037)*
OPENNESS	0.015	(0.009)*	−0.002	(0.009)
CENTRAL GOVT. SURPLUS$_{t-1}$	0.274	(0.163)*	0.242	(0.177)
VETO PLAYERS	−0.003	(0.004)	−0.001	(0.003)
VETO PLAYERS × CENT. GOVT. SURPLUS$_{t-1}$	−0.094	(0.047)**	−0.042	(0.038)
EXECUTIVE ELECTION YEAR	−0.010	(0.011)	−0.014	(0.010)
SYSTEM (pres/parl)	0.321	(0.411)	0.027	(0.017)
PARTISANSHIP OF EXECUTIVE	0.003	(0.003)	0.003	(0.003)
LOG TOTAL EXPENDITURE/GDP$_{t-1}$	−0.239	(0.062)***	−0.091	(0.026)***
Constant	−1.852	(2.372)	0.058	(0.357)
Observations	219		219	
Number of countries	18		18	
R^2	0.54		0.46	

Note: Panel-corrected standard errors in parentheses. Model 6 includes fixed country effects (not reported). Model 7 includes a panel of region dummies (not reported).
***$p < .01$, **$p < .05$, *$p < .1$.

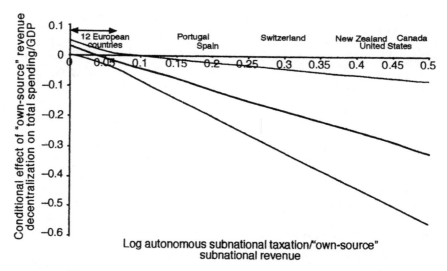

FIGURE 5. *The conditional effect of "own-source" decentralization on the size of government (model 7, time series cross-section)*

ples above), long-term "own-source" fiscal decentralization has a large negative effect on the growth of government in Canada, Switzerland, New Zealand, and the United States, and a positive (though not quite statistically significant) effect elsewhere.[59]

Another approach is taken in model (7), which uses the full range of variation in the (logged) tax autonomy index by interacting AUTONOMOUS SUBNATIONAL TAXATION/SUBNATIONAL "OWN-SOURCE" REVENUE with the lag of SUBNATIONAL "OWN-SOURCE REVENUE"/TOTAL REVENUE. This allows for the calculation of conditional coefficients that capture the estimated long-term effect of "own-source" decentralization at different levels of tax autonomy.[60] Figure 5 plots the conditional coefficients over the sample range, showing that the effect of decentralization is neutral or slightly positive for the majority of OECD countries where most

59. This result has been subjected to the same alternative specifications, sensitivity analysis, and sample restrictions as described above. The result is similar with or without the United States or Canada, but the significance falls below the 10 percent level if the most influential case—Switzerland—is dropped.

60. A disadvantage of this approach is that it is not possible to include fixed country effects because of their correlation with the tax autonomy variable. Model (7) includes a panel of region dummies instead. The results are not substantially altered by the inclusion of dummy variables for influential cases or simply dropping influential cases from the analysis.

subnational revenue generation is regulated by the center. Moving to the right—where state and local governments obtain larger portions of their "own-source" revenues from taxes over which they directly control the base and rate—tax decentralization is associated with smaller government.

Although falling short of incontrovertible proof, the results presented in this section should at least revive the Leviathan debate. But as with the positive effect of intergovernmental grants, the results do not suggest how to discriminate among the possible causal mechanisms. Tax competition might suppress government spending by limiting the taxation of mobile assets. Or if one adopts the perspective that democratic governments naturally tend toward excess, greater reliance on local taxation might reduce fiscal illusion, tighten the tax-benefit link, and strengthen incentives for oversight, perhaps through benchmark competition. Alternatively decentralization might simply resolve the common pool problem associated with centralized budgeting, though in this case one might expect to find that any tax decentralization would reduce the size of government regardless of how the base and rate are determined, which is apparently not the case.

The most important weakness of the analysis conducted in this section is its reliance on three cases—the United States, Switzerland, and Canada—that might be "special" for some reason other than tax decentralization, or that may have something in common that drives both tax decentralization and smaller government.[61] If so, one must go beyond the simple common thread of "federalism," traditionally defined as special rights and protections for provinces in the constitution and representation in an upper legislative chamber. For example, Germany and Austria have these features without tax decentralization or small public sectors. The introduction of a federalism dummy variable does not change any of the results in this article, nor does it approach statistical significance.[62] A more likely omitted variable has something to do with mutual suspicions owing to past civil wars or racial and linguistic differences that may have had a role in suppressing both the centralization of taxation and the growth of government. Perhaps the next step in this literature—both as a solution to the endogeneity problem and a way of choosing among the various causal mechanisms described above—is to go beyond the recent time slice and conduct a comparative historical analysis of (de)centralized taxation and the growth of government.

61. Of course, the results are also only as trustworthy as the quality of the tax autonomy variable, which is still a very rough approximation. For example, subnational governments in some countries, such as Sweden, have considerable autonomy over the tax rate but not the base, which may nevertheless facilitate competition. When autonomy over the rate only is used to construct the variable, the results are not statistically significant.

62. Another possible omitted variable concerns the size and structure of jurisdictions. One possibility raised in the Leviathan literature is that tax competition is more intense when jurisdictions are small and plentiful. In practice, however, smaller jurisdictions are less likely to have tax autonomy. Variables such as the number of jurisdictions, kilometers per jurisdiction, and persons per jurisdiction have been introduced the regressions above without producing significant results.

Conclusions

Those who are alarmed that the global trend toward fiscal decentralization entails dangerous tax competition have little to fear, and those who envision smaller, more efficient government have little to celebrate. Even in the most developed countries, subnational expenditures are most often funded by revenue-sharing schemes, taxes that are controlled by the central government, or outright intergovernmental transfers. In general, the trend toward fiscal decentralization is not moving countries closer to Hayek's "economic conditions of interstate federalism" or Weingast's "market-preserving federalism." These envision powerful, self-financing local governments and a credibly limited central government. If anything, decentralizing countries are moving closer to the overlapping, intertwined multitiered state described by Fritz Scharpf,[63] in which the finances of the central and local governments are increasingly difficult to disentangle.

However, neither the rarity of subnational tax autonomy in practice nor skepticism about revenue-hungry monsters implies that the link between tax decentralization and smaller government should be rejected. Rent-seeking assumptions are not necessary to see that interjurisdictional tax competition limits the ability of immobile asset owners to tax more mobile asset owners. Previous cross-national studies may have been looking for Leviathan in the wrong places using the wrong techniques. Using a limited OECD sample, this article presents evidence that decentralization—when funded primarily by autonomous local taxation—is associated with a smaller public sector. This helps explain why support has been found for the Leviathan hypothesis in time-series case studies of the United States, Canada, and Switzerland but not in larger cross-national studies. When funded by revenue-sharing, grants, or centrally regulated subnational taxation, fiscal decentralization is, if anything, associated with larger government in the OECD sample examined in this article. Using a much larger global sample, this article has also shown that decentralization funded by direct intergovernmental transfers is associated with a larger public sector—a heretofore untold part of the story of government growth around the world during the past twenty years.[64] When central governments increase transfers to subnational governments, they do not reduce their own direct expenditures, and subnational governments spend virtually every dollar of increased transfers.

One should be careful about divining normative or policy implications from these results. Both of the main results are consistent with "responsive" and "excessive" notions of government expenditure, and both are consistent with fiscal decentralization either improving or diminishing the welfare of the representative voter. Perhaps tax decentralization unjustly favors owners of mobile capital and leads to the underprovision of public goods or redistribution, but it might also

---

63. Scharpf 1976.
64. For individual case studies see Borge and Rattsø 2002; and Winer 1980.

eliminate waste, improve accountability, and help government commit to a policy of nonconfiscatory capital taxation. Moreover, decentralization that is funded by intergovernmental grants or revenue-sharing might reflect an efficient response to new demands for public goods that local governments are well positioned to provide but poorly equipped to fund. Demands for decentralization—especially when part of the process of democratization—might be accompanied by demands for increased redistribution and risk sharing that can only be funded by the central government. But on the other hand, there are good reasons for concern that increased reliance on intergovernmental transfers generates agency and common pool problems, especially when subnational governments have access to credit markets and the central government is politically weak.[65]

Given the problems associated with fiscal indiscipline and debt in countries that have decentralized by expanding intergovernmental transfers, it is tempting to conclude that the correlation between grants and larger government is indicative of the inefficiencies highlighted in theories of "excessive" government. However, such a conclusion would require theory and evidence about why countries choose decentralization in the first place, and how they choose their mixtures of grants, revenue-sharing, and local taxes. An increase in grants or revenue-sharing might represent an attempt by the center to shed uncomfortable responsibilities or a strategy in the game of distributive politics, but it might also represent a response to citizens' demands for better local services.

In short, this article has presented some interesting correlations, but the empirical setup does not allow for strong conclusions about causality. This is often the case with cross-country regressions, which are most useful when they shape—and in turn are shaped by—careful case studies. Explicitly comparative county studies are the best way to clarify the causal mechanisms linking intergovernmental fiscal structure and governmental spending. To sort out the causal mechanisms behind the results in this article and get a clearer picture of their normative and policy implications, it is necessary to make cross-national and time-series variations in the vertical fiscal structure of government endogenous. A difficult, but rewarding, further step for cross-national research is to explore political and economic history to find instruments for the relative centralization of taxation and expenditures across countries and over time.[66]

Fiscal decentralization likely has far-reaching implications not only for government's size, but also for its quality and accountability. The devil is in the details, and many questions remain unanswered. But in the final analysis, empirical investigation cannot answer a question that is at its heart ideological. Leviathan will always be a dangerous beast for some and a figment of the imagination for others.

---

65. Rodden 2002, 2003.
66. For first attempts that ignore the distinction between grants and subnational taxation and focus on recent decades, see Panizza 1999; and Garrett and Rodden 2003.

Appendix: Descriptive Statistics and Country Coverage

	Mean	Std. Dev.	Min.	Max.
Forty-four-country sample (models 1, 3, 4)				
TOTAL EXPENDITURE/GDP	0.41	0.15	0.07	1.02
SUBNATIONAL EXPENDITURE/GDP	0.12	0.09	0.002	0.36
NON-GRANT CENTRAL GOVT. EXPENDITURE/GDP	0.30	0.12	0.07	0.95
INTERGOVERNMENTAL GRANTS/GDP	0.04	0.04	0.0001	0.18
GRANTS/TOTAL REVENUE	0.11	0.09	0.0004	0.42
"OWN-SOURCE" SUBNATIONAL				
REVENUE/TOTAL REVENUE	0.17	0.13	0.02	0.55
GDP PER CAPITA	8651	5178	837	18975
POPULATION (millions)	54.36	132.43	0.25	913.60
AREA (log square km)	173174	183339	2639	741570
DEPENDENCY RATIO	0.61	0.14	0.44	0.98
TRADE/GDP	0.67	0.39	0.09	2.09
OPENNESS	0.41	0.49	0	1
DEMOCRACY	6.37	5.77	−10	10
VETO PLAYERS	2.95	1.71	1	13
CENTRAL GOVT. SURPLUS/GDP	−0.04	0.05	−0.30	0.05
SYSTEM (pres/parl)	1.45	0.85	0	2
EXECUTIVE ELECTION YEAR	0.06	0.23	0	1
PARTISANSHIP OF EXECUTIVE	0.10	0.85	−1	1
OECD sample (models 5, 6, 7)				
AUTONOMOUS SUBNATIONAL TAX REVENUE/				
SUBNATIONAL REVENUE	0.09	0.16	0	0.52
SUBNATIONAL REVENUE/TOTAL REVENUE	0.37	0.16	0.09	0.73
AUTONOMOUS SUBNATIONAL TAX REVENUE/				
TOTAL REVENUE	0.04	0.08	0	0.30

Note: The forty-four-country sample used in models 1, 3, and 4 includes all of the following countries, while the smaller "balanced panel" sample used in model 2 includes only the countries in italics: *Australia, Austria, Belgium,* Bolivia, Brazil, Bulgaria, *Canada,* Chile, Colombia, Costa Rica, *Denmark,* Fiji, *Finland, France, Germany,* Greece, Iceland, *India,* Indonesia, Iran, *Ireland, Israel,* Italy, Kenya, *Luxembourg,* Malaysia, *Mexico, Netherlands,* New Zealand, Nicaragua, *Norway,* Panama, Paraguay, Peru, *Philippines,* Romania, *South Africa, Spain, Sweden,* Switzerland, *Thailand, UK, United States,* and Zimbabwe. The countries included in the smaller OECD sample used in models 5, 6, and 7 are displayed in Figure 3.

References

Alesina, Alberto, and Allan Drazen. 1998. Why Are Stabilizations Delayed? In *The Political Economy of Reform*, edited by Federico Sturzenegger and Mariano Tommasi, 77–103. Cambridge, Mass.: MIT Press.

Arellano, Manuel, and Stephen Bond. 1991. Some Tests of Specification for Panel Data: Monte Carlo Evidence and an Application in Employment Equations. *Review of Economic Studies* 58 (2):277–97.

Bardhan, Pranab, and Dilip Mookherjee. 2000. Capture and Governance at Local and National Levels. *American Economic Review* 90 (2):135–39.

Berry, William, and David Lowery. 1987. Explaining the Size of the Public Sector: Responsive and Excessive Government Interpretations. *Journal of Politics* 49 (2):401–40.

Fiscal Federalism and the Growth of Government **727**

Besley, Timothy, and Ann Case. 1995. Incumbent Behavior: Vote-Seeking, Tax-Setting, and Yardstick Competition. *American Economic Review* 85 (1):25–45.

Bolton, Patrick, and Gerard Roland. 1997. The Breakup of Nations: A Political Economy Analysis. *Quarterly Journal of Economics* 112 (4):1057–90.

Borge, Lars-Erik, and Jørn Rattsø. 2002. Spending Growth with Vertical Fiscal Imbalance: Decentralized Government Spending in Norway: 1880–1990. *Economics and Politics* 14 (3):351–73.

Bradford, David, and Wallace Oates. 1971. Towards a Predictive Theory of Intergovernmental Grants. *American Economic Review* 61 (2):440–48.

Brennnan, Geoffrey, and James Buchanan. 1980. *The Power to Tax: Analytical Foundations of a Fiscal Constitution*. Cambridge: Cambridge University Press.

Buchanan, James. 1977. Why Does Government Grow? In *Budgets and Bureaucrats*, edited by Thomas Borcherding, 3–18. Durham, N.C.: Duke University Press.

———. 1995. Federalism as an Ideal Political Order and an Objective for Constitutional Reform. *Publius* 25 (2):19–27.

Buchanan, James, and Richard Musgrave. 1999. *Public Finance and Public Choice: Two Contrasting Visions of the State*. Cambridge, Mass.: MIT Press.

Buchanan, James, and Richard Wagner. 1977. *Democracy in Deficit: The Political Legacy of Lord Keynes*. New York: Academic Press.

Cameron, David R. 1978. The Expansion of the Public Economy: A Comparative Analysis. *American Political Science Review* 72 (4):1243–61.

Careaga, Maite, and Barry R. Weingast. 2000. The Fiscal Pact with the Devil: A Positive Approach to Fiscal Federalism, Revenue Sharing, and Good Governance. Paper presented at the Conference on Political Institutions and Economic Growth in Latin America, April, Stanford, Calif.

Easterly, William, and Ross Levine. 1997. Africa's Growth Tragedy: Policies and Ethnic Divisions. *Quarterly Journal of Economics* 112 (4):1203–50.

Eichengreen, Barry, and Jürgen von Hagen. 1996. Fiscal Restrictions and Monetary Union: Rationales, Repercussions, Reforms. *Empirica* 23 (1):3–23.

Feld, Lars, Gebhard Kirchgässner, and Christoph Schaltegger. Decentralized Taxation and the Size of Government: Evidence from Swiss State and Local Governments. Unpublished manuscript, University of St. Gallen, Switzerland.

Franzese, Robert. 2001. The Positive Political Economy of Public Debt: An Empirical Examination of the Postwar OECD Experience. Unpublished paper, University of Michigan, Ann Arbor.

Garrett, Geoffrey. 2001. Globalization and Government Spending Around the World. *Studies in Comparative International Development* 35 (4):3–29.

Garrett, Geoffrey, and Jonathan Rodden. 2003. Globalization and Fiscal Decentralization? In *Governance in a Global Economy: Political Authority in Transition*, edited by Miles Kahler and David Lake. Princeton, N.J.: Princeton University Press (forthcoming).

Grossman, Philip J. 1989. Fiscal Decentralization and Government Size: An Extension. *Public Choice* 62 (1):63–69.

Grossman, Philip J., and Edwin G. West. 1994. Federalism and the Growth of Government Revisited. *Public Choice* 79 (1–2):19–32.

Hayek, Friedrich von. 1939. The Economic Conditions of Interstate Federalism. *New Commonwealth Quarterly* V (2):131–49. Reprinted in Friedrich von Hayek. 1957. *Individualism and Economic Order*. Chicago: University of Chicago Press.

Hines, James R., Jr., and Richard H. Thaler. 1995. Anomalies: The Flypaper Effect. *Journal of Economic Perspectives* 9 (4):217–26.

Inman, Robert, and Daniel Rubinfeld. 1997. The Political Economy of Federalism. In *Perspectives on Public Choice: A Handbook*, edited by Dennis Mueller, 73–105. Cambridge: Cambridge University Press.

Inter-American Development Bank. 1997. Fiscal Decision Making in Decentralized Democracies. In *Latin America After a Decade of Reforms, Economic and Social Progress in Latin America Report*. Washington, D.C.: Johns Hopkins.

Joulfaian, David, and Michael Marlow. 1990. Government Size and Decentralization: Evidence from Disaggregated Data. *Southern Economic Journal* 56 (4):1094–1102.

Marlow, Michael. 1988. Fiscal Decentralization and Government Size. *Public Choice* 56 (3):259–69.

Meltzer, Allan, and Scott Richard. 1981. A Rational Theory of the Size of Government. *Journal of Political Economy* 89 (5):914–27.

Milesi-Ferretti, Gian Maria, Roberto Perotti, and Massimo Rostagno. 2001. Electoral Systems and Public Spending. Working Paper 01/22. Washington, D.C.: International Monetary Fund.

Musgrave, Richard. 1959. *The Theory of Public Finance: A Study in Public Economy.* New York: McGraw-Hill.

Oates, Wallace. 1972. *Fiscal Federalism.* New York: Harcourt Brace Jovanovich.

———. 1979. Lump-Sum Intergovernmental Grants Have Price Effects. In *Fiscal Federalism and Grants-in-Aid,* edited by P. Mieszkowski and W. Oakland, 23–30. Washington, D.C.: Urban Institute.

———. 1985. Searching for Leviathan: An Empirical Study. *American Economic Review* 75:748–57.

———. 1991. On the Nature and Measurement of Fiscal Illusion: A Survey. In *Studies in Fiscal Federalism,* edited by Wallace Oates, 431–48. Brookfield, Vt.: Edward Elgar.

Organization of Economic Cooperation and Development (OECD). 1999. *Taxing Powers of State and Local Government.* OECD Tax Policy Studies No. 1. Paris: OECD.

Panizza, Ugo. 1999. On the Determinants of Fiscal Centralization: Theory and Evidence. *Journal of Public Economics* 74 (1):97–139.

Persson, Torsten, and Guido Tabellini. 1994. Does Centralization Increase the Size of Government? *European Economic Review* 38 (3–4):765–73.

———. 2000. *Political Economics: Explaining Economic Policy.* Cambridge, Mass.: MIT Press.

Quinn, Dennis. 1997. The Correlates of Change in International Financial Regulation. *American Political Science Review* 91 (3):531–51.

Rodden, Jonathan. 2002. The Dilemma of Fiscal Federalism: Grants and Fiscal Performance Around the World. *American Journal of Political Science* 46 (3):670–87.

———. 2003. *Hamilton's Paradox: The Promise and Peril of Federalism.* Unpublished book manuscript, MIT, Cambridge, Mass.

Rodden, Jonathan, Gunnar Eskeland, and Jennie Litvack. 2003. *Fiscal Decentralization and the Challenge of Hard Budget Constraints.* Cambridge, Mass.: MIT Press.

Rodden, Jonathan, and Susan Rose-Ackerman. 1997. Does Federalism Preserve Markets? *Virginia Law Review* 83 (7):1521–72.

Roubini, Nouriel, and Jeffrey Sachs. 1989. Political and Economic Determinants of Budget Deficits in the Industrial Democracies. *European Economic Review* 33 (5):903–33.

Rodrik, Dani. 1998. Why Do More Open Economies Have Bigger Governments? *Journal of Political Economy* 106 (5):997–1032.

Scharpf, Fritz, Bernd Reissert, and Fritz Schnabel. 1976. *Politikverflechtung: Theorie und Empirie des kooperativen Föderalismus in der Bundesrepublik.* Kronberg, Germany: Scriptor Verlag.

Stein, Ernesto. 1999. Fiscal Decentralization and Government Size in Latin America. *Journal of Applied Economics* 2 (2):357–91.

Taylor, Charles, and Michael Hudson. 1972. *World Handbook of Political and Social Indicators,* 2d ed. New Haven, Conn.: Yale University Press.

Treisman, Daniel. 2001. The Causes of Corruption: A Cross-National Study. *Journal of Public Economics* 76 (3):399–457.

Von Hagen, Jürgen. 1998. Budgeting Institutions for Aggregate Fiscal Discipline. Working Paper B01-1998. Bonn: Center for European Integration Research.

Weingast, Barry. 1995. The Economic Role of Political Institutions: Market-Preserving Federalism and Economic Development. *Journal of Law, Economics, and Organization* 11 (1):1–31.

Weingast, Barry, Kenneth Shepsle, and Christopher Johnsen. 1981. The Political Economy of Benefits and Costs: A Neoclassical Approach to Distributive Politics. *Journal of Political Economy* 89 (4):642–64.

Fiscal Federalism and the Growth of Government   **729**

Wilson, John. 1986. A Theory of Interregional Tax Competition. *Journal of Urban Economics* 19 (3):296–315.
———. 1999. Theories of Tax Competition. *National Tax Journal* 52 (2):269–304.
Winer, Stanley. 1980. Some Evidence on the Effect of the Separation of Spending and Taxing Decisions. *Journal of Political Economy*, 91 (1):126–40.
World Bank. 2000. *World Development Indicators on CD-ROM*. Washington, D.C.: World Bank.
Zodrow, George, and Peter Mieszkowski. 1986. Pigou, Tiebout, Property Taxation, and the Underprovision of Local Public Goods. *Journal of Urban Economics* 19 (3):356–70.

H
Distribution

Journal of Economic Perspectives—Volume 11, Number 4—Fall 1997—Pages 73–82

Tiebout? Or Not Tiebout? The Market Metaphor and America's Devolution Debate

John D. Donahue

T he idea of improving America's public sector by shifting resources and authority to lower levels of government has tremendous intuitive appeal, particularly when so many citizens view government as alien, unaccountable, and inefficient. Competition among rival jurisdictions promises to wring out waste and tighten management by forcing officials to respond to citizens' priorities and deliver more value for taxpayers' money. Decentralization and interjurisdictional mobility gives the individual power over government that can be exercised on the citizens' terms, at the citizens' own initiative, at any time. If public authority is pushed down to levels where choice and competition can operate, every citizen can stage a personal revolution armed with only a moving van.

The proposition that over-centralization is a substantial element of what ails American government, and devolution to the states a potent corrective, inspires periodic calls for a "new federalism" to bolster the role of the separate states and constrict Washington's domain. These proposals—including partly overlapping policy initiatives from the Nixon and Reagan administrations, and more recently from an uneasy alliance of Republican legislators and executive-branch Democrats—have had some success. Over the last few decades, the trend has been mildly toward decentralization within overall public spending, and strongly so within the narrower category of domestic governmental operations (excluding transfers and debt service). Since 1970, total spending by all levels of government has wandered within the fairly narrow range of 27 to 32 percent of gross domestic product; in 1996, it was 29.6 percent (Office of Management and Budget, 1997,

■ *John D. Donahue is Associate Professor of Public Policy, John F. Kennedy School of Government, Harvard University, Cambridge, Massachusetts. His e-mail address is jack_donahue@harvard.edu.*

table 15.3). But there have been striking changes in composition. The sum of all federal spending other than defense, interest, and transfers dropped from 4.2 percent of GDP in 1980 to just 1.7 percent in 1996. Over the same period, state and local spending funded by state and local tax revenues has grown from 8.5 percent to 10.3 percent of GDP. (This actually understates the share of public expenditure under subnational control; roughly one-fifth of state and local spending is covered not by subnational revenues but by federal grants. Meanwhile, the state share of the state-local total has been growing as well.) Expenditure is not the only metric of relative importance, to be sure, but other gauges—like Supreme Court decisions augmenting state autonomy and popular support as signaled in opinion polls—also mark a trend away from Washington.

Government weighted toward the separate states has important generic advantages, many of which Inman and Rubinfeld perceptively detail in their contribution to this symposium. Diverse policy regimes can cater to heterogeneous preferences and accommodate varying conditions. Collective choices are less error-prone, and public administration less plagued by agency problems, with a smaller polity and simpler policy agenda. Interstate competition can discipline government, augmenting the "voice" of the ballot box with the "exit" of mobility. Centralization has its characteristic virtues as well. Costs and benefits falling beyond state borders can be incorporated into policy decisions without interjurisdictional negotiation. There is greater potential for risk spreading and redistribution. Scale and scope bolster bargaining leverage with external actors.

While the optimal degree of centralization yielded by balancing such factors will vary from issue to issue and from period to period, both scholarly and popular commentary increasingly lean toward decentralization. My goal in this comment is to raise some doubts about this intellectual vogue—and the real-world trends it is helping to propel—and to suggest that at America's current margin of public-sector centralization, the disadvantages of a further shift toward state-centered government are likely to outweigh the advantages.

The Market Metaphor

The basic theme of governmental competition as a check on official power is neither new nor restricted to economics. It is central to the U.S. Constitution, and figures explicitly in the political rhetoric promoting that charter's ratification. When economists invoke consumer choice among rival purveyors as a metaphor for improving government through decentralization and competition, however, they usually begin with Tiebout's (1956) brief essay, which is among the most-cited publications in economics. A vast chorus echoes this theme. The Advisory Commission on Intergovernmental Relations (1991, p. 4) declares, "Just as market competition produces an economic system responsive to consumer needs, interjurisdictional competition can produce a government system responsive to voter desires." The authors of one public finance textbook take it as axiomatic that interjurisdictional competition "is a spur to efficiency because it forces government officials to keep benefits in line with taxes paid" (Browning and Browning, 1983, p. 469). Similar sentiments could be cited almost endlessly.

Every economist appreciates, however, that even in the private sector—the home turf of the efficient competition model—the textbook ideal of perfect competition is only a rough approximation of reality, and the merits of market rivalry are contingent on a well-known set of conditions (Scherer and Ross, 1990, p. 18). In this tradition, Tiebout (1956) was scrupulous about listing the conditions under which the potential benefits of jurisdictional competition would be realized.

The conditions hold well enough, for a wide enough range of transactions, to amply justify popular and scholarly enthusiasm for market competition. But extending the logic to government competition requires far more intrepid conceptual leaps. For example, all but a few private markets display an ease of entry and exit that all but a few governmental settings conspicuously lack. If forming and maintaining polities were costless, it would be silly to restrict ourselves to the meager jurisdictional menu of nation, state, and city (Scharpf, 1976, p. 28; Breton and Scott, 1978, pp. 37–39; Tullock, 1969, p. 27; Olson, 1969). In principle, a custom-tailored government should be matched to each collective purpose. But the cost of forming, maintaining, and restructuring polities is often high, and governmental mergers, spin-offs, and liquidations tend to be more traumatic transactions than their private sector analogues. Thus the number and configuration of public sector entities have more to do with the accidents of a capricious history than with the shifting dictates of economic rationality.

The remainder of this comment will take up three more general grounds for hesitation about applying the market metaphor to America's devolution debate.

The Case for Collusion

Market competition both curbs waste (augmenting the total surplus) and tilts that surplus toward purchasers. Only in the most exotic cases can business collusion benefit the average individual. But (except for those who see public institutions as irredeemably wasteful) there is often a reasonable case for governmental collusion.

Consider state efforts to attract mobile business. While such efforts form a perennial theme of American economic history, there is evidence of an intensification in interstate competition for investment since, roughly, the mid-1970s (Chi and Leatherby, 1997; Koropeckyj, 1996; KPMG Peat Marwick, 1995, p. 5). The history of nine major automobile-plant deals, for example, traces the progressive transfer of rents from states and cities to Japanese and European automakers as subsidy packages rose from roughly $4,000 per job for Honda's 1980 investment in Ohio, to roughly $168,000 per job when Daimler Benz selected Alabama after a 30-state bidding war.[1]

---

[1] These are very coarse figures, unadjusted for the time value of money and based on shaky employment projections, but the trend is clear.

Given a competitive setting, it can be entirely rational for states to bid aggressively for major investments offering good jobs. The consequences, however, include higher taxes and shrunken spending for other constituents and a disproportionate solicitude for the more mobile kinds of business. The demonstrated fragility of interstate compacts to curb such competition (due to classic prisoner's dilemma dynamics) shows the difficulty of engineering collusion, but doesn't disprove its desirability. As Graham and Krugman (1989, p. 119) observe, "States would be well served if their power to grant investment incentives were simply abolished."[2] Indeed, there are periodic calls for federal measures to enforce interstate collusion, although the political and practical impediments are formidable.

A comparable collective-action problem arises in a quite different policy area— the regulation of gambling. As recently as 1988, Nevada and New Jersey were alone in allowing casino gambling; eight years later there were 500 casinos operating in 27 states, and some form of gambling was legal in all but two states. Gambling's migration from the margins to the mainstream, one of the more notable economic and social developments of the past decade, is almost wholly the product of changes in state law. Permissive state rules on gambling gratify those who deplore paternalism, and also bring obvious benefits to the state that runs the lottery or hosts the casinos, including relatively high-paying unskilled jobs and revenues for the state treasury. But there are costs as well. Access to legal gambling has been found to increase the number of people who develop a gambling problem, with consequences ranging from mild economic inconvenience to bankruptcy, embezzlement, divorce and suicide. More generally, some see gambling as immoral, or corrosive of the work ethic.

The real question is whether the wholesale liberalization of gambling laws reflects popular judgments about the proper balance of these factors. The logic of interstate competition suggests some cause for doubt on this score. If a state loosens its own restrictions on gambling, it gains the benefits in jobs and tax revenues. It also suffers costs—but not *all* the costs. When citizens of other states buy the lottery tickets and visit the casinos, they leave their money behind when they return home, but take their gambling-related problems back with them. Conversely, states that retain restrictions on gambling will share in the costs as their citizens gamble out of state, but will not receive any of the benefits, and may rationally liberalize their laws in turn. Permissive gambling legislation in Iowa and Wisconsin was aimed at attracting citizens from the Chicago area; Illinois responded by loosening its own laws (Johnson, 1995; Goodman, 1995). New York's governor, calling for laxer gambling laws, emphasized "the most important thing is to be able to stop losing billions

---

[2] A similar problem was faced in the 1780s as state after state—hoping to channel commerce through its own ports—bypassed the national government to strike its own trade agreements with Great Britain. This led Alexander Hamilton (1961, pp. 91) to argue in Federalist 11 for centralized trade policy. He wrote: "Let the thirteen States, bound together in a strict and indissoluble Union, concur in erecting one great American system superior to the control of all transatlantic force or influence and able to dictate the terms of the connection between the old and the new world!"

of dollars to surrounding states'' (Hernandez, 1996). A lobbying firm promoting casino gambling in Florida found that survey responses flipped from majority-opposition to majority-support when a question was reframed to emphasize that gambling was already widespread in the region, so that voting down legalization would only make Florida "miss out on the revenue and economic development casinos generate." The equilibrium under interstate competition, in short, may feature more liberal gambling laws than the average citizen would prefer.

Heterogeneous Mobility and "Citizen's Surplus"

The market metaphor for governmental efficiency requires that location choices respond to state policies. What might be called the "elasticity of location" for individuals and institutions with respect to taxes, public services, and regulatory regimes must be sufficiently high, for a sufficiently large fraction of constituents, to motivate government officials, whether directly or indirectly.

This elasticity varies widely among constituents. For individuals, the rate of interstate migration in the postwar era has usually been in the range of 3.0–3.5 percent per year, dropping to below 3 percent throughout the 1990s (U.S. Bureau of the Census, website). In principle, such rates could still be high enough to affect policy deliberations. A 3 percent average rate could mask much higher inflows into well-run states and away from inefficient governments. Or it could be an equilibrium figure, reflecting the discipline imposed on state governments by much larger numbers poised to move if their state departs from the preferred tax and service portfolio.

But individuals typically make their interstate migration decisions for reasons that have little or nothing to do with the performance of current officeholders. In part, this is because most state policy decisions have indirect and lagged effects on the average citizen's welfare. But more fundamental is the fact that individuals enjoy a large "citizen's surplus"—analogous to the "consumer's surplus" of valuation in excess of the price paid in private exchanges—composed of cultural affinities, ties to friends and family, and economic connections. In most cases, the quality of state government could deteriorate sharply, in terms of the portfolio of policies offered or the efficiency with which they are delivered relative to alternatives in other states, before a citizen's locational surplus is whittled away and migration becomes rational.

Business, educational, and other institutions lack the personal dimensions of citizen's surplus, but vary widely in the other factors that condition their locational elasticity with respect to state policies. Some institutions are powerfully anchored by investments in a current locale or by location-specific access to inputs or markets. But as transport and communication costs fall, states are becoming increasingly close substitutes for the purposes of the typical economic institution. While the issue remains controversial, the weight of state policy in industry location decisions does appear to be rising (Donahue, 1997, Appendix.)

This heterogeneity of locational elasticity with respect to state policy has several implications. First, the promised efficiency benefits of interjurisdictional competition are more likely to be found at the local level, where migration is much more common and usually requires surrendering less surplus. Second, migration is a far more credible response to state policies for most institutions, and for a subset of individuals whose "citizen's surplus" is a particularly light counterweight to state policies. But those at the margin of migration may be quite different from the median citizen. For example, retirees with substantial financial assets may have earnings that are invariant with respect to location and relatively light family burdens, while their expected after-tax wealth may be strongly affected by state taxation of capital income or estates, making them differentially ready to incorporate state policies into their location decisions. Evidence from Australia and the United States is consistent with this conjecture (Grossman, 1990; Cebula, 1990; Hansen, 1995, table 16). Loners, the childless, divorced non-custodial parents, and those with too many or too few economic resources to be much concerned about established careers may also have a smaller-than-average citizen's surplus. It is not obvious that the signals sent by the migration of such constituents will provide the right incentives to state officials from the perspective of the population as a whole.

A general implication is that as state government grows more important within America's public sector and interstate competition intensifies, policies can be expected to evolve to favor constituencies that are more mobile and more desirable, at the expense of constituencies that are less mobile and less desirable. Taken to the limit, as Oates and Schwab (1991, pp. 140–141) write, "[T]he outcome under interjurisdictional competition is identical to the outcome that would emerge if one were to replace local governments with perfectly competitive firms that supplied local public goods to firms and households at marginal cost." By some measures, of course, such an arrangement is highly efficient, but the implied transformation in what we mean by governmental accountability may warrant broader debate than it has so far received.

Distribution, Income Inequality and Welfare Reform

Theorists from Tiebout (1956) onward have conditioned their predictions of efficiency gains through intergovernmental competition on the pre-existence of an optimal income distribution, or on the existence of an overarching level of government responsible for redistribution. The distributional perspective highlights two remarkable things about the shift toward the states. First, it coincides with sharply rising wage inequality (as discussed in a symposium in the Spring 1997 issue of this journal). Second, it has been pushed farthest and fastest in anti-poverty policy, rather than in areas less freighted with distributional issues, like criminal justice or infrastructure finance.

The effects of the Personal Responsibility and Work Opportunities Reconciliation Act of 1996 will remain a matter of conjecture for some time to come. It is difficult to defend the pre-reform welfare system, or to deny the potential gains from experimentation, innovation, and tailoring programs to fit state-specific conditions and priorities. And it is conceivable that the new arrangements will perform as advertised, even after the next recession tightens state budgets and makes it harder to put former recipients into private-sector jobs. But the post-reform system also features built-in incentives for state austerity (Blank, 1996).

Despite long-standing predictions of competitive benefit cuts by states anxious to avoid attracting the dependency-prone, previous studies have found limited evidence of a "welfare magnet" effect that would drive a "race to the bottom" (Brown and Oates, 1987; Levine and Zimmerman, 1995; Gramlich and Laren, 1984). But this research scanned a world with a federal floor under benefits and (more important) a large federal share in the marginal welfare dollar. In that context, neither beneficiaries nor state officials had strong incentives to pursue the strategies triggering a race to the bottom. As new policies alter incentives, warnings of such a race may well turn out to have been (in a precise sense of the term) premature.

Inman and Rubinfeld's essay stumbles somewhat on this point. They describe welfare reform's partly offsetting provisions of a "price effect" sharply raising the real cost to the state of each dollar spent on welfare as federal matching is abolished, and an "income effect" of block grants that exceed for most states the sums they would have received under the prior regime through 2002. But the price effect is permanent, and the income effect is transitory. Block grants from 2002 onward will be set at whatever level future Congresses decide, and it seems less than likely that in the early years of the next century—as federal budget constraints tighten and after anti-poverty policy has been declared the states' domain—Congress will be eager to ease the governors' welfare problems through comparably generous transfers.

Rendering the poor immobile across states can defuse the race-to-the-bottom scenario, as has long been recognized. The nineteenth-century English poor laws restricted the poor to their home parishes (Polanyi, 1944; Stewart, 1985), and America's pre-Constitution Articles of Confederation specifically excluded "paupers" from the provision that "the people of each state shall have free ingress and regress to and from any other state" (Morison, 1923, p. 178). The 1996 legislation does gives states some tools to deter the immigration of the poor—notably the option to limit newly-arrived residents to the benefits they would have received in their previous state, for up to one year—but the durability of this bulwark remains to be tested in practice, and its constitutionality remains to be tested by the courts.[3]

Skepticism about the net improvements to be anticipated from increased interstate competition does not mean dismissing the role of rivalry in enforcing ac-

---

[3] Under the prior welfare system, the courts had barred differential treatment of citizens newly arrived from other states as a barrier to citizens' mobility; it is unclear whether this standard will hold as welfare loses its status as an entitlement. I am grateful to Mary Jo Bane for information on this issue. Relevant court cases are *Shapiro v. Thompson* (394 U.S. 618 [1969]) and *Memorial Hospital v. Maricopa County* (415 U.S. 250 [1974]). (The first court case, in October 1997, ruled Pennsylvania's efforts to deter welfare immigration unconstitutional.)

countability on public officials. Rather, it reflects doubt that interstate competition for constituents is a superior alternative—or even on balance a beneficial adjunct— to *intrastate* competition for electoral support. The diffusion of governmental innovations, for example, appears to be driven by rivalry among current and aspiring officials to present voters with new ideas (Walter, 1969, p. 890; Carpenter, 1991), rather than by interstate rivalry for constituents. The efficiency benefits for most Americans from elevating "exit" over "voice" as a device for disciplining government are likely to be smaller than they at first appear to be, while the depressing effect on public-sector capabilities may prove graver and more general. In other settings, with weaker constraints on governmental opportunism, the calculus may well differ. (For example, Qian and Weingast discuss the case of China in this symposium.)

Some observers applaud virtually any measures to augment choice and enfeeble government even in the contemporary American context, and from such a perspective, enthusiasm for devolution is well-founded. But for those who retain a measure of faith in the possibilities of collective action, there are severe limits to the market metaphor's applicability to the problems of American government.

■ *I am grateful to Brad De Long, Alan Krueger, and Timothy Taylor for helpful comments on a previous draft.*

References

Advisory Commission on Intergovernmental Relations, *Interjurisdictional Tax and Policy Competition: Good or Bad for the Federal System?* ACIR, April 1991.

Breton, Albert, and Anthony Scott, *The Economic Constitution of Federal States.* Toronto: University of Toronto Press, 1978.

Brown, Charles C., and Wallace E. Oates, "Assistance to the Poor in a Federal System," *Journal of Public Economics,* 1987, *32*:3, 307–30.

Browning, Edgar K., and Jacqueline M. Browning, *Public Finance and the Price System,* New York: MacMillan, 1983.

Carpenter, Vivian L., "The Influence of Political Competition on the Decision to Adopt GAAP," *Journal of Accounting and Public Policy,* summer 1991, *10*:2, 105–34.

Cebula, Richard J., "A brief empirical note on the Tiebout hypothesis and state income tax policies," *Public Choice,* 1990, *67*:1, 87–9.

Chi, Keon S., and Drew Leatherby, *State Business Incentives: Trends and Options for the Future,*

Council of State Governments, Lexington, KY, 1997.

Donahue, John D., *Disunited States,* Basic Books: New York, 1997.

Goodman, Robert, The Luck Business. New York: Martin Kessler Books, 1995.

Graham, Edward M., and Paul R. Krugman, *Foreign Direct Investment in the United States,* Institute for International Economics: Washington, D.C. 1989.

Gramlich, Edward M., and Deborah S. Laren, "Migration and Income Redistribution Responsibilities," *Journal of Human Resources,* 1984, *19*:4, 489–511.

Grossman, Philip J., "Fiscal Competition Among States in Australia: The Demise of Death Duties," *Publius,* Fall 1990, *20*:4, 145–59.

Hamilton, Alexander, The Federalist Papers, Number 11, NAL edition, New York: Mentor Books, 1961.

Hansen, Kristin, *Geographical Mobility: March 1993 to March 1994,* U.S. Department of Com-

Economics of Federalism I   *515*

Tiebout? Or Not Tiebout? The Market Metaphor and America's Devolution Debate   81

merce, Bureau of the Census, U.S. Government Printing Office 1995.

Hernandez, Raymond, "Pataki Panel Says Casinos Could Bring In $2.6 Billion," *The New York Times,* August 31, 1996.

Johnson, Dirk, "More Casinos, More Players Who Bet Until They Lose All," *New York Times,* September 25, 1995.

Koropeckyj, Sophia, "Do Economic Development Incentives Matter?" *Regional Financial Review,* February 1996, p. 16.

KPMG Peat Marwick LLP, Business Incentives Group, "Business Incentives and Tax Credits: A Boon for Business or Corporate Welfare?" New York, September 1995.

Levine, Philip B., and David Zimmerman, "An Empirical Analysis of the Welfare Magnet Debate Using the NLSY," Cambridge, MA., NBER Working Paper No. 5264, September 1995.

Morison, Samuel Eliot, ed., *Sources and Documents Illustrating the American Revolution.* London: Oxford University Press, 1923.

Oates, Wallace E., and Robert M. Schwab, "Allocative and Distributive Implications of Local Fiscal Competition," in Daphne Kenyon and John Kincaid, editors, *Competition Among States and Local Governments.* Washington, DC: Urban Institute Press, 1991.

Office of Management and Budget, *The Budget of the United States, Fiscal Year 1998,* U.S. Government Printing Office, Washington, D.C, 1997.

Olson, Mancur, Jr., "Strategic Theory and Its Applications; The Principle of "Fiscal Equivalence": The Division of Responsibilities Among Different Levels of Government," *American Economic Review,* May 1969, *59*:2, 479–87.

Polanyi, Karl, *The Great Transformation.* Beacon Press: Boston, 1944.

Scharpf, Fritz, "Theorie der Politikverflechtung," in Fritz W. Scharpf, Bernd Reissert, and Fritz Schnabel, *Politikverflectung: Theorie und Empirie des kooperativen Foederalismus in der Bundesrepublik.* Kronberg: Scriptor Verlag, 1976.

Scherer, F. M., and David Ross, *Industrial Market Structure and Economic Performance.* Boston: Houghton Mifflin Company, Third edition, 1990.

Stewart, Richard B., "Federalism and Rights," *Georgia Law Review,* 1985, *19*, 917–80.

Tiebout, Charles M., "A pure theory of local expenditures," *Journal of Political Economy,* October 1956, *64*:5, 416–24.

Tullock, Gordon, "Federalism: Problems of Scale," *Public Choice,* Spring 1969, *6*:0, 19–29.

U.S. Bureau of the Census, Current Population Survey, Table A-1. Annual Geographical Mobility Rates, By Type of Movement: 1947-1994, *http://www.census.gov/population/socdemo/ migration/tab-a-1.txt.*

Walter, Jack, "The Diffusion of Innovations Among the American States," *American Political Science Review,* September 1969, *63*:3, 880–99.

[18]

Mobility and Redistribution

Dennis Epple and Thomas Romer

Carnegie Mellon University

The ability of individuals to move freely from one jurisdiction to another is generally seen as a constraint on the amount of redistribution that each jurisdiction within a system of governments can undertake. In this paper, we look at this proposition by developing a positive analysis of income redistribution by local governments in a federal system. We ask how much redistribution occurs when only local governments can have tax/transfer instruments, individuals can move freely among jurisdictions, and voters in each jurisdiction are fully aware of the migration effects of redistributive policies. Local redistribution is shown to induce sorting of the population, with the poorest households located in the communities that provide the most redistribution. While the threat of out-migration affects the potential for redistribution, our results suggest that significant local redistribution is nonetheless feasible. Numerical computations indicate that the proportion of residents who are renters is a major factor affecting the local choice of level of redistribution.

I. Introduction

The ability of people to move from one jurisdiction to another is generally seen as a constraint on the amount of redistribution that

This research is supported by grants from the National Science Foundation. Romer thanks the Hoover Institution, Stanford University, for its hospitality during the 1988–89 academic year. We have benefited from the comments of participants at workshops and conferences at which we presented earlier versions of this work. These took place at Carnegie Mellon, California at Santa Barbara and at Berkeley, Michigan, North Carolina at Greensboro, Washington University, Columbia, Chicago, Harvard, Caltech, Pennsylvania, Miami University, National Bureau of Economic Research, Stanford, Princeton, Maryland, Texas A&M, Yale, and the 1988 meetings of the Public Choice Society. We thank Glenn Cassidy for his assistance with some of the computations.

[*Journal of Political Economy*, 1991, vol. 99, no. 4]

each jurisdiction within a system of governments can undertake. In this paper, we look at this proposition by developing a positive analysis of income redistribution by local governments in a federal system. We ask how much redistribution occurs when only local governments can have tax/transfer instruments, people can move freely among jurisdictions, and voters in each jurisdiction are fully aware of the migration effects of redistributive policies.

A model must have several features to make it a useful vehicle for studying redistribution by local governments: (1) Clearly, it must have more than one locality, and households must be able to move among localities. (2) For the study of income redistribution to be interesting, the population must be heterogeneous. Thus the assumption of identical individuals used as a convenient simplification in many investigations of local governments (Courant and Rubinfeld 1978; Epple and Zelenitz 1981; Wilson 1987a; Wildasin 1988) is untenable in studies of local redistribution. (3) Redistributive decisions of localities must be endogenous. In a positive model, it is desirable that decisions of localities emerge from a collective choice process such as majority rule. In existing models of multicommunity equilibrium with voting (Westhoff 1977; Epple, Filimon, and Romer 1984), voters treat the community tax base and population as fixed when voting on the community tax-expenditure policy. This is unsatisfactory in a model focusing on the limits that mobility imposes on redistribution since one would not want results driven by the assumption of voter myopia.[1] A model of local redistribution must endow voters with greater sophistication than models to date have done, and this proves to require a different approach to analyzing voting. (4) The potential importance of differences in incentives faced by homeowners and renters has been emphasized in discussions of local governments (Oates 1986), but previous research has not provided a way of modeling the differing preferences of owners and renters.[2]

These observations lead us to develop a model of multicommunity equilibrium in which the population of each community is endogenously determined. Tax rates and levels of redistribution are chosen by majority vote of residents of each local jurisdiction. Voters anticipate changes in housing prices and the in- or out-migration that will occur in response to changes in the local tax rate and level of redistri-

---

[1] As a technical matter, we show in this paper that no equilibrium exists when voters behave in this myopic fashion.

[2] In a model with only owner-occupants, Yinger (1982) introduces a distinction between "movers" and "stayers." This device serves to contrast choices facing households selecting a community with those facing households residing in a community. The stayers do not plan to change houses, and hence they ignore capital gains and losses when voting.

bution. We distinguish between renters and owners and show this distinction to have a central role in determining preferences for local redistribution. By bringing these features together in a single model, we not only provide a framework for studying the substantive problem of local redistribution but also broaden the set of phenomena that can be encompassed in models of equilibrium among local jurisdictions.

To provide further insight into the limits of redistribution by local governments, we use functional forms and parameters that are consistent with American data to compute equilibria. These computations illuminate the relationships among redistribution, relative community sizes, and patterns of property ownership. They also illustrate the potential usefulness of the analytical framework for further study of questions that arise in the political economy of systems of governments.

This paper draws on several previous lines of research. Important early discussions of the subject of redistribution in a federal system may be found in Stigler (1957) and Oates (1972). They emphasize that mobility of households is likely to undermine attempts by local governments to redistribute income. More recent contributions by Oates (1977) and Ladd and Doolittle (1982) point to migration as the central issue in the normative evaluation of which level of government should undertake redistribution.[3] A positive analysis of redistribution by local governments under direct democracy is offered by Brown and Oates (1987). Following Orr (1976), they emphasize concern by the wealthy for the poor as the factor giving rise to income redistribution policies. The alternative approach, adopted here, treats income redistribution as an outcome of majority rule with self-interested voters. In following this approach, the paper builds on the work of Romer (1975) and Meltzer and Richard (1981). Altruism may be important in practice. In this paper, however, we are concerned with identifying the prospects for redistribution even when altruism is absent. Rather, the motives for redistribution, if any, emerge from the majoritarian nature of the political process. The political side of the model abstracts from explicit consideration of the role of bureaucrats or politicians in determining levels of redistribution. Again, such influences may be important in practice, but valuable insights can be obtained without the complications introduced by attempting to model these influences. As to the analysis of equilibrium among local

---

[3] Empirical studies of migration in response to differentials in local redistribution have been made by Gramlich and Laren (1984), Rosenzweig and Wolpin (1988), Peterson and Rom (1989), and others. A review of some of the empirical evidence is presented in Brown and Oates (1987).

jurisdictions, this paper extends the work of B. Ellickson (1971), Westhoff (1977), Rose-Ackerman (1979), and Epple et al. (1984).[4]

In Sections II and III, we present the model, define equilibrium, and establish some of its properties. We develop a computational model in Section IV and present results based on it. We make some concluding observations in Section V.

II. The Model

Our framework is a two-good, many-community model with a continuum of households. The local government in each community imposes a tax proportional to the value of property and divides the proceeds equally among the residents of the community. The tax rate of each jurisdiction is endogenously determined, as well as the population and tax base of each community. The two goods in the model are housing and a composite good. Thus communities do not supply a distinct local public good; the good they distribute is a perfect substitute for the composite commodity.

The model is sufficiently general to allow a locality to be thought of simply as one of a system of jurisdictions among which households are free to migrate. One natural interpretation is that the locality is one of several municipalities in a metropolitan area. For convenience we shall refer to the collection of localities as a metropolitan area, but it should be understood that the model is not limited to this interpretation. For example, one may think of subunits of a nation among which households are free to locate.

More specifically, consider a metropolitan area inhabited by a continuum of households. There are two goods: housing, h, and a numeraire bundle, b. All households have the same strictly quasiconcave, twice continuously differentiable utility function, $U(h, b)$. We assume that both commodities are normal goods. Households differ only in their endowed income y. The distribution of income over all communities is characterized by a continuous density function $f(y)$, with support $[0, M]$.

[4] Bucovetsky (1982) recognizes the importance of mobility-related effects in analyzing the response of systems of local jurisdictions to changes in public-sector policies. He focuses on exogenous policy changes and is not concerned with community collective choice. In two recent papers, Wilson (1987a, 1987b) has explored the role and patterns of trade in private goods in an economy with mobile factors and multiple jurisdictions. In both papers, he focuses on the efficiency properties of local taxation and public goods provision. For the most part, the analyses deal with a setting in which individuals are identical, so political processes or redistributive issues play no role. Goodspeed (1988) uses a simulation model to investigate the welfare losses and extent of redistribution in decentralized provision of a "congestable" local public good. Steen (1987a, 1987b) looks at multicommunity equilibrium in a spatial setting, with the level of public services in each community set exogenously.

A look at U.S. data reveals that once boundaries dividing the land area of a region among a set of local jurisdictions are drawn, they are rarely redrawn (Epple and Romer 1989b). Hence, we assume that the homogeneous land in the metropolitan area is divided among J jurisdictions, each of which has fixed boundaries.

Jurisdictions may differ in the amount of land contained within their boundaries. Each jurisdiction may impose a proportional tax, t, on the value of housing and use the proceeds to pay a lump sum, g, to each resident. Hence, the budget constraint faced by a household with income y located in community j is

$$y + g^j = p^j h + b,$$

where p^j is the gross-of-tax price in community j. From now on, the household with income y will be named y.

From a household's viewpoint, a community is characterized by the grant/housing price pair (g, p). For given g and p, the utility of a household is given by the indirect utility function V:

$$V(p, g, y) = U(h(p, y + g), y + g - ph(p, y + g)). \tag{1}$$

On the right-hand side of (1), $h(p, y + g)$ is y's demand function for housing, capturing the way consumption of housing services responds to changes in the gross-of-tax price of housing and gross-of-grant income. With the assumption that housing is a normal good, y's indifference curves in the (g, p) plane are upward sloping:

$$\left. \frac{dp}{dg} \right|_{V = \bar{V}} = -\frac{\partial V / \partial g}{\partial V / \partial p} = \frac{1}{h(p, y + g)} > 0. \tag{2}$$

The slope of an indifference curve through a point (g, p) decreases with y:

$$\frac{\partial (dp/dg|_{V = \bar{V}})}{\partial y} = -\frac{1}{[h(p, y + g)]^2} h_2 < 0, \tag{3}$$

where h_2 is the derivative of $h(\cdot)$ with respect to its second argument. (Since housing is a normal good, h_2 is positive.)

We define *equilibrium* in the system of communities as an allocation such that

1. all communities are in internal equilibrium; that is, within each community
   a) the housing market clears,
   b) the community budget is in balance, and
   c) there is a majority rule voting equilibrium, and
2. no one wants to move.

We begin by developing the implications of part 2 of this definition. The requirement that no one wishes to move is natural in any static model of residential location. With costless mobility, a household's locational choice must maximize $V(p^j, g^j, y)$ over $j = 1, \ldots, J$.

Consider two points (g^i, p^i) and (g^j, p^j) such that $g^j > g^i$. Then (2) and (3) imply that

$$V(p^i, g^i, y) \geq V(p^j, g^j, y) \Rightarrow V(p^i, g^i, y') > V(p^j, g^j, y') \quad \text{for } y' > y \quad \text{(4a)}$$

and

$$V(p^i, g^i, y) \leq V(p^j, g^j, y) \Rightarrow V(p^i, g^i, y') < V(p^j, g^j, y') \quad \text{for } y' < y. \quad \text{(4b)}$$

This ordering of preferences by income means that locational equilibrium generates considerable structure on community characteristics.[5] These are summarized in the following proposition. (The proposition follows readily from the properties of $V(\cdot)$. For more details, see Epple et al. [1984].)

PROPOSITION 1. Consider an allocation in which no two communities have the same housing price. Necessary conditions for such an allocation to be one in which no one wishes to move to another community follow:

a) *Stratification:* Each community is formed of households with incomes in a single interval. If y and y' live in the same community, with $y' > y$, then $y'' \in [y, y']$ also lives in that community.

b) *Boundary indifference:* Communities can be ordered from lowest to highest income levels. When they are ordered this way, there is a "boundary" income between two successive communities. The "border" household (i.e., one with the boundary income) between any two adjacent communities is indifferent between the communities.

---

[5] Conditions (2) and (3) imply that the indifference curve of a given household crosses the indifference curve of any other household at most once and that the indifference curve of the poorer of any two households cuts the indifference curve of the wealthier of the two from below. Models in which indifference curves are assumed to have these monotonicity and single-crossing properties have been studied in a variety of contexts. B. Ellickson (1971), Westhoff (1977), and Epple et al. (1984), among others, use such an assumption to study equilibrium in models of local jurisdictions. Matthews and Moore (1987) provide an illuminating review and discussion of the use of analogous marginal rate of substitution assumptions in screening models. In these models, the marginal rate of substitution property is employed to demonstrate that certain self-selection constraints are satisfied. In our model, the marginal rate of substitution condition plays this role (proposition 1), and it also plays a key role in characterizing the outcome of the voting problem (proposition 2). In the context of voting, Roberts (1977) named this condition "hierarchical adherence" and relied on it to prove the existence of a voting equilibrium. An attractive feature of the model we study in this paper is that the marginal rate of substitution condition relevant to our analysis, condition (3), emerges naturally from the economics of the problem.

c) *Decreasing bundles:* If y^i is the highest income in community i and y^j is the highest income in community j, then, in equilibrium, $p^i < p^j$ and $g^i < g^j$ if $y^i > y^j$.

Proposition 1 focuses on allocations in which no two communities have the same housing price. Next, we consider allocations in which this is not so, that is, allocations in which at least one pair of communities has the same housing price. For such an allocation to be an equilibrium, it must be the case that any two communities with the same housing price also have the same grant, g. Otherwise, all households would prefer the member of the pair with the higher g. Hence, in equilibrium, households will be indifferent between two communities with the same housing price. Thus to generalize proposition 1 to the case in which more than one community has the same price, assign all communities with the same price to a group. Proposition 1 then applies, with "community group" replacing "community" in the statement of the proposition. The population will be stratified across community groups, but there is no necessary stratification within community groups. There is no loss of generality, however, for the analysis that follows in assuming that households are stratified within community groups as well. For convenience, we shall adopt this convention.

Part a of proposition 1 implies that redistributive taxation will induce sorting by income groups. Part c predicts that redistributive expenditure per household will be inversely related to household income in a comparison across communities. These are precisely the outcomes hypothesized by Oates (1977, p. 5): "an aggressive policy to redistribute income from the rich to the poor in a particular locality may, in the end, simply chase the relatively wealthy to other jurisdictions and attract those with low incomes."

By condition a of proposition 1, in any equilibrium the total population must be partitioned into a set of single-interval communities. We shall therefore restrict our attention to such communities. Henceforth, let y^j denote the income of the household at the border between communities j and $j + 1$, with $y^j < y^{j+1}$, and let $y^0 = 0$ and $y^J = M$. From part b of the proposition it must be the case that

$$V(p^j, g^j, y^j) = V(p^{j+1}, g^{j+1}, y^j), \quad j = 1, 2, \ldots, J - 1. \tag{5}$$

Next, we turn to *internal equilibrium*, that is, equilibrium within a community (pt. 1 of the definition of equilibrium). We begin with the housing market. Aggregate demand in each community is determined by integrating the household demand function over the income interval of households in the community, so for community j we have

$$H_d(p^j, g^j, y^j, y^{j-1}) = \int_{y^{j-1}}^{y^j} h(p^j, y + g^j) f(y) dy. \tag{6}$$

We assume that the housing supply function, $H_s^j(p_h^j)$, for a community with fixed land area is continuous and strictly increasing for $p_h \geq 0$, for all $j = 1, \ldots, J$. The gross-of-tax price of housing is determined by the identity

$$p^j = p_h^j(1 + t^j). \tag{7}$$

In equilibrium the housing market must clear:

$$H_d(p^j, g^j, y^j, y^{j-1}) = H_s^j(p_h^j). \tag{8}$$

It is also necessary that the community's budget balance:

$$g^j \int_{y^{j-1}}^{y^j} f(y)dy = t^j p_h^j H_s^j(p_h^j). \tag{9}$$

Voting on Local Grants

Finally, we need to characterize the way that public-sector choices are determined in each community. We assume that the (t, g) pair in each community is chosen by majority rule. In each community, voters assume that the (t, g) pairs in all other communities are fixed. Since we are interested in the limits to redistribution in the face of mobility among jurisdictions, we assume that voters are sophisticated about the impact of taxes and grants in their community. They recognize two types of effects of changing (t, g) in their own community. First, changing taxes and transfers affect housing prices and, hence, housing consumption of current inhabitants. Second, a change in the (t, g) pair in the community (given policies in other jurisdictions) will induce migration into or out of the community.

Let $t^{-k} = (t^1, \ldots, t^{k-1}, t^{k+1}, \ldots, t^J)$ and $g^{-k} = (g^1, \ldots, g^{k-1}, g^{k+1}, \ldots, g^J)$. The alternatives facing voters in community k when other communities' tax-transfer policies are (t^{-k}, g^{-k}) are defined as follows: (i) equations (5)–(8) hold for all communities, and (ii) community k's budget is in balance; that is, equation (9) holds for community k. Together, parts i and ii determine a relationship between the gross-of-tax housing price p^k and the feasible levels of the grant g^k perceived by the voters in community k, given (t^{-k}, g^{-k}). We shall call this relationship the *redistribution possibility frontier* (RPF).

For a given community, a point (g^*, p^*) is a majority voting equilibrium if and only if it is on the community's RPF and there is no point on the RPF strictly preferred to (g^*, p^*) by a majority of the community's residents. In general, neither voter indifference curves in the (g, p) plane nor the RPF will be concave or convex. Consequently, voters' preferences over points on the RPF (and, effectively, over tax-transfer policies) will not be single-peaked. In the absence of single-peakedness, it is usually the case that majority voting equilib-

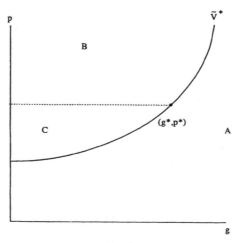

FIG. 1

rium fails to exist: voting cycles occur. An attractive feature of this model, however, is that we can show the existence of voting equilibrium even without single-peaked preferences.[6]

PROPOSITION 2. A point on the community RPF that maximizes the utility of the median-income voter in the community is a majority voting equilibrium.

To prove the proposition, consider an arbitrary community. Suppose that the point (g^*, p^*) in figure 1 is a point on the community RPF that maximizes the utility of the median-income voter in the community. Let $\tilde{V}^*$ be the indifference curve of the median-income voter through this point. There are no points on the community RPF anywhere in region A of figure 1. The existence of such a point would contradict the assumption that (g^*, p^*) is a point on the community RPF that maximizes the utility of the median-income voter. Thus points on the community RPF must fall in regions B and C or on their boundaries.

We can apply (4a) and (4b) to comparisons of points within a single community. By (4a), all voters with incomes greater than the median, $\tilde{y}$, strictly prefer (g^*, p^*) to any other point within region B or on its boundary.[7] Since the median-income voter will also vote for (g^*, p^*) over any other point within or on the boundary of region B, a majority will vote for (g^*, p^*) over any other point within or on the bound-

---

[6] Proposition 2 is based on a result of Roberts (1977).

[7] All voters strictly prefer (g^*, p^*) to points in B such that $g < g^*$ and $p > p^*$. By (4a) we can compare (g^*, p^*) to other points in region B, for voters with $y > \tilde{y}$.

ary of region B. Similarly, by (4b), all voters with incomes less than $\bar{y}$ strictly prefer (g^*, p^*) to any other point within or on the boundary of region C. Thus a majority will vote for (g^*, p^*) over any other point within or on the boundary of region C. Thus no point on the community RPF is preferred to (g^*, p^*) by a majority, and so (g^*, p^*) is a majority voting equilibrium.[8] Q.E.D.

The analysis thus far has established sufficient conditions for a proposed allocation to satisfy our definition of equilibrium. With the results in propositions 1 and 2 combined, an allocation is an equilibrium if it satisfies stratification, boundary indifference, decreasing bundles, and, within each community, the allocation yields a (g, p) pair that is a point on the community RPF that maximizes the utility of the median-income voter in the community. These results thus embody the implications of our definition of equilibrium in the context of the model we are studying.

An Aside on Voter Myopia

We have taken voters to be quite sophisticated in their assumption about how others adjust. Had we assumed myopic voters, the analysis of voting in a pure redistribution context would not be particularly illuminating. Suppose that voters take no account of adjustments in aggregate housing demand, from either current residents or possible migrants. This means that, when voting, they take p_h as fixed and assume that the aggregate housing stock stays constant at H and community population at N. The perceived community budget constraint then is $tp_hH = Ng$, so that the perceived RPF is given by

$$p = p_h + \frac{Ng}{H} = p_h + \frac{g}{\bar{h}},$$

where $\bar{h}$ is average perceived housing consumption. The perceived RPF is linear with slope $1/\bar{h}$. As an illustration of voting outcomes, consider the case in which $U(h, b)$ is homothetic, so that the income elasticity of demand for housing equals one. Then for income distributions skewed the usual way, the housing consumption of the median-income voter, $\tilde{h}$, is less than the average housing consumption, $\bar{h}$. For any pair (g, p), the slope of the decisive voter's indifference curve $(1/\tilde{h})$ is greater than the slope of the perceived RPF at that (g, p), which is $1/\bar{h}$. This implies that any value of g would be defeated

---

[8] There may be more than one point on the community RPF that yields global maximum utility for the median-income voter. Let E be the set of such points. Any point in E will defeat all points not in E, so E is the set of majority voting equilibria. (In our computations, E was always a singleton.)

by a higher value: no voting equilibrium would exist. Or if there were an arbitrary limit set on the magnitude of g, the voting equilibrium would occur at that limit. With more general preferences, nonextreme values of g could be equilibria only in the unlikely case in which $\bar{h} \geq \bar{h}$.

One might foresee other formulations with voter myopia. For example, voters might be assumed to take community population as fixed when making their assessments of the effects of changing the community tax rate. Any such characterization of voter myopia is inherently arbitrary. To guard against the possibility that some such arbitrary assumption about myopia might drive our results, we have opted for a formulation in which voters correctly anticipate the consequences of changes in their community's tax-grant package.

A Two-Community Illustration of Equilibrium

A two-community example will serve to clarify equilibrium in the model. The opportunities facing voters in community 1 may be determined as follows. Community 1 takes the tax rate and grant (t^2, g^2) in community 2 as given. For given (t^2, g^2), the choice of a tax rate in community 1 determines prices in both communities, the population in both communities, and the grant in community 1. To see this, recall that equation (5) must be satisfied, that (7) and (8) must be satisfied in each community, and that community 1's budget must be in balance: equation (9) must hold for $j = 1$. Thus, given (t^2, g^2) and a choice of t^1, all remaining variables are determined by the equations above. By varying t^1 over the set of feasible (i.e., nonnegative) values, we can trace out the opportunities perceived by voters in community 1. Notice from the indirect utility function (1) that voters' utility depends on p and g but not on t. Voters care about t only as it affects the values of p and g that emerge.

The top half of figure 2 illustrates the (g^1, p^1) pairs traced out as community 1 (assumed to be the poor community) varies its tax rate over the set of feasible values. This is community 1's RPF, given (t^2, g^2). The lowest point at which the RPF intersects the vertical axis corresponds to $t^1 = 0$. Clearly, when $t^1 = 0$, $g^1 = 0$. As t^1 is increased, g^1 rises, and the gross-of-tax price p^1 rises. Eventually, a point is reached at which the increase in revenue from further tax increases does not offset the loss in tax base due to out-migration. At that point, the RPF in figure 2 begins to bend back. In general, the RPF need not be as "well behaved" as we have drawn it here and may be neither concave nor convex.

The community's housing market clears and the community's budget is in balance for all points on the community RPF. Hence, a point

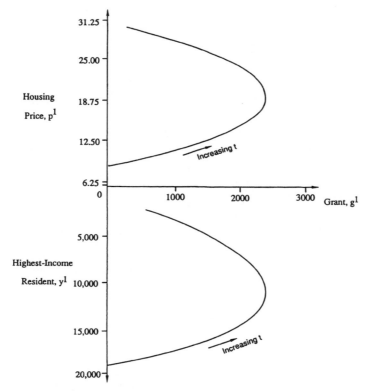

Fɪɢ. 2.—Effects of redistributive taxation in community 1 on housing prices, grant level, and migration.

on the community RPF that is a majority voting equilibrium will be an internal equilibrium in the community. An example of such an equilibrium with an interior solution is shown in figure 3 as a point at which the indifference curve of the decisive voter in community 1, labeled $\bar{V}$, is tangent to the RPF of community 1. (The equilibrium may, in some cases, involve a corner solution, with $g = 0$.) By proposition 2, the income of the decisive voter, $\bar{y}^1$, is the median income in community 1.

In general, the RPF in community 1 will differ for different (t^2, g^2) pairs in community 2, and the decisive voter in community 1 will differ as well. Figure 4 shows a two-community equilibrium. The utility of the decisive voter $\bar{y}^i$ is maximized over points on RPF^i. The RPF in community 1 is drawn with the (t^2, g^2) pair corresponding to (g^2, p^2) taken as given, and the RPF in community 2 is drawn with the (t^1, g^1) pair that corresponds to (g^1, p^1) taken as given. The border

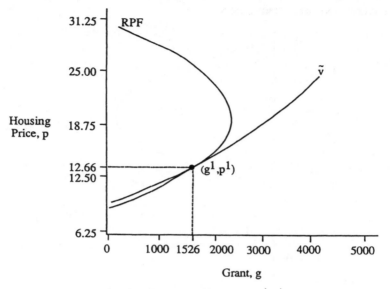

FIG. 3.—Voting equilibrium at (g^1, p^1)

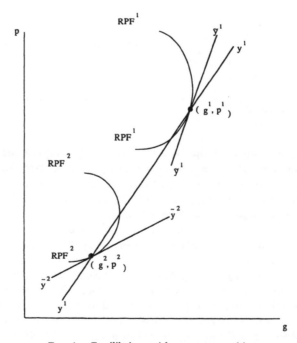

FIG. 4.—Equilibrium with two communities

household is indifferent between the two communities. For this to be a two-community equilibrium, proposition 1 requires that all residents in community 1 have incomes less than y^1 and all residents in community 2 have incomes greater than or equal to y^1. If this is the case, the stratification and "decreasing bundles" conditions will be satisfied. These conditions, the "boundary indifference" condition, and internal equilibrium within each community are sufficient for the existence of a two-community equilibrium.

With more than two communities, equilibrium is determined in a similar fashion. The RPF of community j is the (g^j, p^j) frontier traced out as community j varies t^j over the set of feasible values (the nonnegative real line). Tax rates and spending levels in other communities (t^{-j}, g^{-j}) are held fixed while t^j is varied. Housing markets in all communities clear, and the budget constraint in community j is balanced for each t^j. As in the two-community case, a point on the community RPF that is a majority voting equilibrium is an internal equilibrium. An allocation that satisfies proposition 1 in which all communities are in internal equilibrium is a J-community equilibrium.

Effects of Changing Relative Land Areas

One would expect the community's RPF to expand if the community's share of metropolitan land area were increased. Expansion of the community's share of land will tend to increase its share of total population. Since community 1 in our two-community example is occupied by the low-income portion of the income distribution, expansion of its population will increase the income of the border household, y^1. It follows that the average income level of the community will rise. Ceteris paribus, this will increase the tax base per capita. In addition, an increase in the share of metropolitan land occupied by the community will increase the community's "market power," in that land outside the community becomes scarcer and housing relatively more expensive. The increase in market power provides greater latitude for the community to engage in redistributive policies.

The net effect of an increase in the share of land area depends not only on the expansion of the RPF but also on how the income of the pivotal voter changes. These effects may be offsetting. With two communities, for example, the RPF of the poor community may well expand as the community's share of land increases, making higher grants per household feasible. But, for any given (g^1, p^1, g^2, p^2), a higher fraction of the total population occupies the low-income community when that community's share of total land area increases. Thus, for any given (g^1, p^1, g^2, p^2), the income of the decisive voter increases as the community's share of total land area increases. Ceteris paribus, higher-income voters prefer lower g. As a result, although higher grants are *feasible,* the political process may limit the increase in transfers.

III. The Contrasting Preferences of Owners and Renters

The discussion so far has treated all residents of local jurisdictions as renters. Rents are paid to absentee landlords who do not vote in any of the communities.[9] Suppose, by contrast, that all residents of local jurisdictions are owner-occupants. They locate in a jurisdiction and purchase housing there before participating in the voting process that determines the level of redistributive taxation. There are no transactions costs in the purchase and sale of housing. Households can adjust their level of housing consumption (i.e., sell their current house and purchase another dwelling) in response to price changes without incurring transaction costs. As in the preceding model with rental housing, households correctly anticipate how their housing consumption will change in response to a change in the price of housing induced by a change in redistributive taxation. Households also anticipate the capital gain or loss that they will incur as a result of a change in the net-of-tax price of housing induced by a change in the level of redistributive taxation.

Let h_0 be the amount of housing purchased at price $p_{h,0}$ by a household with endowed income y. When making decisions about whether to change their consumption bundle, homeowners face the budget constraint

$$y + g + (p_h - p_{h,0})h_0 = ph + b,$$

with h_0 and $p_{h,0}$ fixed. The third term on the left-hand side is the capital gain from selling the household's existing dwelling.[10] The demand function for housing for such a household is of the form

$$h = h(p, y + g + (p_h - p_{h,0})h_0).$$

[9] This treatment of absentee landlords is consistent with a strict interpretation of current legal doctrine. R. Ellickson (1982) has noted that cities generally have one-resident, one-vote rule. Challenges by nonresident landowners to this voting rule have typically met with failure, at least since Avery v. Midland County, 390 U.S. 474 (1968).

[10] Suppose that housing does not depreciate and that the real rate of interest is r. Then the capital gain from sale of the house is the present value of the change in annual implicit rentals on the house: $(p_h - p_{h,0})h_0/r$. This increase in wealth will pay an annuity of $(p_h - p_{h,0})h_0$. This annuity is added to the household's annual endowed income y and grant g to obtain its total annual income.

Substituting this demand function into the budget constraint and substituting both into the utility function yields the indirect utility function $V(p, g, y + (p_h - p_{h,0})h_0)$. The slope of the indifference curve through a point (g, p) is

$$\left. \frac{dp}{dg} \right|_{V = \bar{V}} = \frac{1}{h} + \frac{h_0}{h} \left. \frac{dp_h}{dg} \right|_{\text{RPF}}. \tag{10}$$

In contrast to the renter case, dp/dg for a homeowner depends on the net-of-tax price of housing as well as its gross-of-tax price, because capital gains depend on p_h. In characterizing voting equilibrium when all voters are owner-occupants, we assume that dp/dg given in (10) is decreasing in y for all $p \geq 0$ and g such that p_h and dp_h/dg are defined along the RPF. It can be shown that a point on the RPF that maximizes the utility of an owner-occupant with median endowed income is a majority voting equilibrium among points such that this assumption holds (Epple and Romer 1989a, app. 1).

As is standard in static models, we assume that all transactions occur in equilibrium.[11] Evaluating (10) for $h_0 = h$ and $p_{h,0} = p_h$ yields

$$\left. \frac{dp}{dg} \right|_{V = \bar{V}} = \frac{1}{h} + \left. \frac{dp_h}{dg} \right|_{\text{RPF}}. \tag{11}$$

Since all transactions occur in equilibrium, the results in proposition 1 continue to hold as in the renter case. Thus when the assumption in the previous paragraph holds, sufficient conditions for equilibrium in this owner-occupancy model are the same as in the renter model: stratification, boundary indifference, decreasing bundles, and maximization (given the RPF constraint) of the utility of the median-income voter in each community.

An increase in the grant (and the associated tax rate) will typically lead to a reduction in the net-of-tax price of housing. Hence, the second term on the right-hand side of (11) will normally be negative.

---

[11] While the actual process of achieving equilibrium is not typically captured in static models, a heuristic "story" about how equilibrium might emerge may be useful. In our models with only renters, this requires no elaboration. In the model with owners, perhaps the easiest process to visualize is the one in which all land is initially owned by price-taking absentee owners. When they locate in a community, households in the model buy from these absentee owners. Since there is no uncertainty, transactions occur at equilibrium prices.

The key difference between owners and renters in the model is that owners would suffer any capital gains or losses that would arise from a change in the tax rate or grant level in the community in which they choose to locate. As voters, they take account of such potential gains and losses when choosing among feasible tax rates and spending levels. Since they choose not to vote for departures from the equilibrium tax rate and grant in the community in which they live, such capital gains and losses do not arise in equilibrium.

Thus a homeowner with a given level of income will normally have a flatter indifference curve through the point (g, p) where (11) holds than a renter with the same level of income (for whom $dp/dg = 1/h$). Hence, for a given RPF, *an owner with a given endowed income will prefer a lower level of redistributive taxation than a renter with the same income.*

In summary, the theoretical analysis thus far gives insight into the general structure of equilibrium in our model. Comparative-static analysis yields ambiguous results, as often happens with equilibrium models. Development of more specific implications about the features of equilibrium requires more specific information about preferences, technology, the distributions of income and housing tenure, the number of communities, and the land area of each. We therefore turn to numerical computations based on the structure we have presented. To do this we have chosen functional forms and parameter values that are broadly consistent with empirical evidence on housing supply and demand functions and the distribution of income in the United States.

IV. Computed Equilibria

Households have the Cobb-Douglas utility function $U(h, b) = h^\alpha b^{1-\alpha}$. The unitary price and income elasticities implied by this utility function are well within the range of values found in empirical studies (Polinsky 1977; Harmon 1988). This utility function implies the following indirect utility function for a household with income y in a community with housing price p and grant g:

$$V(p, g, y) = \alpha^\alpha (1 - \alpha)^{1-\alpha} p^{-\alpha} (y + g).$$

Net-of-tax expenditure shares on housing of 25–30 percent coupled with property tax rates (as a percentage of annual implicit rent) of 20–30 percent suggest a gross-of-tax expenditure share for housing on the order of one-third. Hence, we chose a value of $\alpha = .33$.

We assume the following constant-elasticity housing supply function: $H_s^j(p_h^j) = L^j(p_h^j)^\theta$. This supply function is implied by a constant returns to scale Cobb-Douglas production function, with θ being the ratio of the value of nonland to land inputs in production. On the basis of a land share of roughly 25 percent (Mills 1972), we set $\theta = 3$.

A lognormal distribution is generally considered to be a reasonably good characterization of the U.S. income distribution (except possibly for the upper tail). The parameters of a lognormal distribution can be calculated using data on the mean and median from the population (Lindgren 1962, p. 89). With 1979 mean ($21,418) and median ($17,880) income for households in U.S. standard metropolitan statistical areas (SMSAs) (U.S. Bureau of the Census 1980*a*, table 107), the implied mean for the distribution of the logarithm of income is 9.8 and the variance is 0.36. Hence, in our computations, incomes are assumed lognormally distributed with $\ln(y) \sim N(9.8, 0.36)$.

The computations assume three communities: a poor community, a middle-income community, and a wealthy community. We assume throughout that one community does not redistribute income (i.e., for this community $t = g = 0$). We know from the descending bundles condition of proposition 1 that in any equilibrium this community will be the one in which the highest-income people live. Land areas of the three communities are varied in the computations to illustrate the effects of changing relative community sizes. We chose units of land so that the combined amount of land in all three communities sums to one unit.

The structure of our three-community examples should not be interpreted literally as meaning that all the wealthy households live in a single community, although for computational reasons it makes sense to do so. The spirit of these examples is better captured by thinking of the wealthy as living in many small communities that do not redistribute and that in the aggregate occupy a given fraction of the available land area. These nonredistributing communities provide the opportunity for anyone who wishes to migrate to a jurisdiction in which no redistribution occurs. (In equilibrium, by proposition 1, this must be the one in which those with highest income locate.) Since we are interested in how much redistribution occurs even when it is possible to escape taxation altogether, we have allowed in our examples for half the land area to be occupied by the jurisdictions that are constrained to have zero taxes.

All-Renter Communities

We look first at the case in which all residents are renters. To compute equilibria, we rely on the results of propositions 1 and 2.[12] To provide an intuitive feel for the behavior of the model, we first present results for the case in which at most one community engages in redistribution. (By proposition 1, this will be the low-income community.) The top half of figure 2 shows the RPF of community 1 when $L^1 = .25$ and $L^2 + L^3 = .75$. The bottom part depicts the out-migration (decline in y^1) that occurs as community 1's tax rate increases.

Figure 5 shows the RPFs obtained with four different values for community 1's share of metropolitan land area: $L^1 = .1, .25, .5,$ and

---

[12] Details of our computational procedure appear in Epple and Romer (1989*a*, app. 2).

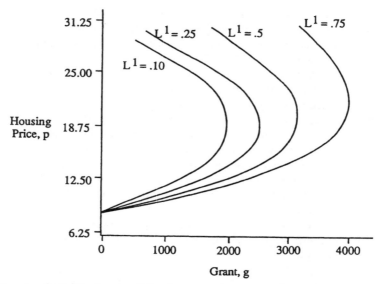

FIG. 5.—Redistribution possibility frontiers for four different community 1 shares of metropolitan land area.

.75. In addition to having the anticipated shape, the RPF does indeed expand as community size increases.

Voting equilibrium in community 1 when $L^1 = .25$ is shown in figure 3. This is the point on the RPF most preferred by a voter with income $y = \$10,542$, the median in community 1. Since, by assumption, the other communities do not undertake redistribution, the outcome in figure 3 is an equilibrium. In this equilibrium, $g^1 = \$1,526$ and 37 percent of the metropolitan area population lives in community 1. The gross-of-tax price of housing in community 1 is $12.66, and in the other communities it is $9.41.

An investigation of equilibrium with various values of L^1 reveals that the outward shift of the RPF slightly outweighs the effect of increasing the income of the pivotal voter as the population of community 1 rises. The equilibrium level of grants per household rises as the land area of the poor community rises. For example, increasing the land area of the poor community from .25 to .45 results in an increase in the equilibrium grant per household from $1,526 to $1,744.

Results for the case in which both communities 1 and 2 may redistribute income are presented in table 1. For these results, the land area of the community constrained to have $g = 0$ is fixed at $L^3 = .5$, and the relative land areas of the low- and middle-income communi-

TABLE 1

EFFECTS OF VARYING THE RELATIVE AMOUNTS OF LAND OCCUPIED BY THE LOW- AND MIDDLE-INCOME COMMUNITIES
FOR TWO ALTERNATIVE TENURE ARRANGEMENTS

	ALL HOUSEHOLDS RENT			ALL HOUSEHOLDS ARE OWNER-OCCUPANTS		
	(1)	(2)	(3)	(4)	(5)	(6)
p^1	12.40	12.39	12.39	9.28	9.35	9.37
p^2	12.28	12.21	12.18	9.21	9.22	9.22
p^3	9.72	9.70	9.70	9.20	9.22	9.22
g^1	1,780	1,799	1,804	68	120	133
g^2	1,711	1,684	1,676	5	0	0
t^1	.62	.58	.57	.014	.025	.028
t^2	.31	.29	.28	.0006	0	0
N^1	.54	.60	.61	.68	.71	.72
N^2	.07	.01	.000013	.04	.009	8×10^{-6}
y^1	19,145	20,980	21,459	23,844	25,222	25,574
y^2	21,213	21,436	21,460	27,725	25,609	25,575
L^1	.45	.49	.49999	.45	.49	.49999
L^2	.05	.01	.00001	.05	.01	.00001

NOTE.—$L^3 = .50$ in all cases. N^j is community j's share of the total population ($j = 1, 2, 3$). $N^3 = 1 - N^1 - N^2$.

ties are varied. In this and other tables, the tax rates should be interpreted as rates *per dollar of rental price*. To obtain the more familiar tax rates per dollar of *property value*, the rental value of housing must be capitalized at some discount rate. With a 10 percent discount rate, this would imply property tax rates of *one-tenth* the rates listed in the tables.

The most striking finding of the model with only renters is that relatively high levels of redistribution are chosen by the middle-income community when that community has a comparatively small land area.[13] This is illustrated in columns 1–3 of table 1, where we present equilibria for cases in which community 2 has 5 percent, 1 percent, and 0.001 percent of the metropolitan land area. Another striking observation about these results is that the levels of local redistributive expenditures are quite high compared to levels observed in U.S. municipalities.[14]

Consider column 3 of table 1. The land area of the middle-income community is a small fraction (.00001) of total land in the metropolitan area. In equilibrium, the population is a comparably small fraction (.000013) of the metropolitan area population. The residents of the community are essentially homogeneous; the range of incomes between the wealthiest and poorest households in the community is less than $1.00. Household income in the community ($21,560) is well above the median ($17,880) and mean ($21,418) income for the metropolitan area. Roughly 39 percent of the households in the metropolitan area live in communities that do not tax or redistribute income. Nonetheless, households in the middle-income community

---

[13] There may be multiple intercommunity equilibria (Epple and Romer 1989a, app. 2). Since (along with much of the literature) we expected that mobility considerations would rule out equilibria with *g* much greater than zero, it is instructive that such equilibria are possible.

[14] Data on local redistributive taxation and expenditure are difficult to obtain for two reasons. First, redistribution often takes the form of goods and services rather than money, and the selection of the set of expenditures to classify as redistribution is not entirely straightforward. Second, local expenditures for redistribution may be financed by contributions from several levels of government so that the local revenue contribution is often hard to isolate. Taking an expansive definition of local government redistributive expenditures—including all items classified by the census as public welfare, health, and hospitals—and counting all local government expenditures in these categories regardless of source of funds, one can obtain an upper-bound estimate of local redistributive expenditures. The per capita average of these expenditures across all municipalities in the United States in fiscal year 1985 was $84. The average in municipalities with a population greater than 1 million was $389, while in municipalities with a population under 50,000 it was $26. For all local governments in 75 major SMSAs, the fiscal year 1983 figure was $192 per capita. For amounts per household, the per capita numbers should be multiplied by approximately three. There is great variability across states and municipalities, but these numbers suggest the order of magnitude (see Tax Foundation 1988, tables F2, F9).

vote to impose a 28 percent tax on the value of housing services and use the proceeds to finance grants per household of $1,676. (This would correspond to a 2.8 percent tax on property value if one uses a 10 percent rate for discounting.) They do this recognizing that it will induce migration out of the community and increase the equilibrium housing price to $12.18—26 percent higher than the no-tax equilibrium price of $9.70.

These results contradict the widely held belief that small communities cannot opt for high levels of transfers. The results show that they can, and that the decisive voter may well prefer a high level of grants. Moreover, the RPFs reveal that the politically chosen grants are significantly lower than the highest feasible grant. In other words, were the communities interested in maximizing the level of grants per household, they could choose higher g than those shown in the table, even given all the mobility considerations.

Why do residents of small and relatively high-income jurisdictions opt for such high grants in this model? Taxation for redistribution increases the gross-of-tax price of housing and decreases the net-of-tax price of housing relative to the no-tax level. The reduction in the net-of-tax housing price implies that a portion of the cost of redistribution is borne by property owners. Since land is immobile and jurisdictional boundaries are fixed, landowners cannot move their land to avoid paying a portion of the redistributive tax. Again, consider column 3 of table 1. The net-of-tax price of housing in the middle-income community is $9.51. This compares to a no-tax price of $9.70. Thus owners of land in the community receive a lower net-of-tax price than that obtained by those who own land outside the community. Landowners pay $0.19 (= $9.70 − $9.51) of the $2.67 difference ($12.18 − $9.51) between the gross- and net-of-tax price of housing in community 2. The incidence of the tax is such that landowners pay roughly 7 percent of the tax, and this is sufficient to induce residents of the community to adopt a relatively high redistributive tax.[15] Thus even in small, relatively high-income jurisdictions, residents find comparatively high levels of redistributive taxation to be attractive. These results echo the finding by Epple and Zelenitz (1981) that governments in small local jurisdictions can follow discretionary policies that expropriate a portion of land rent.

A key message of the computations in this section is that "smallness" of local jurisdictions need not prevent relatively high transfers. We should stress that the results are not due to voter myopia; voters

[15] Thus a portion of the tax is exported to nonresidents (absentee landlords). Johnson (1988) discusses tax exporting as a possible source of redistributive motives in a federal system.

correctly perceive how taxation for redistribution will affect migration and housing prices. The functional forms and parameter values in these computations are realistic enough that the results are not likely to be an artifact of the specification. The argument presented above suggests that these results arise because residents are renters who shift a portion of the burden of redistribution to property owners.

Owners-Only Communities

We used the functional forms and parameter values of the renter model to solve the owner-occupancy model.[16] The results, shown in columns 4–6 of table 1, change dramatically. *In this table, for all values of relative community size for the poor and middle-income communities, the equilibrium level of redistributive taxation is quite modest.* The change in results from those in columns 1–3 is due entirely to the change in voter preferences induced by homeownership. With owner-occupancy, any reduction in the net-of-tax price of housing caused by an increase in redistributive taxation leads to a capital loss for the owner-occupant. This capital loss is sufficient to offset almost completely the benefits of redistribution for median voters in communities of the sizes shown in table 1.

Investigation of the preferences of nonmedian voters in the case in which $L^1 = L^2 = .25$ reveals that there is a large majority of voters (roughly 47.5 percent) in the low-income community who prefer positive levels of redistribution. Since the observed proportion of owners in the United States is lower at low incomes than at high ones, this suggests that a model with both owner-occupants and renters might yield results quite different from those with only renters or owners. We discuss this next.

Equilibrium with Both Renters and Owner-Occupants

In order to consider communities with a mix of renters and owners, let $\rho(y)$ be the proportion of residents with income y who are renters. Since transactions occur only in equilibrium, the choice of community depends only on income, not on whether the household will own or rent. Proposition 1 holds for a model with both owners and renters.

For owners, assume that dp/dg as given in (10) is decreasing in y. Then it can be shown (Epple and Romer 1989a, app. 1) that the

---

[16] In our computations, we verified that dp/dg as given by (10) is decreasing in y and that proposition 2 can be applied over all the points on the RPF. For details, see Epple and Romer (1989a, app. 1).

preferences of owners as a subgroup vary systematically with income, as do the preferences of renters. It is therefore possible to determine the identity of pivotal voters in each community in equilibrium even when there are both owners and renters, and both are free to move among jurisdictions.

Since there are two types of voters, we shall be looking for voting equilibrium in each community, such that it is a point on the community RPF that maximizes the utility of renter-voter $\bar{y}_r$ and owner-voter $\bar{y}_o$, where $\bar{y}_r$ and $\bar{y}_o$ satisfy

$$\int_{\underline{y}}^{\bar{y}_r} \rho(y)f(y)dy + \int_{\underline{y}}^{\bar{y}_o} [1 - \rho(y)]f(y)dy = \frac{1}{2}\int_{\underline{y}}^{\bar{y}} f(y)dy, \qquad (12)$$

and $\underline{y}$ and $\bar{y}$ are, respectively, the lowest and highest endowed incomes of residents of the community.

Equation (12) indicates that a majority voting equilibrium will be an allocation in which an owner ($\bar{y}_o$) with income below the community median income and a renter ($\bar{y}_r$) with income above the community median are both pivotal voters. They are pivotal since one-half of the voters in the community prefer a lower point on the community RPF and one-half prefer a higher point on the community RPF than $\bar{y}_o$ and $\bar{y}_r$ do.

To investigate the model with both owners and renters, we need to specify the function $\rho(y)$ parametrically. We adopted the specification

$$\rho(y) = \begin{cases} \gamma y^{-\delta} & \text{for } y > \gamma^{1/\delta} \\ 1 & \text{for } y \leq \gamma^{1/\delta}. \end{cases}$$

We chose this function for analytic convenience, but it provides a good fit to the available data. We estimated the parameters γ and δ as follows. The U.S. Bureau of the Census (1980b, tables B-3, B-4) presents the number of renter- and owner-occupied housing units in U.S. SMSAs for nine household income classes. We computed average income, $\overline{Y}$, in each income class, using the lognormal distribution of household income presented in Section III. Regressing the log of the proportion of households that are renters, $\overline{\rho}$, against the log of $\overline{Y}$ gives estimates of γ and δ. The resulting regression, with t-statistics in parentheses, is

$$\ln \overline{\rho} = 5.98 - .729 \ln \overline{Y}, \quad R^2 = .89.$$
$$(6.43)\,(7.69)$$

This regression confirms that the proportion of households that are renters declines as income rises ($\gamma = \exp[5.98] = 395$, $\delta = .729$).[17]

---

[17] Using time-series data, Rosen, Rosen, and Holtz-Eakin (1984) obtain an estimate of .707 for the elasticity of homeownership with respect to permanent income. This is remarkably close to our estimate of δ.

As in the all-renter and all-owner cases, increasing the relative size of the lowest-income community will tend to cause the community's RPF to expand. As before, this effect tends to favor an increase in the level of redistribution. An opposing effect, also present in the renter model, is that more high-income voters occupy the community when the community expands. Those voters oppose high levels of redistribution. A second opposing effect, which is not present in the renter model, is that the proportion of residents who are homeowners increases as the share of land occupied by the low-income community rises and, ceteris paribus, homeowners prefer less redistribution than renters.

Results of our computations for the mixed-tenure cases are shown in table 2.[18] Comparing these results to those in table 1 reveals that the equilibrium grant levels are lower in the model with both owners and renters than in the model with only renters. It is interesting to note that increasing the size of the low-income community results in a decrease rather than an increase in the equilibrium level of redistribution. The changes in community 1's composition as its share of land area increases are sufficient to offset the effect of the expansion of the community RPF, with the result that the equilibrium level of grants falls as the size of the community increases. (In the low-income community, the proportion of renters falls from 64 percent in table 2 to 41 percent as community size increases. The community's median income rises.)

Looking across the columns of table 2, one sees that the amount of redistribution in community 2 falls as the size of community 1 increases relative to community 2. This result is due in part to the declining size of community 2. However, the major factor causing the decline in redistribution in community 2 is the increase in household income and owner-occupancy in community 2 as the size of community 1 rises relative to community 2. This is evident in the increase in income of the poorest resident in community 2 (y^1) as the share of metropolitan land area occupied by community 1 rises. These results are in sharp contrast to those in columns 1–3 of table 1.

Finally, we varied the parameter δ that determines the proportion of renters at each income level.[19] The results are graphed in figure

---

[18] An interesting feature of our computations is that in both the all-owners model and the all-renters model, for values of L^1 on the order of .34 or less, our computations find allocations satisfying stratification, boundary indifference, and internal equilibrium. However, these allocations do not satisfy decreasing bundles, and, hence, they are not equilibria. By contrast, in the more realistic mixed-tenure case, our computations yield equilibrium allocations for the full range of values of L^1 that we investigate, as illustrated in table 2.

[19] We thank an anonymous referee for suggesting these computations.

TABLE 2

EFFECTS OF VARYING THE RELATIVE AMOUNTS OF LAND OCCUPIED BY THE LOW- AND
MIDDLE-INCOME COMMUNITIES IN THE MODEL WITH BOTH RENTERS AND
OWNER-OCCUPANTS

	(1)	(2)	(3)	(4)	(5)	(6)	(7)
p^1	12.09	11.31	10.87	10.71	10.65	10.64	10.64
p^2	10.22	10.01	9.78	9.62	9.49	9.45	9.44
p^3	9.42	9.38	9.36	9.36	9.40	9.43	9.44
g^1	1,213	1,030	920	904	933	954	960
g^2	647	528	359	215	74	15	0
t^1	.80	.48	.32	.26	.24	.23	.23
t^2	.13	.10	.06	.03	.01	.002	0
N^1	.13	.24	.40	.53	.63	.67	.68
N^2	.55	.45	.29	.16	.05	.01	.00001
y^1	9,284	11,756	15,473	18,796	22,072	23,405	23,741.0
y^2	23,868	24,210	24,423	24,350	24,019	23,804	23,741.4
$\bar{y}_o^1$	4,250	6,454	8,777	10,377	11,642	12,082	12,187
$\bar{y}_r^1$	8,322	10,515	13,264	15,273	16,876	17,432	17,564
$\bar{y}_o^2$	14,189	15,859	18,538	20,843	22,856	23,572	23,741.2
$\bar{y}_r^2$	18,914	19,976	21,504	22,647	23,464	23,694	23,741.3
PR^1	.64	.56	.49	.45	.42	.41	.41
PR^2	.35	.33	.30	.28	.26	.25	.25
L^1	.10	.15	.25	.35	.45	.49	.49999
L^2	.40	.35	.25	.15	.05	.01	.00001

NOTE.—L^3 = .50 in all cases. PR^J is the proportion of community J's population that are renters. N^J is community J's share of the total population (J = 1, 2, 3). N^3 = $1 - N^1 - N^2$.

6, for L^1 = .45 and L^2 = .05. In the figure, PR^1, PR^2, and PR^T are the proportions of renters in community 1, community 2, and the total population, respectively. As δ increases, the proportion of households at each income level that are owners increases. (The dashed line in fig. 6 indicates the case corresponding to col. 5 of table 2.) The all-renters and all-owners equilibria emerge at extreme values of δ. Parametrically varying δ illustrates the decline in the level of the grant in each community as the fraction of households that are owners increases.

The striking differences in equilibrium grant levels among the all-renters, all-owners, and mixed-tenure settings make a compelling case that housing tenure plays a central role in local redistribution. The effects of tenure arise not by changing what is feasible but by changing what voters prefer. The computational results thus highlight the interplay between individual incentives and collective actions that is a central focus of our model.

V. Conclusions

Some results of the analysis in this paper accord very well with prior expectations. Local redistribution leads to a sorting of the population,

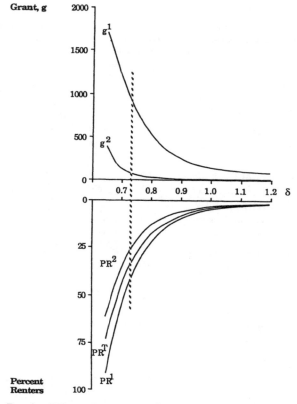

FIG. 6.—Effects of varying δ; $L^1 = .45$, $L^2 = .05$, $L^3 = .50$

with the poorest households located in the communities that provide the highest levels of redistribution (proposition 1). Larger communities within a system of jurisdictions have greater scope for redistribution than smaller ones do.

Some results of the analysis are unexpected. Even though mobility is costless in this model, high levels of transfers can emerge in equilibrium in computations with reasonable parameter values. Indeed, as shown in Section IV, even small, relatively high-income communities opt for high grant levels if all voters are renters. Results with owner-occupancy contrast sharply with those with only renters. Owner-occupants prefer less redistribution than renters. It therefore appears that it is not the threat of out-migration that leads to observed low levels of local redistribution in most municipalities in U.S. metropolitan areas. Costless mobility does not shrink the feasible set of grants sufficiently to prevent local redistribution. Instead, our results suggest that the preference for low levels of redistribution is a political one, and it is closely linked to the relatively high proportion of owner-occupants in most municipalities. The results in the model with both owners and renters suggest that the proportion of residents who are renters is a major factor affecting the local choice of level of redistribution. It would be worthwhile to explore this implication of our model more directly with data on U.S. municipalities.

A central assumption of our model is that moving is costless. Empirical evidence suggests that households do migrate in response to differentials in welfare payments (Gramlich and Laren 1984; Peterson and Rom 1989). However, the evidence also suggests that the response is not instantaneous, and it is clear that perfect stratification does not emerge in practice. Hence, it would be desirable to extend the model in this paper by introducing factors that lead households to be attached to particular locations. Perhaps the most straightforward way to do this would be to endow households with preferences for some locations relative to others. Another approach is to have the system of jurisdictions vary in location relative to a central area, so that communities would differ in some important respect, such as the amount of time required to commute to the center. As we show in Cassidy, Epple, and Romer (1989), our framework is quite amenable to incorporating a spatial dimension to the analysis.

The debate about local redistribution has focused on whether mobility makes local redistribution infeasible. In our model, local redistribution proves to be feasible. The amount of redistribution turns out to be relatively modest in the empirically most relevant cases because anticipated capital losses by homeowners deter them from voting for high grant levels per household. It is likely that local redistribution would be limited further by demands for other services from local governments. A useful direction to develop the model would be to introduce a local public good in addition to local redistribution. This would permit investigation of the allocation of public expenditures between redistribution and the provision of services. This extension poses a substantial challenge since the voting problem becomes more complex.

Our model focuses on the implications of one resident, one vote and ignores the possibility that absentee owners may attempt to influence the political process within the jurisdiction through means other than by casting a vote directly. The introduction of these more indirect channels of political influence in the context of a model of mobile households is an intriguing problem for future work.

Our existing model or its straightforward modifications can readily be applied to a variety of policy issues. The level of redistribution that would be chosen with a single central government can be compared to the case in which only local governments redistribute. When both central and local governments redistribute, one can investigate how changes in redistribution by the central government affect the amount of redistribution done locally. The effect of intergovernmental grants on the level of local redistribution can be studied. The model can be used to determine how consolidation of local governments affects the amount of local redistribution. Our framework, in sum, provides a useful way of combining the essential features we enumerated in the Introduction. The computed equilibria provide insight into the way these features interact and suggest the value of addressing other issues in fiscal federalism using extensions of this structure.

References

Brown, Charles C., and Oates, Wallace E. "Assistance to the Poor in a Federal System." *J. Public Econ.* 32 (April 1987): 307–30.
Bucovetsky, Sam. "Inequality in the Local Public Sector." *J.P.E.* 90 (February 1982): 128–45.
Cassidy, Glenn; Epple, Dennis; and Romer, Thomas. "Redistribution by Local Governments in a Monocentric Urban Area." *Regional Sci. and Urban Econ.* 19 (August 1989): 421–54.
Courant, Paul N., and Rubinfeld, Daniel L. "On the Measurement of Benefits in an Urban Context: Some General Equilibrium Issues." *J. Urban Econ.* 5 (July 1978): 346–56.
Ellickson, Bryan. "Jurisdictional Fragmentation and Residential Choice." *A.E.R. Papers and Proc.* 61 (May 1971): 334–39.
Ellickson, Robert C. "Cities and Homeowners Associations." *Univ. Pennsylvania Law Rev.* 130 (June 1982): 1519–80.
Epple, Dennis; Filimon, Radu; and Romer, Thomas. "Equilibrium among Local Jurisdictions: Toward an Integrated Treatment of Voting and Residential Choice." *J. Public Econ.* 24 (August 1984): 281–308.
Epple, Dennis, and Romer, Thomas. "Mobility and Redistribution." Working Paper no. E-89-26. Stanford, Calif.: Stanford Univ., Hoover Inst., August 1989. (a)
———. "On the Flexibility of Municipal Boundaries." *J. Urban Econ.* 26 (November 1989): 307–19. (b)
Epple, Dennis, and Zelenitz, Allan. "The Implications of Competition among Jurisdictions: Does Tiebout Need Politics?" *J.P.E.* 89 (December 1981): 1197–1217.
Goodspeed, Timothy J. "A Reexamination of the Use of Ability-to-Pay Taxes by Local Governments." Working paper. Washington: U.S. Treasury Dept., January 1988.
Gramlich, Edward M., and Laren, Deborah S. "Migration and Income Redistribution Responsibilities." *J. Human Resources* 19 (Fall 1984): 489–511.
Harmon, Oskar R. "The Income Elasticity of Demand for Single-Family Owner-Occupied Housing: An Empirical Reconciliation." *J. Urban Econ.* 24 (September 1988): 173–85.

Johnson, William R. "Income Redistribution in a Federal System." *A.E.R.* 78 (June 1988): 570–73.

Ladd, Helen F., and Doolittle, Fred C. "Which Level of Government Should Assist the Poor?" *Nat. Tax J.* 35 (September 1982): 323–36.

Lindgren, Bernard W. *Statistical Theory.* New York: Macmillan, 1962.

Matthews, Steven, and Moore, John. "Monopoly Provision of Quality and Warranties: An Exploration in the Theory of Multidimensional Screening." *Econometrica* 55 (March 1987): 441–67.

Meltzer, Allan H., and Richard, Scott F. "A Rational Theory of the Size of Government." *J.P.E.* 89 (October 1981): 914–27.

Mills, Edwin S. *Urban Economics.* Glenview, Ill.: Scott, Foresman, 1972.

Mills, Edwin S., and Oates, Wallace E., eds. *Fiscal Zoning and Land Use Controls: The Economic Issues.* Lexington, Mass.: Heath, 1975.

Oates, Wallace E. *Fiscal Federalism.* New York: Harcourt Brace Jovanovich, 1972.

———. "An Economist's Perspective on Fiscal Federalism." In *The Political Economy of Fiscal Federalism,* edited by Wallace E. Oates. Lexington, Mass.: Heath, 1977.

———. "The Estimation of Demand Functions for Local Public Goods: Issues in Specification and Interpretation." Working paper. College Park: Univ. Maryland, 1986.

Orr, Larry L. "Income Transfers as a Public Good: An Application to AFDC." *A.E.R.* 66 (June 1976): 359–71.

Peterson, Paul E., and Rom, Mark C. "American Federalism, Welfare Policy, and Residential Choices." *American Polit. Sci. Rev.* 83 (September 1989): 711–28.

Polinsky, A. Mitchell. "The Demand for Housing: A Study in Specification and Grouping." *Econometrica* 45 (March 1977): 447–61.

Roberts, Kevin W. S. "Voting over Income Tax Schedules." *J. Public Econ.* 8 (December 1977): 329–40.

Romer, Thomas. "Individual Welfare, Majority Voting, and the Properties of a Linear Income Tax." *J. Public Econ.* 4 (February 1975): 163–85.

Rose-Ackerman, Susan. "Market Models of Local Government: Exit, Voting and the Land Market." *J. Urban Econ.* 6 (July 1979): 319–37.

Rosen, Harvey S.; Rosen, Kenneth T.; and Holtz-Eakin, Douglas. "Housing Tenure, Uncertainty, and Taxation." *Rev. Econ. and Statis.* 66 (August 1984): 405–16.

Rosenzweig, Mark R., and Wolpin, Kenneth I. "Migration Selectivity and the Effects of Public Programs." *J. Public Econ.* 37 (December 1988): 265–89.

Steen, Robert C. "Effects of Governmental Structure in Urban Areas." *J. Urban Econ.* 21 (March 1987): 166–79. (a)

———. "Effects of the Property Tax in Urban Areas." *J. Urban Econ.* 21 (March 1987): 146–65. (b)

Stigler, George J. "The Tenable Range of Functions of Local Government." In *Federal Expenditure Policy for Economic Growth and Stability,* by the Joint Economic Committee. Washington: Government Printing Office, 1957.

Tax Foundation. *Facts and Figures on Government Finance.* 24th ed. Baltimore: Johns Hopkins Univ. Press, 1988.

U.S. Bureau of the Census. *Census of Population: Characteristics of the Population: General, Social and Economic Characteristics, U.S. Summary.* Washington: Government Printing Office, 1980. (a)

———. *Census of Housing: Metropolitan Housing Characteristics, U.S. Summary.* Vol. 2. Washington: Government Printing Office, 1980. (b)

Westhoff, Frank. "Existence of Equilibria in Economies with a Local Public Good." *J. Econ. Theory* 14 (February 1977): 84–112.

Wildasin, David E. "Nash Equilibria in Models of Fiscal Competition." *J. Public Econ.* 35 (March 1988): 229–40.

Wilson, John D. "Trade, Capital Mobility, and Tax Competition." *J.P.E.* 95 (August 1987): 835–56. (*a*)

———. "Trade in a Tiebout Economy." *A.E.R.* 77 (June 1987): 431–41. (*b*)

Yinger, John. "Capitalization and the Theory of Local Public Finance." *J.P.E.* 90 (October 1982): 917–43.

Name Index

Economic Approaches to Law

Economics of International Trade Law
Alan O. Sykes

Economics of Public International Law
Jack Landman Goldsmith

Economics of Constitutional Law
Richard A. Epstein

Economics of Comparative Law
Gerrit De Geest

Economics of Commercial Arbitration and
Dispute Resolution
Orley C. Ashenfelter and Radha K. Iyengar

Economics of Corporate Law
Jonathan Macey

Behavioral Law and Economics
Jeffrey J. Rachlinsky

Austrian Law and Economics
Mario J. Rizzo

Institutional Law and Economics
Pablo T. Spiller